McGRAW-HILL SERIES IN ADVERTISING AND SELLING

STEUART HENDERSON BRITT, *Consulting Editor*

Marketing Research

MARKETING RESEARCH

MARKETING RESEARCH

by Richard D. Crisp

PRESIDENT, RICHARD D. CRISP AND ASSOCIATES, INC., CHICAGO,
CONSULTANTS IN ADVERTISING AND MARKETING MANAGEMENT,
MARKETING RESEARCH, AND NEW PRODUCT DEVELOPMENT;
LECTURER IN MARKETING, NORTHWESTERN UNIVERSITY

McGRAW-HILL BOOK COMPANY, INC.
1957   NEW YORK   TORONTO   LONDON

TO MY WIFE

Preface

The purpose of this book is to introduce the field of marketing research as it exists in professional practice. Marketing research is a management tool which is increasingly important as the marketing management area becomes a more and more vital determinant of business success or failure.

This book is problem-oriented. It identifies the types of problems to which marketing research is most frequently applied. It then describes in some detail the processes by which a marketing research man gathers, analyzes, and interprets those facts which management executives need to help them arrive at important decisions.

In both approach and emphasis, this book differs strikingly from most others on this subject. The approach taken is essentially practical rather than theoretical. Emphasis on various areas of marketing research activity in this book reflects existing practices in the field. The major difference in emphasis between this and other books on the subject lies in the much greater emphasis the latter place on the survey technique. This book covers the survey technique, but accords that single tool the emphasis it warrants as merely one important element in the broad marketing research picture.

There is a tendency for anyone who has been continually active in a field as long as I have been active in marketing research to develop a picture of the field which is heavily influenced by individual background and interest. As a safeguard against describing marketing research as I think it is rather than as it really is, I conducted for the American Management Association a comprehensive survey. That survey provided an objective and detailed picture of what marketing research *really* includes. I am indebted to the AMA for permission to reproduce here portions of the report I prepared for them.

This book is intended to develop familiarity with two viewpoints toward marketing research. One viewpoint is that of a top-management executive, who properly looks on research as only one of the tools available to him in securing the facts needed to guide an important decision. In its attention to the viewpoint of top management, this book parallels many other books, including those which use the case approach to management problems. The second viewpoint—which receives greater emphasis than the first—is that of the marketing research practitioner, who must accept assignments given to him and execute them to the best of his ability with the resources at his command. The latter viewpoint is emphasized because it is likely to be of more immediate use to those who read this book.

Space requirements force the writer of a book about marketing research today to make many difficult decisions as to what material should be included and what excluded. A point of view which has influenced many of my decisions on content should be noted. The *general* subject of research methodology in the social sciences is far more fully and adequately covered in available books than is the *specific* subject of how those research techniques can be and are applied in the solution of *marketing* problems. The marketing viewpoint is more heavily emphasized here than is research in any general or abstract sense.

A competent marketing research man today is required to be familiar with and draw upon many different disciplines. It is unfortunately no longer possible for the writer of a book about marketing research to undertake to supply all required information from such relevant fields as statistics, as part of his treatment of the subject. In this book subjects like graphic presentation and the like, which are adequately covered elsewhere, are therefore not included. Where background information is needed, appropriate sources are suggested. The pages which might be devoted to such subjects are instead concentrated on expanding the treatment of those aspects of marketing research which would otherwise receive inadequate attention.

One overlap between marketing research and an allied field is inescapable. Sampling is covered at considerable length in this book, even though it is also included in most elementary books about statistical methods. Sampling is treated at such great length here because it is of paramount importance as an element of a marketing research education. The sampling discussion offered here is confined to practical applications in the field of marketing research, with a minimum treatment of the theoretical aspects which are so well covered elsewhere.

An attempt is made in this book to encourage the reader to participate in the actual analytical processes involved, first in crystallizing and then subdividing actual marketing problems, and then in determining the research approach most suitable. I feel that such participation is far more rewarding and helpful to the reader in understanding the research process than the descriptive approach which is more commonly used.

Throughout the book an attempt has been made to share with the reader many of the judgments and conclusions which have emerged from my years of work in marketing research. Case material has been included to provide more specific and detailed illustrations of *marketing research in action* than it would be possible to develop through text alone. Note that important concepts are presented in the cases as well as in the text. Therefore the reader who skips the cases through a feeling that they are a pedagogic device of interest primarily to teachers and students in formal classes will thereby deprive himself of much of the meat of this book.

All examples used in the text and cases are drawn from actual situations. No hypothetical or fictitious companies are included. Where company sales data are presented, they have been adjusted to avoid disclosure of confidential material. A fictitious company name is often required to preserve the anonymity of the company. Occasional modification of product identity to serve the same purpose has also been necessary.

With a full recognition of the difficulties that objective involves, an attempt has been made to make this book useful both as a college text and as a guide to workers in the field. Most authors hope to achieve that dual objective, yet few succeed. It is particularly important in a book about marketing research, because the classroom and practice are so close together. Many advances in practice have stemmed directly from the classroom and from the extracurricular activities of teachers of the subject. To aid teachers in using this book as a text, a considerable amount of supplementary material has been presented in a separate Manual for Teachers.

This book has been in preparation for more than five years. Those have been years of great activity in marketing research, and frequent revision of already-written material has been necessary to keep the book abreast of developments. Over those years, many contributions to its emphasis and direction have been made by more individuals than it is possible to mention by name. In some instances credit is given in the text to those who have helped in sharpening a viewpoint or an example. I am sorry that it is not possible to credit specifically all those who have helped me.

There are four groups of individuals to whom I am especially grateful.

The first group consists of the "elder statesmen" in marketing research. Some of them have moved on to broader management responsibilities. Some have retired, others have died. Some are still contributing effectively to the growing importance of the field. In this group are Wroe Alderson, Theodore H. Brown, John Caples, Frank Conant, Don Hobart, Paul Lazarsfeld, Henry C. Link, William J. Riley, Everett R. Smith, Daniel Starch, L. D. H. Weld, Henry G. Weaver, and many others. My indebtedness is particularly great to Donald R. G. Cowan for his advice and encouragement; to Fred Clark, to Robert Elder, to George Gallup, and to Harry Deane Wolfe.

The second group includes many practitioners of marketing research.

Those who have been especially helpful include Paul E. J. Gerhold, A. W. Harding, Fred Haviland, Jr., William Huesner, Gordon A. Hughes, James F. Merriman, Gene Olson, Ralph Stevens, Palmer Waterbury, Fred Willis, and Stanley Womer. Lee McDonald read the sampling chapters and made many helpful suggestions for their improvement.

The third group is made up of teachers of marketing subjects. My colleagues on the faculty of Northwestern University who have been especially helpful on many occasions include Ira Anderson, Richard Clewett, Harper Boyd, Ralph Westfall, and James R. Hawkinson. Other teachers who have given generously of their time and counsel include Helen G. Canoyer, Lincoln Clark, Joel Dean, Robert Ferber, Albert W. Frey, Lawrence C. Lockley, Glenn N. Merry, Joseph Seibert, and Roland S. Vaile.

The fourth group includes my associates William F. Suhring, Sharon Siegan, and Ruth Ebeling.

My indebtedness to Steuart Henderson Britt for his patient encouragement and friendly, helpful counsel is especially great. Without his aid, this book would never have been completed.

This inadequate recognition of my very considerable indebtedness to colleagues in the field is not intended to saddle them with the limitations of this book, for which my own responsibility is complete.

Marketing research is my business. It is a challenging, exciting field in which a day's work is typically spiced by an endless succession of new problems. It is in my opinion one of the last frontiers among business skills. It holds out a rich promise of intellectual stimulation and reward to those who take the not-inconsiderable trouble required to achieve competence in it. If this book communicates to its readers even in a partial sense some of the challenges marketing research can offer a serious worker in the field, the time spent in its preparation will have been richly repaid.

Richard D. Crisp.

18 Yorkshire Woods
Elmhurst, Ill.

Contents

IV. MAJOR AREAS OF RESEARCH APPLICATION IN MARKETING

V. RESEARCH IN NONMANUFACTURING ORGANIZATIONS

Introduction to the Marketing Research Process

CHAPTER 1

Nature and Scope of Marketing Research

Business activity today may be divided on a functional basis into three major phases—production, finance, and marketing. *Marketing* includes all business activities required to move goods or services from the hands of manufacturers or producers into the hands of the final consumer. *Research* connotes critical and searching study and investigation, whether of a problem, a proposed course of action, a hypothesis, or a theory. A definition of marketing research which is suitable for the purposes of this book may be synthesized from the above comments:

> *Marketing research is the systematic, objective, and exhaustive search for and study of the facts relevant to any problem in the field of marketing.*

While this is *a* definition of marketing research, it should not be regarded as *the* definition. At this stage in its development, marketing research is still pushing forward its frontiers in many directions. Therefore no single definition is yet accepted by all who are active in the field as delineating the true nature and scope of marketing research.[1]

[1] Some of the terms used to describe the field of marketing research, or parts of that field, have been used in published material in ways that are likely to be confusing to a newcomer to the field. The American Marketing Association has focused a considerable amount of constructive attention on the problem of definitions in an attempt to eliminate or reduce that confusion. The following comment by a committee of the Association may be helpful in clarifying the relationships between some of the terms occasionally used in marketing research literature:

> *Marketing Research* is the inclusive term which embraces all research activities carried on in connection with the management of marketing work. It includes various subsidiary types of research such as *Market Analysis, Sales Research* which is largely an analysis of the sales records of a company, *Consumer Research* which is concerned chiefly with the discovery and analysis of consumer attitudes, reactions and preferences, and *Advertising Research* which is carried

WHAT DOES MARKETING RESEARCH INCLUDE?

Marketing research encompasses a wide range of activities. Those activities are sometimes divided for convenience into research on *products or services,* research on *markets,* and research on *sales methods or policies.* That basis of classification identifies the three general areas within which most specific marketing research projects fall, and thus helps to provide a frame of reference helpful to newcomers to the field in achieving a general perspective as to the nature and scope of marketing research.

There is some danger, however, that the importance of this subdivision of the field may be overemphasized. In practice the border lines separating those three areas are often blurred almost beyond recognition. It is not unusual for an individual research project to include work in all three of those areas.

Research on Products or Services

Here are examples of the type of research projects usually included in this category:

1. Studies of the competitive position of a company's products in its industry or industries. For example, what share of the total ready-to-eat cereal market does Wheaties control? What proportion of the total market for portable saws do the products of Skil, Inc., represent?

2. Economic research, including the study of trends in industry volume and of the relationship between company or industry sales and economic indicators. For example, forecasts of the level of building activity generally are often used as guides to sales opportunities by manufacturers of building materials. Trends in the level of consumer incomes have a bearing on the future sales expectations of most consumer products. Studies of business plans for expansion provide clues to future market opportunities for many types of industrial products.

3. Studies comparing the consumer or customer acceptance of a company's products or services with that of similar products or services offered by competitors. For example, how well do consumers like a variety of Swanson's canned whole chicken packed in butter gravy, compared with a Banquet product packed in broth?

4. Studies of the dissatisfaction, and the sources of that dissatisfaction, with a company's products, among present or former customers. When sales volume declines on a product, this type of research is often indi-

---

on chiefly as an aid to the management of advertising work. The term *market research* is often loosely used as synonymous with *marketing research.*

From the 1948 Report of the Definitions Committee, American Marketing Association, *The Journal of Marketing,* October, 1948, p. 211.

cated as one clue to a possible cause of the sales decline. It is also widely used to guide product-improvement research of a technical nature.

5. Studies of present or new uses for the company's products. There are many instances in marketing of significant market expansion for a product or type of product resulting from the discovery and/or promotion of one or more new uses for the product. For example, sales of Kraft's Philadelphia brand cream cheese shot upward when advertising was used to promote the product as an ingredient in a recipe for cake frosting. This expanded the potential volume for that type of product tremendously. Studies of product uses (or applications) are especially important among manufacturers of industrial products.

6. Appraisals of new competitive products or of competitive new-product developments or modifications. Management must be ever alert to the threat posed by any new-product development by a competitor. Marketing research helps to identify significant product innovations, as distinguished from those which are minor in their impact on the consumer or customer. When Lever Brothers introduced Chlorodent tooth paste, with chlorophyll as an ingredient, and promoted it with a breath-deodorizing story, every dentifrice manufacturer had to appraise that development. Subsequent major innovations in dentifrices—enzyme-containing formulations, fluoride formulas, etc.—posed the same type of problem. Similarly, the growing use of detergents for washing dishes and clothes posed a problem for each producer of a soap product used for those purposes.

7. Studies aimed at product elimination or line simplification. As a result of continuing new-product developments, the product line of a manufacturer sometimes becomes too complex, volume per item declines, and unit production costs tend to rise. At such times, an objective reappraisal of the present and potential volume opportunities which each product represents is often a helpful guide in simplifying and pruning the product line.

8. Packaging research including design or physical characteristics. The trend to self-service in grocery and drug retailing made a re-examination of the characteristics of products sold through those outlets desirable. Product characteristics (like the length of shelf life of a food product) often pose important packaging problems which research can help to answer. Determining the consumer acceptance of a packaging innovation (such as the spray-type container for shaving cream) is another illustration of packaging research.

Research on Markets

Here are some of the more important specific activities usually included in this classification:

1. Analysis of the size of the market for specific products. It is necessary to know the size of the total market, or industry volume, before one can determine how large a competitive share a particular company's volume represents. This type of analysis is used as an aid in sales forecasting, which is itself a most important area of marketing research activity.

2. Analysis of territorial sales opportunities or potentials. This includes general studies, which might be used to help determine whether a company should expand into a particular geographical area or whether to build a warehouse in some specific city or section. Also included are more specific studies in which an attempt is made to break down the national total market for a particular product into its territorial components.

3. Analysis of characteristics of the market for specific products. A detailed knowledge of the characteristics of the market for a product has many applications. For example, attempts to secure distribution in retail outlets in low-income neighborhoods for a consumer product used mostly by high-income families would be relatively wasteful. Similarly, the knowledge that corn syrups like Karo are used to a far greater extent by families living in small towns and on farms than by big-city families is useful in many aspects of marketing and advertising planning.

4. Studies of trends in market size by products. Shifts are constantly taking place in consumer and customer preferences which have significant marketing implications. A decline in the proportion of women who used cake-type make-up produced problems for an organization like Max Factor & Co. which controlled a dominant share of total consumption of such products. The long-continuing decline in consumption of family flour and the rapid expansion in volume on prepared cake mixes are other examples.

5. Studies of economic factors affecting sales volume and opportunities. This might include analyses of the level of consumer credit, which would have a bearing on sales expectations for products with a large purchase price like automobiles or color-television sets. Similarly, the level of interest rates might influence business-expansion plans and sales opportunities on many types of products. This area is closely related to the more general area of economic research already mentioned.

6. Studies of shifts in the nature of the market. Included would be shifts in the relative importance of different sections of the country as markets (with the South and West long gaining at a more rapid rate than the rest of the country). Studies of trends in the age distribution of the population, which led the H. J. Heinz Co. to explore a line of geriatric foods, would also fall under this heading.

7. Studies of changes in customer-type importance. Steel producers

know how their output is divided among various types of customers. Shifts in the relative importance of different types of customers might necessitate adjustments in production capacity to produce a different "product mix." In consumer-product marketing, the increase in the sale of nonfood products like shampoos through grocery supermarkets required readjustment of sales-coverage plans.

Research on Sales Methods and Policies

Marketing research activities in this area typically include such specific functions as these:

1. Measuring territorial variations in sales yield, market share, sales effectiveness. If we define a sales territory as the area covered by a single salesman, it is apparent that many sales-management decisions require detailed knowledge extending down to the sales territorial level. Without a knowledge of territorial variations in sales yield, management has no way of separating its strong territories from its weak ones, hence no way of concentrating remedial attention where it is most needed.

2. Establishment or revision of sales territories. This is a never-ending sales-management task, as growth increases volume and requires a larger sales force or as market shifts occur making a former territorial assignment unprofitable or otherwise undesirable. Marketing research supplies facts helpful in establishing or revising sales territories.

3. Studies of the distribution of products. Lack of product availability is an element in many sales problems. Studies of the extent to which a company's products have distribution, often related to the extent to which competitive products are available, are a widely performed marketing research activity.

4. Measuring the effectiveness of individual salesmen. Where a substantial part of a company's selling expense consists of the salaries and expenses of its field sales organization, it is standard practice to use marketing research to measure the extent to which those salesmen are contributing to the company's progress.

5. Evaluation of existing sales methods. There are many alternative ways of accomplishing a sales goal. A company making industrial products, for example, might sell direct to customers or instead choose to sell through one or more types of middlemen such as mill-supply houses. An evaluation of the sales volume and profit expectations which such alternatives present is aided by facts developed through marketing research.

Research on New Products

Marketing research plays an important role in developing and launching new products. Such research includes activities in all three of the areas indentified above. Here is a brief indication of some of the more important marketing research activities in the field of new-product development:

1. Estimating demand for new products. A decision to launch a new product is ordinarily preceded by an evaluation of the sales opportunities such a product represents. Marketing research contributes by developing estimates of demand and by determining the characteristics of the market for the proposed product. The latter point is particularly important because the "fit" between the proposed new product and existing products is likely to influence sales costs and profitability. The makers of Johnson's wax considered the possibility of adding shoe polish to their line, but decided not to enter that market when research revealed that it would require sales coverage of entirely new types of customers, with resulting increases in selling expenses.

2. Determining consumer or customer acceptance of proposed new product or service. Marketing research is used to determine whether a proposed new product has the characteristics consumers or customers seek and whether it can compete effectively with existing products in building customer acceptance.

3. Evaluating elements in the proposed new-product introductory program. When the consumer acceptance of a proposed new product or service has been found to be satisfactory, detailed plans for its introduction must be created. Management must decide where, how, and when the new product should be launched. Answering the "where" question requires a knowledge of variations in consumption patterns. In the case of consumer products, sectional and city-size variations are often important. In the case of industrial products, a knowledge of relative potential consumption by different industries and of the geographic distribution of potential customers in each industry is required. The "when" question requires a knowledge of seasonal variations in sales in some cases. The "how" question may involve tests of different promotional devices like "deals," premiums, and the like.

4. Measuring progress in the sale of a new product. After the new product has been launched, marketing research continues to appraise progress and to provide management with facts about its success in achieving planned-for volume on the new product.

Two comments about the above list of activities may be helpful in providing additional perspective. First, this list includes the most widely performed marketing research activities reported in an actual study of the marketing research practices of 180 organizations.[2] Second, this list somewhat overemphasizes marketing research activities from the view-

---

[2] Richard D. Crisp, *Company Practices in Marketing Research,* American Management Association Research Report 22, New York, 1953.

point of manufacturers. That emphasis is desirable at this point because manufacturers are the dominant source of marketing research and provide a sound starting point in developing familiarity with practices in the field. Differences between manufacturing and nonmanufacturing organizations in marketing research activities and practices will be described in detail in later chapters.

MARKETING RESEARCH IS A MANAGEMENT TOOL

Growth in the size of business enterprises has increased the complexity of management's task. There have been changes both in the scale and in the nature of the problems with which management must deal. Specialized tools have been developed to aid management in coping with its increasingly complex problems. Marketing research is one such tool. Cost accounting is another. Industrial engineering, which includes time-and-motion study and methods analysis, is a third. In the interest of balanced perspective, it is desirable to remember that marketing research represents only one small but increasingly important part of the broad spectrum of specialized skills which together constitute business management.

It may be helpful to remember that marketing research is by no means unique as a *type* of management tool. It closely parallels in its objectives and in its approach to marketing problems other very similar functions in other divisions of a business. The primary difference between industrial engineering and marketing research, for example, is that industrial engineering is concerned with production problems and techniques while marketing research is focused on marketing problems. Industrial engineering and marketing research do differ in their techniques, because the particular approaches each uses have been developed to fit the characteristics of the problems studied.

PRIMARY FUNCTION: TO AID EXECUTIVE JUDGMENT

The job of today's executive is a complex one which involves a vast number of appraisals and decisions. Marketing research helps executives to do their jobs better and helps to make their jobs easier by providing facts upon which to base executive decisions. Marketing research is essentially an advisory function, which helps to raise the level of executive performance by narrowing the area within which the executive must rely on judgment alone.

Marketing research *supplements* executive judgment. It is *not* a substitute for that judgment. Perspective on this point is extremely important. It cannot be stated too emphatically that marketing research ordinarily provides *only part* of the answer to most marketing problems. Executive judgment, based on a combination of experience, training, and intuition, must arrive at decisions. Marketing research provides facts which help to make those decisions sound.

AREAS OF CONTRIBUTION

Here is an outline of the executive job, as developed by Dr. Richard Donham and Dr. Leon A. Bosch at Northwestern University:

1. Sizing up the situation. What's the problem?
2. Drawing up a plan:
    a. Defining the objective. What should be done?
    b. Visualizing the job. How can we do it?
3. Setting up the administrative organization. Who is going to do it?
4. Following through: Executive control. Are they doing it, and with what results?

This outline is helpful in illustrating some of the points at which marketing research can and does contribute to the performance of executives. In the process of sizing up the situation and defining the problem, many questions must be asked. Some of those questions can be answered by marketing research. In defining the objective, the executive is confronted by the task of appraising a number of possible alternative courses of action. Marketing research can help with that appraisal. In visualizing the job, alternatives must again be weighed. Marketing research can contribute facts to aid in that evaluation. In the follow-through step, marketing research can provide facts helpful in measuring the degree of success achieved in the earlier steps.

AREAS OF APPLICATION

As a management tool, marketing research is characterized by great versatility. It can be used with profit by firms making and selling consumer products, industrial products, or both consumer and industrial products. It can be used on tangible products or on intangibles, including most types of services. It can be used by retailers and wholesalers as well as by manufacturers. The fact is not widely recognized, but marketing research can be used effectively even in a *part* of the activities of an organization as well as in the whole.

The last point is an important one. It means that an executive with marketing responsibilities need not be in the top-management bracket to apply marketing research methods. Someone farther down the management ladder—say at the district manager's level, with a staff of several salesmen under his supervision—can profitably apply marketing research to his own area of responsibilities.

As a direct corollary of its versatility, marketing research as a field of study is very complex. As defined above, marketing research consists of the search for and study of the facts relevant to a problem in the field of marketing. Since marketing research can be applied in so many different types of business situations, each with its own galaxy of problems and elements of uniqueness, that complexity is inescapable.

CHARACTERISTICS OF APPROACH USED

Because of its inherent complexity, it is not possible to cover all the combinations and permutations of marketing research applications in a single book. The approach used in this book has these characteristics:

1. Primary emphasis is placed on the broad field of marketing research and on developing a picture of marketing research in action rather than on parts of the field.

2. An approach to marketing problems and their solution is described and developed which is applicable, with some modification, in most types of business situations.

3. The major specific areas of marketing research activity are described at considerable length.

4. The influence of variations in the situation of a particular research worker on the approach taken to a particular problem is pointed out wherever such variations are of significance.

WHAT IS THE STATE OF THE ART?

Fields of management skills, like individuals, move through certain well-defined stages in their progress from early beginnings toward maturity. Where does marketing research stand, on that progressive scale? Certainly marketing research is no longer in its infancy. The past decade or two might be described as a period of rather troubled adolescence. Today marketing research evidences unmistakable signs of growth in stature and maturity. While still perhaps not fully mature, marketing research clearly stands at the threshold of its most productive years. Many years of vigorous and significant progress, through ever-increasing contributions to the progress of management skills, lie ahead.

In moving out of its period of adolescence, marketing research has undergone a major transition. With marketing research as with individuals, a lack of perspective was one of the more marked symptoms of adolescence. That lack of perspective is evident in much of the early and even relatively recent literature of the subject. Distortion of parts of the picture occurred. An example is provided by the great emphasis which has been placed on the survey technique. Some of the textbooks in marketing research were completely devoted to the survey or questionnaire approach. Others, while adopting a somewhat broader frame of reference, placed tremendous emphasis on consumer surveys. Still other books placed their major stress on sampling methods, which are useful primarily in the execution of formal surveys. This represented emphasis on *a part of a part* of the broad field of marketing research.

AN INTEGRATED VIEWPOINT EMERGES

What change has occurred to support the conclusion that adolescence is now behind marketing research, and a period of powerful growth and increasing contribution ahead? That change is signaled by the emergence of a marketing research function—not yet in textbooks, but certainly in business practice—which has crystallized into a unified whole and which has demonstrated its ability to improve marketing management practice. The viewpoint of marketing research in practice is one which can perhaps best be described as an integrated one.

In the period of its adolescence, marketing research placed emphasis on this or that technique, its advantages and limitations; on this or that sampling approach, with its advantages and limitations. With the emergence of an integrated approach, the focus has changed. Instead of its past preoccupation with techniques, marketing research today is primarily concerned with the problem or problems to which it can contribute. Depending on the nature of the problem, various types of information are necessary. Depending on the types of information sought and the importance of the problem, various techniques may be used. The techniques are the tools of the marketing research practitioner. It is only by knowing all his tools intimately that he has the background needed to select those best suited to a particular assignment. But the technique tools are only means to an end. *The problem to be solved is the starting point.* Today's marketing research executive begins with a study of the problem and then selects from his technique tool chest those tools which fit the requirements of the problem at hand.

Since that is the way marketing research is carried on in practice, that is the way marketing research is described in this book. The starting point is the problem. Techniques are described, but always against the background of the types of problems for which they are best suited and most frequently employed.

Perhaps the relationships might be clarified by use of a more familiar field as an illustration. A golfer steps up to the tee. *His problem* is to get the ball into the hole with the smallest possible number of strokes. He has a bag of clubs, each different, designed for a different set of circumstances. The golfer must know what each club can do, in order to select the proper club for each shot. He chooses the club for a particular shot only after studying such factors as distance to the hole, wind, size of green, location and type of traps, etc. After study, he uses the club for each stroke that seems best suited to the situation.

The golf illustration can be extended to illustrate some additional points inherent in marketing research practice. The problem, as noted, is to get the ball into the hole. But the golfer subdivides that problem. Each stroke becomes a separate subproblem in itself. Similarly in marketing research, subdivision of major problems is standard practice. Until after a golfer plays one shot and sees where the ball stops rolling, he often doesn't know what club he'll use on the following stroke. Similarly in marketing research, the results of one phase of the analysis of a complex problem often influence the nature of the next step in the research. To hole out this illustration, past overemphasis on surveys represents a tendency to use one club too much while failing to use other clubs often better adapted to some problem situations. A shift to an integrated approach to marketing research has resulted in a better-balanced game and a reduced handicap!

CONTINUING GROWTH LIKELY

The depression years following 1929 demonstrated the inability of the marketing methods then in use to move merchandise and keep factory wheels turning against the current of an economic depression. The search for more effective marketing methods stimulated by depression experiences has continued, with some wartime relaxation, to the present day. The use of marketing research as a management tool has been undergoing irregular but continuing growth since the early 1930s. A continuing expansion of marketing research activities in the future may be predicted confidently.

That expansion appears inevitable partly because the growth of marketing research is not an isolated phenomenon. Rather, it is part of a much broader expansion—the expansion of the staff function, which has been stimulated by growth in the size and complexity of modern business. The Graduate School of Business of Stanford University intensively studied the management policies and practices of thirty-one leading industrial corporations in 1939 and 1940. The report[3] of their research included this comment on the place of staff specialists in the organization picture:

[3] Paul E. Holden, Lounsbury S. Fish, and Hubert L. Smith, *Top-management Organization and Control*, McGraw-Hill, New York, 1951, p. 36.

As the managerial process grows in complexity, the time, ability and comprehension of single executives become increasingly inadequate and must be supplemented by staff agencies able to furnish specialized assistance and advice. An adequate staff organization, designed to take full advantage of specialized knowledge, concentrated attention, unified effort and definite accountability for results within its appropriate fields, can go a long way toward relieving the burden and increasing the effectiveness of management.

The same study emphasized another point which is frequently overlooked in discussing the extent to which a staff function like marketing research is used by business. The authors pointed out that setting up a staff department does not necessarily create a new function, but rather often concentrates specialized attention upon certain phases of management problems as those reach extensive proportions. They commented:[4]

> Before emerging as the specific activities of full-fledged staff agencies, the same functions are found scattered among various individuals in different departments. As the business grows in size and complexity, it becomes increasingly necessary and profitable to set up a well-qualified agency to concentrate upon achievement of desired objectives within each logical field, rather than to rely upon the casual interest and variable understanding of individuals and agencies to whom it is often of secondary concern. In many cases a company does not realize that is is overdue for specialization in some such field, and that it is already paying the price of a fully effective staff agency without securing the benefits of specialized attention.

IS IT SCIENTIFIC?

The existence of basic differences in viewpoint within a rapidly developing field like marketing research is to be expected. Such differences are usually a healthy sign. Disagreement serves to stimulate study and to accelerate progress. A brief review at this point of one controversial aspect of marketing research may provide helpful background for subsequent discussion. The controversy revolves around the question of whether or not marketing research is scientific. A subsidiary but related controversy is concerned with the importance of *scientific method* in marketing research.

One school of thought considers scientific method to be an important and essential element in marketing research. That viewpoint is apparent from the fact that some writers incorporate scientific method as an element in their definition of marketing research. Lyndon O. Brown,[5] for example, defines marketing and distribution research as "the use of

[4] *Ibid.*, p. 36.
[5] *Marketing and Distribution Research*, Ronald, New York, 1955.

scientific method in the solution of marketing or distribution problems."
Other writers[6] reveal their appraisal of the importance of scientific
method to a study of marketing research by devoting considerable space
to the characteristics of scientific method in their description of the
methods of marketing research.

An opposed viewpoint is held by many thoughtful students of the
subject who have concluded that marketing today is not a science. In
discussing the field of sales management, which he defines so broadly
that it is nearly synonymous with marketing, Harry R. Tosdal of Harvard
University commented:[7]

> Sales management is an art, not a science. No classified body of knowl-
> edge has been developed apart from other sciences which would enable
> one to speak logically of the science of sales management.

Most marketing practitioners are likely to agree with Dr. Tosdal that
marketing today is not a science. Neither is marketing research a
science. Although there is rather wide agreement on the latter point, it
is often tinged with regret. If marketing research is not a science, how
may workers in the field benefit from the high regard in which things
scientific are widely held? How may they share in the honorific status
of scientists? One approach is to adopt the method or methods of
science. The line of reasoning involved goes something like this: What
distinguishes the world of science from nonscientific fields is its method.
Let us adopt scientific method as our own and apply it in our field. By
the process of adoption, then, marketing research becomes, if not a
science, at least "scientific."

It may be worth noting in passing that not all scientists agree that
there *is* such a thing as scientific method in this sense. To some extent
the controversy over the place of scientific method in marketing research
is little more than a ripple on a far broader and more turbulent controversy. The opinions on this subject of James B. Conant, expressed
while he was president of Harvard University, have more authoritative
weight than those of most writers on marketing research. Dr. Conant
pointed out:[8]

> One of the most significant discussions now in progress turns on how
> far the methods by which the astonishing results in pure and applied
> science have been achieved may be transferred to other human activities.
> Among the questions on which learned and sincere men now disagree are

[6] James H. Lorie and Harry V. Roberts, *Basic Methods of Marketing Research*,
McGraw-Hill, New York, 1951.

[7] Harry R. Tosdal, *Introduction to Sales Management*, 4th ed., McGraw-Hill, New
York, 1957, p. 4.

[8] James B. Conant, *On Understanding Science*, Yale University Press, New Haven,
Conn., 1947, p. 20.

the following: Is there such a thing as scientific method of wide applicability in the solution of human problems? Is there any significant difference between research in basic science (or pure science) and in applied science? Are the social sciences (psychology, anthropology, political economy, economics and history) really sciences? If not, can they become so?

Unquestionably marketing research has much in common with scientific research in other fields. For example, the characteristics which the skilled worker in marketing research requires—notably including objectivity, freedom from bias, a searching, challenging curiosity, a knowledge of the limitations of his data, and a creative mind—are the characteristics found among successful research workers in pure science. There are close similarities of method as well. Some of the methods of marketing research are nearly identical with methods used in research in some sciences. Yet those resemblances are insufficient, in the opinion of many workers in the field, to support adequately the claim or viewpoint that marketing research consists of the application of scientific method to marketing problems. As Dr. Conant adds:[9]

> To say that all impartial and accurate analyses of facts are examples of the scientific method is to add confusion beyond measure to the problems of understanding science.

ADVANTAGES OF A DIRECT APPROACH

The above discussion of the controversial question of the role of scientific method in marketing research was included to help clarify an understanding of the approach to marketing research methods used in this book. Emphasis here is primarily on the practice of marketing research, and only in a secondary and minor way on its theory, which is still in its formative stages. This book has been prepared both as a guide to the student and as a useful handbook for workers in the field. The approaches and methods which are here described are widely used in marketing research practice. Those methods have some advantages and many limitations. The fact that they are being widely used indicates that *under the circumstances actually existing in marketing research practice,* the advantages often outweigh the limitations.

The methods are presented in this book and recommended to your attention because they have met and passed the test of practicality. These methods are not "scientific." They do not pretend to be. This represents a direct approach to marketing research which has some advantages for the student of this subject. No background in the history or theory of scientific method is necessary to understand this book. The point has already been made that some of the methods described here have much in common with methods of research used in other fields. A discussion

[9] *Ibid.,* p. 25.

of the similarities and differences would perhaps be appropriate in a book on the comparative methodology of different disciplines. It would be out of place here and would divert valuable space and attention from the main purposes of a book about marketing research practice as it is rather than as someone feels it should be.

FUNDAMENTAL VIEWPOINT TOWARD RESEARCH COSTS

A comment was made above about the fact that marketing research is only one of the tools available to management executives for improving the effectiveness of their operations. Like other tools of the same type, marketing research functions within an essentially cost-conscious business environment. The existence of that environment makes it necessary to introduce a fundamental viewpoint of great importance.

The viewpoint in question pervades the entire field of marketing research and will be referred to at least implicitly in almost every chapter of this book. That viewpoint is an essential ingredient in the planning phase of every soundly conceived marketing research job. It exercises a veto power over many proposed research projects. The viewpoint in question is concerned with the relationship between the *cost* of marketing research and the *results achieved.*

Business uses marketing research primarily as a tool to help increase its marketing efficiency. An increase in the marketing efficiency of a given firm can be achieved in several ways—by selling more goods or services with no increase in marketing costs, by selling the same quantity of goods or services on a reduced investment in marketing costs, and so on. Regardless of the direction in which increased marketing efficiency is sought, this point cannot be overlooked: *The cost of the marketing research is itself one of the components of the total marketing costs.*

The significance of this viewpoint to a businessman concerned with his net-profit position is clear. Unless the benefits achieved by a given research project outweigh the cost of the research itself, that project represents an investment of dubious soundness. *Every expenditure for marketing research represents a calculated risk by the management authorizing the expenditure.* That is as true of the general expense of creating and maintaining a marketing research department as it is for the specific costs of a particular research project.

From the viewpoint of management, an investment in marketing research does not differ significantly from an investment in new machinery or in a new building. In each case, the investment is made *because it is expected to pay off.* Every dollar spent for research is an additional dollar of expense, and decreases net profits by one dollar. Unless the research increases net profits by an amount substantially in excess of its costs, that research is not paying its way.

This does not mean that marketing research can or should be expected to be *immediately* self-liquidating. It is extremely difficult to evaluate the profit contribution of many research jobs. However, this viewpoint does mean that when any specific research project is under consideration the "pay-off period" for that research, or the likelihood that it will *increase profits by substantially more than its costs*, should be carefully considered before the research job is authorized.

This fundamental viewpoint may perhaps seem too obvious to deserve mention. It is almost universally recognized by management executives. Unfortunately, it is not always recognized by those who are closer to the field of marketing research. Men active in marketing research occasionally complain about the relatively small investment made in marketing research, in contrast to the larger investment in other types of research. Typical of this viewpoint was the article entitled "85¢ for Product Research; Only 15¢ for Market Research: Why?" which Philip Salisbury wrote and published in *Sales Management* magazine.[10] The implication of such complaints is that management is short-sighted in spending so little on marketing research. They typically overlook this key point: Management does not spend more for marketing research simply because it has not yet been convinced that larger expenditures for marketing research would *increase net profits*.

SUMMARY

1. For the purposes of this book, marketing research may be defined as the systematic, objective, and exhaustive search for and study of the facts relevant to any problem in the field of marketing.

2. Marketing research activities are sometimes divided for convenience into research on products or services; research on markets; research on sales methods and policies; and research on new products. The latter category overlaps all three of the other areas and warrants individual identification only because of the great and increasing importance of new-product development.

3. A single research project often includes activities within all the major areas identified above. The border line between those areas is often shadowy.

4. Marketing research is a management tool, performing the same functions for marketing management that industrial engineering and methods analysis perform for production management and that cost accounting and internal auditing perform for financial management.

5. The primary function of marketing research is to aid executive judgment by contributing facts upon which to base decisions. Thus marketing research acts to narrow the area within which decisions must be made on judgment alone. But marketing research is *not* a substitute for executive judgment.

6. One characteristic of marketing research is its great versatility. It can be used by many different kinds of organizations.

[10] Mar. 15, 1950, p. 37.

7. Today marketing research is an integrated process which begins with the problem to be solved. The nature of the problem dictates the marketing research approach used.

8. The cost of marketing research represents expense, which like all expense acts to decrease profit. Every expenditure for marketing research represents a calculated risk by the management authorizing the expenditure. The expenditure is authorized in the expectation that the research will contribute more to profit than it costs, within a reasonable period of time. This is as true of the general expense of operating a research department as of the cost of a specific study or project. This is a fundamental viewpoint, which pervades every chapter of this book.

9. Whether marketing research is or is not scientific is a controversial question. The role of scientific method in marketing research is also subject to considerable disagreement. The point of view of this book is that marketing research is not scientific. While a knowledge of scientific methods represents helpful background for a worker in the field, that knowledge is not so essential that it warrants inclusion in an introductory book on the subject of marketing research. Marketing research is so complex that major problems of inclusion and exclusion of material are inescapable. Devoting as large a proportion of available attention as possible to the core of the subject seems a preferable approach.

QUESTIONS

1. Distinguish between marketing research, market research, consumer research, advertising research, and sales research.

2. What are the three major areas of marketing research activity? What is the relationship between research in the different areas?

3. Suggest additional specific activities in the areas of research on products, markets, and sales methods and policies which supplement the examples listed in this chapter.

4. Why do you feel that a distinction between research on *new products* and *product research* is necessary or desirable? Explain.

5. Essentially what type of a management tool is marketing research? What other similar *types* of tools are you familiar with?

6. How would you describe the primary function of marketing research?

7. The observation is sometimes made that marketing research today is *problem-oriented*. What does that mean?

8. Describe in your own words the relationship which exists between the cost of a proposed marketing research project and the profit contribution to be expected from that project. How can an executive estimate in advance what the profit contribution from a study is likely to be? What does the designation of marketing research expenditures as examples of *calculated risks* imply in this context?

CHAPTER 2

The Organization of
Marketing Research Activities

Although marketing research can be used by many different types of organizations, one type—the individual manufacturer—stands out as by far the most important user of marketing research. There are several reasons why manufacturers dominate the marketing research picture. One reason is immediately apparent. Almost every manufacturer continually and inescapably faces complex marketing problems. Manufacturers use more marketing research than nonmanufacturers, just as men with headaches use more aspirin than men without headaches! Another factor contributing to the extensive use of marketing research by manufacturers is the prevalence of relatively large-scale operations in manufacturing.

In the preceding chapter it was pointed out that growth in the use of marketing research is closely associated with and related to growth in the scale and complexity of business activities generally. Large-scale manufacturing leads to sales volume on a scale which permits a moderate investment in marketing research to consume only a very small share of the manufacturer's total income. To extend the illustration above, many manufacturers not only have marketing headaches—they also have the price of the aspirin. A further point worth noting is that functional specialization is a common organizational characteristic in large-scale manufacturing. Since marketing research is simply an additional type of functional specialization, it can be introduced without creating any serious organizational problems.

In addition to their own extensive activities in the field of marketing research, manufacturers also serve as the fountainhead which stimulates directly or indirectly most of the marketing research of a number of other types of organizations, such as trade associations, advertising agencies, and advertising media. This relationship is developed more fully later in this chapter. It is mentioned here as an additional reason why the manufacturer is the dominant element in the over-all picture of marketing research activities.

WHAT PROPORTION OF MANUFACTURERS DO MARKETING RESEARCH?

An important survey of the marketing research practices of manufacturers in the war-to-peace conversion year of 1945 was published in mimeographed form in 1946, under the title "Marketing Research in American Industry."[1] The report summarized the results of a mail survey covering companies that were members of the National Association of Manufacturers.[2] The American Marketing Association, through a committee of outstanding practitioners of marketing research, assumed responsibility for the execution and reporting of this survey of NAM member companies. This NAM-AMA survey reported that almost 38 per cent of the 4,786 companies responding to the questionnaire reported doing marketing research of some kind, either through an organized marketing research department or as one of the responsibilities of a line executive. For the purposes of that study, a company was considered to have a marketing research department if it had one or more employees engaged full time in performing any one or more of the sixteen marketing research functions listed on the questionnaire.

The mail survey indicated that at the time of the study about six companies out of ten were not performing any marketing research. This finding illustrates a problem in definition which deserves comment. Most companies that do marketing must inevitably perform some of the functions which are today widely recognized as falling within the field of marketing research. Sales forecasting, for example, is one of the most widely performed marketing research functions. Few companies can operate without some kind of forward estimate of sales volume. In many cases, especially in smaller companies, sales forecasting is essentially a a process of "guesstimating" rather than one of carefully developing fact-based estimates. Such sales forecasts lack the systematic, objective, and exhaustive search for facts included in the definition in the preceding chapter, hence would not qualify as marketing *research*. There is a sug-

---

[1] *Marketing Research in American Industry*, National Association of Manufacturers, New York, 1946, mimeographed. A slightly condensed version of this report will be found in *The Journal of Marketing*, April, 1947, pp. 338–354, and July, 1947, pp. 25–37. It is also reproduced in McNair and Hansen, *Readings in Marketing*, McGraw-Hill, New York, 1949, pp. 83–118.

[2] Because membership in the NAM involves a membership fee and is somewhat selective in nature, the membership of that association should not be regarded as representative of all manufacturing organizations. In particular, the NAM is likely to underrepresent the very small manufacturing organization.

gestion here that the respondent companies in the survey mentioned might well have had a concept of marketing research not too far from the one defined in this book.

MARKETING RESEARCH VARIES WITH SALES VOLUME

There is a very direct relationship between a company's size as measured by its annual sales volume and that company's marketing research activities. That relationship was illustrated in the report of the NAM-AMA study, as shown in Table 2.1. That table will reward careful

Table 2.1. Marketing Research Activity Reported by Company Sales Volume

(Per Cent)

Marketing research done:	All companies	Annual company sales volume			
		Under $500,000	$500,000– $2,500,000	$2,500,000– $5,000,000	Over $5,000,000
By marketing research department	11.3	1.8	6.7	17.9	44.6
As line-executive function	26.6	21.3	29.7	38.1	27.9
Subtotal performing marketing research	37.9	23.1	36.4	56.0	72.5
No marketing research reported	62.1	76.9	63.6	44.0	27.5
Total	100.0	100.0	100.0	100.0	100.0

SOURCE: *Marketing Research in American Industry*, National Association of Manufacturers, New York, 1946, chart II, p. 6a.

study. Note that only 23.1 per cent of those companies with sales volume below $500,000 annually participating in the survey reported any marketing research and that less than 2 per cent of those smaller companies reported that they had a full-time marketing research department. In contrast, 72.5 per cent of companies with sales volume above 5 million dollars a year reported some marketing research, and 44.6 per cent of the companies in that group reported a full-time marketing research department of one or more individuals.

This relationship is an important and natural one. There are more full-time marketing research departments in organizations with large sales volume just as there are more Cadillacs owned by individuals with large incomes. In each case, presence of the wherewithal is part of the explanation.

Consider this in somewhat more specific terms. Assume a hypothetical marketing research department, consisting of one man who had four or five years' experience in the field. Suppose his salary is $9,000 a year. He has a secretary, plus some additional clerical help occasionally. The total cost of the marketing research function in that company is, let's say, $15,000 a year. (As later chapters will make clear, this figure implies that his activities are almost entirely concerned with the analysis of internal data, but that implication is irrelevant to the present subject.) Translate that $15,000 into the proportion of a company's net sales in a company with $500,000 in annual volume. The expenditure represents 3 per cent of total sales. Another company with sales of 5 million dollars annually could hire the same department yet spend only one-tenth as large a share of its net-sales dollar for marketing research.

HOW MUCH IS SPENT FOR MARKETING RESEARCH?

In the illustration above, two widely varying rates of expenditure for marketing research are indicated—3 per cent of sales for the $500,000 company, and $\frac{3}{10}$ of 1 per cent of sales for the 5-million-dollar company. Which of those expenditure rates is more realistic? Which comes closer to approximating actual expenditure practices found among companies that use marketing research?

One answer to that question is provided by the NAM-AMA survey. That study reported that those companies supplying information on this point spent about .28 per cent of net sales for marketing research. That expenditure *rate* was highest (.37 per cent of sales) among companies with sales under $500,000, and lowest (.21 per cent of sales) among companies with sales over 5 million dollars. However, those expenditure data have two major limitations. First, the sample was made up to so large an extent of companies with relatively low sales volume that the data on expenditure rates among organizations with higher volume was not clear. Second, the survey was made in a period of reconversion to peacetime products and production, a fact which makes generalizations from the data somewhat hazardous.

When this book was planned, the need for a more detailed and current picture of actual practices in marketing research including expenditure rates was recognized. To secure such a picture, a study was planned and conducted under the sponsorship of the American Management Association.[3] The report of that study represents more adequately than did the NAM-AMA study what large companies do in the marketing research field. The expenditure-rate pattern disclosed by that survey is

[3] Richard D. Crisp, *Company Practices in Marketing Research,* American Management Association Research Report 22, 1953.

reproduced in Figure 2.1. That chart illustrates the variations in expenditure rates reported in a number of different sales-volume groups as revealed by that survey. In studying this chart it is very important to remember that the figures shown are *median* figures for the companies within each sales-volume group. There is a great deal of variation among the individual companies in each sales-volume group. This chart should

HOW MUCH DO THEY SPEND?

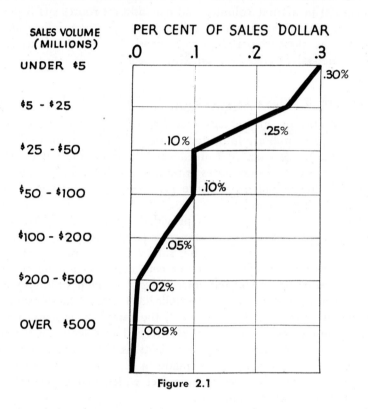

Figure 2.1

be regarded as illustrating the trend in expenditure rates as we move through a sales-volume scale.

INDIVIDUAL RESPONSIBILITY FOR MARKETING RESEARCH

The study by the American Management Association provides an indication of how the marketing research responsibility is assigned within the organization. Each company participating in that study was asked to identify by function the individual who handles marketing research.

The study made it possible to distinguish between cases in which it is the part-time responsibility of a line executive (such as sales manager, vice-president in charge of sales, etc.); the part-time responsibility of a staff executive (typically an "assistant to" a line executive) who spends a larger portion of his time on other types of work; or the full-time responsibility of an individual or department specializing in that activity.

The following table indicates the relative frequency with which those three possibilities were reported where only one was in use, and also the proportion of respondent organizations that contributed multiple replies because they divide responsibility for marketing research:

Table 2.2. How Marketing Research Is Handled

	Number	Per cent
Base: companies that do marketing research...................	168	100.0
Full-time responsibility of a specialized individual or department..	125	74.4
Part-time responsibility of a *line* executive.....................	20	11.9
Part-time responsibility of a *staff* executive.....................	12	7.1
Responsibility shared by two or more of above.................	7	4.2
Other replies..	3	1.8
No response..	1	.6

SOURCE: Richard D. Crisp, *Company Practices in Marketing Research*, American Management Research Report 22, table 5, p. 19, 1953.

Those companies reporting that marketing research was handled as the part-time responsibility of either a line or staff executive naturally tended to be in the lower sales-volume brackets. This relationship is illustrated graphically in Figure 2.2. The "small" companies are those with sales volume below 25 million dollars annually, with "medium" used to designate annual sales volume ranging upward from 25 million to 100 million dollars, and "large" for companies with annual volume above the latter figure. The use of full-time specialists increases, moving up the sales-volume scale, from 62 per cent in the companies with volume below 25 million dollars to 87 per cent in those above 100 million dollars.

The same chart illustrates also that the use of full-time specialists is more prevalent among manufacturers of consumer products than among manufacturers of industrial products. This pattern is related to the size distribution of the two types of manufacturers. Manufacturers of both consumer and industrial products, which tend to be larger companies in terms of annual volume, use specialists at about the same rate as consumer-product manufacturers. The group of nonmanufacturer respondents shown included service organizations, large retailing units (chain-

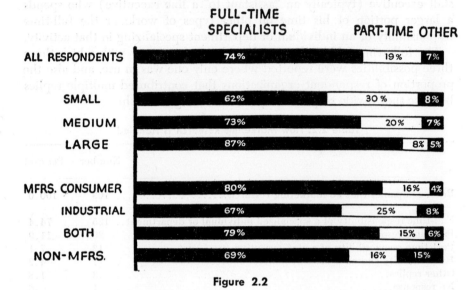

Figure 2.2

store organizations and large department stores), and similar types of businesses.

WHERE DOES MARKETING RESEARCH BELONG
ON THE ORGANIZATION CHART?

We move now to the consideration of a somewhat controversial question: Just where should the marketing research function fit into an organization chart in a manufacturing firm? Although objectivity *in* marketing research is one of the cardinal characteristics of a good marketing research man, objectivity *about* marketing research does not always follow. There is a well-nigh universal tendency for staff specialists to seek the highest possible level on the organization chart. With such a high-level position, both the specialty and the specialization achieve increased organizational stature. To this sort of functional ambition, marketing research men are by no means immune. Many marketing research men feel strongly that marketing research belongs on the highest organizational plane. If they had their way, the marketing research function would almost always report to the president, or perhaps to the executive vice-president, of an organization. The following quotation expresses this viewpoint persuasively and at some length.

Authoritative opinion in the field favors making the director of research responsible to an official with company-wide rather than departmental jurisdiction, as a means of securing a broader sphere of activity and more effective coordination of functions, eliminating self-interest, and encouraging greater objectivity both in the fact-finding process and in subsequent utilization of the facts.

This viewpoint is gaining increasing support from farsighted managerial personnel. Management is learning—from first-hand experience or from the experience of colleagues—that a research activity which is set up in a subordinate position and then expected to work on problems of broad scope and on a high level in the organization is very likely to run into difficulties.

What are the implications of the foregoing for the management which is evaluating its marketing research structure or laying the foundations for the development of this activity on an organized basis? Simply this: A decision must be made as to the level on which the research staff is to function, because fundamentally that may determine the magnitude of the problems properly falling within its scope. If, for example, the data derived from research studies is to assist in the evaluation of vice-presidential actions and decisions—both past and present—and if it is to provide suggestions and recommendations to the vice president, then the research director should be given the independence which reporting to the president affords. Likewise, if the studies are to embrace several divisions of the organization, the research work needs the coordinating influence either of a committee of officers or a senior officer, such as the president or executive vice president.

Those who support this view contend that if, for example, the research activity is set up under a vice president in charge of sales, its critical analyses will be confined to subordinate managerial responsibilities in the sales organization unless the vice president in charge of sales is extremely broad-gauge and welcomes suggestions and criticism, and the research director is unusually courageous. Similarly, if the research director is to report to an assistant sales manager, he cannot work effectively on problems above the level of the latter's managerial responsibility. Thus it follows that the lower the point at which the research function is stationed, the shallower and more superficial its work may be. Conversely, the higher its location and sponsorship, the more far-reaching and penetrating its studies may be.[4]

The student of marketing research will find the field full of borderline decisions. Black and white are rare, grays are everywhere. The definite "principles" and "rules" so easily memorized and so dependable in some other fields seem to be fugitives from marketing research. Is this organizational question one rare area of definiteness? The answer is that

[4] *A Company Guide to Marketing Research,* American Management Association Research Report 5, 1944.

it is not. The quotation above presents the case for "high-level research" and presents it well. But the viewpoint expressed is one which many marketing research men reject. Some of the dissent rests on impressive evidence and comes from authoritative sources.

It is a sound generalization to observe that there is no such thing as any one best place to fit the marketing research function into an organization. *The optimum organizational decision varies from company to company.* Furthermore—and this is important—no one answer necessarily fits any one organization permanently. The best place to fit marketing research into the organization chart when it has been newly set up as a specialized function is not necessarily the point at which the function will be most effective some years later.

There is a considerable body of evidence which supports the opinion that a *newly created* marketing research department should usually be fitted into the organization chart so that the director of marketing research reports to the chief marketing executive. This opinion is based in a large measure on an appraisal of the nature of the specific activities which marketing research is most frequently called upon to perform, discussed in detail in Chapter 3. Successful growth in the acceptance of research in that organizational setup requires a favorable managerial-attitude climate, described below.

Sometimes those who feel that marketing research must fit into the organization at high levels compare the function to the inspection function in production, or to the auditing function in finance. It would be unsound, they argue, for the chief inspector to report to the production manager. That is quite true, but the argument lacks relevance. It tends also to reflect an imperfect appreciation of the true nature of the marketing research function. A marketing research man is not an "inspector," an "auditor," or any other type of policeman or "checker-upper." He is a fact-finding specialist who usually serves a line executive as a staff adviser. He should report to an executive who has the judgment and experience required to appraise his findings and the authority to take whatever action those findings appear to suggest.

MANAGEMENT CLIMATE REQUIRED FOR HEALTHY RESEARCH GROWTH

The importance of personality factors in arriving at a decision on where to fit the marketing research function into an organization should not be overlooked. Often the personality of the individual executive to whom the marketing research function reports—specifically including such attributes as objectivity, open-mindedness, and interest in facts— may well be much more important as a determinant of the effectiveness of the research contribution than the individual's title. This is particularly true in the introductory period of the marketing research function in any organization. As the same American Management Association just quoted above commented:[5]

> . . . The sponsorship of a liberal-minded and significantly informed officer of a company may be such an important factor in the establishment and success of a research department that its formal position in the organization may not be a question of first importance in the initial stages of development. Sooner or later, however, an imperfect setup may seriously impede the continued growth of the research function.

Marketing research is most likely to achieve maximum productivity and to grow in importance as a function when it operates within a management climate with these two characteristics: *top* management that is research-minded—that recognizes the need for research and wants facts on which to base its decisions, whether those decisions concern financial or sales problems; *and sales* management that is openminded—that has the courage necessary to accept facts uncovered through sound research *as* facts, that will *follow where research leads.* Unfortunately some old-school executives tend to pay lip service to the research idea, then to accept some findings and reject others largely on the basis of preconception and prejudice.

ORGANIZATIONAL PRACTICE IN PLACING THE MARKETING RESEARCH FUNCTION

The preface of this book emphasized that it seeks to present marketing research as it actually exists in practice, rather than as someone thinks it *ought* to be. Against the background of the two diverse opinions expressed above about where marketing research should fit on the organizational chart—reporting on a high-level basis to the president or some other executive with company-wide responsibility as against reporting to the marketing vice-president or someone else with divisional authority —where does marketing research *really* fit in the organizations that use it? Facts on this point are provided by the study of *Company Practices in Marketing Research* already cited. The following table from that survey summarizes the practices of 125 different organizations. It is worth remembering that on the average these are *relatively large* organizations in terms of sales volume.

This table makes it clear that in marketing research practice, even in relatively large companies, the marketing research function is likely to report to a vice-president (usually a divisional vice-president with the

[5] *Ibid.,* p. 23.

Table 2.3. Executive to Whom Marketing Research Reports

Marketing research reports to:	Number	Per cent
President of the company	20	16.0
Executive vice-president	6	4.8
Vice-president	56	44.8
Other executives	34	27.2
Miscellaneous replies	15	12.0
Total companies with full-time assignment of responsibility	125*	100.0*

* Columns add to 131 and to a number in excess of 100 per cent because six companies gave multiple answers. This is the first illustration of the familiar marketing research problem of "multiple responses."
SOURCE: Richard D. Crisp, *Company Practices in Marketing Research*, American Management Association Research Report 22, table 10, p. 35, 1953.

title of vice-president in charge of sales, or marketing vice-president) much more frequently than to an executive with company-wide rather than divisional responsibility. The category identified as "other executives" in this table is made up primarily of sales executives, with titles like general sales manager, sales manager, etc.

An additional comment on this organizational question may be helpful. In a number of larger organizations in which marketing research as a function reports to the president or executive vice-president, there is an additional element present which is sometimes overlooked. Some such companies have *marketing* research reporting to the president, but also have a separate *sales* research unit reporting to the chief marketing executive. This represents an advanced evolutionary development in the organization of marketing research. It is in effect a functional subdivision of marketing research responsibilities. This is not likely to be an organizational approach which will prove effective except where there are present two factors: relatively large sales volume (required to support what are, in effect, *two* marketing research departments) and a rather advanced integration of research into the company's marketing management processes.

ADDITIONAL ORGANIZATIONAL GUIDES FROM THE AMA STUDY

Here are some additional helpful guideposts reported in the American Management Association survey report which may round out your picture of the organizational aspects of marketing research:

1. *Job title.* The most frequently reported title for individuals responsible for marketing research on a full-time basis was *director of marketing research.*

2. *Size of department.* In the sample of relatively large-volume organizations covered by the survey, the median department consisted of seven people including the director. It was unfortunately not possible to discriminate between clerical and stenographic employees on one hand and those with marketing research training and experience of a more professional type on the other.

3. *Salary.* The individual responsible for marketing research in these relatively large-volume companies had a median salary *in 1952* which fell in the range between $10,000 and $15,000. Among companies with sales volume below 25 million dollars, the median salary was between $7,000 and $10,000. For a comment on differences in salary between consumer-product and industrial-product manufacturers, see below.

HOW BIG SHOULD A RESEARCH DEPARTMENT BE?

The fact that the average research department of the companies participating in the American Management Association's survey consisted of seven people raises a question. Just how big should a marketing research department be? This again is a question which admits of no easy answer. Within different individual manufacturing concerns, one may find strikingly varied approaches to the task of organizing the marketing research function. In part the approach adopted in any given case is a reflection of the philosophy of the management team involved.

Two extreme examples will illustrate this point. Some companies prefer a *lean* type of organization. They operate a small department, often staffed with highly experienced people, which is supplemented as required by the extensive use of outside research facilities. Other companies have very large marketing research departments and do a high proportion of their own research through their own full-time personnel. The Procter & Gamble Company, for example, took the latter approach for many years. In 1952, P&G had a marketing research department of more than 125 people. That department used its own personnel to do the interviewing, tabulating, and analysis on projects like product tests and test-market operations, which many other organizations chose to handle through outside facilities.

ADVANTAGES OF THE "LEAN" APPROACH

The lean marketing research approach is an attractive and practical choice, especially for a company of small or moderate size. Marketing research should not be thought of as a sales tool which only a blue-chip company can afford. A research department consisting of two people—

an experienced marketing research man and a girl who can make a calculator hum—can make major contributions to the increased marketing effectiveness of any company that has been operating without research guidance. The review of the specific marketing research activities which are most important in practice, in Chapter 3, will confirm that no major investment in expensive surveys or outside services is ordinarily required in the early stages of a program of this type. A marketing research program does not need to be expensive to be sound and adequate. The average manufacturer does not need a department of ten or twenty people in order to enjoy the advantages of a program of fact-guided marketing.

One of the reasons why this lean approach to marketing research organization is a practical one, from the manufacturer's side of the desk, is that there exist a substantial number of specialized marketing research organizations of various types which are readily available as needed to supplement the facilities of the manufacturer's own staff. For a picture of the nature of the major other types of organizations active in marketing research, let's leave the manufacturer now to consider the anatomy of marketing research in broader perspective.

MAJOR TYPES OF RESEARCH CONSUMERS AND AGENCIES

While the individual manufacturer is the most important single type of organization in the field of marketing research, for reasons already indicated, many other different types of organizations also play important roles in marketing research practice. We shift our attention now to those other types of organizations and to the relationships which exist between some of those types. Before doing so, however, an important distinction must be recognized. That is the distinction between companies that are *consumers* of marketing research, or principals in the execution of research, and those which serve as *agencies*, acting simply to execute research assignments for principals.

While this is an important distinction, it is also a confusing one. The confusion arises because the same organization often falls into both categories. A few specific examples may be helpful in indicating the nature of this principal-agency relationship and thus clarifying this important distinction.

1. When General Mills, Inc., wanted to know how consumer attitudes toward Betty Crocker compared with those toward similar corporate personalities maintained by other organizations, they used the facilities of Burke Marketing Research, Inc., to conduct the interviews needed to secure the desired information.

2. When the Admiral Corporation wanted information about the

activities of its retail dealers in several cities, it engaged Market Facts, Inc., to make a shopping survey.

3. When the Campbell Soup Company wanted an evaluation of the relative importance of nutrition as an appeal in advertising soup, as against economy, convenience, appetite appeal, and other alternatives, they engaged Richard D. Crisp and Associates, Inc., to make a qualitative study of homemakers' attitudes.

4. When the Acme Steel Company wanted guidance in setting up a system of sales control and in planning a basis for effective sales analysis, they turned to Gould, Gleiss & Benn, Inc., for help.

5. When the Simoniz Company wanted a comparative study of the consumer acceptance of their Ivalon sponge versus the leading competitive sponge, the assignment was given to Elrick-Lavidge & Co.

6. When an association of carpet manufacturers known as the Carpet Institute, Inc., wanted information about consumer attitudes and buying habits on carpets and rugs, the firm of Elmo Roper was retained to secure that information.

7. When the publishers of LIFE wanted a study made of the audience covered by their publication versus competitive media, they turned the assignment of making "A Study of Four Media" over to Alfred Politz Research, Inc.

All the above illustrations fall into the simplest possible category. In each instance, one organization—the research consumer, or principal—had a problem. The principal engaged the facilities of another organization—the research agency—to help provide the facts needed to help solve that problem. The marketing research in each of the cases cited was conducted *by* the agency *for* the research consumer, or principal. That type of simple two-party relationship exists in much marketing research work. More complex relationships are also common. The same organization may function in different capacities—now as a principal, now as an agency, or again as an intermediate between a principal and some other agency.

THE ANATOMY OF MARKETING RESEARCH:
RESEARCH CONSUMERS, OR PRINCIPALS

Figure 2.3 identifies the more important types of firms active in marketing research work and provides the framework for a more detailed description of the organization of marketing research activities in practice. Listed in the upper portion of the chart are the more important types of research consumers, or principals. A brief discussion of the activities and an indication of the relative importance of these types of research consumers follows. In reading that discussion, it is well to

Figure 2.3. Major Types of Organizations Active in Marketing Research

This is where the problem is..... RESEARCH CONSUMERS, OR PRINCIPAL

    1. Individual company or firm
        a. Manufacturer
        b. Sales company
        c. Merchandising organization
        d. Service organization
    2. Advertising agency
    3. Trade association
    4. Individual advertising media
    5. Group of advertising media
    6. Cooperative mutual-interest group
    7. Government agencies
    8. Educational institutions
    9. Foundations, etc.

This is how the research is done.. RESEARCH AGENCIES

  A. Through the research consumer's own facilities:
    1. Individual company or firm
    2. Advertising agency
    3. Trade association
    4. Individual advertising media
    5. Group of advertising media
    6. Government agencies
    7. Educational institutions
  B. Through the facilities of one or more outside
    agencies, such as:
    1. Specialized marketing research organizations
        a. Complete-service type
        b. Limited-service type
        c. Specialized ("syndicated") service type
    2. Marketing research consultant
    3. Management consulting firm
    4. Advertising agency
    5. Advertising media
    6. Governmental agency
    7. Educational institution

remember that the comments are confined to the role of such organizations as principals in the research process. The discussion of the activities of some of those same types of organizations as research agencies, in the following section, is necessary to round out the picture of the role of each in marketing research.

Individual Manufacturing Companies

The importance of organizations of this type has already been indicated. Manufacturers face and must solve a wide range of types of marketing problems. To get the facts which are needed to help solve those problems, marketing research is used extensively.

Individual Sales Companies

Sometimes manufacturers pass on the selling function to a selling subsidiary or to an independent sales company. Sometimes sales organizations buy merchandise, add their own brand name, and sell it much as manufacturers do. By the process of assuming part or all of the manufacturer's selling task, such organizations necessarily assume also many of the manufacturer's marketing problems as well. Facing similar kinds of problems, sales companies tend to use marketing research much as manufacturers do.

Individual Merchandising Organizations

The category of principals includes wholesalers of various types, chain-store organizations, large department stores, mail-order houses, and other types of companies active in the merchandising field. The organizations in this category have many problems in common with manufacturers, but they have also other kinds of problems which manufacturers do not face. In their use of marketing research, merchandising organizations differ from manufacturers in ways which are described in detail in Chapter 27.

Service Organizations

Companies that sell a service rather than a product—like life-insurance firms or utility companies, for example—fall in this category. Most service organizations have the problem of estimating the size of their market. That problem is particularly acute for utilities, which must foresee future demand and prepare facilities to meet it. In selling a service as in selling a product, marketing problems are inescapable. Marketing research tends to be used in such organizations much as in manufacturing organizations.

Advertising Agencies

Advertising agencies serve and are compensated by advertisers, who are typically manufacturers, but who may be merchandising firms, trade associations, or other types of organizations. The importance of the advertising agency in the over-all marketing research picture has been increasing, as the service offered by agencies has moved in the direction of a broader marketing service. One of the major characteristics of marketing research by advertising agencies is a tremendous variation from agency to agency in the emphasis placed on and utilization of marketing research. That variation makes generalizations about advertising agency research extremely difficult. In total, however, advertising agencies represent a major share of research consumption.

Trade Associations

In many industries, the trade association plays a vigorous role, serving its member companies by providing facts to aid their managements and in other ways. The trade association sometimes helps to focus marketing research on an industry-wide problem on a scale which would be uneconomical for many of the individual members of the association. Some associations—for example the American Dairy Association and the American Meat Institute—conduct their own advertising programs for the benefit of their industry. The trade association represents a more important factor in marketing research practice than is generally realized.

Individual Advertising Media

This category includes individual newspapers, magazines, television or radio stations, and similar organizations which perform the function of serving as media for the delivery of advertising and similar messages. The marketing research activities of advertising media are often broad in scope.

Groups of Advertising Media

This heading includes groups of radio or television stations combined as a network and conducting research as a single unit. It includes also organizations which represent a single type of advertising media, such as the American Newspaper Publishers' Association, whose Bureau of Advertising is active in marketing research. The Magazine Advertising Bureau and the Traffic Audit Bureau in the fields of outdoor and transportation advertising also conduct marketing research activities.

Cooperative Mutual-interest Groups

Groups of individuals or organizations banded together to serve an objective of interest to all are responsible for some marketing research. One example is the Advertising Research Foundation, which combines the interests of advertising agencies, advertisers, and advertising media. Another illustration would be an association of producers of a single agricultural product, such as the apple industry of the Pacific Northwest, which sponsored research to find a profitable market for C grade and cull Delicious apples not suitable for shipping to consumer markets.

Government Agencies

Some units of the Federal government are extremely active in the research field, with a significant proportion of their activities clearly in the field of marketing research. The Division of Special Surveys of the

Bureau of Agricultural Economics, U.S. Department of Agriculture, while under the direction of Forrest E. Clements, was one outstanding example. The U.S. Department of Commerce is another example.

Educational Institutions

Through their bureaus of business research, and as part of the work of graduate students, educational institutions contribute to the marketing research field and participate in activities in that field both as consumers and agencies.

Foundations, Etc.

Various foundations and similar organizations enter into marketing research activities from time to time. Individual differences are so extreme that the marketing research activities of foundations are difficult to pinpoint.

✿　　✿　　✿　　✿

Any categorization such as the one above involves some borderline cases of classification. Since marketing research work involves many such classification problems, it might be well to identify one such problem as preparation for what lies ahead. Where in the above classification listing would you put a group of advertising media under a single ownership? A case in point is provided by the Curtis Publishing Company, which is widely accepted as having been the birthplace of marketing research on an organized basis. That company publishes individual magazines, such as *Saturday Evening Post* and *Ladies Home Journal*. Into which of the two media categories in the list does the very active marketing research department of that company fall? From the viewpoint of this book, the question is largely academic. When a research project is conducted for a single magazine like the *Ladies Home Journal* (as their study of beauty-shop patrons for Breck shampoo was), that project is in the individual-media category. When a project covers their full line of publications (as their study of market areas for shopping goods did), that project falls in the group category. A marketing research man at Curtis Publishing Company would be likely to find himself occasionally with one foot in each of two categories. The same problem of duality of function occurs in other instances, as noted below.

THE ANATOMY OF MARKETING RESEARCH: RESEARCH AGENCIES

The lower portion of Figure 2.3 lists the more important types of organizations active in the agency, or "executor," area of marketing research. The first point to note is that the seven types of organizations under the *A* heading represent duplications of the listing under research consumers, or principals.

The types of organizations included in that portion of the listing are active *both* as principals and as agencies in the execution of marketing research. That duplication occurs because any organization that does much marketing research is likely to have on its staff one or more individuals who specialize in the field and devote their full time to it. Where such an individual is on an organization's payroll, he faces the continually present alternative in the case of every marketing research project of either doing the work himself or of having it done for him by some outside facility. His decision in the case of a specific project depends on many factors, including his own experience in dealing with problems of the particular type under consideration and his existing work load. It is standard practice to use outside facilities to equalize one's work load. In a season of peak activity within a department, a higher proportion of the work is "farmed out" than in less active periods.

The following comments may be helpful in providing perspective on the characteristics of the individual types of organizations which perform the agency, or executor, function, as listed in the lower portion of Figure 2.3.

Individual Company or Firm

This type of organization requires little comment at this point since it is the subject of discussion throughout a major portion of this book. Some companies do their own research, while others rely heavily on outside facilities. Some companies have a research department which serves in a service capacity for various divisions of the company. For example, the Market Analysis Department of General Mills, Inc., often executes product research for the Research and Development Department of that company. It is often the confidential nature of the projects which dictates this approach. Few subjects are more confidential than the nature of a firm's new-product-development activities!

Advertising Agencies

A major share of the marketing research activities of advertising agencies fall in the agency, or executor, category. This is true, of course, of most other activities of advertising agencies also. Those activities are typically carried on primarily *by* the agency *for* the advertisers (clients) it serves. This does not mean that agencies simply execute research for and at the direction of client organizations. On the contrary, advertising agencies play a much more significant part than is generally recognized in determining what research is to be done and how it is to be done, as well as in the actual execution of the research.

Agencies often have a considerable amount of independence in the conception and execution of much of the marketing research they do, despite the fact that that research may be executed primarily for client organizations. Many of the top marketing research men in America today are on the payrolls of the larger advertising agencies.

Trade Associations

Trade associations exist primarily to serve member companies. One of the services provided by many associations is marketing research advice and counsel. Sometimes this is a continuing activity and function of the trade association. On other occasions it may be stimulated by a particularly pressing problem common to all members of the industry association.

There is so much difference in the marketing research activities of different trade associations that it is difficult to generalize about them. The index of this book will be helpful to the reader in understanding the trade association's activities in the field of marketing research. Numerous specific research projects in which a trade association played a part will be found in the index. (See also Chapter 28.)

Advertising Media

Because the research activities of advertising media are described in detail in Chapter 29, it is only necessary at this point to underline the fact that media do research of many different types. Some of that research is executed for their own management guidance; some of it is for sales-promotional purposes, in selling their particular media; some of it is by way of service to their advertisers or potential advertisers. These comments apply both to individual media and to groups of media, which therefore require no further comment at this point.

Government Agencies

A substantial amount of marketing research is executed by government agencies. Especially active in the marketing research field are the U.S. Departments of Commerce and Agriculture. The index of this book will help the reader locate references to specific examples. The "principal" in research by government agencies may be a specific industry (as in the case of the annual report of confectionery sales issued by the U.S. Department of Commerce) or another unit of the government.

It should be noted also that not all marketing research by government agencies is on the national level. Many individual metropolitan areas, through local units concerned with the development of the industry, sanitary facilities, or some other aspect of an area, execute considerable marketing research.

Educational Institutions

Often a college or university will take on a marketing research assignment, sometimes through some such subdivision as a "business problems department." The work of graduate students which is executed in partial fulfillment of the requirements of a doctoral program often represents marketing research of high quality.

Foundations

Some of the larger foundations such as the Ford Foundation sponsor and support a very broad series of research projects, some of which are in the marketing field, hence worthy of note here.

SPECIALIZED MARKETING RESEARCH ORGANIZATIONS

The *B* portion of the list on the lower part of Figure 2.3 identifies some types of organizations which are important primarily as executors of research for others. To make the listing as complete as possible, some of the organizations which are also active as research consumers are again repeated, although further comment about them would be repetitive.

As the use and acceptance of marketing research has increased, there has developed a network of marketing research organizations. All such organizations are in business for the purpose of supplying facilities and rendering service in the field of marketing research to various types of research consumers. It is somewhat difficult to describe such agencies briefly and specifically, because they vary so widely in their type, approach, functions, and emphasis. However, three of the major categories into which specialized marketing research agencies can be divided are described below. That description is intended only to suggest the nature of the organizations in a general way.

Complete Marketing Research Service Organizations

Some of the specialized marketing research agencies offer a complete marketing research service, which sometimes extends into the area of management consulting activities on broad problems. There is usually heavy emphasis on the *marketing* management side in such consulting. Sometimes such organizations subdivide and make available a portion of their broader service as well. Thus one of the larger organizations of this type has a subsidiary firm which confines its activities to the execution of field work and tabulation, some of it done for competitors of the parent organization!

Such companies fill a real need, especially for the company that has no other access to the qualified marketing research personnel needed to help solve a specific major problem. Much of their work is done for companies that do have their own marketing research departments, when those departments are overloaded or face a problem beyond the capabilities of their own personnel.

Limited Service Marketing Research Organizations

Agencies in this category are typically smaller in scale and overhead than the full-service type and often specialize in one or more parts of the marketing research process. Thus many such firms confine their activities to the execution of interviewing; or to tabulating; or to the execution of store-audits for test-market purposes. (Test marketing is the subject of Chapter 25.)

Specialized Marketing Research Service Organizations

The third major category of research agencies is made up of organizations which typically offer a specialized service in the marketing research field, often on something approximating a standardized basis. Sometimes the cost of the service is divided among or spread over the fees charged to all the companies that purchase it, hence the occasional description of such firms as "syndicated services."

Included in the latter category are two of the largest marketing research organizations in America, in terms of the dollar volume of the marketing research they sell—The A. C. Nielsen Co. and the Marketing Research Corporation of America (MRCA for short), which was formerly known as the Industrial Surveys Co. Those two organizations are active particularly in the field of panel research. Their services are described in detail in Chapter 9.

Other organizations in this category provide estimates of the size of radio or television audiences, or estimates of the readership of printed advertisements, or coverage of portions of the national market such as the youth market; and organizations specializing in other subdivisions of marketing research.

Management Consulting Firms

A management consulting organization typically supplements the management manpower of an organization, often diagnosing business problems and recommending action designed to solve such problems. Where the problem in question is in the marketing area, the activities of such firms often include marketing research. That research may be carried on by the consulting organization itself; or it may be executed under the guidance of the consulting firm by one or more of the other types of marketing research agencies which the problem seems to require.

Marketing Research Consultants

The significant difference between this category and the one above is that consultants in marketing research are often active as individuals rather than as part of an organization. More often than not the marketing research consultant confines his activities to a narrower range of problem situations. The consultant often recommends and supervises the facilities of other types of agencies as required.

Marketing research consultants typically move into that work with one of two types of backgrounds: Either they move into consulting after a broad experience in the practice of marketing research, or they offer a primarily academic background, relying on consulting income to supplement compensation from teaching jobs in colleges or universities or to fill in vacation periods.

Other Research Agencies

The agency activities of the other types of organizations listed in the B portion of Figure 2.3 have already been covered in sufficient detail to indicate the nature and scope of their work in the field.

SUMMARY

1. This chapter serves to introduce the reader to the organization of marketing research activities. It identifies the kinds of organizations active in the field and traces the relationship between some of those types. The most important single type of organization in the field of marketing research is the individual manufacturer.

2. The proportion of manufacturing organizations that do marketing research is high and increasing. It is difficult to provide a single percentage figure of any significance on this point because of the close relationship between the size of the organization, as reflected in sales volume, and marketing research activities. Those activities increase with each step up the sales-volume scale. Very few indeed of the really large organizations do no marketing research. Almost all such organizations have their own research departments, some of them very large departments.

3. The proportion of the company's sales dollar devoted to marketing research varies spectacularly and directly with sales volume, as the American Management Association chart illustrated. The organizations whose sales volume was in the below-$5,000,000 bracket spent on a median basis $\frac{3}{10}$ of 1 per cent of their sales dollar for marketing research. At the other sales-volume extreme, the expenditure rate as a proportion of sales dropped near the vanishing point. This does not mean such companies do less research. Rather it means that an infinitesimally small proportion of the sales dollar, in such an organization, is sufficient to provide an adequate marketing research departmental budget.

4. The tendency for marketing research to be done on a full-time basis is greater in large than in small companies, as a corollary of the point above.

5. Where marketing research fits into the organization chart is a somewhat controversial matter, with tremendous variation from company to company reflecting peculiarities in each individual company's situation. The *newly formed marketing* research department is often most effective if the function reports to the organization's chief *marketing* executive.

6. The ideal management climate for the healthy growth and maximum contribution of marketing research is one which combines strong support from the higher top-management levels with a truly open mind among marketing executives, and especially the chief marketing executive.

7. The types of organizations other than the individual manufacturer which play a significant role in marketing research practice are reviewed. This review reveals a considerable amount of flexibility, in that a particular type of organization sometimes does research itself and sometimes "farms out" the research to an outside organization. The types of specialized organizations active to provide the necessary facilities for manufacturers and other types of research consumers are identified and described.

QUESTIONS

1. Among the many different types of organizations using marketing research, which *one* is the most important user? Why would you say it is the most important user?

2. About what percentage of manufacturers reported doing marketing research in the NAM mail survey discussed in this chapter? Why would you say more manufacturers did not report doing marketing research?

3. Where would you say marketing research belongs on the organizational chart?

4. How would you answer the following question: Just how big should a marketing research department be?

5. Who are research consumers, or principals?

6. Who are the "doers" of marketing research?

7. What is the ideal management climate for the healthy growth and maximum contribution of marketing research?

CHAPTER 3

The Marketing-problem Base
of Marketing Research

A marketing research man is concerned not just with marketing research, but rather with the entire broad area of marketing management. This does not mean that he trespasses on or intrudes into the provinces of others—of the sales manager, for example, or of the sales vice-president. It does mean that he must understand the problems his fellow executives face before he can apply his skills productively to the task of helping them by contributing the facts they need to aid them in arriving at key decisions.

This is an extremely important point. Marketing research cannot exist or function effectively in a vacuum, as something apart from marketing management. It is inseparably integrated with the broad base of common marketing problems that exist in most companies which have a product or service to sell. It is literally true that those common marketing problems form the base of all marketing research activities.

Although the number of marketing problems is limitless, those problems can be grouped into a relatively small number of *types* of problems. A useful framework for grouping the major types of marketing problems to which research can be and is profitably applied is needed at this point. Such a framework provides perspective on the specific activities marketing research men do and the relationships between those different activities.

There are many different ways in which marketing problems might be classified. For example, they might be grouped according to their scale, as into major and minor problems. Or they might be classified on the basis of their time component, thus separating short-term problems which require an almost immediate answer or decision from long-term problems. Or they might be classified functionally, thus distinguishing between sales problems and advertising problems, or between product problems and policy problems.

OPERATING PROBLEMS VERSUS NONRECURRING PROBLEMS

A classification base which provides a useful and practical framework for understanding marketing research activities is one which begins by dividing all marketing problems into two major types: *operating problems,* which are continuously present in almost every marketing-management situation, and *nonrecurring problems,* which arise as a result of some specific development or circumstance.

Problems of the first type are found in all marketing situations. The second type of problems is frequently, but not necessarily continuously, present. A review of some of the major specific problems within each of these groups follows.

MAJOR TYPES OF OPERATING PROBLEMS

The outstanding characteristic of problems in this category is that they exist in every organization with a product or service to sell, even though their existence is not always explicitly recognized. Problems of this type are an inescapable element of a management job, as necessary to management practice as breathing is to life. To provide specific illustrations of problems of this type, consider an actual but anonymous company, Allied Products, Inc. At the time of this illustration, the company's annual sales volume was about 10 million dollars. It employed about 300 salesmen, with several levels of sales supervision between the salesmen in the field and the chief sales executive in the company's home office. It spent about $900,000 a year for advertising. It operated more than a dozen warehouses, strategically located in key markets in all sections of the country.

This company was in excellent corporate health. It was a sound, well-managed company. Its business had never been better than at the time of this illustration. This is a type of situation, in short, in which one might perhaps expect to find *no* marketing problems present. If you moved behind the desk of the sales vice-president of this healthy, vigorous business and peeked over his shoulder as he worked, however, you would find that he faced a constant flow of problems. In the course of a full year spent behind his desk, and in front of the desks of some of the executives of the company's major customers, this sales vice-president encountered the following types of operating problems.

Sales Forecasting

Although this company's manufacturing cycle was relatively short— that is, only about three months elapsed between the release of a manufacturing authorization to the production department and the date when the merchandise was available on the shipping platform—the sales vice-president was responsible for the preparation of a *sales forecast* every six months. These forecasts covered a twelve-month period and were reviewed and revised every six months.

In developing estimates of company volume for each future time period, it was necessary to consider the trend of industry volume as well as trends in company volume and to weigh also various economic influences which might tend to stimulate or depress company sales opportunities. The sales vice-president did not have to prepare those sales forecasts personally. He delegated that responsibility to a group of subordinates. But the sales vice-president was personally responsible for reviewing the forecasts and accepting or modifying them.

He was also responsible for presenting those forecasts to the company's management committee, of which he was a member, for approval. He had to explain and justify the forecasts to that committee. Once the forecasts were accepted and approved by the committee as the foundation for the company's production and financial and sales planning, he became responsible for seeing that the volume of merchandise called for by the forecasts was actually sold.

Sales-expense Forecasting

From the viewpoint of top management, a forecast of sales volume is only half the story. That forecast indicates what volume of merchandise the company may expect to sell. It therefore shows anticipated income for the time period covered. But management is concerned primarily with net income or profit rather than gross income. An operating profit results only when the income from sales exceeds the cost of making, financing, and selling the products sold.

With a staff of 300 salesmen, Allied Products, Inc., obviously had a substantial amount of direct-selling expense, to which the $900,000 in advertising costs must be added. The sales vice-president was responsible for all sales costs, including advertising and warehousing expenses. He had to prepare a forecast of those expenses in detail, for the approval of the management committee, along with his forecast of sales volume. It is only when the forecast of sales volume can be equated with the estimated cost of achieving that volume that profit estimates can be made and the performance of the company's marketing management executives appraised.

Forecasts of production and financial expenses, prepared by the production and financial divisions of Allied Products, Inc., and submitted for management-committee approval by the vice-presidents who headed those divisions, were largely contingent on the sales forecast and were typically prepared after the sales forecast had been submitted and approved. This time relationship made it necessary for the sales forecast to be prepared a longer time in advance of the beginning of the sales period covered than would otherwise have been the case.

Comment: The intimate interrelationship of sales-volume responsibility and sales-expense responsibility is illustrated by this excerpt from the job description of the sales vice-president of Allied Products, Inc., as it appeared in the company's organization manual: "The sales vice-president is responsible for determining sales objectives and budgets of sales and advertising expenses and for securing approval of those objectives and expense budgets by the Management Committee." The process of making a carefully considered sales forecast is not a simple one. Chapter 19 describes the process in detail.

Continuing Control of Sales Volume and Expense

Once forecasts of sales volume and sales expenses have been adopted, there exists a continuing need for a comparison of actual sales with planned-for or budgeted sales and for careful control of sales expenses to be sure those expenses do not exceed the forecast. The chief sales executive of any organization needs specific and detailed facts about sales progress at all times. Available data must be maintained in great detail. When actual sales begin to lag behind the sales forecast, such detailed data make it possible to *isolate the problem elements* in the situation quickly.

What individual products are failing to achieve anticipated volume? What territories, districts, or regions are lagging? What types of customers are failing to deliver the volume they were expected to contribute? The answers to questions like these are quickly available through sales-control machinery which ordinarily operates on the exception principle, requiring very little top-executive time.

The sales vice-president is responsible for the creation of that sales-control machinery. He must decide in advance what specific kinds of information he will require, and with what frequency, in order to maintain effective control over sales progress. Planning such control machinery is not a routine or clerical function. On the contrary, as the Stanford University study mentioned in Chapter 1 pointed out, it is "one of the primary responsibilities of top management" to provide "effective means of control, permitting top executives to delegate wide responsibility and authority, thereby freeing themselves of administrative detail in order to concentrate on broad planning and direction."[1]

It might be noted parenthetically that the sales vice-president of Allied

---

[1] Paul E. Holden et al., *Top-Management Organization and Control*, McGraw-Hill, New York, 1951, p. 3.

Products, Inc., is a *divisional-management* executive, directly responsible for one of the major divisions of the company. He is therefore clearly included in the top-management group as defined in the Stanford study.

Appraisal of Territorial Sales Opportunities or Potentials

A national sales forecast for a company like Allied Products, Inc., is simply the sum total of "a lot of little forecasts put together." A detailed and current knowledge of the opportunity to make sales in individual sales territories, districts, and regions—and especially of the *relative* opportunities existing in different geographical units—is an essential element in developing sound marketing plans. This is a continuing problem because territorial potentials change constantly and sometimes rapidly. Changes in territorial buying power and the revisions of a company's sales-territorial boundaries contribute to such changes.

The applications of such knowledge are numerous. You would find the sales vice-president of Allied Products, Inc., using them as a guide in determining how many warehouses his organization requires and where those warehouses should be located. He uses them constantly in planning sales-territorial assignments and in reviewing and revising sales-territorial boundaries. He uses them to help him determine the number of salesmen the company needs and in planning where those salesmen should be positioned for maximum productivity. Again note that the sales vice-president is not personally engaged in this activity, which he delegates to one of his subordinates. But he retains the responsibility for seeing that such appraisals are made and for using the detailed facts about territorial potentials in many aspects of his day-to-day work.

Comment: Because the term *potential,* or *sales potential,* is sometimes used in different ways by different writers, it tends to be confusing. As the term is used in this book, the potential of a territory or a market is *synonymous with the total industry volume* in that territory or market. It is therefore the total within which each competing individual company seeks to build volume. The success of those efforts is reflected in the *market share* achieved. Market share is a percentage figure which relates company sales—either nationally or in a territory—to industry volume nationally or in that territory.

To illustrate this further, one of the products in the Allied Products, Inc., line had industry volume nationally of 10 million dollars at manufacturers' prices. The New York territory was estimated to represent 12 per cent of the national total on that product. The potential of the New York territory thus would be 12 per cent of 10 million dollars, or $1,200,000. If sales by Allied Products, Inc., of that product in the New York territory were $300,-

000, that would represent a 25 per cent market share. In the relatively rare case of a company with a unique product and no competitors, company volume and industry volume would be synonymous and the company's market share would be 100 per cent. Occasionally the term potential is used to describe the total volume which an expanding industry may achieve at some future date. The term is here used in a more limited sense: to identify actual or estimated industry volume in a specific time period—usually this year or next year.

Measuring Territorial Variations in Sales Yield, Market Share, Sales Effectiveness

Facts about territorial sales opportunities provide a useful yardstick which can be used to evaluate the company's actual sales volume and performance, territory by territory. Measuring territorial sales performance and using analysis to find sales soft spots which represent inviting opportunities to achieve volume increases is "standard operating procedure" in well-managed companies like Allied Products, Inc. This type of analysis is usually executed *by* the marketing research director *for* the information and guidance of the sales vice-president and other sales-supervisory personnel. The analytical findings are used as guides in directing sales-supervisory attention where it is most needed and where it is likely to be most productive.

Sales-quota Setting

Sales quotas, which are the individual sales objectives for a salesman or for a territory, are widely used as a tool of marketing management. Such quotas can be set much more accurately when they are built on a foundation of facts about territorial potential and the company's past success in each territory than when they are based on some arbitrary decision or on subjective judgment alone.

Measuring Variations in Individual Salesmen's Performance

With a sales force of 300 individual salesmen, plus supervisory personnel, the sales vice-president of Allied Products, Inc., has a tremendous and continuous task of manpower management. In any group of 300 salesmen, there are likely to be some good salesmen, some who are neither bad nor good, and some who are definitely below average in both ability and performance. Facts are needed to guide management in weeding out the weaker members of the sales organization and in identifying and rewarding the stronger members. Without some objective basis of evaluating the performance of individual salesmen, the sales vice-president would have to rely on judgment alone.

Suppose a sales-supervisory opening developed. Which one, if any, of the 300 salesmen should be promoted? Suppose a competitive firm made one of the 300 salesmen a "better offer." Should the firm meet the offer to retain the man's experience and ability or let him go? The decision requires, among other things, an appraisal of the salesman's abilities and performance. While actual appraisals of individual salesmen are likely to be made first by the direct supervisors of the salesmen, those evaluations must in turn be reviewed by other individuals higher in the sales organization. It is necessary to guard against the tendency of some supervisors to "rate high" and of others to "rate low."

The task of evaluating salesmen's performance *objectively* is as difficult as it is important. Marketing research has made real progress in developing yardsticks which can be used, usually in conjunction with psychological yardsticks as well, to measure the contribution and potential of individual salesmen. Those yardsticks substitute objective measurement for the subjective likes and dislikes of sales executives.

Comment: The need for careful marketing research on this subject is apparent when you consider that there are many variables *other than the individual salesmen* which influence the total sales-volume contributions of two individual salesmen in two widely separated and quite different territories. The job of eliminating the influence of the other variables in so far as possible, so that the salesman's contribution may be evaluated fairly, is an extremely complex one. Differences in such factors as territorial potentials, past sales performance of the company in the territory, competitive weight and activities, and advertising emphasis must be recognized. Many sales managers long considered it impossible to eliminate such influences and to measure salesmen's performance objectively. That viewpoint is gradually being modified as more and more companies report that they have found acceptable ways to apply objective standards to this vital element in the marketing process. The responsibility of the chief sales executive is to see that the tools for such objective measurement are developed and used. He is unlikely to participate personally in this process other than in a supervisory way and by providing guidance and counsel.

Measuring Industry Trends and Company Position in Industry

This activity is implicit within a carefully developed sales forecast, but it is so important that it merits individual attention. Its importance greatly increased in the years following World War II. The postwar expansion of total business volume found some industries growing at a slower and some at a more rapid rate than the economy as a whole. This variable rate of growth, combined with the rather general expansion trend in which most industries participated, led to some new and sometimes acute problems in management control. The danger that a company showing substantial sales-volume increases might actually be losing market position and market share in an industry expanding at a more rapid rate became an almost permanent addition to management's ever-present problems.

An acceleration of mobility in the consumer population and the sweeping changes in the nature of the consumer market in the postwar years also entered the picture. For example, consider the national total number of births each year from the 1920s down through depression-year lows, then up to peaks during and following World War II. That curve has tremendous significance as an industry-volume determinant in many industries. Among the beverage group of industries, sharp expansion in soft-drink sales could be confidently predicted as the bumper baby crop of the early 1940s moved into the teen-age bracket. Brewers of beer had to watch a decline in per capita consumption because the increase in total population became an increase in population of beer-drinking age only after a lag of 18 or 20 years.

Product innovations were an additional major influence in industry trends requiring close attention. The increased importance of liquid-cream shampoos which followed the spectacular success of the Toni Company in introducing White Rain shampoo is an example of the impact of such innovations.

Product-quality and Product-line Review and Evaluation

The chief sales executive of Allied Products, Inc., has the constant task of appraising and reappraising his company's line of products. He is concerned with the quality of the products and with the completeness of the line. If a product in the Allied line were inferior to a competitive product in quality, salesmen would lose orders to the competitor and the difficulty of achieving the company's sales objectives would be increased. If the line were incomplete, so that a major customer had to turn to a competitor for a product not available from Allied, that would ease the competitor's task in selling that customer other products.

Sometimes a product line is too complete, in which case salesmen may be overburdened with the task of selling a large number of small-volume products. This product-line responsibility includes packaging responsibility as well, if the products are packaged, and includes responsibility for exploring the opportunities inherent in ingenious packaging of non-packaged items. There is often a different viewpoint toward product quality in different divisions of a company such as Allied Products, Inc. The people who develop products—perhaps a research and development division, perhaps a part of the production division—have viewpoints which may differ from those of customers. The chief sales executive tends to reflect the customer's point of view in product matters. He wants his salesmen to be selling the kind of products customers want to buy, rather than the kind production executives think they *ought* to want to buy, because in the former case sales friction is reduced and the productivity of the sales force increased.

Comment: The extent to which sales executives have an opportunity to advance the customers' viewpoint in discussion leading to decisions dealing with the product, product line, etc., is increasing sharply. An unpublished study by *Business Week* magazine in 1953 among a group of industrial marketing executives revealed that by that date this trend had progressed to a point at which it was then unusual to find a sales executive who did *not* accept product responsibility and product decisions as part of his duties and responsibilities.

Evaluation of Alternative Promotional Methods

Every sales executive has open to him a wide variety of different promotional methods. In the consumer-product field, for example, a manufacturer may choose to promote through straight product-selling advertising, or he may instead choose to rely on various types of promotional devices such as "deals," premiums, special offers, etc., to move his merchandise into the hands of the final consumer. There are alternatives open even within the latter course. For example, should the deal be aimed at the final consumer or at some intermediate factor such as the retailer or wholesaler? Should promotional funds spent at the retail level be diverted into cooperative advertising, or would the same amount of money be more productive if spent as a commission (sometimes called a "spiff," "push money," or "PM") for retail clerks?

Closely allied to decisions on alternative promotional methods are decisions as to alternative types of distribution channels: Should a company sell direct to consumers, direct to retailers, or rely on wholesalers to sell to retailers and on retailers to sell to consumers? This is a continuing operating problem because of constant shifts and changes in the facts and factors on which decisions of this type are made. Reappraisals of alternatives, in the light of new circumstances developing from day to day, are frequently necessary. Every time a major competitor makes a change, a reappraisal is indicated. Marketing research contributes facts helpful in reappraising the desirability of alternative approaches in this area.

Appraisals of Advertising Effectiveness

Since Allied Products, Inc., spends $900,000, or 9 cents out of each of its sales dollars, for advertising, it is obvious that the advertising responsibility in the company is of major importance. The sales vice-president is responsible for seeing that the advertising expenditures are made in that way which will maximize the company's sales and profit return from its advertising. This is a tremendously complex responsibility, a fact which becomes apparent when some of the major components are reviewed.

It includes an appraisal of the soundness of the story or message told in the advertising; a consideration of the relative productivity of different types of advertising media (for example, of magazine advertising versus newspapers or television or some combination of those or other media); decisions on the geographical or other allocation of advertising efforts; appraisals of different seasonal alternatives for peaking advertising, as against an even, year-around program; and a dozen other basic and important decisions of vital importance to a company spending $900,000 a year for advertising. Primary responsibility for the development of sound advertising plans and recommendations rests with the company's advertising agency. Within the company, the advertising director works with the agency in formulating recommendations. The sales vice-president, to whom the advertising director reports, retains responsibility for the approval of all major advertising commitments. He must of course keep sufficiently well informed on advertising matters to appraise the soundness of the program developed for his approval.

Pricing Policies and Practices

Price policy is a key element in the chief sales executive's job. Decisions must be made on the final selling prices at which individual products will be offered to the company's customers. Where those products are sold for resale (as to wholesalers or retailers), those price decisions must take into consideration the normal operating margins of the distribution channels used. Decisions on other aspects of price policy, such as quantity discounts, are also necessary. When a company's costs rise or fall significantly (as when a new labor contract is negotiated which increases unit production costs), a decision has to be made as to whether the company's prices should be adjusted and to what extent. Where prices are changed, there are additional problems as to whether or not, or to what extent, orders will be accepted at the old price before an increase is put into effect, or whether stocks will be "protected" in the case of a decline. A price change by a competitor may necessitate a review of company pricing. Changes in the relative importance of distribution channels or different customer types may make a re-examination of pricing necessary.

The dozen examples quoted above do not represent anything like a complete listing of marketing problems of the current operating type which the chief sales executive of an organization like Allied Products, Inc., must face. These examples should suffice to illustrate both the general nature and the wide variety of such problems which are always present in a well-managed company.

MAJOR TYPES OF NONRECURRING PROBLEMS

Now let's consider problems typical of those in the nonrecurring category. The primary characteristic of problems of this type is that they usually do not develop gradually and continuously out of the normal day-to-day activities of a business, but are instead typically created by some specific development or circumstance often from outside the company. Because there is usually a specific cause, circumstance, or company objective to which such problems can be traced or attributed, the task of identifying the major types is somewhat complicated. They could be identified by relating them to the types of causes, as well as to the types of effects or results. In the following discussion, an attempt is made both to indicate the nature of the situation out of which the problem developed and to suggest the nature of the action which is likely to be indicated.

Problems of Competitive-product Innovations

One of the most important types of marketing problems is the group which arises out of the necessity of appraising and adjusting operations to fit the changed marketing circumstances which develop when a competitor introduces a new type or modification of product which threatens to make serious inroads into a company's business. Such innovations occur rather frequently in some industries, less frequently in others. The threat of such an innovation is always present in every industry.

The dentifrice field is a classic example of an industry in which major innovations are the rule rather than the exception. Within a very brief period of time, innovations produced several sweeping changes in the nature and competitive division of industry volume. First there were ammoniated formulations, with decay-reducing advertising and promotional claims. The introduction of such products jolted the industry. Established brands with large market shares had to incorporate the ammoniated feature into their formulas and advertising in order to withstand the challenge of newly developed products. Then Lever Brothers Co. introduced Chlorodent, with a newsy breath-purifying advertising story, and the industry had another fast job of product changing to cope with. The impact of chlorophyll as an ingredient is suggested by the fact that *Advertising Age* magazine reported on Aug. 10, 1953, that 35 per cent of the total dentifrice market was then represented by tooth paste containing chlorophyll. There followed development of antienzyme formulations, and the entire industry had to make another product switch. Fluorinated formulas followed, to keep the brand- or market-share boat rocking.

Product innovations may range from the relatively minor influence of a minor product variant introduced by a relatively unimportant firm in an industry to the cataclysmic shock which results when a dominant firm in any industry introduces a product which threatens to make an entire industry's products obsolete. Consider the threat of turbine engines for automobiles to carburetor manufacturers. In adjusting to such innovations, there are many variable circumstances to which marketing research could be effectively applied.

There is always the problem of immediate and potential effect on existing inventories, including both those of the manufacturer which may be finished goods or in process and those at wholesale and retail levels as well if the industry's distribution channels include them. The orderly liquidation of those inventories and a gradual transition to an improved product matching the innovation are sometimes possible; the threat that such a liquidation may be impossible, or that patent or other protection may prevent a duplication of the values present in the innovation, is one of the nightmares every sales executive must constantly face in a competitive industry.

There are dozens of potentially important innovations to each one that actually has a severe impact on an industry. Marketing research is used, in such cases, as a form of "sales intelligence." It permits an objective appraisal of each potential threat. When the innovation is significant, marketing research can sometimes provide a sufficient advance warning to permit management to act more promptly to meet and counter the threat than would otherwise be possible. If the innovation, however promising, is lacking in consumer or customer appeal, research can uncover that fact quickly in many instances. It can thus provide the basis for a confident prediction that what appears to be a competitive cloud on the horizon will fade without storming established industry patterns.

To illustrate, the makers of Servel refrigerators in 1953 introduced a product which made ice cubes automatically, eliminating the need for trays, for difficult ice-cube removal, etc. Was this development destined to revolutionize refrigerators as products? Consumer checks by a competitor indicated that consumer reaction to the new development was mixed to negative. Objections were focused on the fact that the ice-making mechanism took up so much space that it reduced the frozen-food capacity of the Servel units. Frozen-food storage space was more important to housewives at that time than the nuisance value of conventional ice-cube preparation and removal. With the consumer research before them, competitors could safely disregard the competitive threat of the Servel innovation.

Problems of Changes in Competitive Forces

Not all competitive threats grow out of a product innovation. Sometimes the entry into an industry of a new and aggressive competitor, or a change in the operating approach of an established competitor, may be an equally grave threat to the competitive *status quo*. When the Kraft Foods Co. began to build its own distribution facilities for handling such perishable commodities as margarine and salad dressing instead of selling them through independent distributors, the competitive climate in the margarine industry chilled suddenly. When the giant Procter & Gamble organization entered the ranks of makers of home permanents, the threat to Toni's long-dominant share of the market was greater than the addition of one more competitor in an industry including scores of brands would indicate. When Toni in turn moved into the lipstick business, Revlon and Hazel Bishop had to re-examine their own positions and plans in the light of the changed circumstances. Effective marketing management requires constant study and apppraisal of competitive activities. Marketing research contributes facts which aid such appraisals.

Problems Posed by Major Price Changes

Whenever a competitor introduces a major price change into an industry, the impact of that change must be appraised quickly. Often countermeasures must be taken without delay. When Kelvinator brought out its line of refrigerators in 1939, after all major competitors had already introduced theirs, at prices which were spectacularly lower than traditional in the industry, the result was the greatest shift in brand shares in a single year in the history of that dynamic industry. When the makers of Old English self-polishing floor wax changed their prices so that a pint container which had been selling for 59 cents was priced to consumers at 35 cents, the makers of Johnson's Glo-Coat—still at 59 cents—had to decide quickly what counteraction to take, if any.

When Procter & Gamble introduced a new home permanent at a price 25 cents higher than prevailing levels in the industry, the Toni Company faced a major problem. Marketing research was able to evaluate the test markets in which P&G had tested this move and guide Toni to the effective counteraction.

Problems Created by Changes in Competitive Sales Methods or Policies

The analysis of alternative sales methods was mentioned as one of the problems of the operating type in the preceding section. Where such analyses are being made continuously by many of the major firms in an industry, inevitably some shifts in the sales methods or policies of individual competitors develop. Every time such a change occurs, it becomes a new and relevant element in the reappraisals of competitors of the firm making the change. When one major firm in the food field introduced a warehousing discount which enabled chain-store organizations and other volume buyers to purchase at a substantially lower price than smaller customers, each competitor had to re-examine its own pricing and discount practices and policies.

Similarly, when the General Foods Corporation announced, after extensive marketing research, that it would henceforth sell its Maxwell House Coffee through a separate selling organization selling no other product, the increased sales leverage on Maxwell House made it necessary for each competitive coffee marketer to re-examine the sales manpower picture. When the Avco Corporation announced the combined distribution of its two lines of appliances—Bendix and Crosley lines—that decision posed problems and opportunities for competitors and near competitors selling through the same distribution channels. When Avco discontinued the Crosley line and sold Bendix to Philco, reappraisal was again necessary.

Problems Produced by Shifts in Consumption Patterns

When the consumers or customers of an industry change, the result is likely to create opportunities for some sales executives and problems for others. For example, the sharp increase in calorie consciousness proved to be a bonanza for firms selling products accepted as low in calories (like Ry-Krisp and low-calorie carbonated drinks). In contrast, it was a major problem for organizations selling products thought to be fattening, such as candy, cake flour, cookies, and similar products. Such changes may occur quickly or gradually and may be temporary or permanent.

Problems Involving Changes in Distribution Channels

Changes in available distribution channels, or in the relative strength or weakness of various paths from factory to eventual consumer or customer, sometimes pose problems for the sales executive. Changes in types of retailers or wholesalers or in the relative importance of existing types fall in this category. For example, the development of supermarkets reduced the share of total volume moving through smaller outlets and led many manufacturers to shift from direct coverage of such stores by their salesmen to reliance on wholesalers for small-outlet coverage.

The broadening of product lines in supermarkets to include nonfood items like shampoos, dentifrices, and even soft goods like hosiery necessitated reappraisals of distribution channels and of sales emphasis on different customer types. The introduction of drug-type items into supermarkets was stimulated by the development of a new kind of wholesaler known as a "rack jobber," who specialized in servicing stocks of drug-type items in supermarkets. The growth in importance of movie theaters and vending machines as outlets for candy-bar volume illustrates a changed distribution pattern which candy-bar manufacturers had to make plans to serve.

Problems in Developing and Introducing a New Product

New-product development represents one of the most important areas of marketing research application. The importance of research on new products is directly related to the cost-versus-results equation mentioned in Chapter 1. Today the process of developing and launching a new product on a full scale may take years and may involve hundreds of thousands or even millions of dollars. Marketing research within this new-product area embraces a whole galaxy of closely related but individual marketing-research problems. These include estimates of demand for the new product; determination of the characteristics of the market for that product; identification of the product characteristics considered most desirable by customers or consumers, to guide product development; objective measurement of consumer acceptance of the proposed new product against established products of the same type if such products exist; determination of the most effective advertising or promotional approaches to be used; a test-market operation to reproduce on a small scale the planned introductory strategy; and finally, the all-out launching. Because of the vital importance of new-product-development activities within the marketing research picture, that subject is covered at length in Chapter 23. Further comment at this point would be unnecessarily repetitious. ·

Problems of Discontinuing Major Products or Product Lines

The reverse side of the new-product-development coin occasionally comes up, presenting the sales executive with major problems. This is particularly true when a decision to eliminate one or more entire product lines or major products from the company's marketing base is under consideration. Individual products and product lines often have their roots deep in the tradition and history of a company, and a decision to move out of an industry is rarely taken lightly. Thus when the makers of Johnson's wax decided to discontinue the production of a line of wax-fortified paints—thus abandoning a company-developed patent and writing off thousands of dollars' worth of developmental work—the detailed exploration of both sides of the decision required several years.

Problems Arising from Proposed Changes in Sales Methods or Policies

Whenever a major change in a company's sales methods or policies is under consideration, careful study of the possible consequences of the change is indicated. A decision to fair-trade the prices of a company's products, for example, or the decision by a militant supporter of retail-price maintenance like Westinghouse to discontinue fair-trade pricing, requires careful advance study. A contemplated change in distribution channels would fall in the same category. A change in the sales-compensation plan which involves a major policy shift warrants careful study and appraisal. When Max Factor & Co. revised its price and discount policies, months of study on the effects of each proposed change on the company's volume and profit picture and of the likely effects on relative customer-type importance preceded the decision.

Problems Created by Advertising Changes

The development of an important new advertising medium like television makes necessary a complete reappraisal of a company's historic advertising activities. When the cost of advertising increases at a greater rate than the company's appropriation, a similar reconsideration of alternative possibilities is required. An illustration of the latter type of problem is provided by the experience of Congoleum-Nairn, Inc., which had been sponsoring a television program known as "Garroway at Large." When a contract expired, the cost of talent for the show was boosted sharply—reportedly from $7,000 to $17,000 a *week*—which made it necessary for the company to re-examine its advertising program and eventually to decide not to renew the show at the higher rate.

The above list of ten different types of nonrecurring problems is not intended to be exhaustive. Like the earlier list of examples of kinds of continuously present operating problems, these examples are intended only to illustrate in specific terms the types of marketing problems which management executives face and on which they make decisions—often with the aid of marketing research. These two major classifications of problems, as we shall see in the remainder of this chapter, together form *the marketing problem base of marketing research activities.*

COMPANY PRACTICES IN MARKETING RESEARCH

Upon that marketing-problem base there has developed a rather clearly defined structure of specific, interrelated marketing research activities. Information about the nature of those activities is provided by the AMA research report entitled *Company Practices in Marketing Research* which was described and discussed in part Chapter 2. We are concerned here with the portion of the study which deals with the specific marketing research activities performed and the relative importance of those activities.

In that survey, a check list of thirty-seven different specific marketing research activities was included in the questionnaire. After that list was developed, it was reviewed by six outstanding marketing research practitioners before it was converted into final form. In addition to the thirty-seven listed activities, space was provided for respondents to write in any additional activities omitted from the list. The specific list of activities was divided into three different groups, covering research on *products or services,* on *markets,* and on *sales methods and policies.* Figure 3.1 reproduces the listing of the thirty-seven activities just as it appeared in the questionnaire, except that the three sets of blanks for writing in additional activities in each of the three areas have been omitted.[2]

Figures 3.2, 3.3 and 3.4 show graphically the proportion of companies reporting that they performed each of the specific activities listed in the three major research areas. The base of the percentages charted is the total number of companies that do any marketing research. It has been necessary to condense the description of activities on these three charts to maintain legibility. It may therefore be helpful to cross-check between the full description in Figure 3.1 and the capsule descriptions shown on the three charts.

Figures 3.2 and 3.3 show essentially similar patterns, with very high performance of the top-ranking functions. The activities in the sales methods and policies area charted on Figure 3.4 reflect a slightly lower level of activity in this area.

---

[2] In any check list of this type, some problems of communication are likely to develop. Instances in which a description of a specific activity means different things to different respondents are almost inescapable. This problem has a bearing on some of the findings of this study as discussed in this chapter. The sample of companies to which the questionnaire was sent included mostly manufacturers, but many service organizations and large retail organizations were also included. An attempt was made to use terminology that would span the interests and understanding of manufacturers and nonmanufacturers alike. Instead of the activity of *sales forecasting,* which would have been meaningful to manufacturers, the term *general business forecasting* was used in the questionnaire. This compromise was unsuccessful, with the result that the questionnaire failed to provide accurate data on the extent to which sales forecasting is carried on. The relative importance of sales forecasting as a marketing research activity in manufacturing organizations is almost certainly considerably understated in the AMA survey report.

Figure 3.1. Activities of the Marketing Research Function

Please indicate by a check mark those functions which are performed by the executives in charge of marketing research in your organization, or by your marketing research department. Please add to the list any other functions which are not listed.

A. Research on your products or services

_____ 1. Determining consumer or customer acceptance of proposed new products or services.

_____ 2. Comparing consumer or customer acceptance of existing products or services with similar competitive products or services.

_____ 3. Determining present uses of existing products.

_____ 4. Determining or exploring new uses of existing products.

_____ 5. Packaging research, design, or physical characteristics.

_____ 6. Evaluating new competitive products or competitive new-product developments or modifications.

_____ 7. Studies aimed at product elimination or line simplification.

_____ 8. Studies of the competitive position of company's products (market-share analyses, etc.).

_____ 9. Studies of dissatisfaction with existing products or services, among present or former customers.

_____10. Market tests or test-market operations on new or improved products.

_____11. Economic research (determination of industry trends, correlation of company sales with economic indicators, etc.).

_____12. Determining advantages or limitations of proposed new products or services.

B. Research on markets

_____ 1. Analysis of the size of the market for specific products.

_____ 2. Analysis of characteristics of the market for specific products.

_____ 3. Studies of the relative profitability of different markets.

_____ 4. Estimating demand for new products.

_____ 5. Studies of trends in market size by products.

_____ 6. Studies of shifts in the nature of the market (examples: sectional changes, age-distribution trends, etc.).

_____ 7. Studies of economic factors affecting sales volume and opportunities.

_____ 8. General business forecasting.

_____ 9. Analysis of territorial sales opportunities or potentials.

_____10. Studies of changes in customer-type importance.

C. Research on sales methods and policies

_____ 1. Studies of prices and their influence on sales volume.

_____ 2. Studies of price policies, discount structure, etc., in relation to competition.

_____ 3. Evaluation of existing sales methods.

_____ 4. Appraisal of proposed changes in sales methods.

_____ 5. Studies of distribution costs.

_____ 6. Measuring territorial variations in sales yield, market share, sales effectiveness.

_____ 7. Measuring effectiveness of individual salesmen.

_____ 8. Analysis of salesmen's activities.

_____ 9. Studies of effectiveness of promotional devices like "deals," premiums, etc.

_____10. Studies of distribution of products.

_____11. Establishment or revision of sales territories.

_____12. Sales compensation.

_____13. Advertising and selling practices of competitors.

_____14. Selection of advertising media.

_____15. Measuring advertising effectiveness.

SOURCE: Richard D. Crisp, *Company Practices in Marketing Research*, American Management Association Research Report 22, Figure 4, pp. 22-23, 1953.

RESEARCH ON PRODUCTS-SERVICES

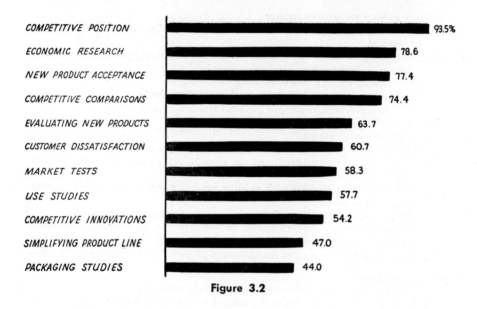

Figure 3.2

RESEARCH ON MARKETS

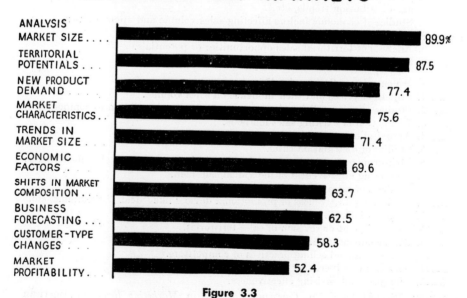

Figure 3.3

RESEARCH ON SALES METHODS AND POLICIES

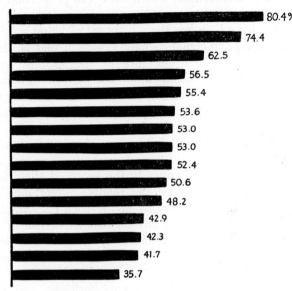

VARIATIONS IN TERRITORIAL YIELD	80.4%
SALES TERRITORIAL REVISIONS	74.4
DISTRIBUTION STUDIES	62.5
SALESMEN'S EFFECTIVENESS	56.5
EVALUATING SALES METHODS	55.4
SALESMEN'S ACTIVITIES	53.6
DISTRIBUTION COST STUDIES	53.0
PRICE STUDIES	53.0
COMPETITIVE PRICING	52.4
ADVERTISING EFFECTIVENESS	50.6
PROPOSED SALES METHODS	48.2
COMPETITIVE PRACTICES	42.9
SALES COMPENSATION	42.3
PROMOTIONAL DEVICES	41.7
ADVERTISING MEDIA	35.7

Figure 3.4

VERSATILITY CLEARLY INDICATED

The three charts reveal an important characteristic of marketing research which is not immediately apparent. That characteristic is the versatility with which marketing research is used in company practices. On each of the three charts, the percentages add to a total far higher than 100 per cent. For the product-services area charted in Figure 3.2, for example, the total is more than 700 per cent. This shows the extent to which multiple answers were recorded; that is, the extent to which companies reported performing more than one activity in each area.

Out of the total of thirty-seven activities listed on the questionnaire, the average (median) respondent company that reported performing *any* marketing research reported performing *twenty-two of the thirty-seven listed functions, or 60 per cent of all of them.* Within the three major areas, the median firm performed almost three-fourths of the functions listed in the area of research on products and services; seven out of ten in the area of research on markets; but only eight out of fifteen, or 53 per cent, of the activities listed in the area of research on sales methods and policies. Further, there is some understatement present in all of these figures because the performance of activities not listed in the questionnaire has been excluded from this summarization.

RELATIVE IMPORTANCE OF SPECIFIC ACTIVITIES

The three charts which show the proportion of companies performing specific activities provide a picture of marketing research in company practice which has the advantage of being specific, but the disadvantage of being somewhat lacking in depth; that is, they provide no indication of the relative importance of the specific individual activities listed. Without such an indication, the picture remains one-dimensional. There is no way to distinguish between the activity regularly performed and considered important and the activity which is performed infrequently and which is somewhat fringe in importance.

With the specific objective of providing a guide for organizations considering the addition of marketing research as a specialized function, or considering changes in the scope of their activities in this field, the AMA study explored the relative importance of the specific activities listed. This was done by giving each respondent an opportunity to rate functions (including any he had written in as "added starters") in five positions ranging from most important to fifth most important.

In filling out their questionnaires, some respondents indicated only the single function they considered most important, some indicated choices for only the first two positions, and so on. The proportion of respondents indicating a first choice was 85 per cent. That proportion declined with each succeeding choice until about 56 per cent designated the activity ranking fifth in importance.

These "most important" designations have a significance so great that it should be underlined before the specific findings are presented.

The percentages of companies performing specific functions reflect a pattern which is partly influenced by the check list itself. Even though it was developed with great care, that list represented essentially an outside judgment. It provided each respondent with a ready-made list of what their marketing research activities *were expected* to include. By indicating their judgment as to the relative importance of the individual activities, the respondents in effect participated in the *creation of a new and much more significant list.* That list represented a distillation of their own experience with marketing research in practice. It is worth remembering also that each respondent had complete freedom to write in specific activities not included on the list and to designate such activities as "most important" if he chose to do so. In point of fact, less than 6 per cent of all choices of activities as "most important" were made from items which were not included in the printed questionnaire.

Figure 3.5 presents a graphic picture of the results of combining two lists of marketing research activities. One is a list of those activities performed by the largest proportion of respondent companies. The other is a list of those activities voted most important by the largest proportion of companies. The charted list was made up, first by taking all activities performed by three-quarters or more of the companies, and then by adding to that list all activities named as important by one-sixth or more of the companies. (Those two cutoff points were arbitrarily chosen to provide a sharper picture of the top-ranking activities.)

Out of the thirty-seven listed activities, there were eight on the first list—performed by three-quarters or more of the companies. There were also eight activities included in the second list. Figure 3.5 shows only

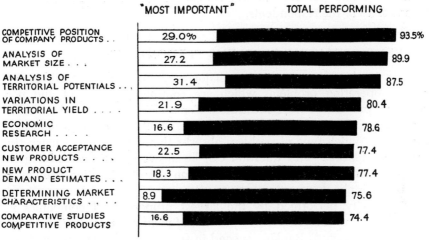

"MOST WIDELY PERFORMED" *and* "MOST IMPORTANT" MARKETING RESEARCH ACTIVITIES

Figure 3.5

nine activities, indicating the extent of overlap between these two lists. There was only one activity on each list which was not on the other. The remaining seven activities were duplicated on *both* lists.

Here are the highlights of this important chart:

1. Determining the competitive position of company products is the most widely performed of the thirty-seven listed functions and is rated as important by more companies than all but one of the listed functions.

2. Analysis of the size of the market for specific products ranked second in frequency of performance—89.9 per cent—and third in frequency of selection as important.

3. Analysis of territorial opportunities or potentials was considered an important marketing research function by more companies than any

of the other thirty-six listed on the questionnaire. This function was performed by almost nine out of ten—87.5 per cent—of the companies that do marketing research.

4. Variations in territorial yield, market share, etc., were studied by eight out of ten companies, and this function was named as important by one-fifth of the companies.

5. Two different activities both specifically concerned with new-product development were included in this list of important functions. Determining customer acceptance of new products and preparing estimates of demand for new products were both reported performed by 77.4 per cent of the companies and named as important by 22.5 and 18.3 per cent, respectively.

6. Product research on existing products, involving comparative studies of company products against competitive products, were reported performed by 74.4 per cent of the companies and considered important by one-sixth of the respondents.

CURRENT OPERATING PROBLEMS PREDOMINANT

Early in this chapter, the two major types of marketing problems—current operating problems which are continuously present and non-recurring problems—were illustrated. For a clear picture of the marketing-problem base of marketing research, this key question must be answered: Which type of problem absorbs the major share of marketing research attention? This question can be answered by reclassifying the nine functions illustrated in Figure 3.5 on the classification framework set up in this chapter.

The activity performed by the largest proportion of companies involves *studies of the competitive position of company's products (market-share analyses, etc.).* Ranking second in frequency of performance is the *analysis of the size of the market for specific products.* These two closely related activities are both in the group of current operating problems.

Ranking third in frequency of performance, but first in the frequency with which it is considered an important activity, is the *analysis of territorial sales opportunities or potentials.* The activity ranking fourth in frequency of performance and fifth in mention as important is the function of *measuring territorial variations in sales yield, market share, sales effectiveness.* These two activities are also closely related. One is concerned with determining territorial potentials, and the other with applying the knowledge of territorial opportunities to evaluate the company's sales performance and to find sales soft spots. These two activities are also clearly examples of current operating problems.

Ranking fifth in frequency of performance is *economic research* (*determination of industry trends, correlation of company sales with economic indicators, etc.*). This activity is another example which belongs in the current operating problem group. It is involved primarily in sales forecasting, although it has other applications as well. For example, economic analysis by individual territories is often used as an aid in determining territorial potentials or in interpreting cases of low territorial sales yields.

The sixth and seventh functions in frequency of performance both are in the area of new-product development: *Determining consumer or customer acceptance of proposed new products or services* and *estimating demand for new products.* Both are examples of the nonrecurring type of problems. (This is true in a strict sense, although increases in the extent of new-product development which are occurring at the time this book went into production give promise of making this a current-operating type of problem in the not-too-distant future.)

Analysis of characteristics of the market for specific products and *comparing consumer or customer acceptance of existing products or services with similar competitive products or services* are both examples of current operating problems.

SUMMARY

1. In summary, then, seven out of the nine top marketing research activities —including all five of the activities ranked highest in importance—fall into the group of current operating problems. The remaining two activities are in the broad area of new-product development.

2. The implications of this pattern are clear:

Marketing research is most frequently used and makes its most important contributions to increased marketing-management effectiveness by aiding in the solution of current operating problems—the kind of problems that are continuously present in almost every well-managed business.

Marketing research also plays an important role in new-product development—a nonrecurring problem area increasing in importance and moving in the direction of becoming a current-operating type of problem.

3. This discussion of the marketing-problem base of marketing research should serve to provide an accurate mental picture of what marketing research practice includes. Applications of marketing research to current operating problems are most frequent and most important. This does not mean that applications to problems of the nonrecurring type are not important. They are. Research on a single complex problem of that type might extend over many months of intensive work. But the more spectacular nature of problems in the nonrecurring category should not lead one to overlook the much greater importance of the more routine type of assignments. Such assignments constitute the bulk of the day-in-day-out work of marketing research men.

4. Because marketing research practice is primarily concerned with current operating problems, the major emphasis in this book has been placed on problems of that type.

QUESTIONS

1. Where is marketing research most frequently applied and where would you say marketing research makes its most important contributions?

2. What are six operating problems a sales vice-president might be confronted with in his duties with a manufacturing concern? Discuss each briefly.

3. What is the primary characteristic of nonrecurring marketing problems?

4. Name and discuss briefly five types of nonrecurring marketing problems.

5. How would you define the following terms: *potential* and *market share?*

CHAPTER 4

Introduction to the Problem-solving Process in Marketing

In the preceding chapter, the marketing-problem base of marketing research was described. The most widely performed marketing research
activities were identified. The activities considered most important by
companies participating in the American Management Association survey were reviewed and were found to be essentially the same activities
which were most widely performed, with some minor variations in rank.
In the last chapter we were concerned with *what* marketing research includes. We now turn our attention from the *what* to the *how* of marketing research.

A systematic, step-by-step approach to the solution of marketing problems is at the core of the skill of an experienced marketing research
man. This chapter will introduce the *how* of marketing research, but it
cannot go beyond that introductory stage. To understand fully and
specifically how marketing research activities are carried on, you must
first know more about the technique tools of marketing research. Those
technique tools are the subject of Section Two of this book, which begins
with the next chapter.

It may be helpful to begin with a clear picture of the relationship
between the step-by-step analytical research approach described in this
chapter and the technique tools introduced in the next section. That
relationship can be illustrated by utilizing the parallel between a complex research job and building a house. In each case, the first step is to
develop a carefully detailed and complete plan. When the plan is complete, how is it to be executed? There are available specific and basic
skills or technique tools in each case. The builder uses crafts such as
carpentry, bricklaying, and plumbing in executing his plan. The research
man uses techniques such as surveys, panels, and sales analysis in executing his plan.

In both cases, the nature of the plan determines the approach taken.
Bricklayers are used only if the plan calls for a brick house. If the house

is entirely of frame construction, no bricklayers are required and none are used. Similarly, there are many basic research techniques which are omitted from consideration in dealing with a specific research problem because the nature of the problem or the plan of attack does not require them. The step-by-step approach introduced in this chapter is used first in developing the plan for a research job, and then as a guide in executing that plan. The technique tools used depend on the nature of the plan.

CASES PERMIT SPECIFIC ILLUSTRATIONS

Many readers of this book are likely to bring to it no personal experience with the actual process of recognizing and diagnosing specific marketing problems. Other readers may be familiar only with certain types of problems or the problems of a single industry. For the benefit of readers in either group, it seems desirable to introduce case material which can be used to focus the discussion of the problem-solving process in specific terms. Cases permit specific analytical illustrations of the marketing research approaches recommended, rather than a more general description of the procedures.

Each case presented has been chosen to illustrate a major *type* of marketing problem. Where a fictitious name is used to protect the actual company against the disclosure of confidential information, a star signals that fact where the company name in question is *first* introduced. The first case describing the problems of a particular company is designated (A), the second reference to the same company with (B), and so on. Although some of the *names* used are fictitious, *all* the companies and problems described are actual.

1. THE DELL-O COMPANY ★ (A)

The Dell-O Company manufactured margarine and other food products of a semiperishable nature including mayonnaise, salad dressings, and a number of different types of shortening products sold to commercial bakers. The company's single factory was located in Chicago. Here are the annual sales of Dell-O brand of margarine in pounds for the years from 1935 through 1940:

Year	Net sales, lb.
1935	37,745,000
1936	32,548,000
1937	34,762,000
1938	27,642,000
1939	17,550,000
1940	15,429,000

Alarmed by the continuing decline in sales of their major product, executives of the Dell-O Company early in 1941 shifted their advertising account to a new advertising agency chosen in part because of its extensive marketing research and merchandising facilities. The new agency was asked to make an objective analysis of the company's sales problem and to recommend a course of action aimed at reversing the long sales decline.

In their indoctrination meeting with Dell-O Company sales executives, the agency's research and merchandising personnel were told that the primary cause of this sales decline was thought to be increased price competition from lower-priced margarines selling for a substantially lower price per pound than Dell-O. Another influence thought to be responsible at least in part for the decline in sales was the price of butter. Company executives explained that the market for margarine was made up in part of a large group of consumers who bought margarine when the price of butter was high, but who switched back to butter when the price of butter declined.

— ★ —

Comment: This case is representative of a large group of frequently encountered major marketing problems. We have here a substantial and continuing sales decline, the causes of which are not known. What is the problem? Note first that the decline in sales is *not* the problem—rather it is a symptom of the problem. The two factors singled out by company executives—increased competition from lower-priced brands and declining butter prices—may or may not actually be important elements in the company's sales problem. That they *are* elements is apparently the hypothesis of company executives.

THE THREE DIMENSIONS OF A MARKETING PROBLEM

The Dell-O example illustrates a marketing problem, not a marketing research problem. A marketing research problem nearly always *grows out of* and *is an element of* a marketing problem. A single marketing problem like that of Dell-O often involves dozens or even scores of different marketing research problems. For reasons that will become apparent as the steps in the problem-solving process are described, a marketing research man usually is unable to make a maximum contribution to the solution of a given marketing research problem unless he is thoroughly familiar with the marketing problem as well as with the specific marketing research assignment or assignments that developed out of the marketing problem.

In dealing with a marketing problem and in preparing to deal with one or more marketing research problems inherent in that marketing problem, the first step is to *establish the dimensions of the problem.* Every marketing problem has three dimensions. All are important. All are intimately interrelated. The first is the *time* dimension. How much time is available for the solution of any given marketing problem? When must the key decisions be made? The second is the *profit* dimension, which establishes the relative importance of the problem. Just how important is the solution of any given marketing problem, in terms of the probable profit contribution that the successful solution may reasonably be expected to make? The third dimension is the *facilities* dimension. Just what facilities are available for use in attempting to develop the solution to a given marketing problem? These three dimensions are so fundamental to successful marketing research work that they warrant closer examination.

THE TIME DIMENSION

The time dimension of either a marketing problem or a marketing research problem is a vital element in planning work on that problem. Until the time dimension has been established, it is not possible even to consider alternative approaches. This is a very practical viewpoint, which is important because it introduces safeguards against wasted effort. If alternative ways of tackling a specific problem were considered without first establishing the time dimension of the problem, some approaches might be considered which would be actually impractical because executing them would require far more time than was available. In many marketing research situations encountered in practice, time is a most essential ingredient.

From the viewpoint of the marketing research man, the ideal situation is one in which he is presented with a problem, plans the research, and then advises how much time will be required. In practice the reverse situation is often encountered. The research man is presented with an assignment and is told that he must have "the answer" by some specified date. Note how that changes the nature of the research assignment. In the former case, the problem is one of determining how certain required facts may be secured most efficiently. In the latter, the problem is one of determining how certain required facts can be secured *by a given date,* with theoretical considerations of research efficiency relegated to a definitely subordinate role.

In thinking about the time dimension of marketing problems, it is sometimes helpful to classify them mentally into one of three groups: *very urgent* problems, on which the nature of the problem or the timing of a decision date requires a crisis type of handling; *urgent* problems, on which time is very short and something beyond normal scheduling is required; or *not-urgent* problems, this becoming a relative term used to identify the kind of problem that takes its place in line and is handled in a normal manner. Very few marketing research problems seem to fall into the latter category!

THE PROFIT DIMENSION

There is both a negative and positive aspect to the profit dimension. The positive aspect is concerned with the added profit a sound solution might be expected to contribute. The negative is concerned with the loss, or decline in profit, which might result from failure to arrive at a correct decision. It is important to remember that the profit dimension of a marketing problem is an extremely relative concept. What would be a tremendously important sum for one company might be far less important to another organization.

In considering the profit dimension of a marketing problem, it is often helpful to classify the problem along these lines: *very important* problems, in which the profit dimension *in relation to the situation of the company facing the problem* is great and the situation therefore grave. As a general guide, this classification is involved whenever a company's actual survival is likely to be at stake or where the rewards of successfully pursuing a given course of action are extremely large. *Important* problems rank below the first group in gravity or in potential rewards, but rank higher than *unimportant problems* which involve an issue that is relatively minor in terms of its potential impact on the company's total situation.

THE FACILITIES DIMENSION

This dimension of a marketing problem is concerned with the actual facilities or resources which are available to a company's management for dealing with a particular specific problem. When a marketing research man appraises the facilities at his command, his appraisal usually begins with himself. The question of the facilities available for dealing with a particular situation may be subdivided into two major parts. Part one is the *ability* of those facilities. Part two is the *availability* of the facilities.

In classifying the facilities dimension of a marketing problem, any of three types of situations is likely to be encountered. The first is one in which *complete* facilities are available. This situation exists where a company has at its disposal the required types of skills or people with the requisite experience and ability *and* where those abilities may be applied to the solution of the problem at hand without diverting them from other equally important problems. Complete facilities exist only where both ability and availability are present. The second situation is one where *partial* facilities exist. This may mean that a company lacks experienced personnel qualified to deal with a particular problem situation. Or it could mean that although the required abilities are present, they are so heavily burdened or committed with other assignments that they cannot be directed to the problem at hand. Less ability or less availability than the problem requires might also warrant this classification. The third situation is the not-uncommon one wherein *no* facilities are available. This situation occurs where a company has no personnel capable of dealing with a particular problem who are in a position to deal with it.

Where a company has complete facilities for tackling a particular marketing problem, those facilities can be and usually are applied to the problem without delay. Companies in either of the other two categories, where a particular problem is concerned, must secure outside assistance to make up for their own limitations in the facilities area or else take no action to solve the problem in question.

DIMENSIONS OF THE DELL-O PROBLEM

The time dimension of the Dell-O situation is clearly in the VERY URGENT category. Continuing sales declines have eroded about 60 per cent of the volume the company had six years earlier. This illustrates the interrelationship of the different dimensions of a problem. The magnitude of the problem, i.e., its profit dimension, creates the great urgency in the time dimension. Note also that the fact that a problem has existed over a long period of time, either unrecognized or apparently unrecognized, does not reduce the urgency of action once the problem *is* recognized and a decision made to take constructive action on it.

In its profit dimension, the Dell-O problem is unmistakably VERY IMPORTANT. The continuing survival of the company is in doubt unless the adverse sales trend could be arrested.

We may safely infer from the facts presented in the Dell-O case that the company had *no* facilities for dealing with a marketing problem of the scope and type of the one it faced. If facilities had been available within the company, they would presumably have been applied without allowing the decline in sales to continue for six years. The management decision to seek outside aid confirms this appraisal. The soundness of the decision to seek that aid from an advertising agency is perhaps open to question, but that question is irrelevant to our discussion here.

STEPS IN RESEARCH ON A MAJOR MARKETING PROBLEM

An experienced marketing research man has at his command a systematic method of attack on marketing problems which can be used on a wide range of different types of problems. That approach is analytical and objective. It involves a planned method of handling a marketing problem which has been proved in practice and which, incidentally, is very similar to the problem-solving approaches used in other fields, including both social and physical sciences. Here are the six steps in that approach:

Step 1. Define the *marketing* problem in specific terms.

Step 2. Refine the problem and subdivide it to isolate the individual marketing *research* problems it presents.

Step 3. Develop a plan for securing the facts or information needed.

Step 4. Execute the plan and secure the facts.

Step 5. Analyze the facts and interpret them in terms of the problem.

Step 6. Summarize the results of the analysis and interpretation and report the findings.

This general six-step approach is applied primarily to marketing problems which have two characteristics. First, the problem area is one which is complex in nature. Both the time dimension and the profit dimension are adequate. Second, the problem cannot be definitely identified as to type on the basis of information available.

The first of those characteristics is essential because step-by-step problem solving is often a tremendously expensive and time-consuming process. If the time is not available, or if the scale of the expenditure involved is unsound when equated with the results which may reasonably be expected, this approach is unlikely to be used.

The second characteristic has this significance: The first two steps indicated—determining what the problem is and then dividing it into its major components—are often the most difficult and time-consuming phase of the task. If the problem can be defined without the need for research, the entire process can often be shortened materially. Note also that this is a *general* approach. There are many types of frequently occurring problems which call for rather clear-cut and *specific* steps. A sales forecast, for example, can be prepared much more efficiently by following the approach outlined in Chapter 19 than by using the general approach above.

INSIDE AND OUTSIDE APPROACHES ESSENTIALLY SIMILAR

To illustrate this approach, let's now apply it to the Dell-O problem. In the following discussion the viewpoint is that of an experienced marketing research man who has been asked to examine the problem in question and to recommend a course of action to secure facts helpful to management in arriving at the indicated decision. In other words, this is the viewpoint of someone outside of the company in which the problem developed.

The problem-solving process in marketing is identical, whether the problem is approached from the inside or the outside of the organization facing that problem. The primary distinction between the inside and the outside approach is that in the former case the research man begins with a backlog of information about the company, its industry, and products. The outsider has no such background. The outside approach is used here because it permits a more complete description of the processes involved.

One might think offhand that the insider who faces a marketing problem brings to the task advantages over the individual approaching it from the outside. That is sometimes true, because of advantages in background and information. Sometimes the insider is deeply steeped in corporate viewpoints, perhaps including some corporate prejudices. The danger of "knowing" things which are not true is far greater in the case of insiders than of outsiders.

STEP 1: DEFINING THE MARKETING PROBLEM IN SPECIFIC TERMS

Once the dimensions of a marketing problem have been established, the actual problem-solving process begins. The first step is to define the marketing problem in specific terms. At this point attention is focused on the *marketing* problem rather than on the marketing *research* problem or problems. This is one of the most important steps in marketing research. Carelessness in defining the problem can and unfortunately often does lead to wasted time and money. After the problem has been specifically defined, one can proceed with confidence and speed to gather the facts relevant to its solution. Until the problem is defined, there is an ever-present risk that any action taken may prove to be wastefully irrelevant to the true problem.

The very urgent time dimension and very important profit dimension of the Dell-O problem have been pointed out. The problem has been turned over by the manufacturer (who apparently had *no* facilities for dealing with it) to an advertising agency where we may assume relatively complete facilities were available. All that is known about the problem is that sales have been declining sharply for six years. That sagging sales curve is an unmistakable symptom of a very serious problem. But what *is* the problem? How can it be defined?

The approach to take is an unspectacular but dependable one which has proved effective in practice. Its major elements are analysis and subdivision. First the problem situation is divided into a number of major elements. Then each element is examined in turn as part of an attempt to *isolate* and *identify* the *problem* elements. This often involves further subdivision of individual elements.

The analytical procedure is largely diagnostic in nature. It is very similar to the approach of a dentist when a new patient turns up with a throbbing toothache. The patient can point out the general area of the pain, but that general information usually isn't enough for the dentist. X rays of all teeth are likely to be his first step. Only after those X rays have been studied can the dentist proceed confidently with his remedial treatment.

MAJOR ELEMENTS IN A MARKETING PROBLEM

A complex marketing problem like the so-far unexplained decline in Dell-O margarine sales calls for a general framework of major marketing elements as a guide to aid in early efforts at defining the problem. Here is such a framework.

1. Industry elements
2. Competitive elements
3. Market elements
4. Company elements

It would of course be possible to offer a far longer list of major areas. This shorter list seems preferable because the roots of a marketing problem which is signaled by a declining sales curve are likely to be found in one or more of those four major areas. Each area can be and usually is further subdivided.

REVIEW OF INDUSTRY ELEMENTS

The industry elements of the Dell-O problem might be explored by seeking answers to questions such as these:

What is the size of the industry's volume? What is the trend of that volume? What economic forces, if any, are active influences affecting the trend of the industry's volume? What are the characteristics of the industry's volume? Are any major changes occurring, or have there been recent changes, in those characteristics?

QUESTIONS ABOUT COMPETITIVE ELEMENTS

In a study of the competitive elements of the Dell-O problem, questions of this type require attention:

Who are the company's major competitors? How do those competitors divide the industry volume? Have there been any recent important changes in market shares within the industry? If there have been such changes, what factor or factors contributed to them? Have any new competitors or new types of competitors entered the industry? Have any competitive product innovations appeared which represent a present or potential threat to the volume of existing firms in the industry? Have any changes in competitive sales methods or policies occurred which represent a present or potential threat to existing industry patterns? Have any changes in pricing occurred which affect the industry's situation? (Note that such changes could be either within the industry itself or in some related industry of competitive or indirectly competitive nature.)

MARKET AND COMPANY ELEMENTS

In subdividing the market elements, attention would be focused on the characteristics of the market for products of the industry and on any major changes in those characteristics.

The company elements of this problem situation would include all matters under the control of the company. The questions which would require answers would include these:

What are the characteristics of the company's products? How do those products compare with those of major competitors, especially in their consumer or customer acceptance? What is the company's pricing practice and philosophy? How do the company's pricing practices, discount structure, etc., compare with those of major competitors? What is the caliber of the company's sales organization? How does that organization compare with those of major competitors? What are the company's sales methods and policies? How do those methods and policies compare with those of major competitors? What are the company's distribution channels? How do those distribution channels compare with those of major competitors? What is the company's customer-type emphasis? How does that emphasis compare with that of major competitors?

The close interrelationship between competitive and company elements should be noted. This interrelationship exists because a competitive problem may develop as a result of positive factors, negative factors, or both. That is, some positive action by a competitor may impel a company into a competitive problem situation; or some negative factor or action of the company itself such as an area or element of weakness in its operations as compared to one or more competitors might have the same effect. Both positive and negative factors of this type could be and often are present in the same problem situation.

OBJECTIVE: ISOLATE AND IDENTIFY PROBLEM ELEMENTS

In the analytical subdivision of a marketing problem situation like the Dell-O one, the constant objective of the research man is to *isolate and identify the problem elements* in each particular situation. Once those elements are identified, further attention can be confined to them, just as the dentist concentrates his attention on the aching tooth and ignores the healthy teeth beside it. It is quite possible that the heart of the Dell-O problem might lie entirely within the area indicated by a single one of the questions above. If this were the case, then all the time and effort spent exploring any of the other questions would be likely to be irrelevant to the problem.

One possibility of such a one-problem-element answer lies in the industry area. If the volume of the entire industry were declining, as the volume of manufacturers of wheat flour did for many, many years, the Dell-O sales decline might reflect the impact of the contracting industry volume on the company's situation. Another possibility is product quality. If the Dell-O product were substantially inferior in its consumer acceptance to the products of one or more competitors, that fact alone might come very close to being the entire cause of the sales decline. It might be well to point out here that *cause* is a word that should be used with extreme caution in marketing research, for reasons which will be made clear in Chapter 17 on the interpretation of data.

Note again the positive-negative possibilities present in this type of analysis. There might be some question as to the likelihood that a single sweeping influence such as this poor-product possibility could be the underlying cause of a long sales decline. That is especially true if the product had been unchanged over the full period of time under discussion. In other words, is it likely that a product acceptable enough to build a 35-million-pound annual volume level could have declined so sharply in acceptance if the product itself was unchanged? The answer is that such a decline might well have occurred as the result of a competitive product improvement, with the Dell-O quality held constant. If a major competitor improved his product and exploited it effectively, such a situation might have resulted.

THE HYPOTHESIS AS AN ANALYTICAL TOOL

If a single element *could* represent *the* problem element in a complex marketing situation like that of Dell-O margarine, and if effort devoted to exploring other elements would therefore be wasteful and irrelevant to the problem, how does one proceed? The answer is that in this step of defining the specific marketing problem some lost motion is inescapable. Each major element must be considered. In doing so, however, the hypothesis is used as an analytical tool to reduce the risk of devoting more than brief attention to elements which are unrelated to the problem.

A hypothesis may be defined as a tentative theory or supposition set up and adopted provisionally as a basis of explaining certain facts or relationships and as a guide in the further investigation of other facts or relationships. In dealing with the problem underlying an unexplained long-continuing decline in sales such as Dell-O experienced, this obvious hypothesis must always be considered:

Hypothesis: *That industry volume has declined sharply over the period during which Dell-O margarine sales have declined.*

There were two other hypotheses advanced by company executives as representing in their opinions complete or partial explanations of the decline in Dell-O margarine sales. These were:

Hypothesis: *That increased competition from low-priced margarine was a major element in the declining sales of Dell-O margarine.*

Hypothesis: *That low butter prices which induced consumers to switch from margarine to butter were a major element in the decline in Dell-O margarine sales.*

Dell-O margarine was priced higher than some other brands. Therefore it was quite conceivable that the effect of a reduction in butter prices on Dell-O sales might be greater than the effect on industry volume or on the sales of one or more competitors with lower-priced products.

The possibility that the decline in company sales might be primarily, if not entirely, a reflection of a contraction in industry volume has already been mentioned. The butter-price question and the closely related question of whether or not changes in consumer income levels might similarly convert margarine users to butter also were both in the industry area. Such influences would be likely to affect sales of all margarine (or of all margarine in the Dell-O price class) with approximately equal force. The question of low-priced competition and the possibility that brands in that price group were capturing an expanding share of industry volume was also closely related. Such low-priced brands might have been expanding their share of an increasing, constant, or decreasing industry total. Again the questions involve industry elements since all margarines in Dell-O's price group would be likely to be affected by any trend of this type within the industry.

SELECTING A STARTING POINT

Now from the viewpoint of the executive responsible for the fact-finding activities within the new advertising agency, what action should be taken to help define the marketing problem? Remember that this is a problem which combines a very urgent time dimension with a very important profit dimension. There is obviously little time to lose. This is a serious problem—the house is on fire! The problem is one of minimizing the risk of wasted time and effort exploring dead-end paths as well as the risk of delaying action which seems to offer real promise. Just what should be done first?

DECISION: EXPLORE INDUSTRY ELEMENTS

When this problem was studied by a team of experienced marketing men, they decided that the industry elements of the problem required immediate clarification. The answers to these six specific questions were felt to be urgently necessary:

1. What is the size and trend of industry volume?
2. What is the Dell-O share of industry volume?
3. What is the trend in Dell-O margarine's market share?
4. How is the margarine industry volume divided among high-priced, medium-priced, and low-priced brands?
5. What trends, if any, are apparent in that price-class division of industry volume?
6. To what extent is industry volume and Dell-O volume influenced by such economic factors as butter prices and consumer income levels?

It is an aside, but an instructive one, to suggest that the above list of six questions be compared with the list of the most widely performed and most important marketing research functions charted in the preceding chapter. In making this comparison, remember that this problem situation was finally recognized and management action taken in 1941, up to which time the Dell-O Company had performed no marketing research.

The executives responsible for the management of the Dell-O Company at that time had *factual* answers to none of these six questions. Lacking facts, they found themselves in serious difficulties. If they had had a fully effective marketing research department, it would be reasonable to expect that they would have had the answers to all six of the questions listed and to many additional important questions as well. The first three of the questions listed above would all be answered if the company had a research department that performed the two most widely performed of all marketing research activities—determining competitive position of company products and determining market size. Questions 4 and 5 would have been answered by research to determine market characteristics. Question 6 would be answered by economic research.

Because our objective at this point is primarily to illustrate how a marketing problem is defined in specific terms, a fully detailed discussion of the actual marketing research approaches used to get the answers to the above six questions would be out of place here. All six questions can easily be answered by marketing research today. The techniques for securing the answers are far more advanced today than they were in 1941.

RESULTS OF EXPLORING INDUSTRY ELEMENTS

When the answers to these questions were secured and analyzed, the following conclusions were reported:

1. Over the period during which Dell-O margarine sales declined, there was a loss in volume for the margarine industry as a whole. But the decline in company sales was much sharper than the decline in industry volume, with the result that Dell-O's share of the total market declined from about 10 per cent of industry volume in 1935 to less than 5 per cent in 1940.

2. Analysis of industry volume by price categories showed that makers of low-priced margarines were *not* increasing their share of industry volume. On the contrary, two major producers of high-priced margarine in the Dell-O price class were recording the only important market-share gains in the industry. Those two firms were in fact increasing their volume, despite the contraction in industry volume.

3. A comprehensive analysis of the relationship between butter prices and national income on one hand and sales volume of Dell-O and all margarine on the other was executed. This analysis used correlation techniques. The following quotation from the report of this analysis summarized the major findings:

> 36 per cent of the variation in the sales of Dell-O Margarine can be attributed to a time trend and to changes in national income. The remaining 61 per cent is due to factors unmeasured in this study.
>
> Butter prices accounted for much more of the variation of sales during 1934–1937 (59 per cent) than for the whole period of January 1934 through April 1941 (36 per cent).
>
> This indicates that other factors (promotion and competition, but not butter prices) have become of dominant importance in the period since 1937.

In summarizing the first phase of its efforts to define the problem in specific terms, the agency reported these findings. Its report pointed out the sharper decline in Dell-O sales and the loss of market share. The fact that the two brands most similar to Dell-O in price, national prestige, and promotion methods had maintained their combined volume and improved their relative position proved that it was possible for higher-priced brands to progress despite low-priced competition. The report concluded:

> In view of all of the foregoing, it is apparent that the Dell-O problem is primarily a competitive problem . . . a problem of taking more business from competitors than they take from Dell-O.
>
> If this final conclusion can be agreed upon, then the next step will be to examine the competitive situation in detail in order to arrive at a diagnosis. We are faced with the problem of a business which is seriously ill. The sole hope of recovery lies in sound diagnosis, which can be made only as a result of weighing objectively the strengths and weaknesses of the business. The examination must be thorough. It must have only one objective—the welfare of the Dell-O Company.

RESEARCH IS SOMETIMES NEEDED TO DEFINE THE PROBLEM

There is a circular relationship in the above illustration which is common to much marketing research work. Start with a marketing problem and with a series of six steps in the problem-solving process. The first of those steps calls for defining the problem in specific terms. But before that first step could be taken on the marketing problem of the Dell-O Company, it was necessary to proceed through all of the remaining five steps on certain specific marketing *research* subproblems (the nature of which was indicated by the six questions which had to be answered).

The first step in the step-by-step approach to the solution of the broad Dell-O margarine problem could not be completed until the results of the exploratory marketing research on subproblems were available for analysis. That analysis led to the conclusion that the problem was competitive in nature.

STEP 2: REFINING AND SUBDIVIDING THE MARKETING PROBLEM

The second step in applying marketing research to a marketing problem like that of the Dell-O Company consists of refining the marketing problem and subdividing it to isolate the individual marketing research problems it presents. In the actual analysis of the Dell-O problem, these key elements were explored:

1. Product
2. Prices and pricing
3. Sales methods and policies
4. Territorial sales potential and market shares
5. Distribution
6. Distributors and their facilities
7. Distribution channels
8. Customer-type emphasis and trends
9. Consumer buying habits
10. Merchandising
11. Displays
12. Promotion and advertising

It would be possible to apply marketing research to each of the above areas and in fact to many different aspects of some areas. In the product area, for example, research could explore the relative consumer acceptance of the Dell-O product compared to the two competitive products which were gaining market share, as to uniformity of product, and packaging. In the prices and pricing area, marketing research could be used to conduct comparative studies of the pricing and discount structure of Dell-O margarine and leading competitors, of pricing flexibility (meaning the speed with which prices were adjusted when raw-material prices changed or when a competitive brand changed its prices), and to actual comparative prices paid by consumers. Each of the remaining ten areas could similarly be subdivided, and marketing research used to explore each subdivision.

THE PROBLEM OF ASSIGNING PRIORITIES

There are clearly many more areas for exploration by marketing research, in a complex problem situation like this, than it would be possible to explore without a budget comparable to the one with which the Manhattan District project developed the atom bomb. In this respect, this problem is more usual than unusual. When a marketing research man faces a complex problem it is necessary for him—as in this case— to confine marketing research at least initially to what appear to be the more important and more promising of the myriad possible marketing research problems. One could easily spend many, many months or even years and many thousands of dollars on the Dell-O problem without exhausting its marketing research possibilities. Remembering the cost-results relationship introduced in Chapter 1, it is apparent that such an approach would be out of line with the realities of the situation.

Since this problem had a very urgent time dimension and a very important profit dimension, what was needed was some kind of a program for pruning the possibilities to a workable number by screening them through a series of questions like these:

1. On the basis of present knowledge, does this seem to be a problem area which is *likely* to represent a *major* element in the marketing problem under study?

2. How much time will it take to explore this area?

3. How much money is it likely to cost?

4. Considering the other elements of this marketing problem to which marketing research might also be applied, and considering the total amount of time, money, and facilities available, is this particular area one that rates a top priority and immediate attention, or should it be considered only after more promising areas are studied?

From among the many possible marketing research problems included within a particular complex marketing problem, the marketing research man must assign priorities and pick the most promising.

IMPORTANCE OF FLEXIBILITY

Two comments should be made regarding this brief series of screening questions. Note carefully the key phrase in question 1—*on the basis of present knowledge*. In his approach to a complex problem like this, a marketing research man must be flexible. The screening questions indicated above may be asked and answered several times, for the answers may change when the results of some step in the research process become available. The golfing illustration in Chapter 1 has a parallel here: You don't always know what club you're going to use on your second shot until you see where the ball stops rolling on your first one. At each step in the research process it is often necessary to re-examine the elements and to reapply the screening questions in the light of the additional information.

The second comment about this screening process is by way of underlining the significance of question 4. Even where there are relatively complete facilities available, those facilities are unlikely to be equal to the task of exploring *all* the promising marketing research possibilities *at once*. It is necessary to weigh different marketing research projects against each other, considering with care the time, cost, and facilities each will consume since inevitably some of these projects will be competing for the same facility.

SEVEN DELL-O MARKETING *RESEARCH* PROBLEMS

To illustrate this problem of assigning priorities, against the background of a now-familiar problem, let's return to the Dell-O situation.

In that case it was decided that these questions—these marketing *research* problems—were entitled to top priority:

1. How does the quality of the Dell-O product compare with that of the two leading competitors in its price group in consumer acceptance?

2. How does Dell-O margarine compare with leading competitors in the size of its consumer franchise, i.e., in the number of using families, and what are the trends by brands? This question was aimed at identifying the brands which were gaining the volume and customers which were slipping away from Dell-O.

3. What is the territorial distribution of Dell-O volume? Of total margarine potential? What are the variations in Dell-O's share of market by areas?

4. How does the sales organization selling Dell-O margarine compare with that of leading competitors in the same price group, both in the quantity and quality of manpower?

5. How does the distributor organization handling Dell-O margarine compare with that of leading competitors? How does the distribution achieved (i.e., proportion of stores handling the product) compare for Dell-O and leading competitors?

6. How do the pricing and discount structures of Dell-O and leading competitors compare?

7. How do the advertising programs of Dell-O and leading competitors compare, both in quantity and quality? What are the relative expenditure rates of each major competitor? How is the advertising divided among different media, and how is it divided through the year seasonally?

Not all the twelve areas identified earlier found their way into this list. The focus has been sharpened down to one or more key points in each area. The single marketing problem has now become at least seven separate marketing *research* problems, although only the first two of the six steps in the problem-solving process have yet been considered.

At this point it is necessary to fan out to cover the larger problem area that has been delineated. The remaining four steps in the six-step approach outlined earlier in this chapter apply to the planning and execution of the marketing research and to the analysis, interpretation, and reporting of the findings. Those four steps would have to be applied *individually* to *every one* of the seven different marketing research problems indicated by the above list of questions. In other words, marketing research would have to be planned and executed and the findings analyzed, interpreted, and reported on *each one* of the seven marketing research problems that grew out of what was initially a single marketing problem.

The time required to complete a given study on any one of those seven marketing research problems could not be estimated until the plan for that study is reduced to specific terms. Therefore, the planning step on all seven of the individual marketing research problems would have to be completed in at least a preliminary way. Only then could the full scope of the combined or total expenditure in time, money, and effort be determined. At that point some of the elements in the marketing research program outlined might have to be combined, eliminated, or deferred, with combination of several questions into a single research project as a real possibility.

The remaining steps in the six-step approach cannot be described meaningfully until the technique tools of marketing research are introduced in the next section. It may be helpful to indicate in a general way what those steps would involve, so that the technique tools as introduced can be associated with portions of the Dell-O problem.

To answer question 1 above would require product research, the subject of Chapter 22. Question 2 might be answered by a consumer survey or by some form of panel research. The survey technique is described in Chapter 8 and panel research in Chapter 9. Question 3 would involve sales analysis and the subject matter of Chapters 6, 20, and 21. It would probably be necessary to complete that analysis *before* a consumer survey (suggested by question 2) could be soundly planned as to its geographic dispersion. Questions 4, 5, and 6 would require field research of the type more likely to involve *informal investigation* (the subject of Chapter 13) by a small number of skilled and experienced people than a more formal survey. It is also possible that the results of the informal study might make a trade-level survey seem desirable.

INTEGRATED VERSUS NONINTEGRATED RESEARCH

In the interest of accurate perspective, it is desirable to underline one aspect of the Dell-O case which is not clear from the above discussion. This situation illustrates the use of marketing research in two phases of the attack on a problem—first as an aid in subdividing a marketing problem, and then in isolating the marketing research aspects of that problem. Marketing research also entered into the planning, execution, analysis, and interpretation steps on each of the individual marketing research problems, of course.

This illustrates the integration of marketing research into the entire marketing problem area, a pattern found in those organizations in which marketing research is used most effectively. It is typical of companies which are relatively advanced in their recognition of the value of marketing research and in their knowledge of how this management tool can be used most productively. There are many organizations in which marketing research is used but is not integrated into the marketing management picture. In such companies, the marketing research executive often operates entirely on the basis of specific assignments which are given to him without the background information which would enable him to become familiar with the entire marketing problem of which the marketing research assignment is a part.

In that kind of nonintegrated situation, a marketing research man might receive the assignment of making a comparative test of the consumer acceptance of Dell-O margarine as against one or more competitive products. That limited and specific assignment would be the only "problem" to which he would be exposed and to the solution of which he could contribute. The difference between integrated and non-integrated marketing research is like the difference in importance of an automobile tire regularly used to propel a fast-moving marketing management machine and one used only as a spare tire. Because the spare tire is only used occasionally, it can contribute to the machine's progress only occasionally instead of regularly.

THE PRICE PAID FOR LACK OF INTEGRATION

The company that spends money for marketing research, yet fails to integrate research into its marketing management activities on a full-time rather than a spare-tire basis, deprives itself of many of the benefits of research. It also reduces its return on an investment in research to a point well below the maximum level. It is easy to see why this is so. Consider the process of subdividing a marketing problem and isolating the elements of that problem to which marketing research can be most effectively applied, as in the Dell-O illustration. In the case of integrated research, that process is carried on by the individual who knows the most about what marketing research can and cannot do.

The marketing research man's knowledge of his technique tools and his knowledge of the sources of marketing facts make it possible for him to visualize many ways in which marketing research might contribute to a particular decision which someone lacking that knowledge might overlook. His skill and training at relating marketing phenomena to each other, at developing hypotheses, and at planning research to span as many aspects of a given marketing problem as possible are partially wasted where there is a lack of integration. The process of fitting together a number of different pieces of a marketing-problem puzzle (like the seven marketing-research elements of the Dell-O problem) calls for a high level of skill. So does the task of planning the fact finding so that the most likely possibilities are explored first. The efficient application of marketing research to a complex marketing problem requires a detailed familiarity with marketing research techniques and processes, a high level of skill in their application which no individual lacking broad experience in the field is likely to possess.

Nonintegrated research is most likely to be found in manufacturing organizations. Since the Dell-O situation described above involved research by an advertising agency, these comments at this point may not seem appropriate. They are introduced here to make it clear that the Dell-O case represents a relatively ideal, and not necessarily a typical, illustration of the role of marketing research in defining a *marketing* problem.

SUMMARY

1. In the solution of a marketing problem, a systematic, step-by-step approach is required. Such an approach permits an efficient application of the available resources to the key elements of the problem with a minimum loss of time. In illustrating such an approach, the use of specific actual problem situations is helpful.

2. One of the first things a marketing research man does when confronted by a problem situation is to establish, at least in his own mind, the *dimensions* of that problem. Every marketing problem has these three vital dimensions:

a. A *time* dimension, which determines the urgency or lack of urgency present in the situation. This dimension is significant because some approaches which might otherwise be indicated may be impossible within the time available for research on the problem. A decision date often determines the time dimension.

b. A *profit* dimension, which determines the relative importance of the particular problem *as related to the situation of the company facing the problem.* This dimension is helpful in assigning priorities to different problems competing for attention at any given time.

c. A *facilities* dimension, which is concerned with the availability of competent personnel and other facilities required for a successful attack on the problem. The evaluation of this dimension varies from problem to problem, because experience with the particular type of problem in question is one determinant of the adequacy of facilities.

3. A problem-solving approach of wide utility in the marketing field involves these six steps:

a. Definition of the marketing problem in specific terms

b. Refinement of the problem and subdivision of the marketing problem into the various individual marketing research problems it presents.

c. Development of a plan for securing the facts or information needed

d. Execution of the plan and collection of the facts or information

e. Analysis and interpretation of the facts in terms of the problem

f. Summarization of the results of the analysis and interpretation into a report

4. The approach taken toward the solution of marketing problems is

essentially similar, whether the responsibility is delegated to an individual or organization outside the firm having the problem or handled from within that firm.

5. In the case of a complex marketing problem, such as an unexplained sales decline, the approach taken is to subdivide the problem situation into elements. In the case of the problem used in this chapter, the first division was into industry, competitive, market, and company elements.

6. An ever-present objective of the problem-solving process is the isolation and identification of the *problem* elements in the situation.

7. Hypotheses are developed and explored, in the search for problem elements. Sometimes research is necessary in this diagnostic stage to help define the problem.

8. There is a problem of assigning priorities to the various approaches and areas which might be explored. Flexibility in this is extremely important. The results of one phase of an exploration may make the next two phases unnecessary and greatly increase the importance of phase 4, for example.

9. Marketing research is much more effective and makes its maximum contribution when it is integrated into the problem-solving process at the marketing problem level than when the research function is simply assigned portions of the problem for exploration without the background required to surround the entire problem.

QUESTIONS

1. What are the three dimensions of a marketing problem? What part does each dimension play in a marketing research man's analysis of a problem situation?

2. Each of the three dimensions of a marketing problem can be divided into priority or situation classifications. What are these classifications and how do they aid the researcher?

3. An experienced marketing research man has at his command a problem-solving approach that is systematic and can be used on a wide range of marketing problems. What is this approach?

4. And this approach is applied primarily to marketing problems which have two characteristics. What are these characteristics?

5. How does the problem-solving process in marketing differ when the problem is approached by someone inside versus someone outside the organization facing the problem?

6. In the Dell-O margarine case in this chapter a general framework of major marketing elements was set up as a guide. What was this framework, and why was it set up?

7. What is a hypothesis? How does a hypothesis fit into the marketing problem-solving area?

8. Why is flexibility such an important factor to consider when assigning priorities to the various approaches and areas which might be explored?

9. Why is marketing research that is integrated into marketing management activities so much more valuable than nonintegrated research?

The Technique Tools of Marketing Research

CHAPTER 5

Introduction to Sampling in Marketing Research

Marketing research is often called upon to answer relatively simple but important questions. For example, when a new Toni hand-care product was under consideration, this question arose: To what extent are products sold as hand lotions used on other parts of the body? The answer was needed to help decide whether the proposed new product should be identified as a hand lotion or should instead be designated as a beauty lotion, skin lotion, hand and body lotion, or all-purpose lotion. Marketing research was asked to answer this specific question: What proportion of the women who buy hand lotions use them on other parts of the body?

To answer such a question, communication would have to be established between those with the problem, on one hand, and those who have the answer to the question—hand-lotion buyers—on the other. There are a number of different ways in which this end might be accomplished, as Chapter 14 will point out. One approach would be to attempt to interview *all* women who buy hand lotions. That approach would be extremely expensive and almost unbelievably time-consuming. If the cost of that approach were weighed against the potential benefits of getting and applying the information, the idea would be likely to be discarded immediately. Such a *census,* or *complete coverage,* would be likely to cost more than the total annual expenditure of *all* consumers for *all* brands of hand lotions over a period of several years. Judgment alone would tell you that in this case the cost of getting the answer would be likely to be far greater than the benefits to be derived from having and applying that answer.

An experienced marketing research man, presented with this problem, would never seriously consider the census, or complete-coverage, approach. He would instead think in terms of determining the habits of *some* of the women who use hand lotions. He would plan to infer from a relatively small group—*some* users—some of the characteristics of *all* hand-lotion users. He would thus use the small group as the basis of certain generalizations about the larger group of which it was a part.

In this example, all the women in the United States who buy hand lotions would constitute the *whole* from which a *part* was selected. The whole is called the *universe,* or *population,*[1] in statistical terminology, and the selected part is called a *sample.* Under certain conditions—mark those words well!—a part can provide much information about the whole. The process of determining *how large* a part and *what* part to select in order to estimate with confidence some characteristics of the whole is called sampling.

Sampling theory is a subdivision of the field of statistics. You will therefore find elements of sampling discussed in most elementary textbooks about statistical methods. But sampling is also a major element— unquestionably one of the most important elements—in marketing research practice. *Today* no one can achieve competence in the field of marketing research without first acquiring a *thorough* working knowledge of *some* of the important concepts of sampling theory. It is interesting to note that sampling has been a major element in marketing research practice for only a relatively brief period of time, as the following discussion will show.

LIMITATIONS OF THIS SAMPLING DISCUSSION

It seems desirable to recognize at the outset some major limitations of the sampling discussion which follows. It is no longer possible to cover the highly technical and extremely complex subject of sampling adequately and completely in a book about marketing research, of which sampling represents only one part. Whole books much larger than this one have been written about sampling, and especially about sampling as applied to various applications of the survey technique.[2] Because sampling is the most complex and technically the most advanced portion of the marketing research field, it would be easy to carry the discussion of

---

[1] In sampling, the word population is often used to describe all individuals, households, families, items, or things within a specifically and precisely defined group. A population might be all the people living in Cuyahoga County, Ohio; or all the readers of LIFE; or all 1957 Chevrolet automobiles (in an observational study of the wearing quality of paint).

[2] See, for example, W. E. Deming, *Some Theory of Sampling,* Wiley, New York, 1950; William G. Cochran, *Sampling Techniques,* Wiley, New York, 1953; and Morris H. Hansen, William N. Hurwitz, and William G. Madow, *Sample Survey Methods and Theory,* 2 vol., Wiley, New York, 1953. The Hansen et al. volumes cited are definitive works with which every serious student of marketing research should be familiar.

sampling here to lengths quite out of balance with the remainder of the book.

To keep the subject of sampling here in balance, the material which follows has been confined to nontechnical aspects of sampling. The discussion has been rather rigorously confined to those aspects of sampling which clearly constitute basic tools of the marketing research man. It is worth noting also that where sampling is concerned, that marketing research man is a general practitioner and not a sampling specialist.

HISTORICAL APPROACH PROVIDES PERSPECTIVE

The path to an understanding of sampling practice in marketing research today which seems to offer the most promise of providing a continually useful perspective on this subject is historical. In parts of this chapter, that approach is used. First the relatively unimportant role of sampling in marketing research even in the rather recent past is indicated. Then growth in sampling knowledge is traced, and the various sampling approaches widely used in current practice are presented against this historical background. Some significant advances in sampling may confidently be predicted for any given period of time, including the interval between the release of the manuscript of this book to the publisher and its eventual publication. The approach taken here is one which is likely to provide a foundation for understanding and appraising such advances with a minimum risk of obsolescence.

There are a number of basic sampling concepts with which every marketing research man should be familiar. Most of those concepts are introduced into the following discussion in a progressive way. For the benefit of readers who bring to this chapter a familiarity with sampling, such basic concepts have been typographically identified so that they may be skipped.

FUNDAMENTAL SAMPLING CONCEPT

All sampling in marketing research is based upon this fundamental concept:

Fundamental sampling concept. If a small number of items or parts (called a sample) are chosen at random from a larger number of items or a whole (called a universe, or population) the sample will tend to have the same characteristics, and to have them in approximately the same proportion, as the universe.

Some key elements of that statement should be underlined. The first is that the sample must be chosen *at random*. This is an extremely important point, for in sampling "random" has a very specific meaning which is very different from "haphazard" or other words that might be considered loosely synonymous with random as that term is used in informal conversation. The second key element is the word *tend*, which identifies one of the fundamentals of sampling. That is the fact that a value developed from a sample is only an approximation of the value that would be found if a complete coverage, or census, were available instead of a sample.

Basic sampling concepts: Elementary sampling units. An elementary sampling unit is a single entity, or element, of the population from which the sample is selected, for which characteristics are to be measured from the sample. An elementary sampling unit might be an individual person, an individual household, an individual family, an individual retail store, or any other type of element.

Basic sampling concepts: Random, randomness. The word random is used in sampling to communicate this specific and precise meaning which it is extremely important to understand and grasp thoroughly: A sample may be accurately described as a random sample only if every single individual unit in the whole, or universe, from which the sample was chosen had a full and equal chance of being included in the sample.

In all subsequent references to random and randomness in this book, the terms are used in the statistical sense to describe true randomness.

The most common failure in achieving randomness is the use of a method of selection which deprives *some* individual units or *some types* of individual units of their chance of being included in the sample. Such failures may occur because of a lack of technical competence in planning the sample, or through faulty execution of the sample plan or design, or through corner cutting to reduce costs. To illustrate the difference between random and nonrandom methods of sample selection, here are three examples of sample selection which might appear to be random but which are not truly random. In these examples, assume that the sampling unit is an individual. The comments would apply to other types of sampling units. Note that *before you can evaluate the randomness of any sampling approach, you must have a clear definition of the universe which the sample is intended to represent.*

1. Objective: a random sample of women living in New York City. Could you get such a random sample by going to one or more high-traffic locations like Times Square or West 34th Street and there selecting from the women who passed you "at random"? The answer is that you could not. Such a selection process would exclude women living

in the other four boroughs of New York City who did not happen to come to Manhattan on your interviewing day. Women with one or more small children who were "confined to quarters" by their brood would similarly tend to be excluded or underrepresented. So would women working in factories at the time of your interviewing.

2. Objective: a random sample of Chicago housewives, from which you seek to determine what proportion buy and use canned chicken broth. Could you get a random sample by selecting phone numbers "at random" from the phone book and then making a daytime telephone interview? You could not. Such an approach would exclude households without telephones. It would also exclude housewives who work during the day outside their homes. Such housewives would be represented in the sample only as so many "do not answers."

3. Objective: a sample of women, from which the publishers of a women's magazine sought to learn about photographic practices. The sample to which questionnaires were mailed was chosen from a list of those who had written in for booklets of one type or another offered by the magazine. Would that constitute a random sample of all women? Of readers of that magazine? It would not represent a *random* sample of *either* group. Women who did not read the publication were of course excluded from the population sampled. Readers who did not write in for booklets were also excluded. Since this was a mail study, with returns from some but not all of those to whom questionnaires were mailed, there is a further problem of loss of representativeness as a result of the nonresponse factor.

It is important to remember the precise sampling meaning of the term random, because it is sometimes *mis*used in sampling discussions. Careless use of the word random in describing a sample is often a vital clue to slipshod or incompetent research.

SAMPLING WAS ONCE SIMPLE

To provide perspective on the dynamic nature of sampling in marketing research, let's now take a brief look backward. How simple sampling was for the marketing research man in the 1930s! In the years 1932 through 1936, a committee of distinguished marketing research experts wrote a book about this then-fledgling subject, which was published in 1937.[3] Written by a committee on marketing research technique of the American Marketing Association, that book summarized the best thinking and practice in the field of marketing research as of that

[3] *The Technique of Marketing Research,* American Marketing Association, McGraw-Hill, New York, 1937.

time. Sampling as an element in planning a research project in marketing was allocated only three of the 402 text pages in the book. There was in addition a seven-page chapter on the problem of determining sample size, adapted from a significant monograph by Theodore H. Brown.[4]

The discussion of the control of samples in *The Technique of Marketing Research* was divided into two parts. One was concerned with sample size and the use of stabilization curves to avoid the use of samples which were uneconomical because they were larger than they needed to be. (Stabilization curves are defined and described later in this chapter.) The other was a single sentence, quoted below in full, plus a brief illustration which it is not necessary to repeat here:

> (*Sample*) *Distribution*. It must be remembered, however, that in any system of determining the adequacy of sample, careful planning is necessary to insure the taking of samples from all groups and all territories, within the area being surveyed, in the approximate ratio which those groups or those territories bear to the whole field.[5]

The sentence quoted identifies two characteristics of samples that remain extremely important in all marketing research. One is the *representativeness* of the sample. The other is the *proportionality* of the sample.

Basic sampling concepts: Representativeness, proportionality. Representativeness refers to the inclusion within a sample of all the important kinds of units which are included in the universe, or population, from which the sample was selected. Unless all the types of units found in the population are found also in the sample, the sample is not representative of the population. Proportionality refers to the relative frequency with which various types of units found in the sample occur in the population. In a proportional sample each of the important types of units in the population is approximately the same proportion of the sample as it is of the universe.

ILLUSTRATION OF TYPES OF "ANSWERS" SOUGHT IN SAMPLING

Up to this point the kinds of information which are most frequently sought in sampling studies in marketing have not been fully illustrated. A knowledge of the nature of the answers sought makes it easier to understand the importance of representativeness and proportionality in

---

[4] Theodore H. Brown, *The Use of Statistical Techniques in Certain Problems of Marketing Research*, Harvard University Business Research Studies 12, 1935.

[5] *The Technique of Marketing Research*, p. 55.

sampling. Sampling studies in marketing usually seek one or both of these kinds of information:

1. The proportion of sampling units which do or do not have some *attribute.* An attribute is a characteristic of the population which each sampling unit does or does not have. For example, what proportion of households in a given market own television sets or home freezers? The attribute in question (ownership of a specific appliance) is present or absent in the case of each household.

2. The magnitude of some measurement, such as the mean, of some *variate,* or *variable value,* of the sampling units. For example, what is the average income of families in Chicago? What is the average weekly volume of canned soup sold by a population of retail stores? What is the average consumption of machine cutting oils per lathe per shift among a population of metalworking factories? What is the average consumption rate of ready-to-eat cereals among Chicago families?

Where your sampling objective is the determination of the quantitative value of a variate, sampling for an attribute is often a necessary first step. Thus in the ready-to-eat cereal example above you would first have to determine what proportion of families do or do not possess the attribute—eat *any* ready-to-eat cereals within a definitely specified time period—and then would proceed to develop estimates of the consumption rate among those families that did consume any. The objective of sampling is to develop *estimates* of the proportion of the population usually with some attribute, or to develop *estimates* of the quantitative value of some characteristic of the whole population from the value found in the sample.

Now consider the importance of proportionality in a sample in the same ready-to-eat cereal example. Families with children tend to consume ready-to-eat cereal at a substantially above-average rate (partly because there are more members in the average family with children, hence more mouths to feed), while families of only one and two members are far below the average family in their consumption of such cereals. A sample higher in its proportion of small families and lower in its proportion of larger families with children than the entire population would provide an estimate of consumption rates on cereal which would be substantially lower than the *true* consumption rate.

ADEQUACY OF SAMPLE SIZE; APPROXIMATION

We noted above that sampling values have a *tendency* to *approximate* the values which exist in the entire population from which the sample was taken. The reason for that tendency is that sampling is based on *probabilities*—on the probability that a unit in the sample will represent a larger number of units in the universe, and on the probability that a value of the sample (such as an average, or the proportion of respondents who use a particular kind of product) will approximate the same value of the universe. From everyday experience it is clear that the probability of heads turning up on a single toss of a coin is equal to the chance that tails will turn up. But if a single coin is tossed many times, there is likely to be *runs* of various length of consecutive heads or consecutive tails. It is only *over a relatively large number of tosses* that one can be confident that nearly half of the tosses would be heads and nearly half would be tails.

It is because chance often diverts a statistic from its true value that we need a reasonably long series of trials (or, in sampling, a reasonably large sample) to *average out* such *chance variations. A sample must be adequate in size* before we can be confident that chance variations which we know *can* occur are not producing a result markedly different from the result we would expect if the number of cases in the sample were much larger. The question of just how big a sample must be to be adequate in size is a complex one, to be discussed in Chapter 11.

Closely related to the need for a sample of adequate size is the notion of *approximation.* The value derived from a sample (such as the proportion of people owning color-television sets) *tends to approximate* and *not necessarily to equal exactly* the *true* value as it exists in the universe from which the sample was chosen.

Basic sampling concepts: Precision, or reliability. A sample value tends to fluctuate about the true value which exists in the universe. The difference between the sample value and the true value (remembering that we often do not know the true value in marketing research) is called the *sampling variation.* That is the variation which is produced *entirely* by chance influences in sampling. As the size of the sample increases, the sampling variation tends to decrease until— as the size of the sample finally equals the entire universe—the sampling variation is reduced to zero for all practical purposes. This statement excludes the effects of *bias,* which is discussed below. *Precision, or reliability, is entirely a function of the size of the sample. The larger the sample size, the greater its precision or reliability.*

STABILIZATION OF DATA

There are two ways in which the precision, or reliability, of a sample value may be appraised. One is mathematical and will be discussed in Chapter 11. The other is an empirical approach which utilizes *stabilization curves.* A stabilization curve is a device for illustrating graphically the effect which an increase in the size of the sample has on a value based on sample data. Such a curve is illustrated in Figure 5.1. The charted value is the proportion of women in a sample who recalled each of these advertisements after they looked through a folder of ten different advertisements. When the first 50 interviews in this study were completed, 44 women, or 88 per cent, recalled the Toni ad, 39, or 78 per cent, recalled the Lady Esther ad, and 38, or 76 per cent, recalled the Ovaltine ad. When the sample size had been increased to 100 interviews, the Toni ad recall was 89 per cent, the Lady Esther ad recall

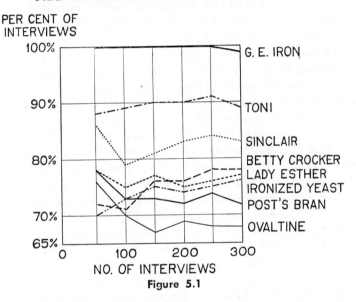

EFFECT OF INCREASED SAMPLE SIZE ON RECALL OF CONTROL ADS

Figure 5.1

was 75 per cent, and the Ovaltine ad recall dipped rather sharply to 70 per cent. (Remember that the first 50 interviews were included within the 100, thus providing *cumulative* percentages. Since the Ovaltine ad had 76 per cent recall on 50 interviews but only 70 per cent on 100, it is apparent that the second 50 interviews added only 32 women, or 64 per cent who recalled that ad.) As successive additions of 50 interviews each were accumulated, the Toni recall figure *stabilized* near the 90 per cent mark, the Lady Esther figure near the 76 per cent level, while the Ovaltine ad recall leveled out at 68 per cent by the time the sample size had reached 300.

The fact that the sample data tend to stabilize as shown on this chart has a very practical value for a marketing research man. It means that by constructing such charts and determining *key* values cumulatively, one can sometimes "chop off" the sample size at any given point when the data have stabilized with confidence that a substantially larger sample *with no change in procedures* would not materially affect the level of the values charted.

LESSONS FROM THE *LITERARY DIGEST* POLL

The relatively minor importance of sampling in marketing research in the 1930s is clear from the scant attention to the subject in *The Technique of Marketing Research*. Today the great importance of sound sampling is widely recognized. That recognition was accelerated by a dramatic demonstration of the dangers of careless sampling in the 1936 Presidential election, when the failure of a pre-election poll by a magazine called the *Literary Digest* to reflect the vote division by candidates marked a milestone in sampling history.

The *Literary Digest* was a weekly magazine which conducted an extensive *mail* poll of voters before national elections and reported the candidate division of total vote returns in the last pre-election issue. In 1936, more than *ten million ballots* were mailed, out of which 2,350,176 were returned and included in the summary published in the issue of Oct. 31, 1936. Of the ballots mailed back to the *Digest,* 55 per cent favored Landon and 41 per cent were for Roosevelt. In the actual election, Roosevelt polled 60 per cent of the vote cast. The difference between Roosevelt's proportion of *Digest* poll votes and his actual percentage was a "sampling variation" of about 50 per cent!

Dr. George Gallup's Institute of Public Opinion used a sample of only a few thousand interviews with voters, yet accurately predicted Roosevelt's election. To sampling students it is interesting to note that more than three months *before* the *Literary Digest* poll fiasco, Dr. Gallup accurately predicted that the *Literary Digest* poll would be in error, in this release:[6]

> If the *Literary Digest* were conducting its poll at the present time, following its usual procedure, Landon would be shown in the lead. The actual figure would be in the neighborhood of 44% for Roosevelt, 56% for Landon.
>
> Since the Institute of Public Opinion sends part of its ballots to the same lists covered by the *Literary Digest*, it is possible to predict with a high degree of accuracy the sentiment which the *Digest* will find. The lists comprise telephone subscribers, automobile owners and registered voters. The upper economic levels are represented to a much greater extent than the lower levels in such lists, and particularly in the returned

[6] Release of the Institute of Public Opinion, July 11, 1936.

ballots. People at the upper levels are more inclined to answer ballots than people at the lower end of the economic scale. When the lower one-third of the voting population is fully represented, Roosevelt's percentage changes from 44% to 56%.

Although there have been great advances in sampling knowledge since 1936, those advances do not invalidate certain lessons underlined by the experience of the *Literary Digest*. The 1936 experience of the *Digest* poll provides the basis for these currently useful generalizations about sampling in marketing research:

1. With 2 million sampling units, the *Literary Digest* sample had tremendous precision or reliability. But although it had precision, the *Digest's* sample was extremely inaccurate, with an estimate of Roosevelt's share of the total vote which proved in error by about 50 per cent. This emphasizes that there is no necessary relationship between the precision or reliability of an estimate from sample data and the accuracy of that estimate.

2. With a far smaller sample, Dr. Gallup's interviewers estimated the vote distribution with far less precision, but with far greater accuracy. It is still true today that a small sample which is carefully planned and executed can sometimes provide far more accurate estimates of population values than a much larger sample which is less carefully designed. Since cost is closely related to sample size, this is obviously a point worth remembering.

3. Over a quarter of a century, the *Literary Digest* had never failed to reflect the distribution of actual vote in its pre-election polls. Yet the identical approach in 1936 produced figures grossly in error. This shows that although unsound sampling methods *may* produce relatively accurate data, such past good fortune is no guarantee that an identical approach will be equally fortunate if it is repeated.

BIAS

Exactly what went wrong with the *Literary Digest's* 1936 poll? There are two ways to answer that question in sampling terminology. Since this is an introduction to sampling in marketing research, it may be instructive to consider both. The first was that the sample was *not proportional*. It included an overrepresentation of upper economic levels and an inadequate representation of the voters at the lower end of the economic scale. In earlier years the *Digest* predicted election outcomes with a sample similarly heavy in upper-income coverage. That lack of proportionality in earlier years did not affect poll accuracy because there was then no marked difference in candidate preference by economic levels. As Gallup commented:

. . . The *Literary Digest* has never had to predict a really close national election, nor to meet a situation such as prevails today with the lower economic levels voting almost solidly for Roosevelt and the upper economic levels voting for Landon.

The important marketing-research moral here is this: Where there are major variations between groups or parts of the population *with regard to the subject being studied,* a lack of proportionality can result in a sharp reduction in the accuracy of a sample estimate.

The second way to describe the cause of the *Literary Digest's* gross error in sampling terminology is to identify it as an example of *bias.* This is the first of many references to bias in this book. Bias is a term and a subject with which every marketing research man is intimately familiar, even though it is often extremely difficult to define precisely. Bias takes many different forms. The dictionary defines bias as a tendency, a leaning, an inclination, or a prejudice. In marketing research, *a bias is any force, tendency, or procedural error in the collection, analysis, or interpretation of data which produces distortion.* Suppose you know that in a given county 60 per cent of the homes have television receivers. In a sample of several hundred homes from that county used in a marketing research study, 95 per cent are reported to own television sets. One does not have to be an expert in marketing research or in statistics to sense that "something is wrong" with that sample. What is wrong, most likely, is that the sample is biased.

In sampling studies, there are two types of influences which introduce variation between a value found in a sample and the same value as it exists in the entire population. One type of influence is benign, the other malignant. The benign influence is sampling variation, which reflects the action of chance influences alone and which diminishes in effect as the size of the sample is increased. The malignant influence is bias. Sampling variation resulting from chance influences alone *can be measured* in random sampling, and the magnitude of such variations can be controlled to hold them within predetermined limits. Bias, by contrast, *cannot be measured,* and the scale of distortion it produces is sometimes very great, as in the case of the *Literary Digest* poll. Bias in sampling is discussed in more detail later in this chapter and in Chapter 11. It is important to recognize that sampling bias is only one of many different types of bias frequently encountered in marketing research.

Comment: The *Literary Digest* poll had a heavy sample-selection bias. Because the sample was selected from sources overweighted with upper-income families (which happened to be predominantly Republican in their candidate preference), the poll results were biased in favor of Landon. Also present was *nonresponse bias,* which exists in most surveys to some extent and which is especially important in mail surveys. If the sample of voters *to whom ballots were sent* had been proportional by economic levels, but if the rate of return was sharply higher in the upper-income levels, the resulting division of *returned* ballots would still have been biased in favor of the Republican candidate. In this case, both sample-selection bias and nonresponse bias were active in the same direction. One bias added to and accentuated the other. Sometimes different biases are offsetting, tending to "average out" like chance variations. A competent research man normally seeks to eliminate all bias, or to reduce inescapable biases to an absolute minimum, because he knows bias cannot be measured and knows that the direction of its influence often cannot be determined.

MAJOR SAMPLING APPROACHES USED IN MARKETING RESEARCH

In sampling literature there are many simple and compound adjectives used to identify different kinds of samples and different sampling approaches.[7] This profuse nomenclature is often frightening to a newcomer to marketing research. It can also be confusing—unnecessarily so, because many of these terms are used by different writers in different ways. The discussion which follows has been planned to introduce and identify the more important types of sampling approaches or sampling designs used in marketing research. Minor or rarely encountered variations have been omitted since such variations are so well covered in advanced books, especially those on sampling alone. The characteristics of samples of different types are stressed here in the hope that the various approaches may thus become more meaningful than if we relied on definitions, which sometimes depend upon fine shades of distinction.

Simple Random Sampling

Simple random sampling involves the selection of sampling units from a predetermined universe in such a way that *every* elementary sampling unit has a *full and equal* chance of being selected and included in the sample. This is sometimes called random sampling. If "random" were always understood as it is defined earlier in this chapter, there would be no need to add the *simple*. Because random is used in so many different ways in sampling literature, an additional adjective is desirable Some writers call this *unrestricted random sampling*. The terms are synonymous.

[7] For example, here are some of the single-adjective designations: quota, random probability, judgment, purposive, cluster, stratified, systematic, proportional, area, block, multistage, double; and there are many more.

In using simple random sampling, the procedure is usually to list and number all sampling units in the universe. The sample is then chosen from the listed, numbered universe. Random numbers are often relied on to ensure true randomness. Simple random sampling is the type of sampling design on which most of the mathematical formulas for measuring sampling variations have been based, and it is therefore of great importance in sampling theory.

This approach is not widely used in marketing research, especially in human population sampling, because of difficulties which are nearly insurmountable in practice. Suppose you wanted to sample the entire United States population. Could you use a simple random sample? Where would you get the accurate, complete, and up-to-date listing of all the individuals in the country? Even if you had such a list, there would remain the monumental task of somehow numbering the more than 170 million potential respondents, so that truly random selection could be ensured. Consider further the problem of *reaching* the respondents thus randomly selected. One respondent might be an Indian guide in the Everglades of southern Florida, another a lighthouse keeper in Maine, another a housewife deep in the Kentucky hills, and so on. Individual respondents chosen randomly might turn out to be hundreds of miles from the nearest other respondent. Extremely high travel and interview costs would be inevitable.

Simple random sampling is sometimes used where the sample-design problem is on a more limited geographic scale so that the problems indicated are reduced to manageable proportions. The existence of a complete list of the universe, or population, in question occasionally makes this approach much more practicable than it would otherwise be. Availability of a list was a factor in a simple random sample of individuals living in Washington, D.C., which H. M. Beville, Jr., described as follows:[8]

The study was conducted during the months of February and March of 1948. . . . Late in 1947, the R. L. Polk Company of Detroit had completed the field work for constructing a city directory for Washington, D.C. The names were still on slips of paper in file drawers and had not yet been alphabetized. . . . From 175 file trays, they pulled 830 names. . . . Since 4.5 names per tray were needed, they pulled four names out of the even numbered trays and five names out of the odd numbered trays, thus getting 780 names. Then they pulled a few more trays by random numbers and took four or five names from each of these trays so that they ended up with 830 names. In order that no biases would result in pulling the names from the trays, the investigators followed

[8] Quotations by permission from H. M. Beville, Jr., "Surveying Radio Listeners by Use of a Probability Sample," *The Journal of Marketing*, October, 1949, p. 374.

this system: each tray was 24 inches deep; they drew random numbers from 0 to 24 allocated consecutive numbers in four's and five's, according to whether the trays were even- or odd-numbered; they then went into the individual tray the number of inches specified by the random number and pulled out a name. This procedure eliminated any "position bias" which the samplers might have had, had they not followed this mechanical system.

Quota Sampling

In a simple random sample, any given value—such as the proportion of individuals using a given type of product—varies from the same value in the full universe. Part of the variation reflects the *approximation of proportionality* of different types of respondents within the sample. Thus the proportion of men or women or of respondents of any given age group in a simple random sample *approximates* within measurable limits the proportion which each of those population segments represents in the total population. The remainder[9] of the variation occurs through the *approximation,* within any segment of the sample, of the value in question. Consider a specific illustration: A survey indicated that about 80 per cent of the individuals aged thirteen to eighteen in a sample of families were reported to have used a food drink (like Ovaltine) within a specified time period prior to the interview. Among individuals aged fifty or over, however, the proportion using this type of product was about 35 per cent. Where such extreme variations exist in the value being measured (i.e., proportion using the product type), the importance of proportionality in the sample is obvious. If the thirteen-to-eighteen-year age group were overrepresented in the sample, the total-sample level of use of the product type would be higher in the sample than in the whole population. Or if those over fifty were underrepresented in the sample, that would also tend to inflate the value from the sample as a whole.

In a carefully designed and executed simple random sample, each age group *will tend to be* approximately the same proportion of the sample as it is of the whole population. However, in an occasional sample— through the natural processes of the laws of chance—the proportionality might vary rather widely from that in the whole population. Partly as a precaution against such a rare but possible circumstance and partly to eliminate some of the difficulties inherent in the careful design and execution of a simple random sample, marketing research has long relied

[9] Bias at any point or of any type might introduce further variation between the sample value and the true value as it exists in the whole population. To simplify this discussion, bias is not considered at this point. It is well to remember, however, that the range of sampling variations caused by chance factors *can* be measured in a simple random sample, while *bias cannot be measured.*

on a sampling approach now widely known as quota sampling. This was almost the only sampling approach used in marketing research until the late 1930s. George Gallup's advance prediction of the error of the *Literary Digest* poll was based on a quota sample.

Basic sampling concepts: Stratification. A quota sample is one type of *stratified sample.* In the simple random sample, the sample is selected from the population as a single whole unit. In a stratified sample, the whole population is first divided into two or more parts (called strata), and then a sample (technically, a *sub*sample) is taken from each of the strata. The resulting stratified sample is a combination of two or more samples from different parts, or strata, of the population. Suppose you were making a survey of individuals in a major metropolitan market in which you knew from a recently completed census that the total population was 52 per cent female and 48 per cent male. If in your survey you *controlled* your sample so that it was divided in those same proportions, instead of relying on probability to approximate the proportions, you would have a stratified sample of male and female respondents and you would *know* that your sample was proportional *as far as sex was concerned.*

In a quota sample, the sample is stratified in its planning phase, using two or more *sample controls.* Proportionality is achieved by dividing the sample in the planning stage into two or more strata and establishing a sample size for each strata with the same proportionate relationship to the total sample as each strata had to be the total population.[10] In the sample of Washington, D.C., discussed in the preceding section, stratification was used to achieve proportionality between residents of Washington, D.C., and the surrounding suburban area. The relative population of the two strata was known, and that fact was used to predetermine the size of the sample from each. (Note that this illustrates stratification but does not make that a quota sample.)

EXAMPLES OF QUOTA-SAMPLING APPROACHES

The literature of sampling contains many comments which are sharply critical of quota sampling. Despite the impressive volume of criticism, quota sampling remains important in marketing research practice. This does not mean that the adverse comments are ignored and that practitioners are clinging to an obsolete approach. Instead it reflects the fact

[10] As a deliberate oversimplification, proportionality is assumed in quota samples in the discussion in this section. Most quota samples are proportional. Disproportional sampling is discussed in Chapter 11. A quota sample is *not necessarily* a proportional sample.

that there have been major technique refinements within the quota-sampling framework which have helped to overcome substantially or to reduce greatly the importance of many specific limitations of quota sampling. It would be reasonably accurate to describe much criticism of quota sampling as obsolete, since it is largely focused on limitations which have long since been recognized and largely removed in professional practice.

Because sampling is an extremely important element in marketing research practice, it is highly desirable for a newcomer to understand in specific detail some of the common problems of sampling. It would be especially helpful to begin with some awareness of the elements in the controversy about sampling methodology. As an introduction to practical sampling problems, and as a contribution toward that understanding, the following pages present the specific steps involved in planning a quota sample. Two different case examples are used to illustrate each step. The limitations of quota sampling and the steps now usually taken to reduce those limitations are presented against the background of these specific cases.

The first of the two examples is an actual consumer survey conducted *in 1936* by one of the largest advertising agencies for one of its clients. The second is a survey of magazine audiences executed *in 1938*[11] under the sponsorship of LIFE magazine. Two examples are necessary to illustrate the variations in approach in two studies which differed markedly in scope and resources. The first survey was a relatively small-scale study involving about 1,500 interviews. It was planned and executed as a routine assignment by a single marketing research man. The second was a far larger study, with 8,000 interviews. Field work was conducted by Crossley, Inc., under the guidance of a committee of distinguished experts in the field of marketing research.[12] The two studies will be identified in the subsequent discussion as the Pekin survey and the LIFE survey.

Step 1. *Definition of the Universe or Population to Be Covered*

This is the first step in almost every sampling study. The Pekin survey involved a household device, bought and used by housewives. The objective of the Pekin survey was to sample "a representative cross-section of American housewives." Because the budget for this survey was limited

[11] *LIFE'S Continuing Study of Magazine Audiences: Report No. 1*, Dec. 1, 1938.
[12] The committee consisted of Paul T. Cherington, Archibald M. Crossley, Samuel Gill, and Darrell B. Lucas. Elmo Roper also took an active part in planning the study. S. S. Wilks, then professor of statistics at Princeton University, examined and analyzed the statistical methods used and the statistics themselves. Cornelius DuBois, who was then LIFE's director of research, also contributed to this project.

to a maximum expenditure figure set before the planning began, alternative approaches had to be explored with more than usual care. Just how could the maximum amount of useful information be secured within the fixed budget available? This question often occurs in marketing research practice today. Where planning begins after a cost ceiling already has been established *for* instead of *by* the research man, the amount of freedom of decision or scope in planning is reduced. The research man responsible for this study weighed various alternatives against his maximum budget, then decided to eliminate from the sample all housewives who lived on farms or in rural areas. Concentration of product use in urban homes was a factor in this decision.

In the LIFE study, both urban and rural segments of the national population were covered. It was decided, however, to eliminate from the sample all individuals below ten years of age.

Comment: Sampling from a predetermined population which is less than the total population is not unusual. Objectives of the study help to determine what segments of the population to include. Cost considerations often influence the decision, as in the Pekin case. It is extremely important to remember that no sample can be representative of population groups excluded from the universe studied. Eliminating rural interviews changed the Pekin sample to one of urban housewives only. Since rural housewives were excluded from the sample, the survey findings could provide no information about such housewives.

Step 2. *Decision on Sample Size*

The decision on the size of the sample in the Pekin case was made by determining the number of interviews that could be completed, tabulated, analyzed, and reported within the limits of the given total-cost figure. Experience with recently completed surveys was used to estimate that about 1,500 interviews could be completed for the budget available. The LIFE study sample size was based on a consideration of the number of breakdowns or subdivisions of the total sample for which values would have to be reported separately.[13]

Comment: Determining sample size in a survey is an extremely difficult and complex problem. The approach recommended in most situations is detailed in Chapter 11. The Pekin case exactly reverses theoretically sound

[13] Published research studies in the 1930s not uncommonly included samples of as many as 15,000 respondents. The *Literary Digest* fiasco blasted the widely held but erroneous notion that sample size and sample quality are necessarily related. Today a national sample in excess of 10,000 cases is rarely encountered, and samples in the range from 4,000 to 6,000 are far more common, with 2,500-interview studies not infrequent.

practice as usually described. It is preferable first to determine the sample requirements with the survey objectives in mind, and *then* to determine sample size and estimated cost. Note that in practice it is not unusual for a fixed-cost ceiling to be set in advance by executive decision. Such an apparently arbitrary decision reflects executive judgment on the profit potential of the facts likely to emerge from the study and thus is consistent with the viewpoint toward research costs described in Chapter 1. If a research man feels that such a cost ceiling is too low for an adequate and sound research job, he would normally recommend against any action on the project.

Step 3. *Decision on Sample Controls to Be Used*

The next step was a decision on the bases on which the sample would be "controlled" and the sample quotas established. The control decision had two parts: *How many* and *which* control bases to use. A control base is any characteristic of the sampling units on which the total sample may be divided into subsamples. The objectives and characteristics of a particular study influence the control-base decision.

Basic sampling concept: Sample cells. When a strata of a sample is further subdivided, the result is two or more subdivisions of the sample having common characteristics, known as *sample cells*. Thus in a food-drink study, individuals in the sample were first divided into two major strata by sex and then those strata were subdivided on an age basis into adults and children. This produced four *cells*, containing respectively, males twenty-one and over; males under twenty-one, females twenty-one and over; and females under twenty-one. If it is anticipated in the planning stage that individual figures (for example, proportion of individuals using food drinks) for each cell will be required from the study, then the sample must be so planned that the number of respondents in *each cell* is large enough to provide the desired precision. As the number of control bases is increased, the number of cells increases rapidly. Example: With one control base (sex), there are two cells. If five city-size groups are added as a control base, the number of cells becomes ten. If nine geographic sections are added as an additional control base, the number of cells increases to ninety. Each cell then includes respondents who are alike in sex, in the city-size group in which they live and in the geographical section in which they live. It is because of this rapid rate of increase in the number of cells that the control bases used in practice are limited, usually varying from two to four in number.

In the 1,500-interview Pekin survey, three control bases were selected. The sample was divided into seven different geographical section subsamples, into five different city-size groups, and into four different income-class, or socioeconomic, groups identified as "high," "upper middle," "lower middle," and "low." With a sample of 8,000, the LIFE study could and did use more control bases: sex; age, with respondents in seven different groups; economic level, with five different groups of equal size; and nine different geographic regions.

Step 4. *Developing Control Data on Each Control Base*

To determine how to divide the sample into geographic sections and city-size groups, the latest information available—usually published census reports—is used to determine the distribution of the total population. In 1936 and 1938, the latest data were from the 1930 Census, updated to some extent by later governmentally developed information on migration trends. In the Pekin study, the marketing research man divided his sample of 1,500 interviews between sections in these proportions:

Geographic section	Per cent of U.S. total
New England	9.2
Middle Atlantic	29.5
South Atlantic	8.3
East North Central	24.4
West North Central	8.1
East and West South Central	10.4
Mountain and Pacific	10.1
Urban total	100.0

Instead of nine census regions, the seven combined sections listed above were used. The final survey report explained the combinations in these words:

> It will be noticed that the East and West South Central sections are combined and that the Mountain and Pacific sections are similarly handled. This combining is considered permissible because the groups involved have similar population characteristics, and because the resulting total makes possible a larger sample upon which to base percentages.

The second point in the above explanation should be noted. Each increase in the number of cells in a sample decreases the average size of the individual subsample. The Pekin sample of 1,500 interviews divided into 35 major cells (7 sections times 5 city-size groups) had an average of 43 interviews per cell. The two pairs of combined sections mentioned would each contribute about 10 per cent of total interviews. Thus the combined sections would contribute only about 150 interviews, which would then be expected to represent the entire geographical area. If these sections had not been combined, the subsamples would have been even smaller.

The process of developing control data for the LIFE study proceeded along parallel lines, with 1930 Census data as the primary source of information. The LIFE report[14] pointed out that "weight has also been given to the Scripps Foundation's estimated shifts within the population since the census of eight years ago."

Comment: The use of noncurrent data as the basis of planning controls in a sample is a source of bias in sampling. Suppose that the combined Mountain and Pacific sections had represented 10.1 per cent of the United States population in 1930 but had increased to 12.7 per cent by the time of the survey. If the proportionality of the sample were based on the 10.1 figure, the two sections named would have been underrepresented in the sample to the extent of almost 20 per cent of their "true" proportion. Whether this lack of sectional proportionality would have resulted in a major or minor bias in the quantitative "answers" provided by the survey would depend on whether or not those sections differed significantly from other sections *with regard to the subject matter of this survey.* Remember the pre-1936 experience of the *Literary Digest* poll: Because there was no sharp difference between economic levels in candidate preference prior to 1936, the bias introduced by lack of economic-level proportionality did not materially reduce the accuracy with which these polls reflected the division of popular vote. This demonstrates the insidiousness of bias, which introduces unmeasurable distortions which may be major or minor.

Step 5. *Breakdown of Total Sample into Major Cells*

Now using the control data developed in the preceding step, and the total sample size from step 2, the sample is broken down into subsamples. The *total sample* in the case of the Pekin study was planned so that it was proportional both by sections and by city-size groups. No attempt was made, in the case of this relatively small sample, to establish city-size proportionality *within* geographic sections. In the case of the LIFE study, the larger sample size and greater resources available made it possible to maintain proportionality both by sections and by city-size groups in total and by city-size groups within sections.

Step 6. *Selection of Sampling Points (Interviewing Locations)*

The next step was the selection of the specific cities and smaller places in each sectional and city-size group which would be used as sampling points for the interviews in these two studies. In the case of

---

[14] Dec. 1, 1938, p. 11.

Figure 5.2. Sample-cell Framework in the Pekin Study

City-size groups	New England	Middle Atlantic	South Atlantic	East North Central	West North Central	East and West South Central	Mountain and Pacific
500,001 and over	Boston, Mass.	Philadelphia, Pa. Buffalo, N.Y.	Baltimore, Md.	Cleveland, Ohio	Chicago, Ill.	St. Louis, Mo.	Los Angeles, Calif.
100,001–500,000	Providence, R.I.	Syracuse, N.Y. Reading, Pa.	Atlanta, Ga.	Indianapolis, Ind.	Minneapolis, Minn.	Dallas, Tex.	Denver, Colo.
25,001–100,000	Portland, Me.	Allentown, Pa. Passaic, N.J.	Charlotte, N.C.	Lansing, Mich.	Cedar Rapids, Iowa	Shreveport, La. Montgomery, Ala.	Bellingham, Wash.
10,001–25,000	Danbury, Conn.	Middletown, N.Y. Bridgeton, N.J.	Gastonia, N.C.	New Castle, Ind.	Watertown, Wis. Keokuk, Iowa	McKinney, Tex.	Boulder, Colo.
Less than 10,000	Waverly, Mass.	Quakertown, Pa. Hamburg, N.Y.	Marietta, Ga.	Bedford, Ohio Berea, Ohio	Anoka, Minn.	Old Hickory, Tenn. Springfield, Tenn.	Mesa, Ariz.

the Pekin survey, the minimum number of such sampling points was determined by the earlier selection of control bases. With five different city-size groups and seven different geographic divisions to the framework of the sample, there had to be a minimum of thirty-five different major cells. (Within each of those thirty-five major cells there was to be a further subdivision of the sample into four income-level cells, but that factor did not enter into the sampling-point selection step.)

The first step in selection of sampling points for the Pekin study was to set up a framework of the thirty-five cells as illustrated in Figure 5.2. The seven geographic sections were listed across the top of the column, and the five city-size groups were listed down the side. The next step was to select one or more cities to "represent" each cell. In the Middle Atlantic group, which included 29.5 per cent of the total population, two cities, or sampling points, were included in each cell in that section. In the case of four other cells, two sampling points were used. The decision on this point was made after a careful study of the characteristics of the individual cities chosen in comparison with the characteristics of the geographic section which that city was expected to represent. Thus if sectional summaries showed that a section had 25 per cent of its population employed in factories, an attempt would be made to achieve that proportion for the selected sampling points. The secondary sampling points in the cells shown were chosen in part to balance characteristics of the sectional sample with those of the sectional total population.

In the selection of specific sampling places, one of the major influences was the availability of experienced field interviewers who were usually local residents.

Sampling planning in the LIFE survey was far more detailed than in the Pekin case. (Economic influence: Note that the cost of planning was part of the total cost of the job, thus limiting planning.) A total of 115 different interviewing points was selected for the LIFE study.

Step 7. *Developing and Assigning Quotas to Interviewers*

The next and final step in planning the sample was to translate the plans into specific assignments for individual interviewers. Since an interviewer ordinarily conducts interviews in the area in which he or she lives, many of the sample controls are superfluous in developing a specific quota of interviews for a given interviewer. A Boston interviewer is in and a part of the largest city-size group in the New England section automatically. The interviewer need only be told how many interviews to make and how that total number is to be divided by control bases. A Boston interviewer in the Pekin study received a quota of thirty interviews, with instructions to make three of them high-, six in upper-middle-, twelve in lower-middle-, and nine in low-income neighborhoods.

Instructions for identifying the income classes in question were provided to the interviewers. The experts planning the LIFE study had less confidence in the ability of interviewers to identify and secure an accurate cross section of the different economic groups. In describing their sampling plan in this respect, they commented:[15]

> It took no discussion to decide that dividing the sample arbitrarily by standards of living would be little better than guesswork. After discarding many suggested methods, we concluded that trial and error was the only sound procedure.
>
> Certain economic facts that make up standards of living are known quantities. It was up to us to make our sample check these known quantities. That meant, with a sample of 8,000 a schedule that went as follows: (1) assign quotas for the standard-of-living groups; (2) make 2,000 interviews; (3) pause, check against known economic data, revise the standard-of-living quotas; (4) make 4,000 more interviews; (5) pause, check the total 6,000, revise again; (6) make the final 2,000 interviews.

THE PROBLEM OF IDENTIFYING QUOTA CHARACTERISTICS

Consider the ideal quota sample: It would be based on up-to-date information as to the distribution within the population of the characteristics used as control bases. It would be perfectly accurate as to the fulfillment of quotas on all control bases. Under those circumstances, a quota sample might well provide a completely representative and proportional sample of the population under study. One extremely important practical limitation of quota sampling is the difficulty of achieving accurate classification of respondents by interviewers. The magnitude of this difficulty varies with the control base used. Thus no problems are involved in the case of geographic sections or city-size control bases. A respondent can be accurately identified as living in a given section or in a city of a given size. In the case of control bases such as age of respondent, occupational classification, or socioeconomic classification of respondent, however, there is a real problem in achieving an accurate classification of respondents (and hence an accurate fulfillment of the assigned quota) by interviewers who are working on a quota sample. Inaccurate classification of respondents, or a lack of accuracy in the fulfillment of assigned quotas, introduces a bias into quota samples.

The particular control bases used in a quota sample are normally those which are thought in advance of the study to be most likely to exert the greatest influence on the particular subject under study. When the Toni Company was studying the market for Silver Curl—a home permanent created especially for women with gray hair—their samples

[15] *Ibid*, p. 8.

were carefully controlled to ensure proportionality by age of respondent. If the samples were overweighted with younger women, the potential for Silver Curl would have been understated, while a sample with too large a proportion of respondents in upper age brackets would bias the findings in the reverse direction. In that case, it was known in advance that the age of the respondent was likely to be a significant control base. In many cases, *one does not know in advance* which factors will prove important in their relationship to the subject under study. The importance of income-class or socioeconomic groups, and especially of the variation in the characteristics of the different groups, is an example. On some products, there is a sharp variation in consumption rate between families in different income levels. On other products a very "flat" profile exists, with high- and low-income families using nearly equal quantities.

Suppose you were studying the consumption rate on a given product and that your sample was (unknown to you) biased in such a way that upper-income families were overrepresented and low-income families heavily underrepresented. If your product had sharp consumption-rate variations between economic groups, that sample would be heavily biased and would be likely to yield very inaccurate data. But if the variation between groups were slight, the resulting bias might be inconsequential. Since you would not know whether such a sample would be slightly or greatly biased, you would exercise extreme care *in the planning stages* to be sure that your sample was as unbiased as possible.

CHANGING ECONOMIC PATTERNS POSE A PROBLEM

Users of quota samples divide the population in different ways on a socioeconomic or standard-of-living, basis and then try through careful instruction of interviewers and through close supervision to see that the particular classification plan adopted is applied consistently and uniformly by all interviewers. Consistent classification of respondents in the case of a single (or "one-shot") study can be achieved through careful training and supervision. Consistent classification of respondents for a series of surveys spanning an interval of time, especially a time period in which there have been major changes in the nature of the population, is far more difficult. The difficulty of maintaining comparability between quota samples taken at different time periods was dramatically demonstrated by a wartime experience in connection with a later LIFE study very similar to the one described above.

The study in question was No. 8 in LIFE's series of Continuing Studies of Magazine Audiences. That study was finally reported long after its initial scheduled release date. The following letter from LIFE's research director, dated Nov. 2, 1944, explains the delay:

Under normal conditions, we would be passing along to you shortly a copy of Report #8 in LIFE's Continuing Study of Magazine Audiences. Because of economic factors which have arisen from the war, Report #8 will be considerably delayed.

Several months ago, when the Magazine Audience Group started analyzing its first 4,000 interviews for the new report, it was found that something had happened to upset the basic sampling procedure which had been used with such accuracy in the seven previous reports. That "something" was the greatly changed money factor in the United States: Interviewers were suddenly classifying in the "C" economic group, for example, people who only a few months before had been classified as "D." This one matter of differences in judgment on the part of the interviewers was distorting the accuracy of the entire #8 study. How great the distortion was you may see in the figures submitted by Dr. Theodore H. Brown, Chairman of the Magazine Audience Group, in the attached letter.

For the past many months, the Magazine Audience Group has been experimenting, on our behalf, with new sampling techniques which will rely less, or not at all, on the personal judgment of interviewers. The work is still in the testing stage, but we are confident that when the new Study is finally made it will have the same high degree of accuracy which has characterized previous reports.

The letter from Theodore H. Brown referred to above is quoted below. This lengthy quotation is included here for two reasons. First, it illustrates in specific terms the sampling problem under discussion. Second, and more importantly, it illustrates how research men study the data they gather, detect any discrepancies or peculiarities of that data, develop hypotheses to explain those unanticipated characteristics of the data, and then proceed to test their hypotheses. Dr. Brown's letter, dated Oct. 30, 1944, included these comments:

When we started interviewing for Report #8, toward the end of 1943, it became immediately apparent that something had happened to upset our sampling technique. In all previous studies, to check the results from interviews, there was included a series of control questions to measure things which were already known quantities: home ownership, telephones, mechanical refrigeration, etc. If the sampling could produce correct figures for these known quantities, it would be reasonable to assume that our sample was pretty close to right on the unknown quantities. Suddenly, only six months after Report #7, these control factors showed marked declines.

There was no reasonable explanation for this discrepancy—except one:

The apparent changes could be explained if the interviewers, because of the new wartime prosperity plateau, were applying economic level standards in a different manner from before.

The first problem was that of testing this hypothesis. To do so, we re-interviewed in May, 1944, one-fourth of the people who had been interviewed a year before.

By comparing 1944 economic level ratings with the 1943 ratings of the same people, we found our hypothesis confirmed. Of the people classified by the interviewers this year as "B," 36% had been rated as "C" a year earlier. And of those now classified as "C," 43% had previously been classified as "D" or "E."

It was obviously necessary to find a procedure which would work equally well at *all* times and in *all* economic conditions.

We have been experimenting—simultaneously—with two improved procedures.

One of these is based on a technique of the Current Surveys Division of the Census. This technique, wholly different from the "quota system" used in surveys like LIFE's Continuing Study and the public opinion polls, selects the persons to be interviewed by strict mathematical rotation —the interviewer has no freedom of choice whatever.

Along with this strict rotation method, we are testing an improvement over our regular quota system—limiting but not entirely removing the interviewer's freedom to choose individuals within economic levels.

While the results are nowhere near complete, the testing of both these new methods is now under way in the field.

It should be emphasized that the current experiments were undertaken because of changed conditions rather than because of dissatisfaction with our older methods. These older methods had worked very well under the relatively stable pre-war conditions. In designing new methods we were looking for procedures which will work under the present war-time conditions and which will work equally well during the changing conditions we anticipate after the war.

AREA SAMPLING

The sampling technique "wholly different from the quota system" described in Theodore Brown's letter above is today usually known as *area sampling*. Area sampling is an approach which, from the practitioner's viewpoint, combines some characteristics of unrestricted random sampling and quota sampling. Like unrestricted random sampling, it provides sample values which are within measurable limits of the same values as they exist in the whole population. Like quota sampling, it is an approach which can be and is widely used on a practical basis.

Both area sampling and quota sampling involve stratification (as distinguished from the complete lack of strata or other restrictions found in simple random sampling), hence both are subtypes of *stratified sampling*. But there is this important distinction between quota sampling and area sampling: Quota sampling relies on *judgment*—in the development of the sampling design, in the selection of controls, in the selection of interview points, and finally in the selection of respondents. Area sampling, by contrast, relies largely if not exclusively on *probability*. Where there is judgment, there is likely to be bias. The reduction of bias by eliminating or very greatly reducing the influence of judgment is one of the major benefits of using an area or other type of probability sample.

Credit for leadership in the development of area sampling as it is used in marketing research today must be given largely to the sampling staff of the Bureau of the Census. Among those recognized for major contributions to area sampling and other probability-sampling approaches are Morris H. Hansen, W. Edward Deming, and William N. Hurwitz. Alfred Politz of Alfred Politz Research, Inc., played a major role in accelerating the acceptance and widespread use of probability sampling in commercial practice. By vigorous and articulate presentation of the advantages of sound sampling and of the perils and pitfalls in inadequate sampling, Mr. Politz focused major critical attention on an area which had previously been grossly underestimated in commercial research. A competently designed and carefully executed area sample provides data almost completely free from many important types of bias which are sometimes present in quota samples. The sampling variations in an area sample can be measured accurately and can be predicted in advance. This technique represents a significant contribution to marketing research knowledge.

To make the contrast between an area sample and a quota sample as specific as possible, the following description of a national area sample has been reduced to a step-by-step basis to parallel the quota sampling discussion above. Since the sample in question was designed for use in a national study of magazine audiences,[16] the objective for which the sample was developed was almost exactly the same as for the LIFE survey described above. Although the area sampling has been reduced in the following to specific steps for your information, the reader is warned that the design of a national area or other type of probability sample calls for an extremely high level of statistical skill and experience. Samples of this type are usually developed by or in close cooperation with a small number of centers of sampling skill, such as the Bureau of the Census, the Survey Research Center of the University of Michigan, or the Statistical Laboratory of Iowa State College. The sample in the case described below was designed by the Bureau of the Census.

Step 1. *Decision on the Number of Primary Sampling Units*

There are administrative requirements, involving the ability of an organization to train and supervise interviewers, the time available for

[16] *National Study of Magazine Audiences 1952*, conducted for *Look* Magazine by Crossley, Inc.

the completion of field work, and other considerations (including a cost-accuracy relationship with which the Bureau of the Census had a great deal of experience). Those requirements influence a decision on the number of sampling points to be used, or, in probability-sampling terms, the number *of primary sampling units* (PSU's) to be used. In the case of this magazine-audience study, the sponsoring organization asked the Bureau of the Census to set a maximum of seventy interviewing centers. The actual sample design included sixty-six different PSU's. Area samples with between sixty-five and seventy PSU's are relatively common. For example, the Current Population Survey conducted monthly by the Bureau of the Census to obtain estimates of employment and unemployment and other data on the labor force had a sample with sixty-eight PSU's. The Survey of Consumer Finances conducted for the Federal Reserve Board by the Survey Research Center, University of Michigan, had a sample base of sixty-six PSU's.

Step 2. *Decision on Nature of Primary Sampling Units*

The primary sampling units used in the survey of magazine audiences were specific areas within the United States. In the case of all cities of 50,000 population and over, standard metropolitan areas have been designated by the Bureau of the Census. All such areas were included in the list from which the primary sampling units were chosen. For the remainder of the country, individual counties were used as PSU's.

Step 3. *Stratification of Primary Sampling Units*

All the primary sampling units were grouped and the stratification and sample selection were handled separately in each of five universes:

I. Standard metropolitan areas with central cities of more than 750,000
II. Standard metropolitan areas with central cities of 100,000–750,000
III. Standard metropolitan areas with central cities of 50,000–100,000
IV. Cities over 10,000 not included above
V. Remainder of the United States

In describing its sample design for this survey, the Bureau of the Census stated:

> Primary sampling units (PSU) were set up in each universe. In Universes I, II, III, each area was a separate PSU. In Universe IV, each city of over 10,000 not included in a Standard Metropolitan Area was a separate PSU. Each of the remaining counties and parts of counties constituted the primary sampling units in Universe V.
>
> The PSU's in each of Universes II–V were combined into as many strata as the total number of enumeration district cluster centers desired in that Universe. The following considerations were used in stratification:

1. The number of cluster centers desired in a geographic section for each Universe.

2. The strata as equal in population as practical.

3. For Universe IV, the population of the city.

4. For Universe V, the per cent of the 1940 population of a county engaged in agriculture.

Step 4. *Selection of Specific Primary Sampling Units for Sample*

The next step was the selection of the specific primary sampling units to be included in the sample. That selection began with the inclusion within the sample of all twelve of the Standard Metropolitan Areas in universe I, each of which had a population of 1 million or more. To select the remaining PSU's, the Bureau of the Census reported that "One PSU was then selected from each stratum with probability proportionate to a measure of size, the measure consisting of the 1950 population of the PSU." This selection resulted in a total of sixty-six different areas as PSU's, as we have already indicated.

Step 5. *Subdivision of Primary Sampling Units and Selection of Smaller Areas*

The primary sampling units—Standard Metropolitan Areas and counties—were next subdivided into enumeration districts (ED's). A typical (not average) enumeration district is roughly a cluster of some 250 family units or about 825 population. There are in the United States about 230,000 such districts. In a city of 500,000 there might be 600, or in a city of 50,000 there might be 60, or in a rural county of 5,000 there might be approximately 6. The ED's within the selected primary sampling units were grouped into clusters of approximately equal numbers of ED's located fairly closely geographically.

In universe I, which included the twelve largest metropolitan areas in the country, the "clusters were arranged in sequence and 40 clusters were chosen in a systematic fashion using the measures of size in the selection. . . . In the remaining Universes, one cluster of ED's was chosen from each PSU with probability proportionate to the measure of size of the cluster. Within the selected clusters, ED's were then chosen, again with probability proportionate to the ED population."

Comment: This area sample involves a process known as multistage area sampling. That simply means that the process of selection has several stages. At each stage, the area to be sampled is divided into several parts with designated boundaries, and some of those parts are selected for the sample. In this case, metropolitan areas and counties were first chosen as primary sampling units. Then as the second stage in sample selection, each PSU was further subdivided into clusters of smaller area units, known as enumeration districts. As a third stage in the sample selection, some of those specific ED's were chosen from each cluster.

A total of 580 ED's were selected in the sixty-six different PSU's. Note that all ED's were chosen on a random basis with judgment eliminated as a factor.

Step 6. *Selection of Household in Which Interviews Were to Be Conducted and of Individuals to Be Interviewed*

The last step in this sample design involved the selection of individual households at which interviews were to be conducted and selection of the individuals in each such household who were to be interviewed. The Bureau of the Census provided starting points and rotation rates which would establish the number of interviews as well as the basis for their distribution within the ED. First, the Bureau randomized starting points, among the 580 districts, so that the distance where the work began from the boundary of an ED varied from district to district. The Bureau cannot designate specific individuals, but can indicate that if every so many households are covered, the result will be a fair representation of types of people in that ED. For example, if their instructions call for a start at the third household, and a rotation thereafter of every tenth, and they report 182 households in the district, then eighteen interviews would be called for in that district.

The fact that the interviewers had absolutely no freedom of choice either as to selection of households or of individuals within those households cannot be emphasized too strongly. The interviewer's procedure was completely controlled by chance factors. She had no choice as to the blocks (or road segments) to cover, for she was required to go to a specified intersection and to work only within the assigned cluster. She had no choice as to where to originate interviews, since her starting points and rotation sequence were fixed. She had no choice as to sex of respondent—that being determined by the sequence in which questionnaires were assembled. If there was more than one person of the sex she was to interview in the household selected for her, she was given an alphabetical code as to which respondent to interview. If the respondent in question were not available, she had to make up to four attempts (original call plus three callbacks) to find that person. She was called upon to work chiefly weekdays after 4 P.M. and week ends, to reduce the proportion of interviews incomplete on the first call because of the not-at-home factor. If, as a result of the absence of the designated individual or refusal of that individual to be interviewed, it became necessary to find a replacement, she had a specified procedure for establishing the characteristics of that individual, including age, size of family, and female-employment characteristics. In finding replacements, the interviewer still had no choice in designating the respondent.

Comment: The process of selecting households or other sampling units by using a fixed numerical sequence, as choosing every tenth household in this case, is known as *systematic sampling.* Systematic sampling is not strictly synonymous with probability sampling, although it is often considered as synonymous in marketing research practice. The major limitation of systematic sampling is the problem of *periodicity*—a relationship between the numerical unit used in the sampling and some physical characteristic of the population being sampled. Thus if a sample of houses called for an interview at every tenth house, in a section in which there happened to be exactly ten (or a multiple of ten) houses to the block, corner houses would be either underrepresented or overrepresented in a systematic sample, depending on the starting point used. One step often present in area and other probability sampling is not included in the above illustration. This study was made at a time when 1950 Census data were "hot off the press." The Census Bureau knew from its records the number of households in each ED and could, therefore, designate the number of interviews in each without difficulty. In most probability sampling it is necessary to *list all households* (or dwelling units or other sampling units) in the selected blocks, ED's, or other areas. With the list prepared, households are selected from the list either by using a selection-ratio and systematic sampling or by numbering all households and using random numbers for the designation of households to be interviewed. Note that as the time since the latest available census increases, migration may increase or decrease the population of a given area. Listing at the time of the survey ensures that no bias is introduced as a result of such changes. This step is one which tends to increase the cost of the study, of course, since listing takes time, effort, and skill.[17]

REVIEW COMMENT ON LIMITATIONS OF THE SAMPLING DISCUSSION TO THIS POINT

A word of warning is indicated at this point. The objective of this chapter was to provide an *introduction* to sampling in marketing research. In many ways that introduction is still incomplete and will be until Chapter 11 has been used to round out the picture.

There is a very real danger that the newcomer to marketing research may fail to appreciate the importance of sound sampling in marketing

---

[17] For a much more detailed description of area sampling than space permits here, on a very similar approach but with listing included as a step, see "Case Study B: The Current Population Survey," on pp. 559–582 of Hansen, Hurwitz, and Madow, *Sample Survey Methods and Theory,* Wiley, New York, 1953.

research. Step-by-step discussions like those in this chapter tend to increase that danger by seeming to reduce sampling to a series of relatively easy cut-and-dried steps on a sort of cookbook basis. The fact that the survey technique has been emphasized in the preceding sampling discussion, for the purpose of facilitating an introduction to basic sampling concepts, heightens the danger since surveys represent only one of the technique tools of marketing research.

To counteract any such impression and to provide better perspective on the importance of sampling in marketing research practice today, two facts should be recognized and emphasized. First, sampling is an extremely important element in *all* marketing research practice, not just in the use of the survey technique. Second, sampling is an extremely complex subject which cannot be adequately understood without long and diligent study.

Chapter 11 will extend this discussion, first with a review of the relative advantages and disadvantages of the two sampling approaches described in this chapter. It will then describe the considerations underlying decisions on sample size and otherwise complete an introduction to sampling, against the background of the technique tools and data sources described in the next five chapters.

SUMMARY

1. This chapter *begins* the introductory discussion of sampling which is one of the most important elements of marketing research practice.

2. Sampling involves generalization from a small number of cases (the sample) about the characteristics which exist in the large number of cases (the universe, or population) from which the sample was selected. It is an extremely complex area with a very extensive literature and body of theory to which this book can provide only a very superficial introduction.

3. All sampling in marketing research is based on this fundamental concept: If a small number of parts (called a sample) is chosen *at random* from a larger number of items or a whole (called a universe, or population), the sample will *tend to have* the same characteristics, and to have them in approximately the same proportion, as the universe.

4. The precise meaning of the term random as used in sampling should be noted carefully.

5. The present importance of sampling as an element in marketing research practice is of relatively recent origin, as the historical review presented in this chapter shows.

6. Two major sampling approaches widely used in marketing research are described in some detail. One is *quota sampling*, in which judgment plays a major part. The other is *area sampling*, which is one form of probability sampling.

7. A single chapter is inadequate to introduce completely the subject of sampling as it bears on marketing research practice. A knowledge of some of the technique tools of marketing research and of major data sources is required to make a further discussion of the subject of sampling completely understandable. Therefore a discussion of sampling with emphasis on practical applications in marketing research practice is resumed in Chapter 11, after five chapters have been devoted to the technique tools and data sources which provide the background for the chapter.

QUESTIONS

1. How would you explain the following sampling terms?

Census	Attribute
Population	Approximation
Sampling	Sampling variation
Random sampling	Bias
Elementary sampling units	Stratified sample
Tend	Systematic sampling
Representativeness	Fundamental sampling concept
Proportionality	

2. What is the most common failure in achieving randomness? Why may these failures occur?

3. What are two ways in which the precision, or reliability, of a sample value may be appraised?

4. What is the practical value of stabilization curves to a market research man?

5. Name two major sampling approaches and give a brief description of each.

6. What specific steps were presented in this chapter as a guide to planning a quota sample?

7. What is one extremely important practical limitation of quota sampling?

CHAPTER 6

Analysis of Internal Data

Facts are the raw material with which a marketing research man works. Those facts are derived from many sources. A distinction is often made between primary data and data from secondary sources. Primary data is the term used to identify information gathered by an investigator to help him with his study of a problem. Secondary data, or data from secondary sources, are those gathered by other individuals or organizations which, in the judgment of the investigator, are relevant to his study of a particular problem. This is a useful frame of reference in many social-science situations, because it underlines the need for careful scrutiny of all information which an investigator did not personally develop, before that information is accepted as valid, unbiased, and relevant to a given problem situation.

In marketing research, a somewhat different framework for classifying data by types is often more helpful. It is often useful to distinguish between *available information,* which can be examined and analyzed without delay and often without the need to spend money to secure it, and *specially gathered* information. The latter category includes all data which must first be gathered and then analyzed.

The significance of this emphasis on availability of information in marketing research stems in part from the cost-results relationship discussed in Chapter 1, and in part from the dimensions of marketing problems (and especially the often-inadequate time dimension) discussed in Chapter 4. Gathering information takes time and costs money. That fact will be more apparent to the reader after the steps in the research process—planning, execution, analysis, and interpretation—are described in the next section. Both the time and profit dimensions of a marketing problem must be considered with care before a decision is made to gather new information relevant to a particular problem except perhaps on the informal basis discussed in Chapters 12 and 13.

CLASSIFYING DATA BY SOURCE

It is also useful to think about the types of information used in marketing research in terms of the type of source from which they are derived. This distinguishes between facts from *internal sources*—that is, from an organization's own records—and facts from *external sources,* which term includes all other sources of information. A practical framework for classifying the types of information used in marketing research is provided by combining this grouping with the one mentioned above, to produce these four major categories:

1. Information from internal sources
    a. Available data
    b. Specially gathered data
2. Information from external sources
    a. Available data
    b. Specially gathered data

The use of *information* rather than *facts* in the above listing and discussion is intended to alert the reader to the fact that not all the information useful in marketing research is completely factual. This point will be expanded and clarified in Chapter 8, which discusses the survey technique.

Virtually all data used in marketing research come from one or more of these four types of sources. This chapter discusses facts from internal sources, with primary emphasis on sales records. Chapter 7 deals with available information from external sources. Chapters 8, 9, and 10 describe the major techniques used to secure information from external sources when the necessary information is not already available.

WHY SALES ANALYSIS IS SO WIDELY USED

The analysis of facts distilled from an organization's own records—commonly called sales analysis—constitutes an extremely important area of marketing research practice. Sales-analysis activities are often the first step in a new marketing research program and play an important part in almost all established programs. The reasons why sales analysis is so important may be inferred from the earlier discussion of the marketing-problem base of marketing research. That discussion emphasized the importance of current operating problems in the marketing-problem foundation of research activities. Sales analysis provides a major share of the facts used in research on marketing problems of that type. In many organizations, especially smaller ones, it is the *only* source of such information.

An organization's own sales figures are the raw material of sales analysis. Those figures exist in readily available form or can be rather easily converted into such form in most organizations. This is true of large or small organizations, whether manufacturers, wholesalers, retailers, or service organizations. Because internal facts are usually already available, sales analysis is typically the least expensive element of a marketing research program. This does not mean that sales analysis is widely used *because* it is cheap. Despite its relatively low cost, creative sales analysis can make many important and productive contributions to marketing effectiveness. The profit contribution made by increased marketing efficiency resulting from applied sales analysis often far outweighs the costs of the entire marketing research program, including external research.

Other reasons why sales analysis represents so large a share of marketing research today should be noted. Such analytical work does not usually require the high level of technical skill and experience which is needed, for example, in planning and executing a large-scale consumer or dealer survey. Further, the detailed work which is a large share of sales analysis can be and often is delegated to clerical personnel who execute it with a minimum amount of supervision. *The interpretation of sales analyses does require marketing research skill,* but the ability to make such interpretations—particularly when confined to the single industry and/or single company alone—can be acquired rather easily and quickly. Anyone with business administration training at the college level who is prepared to do some intensive studying of published material in the field can be expected to do sales-analysis work with reasonable competence in a rather brief period of time.

RESEARCH STARTS WITH INTERNAL FACTS

There is a further very practical reason why marketing research programs so often begin with sales analysis. In a company which has a marketing problem which is likely to call for research on external sources, careful sales analysis often helps to pinpoint the nature of that problem, thereby helping to reduce the scope and cost of the external research that is required. Some companies have had the unpleasant experience of learning, after they had spent substantial sums for external research, that the research did not cover fully the real problem area or areas. The result was that much of the expenditure was wasted and the problem remained partly unresolved.

The use of careful and inexpensive sales analysis to help define the problem and reduce it to specifics is standard practice in the planning phase of most external research. Such analysis contributes information about the nature of many problem situations which helps to guide and to increase the effectiveness of the more expensive external research.

CHANGING STATUS OF SALES ANALYSIS

The review of the marketing-problem base of marketing research makes it clear why sales analysis plays so important a role in the total marketing research picture. Sales analysis provides basic information which is used in many different marketing research functions. It is worth noting that sales analysis was not always recognized as a respectable member of the marketing research family. It once had much the same status as a poor relation. The following quotation summarizes the views of four prominent marketing research practitioners, as they reported them in the summary of the joint National Association of Manufacturers–American Marketing Association study published in 1946:[1]

Confusion Regarding the Name "Marketing Research"

Many of the responding companies that stated they did Marketing Research and reported only one person in the research department, checked only a few of the sixteen functions, usually those covering appraisal of sales opportunities and measurement of sales results.

Strictly speaking, these are not truly Marketing Research Departments yet they had to be so classified for our tabulation. These are really sales statistical operations and while they perform marketing research functions, a department doing only this work should properly be called a Sales Statistical Department. In the opinion of the Committee, the use of the name "Marketing Research" to cover purely sales statistical functions reflects on Marketing Research as a broad gauge management tool and is likely to fix in the minds of top executives a very low limitation on the number of functions that the Marketing Research Department should perform as well as on the value of those functions to the organization.

It is easy to understand the committee's concern. Their study was made during the reconversion period after World War II, at a time when marketing research activities had been restricted for some years. Postwar growth was hoped for and expected, but the scale of that growth was not yet clear. Sales analysis in a rough and primitive form had long been one of the working tools of sales managers and salesmen. If "marketing research" and "sales analysis" had then been widely con-

---

[1] *Marketing Research in American Industry*, National Association of Manufacturers, New York, 1946. (Mimeographed.) A slightly condensed version of this report will be found in *The Journal of Marketing*, April, 1947, pp. 338–354, and July, 1947, pp. 25–37. It is also reproduced in McNair and Hansen, *Readings in Marketing*, McGraw-Hill, New York, 1949, pp. 83–118.

sidered to be synonymous, the subsequent growth in the acceptance and use of marketing research might well have been reduced.

The study of marketing research practices made six years later for the American Management Association revealed that the committee's fears about restrictions on the number of functions performed within the typical marketing research department were groundless. It revealed also that sales-analysis activities had continued to hold their position as part of the most widely performed and most important areas of marketing research.

Much of the improvement in the status of sales analysis as an area of marketing research practice has been the result of increases in the accuracy and versatility of available data, reflecting improved analytical and processing techniques. A specific company situation will help to illustrate how the application of marketing research background contributes to the increased usefulness of sales analysis as compared to the traditional primarily statistical treatment of sales data.

2. ALLIED PRODUCTS, INC. ★ (A)

Allied Products, Inc., produces and sells a wide variety of household products. Those products are primarily chemical compounds of one kind or another, mostly purchased and used by housewives for various household purposes. The company's single factory is located in Chicago. Its products are distributed nationally through a very wide list of wholesale and retail customer types, including hardware, drug, grocery, paint, automotive, and other outlets.

During World War II the company encountered increasing competition. Immediately before the war froze industry volume, a major competitive change in its industry occurred. Two firms which were important and successful merchandisers in other fields moved into Allied Products' industry. They purchased several smaller competitors. They converted the supply and production facilities of those competitive firms from low-priced to premium-priced products in the same price group as those of Allied Products, Inc. They backed the higher-priced products with strong consumer advertising.

Looking ahead to the postwar period, the management of Allied Products, Inc., recognized the importance of this competitive threat. Allied executives were certain that a return to peacetime operations would find them in an intensely competitive industry. They had no intention of allowing their industry leadership to go by default. They laid plans for a well-integrated program designed to strengthen their sales and merchandising operations.

One element in this program was the creation of a sales research department. The company had long used electrical tabulating equipment for financial control purposes and for production and inventory controls. Some reports of sales progress for the information of the company's top management were prepared by the accounting department. Idle time on the tabulating equipment was used to accumulate sales statistics, but no particular use was made of the statistics so produced. What little sales analysis was done was performed by the secretary to the sales vice-president.

The company hired a director for its new sales research department and made available a secretary and what calculating and other clerical assistance he needed from a clerical pool within the accounting department. He was in effect given a free hand as to the types of analyses and reports he was to prepare. He was presented with towering piles of tabulated sales reports covering the years since the tabulating equipment had been installed and was told to begin by summarizing and interpreting those reports.

— ★ —

MODIFICATION OF RECORDS SOMETIMES FIRST STEP

The starting point in a sales analysis program, as in the Allied Products, Inc., situation, is usually a detailed and searching examination of the records which provide the information to be analyzed. In the Allied case, sales figures were available which showed sales in each month, on each product the company produced, and for each size of that product, for each of the 3,000-odd counties in the United States.

So voluminous were the resulting records that they were almost useless until processed into summary form.

Because of the requirements of tax laws, no organization can long stay in business today without permanent financial records of one sort or another. Those records have often been developed primarily for accounting, tax, inventory-control, or similar purposes. Such records provide some but rarely all of the facts needed by alert marketing management executives.

An effective practical program of sales analysis which goes beyond the most elementary steps in developing and analyzing sales data doesn't just happen. It exists because a planned attempt has been made to *get and use* facts for the guidance of marketing management executives. Such an attempt usually begins with a consideration of the types of information likely to be required and proceeds into the more detailed phase of determining exactly how those types of information can be made available. It is often necessary to modify records originally set up for some purpose other than sales control, in order to secure the types and kinds of information effective control requires.

The sales research man at Allied Products, Inc., reviewed the company's sales organization briefly. He found that there were nineteen different sales districts and that sales were reported and summarized by districts. He examined a map of those districts and found that district boundaries tended to follow state lines. Inquiry developed the information that the financial division of the company had recommended using state lines as district boundaries, because that facilitated their state tax record keeping.

In some companies a single set of records is made to serve both financial and marketing purposes. In others, dual or parallel record keeping becomes necessary. What is essential in working out this problem of developing the information needed for sales-analysis purposes is cooperation between the functional divisions of an organization (as between the financial and sales divisions) and an appreciation by each division of the fact that other divisions have certain *must* requirements which should be considered. The particular needs of marketing executives in the sales record area are discussed in this chapter.

The fact that Allied's district boundaries were set following state lines illustrates the conflicting needs of financial and marketing management. For sales-control purposes, a breakdown along state lines is rarely satisfactory. Many of the largest markets in the country—for example, New York, Chicago, Philadelphia, St. Louis, and Cincinnati, to name only a few—are on or near state lines. If district boundaries follow state lines, this is likely to mean that some or all of those markets are divided and no total for the market can be developed without manual combination of data. The first step taken by the Allied Products, Inc., sales research director was to secure authorization to revise district boundaries. The nature of this revision is discussed below.

MAJOR APPROACHES IN SALES ANALYSIS

One of the important approaches to sales analysis is the grouping and analysis of sales by geographical or territorial units. While this is a basic and widely used approach, it is only one of several which belong in the repertoire of a skilled sales analyst. The following brief description identifies the major approaches which are widely used:

Product Analysis

This analysis is concerned with the variations between different products sold by the same organization. "Product" is used here in a broad and flexible way. It may describe different sizes or varieties of a single product, or specific and distinct individual products, or a complete line of related products. The complexity of the company's product line and the relative importance of different individual products as a proportion of total sales are among the influences which determine the amount of detail carried into product analysis.

Territorial or Geographical Analysis

Emphasis in this approach is on the variations which exist between different geographical or territorial units. It is applicable in a wide variety of situations, over an extremely wide range of geographical scale.

Customer or Customer-type Analysis

This approach is concerned with the variations which occur between customers of different types or individual customers. The extent to which this type of analysis is carried on in any given organization and its relative importance depend on the complexity and length of the company's customer list. It is especially widely used in industrial marketing.

Time Analysis

This analysis concentrates on the timing of sales. Major subtypes include *seasonal* and *trend* analysis.

Type-of-purchase Analysis

Although this approach is generally less important than the others mentioned above, it is an important element in many sales-analysis problems. It is concerned with variations in the manner in which either a sale was made or physical delivery occurred. An example would be the distinction between sales made by salesmen and mail orders.

HOW MAJOR APPROACHES ARE INTERRELATED

Each of these sales-analysis approaches is concerned with the answer to a different question. Product analysis is concerned with *what* is sold. Territorial, or geographic, analysis considers *where* it was sold. In customer or customer-type analysis, the question is *who* was the customer. Time analysis considers *when* the sale was made. Type-of-purchase analysis deals with *how* the sale was made or delivery effected. These are not separate and distinct analytical approaches which are used in practice on anything like an either-or basis. On the contrary, all are intimately interrelated. A single sales-analysis program typically combines several of them, on a continuing basis. Further, the remaining approaches are likely to be used at least occasionally, if only in the diagnosis of a problem situation or for guidance in the case of a particular policy decision.

Thus territorial analysis is often used as the first approach, to provide an indication of the relative sales strength or weakness existing in different sales territories. In consumer-product marketing in particular, this is the fundamental sales-analysis approach warranting first consideration. Territorial analysis may be followed by product-type analysis, either for the company as a whole or on a more limited basis to pinpoint differences in relative product-type importance in weak versus strong territories. Customer-type analysis might provide additional information about key differences in the company's sales patterns, again either in total or for some subdivision like a particular product or particular territories. Trend analysis almost always overlaps the other types, since management is constantly concerned with changes in the relative importance of particular territories, products, customer types, etc.

The above discussion of the interrelationships between different types of sales analysis anticipates slightly the introduction of the standard sales-analytical approach which, like the problem-solving approach described in Chapter 4, has the *isolation of problem elements* as its objective.

MECHANICAL TABULATION WIDELY USED

Summarizing and cross-tabulating sales records is an immensely involved detail task. The complexity of that task increases disproportionately as sales volume and product lines expand. If the job were done by hand, it would require many, many hours of clerical time, even in a small company. Sometimes the amount of time required to answer a given question through manual analysis or summarization of data would make it impossible for a key decision to be made before a deadline. It is fortunately no longer necessary to depend on the traditional bookkeeper on a high stool wearing an eye shade for sales summaries. A complete assortment of fast, versatile electronically operated tabulating machinery is available which permits sales analysis on a basis incorporating great advantages in economy, speed, flexibility, and accuracy.

Tabulating equipment can be rented or purchased by manufacturers or other organizations. For those whose need is insufficient to make the full-time use of such equipment economically desirable, there are service bureaus and specialized tabulating services in many large cities. Those service organizations are useful to handle overload work and special assignments or to do continuing tabulations of sales data for management use. In most of the discussion which follows, the availability of mechanically processed data is assumed. The assumption is a

more and more realistic one, as continuing developments in the tabulat-
ing-equipment field make the use of mechanical tabulation more and
more widespread.

At the risk of excessive repetition, it should be pointed out again that
all costs of maintaining sales records represent additions to marketing
costs. The benefits to be derived from the maintenance of such records
should far outweigh the costs involved. The expanded use of electronic
tabulating equipment makes it clear that an increasing number of companies have found that the benefits do far outweigh the costs. The full
cost of tabulating equipment rarely represents a charge to the marketing
division of a company alone. More frequently the equipment is added
as a step in mechanizing the company's entire record-keeping activities,
with accounting, inventory control, production control, invoicing, traffic,
and other applications sharing both the benefits and the costs.

VARIATIONS IN STARTING POINT

The level of development of sales records from which sales-analysis
programs start in different organizations varies widely. This makes it
difficult to discuss sales analysis in a way which has complete applicability to different situations. Consider two extreme illustrations. The only
records available for an analysis of canned-meat sales in a very large
meat-packing organization consisted of penciled figures for each territory
on a set of control cards maintained by hand. There were nearly one
hundred different varieties of canned meat in the line, many of them
available in as many as five different sizes, packed in varying numbers
of units to the case—and the records were entirely on a case basis!
Nearly three months of intensive work by a staff of four people was
required to prepare those records for analysis. At the other extreme is a
situation like that of the sales analyst at Allied Products, Inc., whose
problem was that there were too many records in much too much
detail for analysis without first reprocessing and summarizing the data.

A useful lesson to be learned from this contrast is that either too few
and too primitive or too detailed and too voluminous records are less
valuable than records somewhere between those two extremes. In the
Allied Products, Inc., case, however, the fact that the basic data were
already punched onto tabulating cards meant that condensed and
summarized records could be made available for analysis in a matter
of days, in contrast to the long delay which was inescapable in the meat-
packing example.

Variations in starting point like those mentioned make it necessary
to exercise a high degree of flexibility in approaching the problem of
developing a program of sales analysis to fit a specific organizational

situation. Care must always be taken to avoid unnecessary and expensive repetition of work that has already been done. An experienced sales analyst tries to exhaust all possible uses of available information before devoting time and effort to the task of securing new data. In the Allied Products, Inc., situation, one of the first steps was in the direction of reducing and simplifying the huge volume of record keeping that had previously been carried on.

Despite the fact that different companies begin a program of sales analysis from widely varying starting points, there are certain general guides, or principles, in the preparation and maintenance of sales records that apply in most situations. It is with the introduction and explanation of those guides that the immediately following paragraphs are primarily concerned.

INVOICE FORM SERVES AS SOURCE OF DATA

The information which is translated into the punched cards which tabulating equipment then processes and summarizes usually originates from a company invoice. At the time the invoice is made out, the necessary classification data are included. An invoice typically combines two types of information—data identifying and describing the customer and data referring to the specific transaction. The former type remains the same on all invoices to that customer. It is therefore continually maintained on a master, or control, card from which it can be transferred to the invoice form, either mechanically or by hand.

For a familiar illustration, consider the subscription plates used by a magazine publisher. Each plate carries the subscriber's name and address, plus additional information such as the subscriber's business classification in the case of business publications, the expiration date of the subscription, and so on. The master card used in invoicing simply extends the amount of information carried on a control card or plate beyond the brief data on a subscription card to whatever lengths are required in a given situation.

Various mechanical methods are available for registering information about a particular customer on the invoice form without requiring much clerical time. One relatively advanced approach uses the tabulating equipment as the source of the invoice itself. Into the machinery are fed a series of cards. One carries all classification data about the customer, including name, address, and territorial designation. Other cards refer to each "line" of the invoice, showing the product shipped, quantity, unit price, discount, extension, etc. From the tabulating equipment the invoice itself is produced, while the tabulating cards required to carry the transaction into the company's permanent records for sales-analysis purposes are also mechanically and accurately reproduced. With the growing trend toward automation of paper-handling procedures, further developments in this area may confidently be predicted. A more detailed discussion of this subject, however, would be beyond the scope of this book.

NEED FOR ADVANCE PLANNING

The subscription-plate illustration above may serve also to illustrate the need for advance planning in sales analysis, particularly in the initial setup of the tabulating cards. If the publisher wished to screen out all subscriptions expiring in January, one run through the sorting machine would suffice. If all subscriptions expiring in the first three months of the year were needed and no quarterly code were included on the plate, three complete trips through the sorter would be necessary. If the need for a quarterly sort had been anticipated in advance, it would have been relatively simple to have included a quarterly as well as a monthly code, thus eliminating the need for additional sortings. A code in this sense is simply a numbered position or column by which the machine sorts. Thus in sales analysis, the tabulating-time requirements can be reduced and more data made available by careful advance planning.

Again a specific illustration may help to make this clear. Suppose in the case of Allied Products, Inc., the many different types of wholesale and retail customers were to be identified on the records. A wholesale grocer might be coded 26, a retail grocer 27, a chain grocer 28, wholesale druggists 29, and so on. Then suppose a question arose as to the relative importance on a particular product of wholesalers versus retailers and chains. To get the information needed to illuminate that question, it would be necessary to run all cards through once for each wholesale customer type and then to combine the various types. Since Allied identified eleven different types of wholesale customers, this was a complex sorting job. If a single designation had been used to identify wholesalers, as distinguished from retailers and chains, and another for the *type* as grocer, drug, etc., a single run would have provided the information needed in this case.

In planning for sales analysis, the normal procedure is to work backward from the types and kinds of reports that it is planned to use for sales planning and control, determine the optimum frequency with which each report should be prepared, and then develop on the tabulating card the particular coding, etc., which will provide the needed reports most efficiently. In this advance planning it is desirable to look one additional step ahead—to consider what diagnostic additional breakdowns of data may be required to isolate a problem revealed by the regular reports. The differences in relative efficiency of a properly planned versus a poorly planned sales-record program are staggering.

POLICY ON TERRITORIAL CREDITING OF SALES VOLUME

One of the major applications of sales analysis is in the determination of territorial variations in sales performance. The methods used to achieve that objective are described in Chapter 21. Anticipating that discussion, it is obvious that no territorial analysis of sales performance can be more accurate than the actual territorial sales credits upon which it is based.

How accurately and precisely can a company credit its sales to specific territorial or geographic units or areas? The answer varies with the type of selling in which the company is engaged. With each increase in the number of intermediate links, if any, between the point at which the company loses sight of its merchandise and the point at which the merchandise is finally consumed or used, the relative accuracy of territorial sales credits declines. At one extreme are firms selling on a house-to-house basis to consumers, like Avon Products, Inc., or the Fuller Brush Company. An industrial-marketing organization which similarly sells direct to its customers is in essentially the same position. Such an organization can credit its sales accurately to the marketing area, county, city, and even block in which they are finally sold. At the other extreme is the consumer-product manufacturer selling entirely to and through wholesalers, all of whom take physical possession of the merchandise. Such a manufacturer loses sight of his products at the wholesaler's receiving platform or warehouse. They are subsequently resold and reshipped to manufacturers, retailers, or institutions, in locations at varying distances from the wholesaler's headquarters, and may be again resold by retailers to consumers who may live at varying distances from the retailers.

The question of territorial sales credit is less important in industrial-product marketing than in consumer-product marketing. In industrial marketing, individual-customer control is usually the primary approach rather than geographic, or territorial, control.

CREDIT SHIPPING NOT BILLING POINT

The question of how to handle territorial credits of sales of consumer products to maximize the value of the resulting records *for sales-analysis purposes* requires early attention in most companies. A clarification of policy on this point was one of the first things the Allied Products, Inc., analyst considered. Policy on crediting of sales shipped to one territorial unit but billed to another is an example of the type of clarification required. A shipment of merchandise made to the Chicago warehouse of the F. W. Woolworth Company was billed to the company at its New York office. Should the sale be credited in the sales records to Chicago or to New York? From the financial-division viewpoint, the sales should be and often are credited to the billing point, New York in this case. For sales-analysis purposes, *sales should be credited almost without exception to the point closest to the final consumer*, that is, to the point at which the company's knowledge of their eventual destination or consumption point terminates. In the case cited, the credit should be made to Chicago for sales-control and sales-analysis purposes.

If the sales were credited in this instance to New York, the effect would be to make it necessary to compare the *potential* of the New York territory with actual sales volume which had been fictitiously credited to that territory because of the "happenstance" of the location of the chain-store headquarters. The effect would be to inflate apparent New York volume, to deflate actual Chicago volume, and to introduce unnecessary and undesirable error into the sales performance of both territories.

A parallel but less obvious problem occurs in the case of sales made to a wholesaler in, say, Louisville, who buys merchandise which is shipped to him there but who also has some merchandise drop-shipped to retailers in other markets. The Louisville-shipped merchandise is credited to Louisville, because Allied cannot tell where it goes after it is shipped there; but drop shipments are credited to the point *to which they are shipped*.

DECISION ON UNIT OF MEASUREMENT

It is necessary to decide in setting up a sales-analysis program whether sales volume will be reported on the basis of physical volume (cases, pounds, units) or dollar volume. Since the invoice form which is ordinarily the source of data for tabulating cards usually shows both unit and dollar figures, there is ordinarily no problem of the availability of information on either base chosen. As a general rule it is not desirable to carry *both* dollar and unit volume through all detailed tabulations, because of the increased cost, tabulating time, and analytical burden that it would involve. The selection of the measurement base which is to be used for most analytical purposes must therefore be a carefully considered decision. This decision is fortunately not one which must be made irrevocably or on an either-or basis. A decision to use either dollars or physical volume as the normal analytical base can be supplemented under special circumstances or periodically by tabulations on the other basis.

Again a consideration of the requirements of other divisions of the company may be an important factor. If the tabulating equipment is used for inventory-control purposes, physical-volume counts will be required for those purposes. If the financial division maintains detailed figures on dollar volume by territories, by products, etc., for territorial cost-control analysis and reporting, that also will influence the sales-analysis decision.

As a general rule, the use of dollar figures is preferable. Dollar figures serve to reduce to a common denominator the various sizes, etc., of different product and to eliminate the large amount of calculation which would be necessary to combine volume of products in different sizes, packed in different numbers of units to the case. For example, the makers of Johnson's wax at one time packed Glo-Coat in pints, sold in both 12-unit and 24-unit cases; in quarts packed 12 to a case; and in half gallons and gallons, both packed 4 to a case. To determine Glo-Coat trends, the dollar equivalents of these various components were used and combined.

Comparability of data between different time periods is always an objective in developing sales data. In the Glo-Coat illustration above, note that if physical volume had been used a shift from one package size to another might *increase* the number of cases sold or gallons sold but *decrease* the dollar volume. Similarly in dealing with complex product lines, dollars provide the only realistic choice for use in sales analysis. The fact that territorial sales expenses are often compared with and related to territorial volume is another consideration which inclines the sales analyst toward a preference of the value base.

The use of units as a base is often desirable in organizations in which the product line is relatively simple and/or where the average price per unit is high (as in the appliance or automotive fields).

Sales analysis, and particularly territorial analysis on a dollar basis, is often supplemented by an analysis of average-price trends on a national or regional basis. Such an analysis provides a background against which the territorial analysis can be more accurately evaluated.

SPECIAL PROBLEMS IN DOLLAR-UNIT RELATIONSHIPS

Wherever there is a choice between dollars and units as a basis for sales analysis, a set of special circumstances requiring individual study is likely to be found. The experience of a refrigerator manufacturer provides a case in point. In one year, this manufacturer's sales were concentrated in a small-sized unit with a resulting low figure for the average price realized per unit. The following year, a sharp increase occurred in the relative importance of larger, higher-priced units. There was a decline in the number of units sold, but a sharp increase in the average price per unit and in total dollar volume. The shift in question was by no means uniform by territories. It was necessary to analyze both unit and dollar volume and average price per unit, by territories, for both years, in order to reveal clearly the true sales trend in individual territories.

The problems which arise with rapidly shifting price levels also should be mentioned here. Where price levels are changing, it is highly desirable in analysis to distinguish between any increases or decreases which reflect a change in physical volume as separate from increases or decreases reflecting price changes alone. As in the case of the refrigerator manufacturer cited, this may not be a uniform relationship, and detailed analysis by territories, customer types, etc., may be necessary.

NEED FOR DETAILED INFORMATION

In order to analyze sales data effectively, it is important to have a clear mental picture of just how sales figures are put together. It is especially important to recognize and guard against the loss in detail which occurs every time two sales figures are combined. Consider the mouth of the Mississippi as it flows into the Gulf of Mexico. At that point you could measure the width and depth of the stream on two dates a year apart. From your measurements you could tell whether the volume of water in the river was larger or smaller than it was a year earlier. But if the volume had increased, you could not tell just where the additional water came from. You couldn't tell which tributary streams had contributed more and which less than at the earlier date.

Similarly, when you examine a total sales figure you face a nearly identical problem. You see only the *net* result of pouring a large number of smaller sales figures into a broad stream of total sales. Marketing management executives need detailed information before they can exert positive control over sales volume.

Sales to individual customers in the Chicago market are combined to provide a Chicago market total. That combined total is likely to conceal the fact that some customers have increased and some have decreased their volume. When Chicago is combined with other areas to build up totals for larger geographic units—territories, districts, regions—there is a similar loss of detail. That is just the geographical aspect of the problem. There are other aspects, such as the product phase. Sales to a single Chicago customer may be up on one product, down on another. If total sales to that customer are all that are available, that revealing and perhaps important fact—that sales of one product to that customer are declining—is buried in the net figures.

It is this fact—that *combined* figures are *net* figures, which permits a loss in volume in one element of the sales picture to be offset and hidden by a gain in another element—that makes the need for detailed figures so essential in sales analysis.

ISOLATING THE PROBLEM ELEMENTS

In introducing the problem-solving process in marketing in Chapter 4, the need to isolate the problem elements was stressed. The same approach is used continually in sales analysis. The fact that detailed figures are available, or can be made available when needed, permits the sales analyst to isolate the problem elements in a sales situation. A specific example will illustrate this approach.

One sales manager received a quarterly report of sales in total. For the first quarter of a particular fiscal year, this report showed, his sales were running $60,000 behind the planned-for sales level on which sales and production budgets were based. Lacking any additional detail, that sales manager tried to make up the deficiency by increased pressure all along the line. He could push harder in all territories and on all products, and he had to because he did not know specifically which territories or which products were lagging. His only alternative was to spend valuable time trying to find out just where or why the sales were running behind the budget.

Now contrast that sales executive's situation with that of another whose sales were also behind his budget. This executive's records had been planned to facilitate sales analysis. There were four product lines involved. Comparing sales of each product line with the budget, he found this picture:

Product line	Over budget	Under budget
1	$24,000	
2	. . . .	$93,000
3	3.C00	
4	6,000	
Total	$33,000	$93,000

From this examination of sales by product lines, the sales manager learned that the $60,000 gap between actual and budgeted sales was a *net* figure, which represented a $93,000 below-budget performance on one product line which was partially offset and hidden by $33,000 in over-budget sales on the other three product lines. By this simple breakdown, he was able to isolate the single product-line element which was the problem element. If the product-line comparison had not proved revealing, examination of actual and budgeted sales by territories and by product lines by territories would have followed. In the example cited, remedial attention could be focused on the single product line in question, since that was the primary problem element, and more detailed territorial analysis could be confined to that product line.

A SALES PROBLEM IS LIKE AN ICEBERG

The somewhat oversimplified illustration above reveals another characteristic of sales analysis. At the outset, the sales manager was seeking the explanation of a $60,000 problem. When sales were examined in product-line detail, however, the true size of the problem was revealed as $93,000. It would be likely to be even larger when territorial detail on the problem product was examined.

Sales problems are like icebergs in that their full size is often not immediately apparent. When the masking by nonproblem elements is eliminated the iceberg is lifted out of the water. Only then is the full size of the problem revealed. The elimination of nonproblem elements does not increase the size of the problem; it merely reveals that size without permitting it to be hidden by offsetting nonproblem elements.

CONTROL UNITS: KEY TO TERRITORIAL ANALYSIS

One of the first and most important steps to be taken in setting up a practical program for the continuing analysis of sales on a geographic, or territorial, basis is a decision on the *control unit* to be used in that analysis. A control unit may be defined as the smallest territorial unit to which sales are allocated or credited. The selection of the control unit is important because it influences the inherent accuracy of sales records. A thorough grasp of the important concepts underlying the selection and use of a control unit will be helpful in many subsequent steps in developing a territorial sales-analysis program.

It was pointed out above that a company's total sales figure is simply the result of combining a large number of smaller figures. The company's sales volume nationally, or in its operating area in the case of a regional or local operation, simply combines total sales in a number of smaller territorial, or geographic, units. The sales analyst subdivides total sales into a number of parts and examines them individually. The selection of a control unit involves the decision on how many and what kind of "parts" total sales should be divided into.

One essential characteristic of a control unit is that in analysis it is usually treated as a unit. It might be compared to a freight car. A freight train is made up of many cars. The train is often taken apart and reassembled using some or all of the same cars, perhaps combined differently, or one train may be divided into two or more trains, but the in-individual cars are simply moved around and recombined. They are not usually broken up into smaller parts. Similarly, total sales volume is the total of the volume of all the control units combined. While sales may be broken down to their control-unit elements, that is usually as far as the territorial breakdown goes—with the single notable exception of a handful of extremely large territories or markets which may be further subdivided as a continuing process.

One of the important values of the control-unit approach is the help it provides in maintaining sales records which are comparable through time even though sales territories are revised. An illustration will help make this clear. Suppose one of the district managers in the Allied Products, Inc., picture had fourteen salesmen under his direction. Suppose further that the control unit used at the time was a county. Each salesman was responsible for volume in one or more whole counties. There were sixty-nine counties in the entire district. A change in the situation made it desirable to change this district to one with seventeen salesmen instead of fourteen. A revision of sales territories became necessary. The necessary realignment would ordinarily be worked out by developing different combinations of whole counties, to provide the needed number of new territories. It would *not* ordinarily involve *dividing* a county. When the new territorial map had been developed, sales for the preceding year could be combined for all the counties in each new territorial unit. This would provide past sales history on each new territory, which could be used to evaluate present and future sales. If the control units (counties in this case) had been subdivided, the past sales data would have been rendered useless as a basis for comparison with present sales.

The above example is intended to illustrate the concept in simple terms. It is not to be construed as a recommendation that in the situation cited a county would represent an ideal control unit.

CHARACTERISTICS OF IDEAL CONTROL UNIT

In any given company situation, the selection of a control unit should be made from the alternatives available with these two characteristics of an ideal control unit as useful guides:

1. The control unit should be as small as possible and practical.
2. The control unit should be as nearly self-contained as possible.

The advantages of a small control unit are illustrated by the example given. With small control units, sales records are flexible. The number of ways in which territorial revisions can be accomplished is increased. The other reason why smallness is a desirable characteristic of a control unit stems from the reduction of the danger that a sales problem may be concealed by combining a strong territorial unit with a weak one within a single control unit.

The second important characteristic of the ideal control unit is that it should be as nearly self-contained as possible. This characteristic is a relative one, which refers to the characteristic of a particular control-unit possibility as measured against the pattern of a specific company's sales. Each company's problem is different. Although it anticipates the discussion in Chapter 21, it is desirable to spell this out at this point sufficiently to make the control-unit concept clear and understandable.

AN ILLUSTRATION OF "SELF-CONTAINMENT"

A sales analyst in a company like Allied Products, Inc., intends to compare actual sales in his territorial control units with the potential of those units. The comparison is meaningful only if most of the volume sold and shipped into the control unit actually stays there. If much of the merchandise shipped into a control unit and credited to it in a company's sales records was actually reshipped to some other unit, no true comparability exists. In the case of Allied Products, Inc., two sales territories which had been used as control units before the sales analyst was hired were both in the St. Louis area. The Mississippi River was the dividing line between them. East St. Louis was in one control unit, and St. Louis itself was in another.

As noted, wholesalers played an important part in Allied's sales operations. Most of the wholesalers serving the area of both control units were located in St. Louis itself. By crediting sales to the control unit to which they were shipped, Allied's St. Louis volume was inflated by merchandise subsequently resold to retailers in East St. Louis and surrounding Illinois counties. St. Louis sales volume in relation to its potential would be overstated and the East St. Louis volume in relation to its potential would be understated, because the control units used in this case were *not* self-contained for a company like Allied Products, Inc., selling a substantial part of its volume through wholesalers.

Self-containment is not an abstract or theoretical notion. On the contrary, it is of great practical importance in sales analysis. This point will be developed at length in Chapter 21.

TYPES OF CONTROL UNITS

The selection of a control-unit framework to be used in any specific company situation is usually made from alternatives which are of three general types: *political units,* such as cities, counties, states, townships, etc.; *marketing units,* such as consumer trading areas or wholesale trading areas; or *company units,* such as company sales territories, distributor or wholesaler territories, etc.

Political Control-unit Possibilities

The primary characteristic of control units of the political type is their adoption of the boundaries of some established political unit. The county is the political unit most frequently adopted for sales-control purposes. There are more than 3,000 counties in the United States. The county clearly conforms to one of the characteristics of the ideal unit in its size. However, counties have important limitations as control units which should be recognized. The first such limitation is that the county is based on boundaries which are meaningless from a marketing standpoint in many cases. It is both undesirable and impractical to attempt to impose an artificial political boundary upon a sales operation. The second important limitation of counties is numerical. It is extremely difficult for a national manufacturer to maintain effective control over more than 3,000 control units. The third limitation arises because of the pattern of relative importance of counties in the country. A large number of the nation's counties each represent so small a portion of the United States potential that they do not warrant the time and effort required to maintain and analyze sales in them. In contrast, the counties with very high potential often contribute so large a part of the company's volume that each represents too large a block of potential for practical control unless it is subdivided.

These comments on the limitations of counties as control units apply particularly to companies operating on a national scale. A wholesaler operating within a limited area might find counties entirely adequate as control units. In instances such as the department store operating a main store and one or two branches in a single large city, control units much smaller than whole counties would be desirable. The limitations of counties as the primary control-unit framework, however, do not reduce the occasional value of counties as analytical units in those relatively infrequent instances when analysis of a territorial unit smaller than the control unit is necessary or desirable. Also county boundaries are often used as the boundaries of control units which consist of a number of counties, a point discussed below.

Political control units larger than counties, such as states, are usually undesirable as control units because of their extreme size. Within a single state there is usually too much room for offsetting strength and weakness to coexist. A salesman whose territory was the state of Pennsylvania, for example, needs detailed information about his sales volume and trend in such major portions of that territory as the Philadelphia area, the Pittsburgh area, and other specific points. Because state lines so often subdivide major markets as already noted, they are usually a most unsatisfactory boundary between territories or marketing control units.

Many types of statistical information helpful in marketing management are made available only in the form of state totals. This is particularly true of some figures from governmental sources and of some industry-wide data summarized by trade associations and trade publications. The availability of such information often creates a temptation to maintain state totals for a company's sales so the sales may be compared with various statistical indices. Where the state totals are the *only* control-unit totals maintained, the resulting sales-control machinery is intrinsically weak. The use of state totals as a subsidiary control device, or as an intermediate aid in developing accurate figures on potentials for smaller units, may be desirable, always with the proviso that the additional value of the information so developed must exceed substantially the cost of securing it.

Marketing Control-unit Possibilities

The existence of political boundaries like state or county lines usually does not impose a barrier to the flow of trade. Consumers consistently cross county lines and state lines to buy merchandise. Wholesalers often travel salesmen through and sell merchandise in more than one state. In developing a control-unit framework it is usually desirable to rely on boundary lines which do have meaning and significance in marketing planning, rather than to follow meaningless political boundaries. What this involves in effect is redrawing the political map of the United States with its familiar state lines into a *marketing* map which ignores the existence of political boundaries.

The boundary lines on a marketing map are set by established patterns of the flow of trade in a given area. The boundaries in question vary for different types of products, because purchasing habits also vary widely by product types. The marketing map is made up of territorial units which are usually described as *trading areas*. If the trading areas in question reflect the purchasing habits of consumers, they are called *consumer trading areas*. If the trading areas are based instead on the purchasing habits of retailers, and consequently reflect in turn the selling patterns of wholesalers, they are called *wholesale trading areas*.

A consumer trading area is that portion of the territory surrounding a dominant market or trading center from which consumers habitually direct the major share of their purchasing toward that dominant center. The size of the trading area may vary widely, reflecting in part the size of and distance to other large and rival trading centers. Thus the Milwaukee consumer trading area includes a substantial portion of central Wisconsin. It extends in the direction of and far toward Madison but does not include that city, which is itself the hub of a consumer trading area.

Because consumer trading patterns reflect the crystallized habits of consumers, they often seem illogical. The size of the central city is one determinant of the extent of a consumer trading area. The distance to adjoining trading centers and the size of those centers are other influences. Existing transportation facilities, the location and concentration of retail outlets, and the availability of banking and other commercial facilities also help shape the area. Although the boundaries of consumer trading areas are somewhat nebulous, those boundaries do exist. The boundaries were not created by the arbitrary decision of some sales executive. Rather, they evolved over a long period of time, reflecting the effect of many influences on the individual purchasing preferences of consumers. In adopting consumer trading areas as a control unit, the sales executive simply accepts established flow-of-trade patterns as a way to increase the accuracy of his sales records.

Note that there is no such thing as *the* consumer trading area of a given market. The distance consumers travel to buy different types of commodities varies, with the result that the consumer trading area for grocery products is much smaller than for shopping goods like furniture, carpets, etc.

Wholesale trading areas are characteristically larger than consumer areas. One consumer trading-area map of the United States includes more than 600 areas. In contrast, a wholesale-grocery trading-area map divides the country into eighty-odd areas, and a wholesale drug map utilizes only thirty-six areas. Such wholesale trading areas represent desirable aids in sales-analysis work, but they are so large that it is usually desirable to maintain detail beyond the wholesale-trading-area total in basic sales records. One practical approach to this problem is described below.

Company Control-unit Possibilities

There is often a strong temptation for a company to utilize some territorial breakdown already in use within the organization as its control-unit framework. Sales territories or distributor territories are perhaps the most frequently considered possibility. The advantage of such an approach lies in the fact that sales figures are already available for the territories, which would eliminate the need to reprocess past figures into a new control-unit framework. The effectiveness of sales territories as control units depends in a large part on how well planned the sales-territorial map is.

If the map in question has recently been developed "from scratch" utilizing the latest information on territorial potentials and flow-of-trade patterns in setting territorial boundaries, sales territories may prove quite satisfactory. In the more typical situation in which the territorial map has "just growed" and in which its origins are lost in history, sales territories are of dubious use. Even if sales territories—defining a territory as the chunk of geography covered by a single salesman—are used as control units, it is usually desirable to maintain records on five or more subterritorial units within each territory. This makes it possible to isolate problem elements within a territory, through the same approach which is used at higher levels in the sales organization.

It is perhaps worth clarifying some confusion which may arise as a result of the conflict between the earlier definition of a control unit—as the *smallest* territorial unit for which sales data are maintained—and the above comments on the use of sales territories. Given a soundly planned sales-territorial map, it is sometimes possible to build a control-unit framework in which existing sales territories represent one level, with subterritorial control units as the lower, smaller level. It is more usual to find that the control-unit framework is built up from the smallest units, with sales territories revised to conform to the geographic boundaries thus established.

One additional key element in evaluating sales territories as an intermediate step in the control-unit framework is the frequency with which those territories have been revised in the past. Selecting a control-unit framework is an important step. It deserves and requires detailed study. Once a framework has been adopted, it will ordinarily be used over a substantial period of time with only minor modifications. Sales territories which have been revised frequently in the past are likely to require frequent future revision as well, unless a single sweeping revision can eliminate the sources of friction or other influences which required the recurring revisions. Building a semipermanent control-unit framework on such a foundation is like building a house on shifting sands. If the sales-territorial map was strongly influenced by existing sales methods and a possibility of a change in sales methods exists, a further question is raised.

LOGICAL MARKETING UNITS SHOULD BE USED

A further finding which has emerged from years of experience in sales planning and control should be considered in the control-unit selection.

In planning a sales-territorial map and in developing a control-unit framework, attention should be paid to the existence of *logical marketing units* relevant to the business in question. Those marketing units at their smallest are individual markets like St. Louis, Philadelphia, Cincinnati. On a larger scale, they may be wholesale areas. Whatever marketing unit is applicable in a given situation should be *undivided*. Thus in the Allied example above, the St. Louis–East St. Louis area should be combined because it represents a logical marketing unit. So should the Kentucky and Ohio portions of the Cincinnati market and the Pennsylvania and New Jersey portions of the Philadelphia market. This does not mean that records should not be maintained for smaller-than-market portions of the area. It does mean that in all routine analytical work, the portions should be combined so that the total volume in the total market can be examined as an entity.

In practice, companies marketing drug products often plan their sales-territorial boundaries so that they coincide almost completely with established wholesale-drug trading-area lines. Companies in the grocery field similarly observe the existence of wholesale-grocery boundaries in planning their own territories. This makes it possible to combine territorial or other units to arrive at a wholesale area total for periodic analysis and evaluation of progress. The relevance of this to control-unit selection is apparent. Whatever control units are chosen should combine logical marketing units in so far as possible. The type of marketing units in question of course vary with the kind of product marketed and the company's sales and distribution methods.

HOW METROPOLITAN AREAS SAVE ANALYTICAL TIME

A relatively recent development in sales analysis makes the selection of control units both less difficult and less important than it used to be. That development utilizes a concentration pattern in American marketing as a laborsaving device in sales analysis and control. A major element in this approach is the use of *standard metropolitan areas*.[2] Standard metropolitan areas are geographic units consisting of one or more whole countries. Each such area includes at least one city with a population of 50,000 or more. At the time of the 1950 Census, there were 168 such

[2] Standard metropolitan areas are a device created by an interagency committee to insure uniformity in Federal government statistics. They have been widely adopted as a useful marketing control tool by manufacturers, trade associations, and other users of marketing research. Simply stated, a standard metropolitan area is an integrated economic unit. Its hub is one or more central cities. It consists of one or more whole counties. *Sales Management's* annual Survey of Buying Power issue, published May 10 of each year, lists the name and area included in each standard metropolitan area.

areas. Those areas included about 66 per cent of the United States population, but accounted for about 73 per cent of United States retail sales and for about 86 per cent of United States wholesale volume in 1950.

The concentration pattern is used in sales analysis in this way: *Every* metropolitan area is maintained as one control unit, and sales for each are tabulated individually. Within each sales territory or larger unit, sales are summarized first for each individual metropolitan area in the territory, and then with a single residual figure for the remaining non-metropolitan portion of the territory. In the case of a territory which is wholly or partly in two or more states, it is sometimes helpful to have a single figure developed for the nonmetropolitan portion of the territory in *each* state, thus in effect increasing the number of "metropolitan areas" over which control may be maintained to a total consisting of the number of metropolitan areas, plus the number of states within the territory in which there are nonmetropolitan counties. These comments of course assume that no territorial boundary divides any metropolitan area.

By using the concentration pattern indicated, control on this basis makes possible individual and detailed figures for each market representing a major share of total volume and potential (with the possible exception of such special cases as the marketing of farm machinery). It ensures that a very large proportion of the total volume of a company operating nationally is available on a continuing basis for sales-analysis purposes. It means that minor shifts in territorial boundaries introduce only minor inconsistencies in comparative data. It means that when a territorial revision moves a metropolitan area from one territory to another, there is no loss of control since data on the area are simply transferred also for analytical purposes.

Two additional observations about the use of standard metropolitan areas in sales analysis may be helpful. The largest of such areas is the metropolitan New York–northeastern New Jersey area which includes about 10 per cent or more of the national potential in most marketing situations. The area with the lowest population in 1950 was Laredo, Tex., which had *one* resident in that year *for each 231 in the New York area*. This emphasizes the fact that since metropolitan areas vary widely in size, they are not all of equal importance for sales-control purposes. The second point to be noted is that the number of such areas in any census year is set on an arbitrary basis. Thus the 50,000 population point excludes some markets falling just below that point. An expansion of the number of such metropolitan areas included in a particular sales-control program has two advantages. First, it ensures that comparable data are available when and if a later census lifts an area above the arbitrary dividing line. Second, it permits the sales analysis to be extended down to a point which includes any desired proportion of total volume or potential volume.

DUAL-CONTROL-UNIT FRAMEWORK

When a single company operates in different ways, sometimes through different divisions or subsidiaries, selling products of different kinds to different types of customers, it is sometimes necessary to maintain two or more different control-unit frameworks. Each such framework is used only for the particular sales figures to which it is applicable. An example is provided by the Bauer & Black division of the Kendall Company, which makes products sold through drug channels (like Blue Jay corn plasters), also industrial tape products sold to manufacturers and processors for use in their own production, and also surgical dressings sold to hospitals and hospital supply houses. The company used three different control-unit frameworks in its sales-analysis work.

The increasing acceptance of and use of the metropolitan-area approach in sales analysis has greatly reduced the need for such multiple frameworks. The disadvantage of such a dual setup is that *total* sales could never be developed for the company as a whole, since the two frameworks only partially coincide. This has tended to confine the dual approach to completely separated marketing activities, such as are found in different subsidiaries or in quite distinct marketing approaches within a company.

EFFECTIVE DATE OF SALES-RECORD CHANGES

With a control-unit framework established and a decision made on the extent to which the metropolitan-area-concentration pattern is to be used as a control device, a question arises as to the timing of any necessary changes in sales records. It is usually desirable to have the change made at the beginning of an accounting period, preferably either a calendar year or a fiscal year. If such a date is far in the future (say seven or eight months away at the time the decision must be made), it may be desirable to initiate the new program without a long delay.

In this connection it is worth remembering that the full value of the improved sales control which becomes possible with a well-planned sales-analysis program is not realized until revised and exactly comparable figures are available both for a current period and for the same period a year earlier. In some cases, that date is moved closer by going back and reprocessing past data onto the new basis. In other cases, the tabulating cards required for the reprocessing may either not be available or not include the required detailed codes. In such a case, the analyst must simply defer trend analysis until the passage of time makes comparable data available.

This question is one which must be considered at several points in planning a program. For example, the analyst joined Allied Products, Inc., in October and found the company on a calendar-year basis. Extensive revision in the sales-control framework was clearly necessary. By the latest date at which a new sales-control framework could be made effective January 1, he had a framework outlined which was much improved but still far from perfect. He had the choice of putting that framework into work or of allowing more time to pass until he was more completely satisfied with it. The latter choice would have deferred the date at which comparable current and year-ago data would be available. His decision was to use the improved but imperfect framework without a further delay.

TROUBLE SPOTS IN AVAILABLE RECORDS

When the control-unit framework has been set up and is scheduled to go into effect at the beginning of a record period, the process of accumulating sales records which can be analyzed with maximum confidence in their accuracy begins to get under way. This does not mean that it is necessary to spend a sterile year waiting for the comparable data before effective use can be made of sales records. Sound practice calls for the analysis of those figures which are available, and for the speedy application of the results of that analysis, during the time period in which more accurate figures are being accumulated.

There is no great difference in the sales-analysis problems which are encountered when working with figures based on a sound control-unit framework and those based on historical territorial or other breakdowns found in most companies apart from the increased accuracy and greater meaningfulness of figures in the marketing sense. In working with figures developed before a new control-unit framework has been put into effect, it is necessary to exercise constant caution. The greatest danger is that some major distortion or source of error is present which invalidates the apparent conclusions emerging from the analysis. This danger is of course greater in the case of an analyst in a new company or position, as in the Allied Products, Inc., case. Among the major sources of such distortion are the following.

Territorial Changes

A sudden decline in volume in a territory is likely to signal the existence of a major sales problem. On the other hand, it is always possible that some change in the territorial boundaries may have occurred between two time periods or during either of the two periods being com- pared. This possibility should always be checked before much time is devoted to the analysis.

Extraordinary Transactions

Occasionally a single transaction, typically both of unusually large size and a nonrecurring nature, will produce a marked distortion. Thus the sales analyst at Allied Products, Inc., found a sharp sales decline of the Seattle branch, at a time when all other areas were showing gains. A review of the period in question disclosed that a freight embargo in parts of the country resulting from a snowbound situation had resulted in the diversion of far more merchandise to Seattle than usual. This inflated the volume base in the earlier year. Another example from an industrial marketing situation: A Pittsburgh branch had been averaging $150,000 in annual volume. A new branch manager took over. In his second month on the job he closed a single order for $320,000 in special equipment.

Untypical Base Period

Comparisons of sales when a major source of distortion was present in only one of the periods is often nearly meaningless. For example, a Pittsburgh brewery had sales volume far higher than year-ago levels in one year, but far lower in the same months of the following year. A strike at breweries in Milwaukee in the base year sharply reduced the availability of competitive beer and inflated the base-period sales.

Geographical Influences

The distortion which occurs when logical marketing units are divided has already been mentioned. The St. Louis–East St. Louis territorial example is worth remembering as an illustration of this problem.

New-product Introductions or New-market Openings

When a company is introducing a new product, or expanding its operating area by moving into additional territory, it typically chalks up sales volume which is partly of a nonrecurring nature. There is always the danger that volume in existing territories or products may be declining, with the loss offset by the additional volume in the new territories or products. An unusually effective "deal" or promotion may similarly exert a distorting influence.

Change in Customer List or Operating Methods

Loss of a single large customer will often produce a marked change in the volume level of a territory. A knowledge of those changes in customer lists which are important enough to influence total sales in individual territories is desirable to be sure such shifts are considered.

In some of the cases cited above, a real sales-volume change may have occurred, which could be larger or smaller than it at first appears. The peculiar situations identified above explain, in a true sense, some of the changes in sales figures. Throughout sales analysis, the analyst faces the challenging task of separating *real* explanations from the rationalizations, "explanations," and just plain alibis which somehow bubble to the surface when there is an adverse sales trend in a territory. Assurance that all reasonable explanations for an adverse trend have been studied and explored and that the sales decline remains in fact *unexplained* is necessary before the investigation of causal influences can be pushed forward with confidence.

ACTION IS USUALLY PREFERABLE TO DELAY

The problem of dealing with sales figures which have not been carefully and uniformly processed along the lines discussed in this chapter exists in most companies, particularly in the early phases of a sales-analysis program. When the program begins, such figures are all that are available. There are two alternatives: The analyst can wait until figures processed in accordance with accepted procedure are available, or he can proceed to analyze the available figures without delay. The latter course is usually chosen, because there is so much to be gained by getting the program under way. When the figures in question contain unknown elements such as territorial changes, sales credits to billing instead of shipping points, or inconsistent treatment of drop shipments, extensive digging into the figures themselves is desirable as a precaution against an error in interpretation. Such digging can often be profitably confined to those territories which show an extraordinary change in volume, either upward or downward. Explanations of such changes should be sought from those who are most familiar with conditions in each territory.

COMBINING SALES OF DIFFERENT PRODUCTS

In making sales allocations to geographic units, it is desirable to plan carefully how much detail to maintain. The questions at this point are whether sales of different sizes of a given product should be carried as individual totals or combined into a single figure for that product; whether products of the same general type should be carried individually or combined into a product-type total; and whether products which are not alike should be combined into a heterogeneous total. The analyst faces a constant dilemma in making such decisions. He does not want to maintain records in more detail than is required for effective sales analysis, with resulting excessive costs; but at the same time he does not want to boil down records in the interest of simplicity and economy to the point where important details become unavailable because they are buried within a combined figure.

To guide him in arriving at decisions of this type, the analyst is usually concerned with the importance of the sales volume of each product, product size, or product line, both in absolute terms and as a proportion of the company's total volume. The trend of an element or the expectation that what is a minor element today may be a major element tomorrow also enters into his decision. As a general rule it is well to remember that sales of dissimilar products should almost never be combined for analysis purposes with the single exception of the situation in which they are pooled in a catch-all "all other" or "miscellaneous" group. That exception occurs only where they are very minor in relative importance, each representing perhaps less than 1 per cent or $\frac{1}{2}$ of 1 per cent of total sales. If the aggregate of such an "all other" grouping is large, it may perhaps be subdivided into two or more smaller groups which combine the small-volume products or elements on the basis of some common ingredient such as type, distribution channels, etc.

THE PROBLEM OF TRANSSHIPMENT

All sales records inescapably contain certain elements of "built-in inaccuracy." A frank recognition of the existence of such limitations is helpful in approaching the sales analysis in a realistic frame of mind. Part of that inaccuracy results from the problem of transshipment of merchandise. A company sells merchandise to a customer located at one point, and the customer then transships the merchandise to another, perhaps distant, point. Because this problem is especially vexing and relevant when an attempt is made to analyze territorial sales performance, a detailed discussion of it has been deferred to Chapter 21. It is mentioned here simply to indicate that this problem often requires consideration in setting up sales records as well as in analyzing them.

SUMMARY

1. This chapter introduces the reader to the approaches and problems involved in gathering and analyzing facts from an organization's own internal records. This is the major subdivision of marketing research practice which is called sales analysis.

2. In this introduction to sales analysis, the importance of careful planning and of careful scrutiny of records prior to analysis is stressed. It is axiomatic that no sales analysis can be more accurate than the records on which it is based.

3. The major approaches used in sales analysis are reviewed, and the inter-relationships between different approaches are traced.

4. The applications of sales analysis are developed in subsequent chapters, as part of the factual raw material of marketing research activities.

QUESTIONS

1. How would you differentiate between primary and secondary data?

2. In your own words, how would you explain the fact that sales analysis is so widely used?

3. What problems might you, a marketing researcher, encounter if your company keeps a single set of records to serve both financial and marketing purposes?

4. What major approaches, which are widely used, might you consider in setting up your sales-analysis program? Discuss each approach briefly. How are they interrelated?

5. Why is advance planning such an important factor in sales analysis?

6. You have been asked for your opinion on where sales volume should be credited for sales-analysis purposes—to the shipping point or to the billing point? How would you handle this question? Why?

7. At a company meeting the problem has arisen as to whether your company should use a dollar or a unit-volume figure in their sales analysis. What would be your recommendation? What considerations would enter into your decision?

8. What is meant when it is said a sales problem is like an "iceberg"?

9. The question of control units to be used in your company's sales-analysis program has come up. First, what is a control unit? What are the characteristics of an ideal control unit? And what types of control units are there that your firm could consider?

10. Why is the selection of the control unit such an important step in setting up a sales-analysis program?

11. You have been asked to explain during a coming meeting what a standard metropolitan area is; and to explain why this unit should be given consideration by your firm. What are your answers?

12. What trouble spots should you be watching for as you work with figures accumulated prior to the initiation of the new control-unit framework selected?

CHAPTER 7

Locating and Evaluating Available Data from External Sources

Every marketing research man has available to him a vast reservoir of information. Some of that information is published, some is unpublished. Some of it is complete and factual and of unquestioned reliability. Some of it is factual but incomplete. Some of it may be visibly or invisibly biased. Some information is available without charge, some requires a nominal expenditure, and some carries a high price-tag. In the last instance, the decision to make the expenditure and acquire the information or to try to get along without it involves the same careful weighing of its probable values on the cost-versus-results scales that is necessary in so many other marketing research decisions.

The dual tasks of locating and evaluating available data relevant to a particular marketing or marketing research problem usually consume a major share of the marketing research man's working hours. This chapter will serve to indicate some of the types of sources commonly explored in developing marketing research data from available external sources. It will also provide a systematic basis for evaluating the relative dependability (but not the relevance) of that data.

GENERAL VERSUS SPECIFIC DATA SOURCES

It might be well to preface this discussion of data sources by pointing out the important distinction between general and specific data sources. Acquiring a knowledge of *general* sources of marketing information and learning how to locate and evaluate information from such sources is part of the basic education of a marketing research man. Such knowledge becomes part of his technique tool kit and makes it possible for him to work over a period of time on the marketing problems of many different industries. He does not have to acquire new technique tools for each industry. It is enough for him to know the kinds of information which are usually employed in marketing research work and the types of sources from which those kinds of information generally flow. He uses his knowledge of general sources and types of sources, in working on any particular problem, to the extent that that knowledge applies in a specific problem situation.

Moving now to more specific sources of marketing information, we find that there are in many industries specific sources of marketing data which are widely used and accepted within that single industry. In some cases those sources are unique unto that industry. No research man who has not spent a considerable period of time working within an industry can be expected to know all such information sources. He *can* be expected, however, to bring into his work on a marketing problem situation in any industry a knowledge of general sources and an alterness to the possibility that specific sources may exist in that industry. He should be able to locate such sources once the fact of their existence has been established.

There is a very close parallel between the problems faced by marketing research men in two very different situations in this area of knowledge of specific sources. Take on one hand a marketing research man who has been newly hired by a company in a specific industry with which he has had no previous experience. The director of sales research for Allied Products, Inc., for example, falls in this category. Take on the other hand a marketing research man working for an organization that works with many different industries. He might be employed by a marketing research organization, a management consulting firm, or an advertising agency. If we assume he had no previous experience with the margarine business, the marketing research director of the advertising agency hired by the Dell-O Company will serve as an example. Men in both situations face an almost identical and very difficult problem.

As a newcomer to the problems of a particular industry, each man is naturally concerned with seeing that his efforts are applied in such a way that they will have maximum productivity in terms of contribution to his employer. Those efforts will not be productively employed if they are devoted to working over ground that has already been explored or gathering anew information that is already available. That kind of wasted effort, which is sometimes described as "spinning wheels" or "sawing sawdust," is one symptom of inexperience and ineptness in marketing research work.

As a matter of common prudence, one of the first things an experienced marketing research man does in studying a problem situation in what is, for him, a new industry area is to make a determined effort to find out what types and kinds of information are *already available* on the problems and practices in that specific industry. It is apparent immediately that the marketing research man who is an old-timer in any given industry has a substantial initial advantage over a newcomer in his presumably complete familiarity with the available specific information bearing on the industry's problems. There is sometimes an accompanying and offsetting disadvantage present in such a case, however. Preoccupation with a single industry's problems sometimes precludes an awareness of what other industries are doing and of the kinds of information which *should be* but are not available to and used by a particular industry.

To provide a frame of reference which will make the importance of a knowledge of data sources more meaningful, it might be helpful to review briefly some examples of the contribution such data made to specific marketing problem situations.

3. SHOWER-OF-STARS COSMETICS, INC. ★ (A)

This national manufacturer and marketer of a complete line of cosmetic products, with its factory and headquarters in southern California, watched its sales volume expand spectacularly during World War II and then contract sharply and painfully in the years following the war when competitive pressures began to increase. The approximate shape of the company's sales curve may be inferred from these index figures. With 1939 volume as 100, sales climbed to a wartime peak of 750. Ten years later sales had dropped to an index figure of 390—still well above prewar levels, but sharply below the wartime peak and disappointingly low when the national prosperity and the level of consumer spending power were considered. A management consulting firm was engaged to study the company's situation generally and to recommend specific remedial action.

The individual primarily responsible for the company's sales volume told the consultants in their initial meeting with the Shower-of-Stars management group that the entire cosmetic business had been declining from wartime peak levels and that, in his opinion, the company was doing relatively well against an adverse industry trend. As in the Dell-O case, this opinion represented one of the possible hypotheses to be explored.

The consulting organization was given a fixed ceiling on the cost of their initial study, which precluded any extensive survey of the cosmetic market at either the consumer or dealer level. They were forced to confine their activities in the course of their initial study of the company's situation to a study of available information; to an informal investigation (along the lines discussed in Chapter 13) covering informed individuals with a knowledge of trends in the cosmetic industry; and to an analysis of the company's own sales data.

One phase of their study of available information was an extremely searching study of the published data on sales volume and income trends of those companies in the cosmetic industry whose stock was publicly held. From this study it was determined that all those companies were enjoying sales and profit volume which was at or near the wartime peaks. One or two of those companies, in fact, had shown steady growth both in sales and in profit in the postwar years which had seen the sharpest declines in the volume and profit of Shower-of-Stars Cosmetics, Inc. From this phase of their study, the consultants arrived at the tentative conclusion that no industry-wide volume contraction could be blamed for the adverse trend in their client's sales.

Another phase of the study combined sales analysis with a study of available information published by a number of different consumer magazines including the Dell and Fawcett groups, *Good Housekeeping, Women's Home Companion,* and *Cosmopolitan.* The sales analysis revealed that not all the company's major products had suffered sales losses. One major product, in fact, was responsible for the largest share by far of the company's total sales decline. The published studies of the magazines revealed a correspondingly sharp decline in consumer use of that particular type of product and a spectacular expansion of volume in two other closely related product categories. The expanding product types were functionally identical with the type of product on which the company showed the most alarming sales loss, much as tooth powder is functionally identical with tooth paste. The Shower-of-Stars organization had not developed or introduced any new products in those two product-type categories, because it feared that by doing so it would be competing with itself and contributing to its own sales decline.

From this preliminary study, based largely on a combination of sales analysis and an exhaustive and ingenious analysis of available information, the consulting organization was able to report with confidence that in its opinion the company's problem was primarily in the *company* and *competitive* elements of the marketing picture, as detailed in Chapter 4. The combination of growth in new product types with the company's failure to develop or introduce additional product types over a long period of time earmarked laggard new-product development as one likely candidate as a piece of the problem puzzle.

— ★ —

Comment: This marketing problem, like the Dell-O case presented in Chapter 4, is representative of the broad class of problems in which there is a factually unexplained sales decline. Note that the approach in this case, as in the Dell-O case, is initially one of attempting to determine which of the multiplicity of possible elements in this marketing situation seem most likely to be *problem elements.*

4. BISSELL CARPET SWEEPER CO. (A)

The Bissell Carpet Sweeper Co., Grand Rapids, Mich., was the leading national manufacturer of carpet sweepers. Some estimates put Bissell's share of all carpet sweepers in use in American homes as high as 80 per cent. In 1931, the executives of this long-established and successful business faced a major marketing problem. The company's sales volume had declined sharply from the levels enjoyed in 1928 and 1929. The decline was of course in part a cyclical decline, which reflected the lower level of business activities generally. When business activity contracts, the effect on different industries varies widely. Some types of products decline more than other types. Since a Bissell sweeper had a relatively long useful life, the purchase of a new sweeper at least for replacement purposes could more easily be deferred than could purchases of other types of products competing for the restricted number of consumer dollars. This fact tended to accentuate the adverse impact of reduced business volume on the carpet-sweeper industry and on the Bissell organization, the industry leader.

Bissell executives were gravely concerned about the possibility that their sales decline might be much more than cyclical. There were indications that it might be due in part to the impact upon carpet-sweeper sales of a new-product innovation—the electric vacuum cleaner. The first step in the analysis of this problem situation was an attempt to determine the extent to which sales of electric vacuum cleaners, like sales of Bissell sweepers, were declining.

Information on the size of the industry volume for vacuum cleaners proved relatively easy to get. Research disclosed that manufacturers of vacuum cleaners had a trade association which gathered and published figures on industry volume. In the years from 1926 through 1929, according to the Vacuum Cleaners Manufacturers' Association, more than 1,200,000 vacuum cleaners a year were sold to consumers. The acceptance of that type of competitive product seemed to be rising sharply.

— ★ —

Comment: This marketing problem, to which we shall return in later chapters, is also representative of a large group of major marketing problems. The characteristic of this type of problem is that it arises coincidentally with or shortly after the development and introduction of a significant product innovation or of a new type of competitive product.

Such an innovation represents a continual potential threat to established industries and to established companies in those industries.

Don't allow the depression-year timing of this case to lead you to feel that it is "dated" and therefore no longer worth your attention. This is an example of a timeless type of problem which recurs in industry after industry, year after year. As other and more recent illustrations of problems of this type, consider the situation of the leading washing-machine manufacturer—Maytag—when Bendix Home Appliances, Inc., introduced the first automatic washing machine in the late 1930s. Or consider the situation of dentrifice manufacturers, when a significant new-product development provides important news for consumers of such products. Even a new packaging development like the spray-type plastic container introduced by Stopette poses this type of "Is my product obsolete?" problem for established manufacturers in the threatened industry.

5. STRONG PLUMBING AND HEATING CO. ★ (A)

The Strong Plumbing and Heating Co., with headquarters in Philadelphia, Pa., is a manufacturer of a wide variety of different types of plumbing and heating equipment. Product-line obsolescence threatened to reduce the company's volume early in 1950. The company was interested in adding to its line new products which offered a promise of substantial growth potential. Among the product fields under consideration at this time, two looked especially inviting. One was the air-conditioning industry; another was the commercial refrigeration industry, which supplies refrigeration needs for retail stores and other commercial operations.

Because the company had no marketing research facilities of its own at that time, a marketing research organization was invited to make a preliminary examination of the company's existing situation as it applied to the opportunities in those two areas.

The marketing research man who was given this assignment first consulted the published report of the Bureau of the Census covering the 1947 Census of Manufactures. That report covered the air-conditioning field in great detail, reporting the number of units manufactured in various size and other categories, their value, and other information relevant to this problem. (Note that the problem of estimating what the trend in industry volume had been *since* 1947 remained unsolved at that point.)

Because the company was already active in some parts of the air-conditioning field, the research man asked for and received copies of the company's own reports to the government which were part of the industry total reported in the Census of Manufactures reports. An annual report of industry volume for 1949, released by the U.S. Department of

Commerce, was helpful in developing information on basic trends in the industry since the 1947 Census data had been gathered.

Two other important sources of available data were also consulted in the course of this investigation. One involved financial statistics on the corporate sales, earnings trends, and other vital statistics on those organizations in the industry which had publicly held stock. The other source was a business publication, *Heating and Ventilating*, a magazine serving the field under consideration, which summarized industry statistics. These included current estimates of the size of the total market, in units and dollars; trend data showing rate of growth in recent years; names of leading manufacturers in the field; details on the geographic division of industry volume; a description of existing channels of distribution used by different manufacturers; comments on latest product developments; and other helpful information.

Comment: When a company is considering an addition to its line of products, particularly an addition which takes it into a new industry or into an additional portion of an industry which it covers only partly, all available data on the size and characteristics of the industry under consideration are studied as "standard operating procedure." This subject is developed at length in Chapter 23 on new-product development and is explored also in Chapter 20, which deals with the problem involved in determining the size and characteristics of the market for a product.

6. PARKER PEN CO. (A)

The Parker Pen Co., Janesville, Wis., was interested in diversifying its line of products. One product under consideration was a new type of camera. The new-product problem posed by that camera will be developed at length in Chapter 23. As one facet of the investigation of the size of the potential market for a camera, Parker wanted data on the extent to which people took pictures. What proportion of all families included one or more "shutter-bugs"?

Research disclosed that a national consumer survey had recently been completed by Sylvania Electric Products, Inc., whose interest in the photographic field was stimulated by their activities as manufacturers of flash bulbs used by photographers. Sylvania was happy to release to Parker some data from their survey, giving the answer to the market-size question Parker was trying to determine.

Comment: Note that the two organizations involved in this example were essentially noncompetitive. In fact, Sylvania had a purely selfish interest in Parker's possible entry into the camera field, for Parker's promotion of its camera would be likely to expand the market for Sylvania's flash bulbs. The helpful interchange of marketing research data among noncompetitive organizations is on a broader scale than is generally realized.

MAJOR TYPES OF SOURCES FOR AVAILABLE DATA

Against the background of a few specific real-life problem situations, the above cases serve to illustrate how various types of sources were consulted to secure available information relevant to a variety of problem situations. When a marketing research man faces a problem situation, what major *types* of sources should be explored in a search for available data with a bearing on that problem? The following list identifies and comments briefly on the major types of sources which should be considered and explored under most circumstances.

Federal Governmental Sources

One basic and often-used source of data for marketing research purposes is the Federal government. Within the maze of governmental agencies, some are much more prominent as data sources than others. The Bureau of the Census ranks first in importance as a data source. Use of various census releases including the Population Census, Census of Manufactures, Census of Business (which includes retail trade, wholesale trade, and service establishments) is an almost daily practice in any active marketing research operation. In addition to the regularly published reports, the Census Bureau also contributes to marketing research practice by preparing special tabulations of data of various sorts for marketing research purposes. The latter activity is not so widely recognized as its potential value warrants.

Two specific illustrations will help to suggest the type of special information which the Census Bureau can provide. A farm publication wanted a comparison of its list of subscribers with the next-door neighbors of those subscribers who did not subscribe. The publication furnished its subscription list. The Bureau identified the subscribers and their next-door neighbors in census files and tabulated comparisons showing such things as educational level, number of acres farmed, etc., for the two lists. A marketing research organization active in the test-marketing field had a special tabulation run of the number of outlets and total sales volume within four different sales-volume groupings for each of the country's standard metropolitan areas. That tabulation was helpful in developing store-panel samples proportional to the actual distribution pattern in different markets.

Two limitations of this source should be noted: The information supplied cannot violate the legal prohibition against disclosure of data on individuals or individual firms; and the ability of the Bureau to handle such special assignments varies from time to time, depending on their work load on regular reports. Obviously one cannot expect the Bureau to interrupt the scheduled processing of regular census reports to supply information needed by and useful to a single organization, in preference to data valuable to the entire business community.

Ranking second only to the Bureau of the Census as a source of data for marketing research purposes is the U.S. Department of Commerce. The flow of information of vital interest to marketing management from the U.S. Department of Commerce is tremendous, and the field service offices of the Department maintained in principal cities throughout the country are extremely helpful in locating and supplying data relevant to any particular business-information need.

A number of the U.S. Department of Commerce contributions to marketing research data deserve special mention. One is the monthly publication *Survey of Current Business,* which is one of the "statistical bibles" of the research man. It contains current basic data on most phases of national economic and commercial activity. It is supplemented with a biennial publication *Business Statistics,* which substantially expands the usefulness of the data reported monthly. Other supplements such as one on *Regional Trends in the United States Economy* and *Income Distribution in the United States* make the contribution of the Office of Business Economics of the U.S. Department of Commerce a notable one indeed. *County Business Patterns,* an extremely detailed summary of statistics on employment in specific industries, published by the U.S. Department of Commerce and the U.S. Department of Health, Education and Welfare jointly, is another important data source.

Many marketing research men would nominate as the U.S. Department of Commerce's most important single contribution to their needs a publication called *Market Research Sources.* Figure 7.1 reproduces the table of contents from the 1950 edition of that publication, the latest available at the time this book went to press. Since the 1950 issue was the ninth edition of that vital reference book, additional editions are likely. Until those editions are published, the various indexes of governmental publications serve in their stead as clues to the location of data emanating from Federal governmental sources.

The U.S. Department of Agriculture is active in the field of marketing-data publication, as well as in the execution of specific marketing research projects for various areas of agricultural-marketing interest. Typical of the latter type of activity was a survey entitled *Homemakers' Use of and Opinions about Fats and Oils Used in Cooking*[1] and a sub-

---

[1] U.S. Department of Agriculture, Agricultural Marketing Service, Marketing Research Report 67, June, 1954.

Contents

v

Figure 7.1

stantial supplement thereto. The technical competence of the surveys executed by the U.S. Department of Agriculture is outstanding.

In summary, the Federal government is a major source of data useful in marketing research activities. Changes in the nature of the activities of different departments make a specific identification of particular areas rather obsolescent; but the importance of this type of source for data relevant to marketing research problems is far from obsolescent and in fact increases over the years.

In the cases cited above, the Federal government provided a substantial proportion of the data needed to reduce the problem of the Strong Plumbing and Heating Co. to sharper focus. The use of Census of Manufactures data as an element in the analysis of marketing problems of manufacturing organizations is a basic and fundamental tool which no experienced marketing research man overlooks or underrates.

State and Local Governmental Units

The Federal government is not the only governmental body contributing marketing research data. State governments are also an important source of such data. This is particularly true in the case of states collecting retail sales taxes and reporting the source of those taxes in detail by county and store type, as Wisconsin does. Below the state governmental level are county and city units, and other quasi-governmental units of some importance. Thus when a consumer survey of the Detroit market was under consideration and data were needed on the extent of population growth in a between-census year for the city and for various sections of suburban area in the metropolitan area, the Detroit Metropolitan Area Regional Planning Commission was able to provide current and useful data.

Trade Associations and Other Technical and Professional Groups

Many trade associations are active in the field of marketing research, providing aid and guidance to their member organizations. Typical of the activities carried on by an increasing number of associations is the gathering from individual members of data on output, sales, etc., combining the individual company reports, with anonymity of contributing members carefully preserved, and releasing a summary for the entire industry. Such a summary permits each member organization to appraise its progress against the background of the entire industry of which it is a part. The company's market share and the trend of that market share can be determined with the industry volume figure supplied by the association as a base point.

While trade associations are active primarily to serve and to further the interests of their member companies, they are often helpful to marketing research men dealing with other types of problems. Thus in the case of the Bissell problem above, a competitive-industry member gained insight into a marketing research problem by reference to data supplied by the association of vacuum-cleaner manufacturers. This type of cross-industry application of marketing research data is on the increase, partly because the extent to which different industries compete with each other is on the increase. For example, the outstanding sales accomplishments of the automobile manufacturing industry in 1955 substantially reduced the number of consumer dollars for which such other industries as housing, television-set manufacturing, and the like were competing. Thus the automobile-sales data became of some importance in appraising the market outlook for other industries.

Chapter 28 describes in more detail the marketing research activities of trade associations and similar groups. The comments in that chapter on the limitations of data gathered by trade associations are particularly relevant to a consideration of the usefulness of such data which ranges in accuracy from quite dependable to highly questionable.

Financial-data Sources

There are many marketing research problems in which a contribution to the solution of the problem is made by data gathered from financial-data sources. Publicly held companies, reporting their sales, income, and other data to their stockholders, sometimes perform a notable although unintentional service for their competitors as well. It is standard practice to try to combine figures so that the extent of revelation is reduced to a minimum in such releases. For example, sales expense and advertising expense are almost always combined in published reports to prevent competitors from gaining insight into the company's operations. Even so, competitors who entrust the analysis and evaluation of such statements to experienced and skillful personnel can often develop much data of value.

Such data sources were illustrated in the preceding cases by the Shower-of-Stars Cosmetics, Inc., problem. A more usual application of such data was suggested by the Strong Plumbing and Heating Co. case, in which the sales progress and earnings of companies already active in an industry were evaluated as part of the process of attempting to decide whether that industry offered an attractive opportunity.

Consumer and Trade Publications and Other Advertising Media

Another important source of data useful for marketing research purposes is the broad group of advertising media, particularly including specific consumer and business or trade publications and groups of similar media such as the American Newspaper Publishers' Association. In the case of business publications serving a particular industry, such as

Heating and Ventilating in the Strong case above, a substantial back-log of information about the industry in question is a major part of the publication's stock-in-trade. Without that information, the publication would have no way of knowing what the problems or key develop-ments in the industry were, hence would have little basis for planning editorial content interesting to the specialized groups for whom the publication was edited. Without that information, the publication's ad-vertising salesmen would have no planned basis for locating and identify-ing prospective advertisers.

This type of source is one which is particularly important for a marketing research man who is confronted by a problem in what is, for him, a new or strange industry. We might note that such a problem arises in practice with high frequency. Consider some examples. A marketing research man takes a job in a new industry. Or an advertising agency takes on a new account, and the marketing research men in the agency are in a similiar position. Or a marketing research service organization accepts an assignment in an industry in which they have no experience. Or a company is considering launching a new product, as in the Parker case, in what is for it a new industry.

The approach of consulting a business or trade publication for in-formation about a particular industry falls in the general category of seeking expert advice, which is described in detail in Chapter 13.

Consumer advertising media, like magazines and newspapers, are also often used as important sources of marketing research data. In the Shower of Stars case above, surveys conducted by different publications were consulted for guidance in pinpointing the trend in consumer use of products of different types. Some advertising media, such as the Curtis Publishing Company's magazines, the *Chicago Tribune,* and others, pro-vide substantial assistance to their advertisers. This subject is developed at greater length in Chapter 29.

Industrial Organizations

There was illustrated in the Parker Pen Co. case above an approach to the location of available data which is more important in practice than one might expect from the scant attention devoted to it in the literature of the field. One organization—in this case a manufacturer—had a prob-lem. The marketing research man working on that problem asked him-self, "What organizations would be likely to have to gather the kind of information I need for *their own* management guidance?" His answer in this case would of course begin with manufacturers of photographic equipment, such as Eastman Kodak. But the nature of the problem would be likely to place Parker in a competitive position with Eastman, at least where the sale of cameras was concerned. (Parker would also be likely to be a stimulator of Eastman's business in the sale-of-film category, but that is irrelevant to the present point.) Ordinarily business ethics (not to mention the unkind view the antitrust enforcement agencies take of exchanges of information between competitors!) would estop the research man from approaching Eastman Kodak for an answer to the question about extent of picture taking.

However, further thought in the same direction led to the conclusion that a manufacturer of flash bulbs would have an interest in photography to which Parker's present or potential position was in no way opposed. There was an opportunity, therefore, for an exchange of information between noncompetitive firms, which was recognized and acted upon. The same type of opportunity often exists in a customer-supplier situation. A bakery chain in a major market wanted some information about the potential in their market for certain types of products. That chain bought flour from one of the large milling organizations (like General Mills, Inc., or Pillsbury Mills) which had a large and competent marketing research department. For such a company to aid a customer, by making available data it already had, is neither unusual nor remarkable.

General Library Research Sources

This list would be incomplete if it failed to recognize that the task of locating data relevant to a particular marketing research problem is not essentially dissimilar from any other research approach. Such basic data sources as are used in research in the course of college courses are consulted in marketing research practice as a matter of course. The various indexes to publications such as the *Industrial Arts Index,* the index to the *New York Times,* etc., are often helpful. So are the *Statistical Abstract of the United States* and similar summaries of statistical data.

For data on marketing potentials in different geographic units or in different markets, there are four reference sources which deserve special mention. The first is the annual *Survey of Buying Power* issue of *Sales Management* magazine, published each May. This is almost literally the "statistical bible" of the marketing research man whose problems include territorial potential evaluation. Some specific applications of data from the *Survey* will be found in Chapter 21 on territorial-potential estimation. The second is the market guide published annually by *Editor and Publisher* magazine. The third is *Consumer Markets,* a guide published by Standard Rate & Data Service, Inc. The fourth is *Industrial Marketing's* annual market-data issue.

Research Organizations

The final source which should be mentioned includes various types of marketing research organizations. Consider particularly those two organizations to which considerable space is devoted in Chapter 9 on panel research—the A. C. Nielsen Co. and Market Research Corporation of America (MRCA). Those organizations pick up data on a large number of categories of consumer products, which data are for sale to subscribing organizations for a fee. The particular value of those sources is that they often can make available both current and trend data quickly and easily, albeit not inexpensively. There are other organizations which also deserve mention in this category. For example, the Research Company of America prepares an annual survey of the brewing industry which is widely used as a reference source in research touching upon that industry.

AVAILABLE DATA REQUIRES CAREFUL EVALUATION

There is this important distinction which must be drawn between information which is available from outside sources and that which a research man develops himself or which is developed within his own organization. In the former case, the details of the data collection may be unknown or may be reported only fragmentarily. Therefore, the data which are available must be carefully *evaluated* as to their accuracy, soundness of research procedures used to gather them, freedom from bias, and so on, before they are accepted and used as part of the informational basis of the research process.

The range in such data is extreme. Some have been carefully developed and are dependably accurate, and some are completely biased and misleading. The beginner must be especially careful to guard against mistaking form for substance. It is possible to draw just as impressive charts from data which are utterly untrustworthy as it is from the most carefully gathered marketing research data. Such charts, and the superficial polish of smooth presentation, may mislead the uninformed as to the worth of the information contained in the report or presentation. They should not mislead a trained marketing research man.

Because much available data have been developed by the survey technique, the following comments are relevant here.

KEY QUESTIONS TO ASK IN APPRAISING SURVEYS

The Advertising Research Foundation, Inc., a nonprofit corporation discussed at some length in Chapter 28, published in 1953 some *Criteria for Marketing and Advertising Research* which are helpful in appraising some types of studies, especially quantitative consumer studies based on samples of prescribed populations. These criteria were developed by a subcommittee of the committee on research of the American Association of Advertising Agencies (AAAA). Members of the subcommittee were Edward Battey, Peter Langhoff, and David E. Robinson, all experienced and mature marketing research practitioners. The criteria they developed, which were reviewed and revised by the ARF Technical

Committee and approved by the ARF Board of Directors, are reproduced in full below by special permission of the Advertising Research Foundation, Inc.

1. Under what conditions was the study made?

A statement of the methods employed should be made available in such detail that the study could be duplicated therefrom. In addition to the information revealed in answer to questions 2 through 8, the report should provide:

a. Full statement of problems to be resolved by the study.

b. Who financed it.

c. Names of organizations participating in the study, together with their qualifications and extent of their interest, if any, in the findings.

d. Exact period of time covered in collection of data, with a statement as to the representativeness of the time period regarding subjects surveyed.

e. Date of publication of report.

f. Definition of terms used.

g. Copies of questionnaires and instructions to interviewers.

h. Sources of collateral data.

i. Complete statement of methodology to be issued concurrently with findings.

2. Has the questionnaire been well designed?

The questions must clearly convey their meaning uniformly to all, without suggesting answers either by their context or sequence. Unreasonable demands on the memory or on the actual knowledge of the respondent should not be made. Responses to simple "why" questions are often inaccurate and to "why not" questions, more so. Diversification of subject matter tends to reduce the interest bias.

The phrasing should avoid, or compensate for, a choice of responses which would reflect such influences as prestige, embarrassment, reward or retaliation. "Usually or regularly buy or read" questions maximize such biases. Individuals should answer only for themselves.

Monotonous questioning induces antagonism. Lengthy questioning may induce fatigue and cause incomplete responses. If the questionnaire was one of several completed at the same time with a single respondent, the total content of the interview must be revealed to indicate any conditioning induced by questions preceding the questions involved in the study. Limiting of space for replies limits the completeness of the answers. Repeat interviewing also may condition the response. To check on internal consistency of response, "catch" questions may be used. The questionnaire should be pilot tested.

3. Has the interviewing been adequately and reliably done?

Usually a questionnaire form will be used; the interviewer must be well acquainted with it and with the prescribed interview procedure.

Where no form is used, the interviewer must have greater maturity, training and experience; where extended interviews on attitudes are involved, special reporting means such as a tape recorder may well be required. Per interview compensation usually leads to lower quality interviewing; full-time interviewers generally provide more satisfactory work than do part-time interviewers. Unsuitable, ill-trained or irresponsible interviewers are not justified by economy. Even experienced interviewers should be trained and instructed for each survey's problems.

Only interviewers who can be compatible with respondents should be employed, because good rapport must be established. If the sampling plan does not specifically designate those to be interviewed, a bias often is introduced by the interviewer's picking respondents who tend to be like rather than unlike himself. The interviewer should be able to influence the progress of the interview, but must not influence the answers; it is often desirable that the interviewer not know the main purpose of the survey. The identity of the sponsor should not be known to the interviewer nor, least of all, to the respondent.

Not only should spot checks be made of the total interviews, but interviewer by interviewer comparisons should be made as well. More complete checking, to the extent of partially repeating the interview, is required if quota sampling was employed. The interviewing process should be pilot tested. On-the-scene supervisors improve interviewing quality.

4. Has the best sampling plan been followed?

The population being surveyed is most accurately represented when a random sample, in the mathematical sense, is employed. Each unit must have an equal chance or a known relative chance of being included in the sample; listing, enumerating and interviewing in every household in each defined interviewing area are tools for achieving this aim. Stratification and clustering help to make pure area sampling more economical. Disproportionate sampling may be employed to increase sampling reliability in a survey of a given size, but re-weighting must be employed in tabulating. The laws of probability, permitting calculation of error margins, only apply to truly random sampling, not to quota samples or to samples that are "random" only in an accidental or haphazard sense.

Quota sampling is preferable to accidental sampling, but it is still a matter of judgment as to how effectively various pertinent quotas have been introduced and followed in individual surveys. They should be set so as to maximize the range of coverage, especially by geographic and economic groupings. Consistency with census or other basic data is not in itself proof of sampling representativeness unless it can be proven that the subject being investigated, itself, has perfect random distribution.

Other than in the latter case, there are instances where well-constructed quota samples may be acceptable. The rate of non-cooperation in many surveys, especially of the inventory, panel or continuous type, is so high that it liquidates many of the features of random sampling in the end. Copy testing and other instances where the general, rather than the exact answer, is all that is required lend themselves to well-designed quota samples. In general, *qualitative* in contrast to *quantitative* data can be satisfactorily obtained from quota samples. Where doubt exists, random sampling should be used since this gives the maximum reliability per dollar expended.

5. Has the sampling plan been fully executed?

Substitutions for assigned units destroy a probability sample design. In personal interview surveys, refusals can frequently be overcome by repeat efforts. Not-at-homes, who have characteristics known to be different, should be brought into the sample by call-backs, or their answers should be estimated by special statistical formulas. If quotas were assigned, they should be fulfilled exactly. In quota sampling, refusals and not-at-homes are not controllable.

In mail surveys, the response as well as the mail-out must be representative. To reduce biases growing out of personal interests and economic factors, which are common in mail surveys with a low rate of return, it is desirable to get as close to a 100% return as possible. In telephone surveys, refusals, not-at-homes and busy lines must not be ignored.

6. Is the sample large enough?

If a probability sample is properly designed and executed, the reliability of its results can be estimated mathematically. Breakdown data should have a large enough numerical base to keep their larger error margins within usable limits.

The desired degree of reliability should be expressed in the definition of the problem or plan of the study. Increase in sample size does not compensate for deviations from a true probability sample though it may provide a better basis for evaluating the effect of non-response.

If a probability sample is not employed, it is a matter of judgment as to what additional error is introduced as a result of using a non-random sample. The error cannot be measured statistically if the sample is non-random.

7. Was there systematic control of editing, coding and tabulating?

All editing of questionnaires should be completed before any tabulations are made, and a statement to that effect should be made a part of the report.

Editing should not involve guessing as to meaning. Where context rather than form is being edited, the same editor should handle specific related sections of all questionnaires. Local supervisors should edit for form and completeness. Directions for editing should be formulated and explained uniformly to all engaged in the process.

In machine tabulation, pre-coding not only saves time and money but catches errors and incompleteness in questionnaire design. If pre-coding is used, a pilot test should be made to develop the codes; if pre-coding is not used, a sample of the completed questionnaires should be examined to establish the codes, especially on open-end questions.

Questionnaires should be numbered serially to guarantee completeness of card punching and as a check against duplicate punching. Pattern or consistency checking of each separate column of the punched-card should be done to verify that only appropriate codes have been punched. Each column or group code should be separately counted to establish the varying base, and to verify that different tables with the same base actually agree.

In addition in hand tabulating, spot-checking of results by individual tabulators is desired. Each step should be separately spot-checked. All transfers of data should be double-checked.

8. Is the interpretation forthright and logical?

If causal relationship is assigned to one factor, it must be proved that all other factors are held constant or allowance must be made for other variables.

The basic data which underlie percentages, ratios, weighting systems and breakdown groupings of respondents must be shown. Competitive comparisons should be made on the same bases. Since mean averages are often misleading, especially in income studies, the median should also be examined. Any uncommon mathematical manipulation must be fully explained. Error margins and their reliability should be indicated.

Misplaced emphasis may divert attention from weaknesses in research methods or findings. Complete answers to all questions should be uniformly reported. Interpretation, especially of responses involving memory or prediction of behavior, must not overestimate the ability of an individual to give valid responses.

Small differences, considering statistical error margins, should not be over-emphasized. Charts, tables and text should not be distorted or unduly exaggerated. Simplicity and clarity should be the main objective of the analysis and presentation.

Present the results only for what they are and for what they represent.

The above criteria are useful in appraising marketing and advertising research reports. They are presented here in full because they have a far wider usefulness for the student or beginner in marketing research.

No experienced marketing research man can review the criteria quoted without recognizing that they represent a great many hours of intensive and constructive work by the men who prepared them. They are a distillation of their experience in this field. This quote is a short course in the area of survey technique. Whole paragraphs could be (and have been!) written about subjects which they reduced to a single incisive sentence.

One important value of these criteria lies in their double usefulness. They are useful for their intended purpose—as an aid in appraising surveys and other studies made by others. But they have another and even greater usefulness. They can be used by a research man in the planning stage of work on a research project of the type covered; and used again in self-appraisal which may prove to be helpful in raising the quality of a marketing research assignment before it is released in final form.

Incidentally, these criteria again illustrate the tremendous and recent increase in the importance of sampling. The AAAA issued in October, 1938, a guide for appraising market and advertising research, of which the criteria quoted above represent in effect a revision and moderniza-tion. The 1938 release devoted only one brief paragraph to the subject of sampling. Contrast that with the great emphasis on attention to sampling aspects in the criteria quoted above!

SUMMARY

1. Much of the information which is used and useful in marketing research practice is already available. The marketing research man spends considerable time finding and evaluating such information.

2. The specific sources useful in a particular industry are those which the organizations in that industry typically contribute to, know about, and rely on. There would be little point in devoting space to a listing of such sources. A listing of the *types* of sources which are generally useful to the marketing research man has far wider applicability.

3. Specific case studies in which a vital part of the marketing research in-formation total was contributed by one or more types of sources provide a background useful for reviewing the general types of sources which should be explored in the case of any specific problem situation.

4. Eight types of sources which sometimes are useful in providing the data a marketing research man needs were listed in this chapter and commented upon briefly. There will be additional illustrations of the usefulness of such sources in subsequent chapters of this book, in conjunction with specific cases and problem situations.

5. The need for careful and painstaking evaluation of available data was emphasized.

6. Some key questions especially useful in evaluating data gathered by the survey technique were listed, together with the suggestions of a group of seasoned marketing research men on some problems in appraising available data. Many of those same questions and comments apply also to data gathered by other than the survey approach.

QUESTIONS

1. What is the difference between general and specific data sources?

2. What are the major types of sources for available data listed in this chapter? Can you think of any limitations these sources might have?

3. Why do available data require careful attention? What key questions should be asked when you are appraising data from surveys?

CHAPTER 8

The Survey Technique

The analysis of information which is already available or which can rather easily be made available from an organization's own records has been described in the two preceding chapters. This chapter and the two which follow move on to consider the marketing research techniques which are used to gather information which is *not* already available. The survey technique discussed in this chapter is one approach widely used to gather *from external sources* different types of information not otherwise available when such information is needed to aid management appraisal of a marketing problem.

When the Bissell Carpet Sweeper Company[1] sought to evaluate the threat which vacuum cleaners represented, they first explored available information. They found that much important and relevant information was not available. The answers to specific questions were needed: What proportion of all families owned carpet sweepers? What proportion owned vacuum cleaners? What significant differences, if any, existed between the level of ownership of those two products in different sections of the country, in different city-size groups, and in different income levels? How well did the owners of carpet sweepers like them? How well satisfied with the performance of vacuum cleaners were the owners of that appliance? The survey technique is an approach often used to secure answers to questions of this type.

WHAT IS A SURVEY?

Because the word *survey* is used in many different ways, it might be well to specify the meaning of the terms as used in this book. The survey technique and the term survey are here primarily confined to studies intended to secure one or more items of information from a *sample* of respondents representative of a larger group. The information is usually recorded on a form known as a questionnaire, although statistical literature sometimes describes it as a schedule. The informa-

[1] This problem situation is first introduced as Case 4 in Chapter 7.

tion secured is usually either of a quantitative nature, such as average weekly income or expenditures for a particular type of product, or of a type which can be reduced to quantitative terms such as the proportion of families owning carpet sweepers.

The analysis and interpretation of survey results usually involve projection from the sample data. This provides an indication of the situation or condition which exists in the larger population. Although almost always based on a sampling approach, the survey technique may occasionally be used in a complete-coverage or census type of study. For example, this occasionally occurs in industrial marketing where the total number of sampling units in some universes, or populations, is relatively small—like the number of manufacturers of automobile tires.

COMPLEXITY OF THE SURVEY TECHNIQUE

The survey technique is technically one of the most advanced and demanding areas of marketing research practice. As in the case of sampling, space limitations make it quite impossible to cover the survey technique fully and adequately in a book about marketing research. This is especially true if the objective of the discussion is to equip a reader to plan and execute a survey in a competent and professional manner. One might as reasonably expect a medical student to perform an appendectomy after exposure to his first medical text! The scope of the subject matter of survey making is suggested by the fact that an excellent introductory book[2] of 536 text pages plus a bibliography of 1,145 references is devoted entirely to social surveys. Another excellent book of more than 400 pages is devoted entirely to interviewing problems.[3]

The description of the marketing-problem base of marketing research in Chapter 3 underlined the fact that many areas of marketing research are much more important and more widely used than surveys. A book which covered the survey technique in adequate detail and which also treated other aspects of marketing research on a proportionate scale would be at least as large as an unabridged dictionary. Some of the inescapable limitations of the following discussion of the survey technique should therefore be recognized at the outset.

Unfortunately many people with limited marketing research experience do not appreciate how complex the process of conducting a competently planned and executed national consumer survey has become. An actual example, while perhaps extreme, may help to illustrate that complexity.

[2] Mildred Parten, *Surveys, Polls and Samples,* Harper, New York, 1950.
[3] Herbert J. Hyman et al., *Interviewing in Social Research,* University of Chicago Press, Chicago, 1954.

A manufacturer who is a large national advertiser sought to study the audiences of individual advertising media (including newspapers, magazines, radio and television programs) and to relate media habits to the use of the types of products that manufacturer marketed. The study was confined to women over fifteen. It utilized a twelve-page questionnaire and a probability sample.

A list of the actual participants in the planning and execution of that study provides an indication of the manpower and experience required for such a survey. The advertiser's entire marketing research department of eight people participated in the study. That manpower and experience were supplemented by that of the research directors of several advertising agencies serving the advertiser. A large marketing-research organization was hired to execute the field work. Although that research firm had extensive sampling experience, it was found necessary to engage a sampling consultant for more than three months to design the probability sample used in this survey. Special maps had to be purchased to locate specific interviewing points chosen on a true probability basis. A specialist in the tabulation of marketing research data was hired for a period of seven months, to supervise the coding, editing, and tabulating of the data. The out-of-pocket costs of that survey, with the payroll and overhead of the advertiser's own full-time personnel and of the agency research participants *excluded,* were more than $70,000. The cost per interview was more than $10.

While this example is in no sense typical, it does suggest that a national consumer survey today is not a project to be entered into lightly, nor one that can be planned and executed without a substantial amount of actual experience with other marketing research studies on a similar scale. *Without question,* the soundest approach to a national consumer survey for the average manufacturer is to engage the services of one of the large professional organizations in the field. By doing so, a manufacturer can secure specialized skill and experience at each step in the planning and execution of such a study.

DECLINE IN RELATIVE IMPORTANCE OF SURVEYS

The rather striking discrepancy between emphasis on the survey technique in this and earlier books in the field of marketing research has been pointed out already. A further comment at this point on the causes of that discrepancy may be helpful. The survey technique at one time represented almost the only practicable method of securing much vital marketing research data. Today the survey technique has become far less important in the total picture of marketing research practice than it used to be. Of the many factors which contributed to the decline in the relative importance of surveys since the mid-1930s, several deserve specific mention.

The first of those factors was the development and increasing acceptance of other techniques which provide answers to some essentially similar questions with far greater accuracy than the survey technique. Outstanding among such developments was the increased use and versatility of panel research, which is the subject of the following chapter. In addition to greater accuracy in some information-gathering areas, panel research had the virtue of providing *continuing* information useful in illustrating trend data. The marketing picture after World War II proved far more mercurial than in the relatively stable years between the depression of the early 1930s and 1940. As a result, the need for and value of trend data increased immeasurably.

A second factor reducing the relative importance of surveys was the growing recognition of the fact that much of the information provided by surveys as then executed was relatively inaccurate. Improved sampling and advances in other aspects of the survey technique made it possible to overcome that limitation to a considerable extent and to secure some types of information with almost any desired degree of accuracy. However, those improvements increased substantially both the cost of making a survey and the amount of technical background and experience required to conduct a survey. As the illustration above suggests, a professionally executed national consumer survey today requires resources in research manpower and experience rarely found outside of specialized research organizations or *very* large research departments.

Another factor which tended to reduce the relative importance of surveys was the accelerated rapidity with which changes in marketing patterns are taking place. It takes a relatively long time—several months at the very least—to plan and execute a national consumer survey confined to a specific marketing problem. Often it is necessary today to make a decision sooner than a survey could possibly be completed, analyzed, and reported. This precludes serious consideration of the survey technique in many marketing-research situations.

A fourth factor which has played a part in reducing the relative importance of surveys has been the increasing knowledge and research sophistication among marketing men. A consumer survey of the quantitative type was once highly valued. It was a great advance over the complete lack of factual information which was then prevalent. Today a far broader base of marketing facts is available. What is often needed is not more quantitative information, but a *deeper* exploration of limited aspects of the problem. This need has stimulated the development of *qualitative research*, often along motivational lines, which is the subject of Chapter 26.

A SURVEY IS LIKE A PYRAMID

The individual marketing research man in charge of a survey is responsible for the final accuracy and relevance to the survey objectives of all information gathered under his direction. He has the same responsibility in the case of research using other techniques, but the task of discharging that responsibility is made more difficult by the nature of the survey technique. To appreciate this, you might visualize the research man as representing the pinnacle or top layer of a pyramid of four layers. The second layer from the top is composed of field supervisors. The third layer down includes field interviewers, who are of course more numerous than the supervisors. Finally, the broad bottom layer is made up of the actual respondents or interviewees, who in turn are usually much more numerous than the interviewers.

It is helpful to visualize such a pyramid, because the device identifies the source of some of the ever-present complexities of the survey technique. It is the intention of the research man to combine the answers of all respondents, secured by all interviewers, under the direction of all supervisors, into a single, unified, and consistent whole. To do this, he must so plan and execute the survey as to achieve and maintain complete consistency and uniformity throughout every stage in the survey, in order to gather fully comparable data. If some interviewers make their interviews in different ways or select their samples of respondents differently, the results they secure may be inconsistent with those of other interviewers. In those surveys where the interviewer is not a factor —mail surveys, for example—care must be taken to achieve *unmistakable clarity* in the questionnaire, so that the meaning of each question will be the same to all respondents.

STEPS IN THE PLANNING AND EXECUTION
OF A MARKETING SURVEY

Surveys in marketing research are essentially similar to surveys in any of the social sciences. Common to a survey for any purpose are certain rather clearly defined steps. Those steps include:

1. Definition of the problem in specific terms
2. Careful determination of the informational objectives of the survey
3. Selecting the survey approach—personal interview, telephone interview, or mailed questionnaire
4. Planning the sample of respondents to be covered
5. Planning and testing the questionnaire and other forms to be used in the interviewing or mail survey

6. Preparation of detailed instructions for interviewers and supervisors, in the case of personal-interview surveys

7. Instructing and supervising the personnel who conduct the interviews to secure the desired information, and verification of a proportion of the interviews

8. Tabulation and analysis of the information provided by the survey

9. Preparation of a report of the findings of the survey

This relatively simplified general description identifies the steps involved in planning and executing a survey. In any specific single study, additional steps might be required. Thus if the individual or organization executing the survey did not have available an experienced staff of field interviewers, recruiting such a staff would represent an important additional step. Or if the cost of a proposed survey were high, there might be a real question as to the potential value of the information likely to result from the study. This might lead to the introduction of a small-scale exploration (often called a *pilot* study) as an additional step to aid in appraising the profit potential of the proposed large-scale survey.

In the discussion which follows, these steps are used as a framework for presenting comments on various aspects of the survey technique with which marketing research men should be familiar.

DEFINITION OF THE PROBLEM IN SPECIFIC TERMS

This is the first step in *all* marketing research, regardless of the technique employed. It is included here to provide a complete picture of the steps in a survey. Because this project is treated at length in Chapter 12, further discussion of it at this point would be unnecessarily repetitious.

TYPES OF INFORMATION A SURVEY CAN PROVIDE

Once the problem has been reduced to specifics, the marketing research man focuses his attention on the types of information which are needed and the alternative techniques available to him to secure such information. It is necessary to distinguish between *information* and *facts*, in thinking of the survey technique, because surveys provide different types of information, not all of which are factual. Often the same questionnaire secures information of different types. Here are the major types of information which a survey may be expected to provide:

Facts

Surveys often provide factual information. Example: *Do you own an electric washing machine?* in a survey of housewives. The answer to the question could be recorded by checking one of two boxes provided in the space after the question on the questionnaire. One of the boxes was labeled *Yes* and the other *No*. The answer to this question could be regarded as factual.

Comment: This kind of question is sometimes described as *dichotomous*, which merely means that it divides respondents into two and only two subordinate groups. Referring to the discussion in Chapter 5, note that ownership of an electric washing machine is an attribute of the respondent. Replies to a question like this are quantified by determining the proportion of all respondents who fall into each of the two categories.

Quasi Facts

This designation seems appropriate to describe information from surveys which appears to be factual, but which may or may not be accurately factual. One important influence which reduces the accuracy of answers to survey questions is memory loss. The extent of such loss depends on such factors as the amount of time that has elapsed since the event in question took place and the importance of that event to the respondent. The follow-up question to the one quoted above illustrates this point: *Was this washing machine bought new during 195–?* Suppose the survey were made in March of the following year. A respondent would then have to probe her recollection of a period of fifteen months.

In the case of a rare and memorable event like the purchase of a washing machine, most respondents' memories would be equal to the task. But suppose the question were: *In the past two years, how many home permanents have you had?* Here the event remains one of considerable significance to a woman, but the ability of an average respondent to measure off mentally and accurately a twenty-four-month period backward through time from the date of the interview, and then to recall exactly how many home permanents she had had over that period, is open to question.

There is this further source of inaccuracy: Even if the respondent *could* perform the indicated mental calculations and recollections with accuracy *if* that accuracy were sufficiently important *to the respondent,* the proportion of respondents who *would* expend the required mental effort remains doubtful. This is especially true in the not-untypical interviewing situation in which the question is just one of many, many questions on what the respondent can see is a long questionnaire. The natural tendency of many respondents under such circumstances to give an approximate answer "off the top of the head" in an effort to terminate the interview as quickly as possible is one with which every experienced interviewer is familiar.

Inaccuracy is also introduced into survey data when an accurate answer to some question would require that a respondent make an admission which has overtones of social disapproval. Respondents tend to provide the socially acceptable answer to such questions as: *Do you use an underarm deodorant?* That tendency introduces a bias which inflates affirmative responses and reduces accuracy. Against the background of heavy advertising emphasis on the dangers of "offending," an affirmative reply could be expected from a higher proportion of respondents than actually use such a product.

There is a further inflation of replies to the above question as a result of failure to define "use" in terms of a definite and specific recent time interval. Some respondents might consider themselves "users" if they used a deodorant one or two times a year. This human tendency of respondents to seek to make a favorable impression on the stranger interviewing them introduces bias into studies of advertising audiences. In many surveys in which respondents are asked to identify the magazines they read, high-prestige publications (such as *Good Housekeeping, Ladies Home Journal,* and *Better Homes & Gardens*) benefit from inflated claims of readership, while magazines with less social acceptance (such as *True Romances* and *True Confessions*) tend to have their audiences understated.

Awareness, or Penetration of Information

Often consumer surveys seek to determine the proportion of consumers who are aware of something—such as the existence of a new type of product, a new brand, or a new sales feature. If an advertising campaign has stressed some particular sales point or idea, a survey might be used to determine the depth of penetration achieved as of a given date. Another parallel study at a later date could be used to measure the increase in penetration over the time interval between the two studies.

In the years immediately after World War II, the makers of Bendix automatic washers were concerned about adverse comments on the performance of their product. In a consumer survey they asked: *Have you heard any unfavorable comments about automatic washers?* Subsequent questions asked of those who gave affirmative answers (37.6 per cent of those interviewed in this study) established the nature of the unfavorable comments and—in so far as respondents could recall it—the source of such comments. Another Bendix survey attempted to determine what proportion of housewives were aware of the existence of an automatic washing machine, and what proportion of those had personally operated one or had seen one operated or demonstrated.

In evaluating the competitive threat or the promotional opportunity represented by a new or improved product, the level of awareness either of the existence of such an improved product, or of the problem such an improvement is intended to solve, is often explored. This series of questions was asked to determine the level of awareness of quick-cooking rice among housewives:

> *Have you ever heard of quick-cooking rice such as Minute Rice?*
> *Have you ever used any quick-cooking rice?*
> *Did you like it?*
> *What did you particularly like (dislike) about it?*

Opinions

The opinions of consumers are often explored in surveys. This is particularly true in product research and new-product development. Here are two illustrative questions from a study of men's preferences on clothing items:

> *What do you think are the most important things to look for in buying a shirt of this kind?*
> *What are some other things you think it is important to look for?*

The second question in the above pair is often described as a *probe* question. Such probe questions are usually included in the questionnaires so that all interviewers *do exactly the same amount* of probing for additional recall or reasons and *do it in exactly the same way*. In comparative consumer-product tests (see Chapter 22), often the entire objective of the research is first to provide a recent, controlled experience with the product on which an opinion about the products can be based; and then to achieve accurate and uniform communication of that opinion.

Note that *the existence* of any specific opinion, among an established proportion of a population, *is a fact*. Thus it was at one time a fact that among women living in urban places, one out of seven was of the opinion that Bendix washers did not wash clothes clean. Note further that *to the consumer* his or her own opinion is often a fact. It is extremely important for the research man at all times to distinguish between fact and opinion on a careful and objective basis. It is also important for him to recognize that usually no such distinction is drawn by the consumer who holds an opinion.

Attitudes

Lucas and Britt define an attitude as a "mental and neural state of readiness, exerting a directive or dynamic influence upon the individual's response to all objects and situations with which it is related."[4] In less

[4] D. B. Lucas and S. H. Britt, *Advertising Psychology and Research*, McGraw-Hill, New York, 1950, p. 705.

formal language, an attitude is a preparation and tendency to act. An attitude is usually more general than an opinion and may reflect either a conscious or subconscious summation of a number of different opinions. Surveys often seek to determine the attitude of respondents toward a given subject. Sometimes that attempt is confined to a single, direct question; sometimes it is accompanied by a subquestion which seeks to establish the intensity of the attitude; and sometimes it involves a number of questions, each seeking a clue to a different facet of the attitude or approaching it from a different direction.

In a survey on hair care, these questions were asked in an attempt to determine whether the attitudes of respondents toward specific brands of shampoo were favorable or unfavorable:

> *Of all the brands you know about, which ones do you feel are especially good? Any others?*
> *Are there any brands which you definitely would not buy? Which ones? Any others?*

A direct attempt to determine the attitude of consumers toward a ready-to-eat breakfast cereal was made in a survey which asked this question:

> *In comparison with other ready-to-eat breakfast cereals, would you say that Kix is better, about the same, or not as good?*

This question also serves to illustrate the use of a scale for measuring the degree or intensity of feeling on a subject. In this case a discontinuous three-point scale is used.

Future-action Plans

Another category of information often explored in surveys is developed through questions about the respondents' future-action plans. These two questions from a survey questionnaire provide a specific illustration:

> *During the next twelve months or so, do you think you will have a home permanent?*
> *Which brand will you buy for your next home permanent?*

An answer to a question involving a future action is in no sense factual, but is instead an indication of the existence of an attitude or inclination as of a given moment in time. Questions of this type increase in value when they are used in a series of surveys separated by a substantial interval of time, providing data on the trend of intentions. Thus the recurring *Surveys of Consumer Finances* conducted by the Board of Governors of the Federal Reserve System in cooperation with the Survey Research Center of the University of Michigan identified the proportion of the population who reported that they expected to purchase new and used cars and other durable goods in the year ahead.[5]

Reasons

Often consumer surveys ask questions about the reasons why a consumer has or has not taken some action, or asks *why* he or she holds a particular opinion. This pair of questions from a Survey Research Center consumer survey[6] illustrates how this approach was used in an interview:

> *We are interested in how people are getting along financially these days. Would you say you and your family are better off or worse off financially than you were a year ago?*
> *Why do you say so?*

This is a type of question which calls for expert handling, especially in the tabulation, analysis, and interpretation of replies. Any "why" question, and especially those questions asking the reason why a respondent did or did not act in a particular way, is likely to secure answers which range from fact to fantasy. The replies may be accurate and factual, or they may represent completely incorrect and misleading answers. This occurs because respondents sometimes know the correct answer but nevertheless choose to give a more socially acceptable answer rather than the true one. In other instances, the respondent may not know the reason for an action but still supplies some answer rather than admit the lack of knowledge to an interviewer. Research on the reasons or motives underlying actions is discussed at some length in Chapter 26.

A SINGLE SURVEY PROVIDES SEVERAL TYPES OF INFORMATION

To illustrate in specific terms how a single consumer survey may be used to provide a number of different types of information, here are some examples from a single Crowell-Collier Automotive Survey:[7]

Facts

> *Does anyone in your family own a passenger car?*
>
> (If "Yes") *Who? Do you drive?*
>
> (If car owned) *What make and year?*
>
> *Did you buy it (them) new or used?*

---

[5] An interesting discussion of the relationship between *Consumer Attitudes and Demand* is provided by a study with that title by George Katona and Eva Mueller, a Survey Research Center publication, Ann Arbor, Mich., 1953.

[6] *Ibid.*, p. 106.

[7] *Crowell-Collier Automotive Survey Number 13*, December, 1949, p. 47.

Quasi Facts

How many miles was your car driven in 1948?

Taking out what you spent on gas, oil, lubrication, or tires, what would you estimate was the amount spent on the service and repairs for your (each) car during the PAST MONTH?

Opinions

Do you think that next year's cars will be cheaper, more expensive, or about the same?

Which two or three makes do you consider the best-looking cars on the road?

Attitudes

Were you satisfied with your last repair job?

Future-action Plans

Are you planning to buy a car in 1949, 1950, or 1951?

(If "Yes") Will you buy your next car new or used?

What make(s) of car(s) would you be likely to look at or consider buying?

(If more than one) Which make do you think you will actually buy?

Reasons

What are your particular reasons for favoring that make?

The above listing of types of information and illustrative questions indicates the qualitative range within which replies to the questions asked in surveys can move. At one extreme there is the factual reply to a question clearly and unmistakably understood by both respondent and interviewer in identical terms, which is willingly and accurately answered. Communication problems occur because the respondent and interviewer interpret the same question differently, reducing the accuracy of some apparently factual data. Where the ability of the respondent to answer a question is in doubt because of memory loss over the period of time since the event occurred, or because the event itself was too unimportant to the respondent to make accurate recall likely, the questions move in a quasi-factual direction. Unwillingness of respondents to answer a question accurately also reduces the factual content of replies. At the other extreme in factual content is a question about future-action plans. Although replies to such questions are sometimes of dubious validity, they are often asked and painfully interpreted in marketing surveys. Responses giving reasons are especially difficult to analyze and interpret with confidence.

DETERMINING THE SURVEY'S INFORMATIONAL OBJECTIVES

With the problem defined in specific terms, and with a knowledge of the types of information available from a survey to guide him, the research man then proceeds to decide what specific items of information he may expect from the proposed survey. In the course of reducing the informational objectives of the survey to specific terms, he is likely to begin to prepare at least preliminary lists of the questions which might be included in the survey. He is likely at the same time to move into the third step in which the particular type of survey approach is selected, because the approach used influences the types of information sought. For example, in a shampoo survey an attempt was made to determine the relationship between the respondents' opinion of certain characteristics of their own hair and the independent and objective evaluation of their hair characteristics by carefully trained interviewers. In a mail or telephone survey in which the respondents' hair could not be visually examined, this informational objective would have to be discarded as unobtainable.

SELECTING THE SURVEY APPROACH

There are three major approaches open to the marketing research man who is planning a questionnaire-type survey. The first is a *mail survey,* in which questionnaires are sent by mail to a predetermined list of potential respondents. The replies, in the form of completed questionnaires, are returned by mail for tabulation and analysis. The second is a *telephone survey,* in which a sample of respondents is reached by a telephone call. The replies to questions asked by the interviewer are recorded on a questionnaire during a phone conversation. The third is a *personal-interview survey* in which the interviewers ask a series of questions during a face-to-face meeting with the respondent. All three of these approaches are widely used in marketing research practice. While they vary in the method used to reach the respondent, they are alike in that each requires the application of knowledge of sound survey practice. Each approach has both advantages and limitations, resulting from its own peculiar characteristics, with which marketing research men should be familiar.

MAIL SURVEYS

When a survey is conducted by mail, the questionnaire is usually sent out along with a covering letter. The letter explains the purpose of the study, sometimes identifies the sponsoring organization either specifically or as to type, and requests the respondent's cooperation. Sometimes the covering letter offers the potential respondent some kind of gift or incentive. The offer may apply to all respondents (as when an inexpensive premium is sent along with the questionnaires as a gift in appreciation of the respondent's cooperation). Or the gift may be offered only to those returning the completed questionnaire or returning it by a specified date. A stamped or postpaid envelope or reply card is often included.

Not all those to whom questionnaires are sent bother to answer the questionnaires, and not all those who complete the questionnaires follow through to the extent required to mail them back to the surveying organization. The proportion of replies to a mail questionnaire may range from as low as 5 to 10 per cent of the number mailed, where the source of the questionnaire is unknown to the respondents, to as high as 85 per cent or more in the case of mailings to qualified groups set up as "captive" samples, especially for use in mail surveys. The use of premiums with mail questionnaires, or the offer of a gift for a prompt reply, represents an attempt to increase the rate of return.

Advantages of Mail Surveys

The mail survey offers a number of advantages which are largely responsible for its continued use:

1. The economy of this approach is one outstanding advantage. It costs far less to mail 1,000 questionnaires to 1,000 respondents than it would to interview those respondents personally. Since not all the questionnaires mailed out are returned completed, however, cost comparisons should always be made between the *cost per completed questionnaire* rather than on the basis of the number of questionnaires mailed out. Even on such a comparative basis, however, the mail approach often offers economy as one attraction.

2. Closely related to the economy of this approach is the ability to secure widespread geographic dispersion of the sample, thus tending to increase its representativeness.

3. The mail approach eliminates interviewer bias, since no interviewers participate in a mail survey.

4. With a mail questionnaire it is often possible to reach certain types of hard-to-interview respondents. This category would include doctors and other professional people, those who work or live away from home part of the time, and those whose schedules are irregular or unusual, such as workers on a night shift.

5. The elimination of some of the problems found in personal-interview surveys—notably the effect of removing the bias resulting from excluding those not at home at the time of the interview, the need for callbacks, and problems of ensuring uniform sample-selection and field

supervision—make this approach seem attractive under some circumstances.

6. Because respondents can take as much time as they require to answer the questions on a mail questionnaire, more thoughtful answers are sometimes provided. The elimination of hasty and ill-considered replies by respondents temporarily pressed for time is a closely related advantage.

7. Since mailed questionnaires are usually returned anonymously, it is often possible to eliminate the distortion of replies introduced by the respondent's desire to impress the interviewer or to give an answer more socially acceptable than accurate.

8. Finally, in those cases where a suitable list of respondents is available, the sampling requirements of a mail survey are relatively simple.

Disadvantages of Mail Surveys

As offsets against the above advantages of mail surveys, a number of important disadvantages should be recognized.

1. No suitable list may be available covering the universe which the survey seeks to sample. Since no sample in a mail survey can be representative of any universe not covered by the available list or lists, the adequacy of the sample which can be reached in a mail survey depends primarily on the quality of the available list. Under clues to adequacy of list, quality, accuracy, recency, and completeness should be considered. The list may range from a perfect one (as in the case of a department store's list of charge-account customers who are not delinquent in their payments) to a fragmentary and far from representative list. For obvious reasons, the availability or lack of availability of a satisfactory list influences the selection of the survey approach.

2. Even if available lists are completely satisfactory, the mail survey typically has an additional sampling limitation. The sample of respondents who return questionnaires may be representative neither of the full universe (i.e., the list) nor of the sample of potential respondents to whom questionnaires were mailed. Returning a questionnaire requires a positive action and an expenditure of effort by the respondent. Judgment alone suggests that respondents especially interested in the subject matter of the survey are more likely to make the effort than those completely uninterested in the subject. Experimental evidence supports that a priori judgment.

3. Mail surveys are relatively inflexible. If an error in the questionnaire or procedure develops during a personal-interview study, telegrams to supervisors or interviewers can get an adjustment or correction made in time to salvage much of the field work. In the case of a mail study, no such adjustment is possible.

4. The questionnaire used in a mail study must usually be somewhat shorter and simpler than in a personal-interview job. Since the full scope of the question-answering process is obvious to the respondent, there is no opportunity for an interviewer to cover a long questionnaire by maintaining the respondent's interest through exercise of her interviewing skill.

5. The inability of interviewers to supplement answers to questions by observational data was noted above. This is particularly limiting where differences in replies between respondents in different socioeconomic classifications are great or are vital to a particular study.

6. There is limited opportunity in a mail survey to secure qualitative information which is unmistakably clear in meaning. A printed questionnaire cannot probe, as a skilled interviewer can, nor can it do so by asking "What do you mean by that?" where indicated.

7. Finally, the extent to which the replies of a respondent to a mail questionnaire are those of the respondent, or are aided by conversations with other individuals, cannot be determined.

All the above advantages and disadvantages apply primarily to mail surveys covering a cold or strange list of respondents. The use of mail questionnaires among captive samples of respondents, or respondents linked to the survey or survey source by a common interest is discussed in the following chapter on panel research as well as elsewhere in this book. Essentially that represents a special case to which not all the above comments apply. Other references to mail research listed in the index of this book should be consulted by readers to develop a more complete picture of the role of the mail study in marketing.

TELEPHONE SURVEYS

A survey made by telephone resembles a personal-interview study much more closely than it does a mail survey. In both telephone and personal-interview surveys, there is a questionnaire which the interviewee does not see and the questions are asked by an interviewer. The major difference between the two approaches is that the interviewer is stationed at a telephone in one case. This eliminates the travel time required to move to the point of one interview and from that one to the scene of the next. The telephone approach has certain advantages and limitations which should be recognized.

Advantages of Telephone Surveys

Telephone surveys are more widely used in marketing research practice than the attention paid to them in the literature of the field would lead one to expect. Among the advantages which contribute to the continuing use of this approach are these:

1. There is obvious economy, as compared to the personal-interview approach, resulting from the fact that a stationary interviewer can reach and interview respondents at widely separated geographic points without physical travel.

2. There is a closely related advantage in increased speed, since this approach can provide more interviews per interviewer-day than personal interviews can be expected to yield.

3. Telephone surveys provide greater flexibility than mail surveys because a skilled interviewer can first establish rapport and then explain and probe as required. Naturally the level of rapport is typically below what could be achieved in a face-to-face contact.

4. Since the interviewing can be done under close supervision, with a number of interviewers operating from a single office if the volume of interviewing warrants, administrative problems in connection with such a study are relatively minor. Uniformity of interviewer approach, for example, can rather easily be achieved and maintained throughout the survey.

5. Groups of people difficult to reach and interview in person can often be interviewed by telephone. The upper-income and socioeconomic groups, professional people, and apartment dwellers sometimes fall in this category.

6. Respondents interviewed by telephone must answer questions at once, eliminating both the influence of individuals other than the respondent on replies and the elapsed time required to secure questionnaires from a mail study.

7. The ability to use a questionnaire presenting a planned sequence of questions is characteristic both of telephone and personal-interview approaches, representing a marked advantage over a mail questionnaire. This makes it possible to explore preliminary questions before revealing by more specific questions the interest of the interviewer in a particular brand, product type, or subject.

8. The questionnaire used can be somewhat more complex than one developed for use in a mail study.

9. Pretesting a questionnaire is relatively simple.

10. The lack of face-to-face contact makes it possible for interviewers to secure frank answers to some intimate questions which could not be included except for the anonymity provided by the telephone.

11. Finally, if the proportion of the population under study who are telephone subscribers is high and the available directory is recent, sampling is relatively simple.

Disadvantages of Telephone Surveys

The offsetting disadvantages of this approach, especially in comparison with personal-interview studies, include these:

1. A truly representative cross section of the public can almost never be obtained by telephone. Families without telephones, residents of apartment hotels with a single switchboard, families with unlisted numbers, and those whose working hours make them unavailable during the hours when calls would be made tend to be excluded from the sample. The seriousness of the biasing effect of this limitation depends in part on the proportion of households in a community with telephone service.

2. There are major procedural questions, such as the method of classifying "busy signals" and "don't answers" which must be examined and resolved in the light of the particular objectives of the study.

3. The ease with which an interviewee can either refuse to cooperate or can terminate the interview at any point is often cited as a disadvantage of this approach, although personal-interview studies must also cope with this problem to a slightly lesser degree.

4. An attempt is often made to keep the proportion of "hangups" low by confining the study to a short questionnaire. This has the effect of reducing the scope of an interview below that covered in a personal interview by a skilled interviewer.

5. There is no opportunity to secure information by observation. In a study on home-permanent usage in a metropolitan center with a large Negro population, inability to confine the study to white respondents led to indicated levels of usage which were lower than those established in other ways. Dependable information on age, income levels, etc., cannot be obtained in a telephone interview.

6. Where the interviewing is widely dispersed geographically, there are many of the same problems of maintaining uniformity of interviewing procedure that exist with personal-interview studies.

PERSONAL-INTERVIEW SURVEYS

In a personal-interview survey, a series of questions is asked of respondents in a face-to-face interviewing situation. The usual answers secured are short, calling for definite answers easily tabulated, although it is not unusual to include some questions in which a detailed reply is expected to be recorded verbatim or as nearly so as the stenographic ability of the interviewer will permit.

Advantages of Personal-interview Surveys

These are the important advantages which have led to the great popularity of this approach in social surveys.

1. This approach alone makes it possible to plan and execute a sound, well-planned sampling design. Where it is essential to provide data of great and predictable accuracy in terms of sampling errors, no other approach can be seriously considered.

2. The amount of information which can be secured in a single interview is usually greater than in either of the other two approaches. If properly designed, a relatively long questionnaire can be used. The skill of the interviewer makes it possible first to establish rapport, and then to secure and maintain the interest and cooperation of the respondent. Sometimes a gift is used in surveys requiring a very long interview, to reduce the refusal rate and cut down on incompleted interviews. (Sound research practice suggests that in such cases the incentive be played down in importance lest it exert a biasing influence.) In addition to length alone, greater complexity of the questionnaire is possible. Well-instructed interviewers can be taught, "If answer to question 7 is 'no,' skip to question 16," although consumers themselves cannot be expected to follow such instructions or directions.

3. Through uniform phrasing of probe questions, the personal-interview study can often secure more information on a given point than would be elicited by a mail questionnaire. (The telephone approach would fall somewhere between the other two approaches in this regard.)

4. The opportunity for the interviewer to record data by observation and to observe characteristics of home, neighborhood, etc., permits much more accurate classification of respondents, especially as to socioeconomic status, than is otherwise possible.

5. In addition to the verbal question-answer interchange, exhibits, pictures, advertisements, etc., may be submitted to respondents and their views, opinions, and attitudes solicited. There is almost no limitation to the subject matter which can be included in this type of study.

6. As with a telephone survey, the controlled sequence of questions permits inclusion of material which could not be used in a mail questionnaire without risk of serious bias. Example: A direct question about a particular brand, asked only of those who did not name it in earlier questions about brands now and formerly used, etc. This memory jog often increases recall substantially, thus providing more accurate indications of the level of brand experience than could otherwise be secured.

7. One may have greater confidence that the respondent is the actual individual sought for questioning in a personal-interview study than in telephone or mail research. There is less likelihood of interviewing female members of the household other than the housewife or of including in the sample those not actually within the planned universe (as in the permanent-wave study which sought to exclude Negro women).

Disadvantages of Personal-interview Surveys

1. Ranking first among the disadvantages of this approach is its relatively high cost.

2. Closely related to that cost factor is the need for a substantial

amount of technical skill and experience to plan and execute a competent personal-interview survey. This problem increases in importance with the geographic scope of the study.

3. The amount of time required to plan and execute a personal-interview survey is greater than is often appreciated. The time requirement alone eliminates this approach from consideration in the case of many marketing studies.

4. The interviewer is a major element in the process, thus contributing a whole galaxy of subproblems dealing with the selection, training, and supervision of interviewers. The problem of interviewer bias in the selection of respondents to interview is one of those. Where probability sampling is used to remove the interviewer's choice as a factor (at least in theory), the problem is one of securing strict adherence to detailed instructions. Differences in the quality of interviewing, reflecting in part differences in the experience, diligence, and even honesty of different interviewers, occur.

5. Field-force training and supervision is a major element in the research process, requiring an expenditure of time, effort, and painstaking attention to detail which it is difficult to exaggerate.

6. There are technical problems of how to get the "not-at-homes" into the sample, whether to call back and if so how many times, which require skilled attention.

7. Some types of respondents are difficult to reach in personal interviews. Included are professional people, those who work nights, etc.

8. Some neighborhoods are difficult to cover by personal interviews without incurring substantial additional risk or expense. Interviewers in consumer studies are typically female. The problem of sending interviewers into some slum and "tough" neighborhoods in big cities, and the potential liability of the employing organization for any mishaps, should not be overlooked.

9. A personal-interview survey, especially on a broad national basis, is a relatively inflexible process. Once the interviewing instructions and materials have been dispatched to interviewers or supervisors, it becomes rather difficult to modify the procedures substantially, add additional questions, or change the method of handling particular matters. This makes the pretesting of every aspect of large-scale personal-interview study especially important, which in turn contributes to the time and expense elements already mentioned.

IMPORTANCE OF ADVANCE PLANNING

It would be difficult to overestimate the importance of careful and thorough advance planning in the use of the survey technique. A survey secures certain types of information, which are then tabulated, analyzed, and related to each other and to facts from other sources. After the field work has been completed, no additional elements of information can be secured from the same group of respondents except at extremely high cost. Yet it is not unusual to find when the survey results are tabulated and analyzed that one or more vital additional pieces of information—if they were available—would add greatly to the meaning of much of the information that was secured. The experienced research man minimizes the risk of finding himself in such a predicament by the thoroughness and painstaking care with which he does his advance planning.

There is a close parallel between the planning and execution of a survey and the planning and erection of a house. In both cases it is desirable to make all key decisions before the actual execution or construction begins. In that way, the relationship of all parts of the whole can be examined while there is still time to make any necessary changes. In a survey or in building a house, the danger of an oversight is always present. Sometimes amateur house planners put a fireplace on the first floor but neglect to provide space for the inevitable chimney in their second-floor plan. The same kind of obvious oversights crop up in surveys. An actual small-scale model of the proposed project is helpful in both cases. In surveys, the model may be a real and tangible one—as in the case of a small-scale test study, which is often called a pilot study. Such a pilot study serves to provide a realistic check on the adequacy of the planning. In other cases, a research man with extensive experience may find that a mental model of the project may be sufficient.

Planning the study is not presented as a discrete step in the above list of steps in the planning and execution of a survey, because it is an essential and integral part of *every* step. In a book giving golf instructions, details of the grip and swing are covered, but the author is unlikely to tell the reader to breathe while gripping or swinging! Careful planning is as important in conducting a survey as breathing is in playing golf.

Two aspects of survey planning deserve particular mention. One concerns the relationship between a specific proposed survey which is under consideration and other studies which either have been done in the past or which might conceivably be executed in the future. The other is concerned with the level of application of the survey technique.

"ONE SHOT" VERSUS RECURRING SURVEYS

The survey technique usually involves a single (or "one-shot") study of a group of respondents. Sometimes parallel surveys are executed on a recurring basis. Such studies are usually made at different periods of time on matched samples planned to be as nearly identical as possible, although each sample is made up of a *different* group of respondents. One value of such recurring surveys is the light they shed on changes which have occurred over a period of time or as the result of some major stimuli like the introduction of a new brand or new product. In planning a survey, past studies should be examined. Including some few elements from the past surveys in the later one, in identical form, will often add substantially to the perspective provided by the later study.

When General Mills, Inc., was evaluating the effect of sampling one of its cereals, it conducted "before-and-after" surveys. One preceded the sampling; the other followed it by a six-month period. Parallel samples were used which permitted a comparison before and after sampling.

LEVELS OF APPLICATION OF THE SURVEY TECHNIQUE

Surveys in marketing research are made at all levels of the marketing process; that is, the survey may be made among manufacturers (who are the "consumers" to those selling industrial products), or among any of the various types of wholesalers or retailers active in marketing. Where the survey covers units like manufacturers, wholesalers, or retailers, it is necessary to decide and to specify in the planning stage the type of respondent within the given unit who is to be interviewed. In manufacturing establishments, an interview with a purchasing agent would be likely to yield different types of information from those which could be secured in an interview with the plant superintendent or production manager. A survey of retail drug outlets might be confined to pharmacists or to store managers. Some overlap would occur because some pharmacists *are* store managers. A survey among department stores might cover buyers of a particular type of product, merchandising managers, or retail sales clerks. The type of information sought would influence the respondent selection.

Often the survey planner has a choice of levels open to him. Thus to find out relative brand position on a food product, one might survey at either the consumer or retail level.

It is worth remembering that whether one is surveying manufacturers, wholesalers, retailers, or consumers, each interview must be made with an *individual*. The fact that in one instance a consumer may be speaking only for himself as a consumer, or a housewife for her family unit, or in another case for a manufacturing or retailing organization by which the respondent is employed does not alter the fact that any survey is limited by the ability and willingness of an individual to supply information.

PLANNING THE SAMPLE OF RESPONDENTS TO BE COVERED

The subject of sampling, with major emphasis on the use of sampling in surveys, is covered in Chapters 5 and 11. Beyond the observation that this is one of the most important steps in the survey process, further comments at this point would be unnecessarily repetitive.

PLANNING THE QUESTIONNAIRE FORMS

Again it is desirable to recognize how inadequate the space available here is for covering this relatively complex subject. The ability to prepare a questionnaire in a competent manner is a fine art, which can be acquired only through extensive experience on a large number of different studies of different types. An entire book has been devoted to the problems involved in the selection of words and phrases used in single questions in social surveys.[8] The author of that book had no space to devote to the closely related and important problems involved in combining different questions into a completed questionnaire. In the following few paragraphs, the nature of some of the more important types of problems encountered in questionnaire construction can be indicated—nothing more. Other portions of the book—specifically including the earlier portions of this chapter; Chapters 12 and 13 on defining and refining the problem and on the conduct of informal investigations; and the portion of Chapter 7 about the evaluation of research done by others will make additional contributions to the reader's knowledge of this subject.

In a survey, an attempt is made to achieve two-way communication between an interviewer (either present in person or represented by a questionnaire) and a respondent. The two-way nature of this process should be recognized. First, the interviewer must communicate understandably, through a question or a question and preliminary comments or accompanying exhibits, a knowledge on the respondent's part of exactly what it is that he or she wants to know. Second, the respondent must communicate to the interviewer the information requested. The problems in the area of questionnaire development arise because of the difficulties in this communication process. Through years of experience in social surveys, research workers have learned to measure a proposed question and/or questionnaire with certain mental yardsticks and to eliminate or improve either questions or a questionnaire which fail to meet the standards of sound practice.

Consider first the problems encountered in framing individual ques-

---

[8] Stanley L. Payne, *The Art of Asking Questions,* Princeton University Press, Princeton, N.J., 1951.

tions. Research workers have learned that individual words used in a questionnaire must be selected with the characteristics of the sample of respondents in mind. It is generally desirable to keep the words extremely simple and understandable, so that those members of the sample of the respondents who have the least verbal facility can understand them. The questions should be phrased in the conversational language of the respondent. A question asked of doctors would often be phrased differently and would use a different vocabulary from one asked of "typical housewives." Individual words often interfere with communication, not alone because they are unfamiliar and therefore not understood, but also because many words are inherently ambiguous. Questions should usually be confined to requests for types of information which the respondent can supply. Asking the manager of a large supermarket the sales ranking of several brands of soap powders or detergents, for example, characteristically produces little more than guesses, since the answer to the question is unlikely to be known to the respondent. This is easily recognizable if the large number of product lines stocked in such a store is considered. Other research approaches would supply more accurate information of that type.

Questions which include two or more elements are undesirable. If you ask, *Which cake did you think was higher and lighter?* what is the respondent to answer if she thinks one cake was higher and the other lighter? Questions requiring a generalization by the respondent, such as *How many cans of soup do you usually buy in a month?* are of little value. Focusing the respondent's attention on a specific recent occurrence, such as the most recent purchase occasion, or a definitely delimited and specific time period is sounder practice and often provides similar information with greater accuracy than can be secured by generalization-requiring types of questions.

As a general rule, leading questions should be eliminated, although under some circumstances they are both necessary and useful. One should be on guard against questions including words with high emotional loadings or questions phrased in words of such intensity as to influence the answer. Provision should almost always be made for conditional answers (such as "I don't know" or "I don't remember") to eliminate the forcing effect of yes-or-no questions, especially in mail questionnaires.

Turning attention now to the combining of questions into a completed questionnaire, these points are worth noting. The first question or two should be planned to establish rapport between respondent and interviewer. Early questions should be especially simple. Where a series of questions explores different aspects of the same subject, but move through time (such as the brand used last, how long used, brand used before that, etc.), care should be taken to keep the occurrences in chronological order. This should preferably start with the most recent event and move backward.

The questionnaire should be planned to cover a subject, then move on to the next, rather than to jump back and forth so that the respondent must make a mental effort to follow the questioning in addition to the effort required to recall and supply the information desired. It is desirable to remember that the respondent is extending a courtesy to the interviewer in permitting the interview. Every way in which sounder knowledge of research techniques can contribute to making the interviewing process an interesting and easy one *for the respondent* should be utilized.

The influence of earlier questions on replies to later ones must be considered. Thus if you were to ask a question revealing an interest in a particular brand and were subsequently to ask a question about opinions or attitudes on products of that type, the fact that your interest in a particular brand had been "telegraphed" by the earlier question would be likely to lead to an inflationary bias in replies. Where an answer to one question makes it clear that a subsequent series of questions should not be asked of a particular respondent, the questionnaire should be so constructed and interviewers instructed accordingly.

TESTING QUESTIONNAIRE FORMS

Testing questionnaire forms is an integral step in the survey process. It is essentially a precautionary step, a small-scale use of the questionnaire to reveal whether it does in fact secure the kind of information it was planned to secure and to disclose any shortcomings either in individual questions or question sequences before the actual field work is launched. The total cost of the proposed study has a direct bearing on the amount of testing that is desirable and necessary. In the case of the national consumer survey like the $70,000 one mentioned earlier in this chapter, testing should be extremely intensive. *It should be carried to and through tabulation to the actual tables which are likely to be included in the final report,* because only by attempting to apply the information coming from questionnaires can one be sure that there are no missing links in the chain of information.

The importance of adequate testing of the questionnaire is often underestimated, especially by those with limited research experience. Many experienced research men, despite their years of experience and executive status, personally participate in the interviewing which is an inescapable part of questionnaire testing on major surveys. That experience permits them to detect—in such things as the puzzled looks of respondents, offhand comments, hesitation, groping for words—clues to questionnaire limitations which might be overlooked by someone with less experience.

It is especially important that the questionnaire testing be entrusted to research personnel with experience embracing the entire research process, from coding and editing through tabulation and analysis. Limitations in questions and in types of replies sometimes do not become apparent until one knows how they are to be used. In mail studies, an actual small-scale mailing is often used for questionnaire testing.

INSTRUCTING INTERVIEWERS AND SUPERVISORS

In the case of most surveys, the interviewing takes place in many scattered locations. Ideally, each field supervisor should be personally contacted and instructed in the details of each study and the instruction of interviewers should similarly be carried on through the medium of some representative of "headquarters." In practice, it would be impossible in most instances to cover all interviewing points without piling up excessive supervisory travel expense. The time required to execute such a procedure is another obstacle. As a result of these and other obstacles, interviewers often receive their instructions for a particular survey through the mail. The preparation of detailed instructions which interviewers can and do understand calls for a very high degree of skill.

The magnitude of this step as a problem in the total survey process of course varies with the organization making the survey and with the experience of the field personnel. Those organizations which are continually engaged in surveys often develop and publish extremely detailed instruction manuals which are distributed to their field interviewers. These manuals accomplish the first of the three steps involved in a thorough job of interviewer instruction—the step involving general instructions on method of conducting the interview, how to probe, etc. Any reader responsible for the execution of surveys would be well advised to review carefully one or more of the manuals developed and published by experienced organizations.[9]

Assuming that the interviewing staff is experienced both in interviewing generally and in the special characteristics, if any, of the interview-

[9] Three such manuals which are of interest are *Interviewing for NORC*, National Opinion Research Center, 1947, 154 pp.; *Manual for Interviewers*, Survey Research Center, University of Michigan, Ann Arbor, Mich., 1954, 130 pp.; and the manual developed by the U.S. Department of Agriculture. The latter manual is reproduced in full by Lorie and Roberts in *Basic Methods of Marketing Research*, McGraw-Hill, New York, 1951, pp. 351–375, hence is readily available for review by interested readers with access to a large library.

ing approach of the organization executing the survey, two additional steps in the instruction process remain. The first of these involves instructions in the method of selecting the sample of respondents. The second includes specific instructions in the particular questionnaire being used in the study. Both steps are extremely important.

The sampling instructions should be detailed and specific. They include in a typical situation a designation of the starting point, instructions as to route, instructions as to the selection of dwelling units at which interviews should be made, instructions for the selection of the particular respondent to be interviewed in the dwelling unit, and other pertinent sampling information. One point which should be included is what the interviewer should do if no one is at home in the selected dwelling unit. Sometimes a procedure for choosing an alternate is given; more frequently, callbacks with a maximum number specified are required.

The instructions on the questionnaire itself typically begin with some discussion of the purposes of the survey. The name of the sponsoring organization is usually *not* revealed to the interviewers. They then proceed through the questionnaire, question by question. From the pretesting of the questionnaire, the particular pitfalls or trouble spots likely to arise are known. The interviewer is warned of those perils and given specific and detailed instructions in handling each type of problem situation.

Remember that the objective of the instructions is to secure completely uniform questioning in many different places, from many different interviewers who vary in personality, education, and intelligence. The importance of detailed and complete instructions is then apparent. One problem which sometimes arises is that the interviewers used in the pretest are above average in intelligence and/or experience, hence provide a poor basis for evaluating the clarity of instructions. To illustrate the specific detail required, the instructions should indicate where a probe (in the form of a question like "Anything else?") is to be used, the exact form of the probe, how to indicate the location of the probing question on the interview questionnaire itself, how many times to probe, and all other instructions necessary to achieve uniformity.

CHECKING THE FIELD WORK

Two ways of checking the field work are common in practice. One is to tabulate key questions, if not the entire questionnaire, on an interviewer-by-interviewer basis. The comparison of each interviewer's results on each question with those of other interviewers provides a check on the interviewer's work. Faking of interviews by interviewers is always possible in survey work, and precautions against such interviews slipping through into tabulation should be taken even when dealing with a staff of experienced and known interviewers. This check typically aids in detecting such interviewing.

The second check is a verification of an established proportion of all interviews. This check is sometimes made by a double postcard (in which case it is usually confined to establishing that the reported respondent was in fact interviewed, on the day and time reported, on the subject of the study). Or it may be made by phone or by having a complete or partial reinterview made by another interviewer. Where verification of a proportion of interviews is standard practice, as it is in most professional research, that fact should be communicated in advance to the interviewers so that they know their work will be verified.

No survey can rise above the level of the field work on which it is based. Careful supervision of the quality of the field work is one of the characteristics of sound research practice.

TABULATION AND ANALYSIS OF SURVEY INFORMATION

Some of the more important points to observe in the tabulation of survey results have already been indicated by the ARF comments quoted above on the evaluation of surveys in Chapter 7.

The most important single point to keep in mind is the importance of advance planning of tabulation. A marketing research man who is not intimately familiar with the process of electronic tabulation of survey data would be well advised to consult with the representative of the tabulating organization to be used. That consultation should take place while the questionnaire is in the planning stage, so that minor modifications of the questionnaire which would substantially reduce the cost of tabulation, or reduce the likelihood of error, may be considered.

The analysis and interpretation of the results of a survey are basically the same as the analytical and interpretive steps in other research approaches. Chapters 16 and 17 describe those steps in detail.

PREPARATION OF THE REPORT

This is the final step for which all others have been preparation. It would be incorrect to say that this is the most important step in the survey operation, because all the preceding steps contribute importantly to the value of the survey and of its report. No report can make up for deficiencies in the planning or execution of the study itself. Yet the report remains, in the final analysis, the key to whether the survey itself was a success or a failure. The research cost money. It should contribute more to profit than it cost, within a reasonable period of time. Will it in fact make such a profit contribution? The answer to this question is strongly influenced by the quality of the report itself. It is because of the extreme importance of capable reporting, as a determinant of the value of the research on which the report is based, that all of Chapter 18 is devoted to problems of report preparation.

The comments about reporting made in Chapter 18 apply with particular force to the reporting of survey results. The relatively high cost of field work, tabulation, and analysis impose an added responsibility on the survey report. That report must point clearly toward action to be taken or action to be avoided. It must present its evidence, evaluate that evidence objectively, interpret it clearly, and report lucidly on the results of the research.

SUMMARY

1. This chapter introduced the survey technique, one of the most important technique tools of the marketing research practitioner.

2. Surveys are widely used to gather from external sources information not already available, when that information is needed for a vital marketing decision.

3. The most important single point to remember about a survey is that the process of planning and executing a survey with true professional competence is one that requires the highest degree of marketing research skill. That fact is often overlooked by those who are unaware of the full complexity of the survey process.

4. Fortunately for the beginner in marketing research, surveys represent a relatively smaller portion of all marketing research practice than they used to. The reasons for that decline in relative importance are traced in this chapter.

5. The steps in the planning and execution of a survey were listed and commented upon in this chapter. Of particular importance is the determination in specific terms of the kinds of information to be developed by the survey. As illustrations in this chapter show, there are a number of different kinds of information which can be developed by the survey approach. A single survey often contributes several different types of information—such as facts, opinions, attitudes, etc.

6. Surveys can be made by mail, by telephone, or by personal interview. Each approach has definite advantages and disadvantages, which must be weighed as part of the decision on which approach to take in dealing with a specific problem situation.

7. The most important single element in the survey process, if a single element can be so designated, is the *planning* stage. It would be difficult to exaggerate the importance of careful and detailed advance planning.

8. One advantage of the survey approach is that it can be used at any one or more of the levels in the marketing process—at the consumer level, retail level, wholesale level, or manufacturer level.

9. A questionnaire used in a survey should be developed with care and thoroughly pretested before being used on a large-scale study.

10. Careful attention to the problems involved in instructing interviewers is recommended, since the field work is the foundation of the survey and no survey can rise above the level of its field work. Checks on the quality of that field work are standard practice in professional practice.

11. The tabulation and analysis of survey information, and the interpretation of that information, require a high level of skill to be sure that the effort and expense devoted to developing high-quality field work is translated into the informational foundation for a sound report.

12. Reporting the results of a survey can "make or break" all that has preceded the report, in terms of translating the survey into a source of profit contribution to the company paying the bill. No report can make up for deficiencies in planning or execution of the survey; but a poor report can keep a well-planned and soundly executed survey from achieving its maximum contribution.

QUESTIONS

1. In your own words, how would you describe a survey?

2. How would you account for the decline in the relative importance of surveys?

3. What is meant in this chapter when it is said that a survey is like a "pyramid"?

4. What are the steps used in the planning and execution of a marketing survey?

5. What types of information could a survey provide for your company?

6. Briefly discuss the advantages and limitations of the three major survey approaches.

7. How would you explain the importance of advance planning in the survey technique?

8. What is the real value of recurring surveys? And what part does a "matched sample" play in the use of recurring surveys?

9. What would you say the main objective of instructions to interviewers and supervisors is?

10. Describe two ways that you could check on the field work conducted by your interviewers.

11. Why is the report of a survey so important? Explain.

CHAPTER 9

The Use of Panels
in Marketing Research

Two surveys made at different time periods reveal a variation in a key statistic, such as the percentage of families using a particular type of product or a specific brand. The difference between the two figures could represent an actual change over a period of time (i.e., a trend), or it could simply reflect chance influences in sample selection. The marketing research man analyzing and interpreting the results of two such surveys faces the task of deciding—if he can—whether there has in fact been a change in product-usage levels, or whether the apparent change represents a difference between the two samples in question. What this involves is an evaluation of the *significance* of the difference between the two figures.

Ways of evaluating the significance of two such figures will be described in Chapter 11 on practical sampling. At this point it is sufficient to point out that the problem revolves around two variables—the scale of the difference and the size of the sample of respondents involved in each case. In general we may note that the smaller the change involved, the larger the sample size required to be *practically certain* that a true change has occurred, rather than a sampling fluctuation caused by chance.

The problem of evaluating a change occurring over a period of time between two surveys involves some extremely difficult planning problems. The marketing research man has to estimate *in advance* at least the approximate scale of the change to be measured. Without such an estimate, he could not determine how large a sample would be required to provide a basis for confidence that a real shift in usage levels had occurred, rather than simply a chance variation in sampling.

There is another approach to this type of problem which eliminates the possibility that differences between the samples in the two surveys, rather than differences in usage levels, are the cause of the difference between the two percentages. That approach would measure the usage level among *the same sample* of respondents at *two different time periods*. Thus a sample of 1,000 households might be interviewed in January of one year to determine what proportion use a given type of product and/or brand; and the *same* 1,000 households then *re*interviewed the following January to see what change, if any, had occurred over the twelve-month interval.

When a marketing research man interviews the same respondents two or more times, or secures data from them on two or more occasions, he is using an approach known as *panel research*. Remember that "respondents" as used here might be individuals, households, retail stores, wholesale organizations, manufacturers, etc.

RELATIONSHIP BETWEEN SURVEY AND PANEL RESEARCH

This chapter is devoted to panel research, in which the *same* group of respondents contribute information on two or more occasions. The one major difference between the survey technique and the panel technique lies in this matter of the number of contacts between the respondent and the sponsor of the research. While there is that one difference, there are countless points of similarity between the survey and panel approaches. Consider the matter of sampling, for example. There is essentially no difference between the two approaches in the methods of sampling used.

Because survey and panel research are so similar in so many ways, the preceding chapter and this one should be considered in practical terms as a single unit. Many of the observations made about the survey technique in the preceding chapter apply also to panel research. To repeat them would be undesirable, because of space limitations. Similarly, some of the comments about panel research in this chapter will contribute to your understanding of the survey technique. Considering these two chapters as two parts of a unified whole will therefore contribute to your understanding of both research approaches.

PROBLEMS PECULIAR TO PANEL RESEARCH

There are certain problems which are encountered only in panel research or which are more serious in the case of panel research than in the case of the survey approach. A review of such problems will be helpful in suggesting some of the potential trouble spots when this technique is used. The first problem area concerns sampling. As has been indicated, the sampling approach in panel research does not differ essentially from sampling in the survey technique. In making surveys, there is a problem of nonresponse or noncooperation which is always encountered.

Except in the case of studies by the Federal government in which replies are compulsory (such as the various censuses), every survey encounters some individuals who can and do refuse to cooperate by answering questions and supplying information. With a skilled field staff, this problem can be held within moderate proportions, but is almost always present.

In the case of panel research, a greater degree of cooperation is required of respondents. The respondent must not only cooperate once; he or she must cooperate at least one additional time, and in the case of some variations of panel technique continuous cooperation is sought. There are many respondents who will answer the questions in a survey, but who "can't be bothered" by repeated interviews. If the interval between the interviews is long, a second interview can sometimes be completed before the respondent "draws the line."

This sampling problem is the first trouble spot in panel research. More cooperation is required of respondents, with the result that the refusal rate rises. The gap between the planned-for and delivered sample widens. The question as to the representativeness of the cooperative respondents exists and remains unanswered. Often this problem is indicated by a constantly diminishing sample in the later stages of panel research involving more than two respondent contacts. It is possible to put into the initial sample enough excess size to end up with the desired number of completed responses in most cases, but the question of representativeness is not so easily answered.

The second question about panel research is concerned with the conditioning factor. Different panel approaches condition respondents to different degrees, but some conditioning is present in almost all panel research. Repeated questioning on any subject is likely to make a respondent think much more about that subject than he or she did prior to participation in the panel activity. This is likely to result in some modifications of behavior, attitude, etc. The subsequent conclusion that time (rather than conditioning) was responsible for changes which are revealed by the research is open to question.

There are other questions which exist only in the case of some types of panel research. Such questions are raised in the appropriate section of this chapter.

ADVANTAGES OF PANEL RESEARCH

The advantages of the panel approach have already been suggested, but the importance of this technique in marketing research practice makes further comments desirable. The primary advantage of the panel approach is that it permits a research man to trace the changes occurring through time, with differences between matched samples (which in fact are sometimes not very well matched) eliminated as a possible influence. This eliminates the sometimes knotty problem of discriminating between a real change and one which is really only a statistical fluke.

The panel technique is especially useful in the case of experimental approaches, which are the subject of the following chapter. By setting up a panel and then dividing it, exposing one half to a stimulus (such as intensified advertising, a sample of the product, etc.) while keeping the other half free from exposure as a control group, the effect of the stimulus may often be determined experimentally. In such a situation this evaluation compares the pattern in the control portion of the panel with that in the stimulated portion, as a basis for the evaluation of the stimulus.

Reward to panel members as a part of the motivation of cooperation is standard practice. Such rewards may have the negative effect of conditioning the panel and making their reactions less than representative of a larger, unconditioned group. On the other hand, sometimes the reward used is itself an ingredient in the research. A subsequent callback to determine reaction to and/or use of the product used as the "gift" is not uncommon.

In all research among consumers, the problem of establishing rapport is present. That rapport is essential for relaxed and dependable communication between respondent and interviewer, and vice versa. In the case of a panel, that familiarity is established by repeated contacts, and a situation is set up in which it is often possible to explore consumer reactions and attitudes at more length than would be possible on a "cold" approach. This advantage of panel research was more important in the past than it is today. Increasingly skillful tools and techniques in the area of qualitative and motivational research make it possible to get relatively deep probing from respondents who are not panel members.

Now let's consider two major panel-research approaches which together bulk large in the marketing research picture on consumer products.

TWO CONTINUING PANEL-RESEARCH SERVICES

Specific illustrations of panel research in action are provided by two important continuing research services. Both use the panel approach. Those two services have many characteristics in common, notably including these:

1. Each technique was created primarily to provide a continuing measurement of the consumer movement of merchandise. This is a most important point, which is developed below.

2. Each technique was developed, and demonstrated to be commercially feasible, primarily by a single organization.

3. Each technique is available on a cooperative basis. That is, the cost of operating the panel is divided among a number of different sponsoring organizations, who are typically manufacturers of food and drug products with substantial advertising budgets. Note that each service is available to competitive manufacturers in most instances, although for a substantial premium in price a manufacturer might purchase exclusivity in one or more product classes.

4. In addition to supplying the information on consumer movement of merchandise which they were created to provide, each service offers many other useful and significant marketing facts.

The description of the two services given below has a dual function. First, it is intended to acquaint the reader with two services which together represent an extremely important element in consumer-product marketing research practice. Second, the description of each service is intended to illustrate a specific technique variation of panel research— the store-audit approach, on one hand, and the continuing consumer-purchase panel, on the other. Those techniques, and various modifications of them, are useful in many research situations quite apart from the continuing services described below.

THE IMPORTANCE OF MEASURING CONSUMER MOVEMENT

Both of the services described below are highly successful commercial services because they fill a real need in marketing today. That need was first appreciated on a broad scale by A. C. Nielsen, whose classic chart illustrating it graphically is reproduced as Figure 9.1. The chart indicates that in the case of consumer products, the flow of goods is from the factory through wholesale and chain-store warehouses, through retail outlets, to the final consumer. The factory at the top and the consumer at the bottom are separated by what is collectively described as the *pipeline* of trade stocks. What happens at the consumer level eventually is reflected in activity at the factory, but the time lag involved is often excessively long. The two panel services which are described below make it possible for manufacturers to determine rather quickly what is happening at the vital consumer level.

As Figure 9.2 illustrates, it is possible for factory sales to be declining at a time when the purchases of consumers are rising. When that type of contrast in movement trend exists, the manufacturer is headed into stormy weather. Eventually consumer sales will begin to outpace factory production and sales will be lost until balance is restored. The two services described below are especially useful in helping

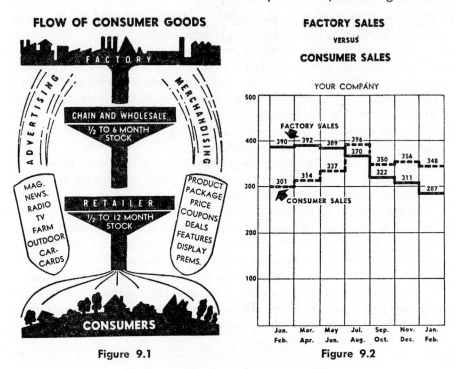

FLOW OF CONSUMER GOODS

FACTORY SALES
VERSUS
CONSUMER SALES

Figure 9.1   Figure 9.2

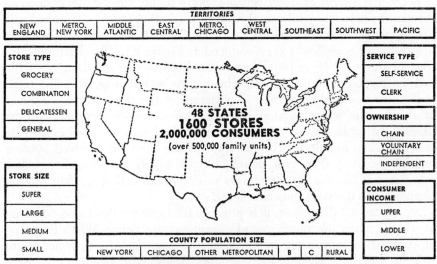

FOOD STORE REPRESENTATION★

BASED ON U. S. CENSUS OF DISTRIBUTION AND OUR OWN CONTINUING STUDIES

48 STATES
1600 STORES
2,000,000 CONSUMERS
(over 500,000 family units)

★ DRUG STORE REPRESENTATION follows identical principles.
(750 stores, 3,000,000 consumers, or over 750,000 family units)

Figure 9.3

their subscribers avoid such difficulties, by keeping factory shipments closely tuned to consumer purchasing shifts.

7. A. C. NIELSEN COMPANY

Since 1933, the A. C. Nielsen Company has been operating a marketing research service designed to supply manufacturers with facts about the consumer sales of their products. This service is called the Nielsen Food-Drug Index. It is based on a research technique known as the store-audit technique.

The Nielsen Food Index utilizes a sample of food outlets, with the characteristics and distribution illustrated in Figure 9.3. Nielsen's field organization measures the consumer movement of a wide variety of different product classes through this sample of retail outlets. Every sample store is audited every two months. A report covering consumer purchases during each two-month period is delivered to clients subscribing to the service. The reports, presented by a Nielsen client service man to a meeting in the client offices in most instances, are largely in chart form supplemented by written analyses of major trends and developments. Copies of the Nielsen reports, including small reproductions of the charts used in the personal presentation, are delivered to the client organization.

The principles of store-auditing are not difficult to understand. A field representative calls on each store in the sample every sixty days. He checks the store's inventory of selected types of products, being careful to count inventory in all locations—shelf stock, floor displays, window displays, back-room stock, basement stock, etc. The store owner or manager saves all invoices covering merchandise received between audits. The store-auditor determines from those invoices and delivery tickets how many units have been added to stock during the two-month period. The store's inventory at the beginning of the sixty-day period is known, for that was the closing inventory of the preceding period. It was the inventory on hand on the previous visit to the store by the field representative. The additions to stock are shown by invoices and delivery tickets. Opening inventory plus additions represent the total available for sale. The closing inventory is checked by physical count. Sales for the sixty-day period are found by subtracting total on hand at the close of the period from the total available for sale.

In addition to the inventory and recording of receipts, the field man determines by observation a number of other facts about the store's activities during the two-month period. He notes whether or not the audited products were featured in special displays, and if so of what type. He determines whether the products audited were included within the store's own local advertising. He checks the price on the product and notes any special-price features or price changes.

The above description of the store-audit operation sounds rather simple. It is simple, in principle; but in practice it can be very complex. Figures for individual stores of the same type are combined to obtain an average movement-per-store figure. Those averages are then projected

COMPLETE LIST OF DATA SECURED EVERY 60 DAYS IN FOOD STORES *

1. SALES to CONSUMERS	7. OUT-OF-STOCK
2. PURCHASES by RETAILERS	8. PRICES (Wholesale and Retail)
3. RETAIL INVENTORIES	9. SPECIAL FACTORY PACKS
4. DAYS' SUPPLY	10. DEALER SUPPORT (Displays, Local Adv., Coupon Redempt.)
5. STORE COUNT DISTRIBUTION	11. SPECIAL OBSERVATIONS (Order Size, Reorders, Direct vs.
6. ALL-COMMODITY DISTRIBUTION	12. TOTAL FOOD STORE SALES (All Commodities) Whlse.)
13. MAJOR MEDIA ADVERTISING (From Other Sources)	

BROKEN DOWN BY:

BRANDS	TERRITORIES	YOUR OWN TERR.		COUNTIES POP. RANGE	STORES		PKG. SIZE	PROD. TYPE
YOURS	NEW ENG.	1	10	MET. NEW YORK			SMALL	
A	MET. NEW YORK	2	11	MET. CHICAGO	CHAIN	SELF-		X
B	MID. ATLANTIC	3	12	OTHER MET.		SER-		
C	EAST CENTRAL	4	13	19 Next Largest Mkts.	INDEP. LARGE	VICE	MEDIUM	
D	MET. CHICAGO	5	14	Other Counties & B Met. Areas Over 100,000				Y
	WEST CENTRAL	6	15		MED.	CLERK	LARGE	
ALL OTHERS	SOUTHEAST	7	16	C Other Counties 30,000-100,000		SER-		
	SOUTHWEST	8	17	RURAL	SMALL	VICE	GIANT	Z
TOTAL	PACIFIC	9	18	Other Under 30,000				

* Substantially the same types of data are collected in DRUG stores.

Figure 9.4

to national figures by using known data on the number of stores of various types in different cells of the sample, such as geographic sections, city-size groups, etc.

The types of information provided by Nielsen's store-audit service are identified in Figure 9.4.

— ★ —

8. MARKET RESEARCH CORPORATION OF AMERICA

This organization, which was formerly known as Industrial Surveys Co., operates a marketing research service which is like the Nielsen service in that it is designed primarily to provide manufacturers with facts about the consumer sales of their products. The MRCA service utilizes a research technique known as the continuous-purchase-record consumer panel. Because the sample is national in its distribution, the service is often referred to as the national consumer panel (NCP).

The consumer-panel technique is based on a sample of households, reporting by mail each week their day-to-day purchases of certain food and personal-care items. The panel is operated continuously, with the same samples of respondents (subject only to a mortality and replacement factor noted below), which makes it possible to compare a given household's purchases at one point in time with the same household's purchasing behavior at an earlier or later point in time. The participating households record their purchases on a printed form called a "diary." One page of the diary used by MRCA in their consumer-panel operation is reproduced as Figure 9.5.

It will be noted from the illustration that for each item purchased in those categories included in the diary, the household through its recording member (usually the housewife) was required to provide information as to the brand, the number of units or quantity purchased, the package size or sizes, the kind of retail outlet through which the purchase was made. In addition other information is supplied in those cases in which some promotional activity such as a coupon, a 1 cent sale, or a combination sale of two different products was involved in a purchase. Most of the product classes included are in the packaged-food and personal-care categories, the latter including items like shampoo, etc.

Basic information is available and on record regarding various characteristics of each panel family. For example, the composition (number and ages of family members) of each family is known, along with the educational level attained by adult members, occupation of principal wage earner, income, etc. This information about the characteristics of panel families makes it possible to break down purchasing of individual products and compare the purchase rate of those with and without any particular characteristic.

— ★ —

TYPES OF INFORMATION AVAILABLE FROM BOTH SERVICES

As we noted above, these two techniques—the store-audit approach and the consumer-panel approach—were both developed primarily to provide a picture of the trends in consumer purchases of certain types of products. Inevitably, there is a substantial degree of overlap between the two techniques in terms of the types of questions that can be answered by each. Here is a brief indication of some of the major questions which *both* services answer, along with some comments on limitations of the services in terms of the particular answers in question.

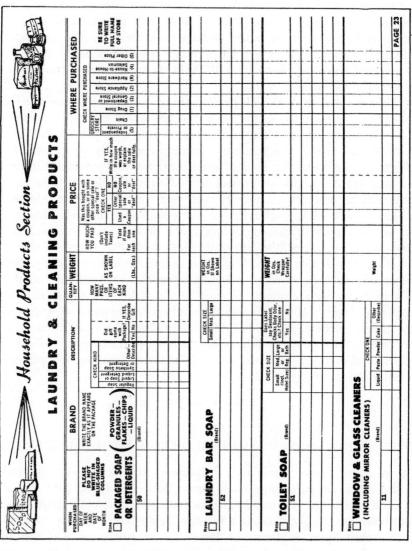

Figure 9.5

218

1. *How Big Is the Market?*

Both the store-audit technique and the consumer-panel techniques provide figures on the size of the total market, that is, industry volume, in dollars and units. The store-audit picks up all sales that are made at the retail level. Therefore it includes purchases made by industrial or institutional users, provided those purchases are made at retail. Since the consumer panel usually covers only *family* purchases, the purchases of nonfamily units including institutional and industrial purchases made through retail outlets are usually excluded. The importance of this omission in panel coverage varies from product class to product class, depending primarily on the relative importance of nonfamily consumption.

Offsetting that advantage of the store-audit approach over the consumer panel is a related and similar problem. The store-audit technique typically provides rather limited coverage of different types of retail outlets. Food outlets are covered by Nielsen, as are drug outlets (although the price of purchasing both food- and drug-outlet coverage is higher than the cost of buying either outlet type alone). There has been a recent trend toward diffusion of different products through a variety of outlet types. Increased distribution of drug and personal-care items through grocery outlets is one symptom of that trend. There are some product types which move through a wide variety of retail outlet types. Wax products, for example, move to consumers through grocery stores, drug stores, hardware stores, variety (i.e., 5¢–10¢ stores) chains, department stores, paint stores, and many other types. In addition, they are sold in substantial volume by house-to-house canvassers, and in the case of the polishes used on automobiles, the service stations and TBA (tire, battery, and accessory stores) category assume importance.

The limitations of estimates of total-market size based on the store-audit approach in the case of such products, are apparent. Nielsen could estimate only the size of that *part* of the total market moving through the types of outlets included in the Nielsen audit. This characteristic of the two services is a vital consideration where a product with a multiple-outlet-type pattern is concerned.

2. *How Is the Market Divided by Product Subtypes?*

An important marketing characteristic of the types of products covered by the Nielsen and MRCA services is a subdivision of total market into various subtype totals which add up to industry volume. Thus in the case of dentifrices, for example, there are pastes and powders; and within the paste category other major subtypes such as ammoniated, chlorophyll, antienzyme, fluoride, etc. Both the store-audit and consumer-panel techniques provide facts on the division of the total market by such product subtypes. Since both techniques are continuing services, both provide important facts about the trends in product-type division of industry volume.

3. What Is the Geographic Pattern of the Market?

Both techniques make it possible to break down the industry volume into various sections of the country. Often the sectional breakdown is based on the manufacturer-client's own sales regions, enhancing the value of the data. Variations in the relative importance of different product types in different sections of the country, and in the purchase rate of families in different sections, help manufacturers to concentrate their marketing activities on known opportunities.

4. What is the City-size Pattern of Consumption?

Both the store-audit and the consumer-panel techniques show how the market is divided among the various city-size groups. There is one important difference between the two techniques in this respect. The store-audit shows the division by where merchandise *is purchased;* the consumer panel shows it by where consumers *live.* This is an important distinction in the case of some product types. Farmers live on farms, but buy in towns and cities of various sizes. The relative importance of the farm market would be reflected more accurately by the consumer panel than by the store-audit approach.

5. What is the Company's Market Share?

In Chapter 3 it was pointed out that the most widely performed of all specific marketing research activities was the task of determining the competitive position of the company's products. This is frequently referred to as *market-share analysis,* the determination of what proportion of industry volume or what share of the market a product controls. Companies making the kind of product included within the Nielsen and MRCA service ranges are fortunate indeed, where such analysis is concerned. The two panel approaches report the company's market share with a high degree of accuracy. The market-share information is provided in considerable meaningful detail. In addition to data on national market share, subscribers to either service receive figures which show also the market-share variations in different sections of the country, in different city-size groups, in the volume sold by different sizes or different types of retail outlets, etc.

6. How Do Competitors Divide the Remaining Industry Volume?

In addition to the figure on their own market share, the companies subscribing to either service receive details on the market share of their major competitors, including the same sectional, city-size, and similiar detail provided on their own sales situation.

7. What is the Seasonal Curve of Consumer Purchasing?

Both techniques provide a picture of the seasonal variations in consumer purchasing. This information is particularly important in the case of products with a marked seasonal difference in consumption levels. By knowing when the *consumer* peak period is seasonally, a manufacturer can key promotion and advertising effort to established habits, thus maximizing their productivity. There is often a marked difference between the factory-shipment seasonal pattern and that at the consumer level. Thus factory shipments often anticipate the consumer-purchasing seasonal peak.

While the overlap in the information provided by the store-audit and consumer-panel techniques is great, there remain some important informational contributions which are exclusive to each approach. The biggest difference between these two panel-research techniques lies in their level of application. One is applied at the consumer or family level, the other at the retail-store level. Each technique contributes some information about the reporting units at its level of operation which the other, applied at a different level, cannot duplicate. Let's examine these exclusive contributions briefly.

EXCLUSIVE CONTRIBUTIONS OF STORE-AUDIT RESEARCH

There are some important contributions of store-audit data not available from consumer-panel research. One is the answer to the question which every manufacturer is concerned with: How much distribution have we? The distribution level, in terms of the proportion of all retail outlets which carry a particular product or size of product "in stock," is reported by the store-audit technique. Distribution translated into the proportion of total business on a type of product done by the outlets stocking it is even more valuable. Thus a product might be stocked by— i.e., have distribution in—30 per cent of all retail outlets. That statistic is much less meaningful than the knowledge that the 30 per cent of outlets in which it is stocked do 60 or 15 per cent of industry volume! The store-audit approach as executed by the A. C. Nielsen Co. can answer both questions.

Other questions dealing with retail-level operations, such as the size of inventories at the retail level of the company's products and of major competitive products, the proportion of stores stocking both sizes of a two-size product, the extent of special retail support in the form of displays, etc., can also be answered by the store-audit approach.

EXCLUSIVE CONTRIBUTIONS OF THE
CONSUMER-PANEL APPROACH

There are many vital marketing questions which can be answered by
consumer-panel research but not by a store-audit. Those questions deal
primarily with consumers—with the kinds of people who buy your
products, with the frequency of their purchasing, with the differences
in purchasing among families of different characteristics, and so on. For

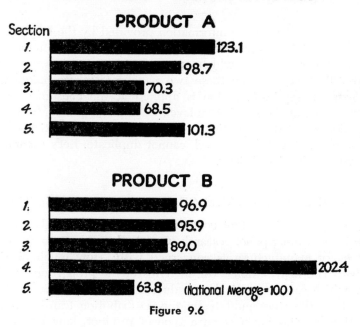

SECTIONAL VARIATIONS
IN CONSUMPTION CHARACTERISTICS

Figure 9.6

example, all economic levels of consumers may patronize a single large
retail outlet audited by Nielsen. Those from lower economic strata buy
different products, and different brands of the same products, from those
with higher incomes. The consumer panel can pinpoint economic-level
variations in purchasing and in brand position. (This type of information
is useful in selecting advertising media, to mention only one of many
applications.) Such discrimination at the consumer level is not possible
with the store-audit approach. Figure 9.6 illustrates the contrast in
geographic use of two very similar products within the wax category,
as revealed by MRCA data. Economic variations are similar.

Since the consumer-panel technique provides records of the same families month after month, it permits measurement of the depth of the market in terms of the proportion of all families buying. There are major differences, even between very similar products. In one month, for example, 69 per cent of all families bought canned soup, while only 18 per cent bought dry-packaged soup. The concentration of buying, established by relating frequency of purchase to number of families, is another important marketing-strategy clue which a consumer panel provides. It is not unusual on some product types to find that a very small proportion of all buying families, buying with high frequency, contribute 60 per cent or more of industry volume.

Brand loyalty, as evidenced by repeat purchasing, and the proportion of buying families reached by a special deal or promotional offer are other informational contributions which a consumer-panel approach can develop.

LIMITATIONS OF THE TWO PANEL APPROACHES

It might be well to underline at this point that there is no perfect marketing research technique. The corollary is that a technique does not have to measure up to theoretical perfection in order to be of tremendous practical value. Both the store-audit technique and the consumer purchase-record panel have been demonstrated beyond question to be dependable sources of marketing research data, *when operated by qualified organizations*. Both techniques are based on sampling, and both have some sampling limitations. It is important to recognize those limitations. It is important also to remember that even with those limitations, these techniques are research tools of great practical value.

The Nielsen service has a major sampling problem. Two of the three largest chain-store organizations in the food field—the Great Atlantic & Pacific Tea Co. and Safeway Stores, Inc.—have so far refused to authorize Nielsen auditing of the movement of products through their outlets, for policy reasons. This is a very serious omission. On some product classes, the private brands of the A&P chain rank among the nation's leading brands. Subscribers to the Nielsen service cannot compare their brand's volume with that of the A&P brands. Some important branded products are much stronger among chain than among independent outlets. Nielsen tends to understate the market share of such brands.

By statistical weighting and control techniques, the Nielsen organization can and does correct their projected estimates of national volume to allow for the (estimated) volume on individual brands and commodity types done by Safeway and A&P. Their estimates of total-market volume are more accurate than are their individual-brand volume and share projections.

The consumer-panel technique, as a function of the record-keeping requirements of the technique itself, tends to have an upward bias on the basis of educational levels. Where pronounced variations exist in the use of a product among groups of different educational attainments, the picture of total-market size projected from consumer-panel data is likely to be less accurate than on products without such a pattern. Operators of consumer panels contend that purchases by families at or near the illiteracy level represent a very small proportion of the United States total volume.

Both techniques have a tendency to understate the size of the total market, but for different reasons. Nielsen understates volume by missing sales through outlet types that are not covered. MRCA's understatement reflects nonfamily consumption and unreported purchases by family members other than the housewife who is typically the family's recorder. For example, consider this situation: The husband of a housewife who maintains a diary for MRCA buys a can of auto polish at a filling station. He polishes the car and throws the can away. The transaction is unlikely to find its way into the diary. As a result, car-polish volume is understated in panel reports by a very substantial margin, whereas the floor-polish category (bought, recorded, and used by the housewife) is relatively accurate.

EXPERIENCE RECRUITING AND MAINTAINING A PANEL

The magnitude of the sampling problem involved in recruiting and maintaining families in a continuous purchase-record panel is indicated by a pair of published reports prepared by MRCA under contract with the U.S. Department of Agriculture. One deals with the problems encountered when an attempt was made to establish a consumer panel in the New York metropolitan area using a probability sample.[1] The other deals with the same problem except that an attempt to establish a national panel was involved.[2] Six months after completion of the training period, 35 per cent of the households successfully contacted were reporting regularly.

This epitomizes the panel sampling problem where a continuing type of operation is concerned. May we safely assume that the 35 per cent

---

[1] *Problems of Establishing a Consumer Panel in the New York Metropolitan Area,* U.S. Department of Agriculture, Bureau of Agricultural Economics, Marketing Research Report 8, May, 1952.

[2] *Establishing a National Consumer Panel from a Probability Sample,* Marketing Research Report 40, June, 1953.

of families who reported regularly are representative of the 100 per cent in the initial probability sample? The study showed that cooperation tended to be best in households in which the housewife was in the younger age groups and in households with more than two members. The resulting sample is far from the theoretical ideal; yet the data developed by MRCA under these sampling limitations have proved accurate enough to be of practical value to an increasing number of large manufacturers, despite substantial cost.

Two other comments are necessary to complete this picture of sampling problems in consumer-panel operations. The first is that the families are rewarded for maintaining diaries by points which are applicable in purchasing prizes from a catalogue supplied. The second is that there is planned "mortality" among panel members and a planned replacement rate in most panel operations. If there were no replacements, the age of panel members would increase each year, with the result that typicality on age distribution would soon be lost. The replacement is intended also to reduce the tendency of panel families to become atypical through conditioning. The success of replacement in achieving the latter objective is problematical.

OTHER CONSUMER-PANEL AND STORE-AUDIT OPERATIONS

The two national organizations whose activities were described above are the most important panel-research operators. There are, however, other smaller-scale panel operations of both the consumer-panel and store-audit type which should be mentioned. Newspapers in key markets operate one-market store-audits and consumer panels in some instances. The exact composition of the list of markets in which such research facilities exist at any given time may be established by contacting the Bureau of Advertising of the American Newspaper Publishers' Association, which maintains offices in New York, Chicago, Los Angeles, Detroit, and San Francisco.

Typical of such newspaper-supported research activities is the consumer panel maintained by the *Chicago Tribune*. With more than 600 families in the Chicago metropolitan area, that well-maintained panel is equivalent to a panel scale which would involve some 12,000 families nationally, roughly double the size of MRCA's national sample. This and other panel facilities operated by advertising media will be accorded the attention they merit in Chapter 29.

Panel operations, especially of the store-audit type, are frequently integrated into a test-market program. Test marketing is the subject of Chapter 25, where such additional panel activities are discussed more fully.

The use of panels is common also in product testing and in comparative product research. This area of application of panel research is developed in Chapter 22, where it concerns product research generally, and in Chapter 23, where it enters into new-product development.

Several organizations maintain relatively large groups of families as present or potential members of panels, both for product testing and other purposes. From those large panel prospects, groups as large as required for a specific study are recruited. There are two advantages in having a much larger group of prospective panel-member families than are required in the case of any particular single study. One is that it is possible, by a postcard preliminary to setting up the panel, to establish use or lack of use of the particular type of product for which the study is to be made. The other is that since panel members from the larger group individually participate in studies relatively infrequently, the effect of conditioning on them is reduced. Specialized research organizations like National Family Opinion, Inc., in Toledo, Ohio, and the Home Testing Institute, Inc., in New York City, are prominent in this phase of panel research.

SUMMARY

1. There are many types of marketing research problems which require repeated or continuing contact with the same sample of respondents (using respondents here in the broad sense to include individuals, households, retail stores, business firms, etc.). This is the province of panel research.

2. Panel research has many points in common with the survey approach. It would be sound practice to consider the chapter on panel research and the preceding chapter on the survey technique as parts of a larger whole.

3. One important value of panel research is that it makes possible the measurement of changes occurring through time among the same group of respondents.

4. Panel research has two ever-present problems: First, the problem of sampling, where the need for securing cooperation tends to provide a sample less completely like the intended design than is possible with a single (survey-type) contact. The other problem involves the conditioning effect of panel membership on the sample included in the sample.

5. Two consumer-product marketing-research applications of panel research were reviewed at length. One is a panel operated at the retail level, using the store-audit technique. The other is a panel operated at the consumer level, using a continuous-purchase-record panel technique.

6. Those two techniques provide essentially similar types of information generally, with some types available only from one of the services. The store-audit approach provides some exclusive information about the retailer; the consumer panel provides some exclusive information about the consumer.

7. In addition to the national panel operations described, panel research

plays a significant part in several areas of research activity, where the research is on a smaller scale. Further references to panel research will be found in the chapters dealing with observation and experiment in marketing research; test marketing; product research; new-product development; and advertising research. Incidental references to panel research will be found in other chapters as well, as reference to the index will show.

QUESTIONS

1. How would you describe *panel research* to someone in your company who is completely unfamiliar with this research approach?

2. Although there are many points of similarity between the survey and the panel approach, what are the problems peculiar to panel research?

3. You have been asked by the comptroller to outline what real advantages the purchase of a continuing panel service could offer your company. How would you answer him?

4. What characteristics do the two major services discussed in this chapter have in common?

5. Describe the types of information offered by the store-audit and the consumer-panel methods that are available from both services.

6. You are asked at this company meeting to briefly describe the A. C. Nielsen and MRCA services. Be sure to cover their exclusive contributions.

7. What are some of the limitations of these two panel approaches?

CHAPTER 10

Observation and Experiment in Marketing Research[1]

Chapter 8 pointed out that the survey technique can be used to provide a marketing research man with different types of information. "Facts" were identified as one type, "opinions" as another. It usually requires some years of experience with the survey technique before the practitioner learns that not all questions intended to secure factual answers in a survey do produce such answers. Shortly after that lesson is learned, the marketing research man is likely to develop a heightened interest in the two technique tools which are the subject of this chapter: the *observational* and *experimental* techniques.

Those two technique tools are far more important in marketing research practice than the scant attention paid to them in the literature of the field would lead you to expect. They are likely to be even more important in the future than they are at present. For of all the technique tools in the research man's kit, those two have one outstanding common advantage: They are *objective* approaches. They are far closer to the methods of physical science than most other marketing research approaches. Under most conditions a result developed by the observational or experimental technique by one marketing research man can be reproduced or duplicated by another. This is true of a relatively minor proportion of marketing research.

The observational approach, as its name implies, is an information-gathering approach in which reliance is placed primarily on the physical observation of one or more phenomena under study. The survey approach seeks to determine what *happened,* or what *was,* by asking questions of a respondent. In contrast, the observational technique seeks to determine what *is happening* or what *is* by watching it happen.

The experimental technique, which is discussed in the later portion of

---

[1] The author is indebted to his associate William F. Suhring for substantial aid in the development of this chapter.

this chapter, involves the use of a small-scale experiment under carefully controlled conditions to evaluate the effect of some variable or proposed course of action. This is a classic research technique in many fields of science It is widely used as a management tool, particularly in production management. What the pilot plant is to production management, the experimental technique is to marketing management.

OBSERVATION USEFUL ALONE OR IN COMBINATION

One of the first points to be made about observation as a technique of marketing research is to emphasize that it is useful in a wide range of situations. It can be used alone; or it can be used (and in practice is used) in conjunction with other techniques, as a useful supplementary tool. There are three sets of circumstances under which the use of the observational approach is strongly indicated. The first is when no other technique tool can supply the desired information. An example would be a traffic count at a proposed store location or in front of an outdoor-advertising display. The second is when there is a question about the accuracy of information provided by some other technique. For example, surveys about magazine readership as made some years ago often simply asked consumers to identify publications read. The high-prestige, high-status publications (like *Good Housekeeping, Better Homes & Gardens, National Geographic,* and *Atlantic Monthly*) picked up a substantial "inflation" in the responses, while publications less well regarded socially (such as some of the confession-type magazines, movie magazines, etc.) were mentioned much less frequently than their circulation figures would lead one to expect. Use of observation as a check on such claims, by asking the respondent to show the most recent issue of publications which were claimed, reduced the replies to a more reasonable basis.

The third situation in which the observational approach should be considered is one in which a high degree of accuracy is extremely important, even though achieving that accuracy adds to the cost of the research.

Some references to the observational approach have been made in earlier chapters, although they were not there so identified. Thus when a field representative of the A. C. Nielsen Co. is checking shelf prices, he uses observation. When he takes a physical inventory, he uses observation. When he locates aisle and window displays and records their presence, he is again using observation.

EXAMPLES OF OBSERVATIONAL APPROACHES

The usefulness of the observational technique in marketing research can best be suggested by some examples. A study made for a chain of retail candy stores in a major metropolitan center had as one objective an evaluation of the chain's standing in its home market compared with three other similar chains. Traffic counts within the stores of all four chains, at scheduled intervals of time, established one observationally measured base line for evaluating the chain's current position. In the same study, observation was used to determine the relative importance of men and women of different age groups in sales of the chain. A study of the extent to which customers in retail drug outlets specified brand names in buying a number of types of products was conducted by stationing an observer in each of a number of different high-traffic retail drug outlets.

Research on fashion and style acceptance often uses observation of the wearing of different innovations in style-setting Southern markets in winter as clues to guide sales forecasting in the more populous Northern markets months later. In a survey conducted for the Toni Company, a division of the Gillette Company, women were asked to describe their hair length (short, medium, or long) and condition (dry, normal, oily). Their responses were recorded on the questionnaire as part of the survey, along with *observations* by interviewers. In the case of the hair-length question, sketches were included in the questionnaire on which the interviewer indicated the hair-length of the respondent.

Many survey questions ask for information which a respondent is not able to supply fully and accurately, even though he or she is cooperative and makes the effort. Suppose you rang the doorbell of your next-door neighbor and asked his wife to tell you what brands of ready-to-eat cereals she had on her shelves at that particular moment. She might make every attempt to answer you fully and accurately. She would probably recall those brands which she almost always keeps in stock—the ones that go on her shopping list when a package is emptied. She might recall some of her once-in-a-while brands. She would be likely to forget brands that are relatively new or that she bought only because one of her youngsters picked a package off a supermarket shelf while "helping" mother shop. The observational approach, in which an interviewer with a check list in hand went with the housewife to the shelf and there took a physical inventory of the brands on hand, would provide an accurate answer to the question asked which would be unlikely to be obtainable by the survey approach alone.

A number of different newspapers conduct annual studies of the usage of different types of products and relative brand standing in their markets. The questionnaire typically asks: *Do you use (name of product)?* If the answer is "Yes," this is followed with: *What brand do you use?* Observational studies made in the same markets in which such "surveys" are made uniformly disclose two strong tendencies in the direction of inaccuracy. First, the proportion of families claiming to use some product types is inflated. This is indicated by inability of families claiming to use the product to produce it or to explain or recall how it happens that the product is not on hand in the home. Second, the brand detail produces a sharp inflation in the claimed usage of the better-known brands and a sharp understatement of the claimed usage of lesser-known brands, especially those in the cut-price categories.

An observational check in one major market made for the Johnson's Wax organization disclosed actual usage slightly less than half as high as was claimed in a study of the type referred to above. This particular approach, in which the product usage is determined by observation, is sometimes called a *pantry check*. In such a case, observation is not completely accurate either. Some products and/or brands of high usage frequency which are usually on hand may have "just run out," hence fail to show up in the check to their true usage extent. In contrast, products of low usage frequency or brands tried and considered unsatisfactory sit almost forever on a pantry shelf, awaiting their opportunity to inflate an observational brand-share total!

In premium and promotional tests, it is not uncommon to use observation to record total traffic past a display; the number out of that total who stopped to read the display or other sign; the number who physically handled the merchandise or premium; and the number who actually purchased. In the absence of data on traffic count, which is obtainable primarily by observation, an evaluation of the pulling power of two or more promotional approaches is difficult except over a substantial period of time.

The use of mechanical recorders connected to radio or television sets constitutes a form of observational research. Those recorders show exactly when the set was turned on, to what station or channel it was tuned, etc., far more accurately than the same information could be secured by the recall of members of the family. (Of course there is no assurance that anyone was in the room listening to the station or channel, but that simply constitutes one of the disadvantages of the recorder approach. It is better to have an *accurate* tally of sets tuned, developed by observation, than to have a "guesstimate" based on variable recall.)

The observational approach is often used in shopping interviews in marketing research. A manufacturer who wanted to know why his sales were declining engaged a marketing-research firm to make shopping interviews among a group of dealers. In some of those shopping calls, the interviewer (who was just another shopper or potential customer, as far as the dealer knew) asked to see an appliance specifying the manufacturer's brand name. In other calls, no brand name was specified. This study disclosed that a strong effort was being made by retail clerks to switch the sale to a competitive appliance, which was running a contest with an expensive "vacation for two" prize which had been heavily promoted to the wives of retail clerks as well as to the clerks themselves!

ADVANTAGES OF OBSERVATIONAL TECHNIQUE

Let's review briefly some of the advantages which make this approach a useful addition to the marketing research man's kit of technique tools. The first advantage is the increased accuracy which can be developed through observation when soundly planned and well executed. The pantry check mentioned above illustrates this advantage. A second advantage is a tendency to reduce the influence, and therefore the possibly biasing effect, of the interviewer. In a survey approach, an interviewer can influence replies by many such factors as tone of voice, emphasis, etc. Reference to the classic example in which an interviewer with prohibitionist leanings reported liquor as an influence in relief cases at a far higher level than other interviewers without such a bias discovered is instructive here. A well-trained field worker using the observational approach typically has no physical contact with the "respondent," hence is not likely to intrude into the research and exert a bias in any direction.

The fact that bias by the interviewer is less in the case of the observational approach does not imply that actual error by the field worker may be considered to be eliminated by shifting to observation as a research technique.

Another advantage of observation is that it can be confined to physically observable actions, hence get behind the generalizations which many survey questions tend to develop as to what the respondent *usually* does or *says* she does. Coupled with the survey approach, observation often extends both the usefulness and accuracy of that approach. Consider a research project in which General Mills, Inc., sought to measure the influence, in the purchase of certain specific brands of ready-to-eat cereals, of various children's premiums and child-audience TV shows. An observer was stationed in a supermarket. Interviews were conducted with shoppers immediately after they had been *observed* purchasing the brands of cereal being studied. That interviewing situation was far more likely to provide a meaningful picture of the influence of premiums, etc., on the purchase than would a call at the same shopper's home a couple of weeks later.

Consider the elements in the above situation which contribute to increased accuracy. In the first place, the interview was sharply focused on a *specific, recent,* and *actual* purchasing experience. This eliminates the tendency toward generalization, which fuzzes up much marketing research data gathered by the survey approach. Further, the interviewer could be sure that the respondent was speaking of a purchase of the actual brand in question. Confusion between brands is far more prevalent than is commonly recognized. As a result, an interview about what influence, if any, the premium offered on a Wheaties package had on the most recent purchase of that cereal occasionally produces a great deal of information all of which adds up to the fact that the respondent was thinking and talking about her last purchase of Cheerios! Finally, the time interval between the specific stimulus of the purchase ("Mom, bring home a box of Wheaties from the store, will you?") and the purchase itself is reduced to a minimum, which makes it possible to pick up some reasons and influences which would have been forgotten a day or so later.

Another characteristic of observational data, under some recording conditions, is that detailed analysis is made possible which extends factual information into new areas. Consider the study of shopping practices at the frozen-food counters and cabinets of supermarkets which the Marathon Corporation, a manufacturer of packaging materials, made with a hidden-camera approach. It was possible through analysis and careful timing of the recorded observations on film to establish the amount of time spent in front of the frozen-food counter, the number of items handled, the amount of time spent reading directions, etc. This study led to considerable activity in the redesign of packages for frozen-food products.

CHARACTERISTICS LIMITING OBSERVATIONAL RESEARCH

There are two characteristics of the observational approach which tend to restrict its usefulness in marketing research. The first of these is primarily a cost consideration. In order to observe behavior, it is necessary for the observer to be present where and when the behavior occurs. That time of occurrence often cannot be determined in advance. As a result, much time by observers is often wasted in nonproductive waiting, which tends to increase the total cost per observation. Consider the General Mills, Inc., approach described above. The proportion of total shoppers buying the cereals in question and the rise and fall of store traffic during the working day would both influence the number of interviews which could be made with women whose observed behavior in buying had been recorded. The cost per interview was relatively high.

The other characteristic is more a characteristic of marketing research generally than of the observational technique, yet it should be mentioned at this point. There are relatively few marketing research studies in which observation alone is sufficient to provide the required information. Observation can identify the behavior, but questions are often required to add depth to the meaning of that behavior in terms of its relevance to a marketing problem. Observation might show, for example, that only three men out of ten passing through a commuting railroad station in June wore hats. That quantitative dimension of the problem would have to be supplemented by other information secured by other techniques before the sales obstacles of a manufacturer of hats could be reduced to specific terms. This is the problem: Observation is most useful in conjunction with other techniques. But experience with the approach is limited, with the result that many cases in which observation could be profitably and effectively used to extend the other techniques' contributions are overlooked by marketing research men.

FORMS FOR OBSERVATIONAL STUDIES

Provision for observational data can be included within a questionnaire used in making a survey, as was the case in the Toni study mentioned above. When the entire study or phase of the study is observational in its approach, special forms must be prepared. There are no essential distinctions between the problems involved in preparing forms for recording observational data and the preparation of questionnaires, but some comments on the observational form may be helpful at this point.

The first requisite in a soundly designed form for recording observations is that it provide adequate space. The tendency to use too small a form, or to crowd observations unnecessarily, reduces the value of some observational work. The second characteristic of the observational form is that it be well organized in terms of the particular problem at hand. The flow of observational detail should be clearly marked, so that it requires a minimum amount of backtracking or searching on the part of the observer. Arrows and other devices useful in speeding the recording process should be used where they ease the observer's task. Remember that often the observations peak in time, and speed in recording is essential.

The forms used in observational studies should be developed and pretested with care. One common approach is to make some preliminary observations without a form, using a shorthand or similar notebook to record all characteristics of behavior or behavior which may be relevant. Then the preliminary forms are developed, to provide space for the requisite data. Finally the actual forms are tested under essentially field conditions, to be sure that all required data are secured and that all that can be done to make the recording process fast and accurate is done. In terms of content, one common limitation of many observational

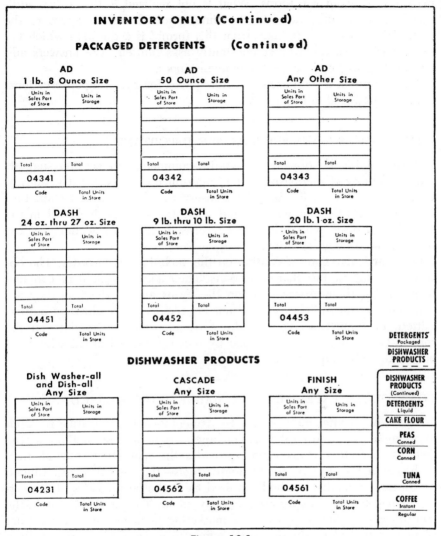

Figure 10.1

forms is their excessive detail. In the step from preliminary to final forms, the research man should ask two questions: Is there any data which I want to record for which the forms do *not* provide space? The second question, which is sometimes overlooked is: What elements of the data on the form *can be eliminated* because they are not actually relevant to the objectives of the study?

The tendency to include excessive detail in a form, whether for a questionnaire or observational study, is often present when inexperienced personnel develop the forms. What is not realized is that every additional item included adds to the time required and therefore to the cost. "What can we eliminate from this form?" is a question which the experienced research worker constantly asks himself. The answers add up to substantial cost savings in many instances.

An example of a form used in a store check for gathering observational data is reproduced in Figure 10.1.

INSTRUCTIONS TO OBSERVERS ARE IMPORTANT

It should be too obvious to require comment, but caution suggests the desirability of emphasizing the importance of careful instructions of observers, in any studies using the observational approach. Detailed attention to spelling out what is and what is not to be included in the record kept often pays substantial returns in increased accuracy of the data gathered by observation.

One particular note of caution on this technique is in order. The observers should be just that—observers. Their activity should be confined to recording their observations on the forms and in the way they are instructed to do so. They should not be asked, nor should they be permitted, to summarize, count, add, subtract, or calculate data on the forms. That work should be done by office personnel about whose accuracy there is no question.

CONTROLLED EXPERIMENT IN MARKETING RESEARCH

The experimental method is a fundamental tool of scientific research in many different disciplines. The application of that method in the field of marketing management provides the marketing research man with one of his most potent technique tools—the controlled experiment. Modifications in that method required to fit the peculiarities of marketing management problems are relatively minor. The parallel between the controlled experiment as a tool of marketing management and the pilot plant as a tool of production management has already been noted. Both tools utilize the same premise: that a small-scale experiment is a useful guide to what may be expected when the experiment is extended in scale.

In both the controlled experiment and the pilot plant, the most important value is essentially the same: The experimental approach contributes small-scale (and therefore limited-risk) experience which is useful in increasing the effectiveness of a larger-scale extension. In production, the pilot plant is helpful in "getting the bugs out" of a product or production technique. In marketing, the controlled experiment provides a factual basis for the decision on whether or not some action should be taken on a larger scale and helps to make the broader-scale activity more productive than it might have been without the lessons learned from the experiment.

EXAMPLES OF EXPERIMENTAL APPROACHES

Probably the most widespread use of the experimental approach in the field of marketing management is in the area of test-market activities. Test marketing typically involves a duplication on a limited geographic scale of the conditions which would obtain in the same geographic units if something were done nationally. This is an extremely important area of marketing research practice. Chapter 25, which is devoted entirely to test marketing, presents a detailed discussion of some problems in experimental work in marketing.

A controlled experiment can be used under many different conditions, with fruitful results. A manufacturer was unable to decide whether to use color comics, rotogravure, or black-and-white newspaper space for an advertising campaign. An experimental approach was indicated. Three markets were chosen, in each of four cells. One group or cell of three markets received color-comic advertising. The second received rotogravure newspaper advertising. The third received black-and-white newspaper advertising. The fourth was a control group of three markets in which there was *no* advertising. The relative effectiveness of the three advertising media was measured, in terms of sales produced with cost as an element in the interpretation, against the control markets which provided an indication of the sales trend under normal or no-advertising circumstances. In an experiment of this type the use of control markets is extremely important, although they are sometimes omitted for reasons of economy. Lacking control-market data, interpretation of a test such as the one described becomes extremely difficult and hazardous.

Of particular significance in a controlled experiment of the type described is provision of an adequate base period prior to introduction of the variable, in each test market. This is sometimes called the pre-promotion period. It indicates whether there were major differences between the markets in different groups in sales of the product being measured, prior to the introduction of the variable, which in the above example was the advertising. It is also vital to continue the test for a substantial period of time. If sales are measured through a panel of stores in which consumer movement is audited, the panel should be maintained for a considerable period of time after the advertising program is terminated. Only in that way can the long-term effects of the experiment be appraised.

Sometimes the primary objective of a controlled experiment in marketing is to determine sales-volume levels. Suppose you ran an experimental campaign or program in markets which represented, according to your best estimate, 4 per cent of the national potential on the product in question. You could then "project" national volume from the experiment by multiplying test-market volume by 25 to determine approximate national volume which would be developed if the experimental situation were expanded to a national scale. Chapter 25 on test marketing will point out some of the hazards in such projections.

The experimental approach is much more useful than is generally recognized. It can be used (and is being used by some forward-looking companies) to answer many questions for which no factual answers now exist. Typical of such questions is this vital one: How much should we spend for advertising? Experimental exploration of the effect of substantially higher and substantially lower advertising expenditure rates on volume and profit often point the way to significant improvements in appropriation-setting procedures.

Another vital area which could be profitably subjected to a great deal more experimental work than it has been in the past is the broad subject of pricing. Would a higher price reduce volume sufficiently to leave the company with lower profit? Would a sharply lower price lead to volume increases which would permit production economies and increased profit? Questions like these can be answered experimentally at relatively slight cost in terms of the potential benefit which the experiments might well deliver.

Retail organizations, especially those operating a chain of stores, are in an especially fortunate position where the experimental method in marketing research is concerned. Will a private brand increase volume and profit in a given commodity class? How wide should the price differential be between a nationally advertised and a store-controlled brand in order to maximize the volume and profit contribution of the former? Erecting a display costs a lot of money, in days of unionized store personnel; does such a display contribute enough additional volume to make it a sound expenditure? Where should the high-traffic departments of the store (like soap and detergent displays) be located, in order to maximize the profit contribution which their traffic makes to an adjoining higher-margin specialty department like personal-care items, dentifrices, etc.? Questions like these can be answered factually relatively easily, when the laboratory which is used to develop the answers—the group of stores in question—is at hand and available.

Experimental evaluation of different premiums and promotional approaches is relatively common. A premium is attached to the package in one group of stores, with a different premium in a second group, and no premium in a third (control) group. Which premium is more effective in stimulating sales of the product in question? The experimental approach provides an answer.

IMPORTANCE OF CONTROLLING VARIABLES

In experimental marketing research, it is extremely important to identify and control all important relevant variables. For example, when an attempt was made to select the best premium to be used to stimulate the sales of Windex, a panel of stores was set up in which different premiums were used. The premiums were rotated from store to store, on a planned and carefully timed schedule. An observational check was made on the number of shoppers exposed to each premium. Without a traffic count, there would be no way to tell whether a premium which sold more units of Windex did so because it was a superior premium or because it was exposed to higher traffic volume.

TECHNIQUE EXPERIMENTS HIGHLY DESIRABLE

One area in which marketing research practice has been relatively backward in its use of the experimental approach is in the evaluation of different marketing research techniques. Consider a specific example. One organization does research on TV commercials by exposing a "captive" audience in a theater to the commercials and then asking them to write down whatever they can recall of what the commercial said about the product. A different organization approaches the same problem—evaluating different commercials—by making interviews in homes the day after the commercial was put on the air in a market. Each organization insists that its particular approach is superior and can marshal the "evidence" on which it rests its case.

Millions and millions of dollars are spent on TV advertising. The commercials used in that advertising are rarely evaluated objectively. Which of the above approaches is a better way to evaluate them? The answer could be provided by a controlled experiment. One advertising agency conducted such an experiment. A series of groups of respondents were exposed to some commercials and immediately thereafter were asked to recall what the commercials said. This was the approach taken by one of the organizations mentioned above. Then there was exposure to an additional group of commercials, with no subsequent recall or interviewing. The following day, a personal interview was conducted at home to see what could be recalled both from the first group and the second group of commercials. This particular experiment was so designed that a comparison was possible between pairs of commercials in the same product class, that is, one commercial for Johnson's Pride versus one for Simoniz' HiLite furniture polish. A comparison was made between the same two commercials among two groups which had been exposed to both and then interviewed; among two groups which had been exposed to both and interviewed the following day; and by the next-day recall of commercials which had been recalled the day before after exposure as well.

The particular experiment in question contributed to that one agency's knowledge of TV research techniques. However, the relatively substantial cost of the research made it extremely unlikely that that agency would share with other competitive agencies the results of their experiments. Those results become part of the agency's stock in trade. One can understand the reluctance of an advertising agency to disclose the findings of experimental research which it paid for. The benefits of that research would ordinarily be confined to the clients of the agency. If the findings were disclosed, the competitors of those clients might also benefit—a highly undesirable development, from the agency's point of view!

NONPROFIT COOPERATIVE RESEARCH PROMISING

There are a number of promising developments which seem likely to accelerate the use of experimental approaches in marketing research. One is the cooperative experimental work being carried on by the Advertising Research Foundation. There are several different commercial organizations which do research on the audience of printed advertisements. Those organizations have different techniques and use different sampling approaches. The ARF sponsored a cooperative experimental duplication of the techniques used by those organizations, on the same issue of the same magazine. This carefully executed and controlled experiment, reported to subscribers to the ARF, made possible the first comparison of techniques. The same group of ads (all those over a certain minimum size in the issue studied) were studied by each method, and a comparison of the results contributed to the knowledge of the advantages and limitations of each technique.

There have been similar contributions to research technique developments as a result of experimental work by governmental organizations. For example, the experimental work by the U.S. Department of Agriculture on discrimination tests and preference ratings of different frozen lemonade concentrates[2] advanced knowledge in the area of product-

[2] *Discrimination Tests and Preliminary Preference Ratings of Frozen Concentrates for Lemonade,* U.S. Department of Agriculture, Bureau of Agricultural Economics, September, 1952.

testing techniques. The published report of test-market operation in the new-product field by the U.S. Department of Agriculture[3] provided a model of a sound approach to controlled experiment in marketing which is likely to contribute to the acceptance of that approach.

Under the sponsorship of a governmental agency, Crossley S-D Surveys, Inc. executed a controlled experiment to determine the effect of various influences on butter sales. Because it illustrates some of the flexibility possible in experimental marketing research, some details of that experiment are relevant here. Seven pairs of stores in a single chain were used for the experiment. Each variable was tested over a four-week period. One factor studied was the location of the butter in the dairy case, with reference to normal traffic flow. Were butter sales higher if consumers reached the butter before they came to margarine, or would the reverse relationship stimulate butter sales more? Another factor studied was the quantity of butter in the case. Specifically, begin with a set amount of butter either in cubic feet or in number of rows or facings; then double that volume. What is the effect on total butter sales? (Since refrigerated space is typically limited, in this instance the loss in sales of the displaced item would have to be considered.) Finally, two different packaging approaches were tested. One was pictorial, the other non-pictorial or "all type."

EXPERIMENTAL RESEARCH RELATIVELY COSTLY

One reason why experimental research is not used more widely in marketing research practice is that such research typically is relatively expensive. Also it often requires a relatively long period of time for execution. In a controlled experiment in marketing, time must be provided for establishing the "normal," or prevariable, level; for introducing the variable; and for continuing the experiment after the variable has been eliminated. Many marketing problem situations have an inadequate time dimension for such an approach.

The point has been made repeatedly in this book that an expenditure for marketing research should be carefully weighed against the profit contribution likely to emerge from that research. This is a viewpoint which tends to restrict much experimental marketing research. It would perhaps be sounder long-run policy to exempt from that method of evaluation and appraisal experimental work, especially in the area of technique development and experiment. It is not too far-fetched to compare experimental technique research in marketing research with pure research in other fields. As distinguished from applied research,

[3] *New Concentrated Apple Juice: Its Appeal to Consumers,* U.S. Department of Agriculture, Bureau of Agricultural Economics, November, 1951.

pure research often requires a longer "pay-off period." The benefits to be derived from pure research are sometimes less definite, less dependable, and less immediate. With its limitations, pure research remains a sound area for the investment of corporate technical-research funds. The soundness of that investment over the long pull has been repeatedly demonstrated in the case of many growth companies. The same kind of long-pull benefit could well emerge from experimental work on marketing research tools and techniques.

Because the potential benefits of the experimental approach are so great, increasing utilization of this technique in marketing research practice can confidently be predicted. As Applebaum and Spears commented in a discussion of this subject in the *Journal of Marketing*, "Controlled experimentation in marketing research is still in its infancy. But it is an infant with a great future."[4]

Further discussion of experimental marketing research will be found in the chapter on test marketing, which is entirely experimental; in the discussion of new-product development in Chapter 23; and in the description of marketing research activities of wholesalers and retailers in Chapter 27.

SUMMARY

1. This chapter introduces two marketing research technique tools which have objectivity as their major characteristic. One is the observational approach; the other is the controlled experiment. Both techniques are used in many areas other than in marketing research, in ways not essentially dissimilar to their marketing applications.

2. Observation is used either alone or in combination with other research approaches. It is often used as a part of a survey. It forms the major part of the fact-gathering function in some phases of panel research, notably including the store-audit approach.

3. Three situations suggest the desirability of considering observation, either alone or integrated with other techniques. The first is the case when no other technique can provide the needed information. The second occurs when other techniques are likely to develop information which is relatively inaccurate. The third is the case in which the importance of the decision involved demands high accuracy, even at relatively low cost.

4. The controlled experiment is widely used in marketing research, especially in test-marketing situations. Chapter 25, which is devoted entirely to test marketing, supplements the discussion of experimental research presented in this chapter.

5. Controlled experiment is used less than it could be and should be in marketing research. Especially promising are the areas of experimental work

[4] William Applebaum and Richard F. Spears, "Controlled Experimentation in Marketing Research," *The Journal of Marketing*, January, 1950, p. 505.

in technique development and technique evaluation and validation. The high cost of such work is one barrier to its expanded use. The tendency of organizations to keep their experimental findings to themselves, with the result that duplicated experiments are carried on continually, is another.

6. Cooperatively sponsored experimental work, with a nonprofit organization or some governmental unit executing the research, is one approach which appears to be increasingly important.

QUESTIONS

1. How would you describe the observational approach and the experimental technique? What outstanding common advantage do these two research tools have?

2. When would you say the use of the observational approach is strongly indicated?

3. What is a *pantry check?*

4. What are the advantages offered by the observational approach? And what are the limiting characteristics of observational research?

5. What is meant by the term *base period?* What is the importance of the base period in the controlled experiment?

6. Can you think of any limitations involved in using the experimental technique?

CHAPTER 11

Practical Aspects of Sampling in Marketing Research Practice

In Chapter 5, which introduced the subject of sampling, a number of the more important basic sampling concepts were introduced. Against the background provided by those concepts, two different sampling approaches were reviewed in step-by-step detail. Space in that chapter did not permit a discussion of the relative advantages and disadvantages of the two approaches. This was so in part because such a discussion must of necessity be a relatively long one. It requires a review and evaluation, from the standpoint of marketing research practice, of a major controversy in the field of sampling methods to which many thousands of words have been devoted in books and professional journals.

PROBABILITY VERSUS JUDGMENT SAMPLING

One of the approaches described in Chapter 5 was quota sampling. The other was area sampling. The difference between those two approaches involves much more than a mere matter of nomenclature; it involves a basic and fundamental difference in approach to sampling. A quota sample is an example of a *judgment* sample. An area sample is an example of a *probability* sample. A comparative discussion of area and quota sampling therefore plunges us into the heart of the judgment–versus–probability sampling controversy.

The idea that there is some kind of sampling which is *not* probability sampling is likely to be confusing to the student, and with reason. As Chapter 5 pointed out, probability is the heart and soul of sampling theory. The literature of sampling theory is extremely extensive. That literature develops the theory of sampling primarily along mathematical lines. The theory of sampling in turn rests on the broad foundation of mathematical-probability theory.

In Chapter 5 it was pointed out that a value from a sample *tends to approximate* the same value as it exists in the total population. The presence of sampling variations which reflect the influence of chance alone results in sample values that tend to fluctuate about the true value as it exists in the total population. Much of the theory of probability and, in turn, much of the theory of sampling are concerned with measuring the range of that fluctuation. To put it in marketing research terms, assume a sample study reveals that out of 1,000 housewives interviewed, 212, or 21.2 per cent, are gainfully employed outside the home. Suppose that study had been made within a city in which there were altogether 100,000 housewives. Suppose further that, simultaneously with the first study, all 100,000 of those housewives had been interviewed, that is, that a complete census of them had been made. What proportion of that total population, or universe, of housewives was gainfully employed outside the home?

That question could not be answered *exactly* without having the results of the complete census as a source. However, sampling theory does make it possible (with one very important "if" noted below) to set an upper and lower limit within which the answer you *would* get *if* you interviewed all 100,000 housewives would fall. Using mathematical approaches described later in this chapter, the marketing research man responsible for this study could report that if the full 100,000 housewives had been interviewed, somewhere between 1,733 and 2,507 of them, that is, between 17.3 and 25.1 per cent of them, would have been found to work outside the home.

FUNDAMENTAL NEED FOR RANDOMNESS

Now for that extremely important "if" mentioned above. The marketing research man could so report with confidence *only* if the sample of 1,000 housewives interviewed were a *true probability sample of all the housewives in the city!*

This is the case because the mathematical formulas which are used to interpret data developed by sample studies are based upon the assumption that the sample in question was a random sample, in which every sampling unit had an equal chance of being included. If the sample were not random, then one of the basic assumptions used in developing the formula would not apply and the formula itself *could not validly be used* to estimate the range above and below the sample value within which the true, or full-population, value could be expected to fall.

In a nonprobability sample, there are biases present—and particularly the bias of sample selection. Remember that bias cannot be measured. Therefore, in addition to the mathematical and measurable variations resulting from chance alone (which are largely a function of the size of the sample, that is, the number of interviews, etc.) there are other unmeasurable variations between the sample value and the true value.

What does this mean in practice? Sticking to the example quoted above, suppose that the sample of 1,000 interviews was a judgment or quota sample. If you were the marketing research man interpreting the findings of that survey to your boss who had paid for it, what could you say? Could you say with confidence that the proportion of housewives working outside the home was between 17.3 and 25.1 per cent? If you were honest, you could *not*. To make that statement truthfully, you would have to know that every housewife out of the 100,000 had an *equal chance of being included* in the 1,000 you surveyed. In the absence of true randomness, there would be present in your sample study a respondent-selection bias (and perhaps other biases as well) which would have to be added to the chance fluctuations in setting the upper and lower limits within which the total-population value could fall. Since bias cannot be measured, the variation between the sample value and the true, or full-population, value *cannot be estimated* except in the case of a probability sample.

To provide a more authoritative statement of this vital and significant point, here is how Robert Ferber puts it:[1]

> The use of this terminology places the need for random selection in its proper perspective, as the implicit and basic requirement of all sampling techniques whose sampling error can be estimated. The importance of random selection derives from the fact that the standard-error formulas used to compare the relative desirability of various sampling techniques are predicated upon this basic sampling assumption of universal equal probability of selection. What this means in practical terms is that *if the sample is selected in an arbitrary manner, the sampling error in the estimate cannot be estimated irrespective of the sampling technique employed*. Consequently, there is no way of evaluating the reliability of estimates based on samples constructed by arbitrary selection.

TREND TO PROBABILITY SAMPLING

Maintaining our historical approach in this sampling discussion, we might note that the judgment sampling approach was "standard operating procedure" in marketing research practice before World War II. George Gallup's advance prediction of the scale and direction of the *Literary Digest* poll's error, for example, was based on a quota (judgment) sample. Much effective marketing research in the prewar period used the same approach.

The major shortcomings in judgment sampling as then practiced be-

[1] Robert Ferber, *Statistical Techniques in Market Research*, McGraw-Hill, New York, 1949, p. 69. (Italics Ferber's.) This book, a most important reference source for mathematical and statistical tools useful in marketing research, belongs in the basic library of every serious student in the field.

came apparent during and after World War II. The letter by Theodore Brown quoted in Chapter 5 tells how the increase in such limitations became apparent. The kaleidoscopic changes in the location and characteristics of the population and in the income-distribution pattern and other social factors led to increasingly great inconsistencies in quota-sampling studies.

By the early 1950s, probability sampling had been almost universally accepted as the more accurate approach to sample surveys. By that time, for example, virtually all sample surveys of the Census Bureau had been shifted to a probability basis. So had the studies made by the U.S. Department of Agriculture and other governmental units. Many surveys in the commercial marketing research field, notably including audience studies sponsored by advertising media, also used a probability sample. The primary reason for the spectacular growth in the acceptance and use of probability sampling has already been identified: the fact that such a sample makes it possible to estimate the reliability of a sample result with accuracy and confidence.

At that point the battle in the field of statistical theory ended. Probability samples emerged with a clear-cut victory over judgment samples. But at that point, too, statistical theory and marketing research practice took different paths. In marketing research practice today, the use of quota samples continues to be common. If it were not for the current and continuing usefulness of quota sampling, there would be no justification for devoting to it the space and attention it has received in this book. To understand why (and, above all, *how*) marketing research practitioners today use judgment samples (which have been repeatedly demonstrated, to the satisfaction of experts in sampling theory, to be essentially inferior to probability samples) it is necessary to review the limitations of quota sampling and the steps that are taken in practice today to overcome those limitations.

LACK OF REPRESENTATIVENESS IN QUOTA SAMPLES

Because it lies at the core of so much criticism of quota sampling, this limitation deserves particular attention. As quota sampling was carried on in the late 1930s, the selection of individual respondents was made entirely by the interviewer. That resulted from the fact that each interviewer had almost complete freedom of choice as to which specific respondents with the quota-specified characteristics he or she would interview.

For a specific example, consider the Pekin survey described in Chapter 5. The interviewer working on the survey in Boston, Mass., had a *quota* of thirty interviews to make. She was told that three of them should be with high-, six with upper-middle-, twelve with lower-middle-, and nine with low-income housewives. Definitions of those groups were provided for her guidance. Within that big city, therefore, the respondent could make her selection of thirty respondents. Since her compensation for interviewing was unaffected, she would naturally tend to interview those respondents easiest for her to interview. The respondents she chose might include her own mother, the next-door neighbor, an aunt across town, the lady who ran the corner grocery store, and so on. The interviews if spotted on a map would tend to be clustered around her house. This was obviously far from a random choice of respondents.

Ideally, the chosen respondents should (and were usually intended to) represent as close as possible an approximation of a random sample of respondents with the desired characteristics. Yet few quota samples in the 1930s would qualify as even approximately random. How closely that ideal was approximated would depend on such factors as the quality of the experience, training, instruction, and supervision of the interviewers used on a particular job. Because those four factors often varied widely, both between interviewers on a single study and between the groups of interviewers used on different studies, the quality of different quota samples also varied widely.

Respondent-selection bias, which we are here discussing, can take many different forms. Interviewers tend to classify respondents into lower economic levels than those to which they actually belong. This point has been demonstrated experimentally. This means that the quotas from lower economic levels are actually filled with respondents of higher economic status. That in turn means that the lower economic strata are underrepresented. As a reflection of the same influence, quota samples in which there is interviewer selection of respondents often include a substantially higher proportion of respondents whose education progressed beyond the grammar-school level than a random sample would be expected to provide. This could represent a result of nonrandom respondent selection; it could also reflect a tendency on the part of respondents to exaggerate their own educational attainments.

EXAMPLES OF OTHER BIASING INFLUENCES

There is also a marked tendency for quota samples to underrepresent extremes around the breaking point of sample cells, or the central values, depending on the particular situation. To illustrate, consider the interviewer whose quota included a specified number of interviews with owners of small farms (that is, those of 15 acres or less) and another number of interviews with owners of medium-sized and large farms. Suppose she chose a farm at which to make an interview, in the expectation that it would be a small farm and a part of her small-farm quota. When the interview was completed, she learned that the farm included 18 acres, hence was a medium-sized farm in terms of her classification data. Would she throw away that interview? Of course not. She would simply credit it to that part of her quota applying to medium-sized farms and move on to the next interview.

Thus the medium-sized-farm quota would tend to include more farms near the 15-acre point and fewer larger farms than a truly representative sample would include. If the quota is of individuals by age, using three age groups (under twenty-five, twenty-six to thirty-five, and thirty-six and over), the tendency of many interviewers is to choose respondents who are clearly within the age group. This produces a sample in which the lower age group includes a disproportionate number of young respondents, while the upper age group would include a substantial overrepresentation of those who were clearly well over thirty-five. The middle age group would tend to include those near the central value, who unmistakably were between the two breaking-point ages.

In the case of interviews made in homes, there is a tendency for the sample to be biased and unrepresentative because certain types of families and individuals are home most of the time, while others are rarely home. For example, the mother of three children all under school age is much more likely to be at home at the time of a daytime interview than a woman who with her husband constitutes a two-member adult family in which both members work during the day. Two families at extremes in terms of the proportion of time they are home do not have an equal chance of being included in the sample. The significance of this particular biasing influence lies in the fact that those families usually at home and more likely to be interviewed differ in a number of key marketing characteristics from families less likely to be at home.

The tendency of interviewers to avoid the lowest-income neighborhoods, especially in big-city interviewing, and to stay out of neighborhoods consisting primarily of members of some racial or other ethnic group which the interviewer happens not to like is a further example of respondent-selection bias.

CHARACTERISTICS OF AN IDEAL QUOTA SAMPLE

There is a substantial body of literature which is sharply critical of quota sampling and of quota samples. The above comments could perhaps be included. Despite that criticism, marketing research practitioners continue to use quota samples extensively. How are we to explain this paradox? Does it mean that marketing research practice is refusing to accept or is resisting a major advance in technology? Or is the controversy about probability-versus-quota sampling actually less black-and-white than much of the literature indicates?

The answer lies in the latter direction. It is true that there was a very wide gap between a quota sample in any theoretical or ideal sense and some quota samples used in practice, especially during and prior to World War II. But this important point is often overlooked: Much of the criticism of quota samples is focused on the shortcomings which develop in practice rather than against an ideal quota sample. The target of the criticism, in fact, was more often than not the gap just mentioned rather than quota sampling itself. Marketing research practitioners are keenly aware of the sampling controversy. Many of them participated vigorously in it. When they use quota samples today, those samples have been planned to eliminate the major sources of criticism by probability-sampling advocates.

In an ideal quota sample, these things would be true. First, the controls selected would be chosen because of their relevance to the objectives of the particular study under consideration. Second, current and accurate data showing exactly how the total population under study was distributed on each control base would be available. Third, the data would be used to plan a sample so distributed into cells that it was exactly proportional on each control base to the population it was expected to represent. Finally, in the execution of the sampling plan the individual sampling units in each cell would be so selected that they would be representative of all units with the cell-defined characteristics. This latter point implies something very closely approximating truly random selection. (In the interests of simplicity, proportionality of a quota sample is assumed in the above comments. Disproportional sampling is discussed later in this chapter.)

As pointed out above, much of the criticism and many of the limitations of quota samples may be traced to the gap between the actual sample and the ideal model described above, in one or more characteristics. Thus one often does not know, before a study is executed, what characteristics will prove to be relevant to the objectives of the study. Thus the selection of controls must rest on a priori judgment in many cases. The 20-20 vision of hindsight sometimes reveals that judgment was a shaky foundation. Second, data on the control bases chosen are often either entirely unavailable or somewhat less than current. Third, the particular respondents chosen within each cell are often not representative of all respondents in that cell. This may be true for any of a number of reasons. The sampling points may be too few; or they may not be representative; or there may be interviewer bias in respondent selection or some other procedural error in the selection of individual respondents.

HOW QUOTA SAMPLING HAS BEEN IMPROVED

Of the above limitations of quota sampling, most experienced marketing research people would rate the third—the biasing effect of interviewer choice of respondents—as the most serious. Much attention has been devoted to ways of eliminating or reducing the respondent-selection bias. In current professional practice in quota sampling, the choice has been largely removed from the interviewer's control.

That has been accomplished in part by providing interviewers with improved and more detailed instructions. Today the instructions given to an interviewer with a quota sample typically specify the exact area within which interviews are to be made. The starting point is usually designated. The route to be followed is described. The exact method of respondent selection is provided. That is usually an entirely objective method, which leaves to the interviewer no freedom of choice.

In effect, this constitutes an introduction into quota sampling of some features of probability sampling. The extent to which those features have been adopted in professional practice is surprisingly high. It is not unusual to find in quota sampling the requirement that the interviewer list dwelling units in a block or section chosen on a judgment basis. Nor is it unusual to find that the dwelling units selected for interviewing from the listing are identified either by a random approach or by a *systematic sampling* approach. In the latter, the starting point for the first interview is often chosen on a random basis, with a specified (and often randomly determined) interval between dwelling units used thereafter.

The lack of representativeness which is created by differences in the extent to which different types of respondent families are at home has also received considerable attention. That problem is now usually reduced in one or more of several ways. The first is to use several callbacks in an attempt to reduce the nonresponse factor. When this is done, the interviewer is often instructed to check with the next-door neighbor of the specified (not-at-home) respondent, for guidance in time of day or day of week at which that respondent is most likely to be at home.

Another approach distributes the timing of interviewing over weekdays and week ends and over morning, afternoon, and evening hours to improve the representativeness of the sample. Still another is the application of a weighting process developed by Alfred Politz and W. R. Simmons.[2]

Improved methods of classifying families on a socioeconomic scale and more careful instruction and supervision of field interviewers to be

[2] Alfred N. Politz and W. R. Simmons, "An Attempt to Get the 'Not-at-homes' into the Sample without Callbacks," *Journal of the American Statistical Association*, March, 1939, pp. 9–31.

sure the methods are uniformly understood and applied have also helped
to reduce the upward socioeconomic bias mentioned above.

SIMPLIFIED DESCRIPTION
OF PROBABILITY-SAMPLING PROCEDURES

When a probability sampling approach is used on a national scale,
it represents a formidable undertaking. That formidability tends to obscure the fact that probability sampling per se need not be so complex
or frightening a process as is sometimes suggested by descriptions of it.
Here is a simplified description of probability sampling which is useful
as a springboard for a closer examination of the advantages and limitations of that process:

> The rules for getting a probability sample require neither a mathe-
> matical formula nor complex procedures. For example, to obtain a prob-
> ability sample of 2 per cent of the blocks in a city, one could number
> serially the blocks of a city map, and draw a random number between
> 1 and 50. Assume this random number is 7. Then if the 7th, 57th, 107th,
> etc. blocks are included in the sample and a census is taken of the popu-
> lation residing in these sample blocks, the result would be a probability
> sample of the people resident in the city. A variation in procedure, still
> simple, would be to take, say, a 10 per cent sample of blocks drawn in
> the manner described above, make a complete listing of the households
> in the selected blocks, and include in the sample every 5th household
> from this listing. Again, the result would be a 2 per cent probability
> sample of people. These are illustrations of probability samples.[3]

As the above comments suggest, the application of a probability
approach is relatively easy when the sample is of a restricted geographical area. This is particularly true where the area in question
is a metropolitan area with block statistics available. However, the
complexities inherent in the probability approach are not fully detailed
in the above description. Those complexities tend to make a probability
sample more expensive than a judgment approach. Hansen and Hurwitz[4]
recognize that fact in the following comments from the same source,
which represent a continuation of the quotation above:

> A cursory examination of the simple steps described above to obtain a
> probability sample might give one cause for wondering why such a simple
> procedure should cost more per interview than the quota or other types
> of judgment sampling commonly used.
> Perhaps a consideration of what probability sampling calls for in the
> way of extra work or inconvenience that is not always called for in the

---

[3] Morris H. Hansen and William N. Hurwitz, "Dependable Samples for Market
Surveys," *The Journal of Marketing,* October, 1949, p. 364.
[4] *Ibid.,* pp. 364–366.

other methods may indicate why one would expect the cost to be higher per interview, that is, higher for a given *size* of sample.

With a probability sample, the enumerator may have to make a number of calls in order to complete an interview. He will have to go to predesignated households to obtain an interview, and is not permitted the discretion of substituting a more accessible household when no one is found at home on first call. He may have to climb stairs and walk through back alleys and go over poor roads in rural areas in order to meet the requirements of the probability sample. The rules for obtaining a probability sample, though they may appear to be arbitrary to the enumerator, must be adhered to closely if one wants to be sure that an unbiased cross-section of the population is covered, and wants to be able to measure the amount of sampling variability in the results.

Another cause for the additional cost in the probability sampling illustrated above is the need for designating the sample blocks and for listing all of the households in these blocks. From these lists the sample required is drawn.

In a quota or judgment sample one faces the risk of not obtaining the appropriate representation of the persons not at home on first call, or of persons living in the relatively harder-to-get-at places, or of any class which is inconvenient or which in the judgment of the enumerator should not be included in the sample. One pays added costs in a probability sample to get the proper representation of classes of the population for which it is impractical to set separate quotas or to depend on the judgment of the enumerator to obtain the proper representation. . . .

. . . Let us consider some of the main aspects of the additional costs that may be involved in a probability sample if the particular sampling methods described above were followed.

One cost is the objective designation of the sample. In the sample design described above, this includes numbering the blocks on a map and listing the households on the selected blocks, and selecting the sample households from this list. Next is the cost of interviewing and of following up households to the point where interviews are obtained from substantially all of the designated households. In the Census Bureau it is usually assumed that if the required information is obtained from more than 95 per cent of the designated households one is entitled to feel fairly secure in assuming that the sample was taken in conformance with sampling theory, even though assumptions may be necessary for the remaining 5 per cent. It has been found that for some purposes trouble arises even when making assumptions for only 5 per cent. A third cost is involved in careful supervision and checking to insure that the specified steps are carried out substantially as specified.

FIELD-WORK COSTS OF PROBABILITY SAMPLING

Hansen and Hurwitz provided an indication of the cost of probability sampling in the same article, citing Census Bureau experience. In considering the following comments, note first, that there have been changes in cost levels since 1947; second, that the Census Bureau has an advantage over commercial marketing research organizations in its ability to use the force of law to compel response; and third, that comparing the cost of work done by governmental employees with that of work done by independent contractors has some booby traps reflecting government–private industry compensation differentials. A tendency for marketing research questionnaires to be somewhat longer than Census Bureau schedules should also be noted. With these limitations in mind, the following comments are of interest:

> There are numerous illustrations in the work of the Census Bureau of the cost of these procedures. As one example, in about 40 surveys of population and dwelling unit characteristics for individual cities taken during 1947, the average cost per household was approximately $2 including both field and office costs. This was for a survey in which the interview could be with a responsible member of the household rather than with a specified individual. Each city involved about 3,500 interviews. In these surveys, the schedule was a relatively simple one. In other surveys, where the schedule is more complex, or if a more complex sampling procedure is used, the average cost per household may run from $3 to $6, or considerably higher. Note that in these higher cost surveys involving long interviews the additional cost required in using a probability sample rather than a judgment sample is less, since the costs of selecting the sample and of calling back becomes smaller in relation to the cost of interviewing.[5]

In the controversy about the relative merits of probability sampling versus quota sampling, the probability case was argued primarily by individuals who approached it from a background of statistical theory. Various individuals in governmental agencies, notably including the Census Bureau, made important contributions to the evidence supporting the probability approach. To some extent, the differences in viewpoint between the probability and quota-sampling advocates may be traced to two important differences between the two groups. The first was the different training and background of the individuals concerned. The second was the difference in the types of problems which the two groups faced and to which they applied their sampling philosophy.

A DISSENTING VIEWPOINT ON PROBABILITY SAMPLING

Drawing on a background which included extensive practical experience with sampling applied to problems essentially similar to those faced daily in marketing research, Clyde W. Hart, Director of the National Opinion Research Center, developed a rather sharply dissenting

[5] Ibid., p. 366.

viewpoint on probability sampling. He presented his views at a meeting of the Chicago Chapter of the American Marketing Association. The following summary of his comments, based on stenographic notes made at the time of his talk, has not been edited by Dr. Hart.

Dr. Hart began by pointing out that his viewpoint was that of an administrator rather than a statistician. He registered the view that quota sampling should not be discussed solely from the standpoint of statistical theory. It was his feeling that many other nonstatistical problems are involved in a balanced consideration of the subject. He commented:[6]

> While sampling theory is extremely important, I think that it is also important to consider other aspects of the whole process of research before attempting to attain the ultimate refinements from the sampling standpoint.
>
> The relative merits of different sampling designs cannot be argued solely on the basis of mathematical criteria. The practitioners of quota sampling have not been loath to publicize the shortcomings of their method, particularly with reference to the problems arising in field work. This leaves quota sampling somewhat unfairly exposed to criticism from the proponents of area sampling. But experience with area sampling has been so limited in market and opinion research that the *practical* difficulties of implementing this type of sampling design are not so well known and have not been so effectively advertised.
>
> At NORC we have always worked with quota samples and we have constantly strived to improve the bases of stratification. But we have also experimented with random and area (or "probability") sampling, using for this work the sampling designs set up by the Bureau of the Census, the leading advocates of area sampling. From this work we have concluded that *if* the universe being sampled is "area-ly" distributed like the population of the United States, *if* you can't determine the relevant variables for use in stratification, *if* there are too many variables for operating purposes, *or if* the relevant variables cannot be adequately defined, then the area sample is the superior design. Most of the problems in the work done by the Census Bureau are of this nature. But even when these conditions prevail, the practical difficulties in administering area sampling are so great that area sampling cannot be given an unqualified decision.

PRACTICAL DIFFICULTIES IN PROBABILITY SAMPLING

Dr. Hart summarized NORC experience in probability sampling work by spelling out in detail some of the practical difficulties involved:[7]

[6] Clyde W. Hart, in a talk to the Chicago Chapter of the American Marketing Association, Nov. 25, 1947.

[7] *Ibid.*

Let me make these practical difficulties more specific:

a. There is no wholly random method for sampling the population of the United States. Quotas and judgment are superimposed on the top of the area sampling design even if, as the men in the Census contend, the choice of respondents within sub-cells is random and the selection of sub-cells is, within limits, random. And in the work done by the Census, more time and money is available than would be available in the case of private businesses.

b. The assertion has been made that there is no need to make a survey if you know perfectly the relationships of the variables used in stratification to the variable you wish to measure in your study. That is if you had all the information necessary for completely adequate stratification, you would automatically have your answer. But even if the distribution of all your variables is known, you still may have to do a study if your objective is the isolation of relationships or dependencies. (I use the latter word to avoid the confusion of causation with statistical covariation.)

c. Expenses are tremendous. Take the question of maps: In the first place, the work involved as a preliminary to your actual sampling is large even if actual maps were always available. But maps contain inaccuracies and they soon become out of date; and there is no way of preventing this difficulty. In a study we made in Cincinnati, fully one-fourth of the maps used were in error, and we have had similar difficulties in a study now going on in Baltimore. We have found it necessary to check and build new maps even before we send out interviewers for the *preliminary* enumeration which precedes the actual opinion survey. In one case, the supervisor had to spend 95 per cent of his time on this stage, and very little was left for anything else. I feel that these difficulties have not been fully brought out.

d. It has also been said that interviewers can be checked better when an area sampling design has been used. . . . I cannot accept this contention as valid because if the supervisory time spent on "address control" in area sampling were spent on *supervision* of interviewers, field work might be of distinctly higher quality under quota sampling than under area sampling. At the present time we are studying the biases which arise in the interviewing process in quota sampling. In area sampling, also, interviewers do make errors. For example, in the preliminary enumeration (listing), it is hard to devise instructions which will be unambiguous. The apartment over the garage or the dwelling in the middle of the block are often missed. It is even hard to define a dwelling unit adequately. Not only have we found errors at this stage in area sampling, but we believe that the opportunity for successful cheating by interviewers is greater than on almost any other phase of survey work. Moreover, a specified respondent must be located and interviewed even if the establishment of rapport is difficult. He may be so suspicious that you may never get the information you want. Besides the things I have mentioned, there are many other errors in area sampling that have not been publicized.

e. While the area sample is superior according to mathematical logic, the mathematical-error formulas cannot always be applied rigorously even here.

In his concluding remarks, Dr. Hart said:

I do not think we should be swept off our feet by the advocates of area sampling. We must approach the problem critically as an operating problem, and we must consider the purposes of the survey, the value of added accuracy, and the costs and time involved if we are to make sensible selections of sampling design.

PROBABILITY SAMPLING ISN'T ALWAYS POSSIBLE

Let us concede, or in legal terms stipulate, that probability sampling is more accurate than judgment sampling. Recognizing and accepting that fact does not mean that probability sampling will be used exclusively in marketing research practice, nor that it will be used more than judgment sampling. For reasons which are traceable to the nature of the animal, judgment sampling will continue to be an important element of marketing research practice. There are many types of situations in marketing research in which a probability-sampling approach is neither possible nor practical.

This is a point which deserves some emphasis. The marketing research man who uses judgment sampling extensively is not necessarily unfavorably disposed toward probability sampling. He may just have a disproportionate number of problem situations which cannot be solved by probability sampling. Let's consider some specific examples for the perspective they provide on this controversial area.

Panel research is one prime example. MRCA, in cooperation with and financially supported by the U.S. Department of Agriculture, made a determined effort to set up first a New York metropolitan area and then a national consumer-purchase-record panel using a probability sample. That effort failed. The proportion of families chosen on a probability basis whose cooperation could be first enlisted and who could then be trained and motivated to provide the necessary information continually, accurately, and on time was relatively low. The use of a judgment sample in that situation is necessary. It is also quite effective, in terms of the practical realities of marketing research requirements.

Still within the panel area, consider the A. C. Nielsen Co. Food Index. Can the sample of stores providing data for which large manufacturers spend millions of marketing research dollars annually be selected on a probability basis? The answer is that it cannot. For years, Nielsen succeeded in operating a successful research service of the retail-panel type in the food field although all three of the largest food chains in America—A&P, Safeway, and Kroger—refused to permit a Nielsen audit of their stores. Subsequently Kroger permitted Nielsen's men to audit some stores. Considerable autonomy at branch and district levels was a characteristic of the Kroger operation. This meant that not all Kroger districts could be tapped for Nielsen's sample. Obviously no probability sample is possible if the largest chains exclude themselves. A judgment sample is the only alternative. Carefully planned and effectively administered, such a sample provides useful information.

Another point to be noted is that in a great deal of marketing, distribution of sampling elements in any population is very heavily skewed. This means that a very small proportion of all sampling units represent a relatively large proportion of total volume. This pattern is found among retail outlets; among consumers of many types of products; among the customer distribution of many manufacturers; and so on. A probability sample would be likely to include large and small stores, high-volume and low-volume customers, etc., in roughly the proportion they represent of total store or customer populations. What is important in many marketing research problems is to develop adequate representation of the high-volume stores, customers, etc. While this can sometimes be achieved by disproportionate or double sampling (both discussed later in this chapter), a carefully stratified judgment sample is often a much more efficient approach to such a problem.

It does no good to have a probability sample of respondents, if there is a high refusal rate, "not at home," or similar factor to create a gap between the initial and (theoretically, at least) probability sample and the actual delivered sample. In Census Bureau work, replies can often be required under threat of legal penalities. In marketing research, the cooperation of the respondent is usually required. Some respondents just won't cooperate. And some marketing research by its nature requires so much from a respondent in the way of cooperation that no probability approach is practical.

As an example, consider a comparative product test of a consumer product along the lines of specific examples presented in Chapter 22. This involves cooperation from a consumer household in following instructions, serving a food product or using some other type of product, noting and reporting reactions, etc. Many households will participate; but many others "can't be bothered." The assumption that the households that do cooperate are like those which do not is open to grave question. What does a marketing research man do in such a situation? He does the best he can—he gets as good a sample as possible, need for cooperation considered. He is careful to see that it is as representative as possible. He identifies characteristics of participating families, so that he can, if necessary, weight the results to adjust the test-panel sample to the proportionality of the total population.

For another example, consider much advertising research. A technique requires that a housewife sit down and devote a considerable period of time to reading a number of advertisements, discussing them with an interviewer, and so on. Such research is impossible without the cooperation of the respondent. You're the research man, and that's your assignment. Would you use a probability sample? Of course not—you'd do the best sampling job you could within the limitations inescapably presented by the demands of your technique.

As a last and important example, consider the whole broad field of qualitative and "motivational" research, which is the subject of Chapter 26. What is required is a group of respondents who will give an interviewer who is (the supervisor of the research hopes!) a stranger to them a very substantial amount of time. An interview running from one to two hours is no rarity in such research. Why should a respondent give such generous cooperation to a stranger? In the case of a probability sample, how could you extract such cooperation? The answer is that you could not—that you would have to do as good a sampling job as possible, circumstances considered. The success of different organizations specializing in qualitative research suggests that their inability to do probability sampling has not resulted in limitations greater than the contributions of their techniques could outweigh.

All aspects of marketing research practice are subjected continually and constantly to experimental evaluation. The search for improvements is never-ending. The area of sampling is no exception. The controversy about judgment–versus–probability sampling stimulated a wholesome and desirable reappraisal of the strengths and limitations of sampling approaches previously used. Out of that controversy, some marked improvements and a great increase in awareness of the importance of sound sampling emerged. These were important developments. They were steps on a path to higher levels of technical competence in marketing research. Further steps may be confidently predicted.

SUMMARY OF THE CURRENT STATUS OF JUDGMENT AND PROBABILITY SAMPLING IN MARKETING RESEARCH PRACTICE

The material presented up to this point indicates the nature of the controversy about the relative merits of judgment and probability sampling. The suggested readings for this chapter will be helpful to those who wish to pursue the subject at greater length. From the standpoint of marketing research practice, these summary comments are in order:

1. Where it is necessary for a marketing research man to make a precise estimate of a population value from a sample, along with a

statement of the reliability of that estimate, probability sampling is necessary. No other sampling approach gives results of known precision objectively established. Judgment sampling rests on a foundation of various assumptions and judgments which are sometimes difficult to defend.

2. Probability sampling is almost always considerably more expensive than judgment sampling. This reflects *cost per interview*, which should not be considered the sole criteria. Cost for a given level of accuracy is often equally important, and such cost comparisons may favor probability sampling.

3. Stimulated in part by attacks of those advocating the probability approach, quota sampling in practice has been improved considerably from the quality levels existing during and prior to World War II. The most important improvements have been those which have greatly reduced or entirely eliminated the factor of interviewer bias in respondent selection. As a result, the randomness of respondent selection in quota sampling has been increased, and the quality of quota samples thereby improved in professional practice.

4. To a considerable extent, the selection of a judgment or probability approach is dictated by the accuracy required in the final sample results. Where a moderate error would not change the action taken on the basis of a research finding, quota sampling is often sufficiently accurate and less expensive. Where a very precise answer is essential, a probability approach is indicated.

Perhaps the most important single observation to be made about this controversy is this: Sampling is *one important part*, but *only a part*, of the marketing research process. It is the net effectiveness of the entire process that is important, rather than of any individual subpart. The most careful sampling plan can produce completely useful or completely useless results, depending on such other factors as the skill, experience, and supervision of field interviewers; the level of competence which participated in the development and pretesting of the questionnaires; and the imagination and intelligence of those who do the analysis, interpretation, and reporting of the research.

INTRODUCTORY COMMENTS ON THE PROBLEM OF DETERMINING SAMPLE SIZE

In the case of any given marketing research problem which involves sampling, this key question must be answered: How big a sample should we use? If there were a single or simple answer to that question, the subject of sampling would be far less complicated than it is.

When you answer that question in the case of a specific question, you execute a complex and difficult process of identifying and weighing a number of interrelated variable factors. In the case of that specific problem, those factors carry different weights; that is, they vary in relative importance. Now move on to the next marketing research problem involving sampling and face the same question again. When you do, you find that some of the factors present last time may be absent; some new ones have perhaps been added; and the relative importance of the factors is often quite different from the preceding problem. This suggests the complexity of this important subject and indicates why considerable attention must be devoted to it in this chapter as well as elsewhere in this book.

It might be well to begin the discussion of the sample-size decision by recognizing two opposing considerations. These are somewhat in the nature of varying *objectives*. One is the influence of *cost*. Of particular significance is the case in which a *practical cost ceiling* exists within which work on a problem must be completed. The other is the influence on sample-size planning of the need for *accuracy*. Those influences are present in most sample-size decisions. Sometimes—as in the case of the Pekin survey described in Chapter 5—a marketing research man begins his sample-size planning with a ceiling on total cost specified in the authorization for work on the study. In such a situation, the question is: How much accuracy can we get for that cost? In another situation— for example, the LIFE study also described in Chapter 5—emphasis was on the need for accuracy in the planning stages, with costs in much the position of a dependent variable.

A specific cost ceiling set before planning on a study began, as in the Pekin example, is undesirable and generally not too frequent in practice. The existence of a *practical cost ceiling* is common in marketing research practice. Planning on sample size much more frequently proceeds from cost toward accuracy than in the opposite direction. Except in the case of studies by the Bureau of the Census, planning to hit a *precise* accuracy criteria is relatively rare.

Planning sample size toward at least an approximate accuracy objective, however, is relatively common in marketing research practice. To indicate the influence of that factor on sample-size planning, let's review briefly the mathematical tools used to measure the accuracy—or the *precision*—of an estimate based on sampling.[8]

---

[8] It is the opinion of the author that an attempt to cover fully the important subject matter of tests of significance within the space limits of an introductory book such as this is likely to result in gross oversimplification. That oversimplification, in turn, may lead to failure on the part of the reader to understand the importance of this vital area. It seems preferable simply to emphasize the importance and complexity of this subject area and to refer interested readers to a source like Ferber's *Statistical Techniques in Marketing Research* (McGraw-Hill, 1949) where tests of significance receive the space and detail they merit.

ILLUSTRATION OF RELATIONSHIP BETWEEN SAMPLE SIZE AND ACCURACY

Let's return now to the example given earlier in this chapter—a sample survey of 1,000 housewives in which 212, or 21.2 per cent, were found to be gainfully employed outside of their home.

The problem is to measure the *standard* error of that *percentage*—21.2 per cent. The formula is:

$$\sigma_p = \sqrt{pq/N}$$

In this formula, p identifies the percentage of housewives who have the *attribute* under study, or employment outside the home; while q identifies the percentage who do *not* have that attribute. The sum of p and q is always 100 per cent, by definition. N is the identification for the *size of the sample,* or the number of cases in the sample, in this case 1,000.

In the case cited, σ_p is 1.29 per cent. The distribution of sample values about the "true value," i.e., of values developed by a series, or succession, of separately drawn samples from the same universe about the value which exists in the entire universe and which would be disclosed by a census, is *normal.* It follows the familiar *normal curve* and the characteristics of that curve as presented in almost every elementary statistics text.

Applying the familiar normal-curve data, this means that in about 68 out of 100 similar samples from the same universe drawn at the same time and in the same way, the sample value would be in the area of 21.2 per cent plus or minus 1.29 per cent, in other words, between 19.9 and 22.5 per cent; in about 95 out of 100 such samples, the sample value would be in the area of 21.2 per cent plus or minus *twice* the standard error, or between 18.6 and 23.8 per cent; and in more than 99 out of 100 such samples, in the range of 21.2 per cent plus or minus *three* times the standard error, or between 17.3 and 25.1 per cent.

This is translated, in the interpretation and reporting of the research, into terms approximately like these: "The chances are about 68 out of 100 that the *true* value in this universe lies between 19.9 and 22.5 per cent; about 95 out of 100 that the true value is between 18.6 and 23.8 per cent; and better than 99 out of 100 that it is between 17.3 and 25.1 per cent."

From this 1,000-interview study, it has thus been established as *practically certain* that the proportion of housewives employed outside the home lies between 17.3 and 25.1 per cent. The study was conducted for a purpose. Is that a narrow enough range within which to pin down the percentage figure? The answer depends on the objectives of the study.

Assume the question was whether or not the employed-housewife part of the market warranted separate advertising attention. That attention might be in the form of special appeals, media particularly well suited to reach them, etc. The information that such a group of housewives represented somewhere between 17 and 25 per cent of the total number of housewives in the market would be likely to be sufficiently accurate to guide the decision on advertising.

LARGER SAMPLES INCREASE ACCURACY

But suppose that it was felt that the range indicated was too wide— that the objectives of the study required that it be narrowed down more precisely. How could that result be accomplished? The answer is relatively simple—by increasing the sample size, i.e., the total number of interviews.

This relationship can be inferred from the formula given above. The size of the sample is the denominator of the fraction under the radical $(\sqrt{})$. Therefore, the larger that figure the smaller the value from which the square root is extracted. It is apparent then that increasing the size of the sample will decrease the size of the standard error, hence narrow the *range* about the *sample* value within which the true value is likely to fall. Because the standard error is a square root, however, the reduction in the error range does not correspond to the increase in the sample size. That is, if the sample size is doubled, the standard error is *not* cut in half; the sample size would have to be increased to *four* times the original figure to accomplish such a reduction. This is illustrated by the standard error which results in the above example when the sample size is increased as shown:

Sample size	σ_p, %
1,000	1.29
2,000	.91
4,000	.65
8,000	.45

Or to translate these figures into the range within the true value may be expected to fall, these values represent the range about the sample value of 21.2 per cent which would exist under the conditions noted:

When the size of the sample in a survey is doubled, not all the costs are thereby increased proportionally. Planning, interpretation, and some other cost elements remain unchanged. However, the field costs of interviewing, etc.; the tabulating costs; and some other cost elements do increase directly with the increase in sample size.

Table 11.1

Sample size.....	1,000		2,000		4,000		8,000	
	Low	High	Low	High	Low	High	Low	High
1σ	19.9	22.5	19.3	22.1	19.6	21.8	20.7	21.7
2σ	18.6	23.8	18.4	23.0	19.0	22.4	20.2	22.2
3σ	17.3	25.1	17.5	23.9	18.4	23.0	19.7	22.7

The above table therefore illuminates a vital area in the sample-size decision. There is an increase in the precision of the sample value, reflected by the narrowing range within which the true value may be estimated to fall, as the sample size is increased. There is also a very substantial increase in the cost of the study—an increase somewhat less than the increase in sample size, but still relatively large—as the size of the sample is increased. *The marketing research man must equate the need for precision in his sample result with the cost of achieving that degree of precision, as against a lesser degree attainable for a lesser cost.*

Attention is again directed to the comment made and confirmed by the Ferber quotation earlier in this chapter. *The above formula can be used to estimate the sampling error only if the sample is a probability sample.* For judgment samples like quota samples, the sampling error cannot be estimated mathematically.

In the above example, the marketing research man derived a percentage figure from sampling data. His problem was one of estimating the range within which the true value existing in the total universe from which the sample was chosen was likely to fall. Remember that in marketing research true value is rarely known. A similar problem occurs in dealing with an absolute value, rather than a percentage. That value might be the mean or average consumption of a product, or mean income or expenditures per family, or some other value. The standard error of the mean would have to be calculated, as explained in any elementary statistics text, and interpreted essentially as the standard error of the percentage was above.

HOW VARIATIONS IN VALUES BEING MEASURED INFLUENCE THE SAMPLE-SIZE DECISION

Other marketing research problems involve the comparison of the significance of two different means, drawn from different samples. For example, suppose that the national average consumption of ready-to-eat cereals in a given year was 5,415 pounds per thousand families or 5.415 pounds per family. Variations in consumption rate in different sections of the country, or in cities of different sizes, would result in different averages for those subsamples. The question of whether such differences are significant can be explored statistically. Ferber presents the formulas involved in his chapter 5 on "The Testing of Hypotheses."

We noted above the influence on the precision of the estimate and on the sample-size decision which resulted from changes in the denominator of the fraction under the radical, that is, the number of interviews. It should be noted also that changes in the numerator of the fraction, that is, in the variation between the p and q values, also enter into the size of the standard error of the percentage and into the sample-size decision.

Let's consider two variations of the example given above to illustrate this point. Instead of the attribute of employment outside the home, assume we are making studies involving two other attributes. Preliminary study of the problem and pilot interviewing suggest that one attribute will be found among about 10 per cent and one among about 50 per cent of the respondents interviewed. In those two cases, the value of pq would be as follows:

10 per cent have attribute, 90 do not: $pq = .09$
50 per cent have attribute, 50 do not: $pq = .25$

The pq values in these two instances show a substantial difference, in the scale of about 2.8 to 1. Given the same denominator under the radical, that is, the same number of interviews, the estimate from the sample value will be more precise in the case of the 10 per cent attribute than in the case of the 50 per cent one. Translated into terms of the sample-size decision, here is what this means: If the particular critical attribute with which the marketing research man is most concerned is shared by about half of all respondents, a larger number of interviews is required to provide an estimate of that value with any given degree of precision than is the case when the attribute is unevenly distributed. The corollary is that the *more uneven the distribution,* i.e., the farther it moves away from a 50-50 distribution in the direction of a 99-1 distribution, *the greater the precision obtainable with a given number of interviews.*

Often the pilot, or testing, phase of work on a research problem provides an indication of the distribution of a particular attribute vital to the purposes of the study. That indication can then be used as an aid in answering the sample-size question.

Where two different attributes with varying distribution, like the 50-50 and 90-10 ones mentioned above, are being explored within the same sample study, standard practice is to make the sample-size decision on the basis of the more evenly distributed attribute. This means that the added precision in the case of the 90-10 attribute is a bonus or safety factor. The above comment assumes that the two attributes are equally important to the objectives of the study. If the 90-10 attribute were the vital one and the other one were secondary in importance, it might be sound practical economy to make the study with the smaller sample required by the 90-10 attribute. It would then be necessary to settle for a lesser degree of precision in the case of the 50-50 attribute. Where no advance knowledge of the distribution of the attribute is available, sample-size planning is usually based on the assumption that there will be a 50-50 distribution of the key attribute. That means that the *maximum* sample size *required to achieve desired precision* is used in planning. Often the actual distribution of that attribute found in the sample is watched as the study progresses. If the attribute proves markedly uneven in its distribution, the size of the sample may be reduced without loss of precision. This is done by terminating the study before the originally planned sample size is reached. Consideration of this possibility in the planning stages of developing the sampling design is usually necessary to permit such sample reduction without a loss in other desirable sample characteristics.

INFLUENCE OF CONFIDENCE LIMITS
ON THE SAMPLE-SIZE DECISION

A third factor affecting the sample-size decision has been suggested by implication in the preceding discussion. This is the influence of *confidence limits* on the decision. Translated into nonstatistical terms, this matter of confidence limits boils down to a subdecision on *how sure one wants to be* that a given sample value is within a specified range of the true value.

Refer back to Table 11.1 above. That table shows that for a sample of 1,000, *one* standard error would embrace a range from 19.9 to 22.5 per cent. From study of normal-curve theory in statistics, we know that the use of a single standard error is likely to include about 68 out of 100 samples. To spell this out a little, assume that a large number of separate samples of the same size were drawn from the same universe in the same way and at the same time. About two-thirds of those samples would be likely to provide a sample value for the attribute in question falling within the 19.9 and 22.5 per cent range. To turn this around, almost one-third of all such samples would be expected to provide a sample value falling *outside* of that range.

Now dropping down to the *two*-standard-error (or 2σ) level, the range widens to embrace the area between 18.6 and 23.8 per cent. This means, as we have already noted, that about 95 out of 100 samples would provide a value in that range. The use of two standard errors is sometimes described as the use of 95 per cent confidence limits. Three standard errors about the value from the sample would define a range within which more than 99 per cent of all those sample values would fall.

ILLUSTRATION OF A CONFIDENCE-LIMIT DECISION

To illustrate the influence of confidence limits in a practical marketing research decision on sample size, let's use an actual example. A large manufacturer of a line of diversified food products uses many premiums in the child-interest area to aid in the promotion of products consumed by children. Before a premium is used, it is subjected to comparative consumer-acceptance research among a sample of 200 children of specified ages. The research procedure used is standardized and de-scribed in a standard-practice manual. That manual specifies that the preference between two premiums compared must be at least 60-40, or the sample size must be increased in accordance with a formula in-cluded in the manual.

Working the standard-error formula above with p as 60 per cent and q as 40 per cent, with the sample size N as 200, provides a σ_p value of 3.464 per cent. Here is the picture of what that means in the case of an actual premium comparison in which premium A was preferred by exactly 60 per cent (or 120) of the children interviewed and premium B was preferred by exactly 40 per cent (or 80):

Table 11.2

	Sample value	1σ	2σ	3σ
Low extreme of value p, or preference for premium A	60.000	56.536	53.072	49.608
High extreme of value q, or preference for premium B	40.000	43.464	46.928	50.392

The "sample-value" column shows the actual results of the survey among 200 children. The other columns show the effect of *decreasing* the value of p successively by one, two, and three standard errors and of *increasing* the value of q accordingly. Before making interpretive comments on this table, it might be well to point out *why* the significance of this particular concept is illustrated by successively decreasing p and increasing q.

EVALUATING A HYPOTHESIS

The problem of the marketing research man in this case is to deter-mine, first, which of the two premiums is preferred. Assuming there is a margin of preference for one over the other, his problem then becomes one of interpreting the indicated preference. Is that a *real* preference, or is it within the range which could result from chance variations in sampling alone. How much *confidence* can he feel in the preference figure resulting from the sample survey?

His *hypothesis* in this case is that *the indicated preference for premium A is a real preference*. He recognizes that a standard error must be applied on *both sides* of a sample value to determine the numerical range within which the normal-curve data apply. In this particular case, however, he is concerned with application of the standard-error figure in only one direction on *each* sample value. He is interested in whether the *decrease* in indicated preference for premium A by increments of standard errors and the *increase* in indicated preference for premium B by increments of standard errors might reverse the preference indicated.

At the 1σ level, he notes that his p value is 56.536 and his q is 43.464. At that point, clearly there is still preference for premium A. At the 2σ level, the range narrows the margin of preference. Now the *lowest* value of p is 53.072, while the *highest* value of q is 46.928. This tells him that in the case of 95 similar surveys out of 100, there would still be a preference for premium A. At the 3σ level, however, the values pass each other and the indicated preference could be transposed.

In terms of the hypothesis stated, considering the margin of preference in the sample (60-40) and the sample size (200), the preference is a real and significant one beyond the 2σ level. It is not significant at the 3σ level. This means that the chances of a similar preference being developed in repeated studies are such that more than 95 out of each 100 such studies could be expected to reflect a preference for premium A.

We could easily state the above conclusion more precisely. We could reduce the significance to a specific number of standard errors by reference to a table of areas under the normal curve. Such a process, at this point, would be completely nonsensical and impractical. Why? Because the sample of children interviewed in this premium research and in all similar studies conducted under the procedure established in the manual is a quota sample—a judgment sample, and not a probability sample. Therefore, the range-of-error formula which we have been applying in this case is *theoretically* inapplicable.

Here is another point at which the theory and practice of marketing research diverge.

SAMPLING ERRORS IN JUDGMENT SAMPLES *ARE* ESTIMATED

The fact that sampling error cannot be measured except in the case of a probability sample has twice been stressed in this chapter.

Theoretically, the truth of that statement is beyond question. However, this is a practical book. We must therefore recognize that *although the formula does not apply, in theory, to a judgment sample, it is applied consistently and continually to such samples in marketing research practice.*

We shall return to this point for more detailed examination after the discussion of sample-size determination is completed. At this point it is sufficient to re-emphasize that sampling error cannot be *measured* except in the case of probability samples. But sampling error in judgment samples can be and is *estimated* in marketing research practice. In that estimation, the same formula used in the case of probability samples is used.

The accuracy of such estimates and their theoretical soundness of unsoundness are open to some question. They are made and used in marketing research practice because many years of work with non-probability samples and the estimation problem have proved beyond doubt to experienced marketing research men that they work very well indeed.

A FURTHER ILLUSTRATION OF CONFIDENCE-LIMIT INFLUENCE ON THE SAMPLE-SIZE DECISION

For a further example of how the confidence limits set exert an influence on the size of the sample required, refer again to Table 11.1 above. Assume that it had been decided that an answer precise within a range from 18.4 to 23.0 per cent would be satisfactory, that is, that an answer plus or minus 2.3 percentage points would fulfill the requirements of precision. The subsequent decision on confidence points would be required. If it were decided that a 95 per cent confidence level (i.e., 2σ) would suffice, the sample size could be set at 2,000; if it were decided that a higher confidence level was needed with the same precision, the size of the sample might have to be doubled to achieve it. Note that the value in the table for 2,000 interviews at a 2σ level and for 4,000 at 3σ level are identical.

BREAKDOWNS PLANNED INFLUENCE SAMPLE SIZE

The next factor which enters importantly into the decision on sample size is the number, type, and characteristics of the breakdowns which are likely to be made from the total sample. Each such subdivision of the sample is a *subsample*. In many practical marketing research situations, the size of the subsamples required are first determined and the size of the total sample then built up or aggregated by combining those sub-samples.

An illustration is provided by a slight variation of the premium-preference problem discussed above. Suppose that one of the premiums under consideration was likely to be stronger in its appeal to boys and the other to be stronger in its appeal to girls. The question as to whether there was a significant preference for either premium within the subsample of respondents of each sex might arise. (Presumably if one premium appealed strongly to boys and the other to girls, *both* might be used.) Recognizing this aspect of the problem in the planning stage, the research man would provide a sufficiently large subsample of boys and another of girls to permit reliance on the indicated preference of the sexes individually. If the requirements in terms of confidence limits, etc., were unchanged from the study described earlier, this would require interviews with 200 boys and 200 girls, for a total sample of 400.

Or suppose the premiums varied in their age appeal. One might be a book, which would be stronger in appeal to children above the age at which reading ability is acquired, while the other might be aimed at the interests of a younger age group. This might call for dependable subsamples in two or more age groups and would similarly require an expanded total sample.

The sample-size decision requires that the marketing research man identify in advance those subsamples, or sample cells, which will be examined individually in the analysis and interpretation of the research. A sufficiently large subsample in each such cell to permit the necessary breakdowns must then be provided. Often this requires disproportionate sampling, discussed later in this chapter.

Figure 11.1 presents an ingenious graphic device which can be used to save time in the process either of approximating sample size or of estimating the standard error of a percentage value in a sampling study. In using this scale, a ruler is placed from the appropriate percentage division of replies in the left-hand scale through the sample-size figure in the center scale. The error limits can then be read in the right-hand scale. Or the chart can be used to determine what sample size would be required to achieve any desired predetermined limit of error, by placing the ruler from the estimated percentage figure on the left-hand scale to the desired error limit on the right-hand scale, and reading the resulting sample-size figure on the center scale.

Note that this scale and the formulas in Ferber to which reference is made elsewhere in this chapter are both based on *random* sampling. The presence of bias, which cannot be measured, introduces variations more extreme, in many instances, than those derived either from the scale or formulas.

SAMPLE   SIZE   CHART

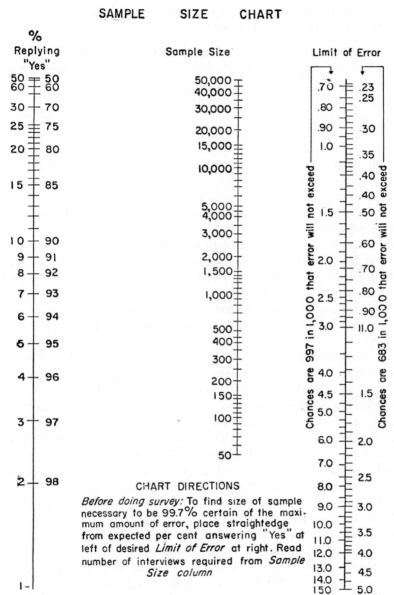

CHART DIRECTIONS

Before doing survey: To find size of sample necessary to be 99.7% certain of the maximum amount of error, place straightedge from expected per cent answering "Yes" at left of desired *Limit of Error* at right. Read number of interviews required from *Sample Size column*

After doing survey: To find error of a percentage replying "Yes," place straightedge from the per cent replying "Yes" at left to number of interviews in *Sample Size* column; read off per cent of maximum error on scale under *Limit of Error* column

Figure 11.1

SOURCE: Adapted from "Let's take some of the gobbledygook out of sampling" by William Reynolds and John H. A. Cross, *Printers' Ink*, February 3, 1950. Reprinted with permission of *Printers' Ink*.

COST CONSIDERATIONS INFLUENCE DECISIONS ON SAMPLE SIZE AND DESIGN

The most important single influence on the size of the sample as well as on the sample design was suggested in the introductory comments on the sample-size decision earlier in this chapter. That influence is the practical-cost ceiling on the research.

A practical marketing research man never loses sight of the vital and fundamental relationship between the cost of a particular marketing research project and the profit contribution that research is likely to make. External research involving sampling, whether of the survey or panel type, is relatively expensive. Therefore, cost considerations play an extremely important role in determining sample size. They influence also the closely related—we might say interrelated—decisions on *sample design* as well.

An example of cost considerations which dominated the sample-size decision has already been presented. In the Pekin example in Chapter 5, the marketing research man had to operate within a cost ceiling which was established before the planning phase of the research was initiated. That same example also illustrated the influence of cost considerations on *sample design,* although the point was not so identified in that chapter.

The sample-design influence was a direct one. For reasons of economy, the marketing research man responsible for the Pekin study decided to eliminate rural and farm interviewing from the study. This represented a redefinition of the population to be studied. In that redefinition cost considerations were of primary importance.

In the design of a sample, the first key decision is a definition of the population, or universe, to be sampled. The second decision is concerned with formulating the strata and cross strata which together constitute the framework of cells into which the sample is divided.

Stratification is almost universal in marketing research sampling. This is true whether the sampling-approach emphasis is on judgment or probability. The most widely used probability sampling approach is area sampling, in which a stratification by areas is involved. Sometimes stratification on other bases, such as city size, age of respondent, socioeconomic or income level, or some combination of such factors is used.

SELECTION OF SAMPLE-DESIGN CRITERIA

Stratification is almost universally accepted as a vital element in sampling in marketing research practice. The need for stratification arises because populations[9] with which marketing research is concerned are complex. Typically such populations are not homogeneous. Random sampling of the type which is possible, e.g., in inspection work in production management, is rarely possible in marketing research.

Instead of a random sample of the whole, marketing research men typically use stratified sampling. The total population is subdivided, or *stratified*, into groups. Random sampling is executed within the groups. In each such stratified group, the population is more nearly homogeneous than in the larger whole. Representation of the various characteristics of the total population is achieved through the combination of the group subsamples into the structure of the whole, or total, sample.

An example from a study of biscuit baking is illustrative. In developing the sample design, previous studies of baking habits were used as guides. Among a sample of more than 3,300 housewives, 86.4 per cent reported that they bake biscuits. Of those interviewed who bake biscuits, 46.4 per cent reported a frequency of biscuit baking which exceeded once a week. In a group of Southern cities, the latter percentage was 75.6 per cent; in the remaining cities, it was near the 35 per cent level. Sample planning to provide a sufficiently large group of the two types of biscuit bakers—the high-frequency Southern housewives, versus the relatively low-frequency housewives in other parts of the country—was essential in this study.

The basis of stratification of a population in marketing research depends primarily on the nature of the problem at hand. It is helpful to recognize that samples used in marketing research divide into two types—general utility samples and samples with a specific and defined survey objective. Samples of the general-utility type are often used by commercial research organizations. They may be modified to fit a particular need, but their main purpose is to serve a variety of ends.

General-utility samples are usually designed with attention focused on a relatively small number of general social criteria, such as geographic area, city size, industrial characteristics, etc. Samples of that type are used in various public-opinion studies as well as in some marketing research investigations. In the latter use, two influences are usually present. One is an absence of specific knowledge about the nature of the variations which exist between different strata in the characteristic or subject being studied. In the biscuit-baking investigation mentioned above, a general-utility sample might have been used, except that pre-

[9] Note again that *population* in sampling terms does not necessarily refer to a sample of *people*. The total number of retail food stores in the country, for example, is a population.

vious studies had disclosed sharp sectional differences in biscuit baking. The other influence which tends to result in use of a general utility sample is either cost pressure, time pressure, or both. If there is no time available to develop a sample tailored to the requirements of the problem, or if that sample development would add excessively to the cost of the study, a general-utility sample might be used. This approach is not recommended, but it does occur.

Field-force availability is another factor which sometimes leads to the use of a general-utility sample where a specially developed sample would be preferable from the standpoint of research considerations alone. Lack of the specialized skill required to develop such a sample, within the organization planning the study, is one additional influence.

In selecting the criteria to be used in developing a sample for a study with a precisely defined objective, emphasis is on the identification of the particular social or other characteristics relevant to the objectives of the study. Thus in a study of the audiences of a number of magazines, these factors were isolated as of critical influence and considered in sample planning:[10]

> *Urbanization,* as indicated by the population of the biggest town in the county;
> *Buying power,* as indicated by retail sales per family or per capita;
> *Cultural or educational levels,* as indicated by the per cent of adults who had more than grade school education; and
> *Housing or living standards,* as indicated by any one of several factors, of which the one chosen was per cent of homes with mechanical refrigeration.

The relationship of these factors to the objectives of that particular study was established by correlation analysis. The fact that circulation figures are available on a county-by-county basis made it possible to pinpoint influential factors more precisely than is typically possible in marketing research. However, allowance for peculiarities in the distribution of product users or usage is common in marketing research studies. Thus a study of antifreeze usage or attitudes would use a sampling approach in which temperature factors were considered. One on fishing-tackle usage or attitudes might consider the number of fishing licenses sold.

Generalizations about sample design are likely to be less instructive than specific examples of the sample-design process. In the cases which make up an increasing proportion of the text material in the chapters following this one, sample design is stressed where applicable.

[10] *Continuing Study of Magazine Audiences: Report No. 9,* November 15, 1947, p. 42. Study sponsored and published by LIFE magazine.

It should be noted that improvements in the theory and practice of sample design are being made constantly. They result in a substantial and expanding literature, with which the individual responsible for sample-design decisions should be familiar. Statistical publications like the *Journal of the American Statistical Association* report such developments and should be consulted for examples of current and improved technique developments.

DISPROPORTIONATE SAMPLING

It is often desirable in marketing research practice to use a sample which is not proportional, i.e., one in which the number of sampling units in some strata is greater than the relative size of the strata would provide in a proportional sample. This is usually the approach indicated where a cell in the sample is more important, in the case of a particular problem, than its size would indicate. A sufficiently large sample of that cell is required because of the analysis planned. In such a situation it is relatively inefficient to increase the size of the total sample to the point where the cell in question has an adequately large number of sampling units. For example, suppose that in a total sample of 1,000 a particular cell was expected to represent 5 per cent, or 50 interviews. The analyses which were anticipated required a minimum of 200 interviews in that cell. It would be far easier to expand the sample within the cell to secure 150 additional interviews than to expand the total sample size to 4,000 so that the cell would include 200 on a proportional basis. In such a case, the number of interviews in an expanded-sample cell is reduced to proportionality in the tabulating process by weighting.

Here are two specific examples. A study of media audiences was made nationally for a large advertiser. That advertiser used television extensively and was particularly interested in the media habits of respondents in rural areas and in some geographic sections where television coverage was relatively low. The size of the sample in such areas was increased, to make possible a detailed analysis of what would otherwise have represented a minor portion of a national sample. In a major-market beer study for a regional brewer, the preferences and attitudes of Negro beer drinkers were especially important. In that case, the size of the sample in those blocks in which more than half of the household heads were Negroes was doubled to provide the requisite number of Negro respondents.

DOUBLE SAMPLING

A similar problem requiring a variation in sampling approach arises when the problem being studied exists among relatively few units of the population. An illustration is provided by a 1955 survey of household air conditioners. At that time, ownership of air conditioners was estimated to exist among about 10 per cent of all households. In the case of a probability national sample, such as was planned for this study, about nine-tenths of all interviews would normally be with families which did *not* own air conditioners. To reduce the costs of that relatively unimportant portion of the survey, a large national sample of households was first designed. Within that sample, a sample of air-conditioned households was taken. This represents *double sampling,* in which *a sample within a sample was used.* The sampling ratio within the two major strata—owners and nonowners of air conditioners—was quite different. A much higher proportion of owners than of nonowners was interviewed.

Other examples of similar situations are found in research on dog-food usage, or usage of detergents made especially for automatic washers. A sample of dog owners must first be designed, and then a sample within that one selected. Or a sample of automatic washer owners must be established, within which interviews are conducted. In practice it is often decided to use quota sampling rather than probability sampling on such problems. In the earlier days of television, for example, a probability sample of television-set owners would involve a considerable amount of wasted effort. An experienced interviewer with a quota of television owners could locate such owners rather easily with outside antennae as one guide.

In double sampling it is not unusual to use a short preliminary questionnaire to establish qualification. A longer questionnaire or interviewing guide is provided to be used only among qualified respondents, numerically in the minority, in the smaller or second stage of the double sample.

CLUSTER SAMPLING

One additional sampling concept of considerable importance in marketing research practice is *cluster sampling.* Cluster sampling occurs frequently in probability sampling. Thus in the air-conditioning survey mentioned above, the first stage in the sample design was the selection of the geographic areas within which interviewing was to be conducted. The second was the designation of specific interviewing areas, or clusters, within the selected geographic areas. A *block* containing forty dwelling units would represent a cluster of forty prospective respondent households. The number of units in the cluster would be determined by listing. The third stage, after listing of the units in the cluster, is the selection of individual households for interviewing.

Often in probability sampling, *all* sampling units in a cluster are included in the sample. In other cases, the number of sample units in the cluster to be included in the sample is indicated and the method of selection specified.

Using the term more loosely, cluster sampling often is used in quota sampling also. This simply means that travel time between interviewing points is reduced by having a specified number of interviews made in a particular locality. The number of sampling units in a cluster is often a function of the length of the interview, with a day's work or a half day's work determining the size of the cluster.

Cluster sampling in probability sampling tends to increase the size of the sampling error of a given size sample. Its offsetting value is that it reduces the cost of the sampling operation, thus increasing the reliability of the estimates developed *per dollar expended.*

BACKGROUND OF ERROR ESTIMATES IN JUDGMENT SAMPLES

Returning now to the substantial contradiction described earlier between what *can* be done, in theory, and what *is* done, in practice, let's examine the background of error estimation in judgment samples. The point was made and reiterated, earlier in this chapter, that the error in a nonprobability sample theoretically cannot be estimated. This is so because the mathematical foundation of the formulas used to measure errors assumed randomness which is not present in judgment samples. Yet marketing research practitioners do estimate the error range in judgment samples. How are we to reconcile this conflict?

Again a historical approach is helpful. It is a slight exaggeration, but fundamentally practitioners estimate the error range in judgment samples simply because they always have! The fundamental contribution to marketing research practice in this area was made in the booklet by Theodore H. Brown already mentioned. That booklet was published in the early 1930s. The fact that it is still in print at the time this book was being prepared for publication is convincing evidence of its durability.

Brown presented in a simple and understandable way the problem of measuring the significance of figures developed in marketing research. He also published a table providing a readily available source of data for rough estimates of error ranges. In the Brown publication, the need for randomness was stressed; but at that time the probability-sampling developments were unknown and he was discussing randomness pretty much as marketing research men then understood it. The formulas he presented were used and are still used in marketing research practice.

There have been major improvements in sampling practice, as described in this chapter, which add considerably to the randomness of judgment samples. That randomness remains, as we have noted, rather far short of the statistical ideal. The Brown formulas for measuring errors have proved over the years to be useful and reasonably accurate yardsticks of the dependability of sampling estimates. Exceptional circumstances, such as the problem encountered in the LIFE study during World War II, have occurred which made the estimates obviously erroneous in a particular case. Such exceptional circumstances have not seemed to be sufficient cause for discarding a useful research tool.

CONFIDENCE-LIMIT PRACTICE

Assume a probability sample in marketing research practice. What confidence limits would you establish? In the case of the majority of practical problems those limits would be set at two standard errors above and below the sample value. Such limits, in 95 cases out of 100, would encompass the value existing in the universe. Where the formulas developed for probability samples are applied in judgment sampling, a three-standard-error limit is often set. The effect of that wider limit is to allow for the existence of some sample-selection bias as an additional source of error.

The value developed by sampling represents the best estimate the research man can make of the value existing in the population sampled. He knows the mathematical basis of error estimation. He knows that other samples would develop values distributed normally about the true value in the universe. He knows that the likelihood of a sample value separated from the universe value by a substantial distance—say more than two standard errors—is relatively slight. Therefore, by the practice of setting an error range on the basis of three standard errors, the practitioner can make allowance for the presence of some sample-selection bias and still be reasonably confident of his research findings.

ADDITIONAL SAMPLING MATERIAL

Although it has been the subject of two extremely long chapters, the subject of sampling in marketing research practice has been covered only in part. There will be subsequent discussions of various facets of sampling in later chapters in this book. Note particularly the material in Chapter 14 on developing the research plan and in Chapter 15 on executing the research plan.

SUMMARY

1. The entire sampling concept rests on the assumption of true randomness, in the statistical sense, in samples. That randomness has been assumed in the

various mathematical formulas which have been developed to measure the sampling errors in various types of samples.

2. There has been a long controversy between advocates of a probability approach to sampling in marketing research and those who rely on a judgment approach, usually of a quota-sample type. The probability-sampling group has stressed that the errors in judgment samples cannot be measured and that a probability sample is the only type in which the range of sampling error can be measured precisely.

3. There is no question about the superiority of a probability sample, where it is necessary to measure error precisely and to make predictably accurate projections from the sample value to the total population.

4. Much of the criticism of judgment samples, and particularly of quota samples, has been focused on the gap which has often been found to exist between the theoretical ideal of a quota sample and the reproduction of that ideal developed in practice. That criticism has often been justified. It has had the positive value of leading to re-examination of judgment sampling practices and to the improvement of such practices.

5. As applied to marketing research practice (and as distinguished from its use by the Bureau of the Census), probability sampling has some marked disadvantages. One is its often spectacularly higher cost. Another is a group of operating problems, which have often been underestimated in theoretical discussions of the two sampling approaches.

6. There are a number of marketing research situations, including panel research and qualitative studies, in which probability sampling is not possible.

7. The decision on sample size is a complex one, in which these influences must be considered:

— The practical cost ceiling on the study
— The accuracy required of the sampling values
— The variation in distribution of the key values being measured
— Confidence limits established, which are a function of how important an error might be in costs or effects
— Number of breakdowns (or cells) which are to be examined individually and need for accuracy within such cells

8. Sampling is so important an element of marketing research practice that two long chapters devoted to it are insufficient to cover it completely even in an introductory way. Further discussions of various aspects of sampling will be found in many later chapters, especially including Chapter 14 on developing the research plan and Chapter 15 on executing the research plan.

QUESTIONS

1. If a sample is not random, what one basic statistical assumption would not apply?

2. What is the primary reason for the spectacular growth in the acceptance and use of probability sampling?

3. What are some of the limitations of quota sampling? And what are the characteristics of an ideal quota sample?

4. In current professional use of quota sampling, what improvements have been instituted to reduce respondent selection bias?

5. What reasons could you give for judgment sampling having a higher cost per interview than a quota or another type of judgment sampling commonly used?

6. What types of situations in marketing research can you describe in which a probability-sampling approach is neither possible nor practical? Discuss each situation briefly.

7. What influences must you consider in order to reach a decision on sample size? Identify and discuss each.

8. Discuss how an increase in sample size affects the sampling error in a probability sample.

9. How would you define *disproportionate sampling, double sampling,* and *cluster sampling?*

Steps in the
Marketing Research Process

CHAPTER 12

Defining and Refining the Problem: Introduction

Now a shift in direction plunges us into the main stream of marketing research practice. This and the next six chapters combine to describe and illustrate the key steps which are at the heart of much of that practice. They show how the technique tools and data sources described in the preceding section are coordinated in the course of the problem-solving process. Together these seven chapters combine to present a picture of *marketing research in action* which is drawn from life. That picture introduces the real problems which are encountered by real companies. Cases constitute an increasing proportion of the material in this and subsequent sections.

This section begins where Chapter 4, which introduced the problem-solving process in marketing, left off. A review of that chapter is recommended as preparation for the comments which follow. It will be recalled that these steps in the process of research *on a major problem* were listed in Chapter 4:

Step 1. Define the *marketing* problem in specific terms.
Step 2. Refine the problem and subdivide it to isolate the individual marketing *research* problems it presents.
Step 3. Develop a plan for securing the facts or information needed.
Step 4. Execute the plan and secure the facts.
Step 5. Analyze the facts and interpret them in terms of the problem.
Step 6. Summarize the results of the analysis and interpretation and report the findings.

The first *two* steps in the above list are both discussed in this chapter. That discussion is continued in the following chapter, which describes the informal investigation—a vital research tool in the problem-defining area. The remaining four steps are the subject of the five chapters which follow the next one, to complete this section of the book.

INTEGRATED APPROACH EMPHASIZED

Marketing research plays a vital part in marketing management practice. It remains, however, only one *part* of marketing management. There is always a tendency in writing about or studying a specialized field like marketing research to become so preoccupied with details of that field that one loses sight of the broader picture of which it is a part. There is a tendency also to think of marketing research as made up of a wide variety of individual activities—like sales analysis, surveys, panel research, and so on—which are related to each other only in a loose, general way. Both tendencies erect obstacles to a full understanding of what marketing research *really* is and *really* does. An integrated approach removes those obstacles and helps to maintain perspective.

In addition to its advantages as a way of providing a realistic picture of marketing research practice, the integrated approach has an additional value. It is closely related to an important marketing trend which merits mention. There is a strong trend toward a broadening and integration of the entire marketing field. In company after company, a single marketing function is being created to replace, draw together, and integrate responsibility for elements in the organization's marketing practices which were formerly divided. Thus we often find a consolidation of responsibility for the management and supervision of the field sales force, the planning and execution of advertising, the broad field of sales promotion, price and product planning and development, and many other areas of related responsibility.

The objective of that consolidation is to provide greater strength for marketing as a function and to help marketing prepare for the increasingly difficult challenge presented by expanded market opportunities coupled with mounting competitive pressure. That trend toward integration of the marketing function represents in essence a basically new and broader marketing concept. In that marketing concept, a coordinated approach and a high degree of integration are key elements. That trend is almost certain to result in an increase in the importance of the marketing function. Integrated marketing research, as part of that concept, is in a position to make substantially increased contributions to the organization's marketing effectiveness just at a time when the need for such contributions is especially great.

STARTING POINT IS THE MARKETING PROBLEM

One important distinction between the integrated and nonintegrated approach to marketing research is the point at which marketing research first enters into the problem-solving process. In the integrated approach, the starting point for marketing research is step 1 above—with the definition of the *marketing* problem. Where research is not integrated, marketing research activities are typically confined to the last five steps. Those activities begin with work on the marketing *research* problem or problems. The difficulty with this latter starting point is that research is often confined to fragments of the total problem. Its potential contribution is thus inevitably minimized, and the return on the research expenditure correspondingly reduced.

A specific illustration of integrated research, drawn from an experience of one of America's merchandising giants, provides an example. The timing of this example is of interest. It indicates that although integrated research is a relatively recent development in most companies, the values of the integrated approach were discovered and applied earlier in some organizations.

9. LEVER BROTHERS COMPANY (A)

Back in 1936, Procter & Gamble's Crisco shortening was enjoying a large and profitable sales volume. Crisco stood almost alone in its field as the only nationally advertised product of its kind. Its brand name had been established as a household word by more than a score of years of able and aggressive promotion. No threat to that leadership was in sight. The margin of Crisco's competitive strength is suggested by a 1936 survey made by *Modern Magazines*. Crisco was named as the brand of shortening used by 58 per cent of a national sample of housewives. No other brand was named by as many as 8 per cent of the women surveyed.

Suddenly, the picture changed. Early in 1936, Lever Brothers introduced Spry, a hydrogenated shortening competing directly with Crisco. Spry was launched with a whirlwind introductory campaign that is still considered a classic in merchandising circles. By the end of 1936, more than nine million homes had been visited by Spry sampling crews. Each housewife visited received a free can of Spry, a cookbook of Spry recipes, a coupon worth 10 cents on a purchase of Spry, and a brief sales message. A major threat to Crisco's leadership had appeared.

Fortune magazine estimated 1937 Spry sales at 12 million dollars, compared to 25 million dollars for long-established Crisco. In subsequent years the margin between the two brands was narrowed markedly.

Spry's marketing success represents a success story also for integrated marketing research. The decision to enter the shortening market was not a sudden one. The product was no spur-of-the-moment creation. Nearly five years were spent developing and perfecting Spry before a factory was built to make the product.

After the decision had been made to enter the shortening market, the marketing research facilities of Lever Brothers Company were focused on the problem. Crisco users were interviewed. Probing interviews sought to identify any product limitations in Crisco which might represent a competitive opportunity for the new product. From these consumer studies, Lever Brothers learned that generally Crisco was an excellent product, well liked by women who used it. But some women who used and liked Crisco still recognized some product shortcomings. Housewives commented on an occasional lack of uniformity in Crisco's color, flavor, and consistency. They also complained that if Crisco were not kept refrigerated, it turned rancid, while if it were cold, it was hard to work into recipes.

Consumer research guided technical research people at Lever Brothers in their product development. The objective was to develop a new product free from the limitations of Crisco. No attempt was made to enter a new product in the shortening market until a new product had been perfected which consumer research demonstrated had clear-cut advantages over Crisco. When such a product was perfected, Lever Brothers built a factory to make it and marketing plans were developed to launch it.

In promotional planning, great emphasis was placed on speed. It was essential to move fast, so that the new product could reach the maximum number of housewives in a minimum period of time. That would permit comparisons of new Spry and old Crisco, in which Spry had a maximum advantage. A slower-moving campaign would have given P&G time to improve Crisco and thus dull the pointed product advantages which spearheaded Spry's invasion of the shortening market.

— ★ —

The above example of integrated marketing research shows how marketing research of many different types was used in the course of work on a single *marketing* problem. Product research began before the decision had been made on what kind of a new product to develop. Panel research, using the Nielsen Food Index facilities, revealed the size and characteristics of the shortening market and the competitive division of that market. Facts on the size and growth of shortening volume contributed to the decision to introduce a new shortening instead of some other type of product. With Crisco identified as the leading brand, Crisco's competitive strongpoints were carefully studied. The geographic distribution of Crisco volume, the city-size pattern of that volume, the relative importance of different store-size groups, etc., were determined.

Consumer research was conducted, especially among Crisco users, to develop the specifications which the proposed new product had to meet or exceed. Various experimental formulations, matched against Crisco in comparative product tests, provided a continuing check on progress in product development. When a product was finally developed which was considered to be ready for production, additional comparative tests confirmed its product advantages. Test results also guided advertising thinking on sales-point emphasis.

In developing the specific marketing plans for the new product, Nielsen data were used extensively. To illustrate just one specific application, consider this question: How big an initial order for Spry should the Lever Brothers' sales organization seek? Remember that the company had no experience of its own in this product category. The size of retail inventories of Crisco in outlets of different types and sizes guided this decision.

VARIATIONS IN ASSIGNMENT OF RESPONSIBILITY

Before examining in detail the steps in the marketing research process, it might be well to review briefly some of the varying circumstances under which this series of steps is likely to be taken. The steps represent action. What triggers or precipitates the action? What influences the decision on how responsibility for the problem-solving process should be assigned? The answer to that pair of questions varies widely both with the nature of the problem and with the facilities available to the organization with the problem. Despite the existence of wide variations, certain generalizations are possible which may help to make the review of the steps more meaningful.

When the marketing problem base of marketing research was described in Chapter 3, the observation was made that marketing research is used most frequently to aid in the solution of current operating problems. The comment was also made that it makes its most important contributions to marketing management effectiveness by contributing to the solution of such problems. These are the types of problems, remember, which are continually present in every well-run, healthy business. The detailed and somewhat formalized step-by-step approach developed in this section is often not entirely necessary in dealing with such problems. Such problems are typically handled as the continuing assignments and responsibilities of the marketing research department of the company. Thus measurement of territorial sales potentials and of territorial variations in market share, sales yield, and sales effectiveness, for example, are activities representative of this broad and important group of problems.

It is important to note that although the specific steps in the problem-solving process described in this section are often not called into action consciously and explicitly in work on current operating problems, they still help solve such problems. This apparent contradiction exists because the steps in the problem-solving process tend to become a deeply ingrained habit, as basic and fundamental to a marketing research man as a set of scales are to a musician. They are near the core of his skill, and represent a major element in his experience and training. They thus tend to form an integral part of the background he brings to his work on all problems.

The steps are called into *conscious* application in the case of major problems, *especially when the nature of the problem is not known. Definition of the problem* is one of the most important elements in the problem-solving process.

INFLUENCES ON THE ASSIGNMENT OF PROBLEM-SOLVING RESPONSIBILITY

Let's consider now some of the major variations in the assignment of responsibility for problem solving in marketing. Primary responsibility for the fact-finding part of the problem-solving process may be and often is assigned to an individual within the company which faces the problem. Assignment of that responsibility to someone outside the company's own organization is also common. In the former case, the responsibility is typically assigned to the company's director of marketing research.

Now consider variations in approach which occur when the problem is assigned to an insider versus an outsider. The insider's approach to the solution of a marketing problem often differs significantly from that of an outsider. A minor qualification of that comment should be noted. That involves a difference in approach of two different types of "insiders." A director of marketing research who has been in a company long enough to have brought his job "under control" is in a quite different position from one who is a newcomer to the job or in a newly created job. The latter approach differs from the former, tending to resemble the approach of the outsider.

OUTSIDE ASSIGNMENT OF PROBLEM-SOLVING RESPONSIBILITY

When the assignment of responsibility to someone outside the company is considered, two types of situations should be distinguished. The first involves a consultant or consulting organization of the marketing research or of the general management consulting type. The role of consultants in marketing research activities is described in detail in Chapter 30. At this point it is sufficient to underline the fact that where a consultant is engaged to work on a specific problem, one of a number of conditions is likely to obtain: The company may have no marketing research department (this being the typical situation in the case of relatively small companies); or the problem is considered by management to be too serious or too difficult for that department to handle; or the department is overloaded and could not work on the problem promptly without sidetracking other projects of equal or greater importance; or the need for an outside viewpoint is recognized. A further variation on that particular theme is the specialized type of problem which makes it desirable to tap specialized experience not available within the company's own research department.

A second broad category of outside assignments are those in which an advertising agency acts for the manufacturer-client with a problem. Whether advertising agencies should be so employed is a highly controversial question. Advertising agencies are usually compensated on some modification of a commission basis. Their total income from an account tends to be proportional to the client's advertising appropriation. An advertising appropriation thus creates a "service bank account" for a manufacturer-client—an account equivalent to about 15 per cent of the appropriation, minus a "slice off the top" which represents the agency's profit on the account.

With such a "bank account" available, a manufacturer can and does influence the types of service delivered. Some manufacturers demand a substantial amount of research work. The cost of that research of course comes out of the service bank account and reduces other types of service to less-than-normal amounts or the total service expenditure by the agency would exceed the balance in the bank account. In most large agencies, some of the service provided is ordinarily of a research nature.

An advertising agency is always in a difficult position when it is called upon to do marketing research work *not directly related to its advertising plans and recommendations*. The findings of agency-executed research are sometimes under attack as less than objective. That is especially likely to occur when they parallel the agency's own interests and indicate, for example, the desirability of increased expenditures for advertising. There is another side to this coin: Many large advertising agencies typically maintain a staff of specialists which includes marketing, merchandising, and research personnel. They have the facilities to execute a competent, professional research job in many instances. The ability of the facilities is often subordinate to the availability of the facilities. The question is whether they can be devoted to the job without conflict with the service commitments for other accounts.

An advertising agency which is newly appointed to an account, or which receives a new-product assignment from an existing client, must often do much research to guide its own thinking and planning in developing advertising and marketing recommendations. A new agency is often appointed when a company is in marketing difficulties. The agency must contribute to the solution of those difficulties and to the improvement of the client's sales trend, if it can. Success in making such contributions may nail down on the account list a satisfied and presumably profitable account. Failure by one agency to reverse a sales decline— *although the decline may stem from other-than-advertising factors*— may be fatal. Another agency may be appointed to show what *it* can contribute to the solution of the company's marketing problem.

LIMITATIONS ON THE USE OF AGENCIES AS "PROBLEM SOLVERS"

In some instances, management executives tend to pass to advertising agencies responsibilities for decisions which the management team itself should make. This is undesirable, but it occurs. For this and other reasons, advertising agencies are often drawn into serious marketing-problem situations. The agency's position, in such a situation, is not essentially dissimilar to that of an independent consultant, except that the agency operates under certain major limitations. One limitation is financial. The agency often cannot afford, within its income from an account, to do the research which the agency executives know should be done.

This means that an advertising agency often faces the task of deciding what research to do with the cost of the research an even more important consideration than is usually the case. If the research required to crack a knotty marketing problem costs more than the agency's visible income from the account, what can an agency do? One answer is to speculate on the future income they *may* get *if* the problem is solved *and if* they keep the account. Ironically, an agency is occasionally in the position of contributing the solution to a marketing problem, and then getting fired for its pains! Where a serious marketing problem has developed in an organization, usually some individual or individuals in the firm are largely responsible. Their ineptitude, or their bad decisions on policy or other questions, have typically contributed to the creation of the problem situation. Effective work by the agency in isolation of the problem elements often incidentally points a finger of blame unmistakably at those responsible. An agency thus often wins the argument but loses the account, if the culpable individual is in a position to say "Off with their heads!"

An additional disadvantage in the use of advertising agencies as a source of problem-solving help is closely related to the one just mentioned. That disadvantage exists where responsibility for engaging the agency's services is placed at some level below the top one in the organization. An advertising agency reporting to an advertising director, who in turn reports to a marketing vice-president, is in a relatively poor position to recommend changes in the organization's sales methods and policies. Those sales methods and responsibilities lie beyond the responsibility of the advertising manager; recommendations affecting them, because of the "channels" involved, must usually be made to the advertising manager. This puts the advertising manager in the position of "seconding" recommendations critical of another executive on his own or a higher level in the organization. If the recommendations are strongly resisted, they may "backfire" and cost the agency the account. Where the problem is clearly in the area of advertising, however, this problem is less likely to develop.

Another limitation on the advertising agency's participation in problem solving is implicit in the agency's basic function. An advertising agency's business is to prepare effective advertising. They do that for a number of different clients. For any agency to have for the solution of a single client's marketing problem the time that problem requires, despite the pressing demands of their other clients, is unusual.

Under most circumstances, a manufacturer should not pass the responsibility for the solution of a major marketing problem *which is not primarily an advertising problem* to his advertising agency. Since the emphasis in this book is on practice rather than theory, it should be noted that often manufacturers do just that, whether they "should" or not. When an agency is handed the responsibility for research on a major marketing problem, it may be in the position of an insider or an outsider. If it has been working for the client organization over a long period of time, it may be in much the position of an insider. If it is a newly appointed agency, it is in about the same position as any other outside organization in approaching the problem.

To summarize the above comments briefly, responsibility for problem solving—for applying the approach outlined in this section—may be assigned inside or outside an organization. The assignment is often to the head of the marketing research department, either as an individual or as a key member of a group or committee. Where internal assignment is made, the research director is typically thoroughly familiar with the company's situation. His approach is somewhat different from that of an outsider, because of the background knowledge he brings to the assignment which an outsider must first acquire. On the other hand, if the research executive is new in his job and/or new in his company, he may take the approach described in this chapter just as an outsider would.

Responsibility for marketing research is often assigned outside the organization. Marketing research consulting organizations, marketing management or general management consulting organizations, and advertising agencies all figure prominently in such outside assignment of problem-solving responsibility. There is an additional difference between the advertising agency's starting point, in such research, and that of the other types of organizations mentioned. Where a consulting organization is called in, the existence of a problem is already recognized. By contrast, sometimes an agency is appointed by a company which has a major marketing problem not yet recognized. The expectation is that a new advertising approach may reverse a sagging sales curve or produce a sales gain for a product with level volume. Thus an agency sometimes has to work with the handicap of operating on a problem when the existence of the problem is not recognized or fully appreciated.

DISTINCTION BETWEEN INSIDE AND OUTSIDE APPROACHES

The fundamental difference between the approach to the solution of a marketing problem taken by an insider and that of someone approaching the same problem from outside the organization lies in this fact: The insider begins with a substantial amount of background information about the company's situation. The outsider may begin with none or some of that information. Therefore there is an additional step which the outsider must take. He must acquire a considerable amount of information about the company, its industry, its products, its competitors, its sales methods and policies, and so on.

It is in the description of this particular step, which is sometimes identified as the *situation analysis,* that some of the older texts in marketing research are farthest from the realities of present-day research practice.

To clarify this point, recall that the marketing problem base of marketing research today was summarized in Chapter 3. The particular research activities which are most important and most widely performed were there identified. As the result of their own execution of those activities, most companies with a competent marketing research department develop and make available for the continuing guidance of their management most of the types of information required for a factual and detailed analysis of the company's situation. Thus we find that today there is routinely available in the majority of well-managed companies most of the types of information which an individual research man often had to develop himself, as part of the problem-solving process, at an earlier day in the development of marketing research.

It is true that a long and detailed situation analysis was sometimes necessary in the days when sales executives ran their jobs "by the seat of their pants." The increasing level of skill and competence in marketing management has been accompanied by a corresponding increase in the factual demands upon marketing research departments. The kinds of facts which are required to do a sound job of marketing management are very nearly identical with the kinds of facts which sometimes had to be developed in an exhaustive situation analysis in the past.

To illustrate this point in specific terms, let's return to an examination of the Dell-O margarine case. That marketing problem situation developed before the present pattern of marketing research practice had emerged and crystallized. It involved a situation analysis of the type now relatively obsolescent, or at least rarely required, in current practice.

REVIEW OF DELL-O MARKETING RESEARCH PROBLEMS

In the discussion of the Dell-O margarine case in Chapter 4, a marketing problem was boiled down to these seven marketing *research* problems:

1. How does the quality of the Dell-O product compare with that of the two leading competitors in its price group in consumer acceptance?

2. How does Dell-O margarine compare with leading competitors in the size of its consumer-franchise, i.e., in the number of using families, and what are the trends by brands?

3. What is the territorial distribution of Dell-O volume and of total margarine potential? What are the variations in Dell-O's share of market by area?

4. How does the selling organization selling Dell-O margarine compare with that of leading competitors in the same price group, both in quantity and quality of manpower?

5. How does the distributor organization handling Dell-O margarine compare with that of leading competitors? How does the distribution achieved by that distributor organization compare with that of leading competitive brands?

6. How do the pricing and discount structures of Dell-O and leading competitors compare?

7. How do the advertising programs of Dell-O and leading competitors compare, both in quantity and quality? What are the relative expenditure rates of each major competitor? How is the advertising divided among different media? What differences exist in seasonal emphasis?

Figure 12.1 presents a recap of the various activities which were required in the step 1 area to define the marketing program of Dell-O

Figure 12.1. Summary of Introductory Steps in Problem-solving Process, as Applied to the Dell-O Margarine Problem

Symptom of the problem: A continuing decline in sales volume on Dell-O Margarine. Dimensions of the problem: Time: very urgent. Profit: very important. Facilities: within company, none; outside (advertising agency), complete.

STEP 1. DEFINE THE MARKETING PROBLEM IN SPECIFIC TERMS

A. Subdivide problem into major elements:
  1. Industry elements.
  2. Competitive elements.
  3. Market elements.
B. Examine existing hypotheses within organization:
  1. Company sales decline reflects lower industry volume.
  2. Company sales decline result of growth in volume of lower-priced margarines.
  3. Company sales decline result of low butter prices.
C. Decision made to explore industry elements, with emphasis on stated hypotheses. Informational objectives include:
  1. Size and trend of industry volume.
  2. Dell-O market share and trend in that market share.
  3. Price-class division of industry volume, and trends in that division.
  4. Influence of butter prices, consumer incomes, and other economic factors on industry volume.
D. Major findings:
  1. Industry volume had declined, but at rate much less than the decline in the company volume.
  2. Dell-O's market share dropped from 10 per cent of industry volume in 1935 to less than 5 per cent in 1940.
  3. Major price-class trend was an increase in the market share of two brands in the same premium-priced group as Dell-O.
  4. Butter prices and consumer incomes had been influential in determining industry and company volume, but that influence had been greatly reduced over the period of Dell-O's sharpest sales-volume decline.

margarine in specific terms. That definition resulted in a recognition of the fact that this was primarily a competitive problem and that two competitors in particular were important to Dell-O. Moving into step 2, in which the *marketing* problem was refined and subdivided to isolate the individual marketing *research* problems it included, the above list of seven different marketing research problems was developed.

Because the type of problem posed by the Dell-O case is one which is frequently encountered in professional marketing research practice, some additional comment on the problem-solving process in this case seems desirable. The basic *symptom* which signals the existence of a problem of this type is a sales decline or a failure by an individual company to match the growth of its industry. When such a problem is studied by a team of experienced marketing people—in a management or marketing research consulting organization, for example—the problem-solving approach taken is usually very similar to the one outlined in this section.

The evidence at hand is first examined in an attempt to determine the nature of the problem. While the nature of the problem is often not completely clear, there are typically clues which suggest a number of specific areas as potential sources of difficulty which are worth exploring. Often a particularly vital piece of information—such as the trend in the price-class division of industry volume in the Dell-O case—is unavailable, and plans to secure it must be made and executed. Here we are again in a situation in which marketing research is used to help define the problem.

The above list of seven marketing-research problems arrived at by such a reduction process therefore represents a realistic base for illustrating the problem-solving process. What is no longer typical in the Dell-O margarine case is the almost complete lack of what we might call vital marketing statistics within the Dell-O organization. An outsider undertaking the problem-solving process for a well-managed company of the Dell-O type today would ordinarily be able to ask for and immediately receive data on size and trend of industry volume, trend in company's market share, etc., without any delay or cost involved in securing such information for use in refining the marketing problem.

NORMAL AGENCY-CLIENT DIVISION OF MARKETING RESEARCH RESPONSIBILITY

Let's move on now to consider an additional illustration of this problem-defining phase of the marketing research process. For the next illustration, a further example of advertising agency activity in this area is used. This example has many points of similarity with the Dell-O margarine case. Even more important than the common characteristics of the two cases, however, are the essential differences between them.

In the following case involving the Toni Co., we find a much more normal picture of the division of marketing research responsibility between a manufacturer (or client) and an advertising agency today.

There are considerable variations in agency-client division of responsibility, but they tend to follow a relatively common pattern. The agency is responsible for developing effective advertising. The research which is necessary to develop such advertising, and to support their recommendations of it, is usually the agency's responsibility. Such research is usually planned, executed, and paid for by the agency; close cooperation with the marketing research department of the client organization is desirable and common. On the other hand, the manufacturer is ordinarily expected to provide, for the agency's guidance, the basic data on market size, characteristics, competitive market shares, etc. The manufacturer is also responsible for product development and product research, and the agency expects to receive data on the characteristics of its client's products and on the comparative consumer acceptance of client and competitive products to guide it in planning advertising.

Where the agency is asked by the client to do marketing research in such areas as market definition or product testing, it is not unusual to find the research executed *by* the agency, but *for* and *at the expense of* the manufacturer. There are exceptional circumstances in which the agency feels a certain type of research, needed to guide advertising planning, is vital. This research is of the type the client is ordinarily expected to provide. The client has no such research available and is not willing to pay for it because, in the judgment of the client, it is not necessary. In such a situation, an agency may decide to do the research itself at its own expense, rather than proceed without it.

In the following case, note particularly the differences which exist in the need for preliminary activity of the situation-analysis type where the manufacturer's marketing research department is active and capable.

10. THE TONI CO. (A)

The Toni Co., Chicago, a division of the Gillette Co., is the leading manufacturer of home-permanent waving kits. The company controls a dominant share of the home-permanent industry's volume and has since the days when Toni pioneered in the aggressive promotion of home permanents and built the industry almost single-handed. Following in Toni's footsteps, many other companies entered the home-permanent field and succeeded in carving out moderate market-share slices for their brands. In addition to home permanents, Toni manufactures and sells a variety of other products in the hair-care and cosmetic field.

After competition for home-permanent volume grew more intense with the entry of such major competitors as Proctor & Gamble Company, Toni embarked on a policy of multiple-brand promotion. In addition to the pioneer Toni home permanent brand, Toni developed and successfully introduced other brands with different brand names, each aimed at a subdivision of the home-permanent market. A product called Prom was one of the brands in the Toni family. A product called Bobbi was another.

The Toni Co. employed several different advertising agencies. Its general policy was to keep competitive products—like different brands of home permanents or different brands of shampoo—in different agencies. Vigorous competition between the company's different brands was encouraged. Advertising responsibility for one of the home-permanent brands—Bobbi home permanent—was assigned to Tatham-Laird, Inc., a Chicago advertising agency which handled two other Toni products' advertising.

A product group within the agency was set up to plan advertising and marketing strategy for Bobbi. That group was under the supervision and guidance of V. T. Mertz, who had spent a business lifetime in the successful promotion of cosmetic-type products. The new agency team set its sights on an expanded volume and market-share peak for Bobbi.

The Toni Co. had a highly competent marketing research department, under the direction of Fred Willis. That department prepared a summary of industry data and trends, which was presented to the new agency team in a briefing session. The data showed the division of the home-permanent market into three subtypes—conventional home permanents like Toni, which required neutralizing with a separate neutralizing solution; self-neutralizing home permanents like the Toni Co.'s Prom, which did not require a separate neutralizer; and pin-curl home permanents like Bobbi, with characteristics described below. At the time of the agency change, Bobbi had about 3 per cent of the home-permanent market on a unit basis, out of about 5 per cent in total for all home permanents of the pin-curl type.

Where would you look if you had the responsibility for defining the marketing problem that held the Bobbi-brand share to only 3 per cent of the total market? The agency team considered various potential problem areas and discarded all but one of them. Was this an industry problem? Hardly—the home-permanent market was expanding. Was this a problem of an inadequate sales organization? It couldn't very well be, since the same sales organization was doing an obviously capable job on Toni and Prom home permanents. Where did the problem lie, then? *The product* seemed to be the logical starting point in reducing this problem to specifics.

Study of the problem revealed these characteristics: A pin-curl type of home permanent like Bobbi had a basically different method of application from either Toni or Prom or their product-type counterparts. In giving herself a Toni or Prom home permanent, a woman had to soak her hair with a waving lotion and then roll it up into tight curls around a spin-curler, which was also made by Toni. In giving herself a Bobbi, the woman would simply put her hair up in pin curls as many women (especially younger women and working women, to whom the appearance of their hair was particularly important) did every night upon going to bed. Then the waving lotion was applied to the pin-curled head for a timed interval, rinsed in clear water, and that was that.

Because it eliminated several steps involved in the other type of home permanent waving, Bobbi was both quicker and easier to give than the other types. At first blush, "Bobbi—the quick and easy home permanent!" seemed to be the advertising approach most likely to sell the product. There were two reasons why that apparently obvious approach seemed to warrant further study. One was historic. The previous advertising agency handling Bobbi advertising had used the quick-and-easy appeal. Sales response had been disappointing, and market share had not been increased. The second objection was that such an approach was selling a type of product—the pin-curl permanent—rather than the particular brand in question. Advertising more sharply fastened to the individual brand name seemed indicated.

Discussions of the characteristics of home-waving products with technical research personnel in the Toni laboratories provided some information which appeared to make the problem even more difficult. A pin curl is traditionally curled around the finger of the woman putting up her hair. The diameter of a finger is greater than that of a spin-type curler. The strength of the wave varies inversely with the diameter of the curl. That is, a curl around a small-diameter curler would make a much stronger (and therefore longer-lasting) wave than one around a larger-diameter finger. Result: Pin-curl permanents like Bobbi produced a looser curl than the standard home permanents that dominated the market. Further, a pin-curl permanent didn't last as long as the regular type. These apparent disadvantages of the product were inherent in its product type and could not be eliminated.

The Toni Co. marketing research department made regular studies of the consumer acceptance of its products and of leading competitive products. One measure of satisfaction with a given brand of home permanent was provided by a survey approach. On a regularly scheduled basis, surveys were made in a number of major markets. In each interview, home-wave users were separated from nonusers; the name of the brand used last was determined; and the date of the last wave was established. (Since a home wave was a relatively infrequent and memorable event, data on date of last wave would be more dependable than similar questions in other types of products.) Then specific questions were asked about satisfaction and dissatisfaction with the last home permanent used. The respondent's opinion as to the brand she thought she would buy next was solicited. If that was a different brand from the one used last, reasons for the change were explored.

By combining out of their total sample of respondents all who used a particular brand last, a relatively large subsample for each individual major Toni Co. and competitive brand was provided. By subdividing into various time groups since last wave (which was vital in establishing satisfaction with the lasting qualities of the wave kit), further detail was provided. On this type of research, Bobbi consistently was reported to have a repeat-purchase-intention figure which was far below that of other Toni Co. home permanents. Competitive pin-curl kits had figures which were similarly much lower than for other types of home permanents. The repeat-purchase-intention figure for Bobbi was higher than for other pin-curl permanents.

— ★ —

The most significant difference between this problem and the one on Dell-O margarine lies in the sharply reduced amount of work required to define and refine the problem. The extensive work which was required in the Dell-O case (and which is recapped in Figure 12.1) was not needed here. The various types of information which had to be gathered at considerable expense in time and effort in the Dell-O case are here available on request from the manufacturer's marketing research department.

The Bobbi problem is in part a product problem. Unlike most product problems, however, this one cannot be solved simply by developing an improved product. Avenues for improvement were being explored by the technical research people at the Toni Co., of course, and some minor improvements could be anticipated. Yet the key product limitations remained, linked inseparably to the nature of the product itself. If this had been the product of a company with no other home-waving product, a change to another type of home-wave kit might have "solved" the problem. Since the market leadership in other larger segments of the home-wave market was already controlled by other brands of the Toni Co., that approach was not applicable here.

AN ILLUSTRATION OF AN INTERNAL APPROACH

For an additional example of the first phase of the marketing research process, let's consider a case in which responsibility was internally assigned. The case presented below is an extension of the discussion of the Allied Products, Inc., case first introduced in Chapter 6. A review of that chapter will be helpful in your understanding of the following material.

The case which follows is an extremely important one for several reasons. The first is that it shows how the steps in the marketing research process are applied when responsibility is assigned to a manufacturer's own marketing research department. This is perhaps the most important single type of problem-solving approach. The second reason is that this case is concerned with a marketing problem of the current operating type. That type of problem constitutes a very large proportion of all marketing research. The third reason is that the particular type of problem involved is one of the most frequently encountered and most important areas of marketing research activity.

11. ALLIED PRODUCTS, INC. (D)

With the revision of sales territories completed, the sales research director of Allied Products, Inc., turned his attention to the activity which ranked first in importance among companies participating in the American Management Association survey—measuring territorial variations in sales yield, market share, and sales effectiveness. He began his work on this problem by reviewing previous activities of the company in that research area. He learned that little previous work had been done on such measurement. What had been done was intermittent and had resulted in a considerable amount of disagreement as to its validity. The result was that the analyses had not been particularly productive.

What had been done was very simple. The population of each district and sales territory had been totaled. "Sales yield" had been calculated by dividing the company's sales in a territory by the population of that territory. The resulting figure was the company's *per capita sales* in each territory, that is, the sales of the company's product *per person* in each territory. In making this analysis, census data had been used. Population figures had not been revised in between census years (every ten years, 1940, 1950, etc.) to make allowances for migration of population, varying birth rates, etc. It had not been felt that adjustment was worth the time it would take in the years prior to World War II. The wartime increase in migration made that evaluation questionable, as the research director reviewed it.

It should be noted that Chapter 21 is devoted entirely to the subject of estimating territorial potentials and analyzing territorial sales performance. That chapter will develop the subject matter of the present case in much greater detail than is possible here.

The sales research director of Allied Products, Inc., had reservations about the validity of population as a *market index*—that is, an indicator of the relative distribution of sales opportunities—for the company's products. The reasons for those reservations will be presented in Chapter 21, where the subject of market indexes is explored in detail. He was sure that migration should be taken into account, if population figures were used.

Despite his reservation about the validity of population as a market index, he decided to proceed with his first analysis of territorial sales performance with that index. This decision was influenced by the fact that *per capita sales* had been used in the past in similar analyses. Since the company's management and sales organization were already some-

Figure 12.2. Work Sheet: Analysis of District and Regional Sales of Allied Products, Inc., 1943

Sales districts and regions	(1) Population	(2) U.S. popula- tion, %	(3) 1943 sales	(4) U.S. sales, %	(5) Sales per capita	(6) Per capita sales index
U.S. total	127,307,883	100.00	$6,184,288	100.00	$.0486	100
ATLANTIC REGION	54,410,472	42.739	2,336,618	37.786	.0429	89
New York.....	15,618,443	12.268	783,619	12.674	.0502	103
Atlanta........	14,210,839	11.162	480,767	7.773	.0338	70
Philadelphia....	12,370,466	9.717	475,414	7.688	.0384	79
Boston.........	6,522,871	5.124	266,401	4.308	.0408	84
Pittsburgh.....	5,687,853	4.468	330,417	5,343	.0581	120
GREAT LAKES REGION	32,843,988	25.798	1,667,581	26.964	.0508	105
Chicago........	10,627,548	8.347	531,137	8.587	.0500	103
Cleveland......	6,524,732	5.125	299,669	4.845	.0459	94
Cincinnati.....	6,177,489	4.852	381,631	6.172	.0618	127
Detroit........	5,806,521	4.561	308,100	4.982	.0531	109
Minneapolis....	3,707,698	2.913	147,044	2.378	.0397	82
SOUTHWESTERN REGION	24,808,358	19.487	1,237,362	20.005	.0499	103
Memphis.......	7,288,475	5.726	207,979	3.362	.0285	59
Dallas.........	5,922,327	4.653	260,523	4.211	.0440	91
Kansas City....	5,037,203	3.957	297,942	4.817	.0591	123
St. Louis.......	3,744,830	2.941	236,120	3.818	.0631	130
Omaha.........	2,815,523	2.210	234,798	3.797	.0834	172
PACIFIC REGION	15,245,065	11.976	942,727	15.245	.0618	127
Los Angeles....	4,875,093	3.830	236,403	3.824	.0485	100
Portland.......	3,853,013	3.025	312,416	5.051	.0811	167
San Francisco..	3,615,034	2.839	231,762	3.748	.0641	132
Denver........	2,901,925	2.282	162,146	2.622	.0559	115

what familiar with such figures, the problem of communicating the results of this analysis to them would be reduced.

He explored the questions which had been raised about previous per capita sales analyses. In this exploration, he was seeking guidance in the conduct, interpretation, and reporting of this, his first major sales analysis for Allied Products, Inc. He was reassured by the fact that many of the objections raised to previous analyses, in his opinion, were valid objections; but the revision of sales territories to eliminate split marketing units had the effect of eliminating many of the problem sources.

Figure 12.2 presents the work sheet developed in this analysis. The company's four regions are identified in capital letters, and the nineteen districts are listed under their respective regions. The analysis applied to 1943 sales, so the population figure for that year was used. In developing the population figures, *Sales Management* magazine's annual *Survey of Buying Power* issue was used. This provided population figures which were increased to show growth in population since the census year and took into consideration migration as well.

Column 1 lists population figures. Column 2 shows the percentage division of the population into districts and regions. Note that the districts add up to regional totals. The company's 1943 sales of consumer products are shown in column 3. The percentage division of that sales volume is presented as column 4. Column 5 shows the *per capita* sales. It represents the result of dividing the sales volume in each district, region, and in total by the population figure.

Column 6 reduces variations in per capita sales to an index basis, using the company's national average of 4.86 cents (or $.0486) as the base figure or 100. The significance of this index figure is developed in Chapter 21.

— ★ —

CHARACTERISTICS OF RESEARCH ON
CURRENT OPERATING PROBLEMS

In the above case we have the normal assignment of responsibility for marketing research to the research director of the company with the problem. The problem in this case of the current operating type. In such research, the first two steps in the research process (which are the subject of this chapter) are often relatively simple. From the viewpoint of the sales research director of Allied Products, Inc., defining and refining such problems is often entirely unnecessary.

Each such problem consists of two parts. One part is general, the other specific. The general part is common to most problems of the current operating type. It therefore provides a sort of omnibus answer to the question: What is the problem? The problem essentially is to answer this question: How can we do our marketing job or some part of it better —more efficiently, more effectively, more profitably, less expensively? The specific part of the problem is the modification of that general part, if any, which the specific problem at hand introduces.

Referring to the above Allied Products, Inc., case, the specific problem within the general framework is a relatively easy one to define. The problem is to identify those sales regions, districts, and territories in which the company's sales performance is strong and those in which that performance is weak. Once that information has been developed, attention will be focused on the weak territories, districts, and regions and on the opportunities that exist there to increase volume and profit by raising the level of their performance.

The only specific modification which the research man introduces into his work on this problem results from previous work done by the company in this general area. The research man recognizes the need to conduct his analysis in such a way that its results will be accepted and used by the management and by the sales organization. There have been past analyses of a somewhat similar type. Those analyses were not uniformly accepted and productively applied. Why not? What are the particular problem areas, the sources of resistance, which must be anticipated?

It is interesting to note that work on this particular research assignment was initiated by the marketing research man himself. This is true of many current operating problems. The research director has general responsibility, usually defined in his job description. Within that general assignment of responsibility, he conceives, plans, and executes much research work. This is only natural. He knows the needs of his company, and he knows the capabilities of the research tools at his command. As a general observation, the higher the proportion of the marketing research work of a department that is initiated within the department, the higher the level of competence of the department as a whole.

The relative simplicity of the problem-defining phase of marketing research work on most current operating problems makes them poor illustrations for this chapter. There are exceptions. Some current operating problems seem to have more in common with nonrecurring problems than with the other problems in the current operating group.

SOME CURRENT OPERATING PROBLEMS RESEMBLE NONRECURRING PROBLEMS

One of the responsibilities of the marketing management team is to appraise the effectiveness of various parts of the company's marketing operation. For example, how effective is the current advertising approach? Such appraisals are current operating problems. Sometimes such an appraisal has many of the key characteristics of a major nonrecurring type of problem. That resemblance is likely to develop when there is evidence that the element subject to appraisal is rather strikingly ineffective.

The following case illustrates such a situation. The similarity of this problem to some of the major nonrecurring problems presented in earlier cases will be apparent.

12. THE MARCINE PAPER COMPANY ★ (A)

The Marcine Paper Company is a small firm in a middle-sized
Wisconsin city. The firm processes paper into a line of products which
includes toilet tissue, paper towels, paper napkins, and cleansing tissue.
Toilet tissue is by far the most important part of the company's sales
volume.

The company manufactures products which are sold under its own
label—the Marcine brand. It also packs products under the private
labels of various organizations, including corporate and voluntary grocery
chains. The private-label business carries a very narrow profit margin.
The management of the company was anxious to convert its entire
capacity to its own brand as quickly as that could be accomplished, to
improve the company's profit picture.

Here are the company's sales of Marcine tissue by years, in cases:

Year	Case sales	Per cent change
1946	779,691	+ 6.6
1947	1,118,378	+43.4
1948	1,071,113	− 4.2
1949	1,302,695	+21.6
1950	1,441,769	+10.7

The company's sales of its own brand of tissue had been developed
through a promotional program which had these major elements:

— A relatively small advertising appropriation
— Spread thinly over a selected list of markets, was
— Heavily "merchandised" to the trade, and
— Supplemented by occasional "loading deals"

The company's sales operations had the following pattern. A salesman
for a given territory was given a schedule of the proposed advertising
in one of the major cities (or "markets" to use the company's designation)
in his territory. He was provided with the name of the newspaper to be
used, the insertion dates, a schedule showing size of the ads, and proofs
of the ads themselves. The salesman then used that proposed schedule
as a tool to persuade chain-store buyers and various wholesale organizations to stock up on Marcine tissue in advance of the date when advertising was to break.

The company used advertising entirely as a sales tool. The advertising
schedule in any given market was worked out to fit the time required
for the salesman to "work" the market.

The "loading deals" were of the nature of 1-cent sales and similar reduced-price offerings. One such deal gave the buyers one roll of Marcine tissues for 1 cent with the purchase of three rolls at the regular price. The "deals" were banded, and the "1-cent roll" identified prominently as such, to discourage dealers from "breaking up" deals and selling the merchandise at full price. The company used large announcement ads in newspapers with such deals. Most of the key retailers "loaded up" on deal merchandise.

The company's sales operations covered an expanding list of markets, in a geographic area spreading outward from the company's Wisconsin mill and headquarters. For sales-control purposes, the company used a consumer trading-area map developed by a magazine publisher. There were more than 600 such areas in the United States. The approximate scope of operations of this regional marketer may be inferred from the fact that the company had sales in 1949 in 180-odd markets out of the total of more than 600.

The company's advertising expenditures were not planned in advance. They were dependent in part on how many markets salesmen could cover. The salesmen's ability to cover markets determined how many markets the company would have to advertise in to develop the volume desired on Marcine tissue. The following figures show the company's advertising expenditures by years:

Year	Advertising expenditure
1946	$175,669
1947	131,603
1948	161,269
1949	162,701
1950	344,685

The above figures cover the cost of space used in newspapers and the charge made for outdoor advertising (billboard) space purchased. They do not include the "art and mechanical" costs of preparing the advertisements and of preparing the material used for posting on billboards. Those "a&m" costs aggregated something less than 10 per cent of the space costs shown and were in addition to those costs.

Early in 1951, the company's executives became concerned about the soundness of the company's sales and advertising program. They noted that the rate of increase in company sales in 1950 was only half as large as in the preceding year. They noted also the sharp increase in the advertising expenditure in total and on a per-case basis. The combination of those two factors—a decline in the rate of gain and an increased expenditure for advertising—indicated the existence of a sales and advertising problem.

A consulting organization in the marketing management field was invited to examine the company's situation and to suggest action which might be taken to guide the company's management in determining future sales and advertising policies.

— ★ —

FIRST STEP: GET THE FACTS IN DETAIL

As a starting point in thinking about the Marcine Paper Company's problem, consider the symptom of that problem. There are two parts to that symptom. The first part is the relatively sharp decline in the *rate* at which sales were increasing. In 1949, there was a 21.6 per cent sales gain. In the next year sales continued to gain, but at a sharply decreasing rate. The annual gain was less than 11 per cent. In itself, a decline in the rate of sales-volume expansion is neither unusual nor necessarily symptomatic of a problem. As gains are piled upon gains, a declining rate of gain simply reflects the growth of the base against which the increase is calculated.

The second part of the symptom, however, made the existence of a problem apparent. There was a very sharp increase in advertising expenditures from 1949 to 1950. From a $162,701 expenditure in 1949, advertising costs climbed to $344,685 in the following year. Thus while advertising expenditures were more than doubled, the rate of sales increase was cut in half! This combination of circumstances added up to a marketing problem.

You are the marketing research man with primary responsibility for the diagnosis of this problem. What would you do? Your first step would ordinarily be a request for more facts. You don't know anything like enough about this problem to begin to do effective work on it.

What do you need to know? Basically you need some specific and detailed answers to questions like these: Was the sales-rate dip uniform in all markets? If some markets gained at a greater and some at a lesser rate than the company's over-all gain, what are the characteristics of the markets in each group? Where was the advertising increase placed? Was it uniformly distributed over all markets, or did some receive greater and some smaller increases in advertising expenditures? What relationship, if any, exists between the advertising expenditure rate, and the change in that rate, and the sales trend in individual markets?

The approach you would be likely to take at least initially in your work on the Marcine problem would be essentially in the area of analysis of sales and advertising expenditure figures. After that analysis had been completed, you would know enough about the problem to decide what additional research, if any, might be appropriate.

SUMMARY

1. This chapter introduces a section in which the major steps in marketing research practice are described and illustrated. It represents in effect an extension of Chapter 4. A review of that chapter as preparation for this section is recommended.

2. For maximum effectiveness, marketing research must be integrated into the problem-solving process. It should be expected to make its first contribution at the point where the existence of a *marketing* problem is recognized or at least suspected. It is far less effective if it is applied only to fragmentary marketing research problems, without being exposed to the entire marketing problem of which those research problems are a part.

3. The detailed, step-by-step approach to the solution, first of a marketing problem and then of the marketing research problems identified as parts of that marketing problem, is applied explicitly in work on a major problem of unknown nature. Essentially the same approach, however, becomes an ingrained part of the working habits of a marketing research man. It is not unusual, therefore, to find these steps used more or less subconsciously in work on less important problems.

4. As Chapter 3 on the marketing-problem base of marketing research pointed out, the most important marketing research applications are those involving current operating problems. Responsibility for the problem-solving process in the case of such problems is usually assigned as part of his primary responsibility to the marketing research director inside an organization. Occasionally there is an outside assignment of problem-solving responsibility, but that is less likely to occur with a current operating problem than with a nonrecurring major problem.

5. Because so much marketing research is done by individuals who work within the company in which the problem develops, the detailed task of familiarizing himself with background on the company, its industry, etc., is often not necessary as a separate step in the research process. When an outside organization is assigned problem-solving responsibility, there is an additional step sometimes necessary in the form of a general analysis of the situation in which the problem exists.

6. In this initial phase of the problem-solving process, emphasis is on securing a *detailed* and *accurate* picture of the problem situation. "Explanations" of the problem advanced by interested individuals are accepted and used, but only as *hypotheses* to guide research planning.

QUESTIONS

1. What are the advantages of using the integrated approach in marketing research?

2. When does marketing research which is integrated enter the problem-solving process? When do research activities usually start under the non-integrated approach? What disadvantage does the nonintegrated approach present?

3. What type of situations exists where the problem-solving responsibility is assigned to someone outside the company? Who might the assignment fall to?

4. Can you think of any limitations to assigning an advertising agency the responsibility of solving marketing management problems?

5. What pattern does advertising agency–client division of marketing research responsibility usually follow?

CHAPTER 13

Defining and Refining the Problem (Continued): Informal Investigation

Defining and refining the problem is one of the most important steps in the entire marketing research process. It is also one of the most difficult. You are the marketing research man with primary responsibility for planning the problem-solving approach to, say, the Dell-O problem. How do you "get your teeth into" the problem? What do you do first? Where do you start?

Your objective initially, remember, is to define the problem. What is the problem, *really?* You are aware of the important distinction between what the problem is and what someone thinks it is. Thus the Dell-O problem really was a problem of declining industry volume, someone thought. The Dell-O problem was really a problem of the increased competition from low-priced margarine, someone else thought. As the marketing research man with the primary problem-solving assignment, you have no opinions on the subject. You enter into a consideration of the problem with a completely open mind. Your job is to find the facts and to report them as you find them.

In the early phases of work on the Dell-O or any other marketing problem, you begin with no opinions of your own. You do your thinking upward from a foundation of facts, not downward from an opinion. You accept the "definitions" of the problem which are offered by those who have greater familiarity with it than you do. You accept them, however, for what they are: the *opinions* of one or more individiuals. What's your own opinion? You have none—yet. You have some hunches, perhaps; some hypotheses of your own, to add to those offered by others.

You proceed to subdivide the problem. Some aspects of that subdivision have already been noted. You decide that the relationship between butter prices and margarine sales can best be explored by a statistical approach which uses correlation techniques. It will take time to get the required basic data and to conduct the analysis. (This was in the days before electronic computers made life more pleasant for statisticians!) So you put that portion of the job on the rails and start it rolling toward completion. You recognize a need for a factual picture of the company's pattern of sales strength and sales weakness. You will need such a picture to guide you in planning the sample of any consumer studies which you subsequently decide may be necessary. You start the sales-analysis procedure.

FUNCTION OF THE INFORMAL INVESTIGATION

You next decide to call upon one of the most potent weapons in the marketing research man's arsenal. That weapon is especially useful in the problem-defining step of the research process. It is known as an *informal investigation*. An informal investigation is a relatively small-scale study. It is planned, and usually much of it is personally executed, by one or more competent and experienced research people.

The objective of the informal investigation is to gather information which is to be used in defining the problem. The findings from that phase of the research are used also in guiding decisions as to what additional research, if any, should be done on a particular problem. The "if any" qualification above should be noted. In many marketing research projects, the research activities begin *and end* with the informal investigation. The results of that investigation are sufficient to indicate that an extension or expansion of the research would be unlikely to meet the required cost-versus-results requirement mentioned in Chapter 1 and frequently thereafter. Result: No additional research is recommended or executed.

WHO CONDUCTS THE INFORMAL INVESTIGATION?

Marketing research includes research into all phases of the marketing process. Marketing takes place almost everywhere. To conduct research into marketing, it is necessary to go where the marketing is done. Products are bought and sold in the field; the problems which develop and which tend to inhibit their sale cannot be analyzed from an ivory tower. These comments are prefatory to the observation that *personal participation in the informal investigation by the individual with primary responsibility for the research is customary.*

The informal investigation is a really important part of the research process. It provides the foundation for all the research which follows, if additional research does follow. It is no place to send a small boy out to do a man's job!

There are two reasons why personal participation in the informal investigation by the most experienced research personnel available is necessary and desirable. The first concerns the scale of the study. It is typically on a relatively small scale. Therefore it is especially important that the evidence gathered in the course of the informal investigation be evaluated by the most seasoned and mature marketing research talent available. There is always a grave danger that too much importance may be attached to a single (and exceptional) bit of evidence. The experienced marketing research man is less likely to go off "half-cocked," or to leap to an unsound conclusion, than is one lacking that experience.

The second reason for personal participation grows out of the objectives of the informal investigation. That investigation is carried on to gather clues, information, opinions, etc., which can be translated into hypotheses. Those hypotheses are then explored and evaluated in subsequent research. Recognizing the significance of key elements, reported or observed, and detecting relationships between apparently unrelated factors call for a high level of research skill. An inexperienced research man might well overlook vital clues which a more experienced researcher would uncover.

EXAMPLE OF AN INFORMAL INVESTIGATION

To provide a specific background for a discussion of informal investigation and its vital role in the research process, let's consider an actual case in which that approach played an unusually vital part.

13. PABST SALES COMPANY (A)

In late 1941, America was accelerating its defense activities. There was an imminent danger that the country might be drawn into full participation in the war then raging in Europe. Strategic materials from Southeast Asia, notably including tin and rubber, were recognized as being inadequate in supply to meet defense requirements. Steps were being taken by defense authorities to conserve existing stocks. One step was a reduction in tinplate used for food canning. Another was an order forbidding the use of cans for products considered nonessential to the defense effort. Canned beer was one of the products so classified. All brewers in the country had to adjust operations accordingly.

A restriction of this type represented a change in the industry's packaging pattern. At first blush, that change would seem to be one which would affect all brewers to about the same extent. If so, it would not represent an important *marketing* problem for any one brewery. Actually, there were important differences in the impact of this development on different breweries. Some brewers had not installed canning facilities. Instead, they continued to put their entire packaged volume (as distinguished from *draft*-beer volume, packed in barrels) into glass bottles. The operations of such brewers were essentially unaffected by the order.

In contrast, other breweries had been aggressively marketing canned beer and had converted a high proportion of their total packaged-beer sales to cans. Breweries in that position rightly interpreted the order as a threat to their competitive position. One brewery which had been especially successful in the promotion of canned beer was the Pabst Brewing Company. Their Pabst Blue Ribbon brand of beer ranked first nationally in volume of *canned*-beer sales. The government order forbidding the use of cans for beer after existing stocks of cans had been used up seemed likely to hit Pabst harder than any other brewery.

The geographic impact of the blow on the Pabst competitive situation seemed likely to be uneven. Through its sales subsidiary, the Pabst Sales Company, Pabst had built substantial volume in the highly competitive New York market. Pabst sales in New York were surprisingly high, especially when the location of the Pabst breweries was considered. Pabst then had only two breweries, one in Milwaukee, Wis., and one in Peoria Heights, Ill.

Thus Pabst was competing successfully against entrenched local brands which did not have to pay a heavy freight bill, as Pabst did, to get its beer to the New York market. With cans eliminated, the Pabst freight burden would increase, for bottles would have to be shipped empty back to the breweries. A breakdown of Pabst volume in the New York market by package types revealed that cans represented a far higher proportion of total packaged-beer sales than was true in other areas. The elimination of cans, therefore, posed a particularly acute competitive threat to Pabst volume in the New York metropolitan market.

The Pabst management faced the problem of evaluating the probable impact of the elimination of canned beer on their New York market volume. The research job had to be completed quickly, so that any action indicated could be taken before the limited supply of cans on hand ran out and Pabst lost distribution in the market on its canned beer.

The assignment was given to the account research supervisor in the advertising agency then handling Pabst advertising. A complete report of his findings had to be available four weeks from the day he received the assignment.

DETAILS OF AN INFORMAL INVESTIGATION

The starting point in this informal investigation, as in most similar projects, was a series of interviews with company executives who could contribute background information helpful in planning the research. Because of the acute time problem, those interviews had to be telescoped into a single day. Some breakdowns of the company's sales by package types were secured. The hypothesis that a shift to a smaller bottle might permit better price comparisons with local beers, hence be a strong competitive weapon, was advanced by one executive.

Detailed and specific information about the situation in the New York market, it developed, could best be secured by an interview with the company's sales representative in that market. Accordingly, the research man went to New York to continue the informal investigation. A discussion with the local representative of the Pabst organization was completed.

Next the research man faced the task of getting a detailed picture of the situation in the New York market, through research he personally planned and executed on the spot. There were a number of different types of retail licenses to sell beer in the New York market. The research man had to determine the characteristics of such licensees and the number of each. Figures on the number of licensees of different types were secured from newspapers in the market. Information on the characteristics of different types of licensees was secured by personal calls on a sample of licensees of each type. In those calls, informal interviews with the license holder were conducted.

The New York market newspapers continually conducted various research studies on beer consumption in the area. The beer-advertising category was important to those newspapers, and they had specialists in beer marketing assigned to the individual breweries and their advertising agencies. Interviews with those informed experts on New York beer marketing were conducted by the research man. The advice of those experts when checked with personal observation provided an indication of the relative importance of a number of different elements in the beer-marketing picture. One paper conducted distribution studies which showed what proportion of grocery stores carried various package sizes and types of individual brands of beer.

Because the expenditures for advertising provided an indication both of relative volume standings and of the aggressiveness of individual competitive beers, figures on the advertising expenditures of major brands over the last several years were desired. A request for such figures was made, this request being channeled through the agency's media department to the individual advertising media involved. This information was secured well within the deadline of the study.

The vast New York market includes a number of major subdivisions. Each of those subdivisions represented more potential volume for Pabst than did the whole of a large number of smaller but still important markets. Because of the nature of the market structure, two subdivisions of the New York market received individual attention in this informal investigation. One was the Jewish portion of the market, which had its own newspapers, radio stations, dietary laws, etc. The Jewish portion of the market was especially important to Pabst because a very high proportion of the small grocery and delicatessen outlets through which Pabst beer was sold were owned and operated by Jewish proprietors. The other market segment to which attention had to be devoted despite the time pressure was the Negro market.

Note how the particular nature of the problem guided the identification of the market segments important enough to need individual attention. It was in part the number of Negroes in the New York market which made special attention to Negro drinkers desirable. It was also the fact that Negroes at that time were somewhat below average in economic status, hence more likely to be beer drinkers than cocktail drinkers, that identified that portion of the market as of potential significance.

The particular characteristics of the Jewish portion of the market were explored, first, by interviews with the experts on that part of the market employed by advertising media which specialized in reaching that market segment; and second, by individual interviews with retail-store proprietors. The Negro portion of the market was studied through the medium of discussions with Pabst's own special representative in that market and by retail calls made with that representative.

Sixteen days and more than 200 interviews later, the agency research man returned to his office in Chicago with the information needed to evaluate the threat to Pabst New York volume of the imminent loss of cans as a beer package. There remained the formidable task of analyzing and coordinating the many pieces of the jigsaw puzzle and developing a report for Pabst management from the informal investigation. By utilizing the existing bits and pieces of information—like the distribution surveys of the newspaper—and filling in the missing links through interviews with informed experts and with retail, wholesale, and other market factors, the informal investigation was completed on time.

— ★ —

INTERVIEWS WITH COMPANY EXECUTIVES

Interviews with executives of the company which has a marketing problem are an integral part of any informal investigation of that problem. This is true whether the problem-solving assignment has been made to someone inside or someone outside of the organization itself. The cases presented up to this point provide many illustrations. Thus in the Dell-O case it was in interviews with company executives, which were part of the informal investigation, that the various hypotheses already mentioned were first presented to the research man. In the Allied Products, Inc., case, interviews with various executives of the company aimed at pinpointing in specific terms the limitations of previous analysis of territorial sales performance were necessary. With that knowledge to guide him, the sales research man at Applied Products, Inc., was in a position to develop an approach which did not face the same roadblocks.

In the case of the Pabst New York market problem, interviews with Pabst sales personnel with a knowledge of the New York situation were part of the informal investigation. In the case of Shower-of-Stars Cosmetics, the observations of various company executives as to probable causes of the sales decline were developed in interviews. In the Bissell case, the reasons why various members of the management team were or were not concerned about the growth in vacuum cleaner sales were explored. The approach in all these cases is essentially the same. The marketing research man asks himself: "Who within the organization has specialized or detailed knowledge of this problem situation?" He then proceeds to interview those who have such knowledge.

In interviews with executives in the company with the problem, an experienced marketing research man is likely to prefer *individual* interviews in which the only participants are himself and one executive of the company. Many times if a group interview or a discussion with a number of respondents is held, there will be aspects of the personal relationships between the participants which would tend to inhibit the free flow of information. The marketing research man wants—and needs —all the information he can get. He naturally prefers a two-man interviewing situation in which he is more likely to secure such information over one with more people present and less likelihood of frank and complete disclosure of facts, opinions, and judgments.

In making interviews with company executives, the marketing research man is alert for *differences in viewpoint*. Thus a respondent may say that thus-and-thus is so. The research man would inquire whether *everyone* agrees that this is the case; whether there are any individuals who disagree; what the basis for that disagreement is; and so on. The results of interviews with company executives made in the course of an informal investigation should almost never be so reported that the respondents can be identified. An executive who is assured and who believes that his comments, observations, and opinions will not be "reported upstairs" and identified as his is much more likely to speak frankly and without reservation than one who is not. In this phase of research work, a marketing research man, like a journalist, should protect his sources. The respondent and the research man who is doing the interviewing have in common one important interest: the ultimate good of the organization within which the problem situation exists. The research man, working from that basis of common interest, should and must establish rapport with his executive respondent. It is essential to gain his confidence and respect, in order to secure from him a full and frank disclosure of whatever information, opinions, facts, or other guidance he may provide.

"A SPONGE ON A FISHING EXPEDITION"

The role of a research man in the informal investigation has been described as similar to that of "a sponge on a fishing expedition." As in the case of a fishing expedition, the research man does not know—at least initially—what he wants to know. He cannot ask direct questions aimed accurately at the heart of the problem, because he does not yet know what the problem is. He has to secure whatever information he can which *may* be relevant to the problem-solving process. He is like a sponge in that he must "soak up" without question as to qualification all the information he can secure. Remember that the information-gathering and the information-organizing and information-evaluating phases of the research are separate and distinct.

In the informal investigation in general, and in interviews with company executives in particular, the information gathered varies tremendously in many key characteristics. Some of it is fact, some is fancy. Some is unsupported opinion. Some is pure hunch. And many of the bits and pieces of information gathered up in this process of applying a vacuum cleaner to executive sources are essentially contradictory. Many "facts" reported to the research man will be in fundamental conflict.

Success in this phase of the research process is likely to depend in part on the acting ability of the research man. He is called upon, in those interviews with executives, to play a role. His role is one of reporter. He is looking for information. What information he can gather he carefully notes. But this is important—his role is *not* that of a judge! The opinions, assertions, and observations of executives interviewed are all accepted as grist for the fact-finding mill. A detached and objective attitude in interviews with executives is essential.

The above comments do not mean that a viewpoint expressed by one respondent which is in fundamental disagreement with one expressed by another respondent should not be questioned. It should be. The comments of the respondent on why some other folks feel differently about a given subject, or on the factors that people holding an opposed or contrary view may be overlooking, should be explored. What is important is that the marketing research man, in such interviews, should not take a firm position either for or against any particular controversial point. He is a seeker after the truth. Each respondent who is interviewed *of course* shares the research man's desire for "the facts" in a particular case!

NEED FOR CAUTION IN ACCEPTING VIEWPOINTS

Anticipating some of the discussions in Chapters 16 and 17 on the analysis and interpretation steps, a vital caution should be introduced at this point. A marketing research man at work is a detached, objective individual, in pursuit of facts. He must retain that detachment and objectivity. In particular he must guard against the too-easy acceptance of any of the viewpoints presented to him by executives whom he interviews as part of the informal investigation.

The company has a problem. The nature of that problem, or some aspects of it, are described by someone working within the company to the individual with problem-solving responsibility. The latter individual, as we have noted, may be a fellow employee of the company or may be an outsider. In either case, this question must be faced: How much credence can you as the research man attach to the information developed in the course of an executive interview? To what extent should you allow your marketing research approach to be guided by it? The answer to those questions has already been suggested by the discussion of the Dell-O case, but it should be repeated here for additional emphasis: *The definition of the problem advanced by someone without marketing research training should be accepted only for what it is—the opinion of an individual.* Such opinions are helpful in marketing research, because they provide a fertile source for hypotheses. As we have seen, hypotheses are extremely useful in marketing research. But a hypothesis, whether developed by a marketing research man or presented to him by someone else, is subject to confirmation, through research; or to nullification, also through research. The hypothesis that the Dell-O sales decline was simply a reflection of a decline in industry volume provides an example of a hypothesis which proved null and void when examined in the light of available evidence.

This is a fundamental viewpoint which pervades all marketing research practice. It should be noted carefully.

The marketing research man has as one outstanding characteristic a questioning mind. He is interested in the opinions of others. He is also (and especially!) interested in the evidence on which those opinions are based. You are in an executive interview, as part of an informal investigation. The executive advances such-and-such as his opinion, or perhaps states it emphatically as representing (in his eyes at least) an unquestioned fact. What is your reaction? A series of questions naturally arise in your mind. You do not necessarily ask them, but you wonder: You say that thus-and-so is the case? How interesting! How do you know? How did you find out? Who told you? How did he find out? What was the nature of the evidence?

You must be especially on guard if the respondent's situation is such that there may be some reason to doubt the objectivity of his comments. You are constantly concerned with deciding whether a respondent is commenting on the basis of his information or opinion, as a disinterested bystander; or whether there is a possibility that he has "an axe to grind" in the matter. It is not unusual to find a respondent who is seeking to *use* the marketing research man as a means of registering his views in certain quarters.

One of the vital differences between different organizations which an experienced marketing research man learns to recognize is in the importance or unimportance of company politics. Some organizations have an essentially harmonious tone. All employees at the executive level are working together toward the common goal of company profit progress. What is good for the company is more important than what may be good for a particular individual. Other organizations are extremely prone to politics, and especially petty politics. Often there is a factionalization within the organization. The views disclosed in an executive interview must be interpreted against a background knowledge of the individual's particular factional alliances and objectives, in the latter case.

SOURCES OF DISTORTION IN INTERNAL VIEWPOINTS

Now let's pause briefly to examine the reasons why a marketing research man is so reluctant to accept the views of insiders without first subjecting them to a searching scrutiny. As well-informed executives, they hold views which are presumably much more expert and therefore acceptable than those of individuals who lack their intimate knowledge of the problem situation. Why then does a marketing research man need such strong reservations against accepting their views? Why is each "definition of the problem" advanced by someone who is not a trained marketing research man regarded with such a jaundiced eye?

The answer to those questions lies in certain characteristics of the insider in a marketing-problem situation. The first characteristic is one which a marketing research man employed by a company must be especially careful to guard against. It's so contagious! That is the tendency of employees of a corporation to acquire as part of their training and indoctrination a viewpoint which is really a corporate prejudice. In some corporations, the process of indoctrinating and training a new employee has some points of similarity with "thought control" in a dictatorship. This is so; this is not so. This is the way to do such-and-such. That competitor is an unimportant example of "cheap competition" unworthy of our notice. And so on.

The questioning mind which is so important a part of the marketing research man's equipment is acquired only through education and training. Most employees lack that training, especially at the time they are hired. They are told that certain basic fundamentals constitute the policy and viewpoint of "the management" and it never occurs to them to question those fundamentals. Many companies operate with reliance on basic assumptions which are never questioned, yet which are fundamentally incorrect.

One area in which this problem is especially likely to be found involves product-quality levels. The tendency to overrate one's own products and to underrate those of competitors is an amazingly uniform one. For a member of a management team to admit out loud that one or more of the company's products is actually inferior to, or even no better than, a competitive product would represent a cross between heresy and treason!

THE DANGER OF BEING TOO CLOSE TO THE FOREST

A second vital characteristic of an insider is that he is likely to be too close to the problems of his company or his industry to see them clearly in accurate perspective. The professional in any industry has certain well-defined tendencies which interfere with his ability to make an accurate appraisal of the elements in a problem situation. For example, to the executive in a company or an industry, the products of that company or industry are extremely important. After all, they are the source of his livelihood. He knows them well. He talks about them to his friends, who also tend to develop an unusually high familiarity with them. This leads to a widespread tendency on the part of executives to overestimate how much their customers know (or care!) about a company, its industry, or its products. It follows that such executives are unable to appraise accurately those facets of a problem situation in which that gap between internal and external viewpoints is a key element. The viewpoint of an insider is often quite significantly different from that of someone outside a company or an industry.

This is entirely natural and understandable. It is also extremely dangerous, from the viewpoint of sound marketing research practice.

THE CUSTOMER'S VIEWPOINT IS MORE IMPORTANT

One of the really fundamental concepts of sound marketing management today is that the really important viewpoint toward a company, an industry, or its products is the viewpoint of the customer. In a long-distant day, manufacturers first made products, and then proceeded to sell them. The selling job was often difficult, because the products the manufacturer wanted to sell were often quite different from the products his customer wanted to buy.

Successful companies no longer proceed on that basis. The needs of customers are consulted before the decision as to the nature of products to be made, their quantity, price, etc., are finalized. The products resulting from that approach are keyed closely to the requirements of customers. As a result, marketing such products is much easier and less expensive.

One important function of an experienced marketing research man working for a manufacturing organization lies in this particular area. It is the marketing research man's job, first, to determine what the particular needs or requirements of customers are; and then to communicate those needs or requirements clearly and accurately to his management. From constant work in this field, marketing research men have learned that there is often a wide gap between what customers want and what someone in the company *thinks* they want (or thinks they *ought* to want!). They have learned also that it is easier and cheaper to sell the products customers want to buy. In the course of his work, a marketing research man is continually exposed to the viewpoint of customers and others outside the organization. It is his job to report that viewpoint to his management and to see that that report is accurate, objective, and clear.

A TOO-EXPERT VIEWPOINT POSES PROBLEMS

There is an additional characteristic of insiders which warrants attention, because it is often revealed in the course of executive interviews which are part of an informal investigation. While it is closely related to the one just mentioned, it remains sufficiently different to require specific identification. Insiders in a company or industry are often too expert or too specialized. In their product planning in particular, they sometimes develop a product to suit their own advanced and expert judgment as to what customers (who are erroneously assumed to be similarly expert, hence to share the insiders' viewpoint) ought to want.

Two specific examples may be helpful in illustrating this viewpoint. One was the marketing problem of a beer company which continued to brew the same kind of beer, year after year. Consumer tastes changed, and a lighter type of beer grew in popular favor. The company's sales declined sharply until a change in the management of the brewery shifted to the kind of beer consumers preferred as against the type preferred by the brewmaster. The other problem was in the field of canned-chicken products. Sales of a single item in the line—canned whole chickens—were lagging. A product test against a competitive product was recommended by a marketing research man. The executives in the chicken-processing firm thought the idea of a test rather absurd. Their product was packed in an expensive butter gravy; the competitive product against which the test was proposed was a much cheaper broth pack. When the test was made, consumers preferred the broth-packed chicken by a wide margin. The most important single reason for preference? Consumers didn't like the butter gravy, which the chicken experts felt represented the finest method of packing a canned whole chicken!

OTHER PRECAUTIONS IN INTERNAL INTERVIEWS

Two other observations about potential trouble spots in the executive interviews which are a part of the informal investigation are necessary. The first concerns the defensive attitudes which some executives exhibit in the course of such interviews.

When a problem situation exists in a company, it is essential to recognize that in most cases the problem did not spring into being full grown. More likely it developed gradually over a period of time. The origins of the problem are unlikely to have been spontaneous. It can probably be traced backward to some decisions which were made in the past; or to some decisions which should have been made, but were not. An effective job of marketing research in some cases unfortunately but inevitably tends to point a finger of blame at one or more individual executives, or at some division or department of the company or some other functional group. Since this is the case, it is natural to find some executives—anticipating either correctly or incorrectly that they may end up as the individuals responsible for a particular problem—with a very defensive attitude toward those exploring that problem.

A defensive attitude on the part of an executive being interviewed in the informal investigation is usually apparent to an experienced research man making that investigation. In some cases it is suggested by the fact that an individual who would normally be expected simply to supply information in answer to questions asked appears to be "selling hard" on one or more points or in general. In other cases the defensive attitude is revealed by a reluctance to disclose information of an authorized nature which the respondent almost certainly possesses. The path is paved for an executive interview by authorization, usually from the superior or superiors of the individuals interviewed. Assuming the authorization and related instructions are clear and complete, there is usually no reason for a respondent to withhold information except in a clearly confidential category. An experienced research man rarely ventures into such a category without authorization.

Where an individual being interviewed is unable or unwilling to disclose requested information about a problem situation, therefore, certain questions are raised which are germane to the investigation. Why the unwillingness to talk frankly? One possibility is that the individual does not have the necessary information. If that information is requisite to his performance on his job, that is in itself a revealing item. Another possibility is that there is a division within the management team as to the nature or importance of the problem itself. That, too, can be a significant finding. A third is the possibility that the individual in question has major responsibility for one or more factors which have contributed to the problem and that he recognizes this and the potential threat which the investigation represents to his status or position.

The other point to be noted about interviews with executives of a company is concerned with the relationship between the position of the man interviewed and the subject matter of the interview. One of the fundamental rules of questionnaire development is that questions should be asked only of those who are in a position to answer them. This applies also in informal investigations. Thus questions about the company's product policy, etc., should be confined to those who have a knowledge of that subject; questions about sales methods and policies should rarely be asked of a financial executive; and so on. Extending this point, where a problem involves a particular portion of the country rather than a national-scale situation, the information should be sought from those with local and specific knowledge of that area. For information about the Pabst situation in New York, it was necessary to go to New York to interview the individual in the sales department with responsibility for that territory.

A closely related observation may be helpful. In organizations which promote from within, the sales executives are often those who have risen up the selling-organization ladder. Strength of personality is often a characteristic of such individuals. They have a high respect for their own judgment, and on their records are entitled to that respect. Such executives sometimes tend to lean heavily on their own experiences as members of the field sales organization in appraising the problems to which they are exposed. There is always a danger that their experiences may have occurred so long ago that they are no longer applicable. This is sometimes a difficult finding to communicate tactfully.

DETAILS OF ANOTHER INFORMAL INVESTIGATION

The point above is illustrated by the following case which provides an additional step-by-step example of an informal investigation.

14. ALLIED PRODUCTS, INC. (C)

As a result of a considerable amount of sales analysis, the sales research director of Allied Products, Inc., reached the conclusion that a major sales weakness existed for the company in the Boston district, which embraced most of New England. When the details of sales performance on a product-by-product basis were reviewed, it became apparent that one major product was primarily responsible for the (apparently) great weakness of the Boston district.

As a newcomer to the company with less than six months of service behind him, the sales research director was naturally careful to qualify his reports on this weakness. He was still using a *general market index* (defined and explained at length in Chapter 21), and he was aware of the possibility that one or more of the company's products might have a sharply defined geographic pattern in consumption. The magnitude of the opportunity for the company to expand sales in Boston seemed so large that he did not feel his report should be delayed until that possibility could be explored.

When he reported on the Boston problem to his boss, the company's sales vice-president, he identified the product which was primarily responsible for that problem according to his analysis. His boss had spent his entire business lifetime working for Allied Products, Inc., and had moved up to the chief sales executive's position after having been salesman, district manager, regional manager, and general sales manager Drawing on his lifetime of experience selling Allied Products, the sales vice-president dismissed the Boston problem as nonexistent. "They just don't use that product type in Boston," he explained. The implication was that the general index was insufficiently accurate to reflect sales performance *by territories by products* with dependable accuracy.

The sales research director asked for permission to make some retail and wholesale calls in the Boston district, to provide him with a first-hand picture of the particular characteristics of that important section of the country. That permission was granted. He was authorized to spend up to three weeks in the Boston district. The exact nature of his activities was left pretty much up to him.

The work which could be done through sales analysis to pinpoint the specific nature of the Boston problem had already been completed. Therefore, the sales research director decided that an informal investigation within the district itself was indicated. Armed with a vast amount of detailed information about the level and trend of the company's sales in that district, including product-type and customer-type detail, he went to Boston.

The Boston district consisted of twelve major sales territories. The largest was the Boston metropolitan area, which represented almost half of the total district potential. There were four other markets which individually represented more than 5 per cent of the Boston district potential. Those five markets were singled out as the area within which the informal investigation would be carried out. Because of its tremendous importance, Boston was given top priority. In view of his limited experience with the company's problems at retail and wholesale levels, the sales research man decided on this approach: First, he was going to do an intensive study in the Boston market; then he was going to do smaller-scale studies in the other four markets, with attention primarily focused on the ways in which those markets differed from the Boston pattern.

Step 1 in this informal investigation was a meeting with the company's Boston district manager. The objectives of this meeting, from the research man's point of view, were two: First, he wanted as much information about the possible origins of the Boston problem as he could secure from the local district manager. Second, he wanted to win the confidence of that district manager and enlist his cooperation to whatever extent it became necessary.

Comment: To those who regard the marketing research function as some kind of gestapo-like device, this direct approach may be difficult to understand. From their viewpoint, it makes about as much sense as a policeman's request to a suspect to provide the information needed to put the latter behind bars! Actually, there is a basic mutuality of interest between the research man and the district manager which can be translated into effective and active cooperation. If Boston sales go up, as they should if the causes of the problem are uncovered, the district manager will thereby gain considerable credit. If the Boston problem has roots in areas beyond the district manager's control (for example, if the manpower authorized is low for the potential in the area), the investigation may well reveal that fact and provide new strength for the district. The need for frankness and sincerity, in such a face-to-face discussion between a research man and someone in the line sales organization, cannot be overemphasized.

The Boston district manager proved to be young, ambitious, and eager to help. He provided a completely detailed and relatively frank appraisal of the strengths and weaknesses of the company in the Boston district. He accompanied the research director to interviews with key buyers in wholesale and chain organizations. After introducing the research man, the district manager left so that the discussion would not be inhibited by his presence. The latter approach had been suggested by the research man. It was intended primarily to guard against the danger that the buyer might use his presence as a "sounding board" for complaints against the company's practices and policies.

Interviews with merchandising executives of leading newspapers in the market provided an informed view of the relative importance of different wholesale and retail forces in the market. The company's own sales to such wholesalers and retailers were part of the analytical ammunition which the research man prepared in advance of his trip to Boston. He was especially careful to try to identify the important *potential* customers of the company which did not show up in important volume as *actual* customers. Unaccompanied by any of the local personnel, he made a large number of wholesale and retail calls personally. On each such call he interviewed the key personnel in the wholesale organization or retail outlet. He also observed the distribution of the company's products and of competitive products in retail outlets, noting size of displays, relative pricing, etc.

After making 114 retail calls on a variety of different types of outlets in the Boston area, plus 26 wholesale calls, the research man moved on to sample the other smaller markets on a smaller scale. In each market visited, he met with the company's salesman covering the market, interviewed him, then made additional wholesale and retail calls. Some of those calls were made with the salesman along, while others were made unaccompanied.

— ★ —

ESSENTIAL SIMILARITY OF APPROACH NOTEWORTHY

In the above informal investigation and in the Pabst study described earlier, there is an essential similarity of approach which provides the pattern for research work of this type.

In each case, executive interviews were the first step. In each case, emphasis was placed on identifying the executive with the particular knowledge of the particular problem situation which the research man sought. This was the local representative of Pabst in the New York market. It was the Boston district manager in the Allied Products situation.

Careful preparation for the informal investigation is essential. In the Pabst case the amount of time for such preparation was limited. However, the research man could and did secure information about what advertising media conducted what types of research on beer marketing, before he left for New York. In the Allied case, a substantial amount of sales analysis was completed before the trip to Boston was proposed.

In each case, the marketing research man *went where the problem was.* He was not content to sit behind a desk in an office, far removed from the problem situation. He was not content to rely on someone else's impression of what the problem was or was not. He went to the problem point, so that he could see for himself.

There is a point here which should be stressed because of its fundamental importance in understanding the marketing research process. Often descriptions of marketing research tend to make it seem extremely complicated. As an offset against that tendency, it is sometimes helpful to go back to fundamentals. *A great deal of marketing research boils down to two essential ingredients: a man and a problem.*

You are a marketing research man, given the responsibility for planning the research work on a major problem. What do you do? In many cases, you simply do as well as you can, following the approach outlined in the case of the Pabst and Allied Products, Inc., informal investigations. That approach involves little razzle-dazzle or glamour, but it involves a great deal of applied common sense. It also often involves a great deal of hard work. "Taking apart" a problem involving the largest market in America with a four-week deadline is a tough assignment. Making 114 retail and 26 wholesale calls in Boston, covering four other markets on a smaller scale, and getting "back home" within the three weeks authorized was no vacation for the Allied Products, Inc., research man.

This is not easy—but this is marketing research practice. One cannot supervise marketing research work without first learning to do that work. This kind of pavement-pounding work is the foundation of the experience of most skilled marketing research men.

EVALUATING INFORMANTS VITAL

Returning to the two informal investigations described above, note that in both cases care was taken to locate those experts informed about the particular problem situation who could be used as sources of authoritative information. Since one of the newspapers in the New York market made a continuing check on distribution, the research man working on the Pabst assignment located the man responsible and interviewed him. In working in the Boston, Springfield, Hartford, and Providence markets, the research man on the Allied Products payroll interviewed newspaper executives and wholesale and retail personnel who could provide the information he needed.

In informal investigation, it is standard practice to find and interview the informed specialists or experts who have relevant knowledge of the nature of any problem situation. Sometimes, as in the cases cited, these are men who know about the particular geographic area where a problem exists. Often those individuals have specialized knowledge of a particular industry or of the problems, practices, and attitudes of a particular group of individuals. The specialists in the Jewish portion of the New York market are representative of such potential respondents. The marketing research man planning an informal investigation asks himself: Who knows something I ought to know about this problem? Where can I find him? How can I get him to tell me what I want to know?

In all marketing research in which there is reliance on a relatively small number of respondents—and especially in the informal investigation—it is essential for the marketing research man to evaluate each individual respondent carefully. So much depends on so small a numerical base that confidence in the reliability of the information provided is essential. That confidence depends, in essence, on confidence in the individual supplying that information.

CLUES TO GUIDE THE APPRAISAL OF A RESPONDENT

The accurate appraisal of the dependability of an informant and of the information he provides is extremely important. How do you make such an appraisal? Few subjects in all of marketing research practice are as difficult to communicate as this one. It depends so heavily on the individual research man's background, education, and experience that it is only possible to provide some rough but perhaps useful clues as guides.

Your starting point is a general appraisal of the individual. Who is he? What is his job? How long has he had it? What do the answers to those questions tell you about his reliability as a source of information? What do you know or can you learn (either in the course of the interview or from other sources) of his previous experience and of his educational background?

Your consideration next moves on to consider the relationship between the respondent and the subject of your inquiry. Is there any reason why you should suspect him of being less than objective in discussing the subject? Does he, as a result of his background or as a function of his position, have some kind of bias which reduces the value of his comments? Does he have an "axe to grind"? Examples are provided by interviews with retailers, who characteristically feel that the manufacturer's marketing problems would be solved if only the margin available for the retailer were widened; or the characteristic view of wholesalers that the way to increase volume is to reduce the extent to which manufacturers compete with wholesalers by selling direct! The fact that such biases are present does not invalidate the interview. It does reduce the significance of reactions to some specific research areas.

In the course of a reasonably long discussion, most respondents tell an experienced research man much more about themselves than they are aware they do. The research man studies the answers made and the way they are made. Are these "off-the-cuff" opinions to which little significance should be attached, or were they developed by referring to records or other sources of information which would suggest a relatively high degree of accuracy? Do the judgments made seem to be sound and the manner of communicating those judgments temperate? Does the respondent point out evidence on both sides of controversial opinions, or is he one to whom everything is black or white?

A final important area concerns the specific rapport and interplay of personality of the interviewer and the respondent. How well do the two seem to "hit it off"? Is there some basis of common interest present which makes the discussion a reasonably frank and relaxed one, or is extracting information "like pulling teeth"? If the respondent quite apparently has taken a dislike to the research man, the value of all that follows is extremely questionable. In general the interviewing process goes best where the research man and the respondent are essentially similar in such matters as age, education, economic status, etc. This is not always possible, of course; but where there are marked differences, a skilled research man can and does try to minimize their influence on the interviewing situation. Thus if there is a substantial age difference, with the respondent the older of the pair, a competent research man will try to evidence more respect or even deference than might be necessary or desirable if the pair were contemporaries. Deliberate errors in English by a better-educated research man are often helpful in establishing rapport with a respondent of substantially less education.

Another area contributing to the appraisal is the breadth of the respondent's interest and information. A well-informed respondent who knows about current significant developments in his field is likely to be a more dependable informant than one whose mental alertness is lower and whose interest in and awareness of current development are limited. Obviously the research man himself must be well informed in order to have a judgment on this point!

ALL OTHER SOURCES OF DATA EXPLORED

There has been considerable emphasis, in this chapter, on the physical activity of gathering information by a marketing research man. That emphasis has been desirable for two reasons. One is that a very substantial part of all informal investigations involve that type of activity. The other is that such activity represents to a considerable extent the new contribution which this discussion of the informal investigation makes to the developing picture of marketing research practice.

It should also be emphasized, although that emphasis should *not* be needed, that a marketing research man engaged in a situation analysis secures relevant data from all other sources as part of his investigation. Thus if there is available relevant data from the company's own records (as there was in the Allied Products, Inc., case) those data are examined as part of the investigation. This ties the informal investigation in with the data source described in Chapter 6. If there is any type of panel data available (along the lines described in Chapter 9), those data should be considered. If surveys made by the company or by anyone else shed light on the problem under investigation, they should be considered. In particular the possibility that there is relevant published or unpublished data available of the types described in Chapter 7 should be explored.

REPORTING INTERVIEWS IN AN INFORMAL INVESTIGATION

Informal investigations normally involve a varying but often substantial number of interviews. Those interviews are made with respondents representative of many different levels in the marketing machinery—with consumers, retailers, wholesalers, and manufacturers. To what extent are the interviews which collectively add up to a substantial part of the informal investigation reported, and to what extent are they simply summarized into a unified report of the whole investigation? The answer to that question depends on a number of factors, of which two should be specifically identified: the skill and experience of the research man responsible for the informal investigation, and the objectives of that investigation.

As a general rule, the more experienced the research man in charge of an informal investigation, the less likely there is to be detailed reporting of individual interviews. The process of conducting an informal investigation and of moving into sharper and sharper focus on the nature of a particular marketing problem is to a surprising extent an intuitive one. With increasing experience, the process of identifying the significant needles in a haystack of evidence becomes easier and easier. In the early days of one's research experience, detailed reports of each interview are highly desirable. Such reports, reviewed by others with more experience in the field, provide one basis for learning what is and what is not important. As one acquires more experience, however, the need for detailed reports of individual interviews diminished.

The objective of the informal investigation, however, enters into this subject. An investigation made for the purpose of aiding an advertising agency in its search for an effective sales appeal or advertising theme may be reported fully and in detail. The effect of the complete reports of the interviews is to reproduce at least roughly the exposure that would have resulted if members of the agency's creative staff had accompanied the researcher on the investigation. The interviews in that case are important for their value as stimulants to the creative process. They should be reported fully, with as much of the feeling tone of the interview included as the interviewer can recapture. Where the informal investigation is part of the problem-solving process, as in the Pabst and Allied Products, Inc., examples given earlier, and where the research man with primary responsibility has extensive experience and the confidence of the principal in the research, detailed reporting is unnecessary. In both those cases, a single report of the findings of the investigation was made, without details on individual interviews within the investigation.

To some extent the scope of the study is a factor here, too. In an informal investigation involving 25 to 50 interviews, preparing detailed interview reports may be feasible. Reporting in detail on the 114 retail and 26 wholesale interviews in Boston in the Allied Products, Inc., example would be a tremendously time-consuming task.

CRITERIA FOR EVALUATING AN INFORMAL INVESTIGATION

An informal investigation is relatively difficult for anyone who does not have a considerable amount of marketing research experience to evaluate. The results of that investigation must be measured against its objective. That objective, you will recall, is to provide the research man with the information needed to define a particular problem in specific terms. If the end result of an informal investigation is to leave the research man with a sharply focused picture of the problem he faces, that investigation must be considered a success. Usually that investigation provides the foundation for subsequent research, for additional steps in the research process. Sometimes it is complete in itself. Since the results of the investigation exist primarily in the mind of the individual who planned and executed it, it is obviously difficult to measure objectively.

It has been said that a problem well defined is half solved. Informal investigations often exceed that level. Many research projects begin and end with an informal investigation. It is not unusual to find that the results of that informal study, intelligently interpreted and lucidly reported, make further research unnecessary.

This type of highly productive informal investigation is illustrated by both the Pabst and Allied Products, Inc., examples presented in this chapter. In both cases, the results of the informal investigation made further research both unnecessary and undesirable. Those examples were chosen to provide full-scale illustrations of the informal investigation. It should be emphasized that many informal investigations are on a much smaller scale.

Remember that the objective of the informal investigation is to provide the information needed to define and refine the problem. That investigation ordinarily provides the foundation for subsequent research. In the next chapter, we shall see how the development of research plans is aided by the results of the informal investigation.

MORE EXTENSIVE PARTICIPATION OCCURS

In the examples given in this chapter, we see a marketing research man charging into an informal investigation to define a problem. Sometimes there is a team of marketing research people working together on an informal investigation. Sometimes a single individual heads up the activity but enlists aid, for example, in developing a series of consumer or retailer interviews which become a part of the total investigation.

While more extensive participation in informal investigation occurs in marketing research practice, the "irreducible minimum" in terms of participation illustrated by both the Pabst and Allied Products, Inc., examples is worth remembering. This is what *one* skilled and experienced marketing research man can do. This is an example of the application of the kind of marketing research know-how which you are reading this book to acquire.

SUMMARY

1. The informal investigation is an approach which is particularly useful in the problem-defining stage of the research process. The objective of such an investigation usually is to gather information useful in defining and refining the marketing and marketing research problems.

2. Personal participation in the informal investigation by the individual with primary responsibility for the research is customary and desirable.

3. Executive interviews are often the first step in an informal investigation. Those interviews provide the research man with background on the nature of the problem. They are helpful to him in developing hypotheses to be explored in subsequent research. They are particularly fruitful where there is substantial disagreement as to the nature of the problem, because they provide a number of different viewpoints toward the problem.

4. In executive interviews, the research man's objective is twofold. First, he wants to secure all the information he can about the problem situation. Second, he wants to evaluate the individuals interviewed as to objectivity, reliability, etc., to guide him in weighing varying views presented to him. Caution in accepting as factual any individual's opinions is always necessary.

5. Another step usually involved in informal investigations is the interviewing of those individuals who have specialized knowledge of the problem area. If the problem has a geographic basis, like the Pabst New York problem, experts on that area are interviewed. If the problem instead involved a particular type of retail or wholesale operation, informed individuals with a knowledge of such an operation would be consulted.

6. The value of an informal investigation accrues primarily in the head of the individual responsible for planning and executing it. It is typically just one step in the research process, completed when the problem is defined. Sometimes research begins and ends with an informal investigation.

7. Whether and how the interviews and other parts of an informal investigation are reported vary in part with the skill and experience of the research man. In general, the more experienced the research man, the less need for and likelihood of reporting on detailed parts of an informal investigation. The subject of over-all reports on an informal investigation is discussed in Chapters 16 and 17 on analysis of data and in Chapter 18 on the preparation of research reports.

8. Although the subject is not discussed at length in this chapter, because it would be repetitive, all the sources of information discussed up to this point are considered and explored in the course of an informal investigation.

QUESTIONS

1. What is an *informal investigation?* What is the objective of the informal investigation? Why is it desirable to have the person with primary responsibility for the research participate personally in the informal investigation?

2. What type of interviews is often the first conducted in the informal investigation? What aid are these interviews to the research man?

3. Why is the role of the research man in the informal investigation described as similar to "a sponge on a fishing expedition"?

4. What is meant in this chapter by the reference to the danger of an insider confusing the "forest" with the "trees"?

5. Is it possible for executives to be "too expert" in their viewpoint? Is there any problem here?

6. How would you appraise the dependability of a person you were interviewing in the informal investigation? And the information he provides?

7. Are the interviews in an informal investigation reported? If so, how? What factors must be considered?

8. How could you judge if the informal investigation has been a success?

CHAPTER 14

Developing the Research Plan

With the informal investigation completed, the problem is specifically defined. The next step in the marketing research process is to develop a detailed plan for securing the information which marketing research can contribute to the solution of the problem.

This is an extremely important part of the research process, for many reasons. One reason is that if the plan is unsound, all subsequent steps in the research process might well represent a complete waste of time and money!

EACH MARKETING RESEARCH PROBLEM REQUIRES AN INDIVIDUAL PLAN

Because we have been discussing both *marketing* problems and marketing *research* problems in the preceding chapters, it is necessary to make one point completely clear. We are here concerned with the task of developing a plan aimed at contributing to the solution of a *marketing research problem*. Often a single marketing problem involves a number of different marketing research problems. The planning process must be carried on individually for each marketing research problem involved. It is sometimes possible for a single plan to encompass two or more marketing research problems, but such a possibility is relatively rare. Even in such a situation, one normally proceeds, first, to develop a plan for each specific marketing research problem, and second, to combine the plans to whatever extent proves possible and feasible.

Where there are many marketing research problems growing out of a single marketing problem, all of which must be tackled more or less simultaneously, it is possible to achieve some economy of time and effort by combined planning. The Dell-O margarine problem is an excellent illustration. Out of a single marketing problem, seven different marketing research problems developed. For planning purposes, those individual problems would be consolidated, as the following discussion indicates.

15. THE DELL-O COMPANY (B)

Reviewing the seven Dell-O margarine marketing research problems already discussed, the team of marketing personnel working on the problem situation consolidated them as follows:

1. *Comparative consumer acceptance of Dell-O margarine and of the two leading competitive products in the same price group.* Questions about the relative acceptance of consumer products can be answered by comparative testing in most instances. The techniques used, as described in Chapter 22, are relatively standardized. This marketing research problem therefore was simple, in so far as the planning phase was concerned.

2. *Analysis of the territorial distribution of Dell-O volume and of total margarine potential.* This analysis would provide an indication, among other things, of Dell-O's market share by area. This, too, is a frequently encountered type of problem requiring relatively little special planning. The techniques used in this analysis are the subject of Chapter 21.

3. *Retail- and wholesale-level research aimed at evaluating Dell-O's competitive strength and weakness at trade levels.* For planning purposes, three of the seven marketing research problems could be and were combined. One of those problems called for an evaluation of the selling organization of the Dell-O company itself, as against leading competitors, in both the quantity and quality of manpower. A second was a similar evaluation of the distributor organization, i.e., of the wholesalers who handled Dell-O margarine. A third was a comparison of the pricing and discount structure of Dell-O and the two leading competitors. It was decided that a single trade-level study could cover all three of those problem areas.

4. *Advertising-program evaluation.* The agency was in a position to get the necessary information on the quantity and type of advertising used in the past by Dell-O and leading competitors, using standard sources of information on expenditures and the ad files of the Daniel Starch research organization for past competitive advertisements in national magazines.

This left only one of the seven problems open—the one of determining how Dell-O compared with leading competitive brands in the size of its consumer franchise. Because it seemed likely that the information growing out of the product test might make additional information from consumers desirable, it was decided to defer planning on this research problem for three weeks while the product test was executed.

— ★ —

IMPORTANCE OF INTEGRATING TIME REQUIREMENTS

Especially where more than one marketing research problem is being studied at approximately the same time, it is necessary for the marketing research man to pay close attention to matters of timing in the planning stage of his research work. Different types of research work require different periods of time to execute, analyze, and report. Some research of one type can be much better performed if the results of an earlier piece of research are available to guide the planning. This adds up to a relatively complex "traffic," or scheduling, problem in many instances.

The Dell-O case provides two examples of such a need. One is the decision to defer the consumer research until the product test had been completed. The reasoning was that the results of that product test might make the consumer research unnecessary; or might reveal important areas which should be included within it. The other illustration is provided by the relationship between the analysis of territorial sales performance and the retail and wholesale study. Without a knowledge of which were strong and which were weak Dell-O territories, distributorships, or areas, it would be virtually impossible to do a sound job of sample planning for the trade study. Therefore, top priority had to be assigned to the sales-analysis job, which was thus delaying the trade study.

There are instances in which this question of how long it will take to do what is the determinant of the sequence in which different types of research work are done. The following case provides such an illustration.

16. SHOWER-OF-STARS COSMETICS, INC. (B)

The report of the preliminary review of the Shower-of-Stars problem was a well-documented one which added up to this conclusion: The company's problem was primarily a competitive one. While the company's sales volume had been declining sharply, the volume of its industry had continued to show increases. After studying the report and the evidence it presented, the management of the cosmetic company authorized further work on the problem by the consulting organization.

In the opinion of the consulting executive with primary responsibility for the account, the Shower-of-Stars marketing problem was an extremely complex one. It appeared to him that the company's marketing management had failed to keep pace with the times. Analytical and control tools which were standard operating aids in well-managed companies even smaller than Shower-of-Stars were unknown to the marketing management of that firm. An objective re-examination and appraisal of almost every element in the marketing operation of the company was indicated.

The problem of the consulting firm was one of selection. Where should they start? One problem area seemed particularly promising as a starting point. That was the area of product policy and new-product-development activities. It seemed an especially desirable starting point for a number of reasons, with time influences prominent among that number.

The company's sales-volume decline had been concentrated to a surprisingly large extent on a single product in the line. There were indications that that product was obsolete, from the consumer's viewpoint, or had been displaced by one or more competitive new-product developments. Although the company was active in a volatile industry in which new-product development was a major source of volume, the company had been relatively inactive in experimental work on new products.

New-product development takes time. It involves a series of steps, beginning with the decision on the type of product to develop. Marketing research was necessary to establish the desirable characteristics of a product in the product-type area selected. Then laboratory research would follow, attempting to build the new product to consumer specifications. Both the marketing and laboratory research would be heavily concerned with the limitations, if any, of competitive products in the target area.

After the product specifications had been set, developmental work could proceed, but that work required considerable time. Various types of product had to be developed experimentally. They had to be tried out by consumers on a small scale, necessary modifications made, and the process repeated. When the product was finally "right," the judgment of technical-research people had to be confirmed by a consumer-acceptance product test. If the test proved the product a winner, marketing plans could begin to move. If the test proved the product unsatisfactory, it was back to the lab, redevelopment, new product, new test, and so on. Other problem areas could be explored while this new-product activity was in progress.

For the reasons indicated, the first marketing research recommended was aimed at determining to what other types of products, if any, the former users of the company's major product had shifted.

— ★ —

SOUND APPROACH COMBINES FLEXIBILITY WITH A USEFUL FRAMEWORK OF MAJOR ELEMENTS

The process of developing a sound research plan is a difficult and exacting one. There are two characteristics which are highly desirable parts of that process. The first is *flexibility*. There is no cut-and-dried method of planning research. Each sound research plan must grow out of the characteristics of the particular problem situation to which it is expected to contribute. A "cookbook approach," in which the steps are listed in order and the ingredients are specified, is inapplicable in marketing research practice. A *single* vital difference between two specific problem situations may call for an entirely different research plan.

But the fact that the planning of marketing research must be kept flexible does not mean that it can or should be haphazard. Of course the research plan must be modified to fit the needs of a particular problem situation. Nevertheless, the planning of research can and should be on a rather systematic basis. It is highly desirable to have available to guide the research man some kind of a *framework of major planning steps* to which he can refer for guidance. This chapter is intended to provide a useful guide to the major steps in the development of a sound research plan. The fact that the research man can and should tailor his planning to fit the particular problem situation he faces is implied in all the comments which follow. That implication—the fundamental importance of flexibility—should not be overlooked!

STEP 1: DETERMINE OBJECTIVES OF THE RESEARCH

Your starting point in developing a research plan is a relatively simple one. All you have to do is to *determine in specific terms the purposes or objectives of the research*. What you want to know at this point is: *Why* is a research plan being developed? What is it expected to accomplish or contribute? Until you have the answers to those questions firmly in mind, sound planning is impossible.

The objectives of the Dell-O research have been established. In the Shower-of-Stars Cosmetics case, however, those objectives have not yet been spelled out. You are responsible for the Shower-of-Stars research. The president of that firm says to you, "Just why are we doing this research? What do we expect it to contribute?" What would you answer?

The first objective of the Shower-of-Stars research is to provide a directional guide for new-product development. You have a pretty clear picture of the problem in mind. The company's volume is down. A single product is responsible for the major share of the decline. It has been established that this is not an industry-wide decline—the cosmetic business generally is holding up well. There are strong indications that this is a competitive problem. The business the company has lost, one or more competitive firms have gained. Apparently customers have been switched away from one of your products. What you want to know is, who gained the business you lost?

There is no question in your mind about how the information will be used after you get it. If users have switched to another product of the same type, your problem is first to find out in what ways that product is superior to yours. Next you face the task of improving your product to shift the margin of superiority to your side of the fence. That may not be easy, of course—but that's the problem! After you improve your product so that yours is superior, you'll try to win back your former users to your "amazingly improved" product. On the other hand, perhaps the problem is one of a product-type shift. Perhaps—to use an allied industry for purposes of illustration—users have moved from a dentrifice which you make in paste form to a powder. You don't make a powder. Your problem then is to find out what kind of product is increasing in importance. After you establish that, your job is to get a product entry into the field which can cut you a slice of that expanding market.

In the Marcine Paper Company case, the objective of the reseach is essentially to determine what kind of marketing problem you face. Advertising costs are up. The rate of sales increase is down. Does this mean your advertising is ineffective? That your advertising and sales activities are not coordinated? Or that there's a competitive mouse gnawing at your rope? If it's a competitive problem, what kind? Is it an increase in the competitive pressure from the same old competitors? Or one or more new firms in the field? Or one or more new and/or improved products? Fundamentally, the objective of the research is to identify the nature of the problem.

HOW INFORMAL INVESTIGATION CONTRIBUTES TO THE PLANNING STEP

The comment above may at first seem confusing. The objective of the Shower-of-Stars' research was to identify the nature of the problem. But isn't that the objective of the informal investigation? Just how does the informal investigation fit into this planning step, anyhow? The answer to the latter question is that the informal investigation is often an integral part of the planning phase of the research. In the informal investigation, your objective is to determine the nature of the problem. In the course of that investigation, you acquire considerable information essential to the research-planning process. From it, for example, you may develop various hypotheses. You then proceed to plan the research needed to confirm or nullify those hypotheses.

Perhaps the best way to clarify the relationship of these parts of the research process is to remind you of the comment made in Chapter 4. It was pointed out there that sometimes marketing research must be executed as part of the problem-defining task of determining what the marketing research problem is. This is the circular relationship within the research process which was mentioned in Chapter 4.

This relationship is so important to an understanding of the research process, and so inherently confusing to newcomers to marketing research practice, that it should be spelled out in a little more detail.

An experienced marketing research man has a kit of technique tools and skills at his disposal. He knows how to use those tools and skills. He knows what each one can and cannot do. He uses them wherever and whenever he can, in the course of his work.

When he is working on a complicated major assignment, he often begins with work on a marketing problem. His first step is to attempt to define that problem. If there are tools in his kit which would be helpful in this process, he uses them. Thus in the description of the Dell-O case back in Chapter 4, one technique tool—correlation analysis—was used to evaluate the influence of butter prices as a contributory force in the sales decline. This tool was used and its results reviewed early in the research process. This was part of the problem-defining process. It was considerably earlier in the broad research picture than the planning step with which we are here concerned.

Thus we see that marketing research practice embraces and includes all phases of marketing research. The actual research does not begin after the planning stage, which is the subject of this chapter, is completed. Research knowledge, techniques, and sometimes actual research itself are used continually and constantly throughout the whole research process—to subdivide marketing problems; to identify and evaluate marketing research problems; in the course of the informal investigation; and sometimes in the planning phase of the research itself as well as subsequently while the plan is being executed. In short, it is sometimes necessary to *do* research before we can *plan* research.

STEP 2: DETERMINE SPECIFIC INFORMATION DESIRED

The next step in developing a marketing research plan is to determine in specific detail exactly what information is necessary. There is a continuing interplay between this step and the preceding one. When a specific piece of information is "nominated" as one which the research should provide, the research man normally refers back to the defined objectives of the research to determine whether, in his judgment, that information is necessary and relevant to those objectives. One of the unmistakable symptoms of inexperienced marketing research is a tendency for the informational objectives, especially of a survey, to be diffuse and often irrelevant to the purposes of the study. In professional marketing research practice, little time is spent developing "interesting information." If the information is not clearly relevant to the objectives of the research, its right to be included should be seriously questioned. There

is little reason or excuse for carrying dead weight in the form of superfluous information through the often expensive steps of marketing research data gathering, tabulation, analysis, and reporting.

17. BISSELL CARPET SWEEPER CO. (B)

After reviewing available information on sales of vacuum cleaners,
Bissell executives felt that further research was indicated. They were
particularly interested in learning whether the sale of a vacuum cleaner
displaced a carpet sweeper. Bissell had recently changed advertising
agencies. The new agency, Young & Rubicam, Inc., had extensive research and merchandising facilities. In soliciting the Bissell account,
Young & Rubicam had indicated that it woud probably begin its Bissell
advertising planning by using marketing research to determine the
nature of the Bissell sales and advertising problem. Advertising recommendations would be based on the research findings.

The Bissell management suggested to their new agency that an
evaluation of the importance of vacuum cleaners as a competitive threat
belonged within the scope of the agency's proposed research. After a
review of the situation, the agency agreed. Responsibility for further
research on this problem thus passed to the research department of
the advertising agency.

Note that this shift in research responsibility had as one effect a
broadening of the informational objectives of the research. While an
evaluation of the vacuum cleaner as a threat to carpet-sweeper sales
remained a prominent objective of the research, it was no longer the
only objective. In addition, the proposed research was now concerned
with securing considerable basic information about the market for carpet
sweepers which the agency could use to guide its advertising copy and
media recommendations.

The first step in the agency-directed research was an informal investigation among consumers. A substantial number of intensive interviews with housewives were conducted. Many of these were conducted
personally by the account research director at the agency. Others were
conducted by other full-time members of the agency's research department.

After studying the results of its informal interviewing, the agency was
in a position to specify the information which it felt was necessary to
achieve the broadened objectives of the research. Here is a partial list
of the informational objectives specified:

1. What proportion of homes now own carpet sweepers? What
proportion own vacuum cleaners? What proportion own both? What
variations exist in ownership of either or both devices in different sec-

tions of the country, different city-size groups, different socioeconomic levels, and among housewives of different age groups?

2. How long have the carpet sweepers now owned been in use? Were they the original sweeper of the housewife, or do they represent replacements? If replacements, what brand was owned before? What reasons are given for a change in brand, where one occurred? When do present carpet-sweeper owners anticipate that they may buy another to replace their present one, if ever? What brand do they think they will buy next, if a future purchase is anticipated?

3. Among housewives not owning carpet sweepers, what is the reason, if any, for failure to purchase a sweeper? Is future purchase considered likely by the housewife? Why or why not? If a future purchase is planned, what brand will be bought, in the housewife's opinion?

4. Among families owning vacuum cleaners, brand detail is not important, but we do want to know how long they have owned a vacuum cleaner. We want to know how well the housewife likes her cleaner. We want to know how she cleaned her rugs before she bought the vacuum and what has happened (if anything) to the device formerly used.

5. What is the usage pattern of vacuum cleaners and of carpet sweepers? How often is each used, and on what occasions?

6. What are the vulnerabilities, if any, of the vacuum cleaner? In other words, what if anything is there about the vacuum cleaner that owners dislike?

Because the informal investigation had disclosed a substantial difference in usage and attitudes among housewives with different-sized houses or apartments and with varying amounts of square footage of rugs and carpets, it was considered important to determine both the exact number of rooms in the house by type (i.e., number of bedrooms, etc.) and also to determine, for each room, whether the floor was covered by a rug or carpet, by a scatter rug, or by a hard-finish (lineoleum) floor covering or was without any covering.

The above case provides an illustration of a fairly specific description of the informational requirements of proposed research. Note that this does not represent and is not intended to represent a questionnaire or other type of formal specification of the way in which the information is to be secured. The research man receives the informational specifications or develops them and has them approved. Then he proceeds, in the subsequent steps in the research, to translate them into the actual form in which they will be used in the research. There is a widespread belief that preparing a questionnaire, for example, is a relatively simple process. The fact is that preparing a questionnaire calls for an extremely high degree of skill and experience.

Therefore responsibility for questionnaire preparation is almost always assigned to a research technician in marketing research practice. A similar assignment of responsibility is made in the case of translations of informational objectives into forms other than a questionnaire, such as forms for observational studies. This is a sound approach.

In this as in so many other areas of marketing research practice, however, problems of communication are sometimes encountered. Ideally the marketing research man participates in developing the informational objectives. Sometimes those informational objectives are handed to him, without his prior knowledge or participation. In such a case, he usually reviews with his superiors, associates, or with the client sponsoring the research the exact approach he proposes to take. A review of the detailed questionnaire, instructions, etc., is desirable. This is especially true in cases where the research man is not intimately familiar with the industry environment of the research problem. An experienced "insider" who knows the characteristics of the industry can often detect a potential source of ambiguity, misunderstanding, or other possible trouble spot, even in a soundly developed questionnaire.

What is called for in this particular area is an attitude of mutual respect. Such an attitude is almost a prerequisite of sound, productive research. The executive who is not a marketing research technician should respect the ability of the marketing research man to develop soundly conceived and well-organized questionnaires or other forms better than someone without technical training could. But the research man, in turn, must respect the experience and knowledge of the nontechnician. There is an opportunity to learn from the experience and greater familiarity of others with a company, an industry, or a problem area. A competent research man respects that knowledge and benefits from it whenever he can.

ADDITIONAL ILLUSTRATION: SPECIFYING INFORMATION

Because of the vital importance of this particular element in the plan-development phase of marketing research work, an additional case example seems desirable.

18. STANDARD FOODS, INC. ★ (A)

Standard Foods, Inc., with headquarters in Boston, Mass., is one of the nation's large, diversified producers and marketers of a wide variety of different food products. The company's volume and the length of its product line had been expanded spectacularly in the years following

World War II, largely through acquisition by purchase or exchange of stock of a large number of smaller firms. The products of such manufacturers were added to the Standard Foods line. Often the purchase of a company involved a sort of mixed blessing. It brought into the Standard Foods family of products a product or group of products in which the company was especially interested. Sometimes it also involved added products in which the company had little or no interest.

One such corporate purchase had resulted in the at least temporary entry of Standard Foods, Inc., into the manufacture and sale of dry packaged soup. The management of the parent company knew nothing about the characteristics of dry-soup marketing or consumption. They were undecided as to whether they should continue to manufacture and sell dry packaged soup or should discontinue the line. They did know, from a review of the sales and profit records of the acquired company, that dry soup had not been a major profit contributor in the past.

A management-consulting organization was called in to appraise the volume and profit opportunity which dry soup represented. The Standard Foods, Inc., management asked the consulting organization to answer two basic questions:

1. Is there an important volume and profit opportunity for Standard Foods, Inc., in the dry-soup business?

2. Can that opportunity be exploited at a cost commensurate with the value of the property to be built?

The partner in the consulting organization who assumed primary responsibility for this assignment reviewed the available information about the size and characteristics of the market for dry packaged soup and decided that information was inadequate. He set about the determination of the specific types of information needed and developed the following preliminary listing of information desired:

1. What is the size of the market for soup? What is the trend in market size? How is that market divided between canned soup and dry packaged soup? What trends, if any, should be considered in that dry-canned market division?

2. What are the competitive factors in the dry-soup field? What companies control what share of market? What trends in market share should be noted?

3. How is the dry-soup market divided sectionally, by city sizes, by socioeconomic groups? How does that pattern of dry-soup consumption compare with the pattern of canned-soup consumption?

4. Is a company that makes and sells dry soup competing with other companies also in the dry-soup field, or is the true competitive framework total soup consumption (canned plus dried) rather than just dried soup?

5. Partly as a guide to the answer to the above question, what are the characteristics of consumers of dry soup as against consumers of canned soup? What is the flavor preference? Purchase frequency? Seasonality of volume?

6. What is the profit arithmetic of dry-soup production and marketing, as against canned soup? What are production costs, advertising and other promotional costs, and reasonable profit expectations? How does the profit promise vary with volume levels? That is, is this a business within which one may do an investment-spending job on advertising and promotion to build business, with the expectation that the profitability at high volume levels will quickly "pay off" on that investment?

7. What is the product-quality picture in the dry-soup field? Are the soups made by the company acquired by Standard Foods, Inc., superior products, about the same as other dry soups, or inferior? How do dry soups compare with canned soups in consumer acceptance? Is that comparison uniform by flavors, or are there some flavors or varieties of canned soups which are inferior and some superior to dry soups in consumer acceptance?

There were some additional questions involved which were not in the marketing research field, involving relative production costs, various production processes, raw-material costs, etc., which need not concern us here.

— ★ —

STEP 3: DETERMINE POSSIBLE SOURCES FOR REQUIRED INFORMATION

With the informational specifications developed, we move on to a consideration of the possible technique tools and approaches which might be used to secure the required information. This step varies tremendously in complexity and difficulty. At one extreme there is a situation reminiscent of the lost motorist who asked a native for directions; the answer seems to be: "You can't get there from here!" In other instances, the nature of the information is such that the technique decision is a cut-and-dried one. An example of such a situation was provided by the consumer-acceptance product-testing aspect of the Dell-O problem.

Between those two extremes lies the situation in which two or more sources provide highly similar information. An important area of marketing research is the selection of a technique approach from two or more alternatives. A careful appraisal of the advantages and disadvantages of each approach is necessary, with frequent reference to the objectives of the research and the informational specifications as guides. In that appraisal, a detailed examination and evaluation of differences in cost, accuracy, time requirements, and completeness of information is typically necessary.

Let's examine some cases in which a marketing research man had to make such an appraisal.

19. C. A. SWANSON & SONS, INC. (A)

C. A. Swanson & Sons, Inc., with home offices in Omaha, Nebr., was one of the pioneer firms in the field of quick-frozen convenience foods. (This organization has since been purchased by and integrated within the Campbell Soup Company.) The company manufactured and marketed a line of frozen meat and poultry pies, and also pioneered in the development of a one-dish frozen dinner. The dinners prepared by the company were marketed as Swanson's TV Brand Dinners. They came in various types, including turkey, beef, and fried-chicken dinners. These dinners were prepared on a throwaway aluminum platter, shaped to provide compartments for the main dish and for two vegetables.

In the development of their existing dinner varieties, and looking toward expansion of their line, the Swanson organization recognized a need for factual guidance in determining the relative consumer acceptability of different types of food products. For example, suppose they had the alternative of using mashed white potatoes, *au gratin* white potatoes, or sweet potatoes as one of the vegetables with their turkey dinner. Which would appeal to a higher proportion of potential consumers?

The research director of Swanson's advertising agency was asked to recommend a method of securing information on the relative popularity of certain foods from a national sample of consumers.

He pointed out that this type of information could be secured rather easily either by a personal-interview or mail consumer survey. If the mail approach were chosen, the use of one of the panel organizations specializing in such research would be recommended.

Along with a summary of the cost and time requirements of the two approaches, the agency research director pointed out that an opportunity existed to broaden the informational base of the study slightly. For very moderately higher costs, he noted, the Swanson organization could determine the extent to which the respondent families had or did not have frozen-food storage capacity in their homes. He suggested that there might be food-preference differences between families with and without frozen-food storage. If such differences were disclosed by the research, the preferences of families with storage facilities would be more important from a Swanson viewpoint. He also suggested that past experience with and attitude toward frozen dinners might provide helpful additional information useful in improving existing products.

Comment: This relatively simple illustration provides an example of a marketing research problem for which at least two technique approaches were easily possible. The broadened informational base is an illustration of a creative contribution in the planning phase of the research.

In some problem situations, the choice of marketing research approaches is an extremely wide one. That type of situation is especially difficult. It involves, first, a decision among a relatively large number of alternatives. A second characteristic is that often the pros and cons of two or more specific approaches are relatively intangible. The following case is illustrative.

20. BENDIX HOME APPLIANCES, INC. (A)

Bendix Home Appliances, Inc., South Bend, Ind., was the organization that first developed the automatic washing machine. (Subsequent to the case here reported, the company was purchased by Avco, Inc., which already manufactured and marketed Crosley appliances. The withdrawal of Avco from the appliance field followed.) The Bendix automatic washer (which at first was called an "automatic home laundry") was introduced in 1937. Here is the company's market share of total washing machines sold, on a *unit* basis, over the period before World War II interrupted production:

1937	.8%	1940	5.4%
1938	5.0%	1941	6.9%
1939	2.7%	1942	11.2%

In its initial year or two, the product developed some major "bugs" which necessitated extremely high service costs and slowed down the rate of sales. With those mechanical problems eliminated, the product, which represented a tremendous laborsaving advance over "conventional" (i.e., wringer-type) washers, began to show real sales promise. The marketing of the product, under the able leadership of Judson S. Sayre, was aggressive and effective. The above figures show the Bendix's market share on a unit basis. On a dollar basis, the Bendix's share was much higher because the Bendix washer had an average selling price which was more than double the average of the remainder of its industry.

During the war years while there was no production of automatic washing machines, consumer acceptance of the automatic-washer idea mushroomed. The late Arthur P. Hirose, who was director of market research for the McCall Corporation, was a keen analyst of appliance-merchandising trends. In a letter to the author he wrote in 1943:

> The automatic washing machine has taken such a hold on the imagination of the American homemaker that after the war, all the emphasis will be on the automatic. Scores of companies are planning to introduce automatic washers. . . .

Bendix moved aggressively to fill the pent-up demand for automatic washing machines in the months after production became possible following World War II. With the dies and other machinery available, Bendix was in a strategically advantageous position as against competitors whose products were still in the planning or pilot-model stage. In more than five years preceding World War II, Bendix sold in total about 250,000 units. In 1948 alone, Bendix sales were in excess of 300,000 units.

As material shortages eased and as more and more competitors launched their automatic washers, Bendix faced the problem of reappraising its competitive situation. That reappraisal began early in the postwar period, but it was relatively unimportant so long as the company could sell every unit it could produce. In 1948, however, competition became a major factor in Bendix's marketing thinking. In that year, a review of the Bendix marketing situation disclosed one extremely important weakness. That was essentially a regional weakness in sales performance. The following figures were presented to a Bendix sales conference in 1948 by the company's director of distribution:

Region	Per cent of U.S. Bendix sales	Per cent of U.S. industry sales	Bendix level of sales performance
Middle West.........	18.571	35.48	52
East...............	31.441	26.47	119
South.............	30.193	22.23	136
Far West..........	19.795	15.46	128
U.S. total..........	100.000	100.00	100

The problem which A. E. Cascino, then research director of Bendix Home Appliances, Inc., faced was one of deciding how much of what kind of research to recommend to his management for the diagnosis of this important problem situation. Should the company conduct a national study, aimed at identifying the differences between the Middle West and the rest of the country? Or should a comparison of the Middle West with one other region be considered sufficient? Should the research be conducted in all parts of the Middle West, which would probably require a relatively small sample in any one major market or other part of the territory, or should selected individual markets within that area be studied? Should the survey approach be used? If it should, would you suggest a personal-interview or mail study?

STEP 4: EVALUATE ALTERNATE SOURCES AND SELECT MOST DESIRABLE

Where there are two or more different research tools or techniques which could be used to develop the information specified in step 2, above, the marketing research man faces the task of evaluating those sources and of selecting the one which seems to him most desirable. The question he must answer, at least to his own satisfaction, is: Which *one* of the approaches open to us represents the best "fit" with this particular problem situation, all things considered?

Just what are "all things" which must be considered in making this appraisal? The number varies from problem to problem, but in almost all cases involves at least three major elements: *Cost considerations; relative accuracy or dependability of the data developed by different approaches; and time requirements to secure the information using different techniques or approaches.*

Cost Considerations

The aspect of cost deserves first consideration because it is often the dominant influence in the technique or data-source decision. An illustration is provided by the C. A. Swanson & Sons case earlier in this chapter. The informational requirements could be fulfilled either by a personal-interview or mail survey. But the personal-interview study would be substantially more expensive, and incidentally it would take longer to plan and execute. Primarily on the basis of the cost factor, it was therefore decided that this particular research should be done by a mail survey.

Cost considerations enter importantly into the selection process also where a wide variety of different approaches are open to the research man. Thus in the case of the Bendix Home Appliances case above, the obvious or the national approach to the problem would most likely be considered by most research men to be relatively inefficient, since the problem is one of diagnosing a problem which is confined to an area representing only a little more than a third of industry volume nationally. Often relative costs are used to narrow down the approaches receiving detailed consideration with a longer list of possibilities as a starting point.

There are important differences in approach between a practical and a theoretical marketing research man in this phase of the research. A theoretical approach might develop the ideal approach to the problem from the marketing research standpoint and incidentally involve a sum of money which would be quite beyond reason for the company involved. Since the ideal research could not be accomplished within the limits of the funds available, a theoretical approach might settle for no research on the problem. Sometimes "no research" is the answer, and sometimes budgetary reasons make that the right answer. A practical approach would be preoccupied with finding out what research could be planned and executed, within the limits of available funds, which would be likely to be worth more than its costs in terms of the contribution it could be expected to make to a specific problem.

If you believe as most experienced marketing research men do that judgment based on facts is better than judgment alone in a particular decision area, then you are likely to share their belief that almost any *good research* is better than *no* research. If you can't afford a Cadillac or a Continental, a lower-priced car may still represent adequate transportation for you!

Relative Accuracy, Dependability, or Completeness of Data

Within those data sources or technique approaches which are feasible from a budgetary standpoint, the research man now moves on to consider the qualitative differences in information provided. The interrelationship of this consideration with the cost elements should be stressed. Thus it was pointed out above that in the Swanson case a decision was made to use a mail-survey approach. The decision was made, as noted, primarily for cost reasons. It should be noted, however, that it was decided that the information provided by a mail survey was considered to be adequately accurate and dependable, or that choice would not have been made.

In the Bissell case, a national consumer survey was chosen as the most desirable way to secure the required information. When the mail and personal-interview approaches were weighed against each other, with the requirements of the study as a factor, it was decided that the more expensive personal-interview study was preferable. Two elements strongly influenced that decision. One was the danger that a mail study might develop a nonrepresentative sample. It was anticipated that those lacking either a carpet sweeper or a vacuum cleaner might not return the questionnaire. The other factor was the relative complexity of the questioning process, along with the difficulty of effectively communicating the meaning of some of the questions to respondents in written form.

Skilled interviewers could do a better job on the subject matter of that study, it was decided.

Sometimes accuracy of data and completeness of data are mutually exclusive characteristics of alternative approaches. In that case, a painful decision must sometimes be made between them. A shampoo manufacturer, looking for a continuing source of information on the size and competitive division of the market for shampoos, provides an illustration. He could purchase the data provided by the Nielsen Drug Index, which would be relatively accurate but which would not cover some important sources of shampoo volume such as variety (5¢–10¢–$1) stores, department stores, mail-order houses, and house-to-house canvassers. Or he could purchase the data provided by the MRCA National Consumer Panel. Those data would provide coverage of all household purchases through all outlet types, hence would tend to be more complete than the Nielsen data. However, it would not cover purchases by nonhousehold units. In some product categories, especially in the cosmetic- and personal-care-item area, the purchases of such nonhousehold groups as residents of sorority houses, groups of working girls sharing an apartment, residents of YWCA's, etc., represent a substantial proportion of total consumption. Here the choice between accuracy in a portion of the market, or broader coverage with less accuracy, would have to be made.

Time Requirements

The time dimension of a marketing problem or of a marketing research problem exerts an important influence on most technique-selection decisions. How much time will it take to get the information if we use the approach which is considered best from the standpoints both of cost and accuracy? Do you have that much time? Is there some less accurate (or perhaps more expensive) approach which could give us the answers we need more quickly? These are the types of questions which a limited time-dimension introduces into the technique-selection decision.

Personal Considerations

Since we are here concerned with practical problems, one additional element entering into the technique decision should be noted. That is the personal element, the influence on that decision of personalities, and various facets of personal or corporate prejudice. A specific example will illustrate. A company had a problem which the continuing consumer-panel approach was ideally suited to. The product type involved was one on which consumer-panel coverage could be expected to be extremely high (i.e., purchased by the housewife for family use, little institutional use). A marketing research consultant was asked to suggest research approaches. He recommended the consumer-panel technique as almost the only one which could supply the required information. The recommendation was vetoed. Reason? The president of the company, while in a previous job, had had an unfortunate experience with a consumer-panel research job. It was his considered opinion that panels were essentially inaccurate, and he refused to consider a recommendation which involved panel research.

Personal considerations of a somewhat similar type enter into marketing research practice at many points. If a key executive, for example, "doesn't believe in small samples," the company's marketing research director may be forced to recommend research using samples larger than he considers necessary, with consequently higher costs. If he does not have a sample size meeting this individual's "mental specifications," the results of the research might be rejected and the total cost wasted. An educational job on such an individual is of course indicated—but some individuals are less susceptible to education, after a certain point on their life span, than others! That's life—and that is also marketing research practice!

SUBDIVISION SOMETIMES INDICATED

Still within the area of practical problems in the development of a marketing research plan, the advantages of subdividing a marketing research problem or the research on a problem should be noted. Suppose, for example, that the research necessary to meet the informational specifications is not possible within the budgetary ceiling in prospect. As noted above, this sometimes means that a less desirable research approach which is within the cost limits operative should be used. There are occasions which should be mentioned when that is not the only or most desirable solution. Perhaps there is no alternative fitting within the budget available. What do you do then? One possibility is to consider doing only part of the research, fulfilling only part of the informational requirements. Obviously the subdivision should be guided by an appraisal of the relative importance of the parts involved. The most important part of the research should be isolated first, and the feasibility of executing it by itself considered.

There are other situations in which one reason why there is insufficient money available for the research is that management or some vital individual or department within management is unconvinced that the research is necessary or desirable. Often a subdivision approach is helpful in dealing with this contingency. If a significant part of the research can be "broken off" of the total problem and executed individually and if the benefit to be derived from the whole can thus be demonstrated with a moderate **investment,** the ceiling can often be raised. This is somewhat akin to using a "pilot-study" approach, along the lines discussed in the following chapter.

STEP 5: FORMULATE A RESEARCH PLAN, IN COMPLETE DETAIL

To include "formulate a plan" as one of the steps in a chapter on how a plan should be developed may seem at first something like a dictionary definition of a word in terms of the word itself. What is involved in this step is a pull-together of the various decisions made prior to this point and a reduction of those decisions to a written basis. A written research plan should be a carefully formulated, completely detailed description of research which is to be done. There is a tremendous difference in scale between different research projects. Some are relatively minor, involving no key decisions to speak of. For example, in the Boston Allied Products, Inc., case in Chapter 13, the sales research man had the company's sales in the Boston district specially tabulated in a number of different ways. One tabulation, for example, was by individual counties in some key areas. Another was a special tabulation of the sales of each of a number of major products by different types of customers. No *research plan* in any formal sense is required for such a relatively simple research step.

Moving on up the scale of complexity and detail, total cost is one useful guide. In many large organizations, the research director has authority to make commitments up to a specified figure, say $500, without any necessity for authorization from his superior. Commitments in a range from $500 to $2,500 might require approval of his superior. Commitments larger than that (and these figures of course vary widely from company to company) might call for approval by an executive vice-president, a management committee, etc. *One* (but only one!) influence on the detail and completeness in which a research plan is developed is of course the individual or group to whom it must be submitted for approval. Even where the authorization involved is within the range which does not require formal approval, however, some kind of written plan is desirable in sound research practice.

FUNCTIONS OF A RESEARCH PLAN

A written research plan has a number of values which make it worthwhile even in the case of relatively minor research projects. One is that the research plan provides, as a matter of record, a *statement of the problem* to which the research is intended to contribute. It also typically states the limitations of the research approach proposed, in so far as those limitations can be predetermined in advance of the research itself. The problem of communication which is prevalent in many research areas has already been mentioned. The research plan, written and distributed to key individuals, is one device which research men can and do use to reduce the danger that a communication failure will reduce their effectiveness.

Here is a fairly typical situation. A piece of research is discussed. It is agreed that this research is desirable, its cost reasonable, and the research is authorized. The research is completed, to the specifications in the research man's mind. The research is reported. A great hullabaloo then is kicked up. This individual or that one says, "I thought the research was going to show so-and-so" or "I thought you were going to do it this way instead of that way." The following comment often is: "I never would have voted for the approval of the research expenditure if I had known you were going to do (or were not going to do) thus and so." That research is likely to produce no action other than controversy, and the time, effort, and money that went into its planning, execution, analysis, and reporting are likely to have been wasted.

Now project yourself into such a "rhubarb." You are the marketing research man in the picture. Whose fault is it that there was so much misunderstanding about the methodology, objectives, and limitations of the research? The answer is simple. The fault is yours. If you had prepared a written discussion of the research—a written *research plan*—and had distributed it in advance of the execution of the research to all interested executives for their information, you would not be in the eye of the typhoon. With such a procedure, it is a relatively simple matter to dig out the plan and review it. Did you or did you not deliver the research the plan promised? If you did, the research department is obviously not responsible for failure of the individuals involved to read with care the plan you sent them and to record their objections while you could still do something about them!

This is an important point, in a day when the trend to committee and other forms of multiple management is a strong one. The research plan is a vital tool of the research director. It is an insurance policy against a failure in communication, on his part or that of someone else. Mark this: The written plan is not an "alibi prepared in advance." It is a way of being sure that there *is* agreement where there *appears to be* agreement on the purposes, method, scope, cost, objectives, and limitations of the research!

This is the first important function of the research plan. It guards against communication problems by stating in writing in advance what has been agreed upon, as the research man understands that agreement. It serves much the same purpose as the familiar expression "Speak now or forever hold your peace!"

The second function of a research plan is the aid it provides in getting research approved and authorized. In the research plan, the research man has an opportunity to state the problem and to point out the contribution which research can make to that problem, along with the cost and applications of the research.

The third function of a research plan is as a guide in the execution of the research. A research project, described in detail in a written plan, is approved. The written plan remains currently available to all who are concerned with that research as a guide in its subsequent planning, execution, and reporting. Often a research director prepares a plan for which one of his subordinates then assumes responsibility. If the plan is complete and clear, the danger of misunderstanding—of a communication failure downward within the research department—is reduced.

The fourth function of a research plan is perhaps its most important. The discipline of reducing a research plan to writing requires that it receive careful thought. The review of that plan before its release gives the research man a last and vital opportunity to review objectively what the problem is and what he proposes to do about it. In this review, an experienced research man is on guard against one problem which often develops. That is the risk of loss, somewhere between the original statement of the problem and the final research plan, of coverage of one or more important elements of the problem. Research men are human, and people forget things. The final review of a research plan before its release is a very important step in the marketing research process.

EXAMPLE OF MATERIAL INCLUDED IN A RESEACH PLAN

We have noted the variation in complexity of research, and accordingly of research plans. A research plan may represent no more than a single paragraph or a single page, stating the problem, what is to be done about it, how much that will cost, and how long it will take. On the other hand, a research plan involving a substantial expenditure, for example, for a national consumer survey or for the purchase of a continuing source of panel research such as the MRCA or Nielsen organizations provide, is often a relatively long and extremely detailed document.

Here, with varying amounts of detail, are some excerpts from an advance research plan, prepared to secure management authorization for a program aimed at contributing facts helpful in the diagnosis of the Bendix Home Appliances, Inc., Middle Western weakness.

Introduction

This proposal outlines a comprehensive research program aimed at identifying the causal factors in Bendix' middle-western problem of low sales performance.

This research program is complex. That complexity is unfortunate, but inescapable. The Bendix middle-western weakness is a major marketing problem. Its solution is extremely important to the company's sales progress. To get the facts needed for current sales and advertising decisions, and perhaps policy decisions as well, it is necessary to surround that problem. Surrounding it requires gathering a number of different kinds of facts, from different sources, using research approaches appropriate to each phase of the problem.

Actual questionnaires are included in this research proposal. Those questionnaires have been made more detailed than it would be desirable to use in the actual field study. They have been so prepared to provide a basis for detailed and specific discussion. It is hoped that that discussion will lead to agreement on some rather extensive pruning of those questionnaires.

As a point of reference in reviewing the proposals which follow, a basic viewpoint should be noted. A well-planned, well-executed survey will involve a substantial capital investment. No survey should be made involving such an expenditure which is not sound enough in every detail to warrant the complete confidence of every Bendix and distributor executive. If budgetary considerations necessitate a compromise with the quality of field-work, it would probably be preferable to make no survey rather than to make one about which serious questions could be raised.

There followed a summary of the proposal, which pointed out that the research program in question involved three different surveys. One was a consumer survey, covering both owners and nonowners of Bendix washers. One was a survey covering retailers, Bendix dealers, and competitive dealers, to be made on a shopping basis, that is, with the investigators unidentified other than as prospective customers so far as the dealer was concerned. The third was an expanded study of Bendix owners, to provide a large enough sample for detailed examination. The cost of each element of the program was estimated. The time required to complete each element was indicated. A calendar starting with "authorization day" and showing exactly when each part of the research would be completed was also included in this summary.

For each of the three individual proposed studies, the specific informational areas to be covered were listed. Here is the list of objectives of the consumer study:

1. *Ownership information on washing machines, dryers and ironers*
   a. Types, brands and age of machines owned.
   b. Likes and dislikes about present machine.
   c. Major reasons for purchase of particular type and brand.
   d. Accessibility to and former use of appliances.
   e. Location in home of owned machines.

2. *Future buying intentions on washing machines, dryers and ironers*
    a. Type and brand chosen to buy next, for those with and without buying intentions.
    b. Reasons for preferring chosen type and brand.
    c. Price expected to pay.
3. *Washing machine market in general*
    a. Present method of handling laundry (at home, part sent out, all sent out).
    b. Rating of most important features when buying a washing machine.
    c. Likes and dislikes of leading machine makes.
    d. Information as to whether or not respondents have ever operated fully automatic washer:

    — Place of operation
    — Brands operated
    — Likes and dislikes of automatic operated.

    e. Information as to whether or not unfavorable comments were ever heard about automatic washers, and if so, details on comments related to specific brands.
4. *Shopping habits of recent washing machine purchasers*
    a. Number of dealers visited before buying, and distance from home to each dealer.
    b. Information as to whether dealer first was visited for shopping purposes or after decision to buy had been made.
    c. Number and names of brands looked at before buying and reasons for not buying rejected brands.
    d. Original brand intended to buy vs. brand actually bought and reasons for changing brands.
    e. Price originally intended to pay vs. price actually paid.
    f. Information on trade-ins: Involved? Discussed? Why or why not?
    g. Reasons for buying particular type and make bought.
    h. Husband's part in washing machine purchase.

The plan went on to describe in detail the breakdowns of the survey data which could be made on the basis of a relatively large sample size. The breakdown bases were presented in two sections, as noted below:

1. *Market segments of general marketing interest*
    a. Sub-divisions of the middle-western area.
    b. City-size groups, including rural farms.
    c. Socio-economic groups.
    d. Home owners vs. renters (with detail on value of home or rent paid).
    e. Single family dwellings vs. multiple-family dwellings.
    f. Age of housewife.
    g. Family size and composition; presence of children.

     h. Presence of domestic help.

     i. Occupational classification.

2. *Market segments related to washer market*

     a. Present washer owners vs. non-owners.

     b. Present method of handling laundry.

     c. Families intending to buy a washer vs. those not contemplating a purchase.

     d. Housewives with a preference for an automatic washer vs. those preferring a conventional washer.

     e. Housewives who have operated a Bendix vs. those who have not.

The interviewing method to be used was then described in detail. Sample size was specified, and the method of selecting the sample described. The timing was reviewed in additional detail. The marketing research organization to be used was identified, reasons for selection of that firm reviewed, and comparative prices and other aspects of the approach recommended versus other approaches suggested by other research organizations which had submitted a proposal on the study were reviewed. Cost components were reviewed. Finally, the actual questionnaires proposed were presented in detail.

STEP 6: FINAL REVIEW OF PLAN

This brings us to the last step in developing a research plan, which is the last step before the actual execution of the plan begins. This is a review of the plan by the marketing research man who has primary responsibility for its development. In this review, emphasis is placed on three aspects of the plan itself.

The first point which requires careful review is the *completeness* of the plan. How completely does it fulfill the informational specifications it was developed to fill? In the course of plan development, it is not unusual to have the problem of "many cooks." This point is added, that one eliminated, that other one modified. It is the responsibility of the marketing research man to review the plan as it has finally developed, to be sure that the various revisions made have not resulted in "holes" in the plan. One way to make this review is to begin with the questionnaires or forms and to review them against the informational specifications. Will they provide all needed information? Anticipating various results from a completed study, will the forms developed be adequate to record such results in all necessary detail? A mental outline of the report which might be written of the research, and a check of that outline against the plan itself, is sometimes helpful.

The second point which requires searching scrutiny should by now be an old friend. This is the ever-present question of the balancing of the cost of the research against the potential profit contributions from the research. It is rather common practice, in this phase of the research process, to assume that the research has been completed with any of a number of different outcomes; and to consider *in specific detail* exactly how the findings of the research would be applied. There is little room in marketing research practice for the routine collection of "interesting information" which is then filed away. Unless something is done about the findings of the research, the entire cost of the research and the time and effort spent in planning it are completely wasted.

One reason why such a review is so important at this late date in the planning process is because constant changes are occurring. Any one of those changes might make what would otherwise be a soundly planned and promising piece of research a complete waste of time and money. There is a danger that failure in communication between someone with specialized or advance information and the marketing research man may result in research authorizations which should have been canceled. It is sound practice in planning the timetable of a complex research job to establish the "last-refusal" or "final-cancellation" date of a research project. The advisability of doing the research, in the light of existing information which has come in since the research planning started, should always be considered at as late a date as possible.

The third and final point receiving emphasis in this review of the research plan is the matter of responsibility. Is it spelled out in specific detail? Are the *what, where, when, why, how,* and *by whom* of the research clearly stated? It is not enough that those vital details should be stated so clearly that they can be understood; they should be stated so clearly and specifically that they *cannot be misunderstood!* Who is responsible for what? At what point does responsibility pass from one individual, department, or organization to another?

FLEXIBILITY REQUIRES RE-EMPHASIS

Early in this chapter the need for flexibility in planning research was emphasized. That need should be re-emphasized at this point in the planning process. Remember that research is a continuing process. Each contribution of additional information may require a change in direction of other research which is, perhaps, already in process. In the case of complex marketing problems to which there are many marketing research parts—the Dell-O example providing a perfect illustration—the careful coordination of different marketing research plans requires constant attention.

The hypothesis is a useful tool in marketing research planning. Each time evidence indicates that a particular hypothesis is null and void, a re-examination of the entire research picture is indicated.

RESEARCH PLAN AND ITS EXECUTION FLOW TOGETHER

All the steps in this six-chapter section on the marketing research process are closely interrelated. Two which are especially close in their linkage and intimate in their interrelationship are the planning step which is the subject of this chapter and the execution of the plan described in the following chapter. As the comment above suggests, flexibility is essential. Often—during the actual execution of a research plan—new evidence makes necessary a modification of that plan, involving what is essentially additional planning.

Therefore, *the following chapter which describes the execution step should be regarded as an extension and continuation of the planning step.*

SUMMARY

1. This chapter describes the process of developing a research plan. It begins by emphasizing that each marketing *research* problem requires its own individual plan. This in turn means that there may be a number of different plans required for work on a single *marketing* problem.

2. Where more than one research plan is involved in the area of a single marketing problem, careful integration of the plans and considerable flexibility are required. Additional evidence at any point may require modification or abandonment of a research plan.

3. The time requirements of different pieces of research all of which contribute to a single marketing problem must be carefully considered. Sometimes the time aspect is the most important single influence in assigning priorities to portions of a complex marketing research problem.

4. A series of steps which combine to provide a framework for the development of a research plan were presented in this chapter. The need for flexibility in applying those steps to any specific planning operation was stressed.

5. A particularly helpful element in the planning process is painstaking attention to the development of a set of informational specifications for the research. These bring the research down out of the "blue sky" and translate the sometimes unrealistically broad generalities of early discussion into concrete terms. One value here is that sometimes a recognition of how much (or how little!) information research can realistically be expected to contribute leads to the termination or expansion of a particular project.

6. It is not unusual to have the planning step reveal a very wide gap between the scope of information desired and what can realistically be secured for the budget available. In such a situation, subdivision of the broad research approach into parts and consideration of the potential value of parts of the whole are helpful.

7. A research plan in specific (and usually written) form is a useful disciplinary device which contributes to sound research practice.

8. Because of the close interrelationship of the step of developing a research plan and the subsequent step of executing that plan, this chapter and the one which follows (on executing research plans) should be regarded as parts of a unified whole.

QUESTIONS

1. What difference is there between a marketing problem and a marketing research problem?

2. What are two characteristics which are highly desirable parts of a sound research plan?

3. What is your starting point in developing a research plan?

4. Who is almost always responsible for the preparation of the questionnaire? Should anyone else be brought into the picture? If so, who might this be?

5. What three major elements must research men consider when there are two or more research tools or techniques which could be used to develop the desired information? Discuss each briefly.

6. Why is it advisable to have a written research plan in complete detail? What is its function? What should be included in the written plan?

7. Who should have the final responsibility of reviewing the research plan? In this review, emphasis should be placed on three aspects of the plan itself. What are these points which require careful review?

CHAPTER 15

Executing the Research Plan

The execution of a research plan sometimes has a circular relationship with the preceding step, in which the plan was developed. That relationship was pointed out at the close of the preceding chapter. It comes about in this way: You develop a plan and begin to execute it. Some results of the execution make it clear that the plan itself should be modified or extended in scope. You circle back through the planning process for that modification. Then you proceed to execute the modified plan.

The possibility that such a circular relationship may develop, in the execution of any specific research plan, should be recognized at the outset. Fortunately it becomes necessary only in a minority of instances. In the majority of research plans, the execution step proceeds in a straightforward manner out of the plan itself. The specific details of the execution are provided by the plan itself.

TWO PHASES OF PLAN EXECUTION

The execution of a research plan involves two distinct phases of activity. In some ways, this step is like driving a car. In order to drive a car you must, first, know the bare mechanical requirements of how to drive. You must know where the starter switch is, where the brake is, where the accelerator is, and so on. These are specific details, subject to specific variation. Thus the location of the starter switch in a Ford is often different from that in a Chevrolet. The controls on the automatic transmission are also different. In the research case, there are similarly specific differences in the execution step which grow out of (and should be spelled out in) the plan.

The second phase is more general. You might know how to drive in the mechanical sense and proceed onto a city street. You would be likely to be in serious trouble shortly thereafter unless you also knew some general safety principles and the traffic regulations and customs in effect. In our research parallel, we may assume generally that the individual who knows enough to develop a research plan knows "how to drive it" through to execution. He knows the objectives of the research, its limitations, the particular hazardous areas present, and so on. To drive the research through safely to its planned conclusion, however, he must know also the "safety principles" in the execution of research. It is those safety principles, which might be described also as fundamentals of sound research procedure, with which this chapter is primarily concerned.

MAJOR GOAL: ELIMINATION OR REDUCTION OF BIAS

One of the major objectives of many of those fundamentals is the elimination or at least the maximum reduction of bias at all phases in the research operation. We have already noted in Chapter 5 that *bias is any force, tendency, or procedural error in the collection, analysis, or interpretation of data which produces distortion.* The illustrations of bias up to this point have been primarily of bias in sampling. Bias may enter at many different points in the execution of research. The fundamentals of sound research procedure mentioned are concerned with keeping bias from producing distortion at any step in the collection, analysis, or interpretation of data.

An additional comment on the above definition is desirable. Note that it emphasizes distortion resulting from an error. What of the distortion which does not reflect an error, that is, of *intentional* distortion or bias?

This brings up a fundamental viewpoint which applies to the execution of research plans and applies with equal force to all other areas of marketing research practice.

THE IMPORTANCE OF INTELLECTUAL HONESTY IN RESEARCH

A competent marketing research man has as part of his equipment for research practice a number of characteristics. One of those characteristics is objectivity—the ability to see things as they are, rather than as someone says they are. Another is integrity. There are many occasions on which it is necessary to report unpleasant findings in research. In a series of seven product tests, for example, conducted for a client organization, *all* the competitive products against which the tests were made proved superior to the client's products. The results of research, pleasant or unpleasant, should be reported with forthright honesty. A research man who lacks the intellectual honesty required to face unpleasant facts as well as pleasant ones is out of place in the field.

Many people feel that marketing research is not dependable. It is their opinion that it can be used (many research men would say misused or abused) to "prove" any point. Unfortunately, the basis for that opinion is not entirely imaginary. John Crosby commented in a column about research on this paradoxical situation: Two surveys were made in 1955 to measure the impact on the audience physically present at a sports event of the telecasting of that event. One survey was sponsored by a collegiate association. Its primary conclusion was that television hurts attendance at sports events. The other was sponsored by a group of television-set manufacturers. That survey "proved" that television of sports events did *not* hurt attendance.

Now contradictory findings are possible in research without the necessity of bias being present. If basically different assumptions or definitions of the problem are the starting point, different research approaches may well develop findings which are in substantial conflict. When the findings of two studies in the same general area are opposed, and when the finding of each study "happens" to coincide with the interests of the sponsoring organization, both studies are suspect. The same suspicions are aroused when a single research study has findings so favorable to the sponsoring organization that it can be used for promotional purposes.

Bad research hurts all research and all research men. It is because of the reflections on their own competent and honest research cast by shoddy and shady incompetent research that marketing research men generally take so dim a view of *promotional research*. This subject is discussed further in Chapter 18 on research reporting and also in Chapter 29 on research by advertising agencies and advertising media.

In every assignment he tackles, a research man puts his professional reputation on a chopping block. To protect that reputation, he executes every step in the research process with all the skill, experience, and integrity he possesses. This applies to the planning of the research, to its execution, to its analysis and interpretation, and to its reporting.

Complete intellectual honesty, combined with uncompromising integrity, is postulated throughout this book as one of the essential characteristics of a competent marketing research man.

A reader who has been exposed at any time to a piece of conspicuously incompetent or apparently dishonest research may conclude from that isolated exposure that the above postulation is unwarranted. We might draw a parallel between this situation and that of the medical profession. The vast majority of the members of that profession adhere to high standards of ethics in their practice. This does not preclude a jackal fringe, whose activities bring discredit upon their professional colleagues.

In established professional fields like medicine and law, there are definite procedures for penalizing and expelling those whose ethics bring discredit upon the profession. Marketing research has no such procedures. Each individual in the field has a responsibility both to himself and to his associates to observe in his own activities the highest standards of ethical practice.

ILLUSTRATIONS OF SOURCES OF BIAS

Now let's illustrate the introduction of bias into research by some specific examples. In the survey approach, bias may be introduced by a single question. There is a strong tendency on the part of respondents to give an interviewer the answer the respondent thinks (or guesses or suspects) that the interviewer wants. This tendency is called by psychologists the *accommodating answer*. Wherever the answer desired is revealed or suggested by a question, the question is considered a leading one which is likely to introduce bias. For example, a question such as: *Do you buy floor wax?* will produce replies in which the level of floor-wax usage is inflated through bias. A question such as: *Have you seen this advertisement?* in which an advertisement is shown has been demonstrated to produce inflation ranging as high as three times the total number of "Yes" answers developed by a less biasing approach.

This tendency to say "Yes" in answer to a question is always present. It is even stronger where there is an element of social acceptance or social approval present. Thus the question: *Do you use deodorants?* as a result of advertising emphasis on the social undesirability of people who do not would be likely to produce results biased upward for both reasons indicated.

It is standard practice in surveys not to show the identity of the sponsoring company, brand, or organization on the questionnaire or in specific questions. Such identification reveals the interest of the sponsoring organization and introduces biases both at the respondent and at the interviewer level. Any questions asked in a survey which reveal the identity of the sponsoring company or brand cast doubt on the dependability of answers to all subsequent questions. The point is sometimes overlooked, but a question *which is interpreted by the respondent* as identifying the sponsor of the survey may also have a biasing effect. This is particularly dangerous because the research man responsible for the study may overlook the implication. Suppose that a brand of refrigerator, for example Frigidaire, were strongly associated in advertising with a product feature given a distinctive name like Meter-miser. Suppose further that a competitor sought to evaluate that feature, identifying it by that name. This might make respondents think the sponsor was Frigidaire and so introduce a bias into all subsequent questions.

An illustration of this is provided by a beer survey conducted in a Middle Western market. The survey had been planned to coincide with the beginning of the seasonal increase in beer consumption. Field work was about to begin when a new brand in the market exploded with a tremendously concentrated and unique advertising campaign about a new kind of beer. The questionnaire used was revised to include some questions designed to determine penetration of that new campaign. Questionnaire testing revealed that unless those questions were placed last in the questionnaire, they led respondents to assume that the new brand of beer was making the study and to supply answers which were strongly influenced by the attitude of each respondent toward the new brand of beer.

In this case, the new brand of beer had a promotional program which combined with highly distinctive product characteristics to split consumers into two groups. One group strongly favored the new beer. The other group just as strongly disliked it. Those standing on a middle ground were few in number. The effect of this pattern on the results which could be expected from the proposed beer survey was dramatically demonstrated by the questionnaire-testing interviews.

To overcome this biasing influence, a decision was made to include the questions about the new beer but to place them last in the questioning process. This reduced (but did not eliminate) the danger of bias from that source. Some bias was still present because the impact of the new beer's promotional program was extremely great. The unarticulated assumption that this beer survey was being sponsored by the new beer tended to influence many of the respondents' answers.

This example illustrates the need to be on guard against an unusual incident or influence which might affect survey results. For example, a proposed survey on attitudes toward major airlines was postponed when one airline had the misfortune to make headlines as a result of two dramatic and fatal crashes within a two-week period.

INTERVIEWER BIAS

There are many illustrations in marketing research and social science literature, some of them experimental, of the extent to which biased interviewers can and do distort survey data. One classic example is provided by the ardent prohibitionist. The down-and-outers he interviewed uniformly blamed liquor for their situation to a much greater extent than did similar respondents interviewed by individuals who brought less prejudice to the interview! It is axiomatic in sound marketing research practice that skilled and experienced interviewers should be used and that those interviewers should be free from bias. Little further comment on this point is required here.

There is a more subtle form of interviewer bias, however, which should be mentioned and which requires attention in executing many research plans. That bias results where there is a marked difference between interviewer and respondent in such matters as age, education, socioeconomic status, and so on. In the case of any particular interviewing assignment, the interviewers chosen should be those who are closest to the respondents in such vital characteristics. It is preferable in most cases to have women interview women and to have Negro interviewers where interviews are to be made in the homes of Negro respondents. Whether it is preferable to have men or women interview men is a point on which many research men disagree. The nature of the subject matter is one influence in a decision on that point.

The use of properly qualified interviewers becomes especially important in the case of industrial marketing research, where the respondents sought are often well-paid executives or highly trained technical specialists. The interviewers used must be able to establish rapport with such respondents. This usually requires that interviewers who are substantially equal to the respondents in socioeconomic level, educational background, and intelligence be used. Such interviewing of course costs more than "run-of-the-mill" interviews by less well qualified and less highly compensated interviewers.

POSITION BIAS

Another bias against which care must constantly be exercised is position bias. If a list of brand names, for example, is supplied to respondents, the sequence in which the names are listed should be rotated to eliminate the bias which the first and last names in a list have as a result of the operation of laws of memory. Similarly in advertising research, the position of ads in a folder under study requires rotation. In experimental store-display tests, such factors as the biasing effect of position in a store (near the check-out counter, for example) must be guarded against. Again, this is a type of bias against which experienced research people are always on guard. The point need not be labored here.

IDENTITY OF SPONSOR SHOULD NOT BE REVEALED TO FIELD PERSONNEL

Introduction of bias at the interviewer level was mentioned above. This is an ever-present danger. If the field interviewers know the identity of the sponsoring company, they may reveal that knowledge by emphasis in a listing of brands or they may use unauthorized probes which include the sponsor's name or brand. Similarly, if the field supervisors know the name of the sponsor, there is no assurance that they will not communicate that knowledge to the field interviewers. *It is axiomatic in sound research practice that there should be no unnecessary revelation of the name of the sponsoring brand or company* or of the name of a brand or company in which the sponsor has a particular interest. Such revelation introduces a bias, or the strong possibility of a bias, into field work.

The explanation of the word *unnecessary* in the italicized statement above lies in the fact that sometimes the purposes of the research cannot be accomplished without revealing the sponsor's identity or particular area of interest. One way to keep the bias in responses to a minimum was noted above—by putting the biasing questions last in the questioning sequence. But obviously where that is done the interviewer cannot always be kept in the dark as to the sponsor. In the beer survey mentioned, field interviewers were told that the study was *not* sponsored by the new brand and were told to inform respondents of that fact *if the respondent revealed such an assumption by a question.*

Where there is a revelation of the sponsor's identity in the questionnaire, for example, in the final sequence of questions, it is typically necessary to strengthen the quality of field supervision and instruction of interviewers to be *as sure as possible* that there is no *interviewer bias* in the responses recorded. Let's consider a case in which the likelihood of interviewer bias was present and relatively strong.

21. THE TONI CO. (B)

The key problem in the case of Bobbi home permanent was a decision on whether or not additional research was needed, and if so of what type. The capable marketing research department of the Toni Co. had already done an exhaustive research job on Bobbi, as well as on the other home permanents in the Toni line. Did this *marketing* problem seem likely to be solved by additional research?

Step 1 was a very detailed study and review of all information available from the company's own marketing research department. A substantial number of users of Bobbi home permanents had been interviewed in the course of Toni's research. One avenue which seemed promising was a reinterview of those Bobbi users. The study which had been conducted by the Toni marketing research department had been of the questionnaire type. It was primarily quantitative. It sought to establish the *proportion* of users of different brands of home permanents who were satisfied and dissatisfied with the results when those permanents were used. It was felt that a qualitative approach, in which a smaller number of much longer and deeper-probing interviews were made, might contribute relevant additional information.

It was decided to explore this approach on a small-scale, or pilot, basis. Initially a relatively small number—about fifty—former Bobbi users were to be interviewed. To make possible a comparison of Bobbi users with other home-permanent users, an equal number of interviews with a matched sample of nonusers was considered desirable. All these interviews would be of the type sometimes described as *depth interviews*. Chapter 26 on qualitative and motivational research describes this approach in detail.

— ★ —

MASKING SPONSORSHIP OR AREA OF SPECIFIC INTEREST

In the execution of this research, the primary objectives of the study were masked by including them within a relatively broad interview on likes and dislikes about the last brand of home permanent used, comparison of that brand with the brand last used before that, what brand would be bought next, when, reasons for that choice, and so on. This is an approach which is often taken to reduce the likelihood that bias will be developed in an interviewing situation. If a single ad is shown to a respondent in advertising research, it is pretty clear that the interviewer is interested in that particular ad. If the ad being researched is "buried" in a portfolio of five or ten ads, and *interviewing on all ads is conducted in an identical manner*, neither the respondent nor the interviewer can tell which of the ads (or which combination of ads) is the subject of the research. The likelihood of bias inflating results on the ad being studied is thereby greatly reduced.

Note that in product research (the subject of Chapter 22, two products are placed with a test participant even though an evaluation of only one is desired. This is another example of a research-technique development designed to reduce the impact of bias.

In summary, then, there are dangers of bias which must be avoided in the development of questionnaires and other forms. Those dangers exist in the case of individual questions, in which one question can and often does contain its own bias which introduces distortion. They exist also in the case of a sequence of questions, in which one question exerts a biasing influence on subsequent questions. The latter type of bias is particularly subtle in some cases and must be watched with care. The danger of intentional or unintentional bias introduced by the interviewer can be reduced if there is no disclosure in questionnaire, instructions, *or in the address to which questionnaires are to be sent upon completion,* of the identity of the sponsoring organization. If there appears to be a likelihood of an incorrect assumption as to sponsor biasing results (as in the beer study mentioned), that likelihood may be reduced by a specific statement that that company is *not* the sponsor, although that approach may in turn simply create an additional bias in the opposite direction.

The influence of the address to which questionnaires are forwarded should be noted. It requires no genius-level intelligence on the part of an interviewer to deduce the identity of the sponsor of a study of photographic practices made by some company in Rochester, N.Y., or of a soup survey emanating from Camden, N.J.! Often a "dummy name" is used as a mailing drop to avoid identification of the sponsoring organization. Some such name as "Cosmetic Research Institute" or "Family Survey Bureau" may provide an effective barrier against sponsor identification.

OTHER PROBLEMS IN QUESTION SEQUENCE

The sequence in which questions are asked in a questionnaire may have an important influence on the quality of the resulting information. Thus it is often helpful to have the first question in the questionnaire chosen with care for that position. Ideally, it should be as interesting as possible a question *from the respondent's viewpoint,* to capture his interest, and should also be relatively easy to answer. Some research men favor an opening question which tends to build the respondent's ego or self-confidence. Sometimes the opening question is a complete "blank" as far as the objectives of the survey are concerned. It is planned solely as a device to capture the interest of the respondent and to establish rapport with him.

Where a particular subject or area is being explored in a questionnaire, it should ordinarily be exhausted before moving on to the next series of questions or area. An interview in which the questions skip from subject to subject and then back again is difficult for a respondent to follow, hence difficult to reply to accurately. The respondent in most cases is doing the interviewer a favor by answering the questions. It is a matter of common courtesy, as well as of sound research practice, to do whatever is possible to make the interview easy for the respondent. A well-organized questionnaire is one step in that direction.

Within a particular subject area, questions should flow logically. If the questions involve time or trend data, they should ordinarily begin with the respondent's most recent experience, purchase, etc., explore it, then move on backward through time. By using normal laws of association to guide the questionnaire development, more accurate (hence less biased) data can be secured.

Where one part of the subject matter in question is rather personal or may be offensive to some respondents, it is sound practice to put that series of questions near the end of the interview. Thus if the respondent terminates at that point, answers to other questions have already been secured and can be tabulated. The interview is incomplete, but it is not a complete loss.

Frequently in a study covering a number of different areas of a subject, there is one area that is much more important to the sponsor of the study than any of the others. Where this is the case, the placement of that particular question or series of questions should be studied carefully. Usually it should not be used too early in the questionnaire; it is better to give the respondent a chance to "warm up" first. Also it should not be placed too far back in the questionnaire, so that respondent fatigue enters into the answers to the key questions. Similarly if there is a possibility of a relatively large number of "terminates" or incomplete interviews, it should be placed before the point at which termination by respondent is most likely to occur.

LENGTH OF QUESTIONNAIRES

One of the earmarks of an amateurish job of questionnaire development is the extremely long questionnaire. In the case of qualitative research where well-trained interviewers are used, it is possible to make a relatively long interview with a respondent. In the case of most quantitative studies, where the level of interviewer competence is sometimes lower, the length of a questionnaire which can be completed without a drop in the quality of replies is definitely limited. One reason for this is the fatigue factor on the part of respondents. It is because there exists a point of diminishing returns in questionnaire length that careful pruning is necessary in the planning phase of questionnaire development.

A notable source of bias, in the area of questionnaire length, is the repetitive questionnaire. Suppose a questionnaire first asks a series of questions, say on product use. Then it asks a question about the time interval since last usage of each product. Then it asks more detailed questions in the case of products used frequently. The respondent is getting tired of "being bothered." He or she notes the pattern of questioning. Anticipating that there will be many follow-up questions if further answers of "Yes" are given on product-use questions, the respondent shifts to the negative in an effort to speed the conclusion of the interview.

Against all of these potential problems, the best insurance is a series of test interviews made by the individual with greatest experience in field work, preferably by the research man himself. This is a point which is not heavily stressed in existing literature, but competent research men who are responsible for the planning and executing of a big research job often participate personally at many phases in the job themselves. It is only by conducting some interviews by himself that the research man can "get the real feel of" the particular survey or study in question. While this sounds at first blush like an inability to delegate, it actually is common practice among skilled and experienced research practitioners.

PROBLEMS IN INDIVIDUAL QUESTIONS

The danger of bias as a result of questions which are leading, which encourage an accommodating answer, or which disclose the survey sponsor's identity or area of interest has already been noted. There are some other danger points in individual questions against which the research man must be on guard.

A multiple-element question is one which occasionally slips into a questionnaire and piles up headaches in tabulation and analysis. Suppose you are making a survey on ready-to-eat breakfast cereals. You ask this question: *Did you eat a ready-to-eat cereal for breakfast yesterday?* This is a complex question. Some people may have eaten ready-to-eat cereals *yesterday* although *not* for breakfast. They answer the question: "No." If your objective is to determine how many people ate ready-to-eat cereals on the preceding day and/or if this was a preliminary question after which you expected to determine brands eaten, you would not get the desired information. Another illustration of bias: Such a question would reduce the apparent consumption of cereals which are widely used as between-meal snacks (such as sweetened cereals) more than it would a cereal used almost entirely for breakfast consumption.

Another pitfall, particularly for the less experienced research man, is the question that asks for a generalization. Questions about how many times such and such a food was served or product was purchased in the last four weeks, or about the proportion of all cakes baked that are made with cake mixes, are illustrations. It is far sounder procedure to ask about a specific recent situation or occurrence. In a questionnaire about the use of a product, for example, it is better to ask when the product was used *last* than how often it is "usually" used. It is better to ask a respondent to think back over the *last ten* cakes she baked and tell you *how many of those ten* cakes were made with cake mixes than to ask for the proportion of cakes made with mixes directly. Information developed by questions which involve a generalization is generally rather inaccurate. When the undependability of such data is not fully recognized in the analysis and interpretation step, misleading conclusions are likely to result.

Questions should ask only for information which the respondent can supply. Thus it is pointless, in most instances, to ask a wife how it.

happened that her husband last purchased such-and-such a brand of candy for a gift to her. She may know ("It's my favorite brand, and he always buys that one"), but often she won't know. In the latter case, if a marketing research man makes the mistake of asking a respondent for information he or she doesn't know, an answer (although not necessarily a correct answer) is likely to be forthcoming.

Another pitfall in question construction is the use of words which are in the "trade" category—with technical meanings understood by those in an industry, but not to ordinary consumers. Thus a question in a survey about washing machines asked whether women owned a "conventional" washing machine. This trade term signifies a wringer-type washer to those familiar with the industry. A far sounder approach is to describe the product type ("a conventional washing machine with a wringer on it") or to show a picture of different types of washing machines as Proctor & Gamble did in a survey on detergents.

Clarity in a question is always essential. Comment on the need for it should not be necessary. The fact is, however, that many questionnaires contain muddied, unclear, and ambiguous questions. Those questions should be identified on a pretest of the questionnaire. Some of them slip through into the field, with sometimes sad results.

For a specific illustration of the problems encountered in questionnaire development, let's consider the following case in which a questionnaire was developed and is reproduced in full.

22. BISSELL CARPET SWEEPER CO. (C)

One limitation of combining the evaluation of vacuum cleaners with the preadvertising research of the advertising agency was that the latter research had a tighter timetable. Carpet-sweeper sales traditionally followed a seasonal curve common to many products which are related to housecleaning practices. There is a seasonal peak in spring at traditional "spring-cleaning time" and a smaller peak in fall. Sales in summer and in winter are below average. The agency had to complete its research, develop the plans based on that research, prepare the necessary advertising, and get the advertisements produced and in the hands of the publications in time to precede the spring-cleaning increase in sales.

The agency recommended a survey of households in urban United States on a national scale. The sample size of the proposed study was established, after careful study of the breakdowns which were likely to be made, at 5,500 interviews.

Farm and rural populations were excluded from the sample design for two reasons. One was the relatively high cost per completed interview of such interviews. The second was the fact that at the time of the study farm and rural households were typically much lower in availability of electricity, ownership of carpets, etc., hence constituted for the most part "second-class prospects" for Bissell.

Guided by the informal investigation, a questionnaire was developed which the agency recommended for use in the survey. There were many suggested revisions, additions, and modifications of this recommended questionnaire. The sampling points were selected and interviewer time reserved. Meanwhile, the time dimension of the problem—with a fixed date by which "answers" were needed—became more binding.

Finally, a questionnaire was approved. The project was now on an extremely tight time schedule. Corner cutting to save time was urgently necessary. One way to trim some time out of the research plan was to proceed without subjecting the final questionnaire to the relatively extensive test which sound research procedure would ordinarily require. This was a study of considerable magnitude; it involved substantial costs; the risk of some undetected imperfections in the questionnaire or in the instructions for interviewers was consequently great. A very small number of "test" interviews were made by the agency's own personnel. Then the questionnaire was "frozen" and the study released to the field.

The questionnaire as it went to the field is reproduced below:

City_____ State_____

NATIONAL URBAN CONSUMER HOUSECLEANING SURVEY

1. Have you one or both of the following appliances in your home?
   Carpet Sweeper_____ Make and Model_____
   Electric Cleaner_____ Make and Model_____
   Neither   _____

(INTERVIEWER: Ask to see the appliances the woman claims to own, and get exact makes and models as stated on the appliances.)

IF A CARPET SWEEPER IS NOT OWNED:

a. Why don't you have a carpet sweeper?_____

---

b. Have you had one in the past? Yes_____ No_____

   IF YES:

   c. What make and model was it?_____

2. Kind of floor covering used in:	All over carpeting	Room size rugs	Scatter rugs	Composition
Living room	_____	_____	_____	_____
Dining room	_____	_____	_____	_____
Hall	_____	_____	_____	_____
Bedrooms	_____	_____	_____	_____

(INTERVIEWER: If neither appliance owned, skip to qualifying data, get that data, and terminate interview.)

IF CARPET SWEEPER IS OWNED:

3. How long have you had this sweeper?_____

4. How did you happen to get this make and model?_____
_____

5. In general, what is your opinion of it?_____
_____

6. What do you particularly like about it?_____
_____

7. Is there anything about it that you dislike?_____
_____

8. Is this your first sweeper or have you had others in the past?
    First one_____   Had others_____

IF OTHERS OWNED PREVIOUSLY:

a. What make and model did you have before your present carpet sweeper?_____
_____

b. Why did you give it up?_____
_____

9. If you were going to buy a new sweeper today, what make would you buy?____
_____

a. Why would you choose this make?_____
_____

b. Where would you buy it?   Department store____ Furniture Store____
    City_____   Hardware store____
                             Other_____
                                       (Describe)

IF A VACUUM CLEANER IS OWNED:

10. For what purposes do you use the vacuum cleaner?_____
_____

(INTERVIEWER: Find out all her uses of the vacuum cleaner—rugs, draperies, thorough housecleaning, etc.)

IF BOTH CARPET SWEEPER AND VACUUM CLEANER ARE OWNED:

11. How many times a week do you use these appliances?
    No. times per week carpet sweeper is used_____
    No. times per week vacuum cleaner is used_____

QUALIFYING DATA (INTERVIEWER: Be sure to fill out the following items completely.)

Class of Home: High____ Upper middle____ Lower middle____ Low____
Age of Housewife: Under 25____ 26–34____ 35–49____ 50 and over____
House wired____ Unwired____   White____ Colored____
Type of house: Detached single family____ 2-family____ 3 or more____
Number in family: Number of adults____ Number of children____
Name of housewife_____
Street address_____
Date_____   _____
                                     Interviewer's signature

COMMENTS ON THE BISSELL QUESTIONNAIRE

The above questionnaire is reproduced just as it was used in this national consumer study. It is *not* offered as an ideal or model of questionnaire construction; but neither is it in the "horrible-example" category. In part because of inadequate pretesting, some aspects of this questionnaire as it was used in the field were open to improvement. In the light of today's knowledge of questionnaire construction, a somewhat different and certainly improved questionnaire would be developed by a research man with comparable experience given the same assignment. A review of this questionnaire is likely to be more instructive than additional generalizations about this phase of research work. In the following discussion, the question under discussion is reproduced in italics. Comments on that question follow with actual questions in italics.

Have you one or both of the following appliances in your home? There is a question as to the use of the word *appliances,* especially as of the time of this questionnaire. It would be sounder to ask: *Do you own a carpet sweeper?* The question could be followed by: *Do you own an electric cleaner?* There is a question also as to the communicating value of the designation "electric cleaner." It is better to spell out such a term, in consumer terminology.

Note that the observation technique was used to verify claimed ownership. This certainly increased the accuracy of information on that vital point.

Why don't you have a carpet sweeper? By today's research standards, this question would be considered rather naive. A sounder approach would be to use some preliminary questions which would qualify respondents as to their knowledge of and interest in a carpet sweeper and as to their past experience with such a product, if any. Then additional questions would be confined to those respondents in the most important categories from the standpoint of the research objectives.

In the Bissell case, two groups of respondents can be identified as of particular importance. One is the respondent who does not have a carpet sweeper because she discarded it when a vacuum cleaner was purchased. That's a "lost customer," and the reasons for the loss—the likes and dislikes of the respondent where each such appliance is concerned— are extremely important. The second is the respondent who weighed the merits of both devices, then decided on a vacuum cleaner in preference to a carpet sweeper. The relative proportion of total respondents falling in each group is important. The reasons which influenced the indicated action are also important.

Other types of respondents are also of especial interest: those (if any) who tried a vacuum cleaner and switched back to a carpet sweeper;

or those who discontinued the use of a carpet sweeper even though they did not replace it with a vacuum cleaner.

Note that the question *Have you had one in the past?* is followed only by a question about the make and model owned. Nothing is asked about how long ago the ownership took place, nor are reason questions asked to explore the sources (if any) of dissatisfaction with the product. This represents an oversight in planning the questionnaire. Note that questions of the type indicated *are* asked of those who now own carpet sweepers (in questions 8*a* and 8*b*).

This questionnaire was planned for an essentially quantitative type of study. It used, as a review of the questionnaire will indicate, a rather large number of *open-end-* or *reason*-type questions. Such questions are typically used much less extensively in quantitative research today. They pose major problems in tabulation and analysis. The tendency is to secure quantitative information which is more easily handled in mechanical tabulation of data on a quantitative-type study, and to turn to qualitative or motivational research (the subject of Chapter 26) on a more intensive basis with a smaller sample to explore qualitative and reason-why areas.

WHY "WHY?" QUESTIONS ARE USED CAUTIOUSLY

As the comment above suggested, it is relatively difficult and expensive to edit, code, and tabulate mechanically the responses to questions of the qualitative or reason type. The trend away from such questions in quantitative studies, or to the more restricted use of them, has been influenced by that difficulty and cost factor. There is another even more important reason for that trend, which should be recognized. That reason is the growing recognition among research men of complexities of a psychological type which were once overlooked.

It was once naively assumed that a single "Why?" question could provide the researcher with a meaningful and dependably accurate response of the reason type. In the light of today's vastly higher level of psychological training among research personnel, the unsoundness of that assumption is widely recognized. A whole battery of direct questions sometimes is inadequate to secure a "Why?" response which a single, simple question would once have been expected to supply. The less direct approaches described in Chapter 26 on qualitative and motivational research are often called upon to supplement the traditional quantitative approaches.

Where open-end or reason types of questions are included in a quantitative type of study, a small-scale pilot test is often used as a preliminary step. A careful tabulation and analysis of those replies are then used to develop a partial check list of the most frequently occurring types of responses. Space is provided on the questionnaire for the check list, which the interviewer or respondent (in mail studies) need only check. Space is also provided for writing in replies which do not fit any of the check-list items. The check-list approach has some limitations, to which we shall return in the next chapter in discussing the analysis and interpretation of data.

CONTINUING NEED FOR FLEXIBILITY

There is a continuing need, in the course of executing a research plan, to maintain a maximum amount of flexibility. Sometimes the results of the early part of the research will disclose a major error, change, or complication which was not anticipated, with the result that a searching reappraisal of the proposed research is urgently necessary. Sometimes a change in the market or within the company (as in the case of an unexpected strike) will make an interruption of the research necessary.

Often a proposed plan will be "approved," but with so many changes, modifications, etc., that it amounts in effect to a completely new research approach. The research man must be alert to the possibility that a plan may be derailed and may require extensive revision. The following case is illustrative.

23. BENDIX HOME APPLIANCES, INC. (B)

The Bendix management team rejected the recommended consumer survey which had been planned to aid in diagnosing Bendix's recognized "Middle Western weakness." Two primary reasons for that rejection were reported to the company's marketing research director. First, the high cost of the proposed research was a major obstacle. It seemed quite likely that, over a period of years, the correction of Bendix's regional weakness would represent far more dollars in profit than the research would cost. Yet it was by no means certain that the research in question would make enough of a contribution to the solution of that problem to represent a sound business risk. Second, the Bendix management team was opposed to a general, broad approach to the Middle Western problem. They asked whether a more specific approach, confined to a limited number of individual markets in the Middle West, might not be more productive and more economical. Not all the markets in the Middle West were weak markets for Bendix. Might not a study of some strong and some weak markets in the Middle West provide a more promising research approach?

The company's research department was asked to reconsider the rejected recommendations. It was made clear that no minor modification in approach would suffice to secure authorization.

This is one of those situations in which a thoroughgoing reappraisal is necessary. So long as it seemed likely that the company might soon make a broad-scale study, the research decision to await vital information from that study was sound. With the proposed study vetoed, alternative sources of at least some of the desired information had to be re-examined. One such source of information was found. It was a national consumer survey conducted for the Crowell-Collier Publishing Company by the Psychological Corporation. The survey was published under the title *The Collier's Market*. It was an 8,000-interview survey made on an extremely well-developed sampling plan.

Much information published as a result of research by advertising media is of limited usefulness for one of two reasons. Either the sample itself is not likely to be a representative one, or the sample is likely to be representative only of those who read a given (sponsoring) publication. This leaves the sometimes impossible task of linking the survey results to the total population. The *Collier's* study, however, reported data in full *both* for the full national sample and for readers of *Collier's*. Included in the survey were questions about present ownership of various appliances, including washing machines. Included also were questions about future purchasing intentions on such appliances, including brand detail. Ray Robinson, who was then research director of *Collier's*, agreed to prepare special tabulations from the *Collier's* survey data. Those tabulations would show ownership of washing machines by brands and types; purchase intentions by brands and types; and would be broken down to show variations on a large number of bases. They would show, for example, sectional variations in washer ownership and in brand position among washers owned. Similar detail on city-size groups, on apartment dwellers versus home renters and home owners, on different economic levels and different occupational groups, would similarly be provided. For the cost of tabulation alone, running to a few hundred dollars, a very substantial amount of the data which would have been provided by the Bendix survey if it had been authorized became available from the *Collier's* survey.

To sharpen focus on the uncovered portions of data with particular emphasis on major Middle Western markets, individual market studies in a number of different markets were authorized. One of the markets to be studied was Chicago; another was Omaha. Both those markets were selected because of specific and pressing Bendix competitive problems in them. In executing the research in those markets, attention was paid to details which might make it possible to use those individual-market studies as small-scale tests or pilot surveys precedent to a larger and broader study which might subsequently become necessary.

WHERE DOES PLANNING STOP AND EXECUTION BEGIN?

In the above case a complete research plan was developed and then replaced by another radically different approach. It would be possible to regard this as an illustration of the planning process and to consider it out of place in a chapter on the execution of a research plan. It is included here to illustrate this key point: that the process of marketing research on a specific problem is a continuing one, with modification of direction or approach possible at each of a large number of points in the course of the research. While a research man might well consider this to be a rejection of one plan and a new planning assignment, management people who are not research specialists would be likely to consider the change in direction as primarily a modification of a research plan rather than as a new plan.

It is important to note also that the original plan, which was rejected, played a very important part in stimulating *some research action* on an important marketing problem. A research plan which represents the end result of dozens of hours of work may well become as dear to a research man as one of his children. He may tend to resist and resent any tendency to modify or change the plan, especially when the changes are imposed by those who lack research training. The important point to note is that any *sound* research *upon which some action is taken* is likely to be superior to *no* research.

Research men often encounter the problem of a closed mind on the part of one or more executives to whom research results are reported. The tendency for executives to accept research which agrees with their own opinions or prejudices and to reject research which is in conflict with their own ideas is rather general. That exposure to the problems which a closed mind on the receiving end of research results can create should serve to reduce the danger that the research man himself may exhibit a closed mind. A "stiff-necked" attitude, resisting and resenting a change in a proposed plan, should be avoided.

Sometimes the changes which are suggested in research approaches by nonresearch people represent major improvements in the plan. It is as a practical matter impossible for the research man to think of all possible approaches or angles in planning the research. The possibility that those more intimately familiar with the problem situation may be able to contribute to the improvement of proposed research is ever present.

The Bendix case above is an illustration of a situation in which the requirements imposed on the research activity by nonresearch personnel (in this case, primarily by top management) contribute to an improvement and strengthening of the research approach.

THE ROLE OF A PILOT STUDY

What was originally proposed in the Bendix case was a rather large-scale study which involved three different areas of research. One prong of the program was a consumer study, planned to cover both owners and nonowners of Bendix washers. The second was a shopping survey of retailers. Both Bendix and competitive dealers would have been included. The third was an expanded study of Bendix owners. As the preceding chapter pointed out, this complete research program would have involved a substantial capital investment for Bendix. The Bendix management group weighed the research contributions (as they saw them) against the costs involved, vetoed the study as originally conceived, and suggested the substitution for that broad study of some individual-market studies.

This is an excellent illustration to use as background for emphasizing this very important and fundamental viewpoint: *There is no one best research approach to use, in tackling any specific marketing problem. Different research men can and do study the same marketing problem and suggest quite radically different research approaches to it.* There is no assurance that the proposed research approach in the Bendix case was the best approach to that problem. There is no basis for concluding that the individual-market approach represented an inferior method of researching that problem.

Because there is so much room for judgment in selecting the most desirable of a number of alternative research approaches to a particular marketing problem, marketing research men often *use research to pretest* a proposed research approach. In such a pretest, they use a small-scale study which duplicates exactly the approach they contemplate on a larger project. The results of the small-scale test provide assurance that the contemplated larger study is sound in concept, complete in every detail, and likely to produce a contribution to profit substantially in excess of its cost.

Such a small-scale duplication of a proposed or contemplated larger-scale research study is often described as a *pilot study*.

Ordinarily a pilot study is planned and executed *on a scale which is no larger than it need to be* to provide a substantial duplication on a practical scale of the problems which would be encountered in executing the larger study and of the types of information the larger study would be likely to contribute.

A pilot study might be conducted everywhere that the proposed large-scale research would be conducted. On the other hand, there is no reason why the major benefits of a pilot study could not be provided by research much less limited in scope. When the Bendix top management suggested the substitution of individual-market studies for the broader research which was proposed, they set up a situation which was perfectly suited to provide the benefits of a soundly conceived pilot test of the larger project.

If the Chicago and Omaha studies following the approach proposed for larger-scale application proved rewarding, that is, if they provided new and useful knowledge of the nature of the Bendix problem in those markets, the likelihood of securing approval on the broader study would be increased. On the other hand, if the individual-market research failed to disclose facts which management could use to develop substantial profit contributions, the broader-scale study in all probability would prove similarly unrewarding.

In the Bendix case, the proposed individual-market studies had certain characteristics common to soundly conceived pilot studies. The small-scale study should be planned within, and as a part of, the larger-scale study. Thus if it were decided to expand from Chicago and Omaha studies to one covering the remainder of the Middle West, the Chicago and Omaha *parts* of the larger study would already be complete and would not have to be duplicated.

The point to note here is that the cost of a pilot study is typically not entirely an *additional* cost. Much of it represents costs which *would be* incurred *if* the broader-scale study were executed. Thus the cost of the entire research project is increased only slightly by the introduction of the pilot-study step. The key "extra cost" which a pilot study entails is usually the *time cost*. There are many situations in which a research man would like to conduct a pilot study but fails to do so because the time dimension of the major problem makes it impossible. Such situations are unfortunate. The results of a pilot study more often than not disclose significant opportunities to increase the effectiveness of broader-scale studies.

WHY A PILOT STUDY IS OFTEN DESIRABLE

The desirability of conducting a pilot study as part of a large-scale research project increases with the cost of the proposed study. The greater the total cost of the study under contemplation, the greater the likelihood that a small-scale pilot study in advance of the all-out effort will contribute more than its costs in terms of increased effectiveness of the large-scale research.

Just as a production pilot-plant serves production management by helping to "get the bugs out" of proposed new products and processes, so does a pilot study in research protect against errors or oversights in research planning. Some research men have great confidence in their own ability and experience and feel that a pilot study is unnecessary before their plans are put into action on a large scale. Where that experience is in substantially similar research projects, their confidence may be warranted. The possibility that it may be unwarranted and that their plans may be incomplete or imperfect in one or more respects is always present.

The pilot study contributes to the improvement and strengthening of the full-scale research project in many ways. Specifically, contributions may usually be anticipated in the following areas.

1. *Improvement in Questionnaires, Forms, and Interviewing Materials*

The pilot study makes it possible to conduct a test of questionnaires, observation forms, instructions, and other interviewing materials under actual field conditions. If there are "bugs" in the forms—and there often are!—the pilot study helps to detect and eliminate them before they have had a chance to affect the bulk of the field work adversely.

The relationship between this contribution and the testing of questionnaires should be noted. In a test of a questionnaire, it is customary to use highly skilled and experienced interviewers who are thoroughly conversant with the objectives of the study. They bring a considerable amount of general research experience plus knowledge of the specific study in question to the questionnaire-testing as background. That background makes it possible for them to spot weaknesses in the questionnaire. Those weaknesses may be of any of a number of types. Perhaps the questions as asked do not develop the basic information the study is being conducted to secure. In that case, what questions would develop such information? The skilled interviewer, in the course of a questionnaire test, can often develop alternate approaches and actually try them out if the original concept proves unworkable. There may be other weaknesses in the questionnaire, in such highly technical areas as question sequence, for example, which a test will disclose. The soundness of the basic assumptions as to the understandability and communicative value of the terminology used is re-examined in the course of a test.

The pilot study, in contrast, typically utilizes field interviewers who are *not* far above average in skill and experience. Ideally, the interviewers used in the pilot study should be *exactly representative* of the levels of competence which would be found in the full field force. There have been cases in which the pilot study's major contribution was the disclosure of the sad fact that the questionnaire developed could not be adequately handled by field interviewers of the experience level it had been planned to use!

2. A Check on "Production," and Hence on Cost Estimates

In estimating the costs of executing a study, especially one involving a substantial amount of field work, some estimates of the average daily production in terms of number of interviews per day must be made. The pilot study provides a basis for checking those estimates under field conditions. An error in such an estimate could easily represent a major discrepancy between planned and actual costs. A study on which costs had been estimated with assumed production of six interviews per day would have total interviewing costs 20 per cent higher than estimated if actual production were only five interviews per day.

It should be remembered that often a cost estimate is prepared and authorized, with the development of the actual questionnaire as a subsequent step. If the temptation to crowd in "just one more question" is insufficiently resisted and the questionnaire grows in length as questionnaires often do, such a difference between estimated and actual production could easily develop. A pilot study would reveal that the total costs would be substantially higher than estimated, permitting either an increase in the authorized expenditure or a pruning of the questionnaire to restore balance before the full costs were incurred.

3. A Review of Understanding of Instructions to Field Personnel and an Indication of the Cost of "Study Time"

Instructions to the field organization represent a vital element in the research process. Those instructions must be clear and complete. They must be thoroughly understood by the field personnel. The proof of their clarity is whether field personnel do in fact understand them.

In developing instructions, some organizations do a very complete and detailed job of "dotting i's and crossing t's," leaving literally nothing to the interviewer's judgment. In theory that is the soundest approach. In point of fact it is desirable in practical marketing activities to recognize an offsetting disadvantage of that approach. If the instructions to the interviewer are too detailed, they are likely to require a relatively long time for the field personnel to "study" and "digest." Note that the "skimming" approach is not possible, because a point of great importance could be buried in a considerable amount of "chaff." Study time costs money. Where the interviewing is widely dispersed, so that many different individuals must study (and study time must be paid for, for each of them), excessively detailed instructions can add very substantially to the cost of the field work.

In summary, the level of competence and experience of the field personnel used should be a known quantity. That level should determine the amount of "spelling out" of relatively obvious points necessary. Where there is a considerable range in experience within the field organization, instructions must be prepared to handle adequately the *least* experienced and intelligent field personnel's requirements. The possible economies of having two different sets of instructions, one more detailed than the other, may merit consideration.

4. *Experience in Coding, Editing, and Tabulating Actual Data*

The research process is a complex one, with a high degree of interdependence of parts. The questionnaire in a survey, for example, is planned to provide certain information. Whether it does or does not successfully deliver that information often cannot be ascertained completely until the questionnaires are processed. Processing involves a number of steps: first, the editing and coding of completed questionnaires; and second, the actual tabulation of the data.

In many cases it is the cross-tabulation of various pieces of information which provides the most significant findings of the research. A pilot study, carried through the actual steps in data processing to final tables, provides insurance against two things: One is an oversight in the questionnaire construction, which makes it impossible to explore vital relationships because some questions were not asked of some respondents. (An illustration was provided in the Bissell questionnaire, where past ownership of carpet sweepers was not explored among nonowners who formerly owned one.) Second, when major cross tabulations are anticipated in advance, and scheduled into the tabulation plan, important economies in tabulation can often be achieved.

An additional possible contribution worth noting is this one: Often a piece of information secured only from a small subsample in a survey is considered of vital importance. It is typically impossible to estimate accurately the size of many subsamples until the actual survey data are received. A pilot study provides an indication of the sample size which will be available for analysis, in the case of a "vital statistic." If the sample is likely to be too small for the planned analysis, it can be expanded without loss of time in the full-scale study.

SAMPLE SIZE IN PILOT STUDIES

The scale of a pilot study need not be very large. A study with a few hundred interviews, precedent to a full-scale study running to several thousand interviews, may be entirely adequate. To achieve the advantages suggested above, it is usually necessary to spread the field work to provide advance experience with the many special circumstances which are likely to be encountered in the full-scale study. The actual number of interviews included may well be arrived at by combining a number of actual elements in the study. For example, if it were felt that the typical interviewer would need three days of interviewing to arrive at her "full speed" and production rate, the number of interviews in a pilot study might proceed upward from x days per interviewer (in the pilot interviewing) extended by the number of types of points (city sizes, etc.) in which interviewing was planned. Provision for recording of starting time and terminal time on each interview, in the pilot phase of the research, may be helpful in securing the contributions from the pilot study which were indicated above.

IMPORTANCE OF TIMING ON COMPLEX ASSIGNMENTS

Individuals differ widely in their ability to work effectively on multiple-facet assignments. In the field of marketing research, there is a very great need for the rather intangible ability to "keep a number of balls in the air" at one time. The need for that ability is most clearly demonstrated in the case of complex assignments. Wherever there are a number of elements to a complex research program, careful attention to the timing of the various phases of the research is necessary. This point has already been mentioned. It is especially important because it is continually necessary to consider the possibility that the results of one or more phases of the research may seriously affect the direction, emphasis, or necessity for one or more other phases of the research.

Because the likelihood that one facet of a complex assignment may affect other phases of the same research cannot be reduced to specific probabilities, exercise of considerable judgment is needed. It is generally desirable to consider the possibility that some one or more perhaps likely results from one phase of the research may make subsequent phases unnecessary. In such a case, it is desirable to expedite the scheduling of the research which might have such an effect. This is simply a precaution against the waste of time, effort, or money on research which hindsight proved to be unnecessary. The following case illustrates such a scheduling problem.

24. THE DELL-O COMPANY (C)

The research planning on the Dell-O problem had been developed to a point at which four distinct problem areas were blocked out for action. The first was in the product area, where a comparative consumer-acceptance test of the product versus leading competitive products was in progress. The second involved an analysis of the territorial distribution of the company's volume and of total potential. The third was research at the retail and wholesale level. The fourth was an evaluation of the advertising program. Of those four areas, we are concerned here only with the second and third.

The sales-analysis activity received top priority, because the results of that analysis were necessary before the areas to be included in the wholesale and retail research could be identified.

The company's distribution of volume and variations in market share were determined territorially. This analysis disclosed a tremendous range in effectiveness for the company from market to market. In particular there was a tendency for the company's market share to decline as distance from the company's factory increased.

It was also found that the company had a number of different types of distributors. The most important type in terms of volume was a specialty distributor, representing about 40 per cent of total volume. Ranking second in importance were two branches owned and operated by the company. One of those was within the company's factory; the other was a distributor whose operation had been taken over by the company under pressure of some extraordinary circumstances. Ranking third were distributors who handled butter, eggs, and cream. There were also distributors who were primarily fruit and produce wholesalers, mayonnaise jobbers, potato-chip jobbers, ice-cream distributors, and several other types.

Efforts to correlate competitive position with type of distributor representation proved futile. There was no apparent relationship. Some distributors of each type were in strong markets, and some of each type in weak markets. However, there were some significant differences in the company's trend over the last year by type of distributor. One type of distributor showed a 22.5 per cent decline in volume. Another type showed a 20.3 per cent increase.

In planning the wholesale and retail research, a number of decisions were made. One was to study both retail and wholesale factors *in the same markets*. This had a practical value, in the reduction of travel time and cost. It had a research value, in that the patterns of wholesale and retail characteristics could be related to each other. That is, if a wholesaler was strong in sales performance, the various specific elements of strength (such as level of distribution, amount of retail display activity, ratio of sales manpower to number of accounts covered, etc.) could be studied at both wholesale and retail levels. It was decided that the wholesale-level research must include wholesalers of each major type, and within each type studied should where possible include a strong and a weak distributor.

While the coverage of the retail and wholesale research was being planned, results of the product test were received. Those results showed, apparently conclusively, that there was no product disadvantage which could explain the sales decline. The Dell-O product was equal to the two leading competitive brands on all points, and even enjoyed an edge of superiority over those brands in some respects. Since the product was not the problem element, it was decided to extend the research area to include a consumer survey as well.

Here is the list of markets in which research was executed, with the type of research in each. The code used is *W* for wholesale, *R* for retail, and *C* for consumer research.

Albany, N.Y., *W, C*	Greenville, S.C., *W, R*	Portland, Maine, *C*
Altanta, Ga., *W, R, C*	Houston, Tex., *W, R, C*	Providence, R.I., *R*
Baltimore, Md., *W, R*	Jackson, Miss., *W, R*	Quincy, Ill., *W, R, C*
Chicago, Ill., *W, R, C*	Kansas City, Mo., *W, C*	Rochester, N.Y., *C*
Cleveland, Ohio, *W*	Lafayette, Ind., *R*	Rockford, Ill., *W, R*
Columbus, Ga., *C*	LaSalle, Ill., *R, C*	Schenectady, N.Y., *R*
Dallas, Tex., *W, R*	Montgomery, Ala., *W,*	Sedalia, Mo., *R, C*
Denver, Colo., *W, R, C*	*R*	South Bend, Ind., *C*
Detroit, Mich., *W, R*	New Orleans, La., *C*	Syracuse, N.Y., *R*
Dixon, Ill., *R*	Philadelphia, Pa., *R*	
Galesburg, Ill., *R*	Pittsburgh, Pa., *R*	

In the execution of this research what might be described as a rolling plan was used. On the basis of sales analysis, certain points were selected for long and detailed interviews with wholesalers. Retail calls were made in the same markets. These relatively intensive calls were subsequently supplemented in several waves by additional calls, especially at the retail level, exploring new areas or exploring the same areas with a broader numerical base. The consumer study was planned to include a number of strong, medium, and weak markets in terms of the company's sales performance.

— ★ —

IMPORTANCE OF INITIATING PROMISING ACTIVITY

In developing an integrated schedule of research activities involved in surrounding a complex problem, the research man often faces this problem: One particular facet of the research will cost substantially more than other parts of the whole program. Pressure to defer the execution of that expensive part of the job is often brought to bear. The soundness of delaying that particular part of the job until other parts have been completed calls for careful individual evaluation. Often the pressure to defer the expensive step in the program is brought to bear by the research man himself.

One of the most frustrating aspects of marketing research work occurs when a carefully formulated plan has been developed and some new element is then produced (or disclosed!) which may require examination or research before the plan itself is launched. This often occurs when the organization with a problem is divided into factional groups which take different views of the gravity of the problem. The time and profit dimensions of the original plan influence reaction to this problem in some cases. It is extremely important (and often terribly difficult!) to distinguish between a bona fide additional element which deserves consideration and a "red herring" introduced in an attempt to defer clearly needed action. The following case provides an illustration.

25. SHOWER-OF-STARS COSMETICS, INC. (C)

To guide the assignment of priorities in the company's product-development activities, published data on trends in the usage of various types of cosmetic products as compiled in research by consumer magazines were carefully reviewed. As indicators of the absolute level of usage of different products, this research was not dependable. The sample of women covered, as is true in much research by individual advertising media, was the audience of the publishing sponsor organization. Since there was no way of relating the readers of any one magazine to the universe of total population, this meant the figures were "floating" on an absolute basis.

However, several of the published studies had been made year after year, using essentially the same sampling approaches and methodology. Therefore, the trend data provided were expected to show which types of products were increasing and which were decreasing in usage levels.

The major product of the company which had declined so sharply in volume was in the make-up field. There were a number of different types of make-up, all performing essentially the same beautifying service for their users, but varying widely in specific characteristics. For example, one type was a *cake* make-up. It came flat in a round case usually and was applied to the skin with a wet sponge in solution. The application process was: apply, let dry. One disadvantage: The wet sponge was somewhat messy. Another type was a *cream* make-up. This was essentially similar to a cake make-up in form, except that it was applied without the need for a sponge. In some brands, the make-up was applied with the fingers and then smoothed on. In others, the make-up came in a large stick form something like a lipstick and the stick itself was rubbed on the skin. In either form, the fingers were likely to become somewhat greasy, which was one disadvantage of that form.

A third type of make-up was *liquid* make-up. It came in a small bottle, was applied with the fingers, and had about the same magnitude of "dirty-finger" problem as cream. A fourth type was the *pressed-powder* form. This also came in a flat round cake, like a compact. It was applied with a powder puff, hence did not get the fingers dirty. It had as one disadvantage that an application lasted a shorter period of time than the other forms.

The company had suffered its major volume decline in one of these four types of make-up products. It had added a product in one of the remaining three categories. While that product sold moderately well, it did not come anywhere near replacement of the volume lost on the original type. Questions existed about the comparative quality and consumer acceptance of the original forms of make-up, which had suffered such a sharp decline in volume. To what other products, if any, had former users switched? Similar questions existed about the second type introduced by the company. Further questions existed as to which if either of the remaining two types the company should try to develop.

In the discussion of product characteristics with the cosmetic firm's development chemists, the consultant in charge of work on the Shower-of-Stars assignment received a shock. The company's technical people were certain, in their own minds, of the reason for the decline in sales of the company's leading product. That product had a characteristic which was relatively undesirable—it had a sensory effect which made it seem to the woman using it as though it were drying to her skin. It had a drawing sensation, in the process of application, which led to that interpretation. This was not actually a product limitation, in their view, because the product actually did not dry women's skins. However, they had developed a product modification which, in their judgment, over-came the drying impression.

This posed a new research problem. Was this improved formulation the answer? If it was, why the delay in putting it into production? Diligent questioning revealed that essentially no consumer-acceptance research on the new formulation had been done, although that formulation had been in existence for a considerable period of time!

The research plan on which agreements was finally secured had these parts:

1. A comparative consumer-acceptance test of new and old formulations of the company's product was initiated without delay.

2. In the course of qualification for the test, present and former make-up usage by type was explored. The placement work on the

product test thus provided as one by-product some information on product-type shifts within the make-up field.

3. Available published data on usage of different types of make-up were to be secured and reviewed for clues on developmental priorities.

4. Experts on trends in the beauty field—the editors and beauty specialists on the various women's magazines covering the subject—were interviewed for their observations on past trends and prediction of future trends.

— ★ —

MOTIVATIONAL PROBLEMS OF THE RESEARCH MAN

There is a whole broad area of relatively complex and interrelated factors, mostly of a motivational type, which should be pointed out in conjunction with the above case and the comment immediately preceding it. The problem area is one involving conflict—between some individuals who want research executed with all possible speed and others who believe the research should be deferred or vetoed entirely. Inevitably, the research man plays a central role in this area of conflict.

Let's begin with the simplest type of relationship. A research man working for and in a manufacturing company is exposed to a marketing problem. He recommends a program of research on that problem. There has been, let us say, no action on his recommendation. To what extent, if at all, should he try to "push" that recommendation? The answer to that question depends upon his considered and (let us hope!) objective judgment as to *the importance of the problem, and the potential research contribution to the problem, to the company from which he receives his pay checks.*

If he believes the research recommendation is vitally important to his company, he should leave no stone unturned in his effort to secure favorable consideration of the proposal. For him to fail to push it as hard as he can would be nothing less than disloyalty to his employer.

One way for him to look at the company's failure to act is to interpret it realistically as his own failure in presentation. If the company understood as well as he does how important that research is, they would certainly lose no time in authorizing it. No action has been taken on it. It therefore seems a reasonable assumption that *he has failed* to present the problem and the proposed research as forcefully and clearly as the value of that research warranted. He should certainly pass up no opportunity to make up for that past failure by supplementing his proposal with whatever oral or other supporting material he can devise which will make his associates appreciate its true value.

On the other hand, some research assignments are much more interesting and challenging than others. A research man would be less than human if he desired to have a larger number of dull and routine and a smaller number of really stimulating projects to work on. It is extremely important (and very difficult!) for a research man to make his "to-push-or-not-to-push" decisions on an objective basis with company benefits as the sole criteria.

Those who oppose a particular research project do so, let us assume, for entirely aboveboard and equally objective reasons, again with the company's own good (as they see it) as the sole influence. In this type of an impasse, reflections on the motivation of the opposition are sometimes cast. The research man in this situation should present his own viewpoints as forcefully and effectively as he can, without heat, and then retire from the fray. He should be content to let the facts speak for themselves.

In the situation indicated, there is no deep basis for concern regarding the research man's motivation in pushing the research. He is on a salary. Whether the research is or is not authorized has no bearing, presumably, on his income. Therefore he cannot be accused of "grinding his own axe."

The situation is very different when the research proposal has been presented by someone outside the company—by a concern selling a marketing research service, for example, or a consulting organization, or occasionally an advertising agency. Unlike the inside research man, the proposer now has a dollars-and-cents reason to want to see the research authorized in many instances. The motivation of the advocate(s) of the research is under considerably more intense scrutiny than is the case in the preceding example. And properly so.

In this type of situation, a marketing research man should act with the same preoccupation with the potential profit contribution of the research as he would if he were on the company's payroll. It is only by strict adherence to the highest ethical standards in his professional conduct, and particularly in the area of formulating and "pushing" recommendations, that he can maintain the intellectual integrity which is so important to success in marketing research.

It would be folly not to recognize that under many circumstances the motivation of the research man may be under scrutiny or even under attack. That cannot be avoided. What the research man can avoid is a situation in which there is a reason why his motivations *should be* suspect!

SUMMARY

1. The execution of a research plan combines two areas of activity. The first is concerned with those particular elements which are unique to a particular research project and which are usually spelled out in the written re-

search plan. Those elements are linked to the objectives of the research or to peculiarities in the product, problem, or area under consideration. The second is concerned with elements common to most research plans.

2. In the execution of the research plan, the marketing research man must be continually and constantly on guard against anything which might introduce bias into the planned research.

3. There are many points at which bias may be introduced into a research study. The research man's responsibility is to recognize the danger of bias in the planning stage and to guard against it in the execution of the plan. Individual questions (in a survey) may be biasing; so may the sequence of questions.

4. The difficulties inherent in securing a dependable answer to a "Why?" type of question have been increasingly recognized over recent years. As a result, there has been a sharply reduced tendency to try to secure complex motivational data—which are often involved in the answer to a simple "Why?" —by a direct approach. Qualitative and motivational approaches which can be used to secure such information are the subject of Chapter 26.

5. Throughout the execution of the research plan, there is a continuing need for flexibility. A development at any time, either disclosed by the plan or introduced from the outside, may require major modifications or perhaps the abandonment of the research.

6. The circular relationship in which research is required to define the problem which is to be researched appears again in the relationship between the planning and execution step. Execution often (and sometimes quickly) reveals elements in the plan itself which require major modification.

7. Where time permits, a small-scale study following the plan of the study itself—called a pilot study—can often make major contributions to the value of the research.

8. Where a research assignment is of a complex, many-faceted nature, it is especially important to have an over-all timetable. In developing that timetable, the possibility or likelihood that one part of the research may necessitate a modification of some other part is a constant consideration.

9. New facts or new possibilities constantly bubble up in the course of research. Such a possibility may threaten to make all previously planned research unnecessary, obsolete, or undesirable. A promising possibility should be explored, whenever time permits and the costs-results relationship makes it seem desirable.

10. The research man's fundamental objective always should be to render the maximum service to the organization he serves. Sometimes that objective cannot be achieved without sacrifice of pride in or interest in planned research. Where such a conflict develops, the research man can and should resolve it without question and without regard to his own interests.

QUESTIONS

1. The execution of a research plan involves two distinct phases of activity. What are these two phases? Briefly discuss each.

2. In the execution of the research plan, what is one of the major objectives? Discuss some of the problems involved.

3. What is the best way to evaluate the length of a questionnaire you are planning to use?

4. What are some of the pitfalls in question construction you should be aware of, and what sound procedures should you follow in questionnaire construction?

5. What are the difficulties inherent in securing a dependable answer to a "Why?"-type question?

6. What is a *pilot study?* What role does it play in the total research study? Why is a pilot study often desirable? What contributions might be expected from the pilot study?

7. Why is an over-all timetable such an important factor in a complex research assignment?

8. As a research man working for a manufacturing company exposed to a marketing problem, no action has been taken on your recommended program of research on that problem. To what extent should you try to "push" your recommendation?

CHAPTER 16

Analysis and Interpretation of Marketing Research Data: Introduction

The end product of the execution of a research plan is a body of information or data. The type and amount of data developed vary widely, depending on the nature of the plan itself. This point is apparent when you contrast the information developed by a national consumer survey, as in the Bissell case, with that gathered in the course of an informal investigation, of the type conducted in studying the New York market problem of Pabst beer. In the former instance, the execution of the research plan provided thousands and thousands of completed questionnaires, which required painstaking tabulation and analysis. In the latter case, all relevant data were detailed in three shorthand notebooks, with some supplementary newspaper survey reports.

No matter what the nature of the research plan and no matter what type and amount of data the execution of that plan developed, the next step in the research process is clear. The data now require analysis and interpretation. It is with the analysis and interpretation of marketing research data that this chapter and the one which follows are concerned.

You may wonder why the discussion of the analysis and interpretation of marketing research data is divided into two separate chapters. That division is desirable to reflect the pattern often found in practice, where the execution of analysis and interpretation is often split into two rather sharply defined areas.

The first of those areas involves *preliminary* analysis and interpretation. Activities involved in the preliminary phase of the analysis and interpretation of data sometimes tend to be somewhat mechanical and are often rather routine. It is with that preliminary portion of the analytical and interpretive step that this chapter deals.

After the preliminary work has been completed, a most important portion of the analysis and interpretation step remains to be accomplished. Further analysis and interpretation are required, of a type which is far from routine. The final stages of the analysis and interpretation of marketing research data call for the highest levels of creative judgment, imagination, and ingenuity of which a marketing research man is capable. It is that advanced, final portion of the step which is discussed in the chapter which follows this one.

RELATIONSHIP BETWEEN ANALYSIS AND INTERPRETATION

The analysis and interpretation of marketing research data are treated as a single step in the research process because it is often difficult if not impossible to draw a line between analysis and interpretation in practice.

The fact that it is difficult to separate analysis from interpretation does not mean, however, that the two terms are synonymous. Rather, they identify two closely interrelated parts of a major step in the research process. A clear mental picture of the difference between analysis and interpretation, as well as of the relationship between them, is necessary to an understanding of this chapter and the one which follows.

As used in marketing research, *analysis* conforms closely to the definition provided in Webster's New Collegiate Dictionary: "Separation of anything into constituent parts or elements; also an examination of anything to distinguish its component parts or elements, separately or in their relation to the whole."[1]

The objective of analysis in marketing research is to reduce data to an organized, integrated, meaningful whole. It is concerned with answering the question: What did we learn from this research? Interpretation picks up where analysis leaves off. It seeks to answer two additional questions: What does that mean? and (usually) What should we do about it?

The intimate interrelationship between analysis and interpretation is illumined if you think of the primary function of analysis as *preparation for interpretation*. This picture then emerges: Analysis is undertaken and "completed." Interpretation begins. But interpretation raises some questions which analysis has not yet clarified. Further analysis takes place, in effect as an integral part of the interpretive step. Additional interpretation follows, which may or may not require additional analysis.

Thus analysis and interpretation illustrate the same kind of circular relationship previously revealed as part of the problem-defining step. It is often necessary to plan and execute research *before* the problem can

[1] *Webster's New Collegiate Dictionary*, G. & C. Merriam Co., 1953.

be defined, although defining the problem is the first step in the research process. Similarly, it is often necessary to begin the interpretation of research data before the analysis may be completed, although analysis (at least in theory) precedes interpretation.

A tight time dimension, which is characteristic of much marketing research, contributes to the relatively high frequency with which analysis precedes and is also a part of interpretation.

ANALYSIS BEGINS WITH THE PLANNING STEP

There is a high degree of interdependence between different elements of the marketing research process. That interdependence extends beyond those elements—like analysis and interpretation—which are so closely linked that they cannot realistically be separated. It may be illustrated by noting the close relationship between the planning step and analysis. Analysis rarely takes place "in a vacuum" or is brought to bear on a problem to which a research man comes "cold." Almost always the analysis follows a planned approach which was developed almost inescapably as part of the process of developing the research plan.

The detailed specification of the objectives of the research and the description of the relationships which the research was designed to explore—included in the written research plan—typically provide the basic framework of the analytical procedures used.

In the process of planning the research, it is usually necessary first to think ahead and crystallize a picture of the specific types of data or information the research is expected to provide. Then with that picture developed, the research man works backward. He selects the technique approaches which can provide the requisite information. He works out the details of using the chosen approaches. Then when the plan has been executed and it is time for actual analysis, he typically proceeds according to the predetermined plan.

The extent to which a soundly developed plan for the execution of research requires specific and detailed planning of the analytical steps in advance varies with the research technique used.

You must develop detailed analytical procedures as a routine part of the planning process in the case of sales analysis and other work on internal company records. It is necessary to know what analytical steps are going to be taken, in order to be sure that the tabulations or summations of data prepared provide the complete required raw material for the planned analysis.

There is an especially great need for detailed advance planning of the analysis where the survey technique is used. The close relationship between that analytical plan and the sample-size decision is illustrative.

In order to be sure that there would be an adequately large subsample available for analytical study, the plan for a survey typically requires a relatively complete analytical plan before the data-gathering step begins.

STEPS IN THE ANALYSIS AND INTERPRETATION OF RESEARCH DATA

A marketing research man's procedure in the analysis and interpretation of research data ordinarily proceeds through a series of carefully planned and integrated steps. Those steps are as follows:

Step 1. *A Careful and Thorough Review of the Statement of the Problem and of the Objectives of the Research*

This step may seem unnecessary where a research man personally formulated the statement of the problem and prepared the written plan in which the objectives of the research were specified in writing. It is a highly desirable precautionary step even in such a case and is absolutely essential if there has been any change in personnel or responsibility during the course of the research process. The urgency of careful attention to this step is particularly great if the research man with primary responsibility for the analysis and interpretation was not in on the very first phases of the discussion and planning of the research.

This step is also indicated whenever there has been, over the course of the execution of the research, some modification in either the nature of the problem or the objectives of the research. Often a change occurring over the period of time when research is in work will make necessary changes in emphasis in the analysis and interpretation. Perhaps the problem is not now exactly as it was when the research was first planned. Perhaps a new element has entered the picture, which resulted in a decision to modify or extend the research area. (Often such a decision is made without revising the earlier written plan.) Care must be taken to see that the analysis and interpretation step is made by an individual who is *fully informed* both as to the initial problem and initial objectives of the research, and as to any subsequent modifications, revisions, extensions or deletions.

Step 2. *A Review of All Data Gathered in the Course of the Research, Conducted to Separate Information Which Is Relevant to the Purposes of the Research and the Problem under Study from That Which Is Not*

A typical research project gathers in a great deal more information than is ordinarily used in the final analysis and interpretation (and report). Some of that information was gathered in the course of exploring this hypothesis or that one. If the exploration proved that the particular area in question was irrelevant to the purposes of the research, that information would be likely to be eliminated from the major analytical and interpretive steps.

This will be clearer if it is presented in more specific terms. Suppose that in the case of the Dell-O margarine study, one hypothesis had been that Dell-O's price to consumers differed from that of the major competitive brands. Suppose, further, that considerable research evidence bearing on that point had been gathered. Analysis of that data indicated that this was a *null hypothesis*—that there was *no* difference in price to consumers between Dell-O and the competitive brands studied.

Information bearing on that price exploration would be set aside as *irrelevant to the main objectives* of the Dell-O research, which were to determine what elements in the picture *were* responsible for the decline in Dell-O sales. In the course of reporting the research, a statement would be included to the effect that price had been explored as a possible influence and that no differences had been disclosed.

Step 3. *Study of the Relevant Data, in a Search for Significant Relationships Bearing on the Objectives of the Research and the Problem Area*

This is perhaps the most difficult element in the analytical and interpretive process to describe, to communicate, or to teach.

The problem itself, and the objectives of the research, are firmly fixed in mind as a result of the first step in this series. The amount of data under consideration is reduced by pruning out any that is clearly irrelevant or that does not contribute to the objectives of the research or the solution of the problem. The research man's problem now is to extract the maximum amount of meaningful and helpful information from the data which remain. Or to put the same point in another way, the research man's task is to evaluate what he found out as a result of the research.

This task is actually considerably more purposive than the above general comments would suggest. Remember that in most cases the research man who is doing the analysis and interpretation actually planned and executed or supervised the execution of the research. He did so because he had certain ideas and/or expectations as to what the research approach in question would contribute to the solution of the problem. The present step involves an examination of the finished results of the research to determine whether the research did or did not contribute.

In this phase of research considerable flexibility of approach on the part of the research man is required. In most instances we do not know, before research is executed, what it will show. When we examine the results of research, it is therefore extremely important not to examine those results too narrowly. It is often the completely unexpected finding which is the flash of fire that makes all the research worthwhile. Whenever one or more indications of the research prove to be markedly at variance with the research man's expectations, a careful study of the implications of that finding is warranted.

The hypothesis as a useful tool in the problem-defining phase of marketing research work has already been mentioned. The hypothesis is also used productively in the analysis and interpretation of research data. It is particularly useful in the search for and interpretation of vital relationships.

A skilled marketing research man may develop and explore anywhere from twenty to fifty different hypotheses, in the course of the analytical and interpretive portion of his work on a complex assignment. Most of those hypotheses will be discarded. Some of them are likely to survive as cores of the final interpretation.

Step 4. *Development of New Combinations of Data, or Use of New Methods of Analysis of Existing Evidence or Data, to Explore New or Surviving Hypotheses*

This is closely related to the preceding step. It is set out separately to underline one vital point. In the earlier step, the research man is dealing with data and information developed in accordance with plans he had when he began the analysis and interpretation. In the course of that analytical and interpretive step, new approaches are suggested and become desirable. Often considerable data reprocessing is necessary to explore them.

It should be emphasized again that flexibility in approach is essential. The "gold" in a vein of data "ore" is often not where it was expected to be. The research man's job is to find it, wherever it is!

Step 5. *Review of All Available Data for Unanticipated Findings or Contributions to the Marketing Problem under Study or Any Other Major Marketing Problem of the Organization Sponsoring the Research*

This particular step is included in this listing more as an insurance policy than anything else. It is not always necessary. The possibility that it may be necessary should always be considered.

One of the characteristics of effective marketing research is that it follows where the facts lead. Facts sometimes prove to be contrary. Often the major contribution of a research study is in some entirely unexpected direction, perhaps to some completely different problem of the sponsoring organization. An example or two will illustrate. A study of the potential value of a particular advertising theme for a major food company disclosed an unmistakable new-product opportunity, which the company quickly and effectively exploited. A study of consumer attitudes toward promotions like coupons, contests, etc., disclosed a tremendous competitive-product vulnerability for one major advertiser which was far more significant and important than the promotional findings of the study.

Step 6. *Integration and Organization of All Available Relevant Data to Make a Maximum Contribution to the Fulfillment of the Objectives of the Research and to the Solution of the Marketing Problem That Inspired It*

Up to this point, emphasis has been on *pieces* of the research and on the relationship of those pieces to each other. Now perspective shifts. It is time to assemble those pieces into a meaningful and coherent whole. The organization of material requires the building of a firm, logical sequence of relationships relevant to the objectives of the research.

The steps which preceded this one have established that this, this, and this have been uncovered. Now comes the pay-off. What do those findings mean? What is the relationship between them? What should we do, now that we know those findings, that we did not previously know enough to do? Or what step that we were planning to take should now be urgently reconsidered?

The first in this series of steps should again be recalled. *The objectives of the research* become the north point which orients the integration and organization of the findings. One characteristic of an inexperienced or incompetent marketing research man is his tendency to line up an unorganized succession of bits and pieces of "interesting information." In contrast, the experienced, skilled marketing research man organizes the bits and pieces into a unified, meaningful whole. Organization of material is discussed at considerable length in the chapter on the preparation of research reports. It is worth emphasizing at this point, however, that the organization of research material must begin long before the report-preparation stage actually gets under way.

In point of fact, an experienced marketing research man begins to think about the organization and reporting step while the research is still being planned. He tries to anticipate the problems which will arise in the understanding and interpretation of the research material by those lacking his specialized education and training and thinks through the organization step many times while the research is in progress.

Each change in direction or emphasis which becomes necessary, whether from some preliminary findings of the research itself or from some change in the basic situation between the time the research is initiated and the time it is completed, may influence the organization plan used. Each time such a change occurs, one natural question which the research man asks himself is: "How does this affect the way I'd planned to organize this material? How should I modify that organization plan in the light of present knowledge?"

ILLUSTRATION OF THE ANALYSIS AND INTERPRETATION OF DATA ON A SPECIFIC RESEARCH ASSIGNMENT

To translate the preceding steps into more specific and meaningful form, let's consider the analysis and interpretation which took place in conjunction with the informal investigation of the Pabst beer problem in the New York market. The problem in this case, and the research step taken, are described in Chapter 13. A brief review of the material there presented will add meaning to the comments which follow.

Step 1. *Review of Problem and Objectives*

The marketing problem in this case was raised by the imminent loss of cans as a package for beer, and specifically the impact of that loss on Pabst's volume in the New York market. The objective of the research was to appraise Pabst's situation in the New York market. In the course of that appraisal any indications of effective action which Pabst might take to offset the loss in can volume should of course be underlined.

Step 2. *Review of Data Gathered*

The first major segment of research data gathered was concerned with developing a detailed picture of the beer marketing picture in the New York market. Three major types of beer-selling licenses were identified and described. The number of licensees of each type was determined.

Against the numerical background of the number of licensees of each type, descriptions of the characteristics of the various types of licensees were given. The relative importance of chain versus independent grocery outlets was explored at length, and the reasons for that relative importance were detailed.

Next, to provide background on the picture of beer licensees, some peculiarities of the New York market retail structure were examined. For example, it was noted that whereas the sales volume of *combination stores* (selling both groceries and meats) exceeded that of grocery-only stores nationally in the ratio of 2.5 to 1, in New York the relative importance was reversed by the same proportions. The importance of independent grocery outlets as against chains, another peculiarity of the New York market at that time, was emphasized. Independents did 70.6 per cent of the grocery business in New York, as compared to 45.3 per cent in Chicago.

Because Pabst volume in the New York market was largely through distributors (while some competitors operated through wholly owned branches), the relative strengths and weaknesses of distributor operation were next examined. The major point which emerged from this review was that a company working through distributors, as Pabst did, had far less control over volume than did a competitor selling direct. The typical distributor handled a long list of brands of beer, of which a single brand like Pabst represented just one apple in the basket. The distributor was most emphatically not under the brewer's control.

A strong tendency for retailers to centralize their purchasing of beer with a single distributor was noted. The reasons for that tendency were detailed.

Two special segments of the New York market with unusual characteristics—the Negro market and the Jewish market—were briefly described.

Advertising-expenditure figures for major brands were reviewed. In that pre-TV year, Pabst spent about $30,000 annually for newspaper advertising in the New York market. That was a larger expenditure than the (then) two other "national shipping premium beers" (Budweiser and Schlitz) made. It was less than one-fifth of the expenditure of the leading local beer, however, and ranked *ninth* in a listing of beer-advertising volume by brands. Pabst was similarly heavily outadvertised by local brands in other media such as radio, outdoor, subway cards, etc. Detailed figures by media were available for study.

Budweiser—the major competitive national premium brand, from Pabst's viewpoint—was being sold directly in the New York market. That brand had its own branch and its own trucks which handled the products of no other brewery.

The package-type division of volume in the market (at a time, remember, when cans were still available) was reviewed. Within the package-beer segment of the market (i.e., excluding draft beer), retailers reported unanimously that bottles outsold cans by a wide margin, with estimates ranging from 3 to 1 up to 5 to 1 superiority for bottles. Further, retailers in general reported a substantial growth in the importance of quart bottles. For beer sold for off-premise consumption, cans were thought to represent about 20 per cent of volume, with 12-ounce bottles representing 40 per cent and quart and larger bottles contributing the remaining 40 per cent.

Three well-defined price levels for beer in the New York market were noted. These may be loosely identified as the prices for "cheap," "popular" (major local brands), and "premium" beer. Here are the prices for those three price types of beer on major packages *in 1941:*

Package	Cheap beer	Popular beer	Premium beer
12-oz. can	3 for 26¢	3 for 31¢	2 for 26¢
12-oz. bottle	4 for 26¢	3 for 26¢	2 for 26¢
Quart	16¢	21¢	26¢

To the bottle prices shown, deposit had to be added. *However, there was one major exception to this clearly defined pricing pattern. Pabst cans were selling everywhere at three for 31 cents, while Pabst 12-oz. bottles were selling at two for 26 cents!*

Careful estimates were developed of the relative volume importance of the three different price levels. It was estimated that between 70 and 80 per cent of the package beer sold was at the central, or popular, price level. Between 15 and 25 per cent of total package-beer gallonage was believed to be moving at the cheap-beer price level. Less than 5 per cent of all beer was being sold at the premium price level.

Newspaper studies of beer distribution by brands, among outlets selling off-premise beer, were reviewed. There were studies by different papers, using different samples of stores. Those studies agreed that the major local brands of beer had distribution of 95 per cent or higher. Pabst distribution was at levels ranging from 92 to 94 per cent. Budweiser, a competitive premium brand, had distribution of only 33 per cent. Schlitz, another premium brand, had distribution of 21 to 23 per cent.

While the above distribution levels existed on the brands in total, there were marked differences—especially in the case of Pabst—between can and bottle distribution levels. Two different newspapers' surveys showed that Pabst bottle distribution was found in less than 9 per cent of a large sample of outlets. Budweiser had distribution ranging from 27 to 29 per cent in the two surveys on its bottles, while Schlitz distribution on bottles was as low as Pabst's 9 per cent level.

Step 3. *Study of Relevant Data in a Search for Significant Relationships*

Step 4. *Developments of New Combinations of Data*

The picture emerging from the research up to this point appeared relatively sharply focused. One additional point in the "new combinations of data" area did suggest itself. For how long a period of time had Pabst's cans been priced with the popular-priced local beers? What distribution levels had been achieved by Pabst on its canned beer when its price was completely in the premium-beer bracket? Fortunately, the newspaper surveys in question ran backward far enough to permit a relatively easy answer to this question.

Step 5. *Review for Unanticipated Findings*

To a far greater extent than is true of most research, even of the informal-investigation type, this research study pinpointed a single element as potentially determining the basic research finding. That element was the peculiar Pabst pricing situation. While the nature of that element had not been anticipated, it was of course one of those included in the plan for the original informal study. Therefore this was a research project in which this step was not necessary in the analysis and interpretation phase of the research.

Step 6. *Integration and Organization of the Relevant Data*

Adding to the research findings some additional information disclosed by Pabst's sales records, the marketing research man who was responsible for this research put the pieces of the puzzle together in this way:

a. Of Pabst's total volume in New York, 30.5 per cent was draft beer and 69.5 per cent was package beer.

b. Of the package-beer volume, 91 per cent was canned beer.

c. In the market in total for all brands, of package-beer volume, bottles represent about 80 per cent and cans about 20 per cent. This means that about 91 per cent of Pabst's package volume is in a package type representing only 20 per cent of total package volume of all brands combined.

d. The price-level division of volume in the market is clear-cut. Premium beer represents no more than 5 per cent of total package gallonage. Popular beer represents 70 to 80 per cent.

e. Four brands of local beer—Schaefer's, Ruppert's, Rheingold, and Ballantine—dominate the New York beer market. All four sell for the same price—cans three for 31 cents, bottles three for 26 cents plus deposit.

f. Pabst pricing straddles two price levels. Pabst bottles at two for 26 cents are in the premium-beer bracket. Pabst cans, at three for 31 cents, are in the popular-beer bracket. This means that *while the major brands in the market have bottles that are cheaper than cans, Pabst alone has cans that are cheaper than bottles!*

g. Pabst has high canned-beer distribution, but relatively low distribution of its bottled beer—especially in contrast to the major local brands.

h. Pabst uses distributors, over whom it has very little control, in contrast to major local competitors and Budweiser, who do direct distributing. Obviously brands of beer with their own distribution facilities are in a far better position to convert canned-beer volume to bottled-beer volume than are brands, like Pabst, that must rely on distributors.

i. This adds up to a situation which is far more serious for Pabst than for any other brand, when cans disappear, because:

— Pabst volume is predominantly canned volume.
— Pabst bottle distribution is low.
— Competition faces a transition to *lower-priced bottles*, while Pabst must switch consumers to *higher-priced bottles*.

— The shift lifts Pabst entirely out of the popular-beer price bracket, from which it had been securing more than 90 per cent of its package-beer volume, into a much smaller market segment.

In this particular case, it was not too difficult to interpret the probable effect of the loss of cans on Pabst's volume in the New York market. Budweiser, in the same price class with Pabst where bottles were concerned, but with the "plus" of direct distribution, had been able to achieve only 31 per cent distribution. Back when Pabst cans were selling at the same prices as Budweiser cans, Pabst's canned-beer distribution had ranged from a high of 29 per cent in 1933 to a low of 15 per cent in 1935. The assumption that Pabst would be able to achieve bottle distribution, in the premium-beer price bracket, not exceeding 31 per cent, seemed sound and safe. That would represent distribution not even one-third as high as Pabst cans had at the time of the study. If Pabst were able to convert one-third of its canned-beer volume to bottled beer—an extremely optimistic estimate, from the Pabst viewpoint—it would lose two thirds of its canned-beer volume, which represented 91 per cent of total package volume!

The conclusion from this informal investigation was reported in a single brief paragraph:

> If Pabst succeeds in converting one-third of its can volume to bottles in New York, which seems extremely optimistic, the total volume will drop to a level between 50 and 60 per cent of 1941 sales. An even greater drop is even more likely.

HOW FAR SHOULD INTERPRETATION BE CARRIED?

In the interests of clarity and of developing a balanced picture of the analysis and interpretation of research data, it seems desirable to repeat with some supplementary comments a point made earlier in this chapter.

Interpretation was described as an extension beyond the analysis stage. It was noted that that extension is concerned with answering two additional questions: What does that mean? and (usually) What should we do about it? In the above example, the first of those questions was answered. The research findings were made more meaningful by translating them into a specific estimate of the impact which the elimination of cans was likely to have on Pabst's New York volume.

But no attempt was made, in the above example, to answer the question: What should we do about it? The extent to which marketing research enters into the development of alternative courses of action, and into evaluating such alternatives, varies widely. The timing of such participation by research is also subject to considerable variation.

One factor which influences research activity in that area is the location of research responsibility. In the Pabst example, it will be recalled, the advertising agency assumed responsibility for the planning, execution, and analysis of the research. Now consider the probable nature of the alternative courses of action open to Pabst. Those alternatives would enter into many different areas of marketing and management policy. Some of those areas would be far removed from the advertising agency's sphere of responsibility. *If specifically invited to do so* by the client's top management, executives of the agency might well make suggestions as to some alternative courses of action or as to some parts of various alternatives. In doing so, they would be discharging the normal agency function of providing advice and counsel on marketing and advertising problems as requested by the client.

For the *research department* of the agency to intrude into those areas of management responsibility *without invitation,* however, would be something else again. In the Pabst example, the agency's research department carried the interpretation as far as the facts available and their assigned responsibility with relation to the gathering and interpretation of those facts permitted.

This is a most important point. Often the findings of a marketing research study enter as one factor into a management decision in which there are many other unknown factors. It does not make sense for a marketing research man to try to extend the findings of his research into areas of unknown problems for which others have responsibility. Few competent research men do so. As a generalization, the development of alternative courses of action is likely to follow naturally from, rather than be a part of, the research. Often the research man is asked to participate in such development. There may be data in the research which was not fully reported or explored but which is relevant to one or more alternative courses of action. If the research man had known such courses were under study, he would have developed the data in his report. These comments should not be interpreted as meaning that if, in the judgment of the research man, the research findings point unmistakably in the direction of a particular management action his report should fail to register that fact.

STATISTICAL TRAINING IS ESSENTIAL PREPARATION FOR MARKETING RESEARCH PRACTICE

Much of the data which the marketing research man is called upon to handle is quantitative. He must examine, appraise, tabulate, summarize, analyze, and interpret that data. When he does so, he is clearly working within the area of the discipline of statistical methods. That closely related discipline is concerned with the reduction of large or small masses of data to more manageable summary form. It is concerned also with developing or extracting various descriptive terms relating to the characteristics of the data. Those descriptive terms are themselves summary in nature. Finally, drawing inferences from summaries of data and from various descriptive terms rests on a foundation of statistical theory and statistical methodology.

A considerable proportion of the marketing resesarch man's kit of technique tools has been drawn in whole or in part from statistical methods. To understand the advantages and limitations of those statistical tools, statistical training is necessary. Today no marketing research man can be considered competent unless his background includes at least a minimum amount of training in the field of statistics. Just what does that minimum amount include? *How much* statistical training is necessary for marketing research work? Those questions cannot be answered without the grave danger of overgeneralization, because there are wide variations in the statistical requirements of work in various specialized areas of marketing research practice.

This much may be stated without risk of overgeneralization and without equivocation: An understanding of the fundamentals of statistical methodology, and of at least the introductory aspects of statistical theory, is absolutely essential to marketing research practice and to any worker in the field who aspires to a position above the most routine and clerical in nature.

Some guidance as to the amount of statistical training necessary is provided by the fact that many marketing research directors include two or three semesters of college-level work in fundamentals of statistical methods as a prerequisite for employment, even of a beginning worker in the field.

Different types of marketing research activity are likely to draw on different portions of the broad field of statistics. In addition to the introductory training in classrooms, most experienced marketing research men have read widely in the field and keep abreast of developments in statistics relevant to their own interests.

A well-thumbed copy of a statistical text is likely to be found on the working bookshelf of most marketing research men. In addition, more advanced books are frequently consulted. The Appendix lists suggested references of both types. One book which belongs in every research man's library is Robert Ferber's *Statistical Techniques in Market Research.*[2]

[2] McGraw-Hill, New York, 1949.

THE LIMITED ROLE OF ADVANCED MATHEMATICAL
AND STATISTICAL ANALYSIS

The preceding comment about the importance of statistical training in the preparation of an individual for work in the field of marketing research should be supplemented by an important additional comment. *Most of the statistical knowledge which is frequently used by the majority of workers in marketing research is of a relatively simple and introductory nature.* The role of advanced mathematical and statistical analysis, and of rather recent developments in the field of statistical theory, is a somewhat limited one.

The charge that that role is too limited, and that marketing research men continue to use techniques long after more advanced and effective techniques have been developed, has often been made. There is a considerable body of literature which indicates that marketing research practitioners *should* use advanced tools of statistical and mathematical analysis to a much greater extent than they do. Ferber in particular has advocated that viewpoint with vigor and eloquence.

Here is Ferber's view on this subject, as expressed in the opening paragraphs of the preface to his book: [3]

> In the field of marketing and market analysis, statistical theory has far outdistanced practice, mainly because practical marketing men do not have the time to sit down and devote long hours to the translation of the abstract mathematical writings of the statistical theorists. As a result, researchers are employing antiquated, and at times faulty, statistical methods in their market studies, resulting in needless expenditure of time, labor, and money.
>
> Market studies have been frequently rendered ineffective by the application of these outmoded techniques because of the misleading and inconclusive findings that have ensued. Their true inaccuracy is often discovered only after long and costly experiences arising from the application of these erroneous findings to existing conditions. The fact that the newer and more powerful statistical procedures can be employed to yield more accurate and reliable results than could be attained by the older methods, *and at less cost*, has not yet been widely realized.

William G. Cochran comments[4] on the same tendency, but with a recognition of the fact that the problem is not a simple one:

> One feature of the growth of theoretical statistics during the past 30 years is the emergence of a substantial body of theory which discusses how to make good estimates from data. In the development of theory specifically for sample surveys, relatively little use has been made of this

[3] *Ibid.*, p. vii.
[4] William G. Cochran, *Sampling Techniques*, Wiley, New York, 1953.

body of knowledge. For this I think there are two principal reasons. First, with routine surveys which contain a large number of items, there is a great advantage in an estimation procedure that requires little more than simple addition, whereas the superior methods of estimation in statistical theory, such as maximum likelihood, may necessitate a series of successive approximations before the estimate can be found. Second, there has been a difference in attitude in the two lines of research. Most of the estimation methods in theoretical statistics take it for granted that we know the functional form of the frequency distribution followed by the data in the sample, and the method of estimation is carefully geared to this type of distribution. The preference in sample survey theory has been to make only limited assumptions about this frequency distribution, e.g. that it is very skew or rather symmetrical, and to leave its specific functional form out of the discussion. The attitude is a reasonable one for handling surveys with many items, where the type of distribution may change from one item to another, and where we do not wish to stop and examine all these distributions before deciding how to make each estimate.

WHY ADVANCED TECHNIQUES ARE NOT MORE WIDELY USED

It would be a grave disservice to the marketing research practitioner to present comments like those above without appending an explanation of the apparent "statistical backwardness" which specialists claim exists in the field.

The first point to note, in that connection, is that no competent marketing research man knowingly or intentionally uses any technique tool—mathematical, statistical, or otherwise—which is obsolete, in preference to a superior tool *which could also be used within the time and cost dimensions of the problem.* Many of the advances and refinements of a statistical nature tend to increase substantially the time required to develop and execute a research plan, or increase the cost of the study, or both. A closely related point is that an individual with the specialized technical knowledge required to adapt a theoretical advance to a specific practical problem situation may not be available. The time and/or cost required to locate such an individual and to acquaint him with the problem and get his advice on technological aspects of it is a component cost of the research.

The observation may perhaps be made that the word *knowingly* in the above paragraph represents a "hedge," or "weasel," word. Why don't marketing research men take pains to keep abreast of advances in such closely related fields as statistical methodology and apply them? Is their failure to do so a sign of intellectual laziness? The answer to these questions lies in the tremendous and increasing complexity of the marketing research field.

As its name suggests, marketing research embraces both marketing and research. A worker in the field must keep abreast of the tremendously volatile and dynamic area of marketing management, with its constant and continuing "revolution." *In addition,* it is necessary for a marketing research man to keep in touch with developments in the whole area of research techniques and methodology in the area of social science. Statistics represents an important part, but only a part, of that area.

The extracurricular time demand on a working marketing research man imposed by the need to keep abreast of developments in and affecting his whole broad area of interest is fantastically high. In the last half dozen years, for example, marketing research men with many years of experience have had to spend hundreds of hours bringing themselves up to date, first, with the striking advances in sampling knowledge which crystallized in the years following World War II; and then with the tremendous volume of literature dealing with advances in psychological and other social-science contributions to marketing research methodology, growing out of the increasing importance of qualitative and motivational research.

An additional vital factor is often overlooked by statistical specialists. Research is valueless unless its findings are applied. Before they can be applied, they must be communicated to and understood by nontechnicians in executive positions. This communication problem is an extremely difficult one. Many marketing research men choose to use a less advanced or complex approach which their superiors can understand and accept, in preference to a more advanced but more complex procedure which would be likely to be rejected as "theoretical" or "impractical" by those with the responsibility for okaying research costs.

Lengthy discussion of principles of statistical inference, characteristics of the normal curve, etc., so well covered in statistical texts, would be out of place here. Other marketing research books which devote considerable space to such subjects are concerned primarily with the survey technique. Since this book covers a broader field of marketing research practice, with correspondingly greater pressure on a limited amount of space, this omission becomes necessary.

TABULATION: THE BROAD AND NARROW VIEW

An extremely important step in the processing of data—particularly quantitative data—developed through marketing research is the *tabulation* of that data. Tabulation is an important element in the analytical and interpretive step in marketing research. Like many other terms in the field, tabulation often means different things to different people.

Two quite dissimilar views of tabulation may be distinguished. One view sees tabulation as a relatively narrow activity. That view is presented in some dictionary definitions. Merriam-Webster's New Collegiate Dictionary, for example, defines tabulation as the process involved when one seeks "to form into a table or synopsis." It is the broader view of tabulation which applies in marketing research practice. Tabulation plays a most important role, which should not be underestimated.

A committee of the American Marketing Association provided accurate perspective on the importance of tabulation in marketing research when they introduced a report on "Tabulation Planning and Tabulation Techniques" with this comment:[5]

> If tabulation were defined as a function in which data are arranged and classified into a form which give them meaning, it should be evident that virtually every phase of marketing research must be subjected to tabulation treatment of one kind or another.
>
> The data under examination may be selective company sales statistics, government statistics, media circulations, radio coverages, various other market indices, or questionnaires, collected by mail or through personal interviews. In every case, the figures being studied must have been summarized and classified for presentation in a form which makes clear their significance. A competently-executed tabulation should produce results which are clear, concise, simple to understand and to interpret.

OBJECTIVE OF TABULATION

A full appreciation of the importance of tabulation can perhaps best be achieved by working backward from the objective of tabulation. Essentially *the objective of tabulation is to arrange and present quantitative data in a form which makes it easy for the reader of the finished report to grasp and understand the significance of the data presented.*

That broad objective can be subdivided into two subobjectives, which correspond to two distinct phases of the tabulation process. The first phase is preliminary in nature. Its objective is to provide the analyst with details of the major findings or results of the research and to permit him to explore relationships which are (or could be) significant. The second phase takes place when the interpretation and analysis have been completed. It is concerned with translating the findings into appropriate form for the final report. In this chapter we are primarily concerned with the first phase of the tabulation procedure. The second phase is discussed in Chapter 18 on report preparation.

[5] "Tabulation Planning and Tabulation Techniques," a committee report of the American Marketing Association, published in *The Journal of Marketing*, January, 1949, p. 330. Joseph S. Boyajy was chairman of a committee of which John W. Barry, Walter P. Kuenstler, and Mary R. Paton were members.

It may be helpful to think of phase 1 of the tabulation, with which we are here concerned, as embracing those activities which enter into the preparation and development of all *working tables*. Those working tables are used by the analyst in his analysis and interpretation of the results of the research. The development of *finished tables* required to communicate the findings of the analysis and interpretation, in the research report, becomes part of the report-preparation step.

RELATIONSHIP BETWEEN WORKING AND FINISHED TABLES

Working tables, which are typically developed either in printed register form where machine tabulation is concerned, or in penciled figures and percentages in the case of hand tabulation, are tools of the analyst. They may be described as the raw material which enter into the analytical process. Working tables are typically far more numerous than are finished tables. They are also, in most cases, more detailed. A single working table may end up as several finished tables in the final report. The process of converting working tables into finished form is likely to involve a certain amount of condensation and consolidation. Finished tables emerge from working tables as the end result of a selection process. Tables carried into finished form are those which proved to be significant and to disclose or illustrate relationships or information relevant to the objectives of the research and to the interpretation of the research findings.

TABULATION PLANNING BEGINS WHEN THE RESEARCH ITSELF IS PLANNED

Planning the tabulation process in at least general terms usually begins early in the planning phase of the research. Most experienced marketing research men develop at least a mental image of the planned tabulation procedure in the course of their work in developing the research plan itself. That is a logical place to start, and very often an essential starting point.

Let's clarify that latter point. When people who are not trained and experienced in marketing research discuss a proposed research study, they often tend to think in "blue sky" terms. It is not unusual to find different individuals expecting a proposed piece of research to contribute a wide range of answers far exceeding the scope of the research itself. In this type of situation, it is the responsibility of the marketing research man to reduce the expectations to realistic terms. He knows that the information developed by research cannot exceed certain limits which are established by the nature and scale of the research. For example, in a simple product study in which two products are compared, it is reasonable to expect to secure a modicum of information about previous usage of products of the same general type. That information is needed to classify the preferences of test participants. But it is not reasonable to expect that limited approach to provide detailed information on such matters as advertising awareness, etc.

What the above comments boil down to is simply this: The research is planned with a specific objective in mind. Information irrelevant to that objective is usually pruned to keep the research sharply focused and to hold down the costs of the study. The written plan spells out in detail what the research can and—sometimes even more importantly—*cannot* be expected to include. In the development of that written plan of the research, the marketing research man usually has to think in definite and specific terms of the tabulations which are possible with the data in question. Only such thinking can lead to an accurate and complete delineation of the information the research can be expected to provide.

Thus we see that the written plan, as noted earlier, serves as an insurance policy against misunderstandings. The detailed plans for tabulation, even if only in general terms in the research-planning stage, in turn serve as the foundation on which the written plan is based.

In terms of the method of processing the data in the tabulation step, two approaches are widely used. One involves hand or manual tabulation. The other involves machine tabulation. The influences which determine which approach to take will be spelled out later in this chapter. Whichever method is chosen, certain fundamentals must be observed in the tabulation process. Let's use a specific case to illustrate those fundamentals. Because the tabulation of data gathered in the survey and panel approaches sometimes poses more problems than less complex data, a case involving a product test provides a useful framework for illustrating the tabulation process and for underlining the fundamentals of that process.

DETAILED REVIEW OF THE TABULATION PROCESS

For purposes of illustrating the steps in the tabulation process, let's consider the comparative product test for Shower-of-Stars Cosmetics, Inc., mentioned in the preceding chapter. That was a product test between an existing formulation of a make-up product and a different formulation. In the opinion of the development chemists of the cosmetic firm, the existing product's decline in volume was primarily attributable to a single negative product characteristic. The other formulation to be tested was an improvement which, in their judgment, offset that negative product characteristic. Their view was that this new and improved formulation represented the weapon by which the company could regain the volume lost on the defective product.

In the marketing research sense, that the different formulation was an improvement with increased consumer acceptance was one hypothesis. That the product limitation which the improved formulation was designed to overcome was the primary cause of the sales decline was another hypothesis. The comparative product test was designed to explore both hypotheses.

Now let's move into the planning phase of this research and see how the planning of the tabulation inevitably grows out of the research-planning step. Sales of the make-up product in question had declined sharply. This set up a potential test situation in which there were three subuniverses of potential test participants: present users of the product, former users who had discontinued it, and those who had never used it. It was extremely important, in the judgment of the research man with responsibility for this assignment, to conduct the product test among both present and former users. Nonusers, he felt, could be dispensed with for the purposes of this initial phase of product research.

The objective of the research was essentially to answer two questions: *Was* the new formulation, in *the opinion of consumers,* an improvement over the existing product? The answer to this question would come from present users of the existing product. The second question was: If the new formulation was an improvement, *was it a sufficiently marked improvement* to return former users to the user fold? Answering the latter question involved a determination of what reasons had led to the decision to discontinue use, what products were used in place of the former product, and so on. This information would all have to come from the former-user category in the product-test sample.

Thinking now in terms of the tabulation problem, it is apparent that whether a test participant is a *present* or *former* user of the present product represents a vital characteristic which must be carried through analysis. Present and former users must be tabulated separately. In terms of sample planning, *an approximately equal number of present and former users* were required in the test sample, to permit comparable breakdowns and comparisons of the two groups in tabulation and analysis.

Sample size of total placements was set at 250. It was hoped that that number of placements would provide subsamples of 125 present and 125 former users. Provided the number of *completed* tests among each subsample exceeded 100, minor differences in the number of users and former users were regarded as acceptable. (Note that there are typically some participants in a product test who do not complete the test. Therefore the number of placements is usually set higher than the minimum sample required to allow for incompletes.)

The product test was completed, and the test material on each respondent was delivered to the research man responsible for this project. In this case, the material included an initial qualifying interview, recorded on one questionnaire; a diary in which reactions to each product in use were recorded; and a final questionnaire, covering the terminal interview which was made when the diary and remaining test product were picked up. (A physical examination of the used products was part of the testing procedure.)

1. *All Forms Were Numbered and Counted When Received*

The first step in the tabulation process was to *establish the base count* of the data. How many completed test participants were included in the research material? A physical count established a total of 239 respondents, after incompleted tests were eliminated.

In a complex study of this type, there is a danger that different parts of the research material referring to a single respondent may become separated. Therefore it is usually standard operating procedure to *assign a serial number* (using a numbering machine) *to each respondent* and to *place that same identifying number on all material* (initial questionnaire, diary, final questionnaire, and classifying data or listing of respondent characteristics) *of that respondent.*

This makes it possible for different individuals to work on the tabulation of different questions without the danger that the identity of the respondent may be confused or lost.

2. *Base Counts Were Extended to Each Major Classification Element*

In addition to the total number of respondents, it was important to determine whether a sufficiently large number of present and former users had been carried through to completion in the testing. After the forms had been counted and numbered, they were divided into two piles. One pile consisted of present users, the other of former users. A count on each pile was made, and the combined total of the two was checked against the total sample-base count. There were 113 present users and 126 former users, a total of 239 which checked against the total base count.

In addition to this division of the sample into the two major categories of present and former users, it was possible to anticipate at this point in tabulation planning that certain other groupings would also be important. Base counts were established for those cells of the sample as well. One of the groupings was on the basis of the age of the individual. Three different age groups were planned. (In this as in most other decisions in the course of tabulating this study, the relatively small sample size involved acted as a limiting factor on the number of divisions it was practical to make on any classification basis.) Another was the skin type of the individual respondent—dividing those with normal, oily, and dry skin into different cells.

On a large-sample study, the cell pattern of the sample would have been more complex. Divisions could then be made within subsamples. Thus the respondents *within each age group* might be divided into each of the skin-type groupings, as they were on a different 8,000-interview study.

A table showing the base counts on each major cell division was developed. Because this was a comparative product test, and product preference was vitally important, each cell was then further subdivided to reflect product preference. There were four possibilities, as product-

Table 16.1. Base-count Total Sheet—Make-up Product Test (Job No. 402)

(Client: Shower-of-Stars Cosmetics, Inc.)

Major sample cells	No.	Product-test preference grouping:				
		Prefer J	Prefer K	Like equally	Like neither	DK, NR
Total sample............	239	119	90	14	16	
A. Product usage						
Present users..........	113	58	41	8	6	
Former users..........	126	61	49	6	10	
B. Age of respondent						
24 and under..........	82	35	47	...		
25–35................	101	58	25	7	11	
36 and over..........	56	26	18	7	5	
C. Skin type						
Dry.................	56	18	25	5	8	
Oily................	70	49	18	2	1	
Medium.............	105	51	42	7	5	
Other (part dry, etc.)...	8	1	5	...	2	

Date: 8/2/5–
Tabbed by: RAE   Checked by: DBT

preference cells: Respondents might prefer the existing product over the proposed formulation; they might prefer the proposed product over the existing one; they might like both equally well; or they might like neither. Table 16.1 shows the working table developed to reflect the base counts for each major sample cell, with the preference division detailed.

That table illustrates several important fundamentals of sound tabulation practice which should be noted, as follows.

3. *The Working Table Has a Clear and Complete Title Which Fully Identifies It*

Note that the nature of this particular working table—"base-count total sheet"—is shown. The nature of the particular research project is indicated—"make-up product test." The job number of the research organization is shown, permitting reference to a job file which includes complete specifications of the research. The name of the client is shown.

4. *The Working Table Is Complete, with Provision for DK and NR Tabulation*

DK is a research abbreviation for "don't know," and NR is a similar abbreviation for "no response," or "no reply." Often a questionnaire will be substantially complete except that to one or more questions no reply is shown, or the respondent simply said "I don't know" in answer to a question. In order to arrive at a total which checks against the base count numerically, each working table should include provision for the tabulation and tallying of all such replies. In the table as set up, provision for a DK-NR tally is provided only vertically. In many cases it should be provided horizontally as well. Thus if a questionnaire were otherwise completely filled out and in good order, but the interviewer had failed to record the age of the respondent, that would be an additional DK-NR category as a fourth subdivision of the age-of-respondent cell division of the sample.

It is extremely important to show on working tables the complete division of replies. Both vertical and horizontal provision for replies which cannot be classified or which are incomplete is usually necessary. In some research projects there is a large and significant group of "don't know" respondents (as in election polls, for example). This makes it desirable to have separate DK and NR tallies made. In the product test under discussion here, skilled interviewers were used and no replies fell into the DK-NR sample cell.

5. *Provision Is Made for All Possible Replies*

In addition to providing for completeness through inclusion of DK-NR tallies, it is necessary to anticipate all possible types of replies and/or classifications of responses or respondents. The division of preference into four categories is illustrative. It might be necessary in some cases of a product test to have additional groupings such as "prefer with qualifications." The normal procedure is to take a group of the forms to be tabulated and develop the tabulation framework necessary on the basis of the way the replies or respondents on that small group of forms divide.

6. Tabulating Responsibility Is Identified

Note that the initials of the individual who did this tabulating are shown on the bottom of the table. Where two or more individuals worked as a team in the tabulation, a rather common practice, initials or names of both should be shown.

7. Arithmetical Accuracy of the Table Is Checked Routinely, and Responsibility for That Check Is Identified

In the table shown, the vertical totals for each major classification of sample cells (i.e., for the A, B, and C groupings on the table) should add to the total-sample figure. The horizontal total of the individual cells in each line should add to the left-hand total figure. Upon completion of tabulation, a routine arithmetical check for accuracy is made and the initials of the individual making that check are shown. It is sounder to have this check made by someone other than the initial tabulator, although self-checked work is sometimes necessary.

8. Mutually Exclusive Classifications Should Be Used in All Possible Sample Cells

Note the age groupings used in this sample. Women 24 and under are in one cell, those 25 through 35 in another, and those 36 and over in a third. Each of those age classifications is mutually exclusive. Sometimes the mistake is made of setting up groupings which are overlapping, as 25 and under, 25 through 35, etc. In such a case, there is an overlap at the breaking point in each classification which makes for ambiguity and "fuzzes up" the classification problem. That should be avoided.

9. Data Should Be Tabulated Separately for Major Sample Groupings

The procedure in tabulating the results of this product test was first to establish the major subdivisions of the sample and to develop base counts for each. Then the major research finding or findings (product preference, in this case) is tabulated separately for each of the major sample cells. This sequence of operations has proved far more effective and efficient in practice than the reverse approach in which a total tabulation is first made, and then individual tabulations for sample cells follow. The total findings are *built up* from the major sample cells into the total, rather than *broken down* from the total into the subtotals.

This approach permits early identification and, perhaps, re-examination of peculiarities of individual cells in the sample. Where different individuals are responsible for the tabulation of different sample cells, the possibility always exists that some variation in tabulation procedure (rather than some variation in the reaction of individuals in a particular cell) may be responsible for variations. That possibility can easily be checked when this sequence of operations is followed.

Where the sample is geographically dispersed, tabulation of the replies from individual cities, individual sections, etc., as an initial step is often desirable. If the research is done by field personnel or supervised by supervisors who are not full-time employees of the organization executing the research, examination of replies by individual interviewers and individual supervisors may be a necessary step.

COROLLARY VALUE OF BASE-COUNT TABLE

The working table showing base counts is usually developed as the first step in the tabulation process. It provides totals against which each succeeding step is regularly and routinely checked for accuracy. When it includes a division in terms of the major objective of the research, as it does in this case (product preference), it has an important corollary value. As a thoughtful examination of Table 16.1 will indicate, the major findings of the research—which product was preferred, by what margin, and among which major subdivisions of the sample—are apparent in the working table on base-count totals, which is usually the first working table prepared.

Other characteristics common to a well-planned tabulation of research data will be developed in the following chapter and in the chapter on preparing the research report.

KEY DECISION: TABULATE BY HAND OR BY MACHINE?

One important decision which must be made (usually in the research-planning stage) is whether data of a particular type, or data produced by a specific research technique or assignment, should be tabulated by hand or by machine. *Machine tabulation* refers to the transfer of data to (usually) punched cards and to the tabulation of the data on those cards by one of the various forms of electronic tabulation equipment. This decision is one which must be made individually in each case. All that is possible here is to identify some of the major influences which enter into that decision and to suggest the direction in which specific characteristics of the study or data incline the research man who must make the decision.

The first consideration is sample size. Where the number of items to be tabulated is small, manual tabulation is likely to be both faster and more efficient. But what is a *small* number of items? That question is difficult to answer because the number of items alone is only one dimension of the problem area. The complexity of the data, and the extent to which cross analysis of it is likely to be necessary, is another. The following quotation from the AMA committee report quoted earlier in this chapter[6] illustrates the point:

> The ever-recurring question in the researcher's mind is when to use machine tabulation and when to use manual tabulation. Obviously, the selection of tabulation method can be determined only on the basis of circumstances and specifications relating to each particular survey. There is no magic formula for classifying surveys as machine or manual tabulation jobs by any combination of set standards.
>
> Broadly generalizing, one might say that with surveys involving less than 500 interviews with long lists of brands, reasons and the like, and not much cross-tabulation, the manual method is more efficient. Surveys using the so-called "depth" interviewing technique (frequently used in industrial distribution problems), where no formal questionnaire is used, are best handled by manual tabulation. Usually they are limited in number of interviews, and there is no set pattern of form and sequence of questions, particularly when several people are doing the interviewing.

As a general rule, the essentially quantitative type of research can and should be tabulated by machine. As the qualitative component increases, the likelihood that manual tabulation will be more efficient increases. Situations in which several different portions of the same questionnaire or schedule must be combined in order to arrive at a rounded picture of the way a given respondent or item should be classified point to the desirability of manual tabulation.

Time is another element in the decision. Generally the machine approach can produce finished tabulations more quickly than can a manual tabulation. However, it is important to consider the time question in full. If data must be slowly coded by hand before it can be tabulated by machine, and the coding task is a complex one, the entire process can sometimes be done by hand within the same amount of elapsed time.

Referring to the above quotation, note that the committee referred to the tabulation problem on "surveys." There is much more to marketing research than the survey technique, and the tabulation step is an important one regardless of the technique used.

SUMMARY

1. This chapter introduces the analytical and interpretive step in the research process. Analysis is here regarded primarily as *preparation for interpretation.*

---

[6] "Tabulation Planning and Tabulation Techniques," *The Journal of Marketing,* January, 1949, p. 354.

2. Analysis of the data gathered in the course of the research is usually anticipated and considered as part of the process of planning the research. Therefore it may be said that analysis begins with the planning step.

3. Steps followed in the analysis and interpretation of data were listed in this chapter. In those steps, the basic objectives of the research serve as the north point in analysis. The written statement of the research plan is a helpful guide in analysis. Care must be taken to consider any changes in the situation being researched, or in the position of the organization sponsoring the research, which have occurred since the research plan was prepared.

4. While the objectives of the research and the plan guide the analysis and interpretation, the analyst must take care not to enter into analysis with blinders on. Often the results of research which seem to have nothing to do with the initial objectives of the research are among the most important and profitable findings.

5. There is room for considerable variation as to the extent to which the findings of the research can and should be carried into the development and appraisal of an alternative course of action suggested by the research.

6. Statistical training is essential to marketing research practice.

7. Advanced mathematical and statistical techniques for analyzing and treating data are used to a very limited extent in marketing research practice. The view that they should be more widely used is held by many statistical specialists. There is much evidence to support that view. There are also some practical obstacles which make progress in that desirable direction somewhat slow.

8. Tabulation—which has as its objective the arrangement and presentation of quantitative data in a form which makes the meaning of that data clear— is an important element in the analytical process. It is helpful to distinguish between the development of *working tables,* used by the analyst in interpreting the data, and *finished tables,* used in the final report to communicate that interpretation to others.

9. The decision to tabulate by hand (manually) or by machine is a complex one. The time available and the nature of the data are key determinants, with sample size often a major consideration.

QUESTIONS

1. When does analysis of the research conducted actually begin? What is the relationship between the analytical and interpretive steps in the research process?

2. What is the objective of analysis in marketing research?

3. A marketing research man's analysis and interpretation of research data ordinarily proceed through a series of carefully planned and integrated steps. What are these steps? Briefly discuss each.

4. How would you answer the question: How far should interpretation be carried?

5. What is the objective of tabulation? When does tabulation planning begin?

6. As a marketing research man, what elements must you consider before deciding on hand or machine tabulation?

CHAPTER 17

Analysis and Interpretation
of Marketing Research Data
(Continued)

We move on now to consider additional aspects of the analysis and interpretation of marketing research data. As we do so, we move into what might be described as advanced areas of marketing research practice. Those areas are advanced in that they involve analytical and interpretive activities and skills which are far from routine in nature.

Because those advanced aspects of analysis and interpretation can be more easily illustrated by example than by description, specific examples and case material constitute the bulk of this chapter.

Before considering those examples, however, it seems desirable to explore at some length the relationships between a marketing research man and those for whom and with whom he works. Such an exploration is relevant at this point for this reason: To a very considerable degree the extent to which a marketing research man can pursue analysis and interpretation beyond a purely routine level depends on his understanding of and effective structuring of those relationships.

VARIATIONS IN ACCEPTANCE OF MARKETING RESEARCH
IN ORGANIZATIONS OF DIFFERENT SIZE

Marketing research today represents an important area of management skill. In the management hierarchy, a marketing research man usually ranks as a skilled technician. He is a specialist whose specialty is accepted because it has earned that acceptance. The important contributions which that specialty can and does make to improved management performance are recognized. That description applies primarily to the status of marketing research in larger organizations. These are typically well-managed firms, in which the latest management techniques

422

are recognized and used. Often they are firms in which the organizational structure and approach are on a rather formalized basis.

In such large, well-managed organizations, the marketing research man is free to do his work. In doing it, he faces no unusual problems. It is not necessary for him to shoulder the additional burden of a continuing battle for recognition and acceptance which was typically necessary only a decade or two ago.

But marketing research as a management tool is rapidly filtering down the organization-size scale. It is being adopted in an ever-increasing number of companies which are medium or small in size. Such companies typically are much less formal in their approach to organization matters. They rely to a greater extent on a more personalized approach to management. It is the informal interaction of ideas and personalities among a small group of key executives that determines basic policy and direction in most such company situations.

A marketing research man who takes a newly created job in such a firm faces problems which no longer exist in larger organizations, or in organizations in which marketing research has been established as a recognized area of specialized skill. It is necessary in most instances to devote a relatively large amount of attention to the matter of personal relationships with other individuals in the organization. Those relationships are of overriding importance in smaller organizations. It is also necessary to devote considerable time and effort to "selling"—to selling the individual's own abilities and to selling the importance and usefulness of the new area of specialization.

The problems which a marketing research man with little or only moderate experience faces in such a situation may appear to him to be new and unique. They are likely to resemble closely and to parallel the problems which were more widely encountered in the recent past when marketing research was less widely accepted. An indication of the nature of some of those problems and of the direction of the change which is occurring in management attitudes toward research as a result of progress toward the solution of those problems is likely to be both reassuring and helpful.

Marketing research findings must be accepted and acted upon by executives with operating responsibility, usually at top-management levels. Those executives have typically achieved success largely as the result of their own efforts. Many of them, typically, are "self-made men." They are characteristically strong-minded and decisive individuals, long accustomed to arriving at decisions primarily based on their own judgment. They have considerable confidence in that judgment. On the record, that confidence is warranted.

Now introduce marketing research into that picture. Marketing research acts to narrow the area within which it is necessary to make decisions based on judgment alone. Resistance to marketing research or to any other approach which might be regarded as intruding into or trespassing upon prerogatives long enjoyed is entirely natural. It is also frequently encountered!

BASIC EDUCATIONAL JOB NEEDED

Those who are too close to a marketing problem often see it in imperfect perspective. Often they bring to it deeply ingrained opinions on "how things are" which are at variance with the facts. Industry-wide assumptions and company-wide prejudices often stand as barriers to an accurate understanding of the problem.

Marketing research can grow and flourish and make a maximum contribution only in a certain climate. That climate is characterized by open-mindedness on the part of those who must accept and act upon research findings. In order to achieve such a climate, an educational job of greater or lesser breadth is usually necessary. That educational job takes time. It eventually registers the viewpoint that it is *what customers or consumers think and want,* and *not* what someone in the company thinks they *ought to* think and want, that is important.

A marketing research man who faces what he considers to be unusual resistance to the acceptance of research findings is often frustrated. He is likely to feel that the situation in which he finds himself is unusually difficult. It is much more likely to be completely "normal." Until the educational job mentioned has been accomplished—usually through a series of demonstrations of the contribution marketing research can make—it is likely to remain continuously difficult.

One important element which speeds the educational job mentioned is the attitude of the company's chief executive. Where the importance of marketing research is recognized at the top of an organization, its penetration and acceptance at lower levels can be much more speedily accomplished than where that recognition is absent.

THE EDUCATIONAL PROCESS IS A TWO-WAY STREET

It is worth emphasizing also that the educational job in question is by no means a unilateral one. The marketing research man faces the task of educating his associates and his superiors as to what marketing research can and cannot do, how it can be most effectively used, how to recognize a problem to which research could contribute, and so on. But that is only one side of the coin. The marketing research man should also be on the receiving end of part of the education which is necessary.

He must develop an awareness of the fundamental interests and needs of the executives to whom he reports. Then he must work continually on the task of bringing his research and his research reports more and more closely into line with their requirements.

People who won't face facts often pose problems for a research man. Sometimes the research man has the same kind of problem with himself and doesn't recognize it. He should and must face up to the fact that responsibility for accomplishing the necessary educational job is primarily his own.

In that connection, the keynote of a sales-training conference of a large company is worth mentioning. On each wall of the conference room, large signs read: "If the student hasn't learned, the teacher hasn't taught." The research man who is having difficulty "getting over" to his associates would be well advised to paste that slogan in his hat. The burden of responsibility for communication and education is on the research man.

CHARACTERISTIC PATTERN OF EARLY, NONPRODUCTIVE RESEARCH PRACTICE

There is a rather well defined series of steps through which marketing research in any company is likely to have to move before it can approach anything like maximum productivity. The early use of marketing research, in particular, is likely to be far less productive than it could be. The following comments by Robert F. Elder describe that characteristic pattern in the early stages of the introduction of research into a marketing operation:[1]

One of the biggest reasons why most companies, though they may get their money's worth, fail to get all they could out of market research is the lack of effective contact between the man responsible for market research and the top-management circle. The usual thing is for the market research man to be given a series of disconnected assignments on specific topics, as management realizes the existence of problems. It is only seldom, in my observation, that the man responsible for market research knows the full background of the problem he is asked to deal with. Lacking full knowledge of top-management thinking and strategy, he is not in a position to contribute his professional ideas as to the directions a sound and comprehensive investigation ought to take. Nor is he in a position to recognize the importance of by-product information, which is sometimes the most valuable fruit of a survey. Nor can he interpret his findings and

[1] Robert F. Elder, "Management Attitudes toward Market Research and Market Research Findings," a talk delivered to the American Marketing Association, May 16, 1948, at a national conference in Boston, Mass.

present them in the way that is most understandable and most useful to management.

In an earlier discussion of the steps in the marketing research process, attention was focused on the difference between a *marketing* problem and a marketing *research* problem. The above comments describe a situation in which marketing research is confined to work on a series of marketing research problems. The marketing research man is not exposed to the marketing problem, of which the specific assignments he receives are a part. As a result, his efforts are necessarily far less productive than they could be. Some of the factors contributing to that loss of effectiveness were mentioned above by Elder.

The heart of the problem of marketing research effectiveness lies in this area: The individual who knows most about what marketing research can and cannot do—i.e., in most instances the marketing research director—should be in a position to help identify the areas to which research should be applied. If someone else preselects those areas, in the process of making assignments to him, there is always the possibility that other, equally important areas may be overlooked. Perhaps their "researchability" is not recognized. There is the further loss of efficiency which often occurs when two or more separate assignments are made to cover an area which could be explored more efficiently and economically in a single, broader research approach.

To a considerable extent it is in the area of determining the relationships between different parts of a marketing-problem puzzle, and the relationships between data gathered in different ways or data (apparently) bearing on unrelated aspects of a problem situation, that is the vital contribution of a trained marketing research man. He may identify those relationships in the early stages, if he is permitted to work on the *marketing* problem on a fully informed basis. Or he may identify them by pulling portions of the findings of two different studies or analyses out of their contexts and relating them.

IMPORTANCE OF THE PERSONALITY FACTOR

There is one facet of the problem of "selling" marketing research, especially in an organization in which it is relatively new, which requires specific comment. To a considerable extent, the selling job in question is a two-pronged one. The individual with marketing research responsibility must sell both marketing research generally and his own ability and competence in the field specifically. It is likely to be of slight value to make only "half the sale." As a generalization, it is usually easier to sell the idea of marketing research than it is to sell one's own abilities in the marketing research field. Failure to make the more personal part of the sale often leads to continuing frustration and to a great loss of marketing research effectiveness. It is essential to realize that to many people the individual who has responsibility for marketing research *is* marketing research. If that individual is categorized as "theoretical" or in some other negative term, marketing research is similarly classified.

Progress from the early pattern of nonproductive research practice to a fully effective and fully accepted pattern of high productivity is usually gradual. It almost always requires more time than the marketing research man feels it should take. Gradual increase in the acceptance of and recognition of the individual with marketing research responsibility is often the first step forward. With that increased acceptance, he has an opportunity to identify more potential areas of marketing research contribution earlier in the research process. Each contribution made contributes to the building job. The acceptance mentioned is usually accelerated by flexibility on the part of the individual responsible for marketing research. He must adjust to those he works with, and to the corporate personality of his organization, so that that organization can find it easier to adjust to him and to the important new area of specialization he represents.

CHARACTERISTIC PATTERN OF MARKETING RESEARCH PRACTICE ON A FULLY EFFECTIVE, INTEGRATED BASIS

What are the characteristics which are usually found in those situations in which marketing research is used productively, with something approaching maximum effectiveness? The following list identifies the major elements which are likely to be found in such a situation:

1. Marketing research is likely to represent the full-time (and essentially the only) responsibility of the individual responsible for it. He may work alone, aided by secretarial assistance; or he may head an organized department. He may represent an outside consulting organization, especially in the case of the research program of smaller organizations. In any case, the individual responsible for marketing research rarely has other responsibilities.

2. Marketing research is recognized by the top-management team of the organization as a helpful and useful tool, which they can and do use whenever its use satisfies the cost-results equation and when time and facilities permit. This means that in addition to a recognition of the desirability of marketing research, the top-management team has some understanding of marketing research, of its advantages and limitations. This in turn presupposes that the educational job mentioned earlier has been done thoroughly and well.

3. The organizational aspects of marketing research are so structured that the individual responsible for research has access to top-management thinking, plans, and intentions in major marketing areas. This may be accomplished through placement of the function on the organization chart; or it may reflect key committee appointments of the research director. The effect is to permit the research director to have a maximum opportunity to recognize potential areas of marketing research contribution. Further, he is able to be sure that all areas of management interest or potential interest are considered in the planning, execution, and reporting of research.

When those three elements are present, marketing research is likely to begin when a marketing problem is recognized. The analysis and interpretation of marketing research findings are carried as far as the data permit. There is a cooperative acceptance of research findings rather than the jealous safeguarding of prerogatives which is typical of situations in which research is rigidly confined to reporting of findings without creative interpretation.

In the illustrations which follow, the more advanced analytical and interpretive thinking which such a climate permits and encourages is assumed. Let's begin with a return to the Bissell problem with emphasis on the analytical and interpretive phases of that problem.

26. BISSELL CARPET SWEEPER CO. (D)

The national urban carpet-sweeper survey for Bissell, with a total sample size of 5,469 completed interviews, was tabulated by machine. Table 17.1 presents the base-count total sheet developed by the machine tabulations. The table identifies the three major classification bases—income level (which would now be more likely to be identified as socio-economic or economic level); the city-size group in which the respondent lived; and the section of the country in which the interview took place. The total number of interviews in each cell in which the major classification bases were divided is shown on the table. Note that the total for the A, B, and C subdivisions of the table corresponds in each case to the total sample size of 5,469 interviews.

One of the most important questions in the analysis and interpretation of this survey was concerned with the level of ownership of the two major devices involved—carpet sweepers and vacuum cleaners—and with the overlap between them. With the importance of that point recognized, the base-count table was so developed that figures on the more important ownership-classification groups were included. As the total-sample figures indicate, 2,027 of the 5,469 housewives interviewed owned carpet sweepers, while 3,283 of them owned vacuum cleaners. The over-

Table 17.1. Base-count Total Sheet: National Urban Carpet Sweeper Survey

Major sample cells	No. of inter- views	Total carpet sweepers	Carpet sweepers only	Carpet sweepers plus vacuum cleaners	Vacuum cleaners only	Total vacuum cleaners
				Number of owners of:		
Total sample.........	5,469	2,027	809	1,218	2,065	3,283
A. Income level						
High..............	585	276	20	256	288	544
Upper middle.......	1,099	491	102	389	544	933
Lower middle.......	2,139	798	398	400	915	1,315
Low..............	1,646	462	289	173	318	491
B. City size						
500,001 and over....	2,194	903	393	510	929	1,439
100,001–500,000....	902	308	116	192	336	528
25,001–100,000.....	733	306	104	202	239	441
10,001–25,000......	552	174	58	116	210	326
Less than 10,000....	1,088	336	138	198	351	549
C. Section						
New England.......	525	175	75	100	238	338
Middle Atlantic....	1,187	571	181	390	456	846
South Atlantic.....	574	137	60	77	194	271
East North Central.	1,099	469	190	279	414	693
West North Central	613	254	122	132	272	404
East and West South Central....	798	133	61	72	240	312
Mountain-Pacific...	673	288	120	168	251	419

lap in ownership between the two devices was surprisingly high. There were 1,218 respondents who owned both.

There are two major values of a base-count table such as is illustrated in Table 17.1. The first is mechanical. It provides totals which serve as check points against which totals developed in various cross tabulations and subtabulations are routinely checked. The second value lies in the fact that it provides a picture of the exact size of each sample and subsample cell. It thus aids the research man in keeping the limitations imposed by sample size constantly in mind in analyzing the data.

From the base-count table, the proportion of the total respondents in each sample cell who fell into each ownership group was next calculated. Table 17.2 illustrates the results of this calculation.

For the benefit of readers with limited experience in the analysis and interpretation of tabular data, some general comments on approach may be desirable at this point. When presented with a table such as Table 17.2 represents, your first step should be to establish clearly in your own mind the nature of the relationships illustrated. Are the percentage figures calculated horizontally or vertically? Thus consider the

Table 17.2. Ownership Proportion of Total Interviews in Major Sample Cells National Urban Carpet Sweeper Survey

Major sample cells		Proportion of respondents interviewed in each cell owning specified devices				
	No. of inter- views	Total carpet sweepers, %	Carpet sweepers only, %	Carpet sweepers plus vacuum cleaners, %	Vacuum cleaners, only, %	Total vacuum cleaners, %
Total sample.........	5,469	37.1	14.8	22.3	37.7	60.0
A. Income level						
High..............	585	47.2	3.4	43.8	49.2	93.0
Upper middle......	1,099	44.7	9.3	35.4	49.5	84.9
Lower middle.......	2,139	37.3	18.6	18.7	42.8	61.5
Low..............	1,646	28.1	17.6	10.5	19.3	29.8
B. City size						
500,001 and over.....	2,194	41.1	17.9	23.2	42.3	65.5
100,001–500,000....	902	34.1	12.8	21.3	37.2	58.5
25,001–100,000.....	733	41.8	14.2	27.6	32.6	60.2
10,001–25,000......	552	31.5	10.5	21.0	38.0	59.0
Less than 10,000....	1,088	30.9	12.7	18.2	32.3	50.5
C. Section						
New England.......	525	33.3	14.3	19.0	45.3	64.3
Middle Atlantic....	1,187	48.1	15.2	32.9	38.4	71.3
South Atlantic......	574	23.9	10.5	13.4	33.8	47.2
East North Central.	1,099	42.7	17.3	25.4	37.7	63.1
West North Central	613	41.4	19.9	21.5	44.4	65.9
East and West South Central....	798	16.6	7.6	9.0	30.1	39.1
Mountain-Pacific...	673	42.8	17.8	25.0	37.3	62.3

47.2 per cent figure for high-income respondents, under the "total carpet sweepers" heading. Does that mean that 47.2 per cent of the owners of carpet sweepers were in the high-income group (i.e., a *vertical* calculation of percentage, with the per cent figures adding to 100 per cent for each sample division), or does it mean that 47.2 per cent of the respondents in the high-income category own carpet sweepers (i.e., a *horizontal* calculation of percentages)?

To be sure that your understanding of the relationships shown is accurate, it is a sound step to state them to yourself and see whether they are consistent with the data. Thus in the case of the first line (high-income cell) of the data shown in Table 17.2, you might state the indications somewhat like this: "There were a total of 585 high-income respondents interviewed, of whom 47.2 per cent reported that they own carpet sweepers, 93.0 per cent reported that they own vacuum cleaners, and 43.8 per cent reported owning both devices. There were 3.4 per cent of the respondents in the high-income group who owned carpet sweepers but not vacuum cleaners, while 49.2 per cent of them owned vacuum cleaners but not carpet sweepers." A check on this interpretation is provided by adding the percentages horizontally. Thus 43.8 per cent owning both carpet sweepers and vacuum cleaners, plus 3.4 per cent owning carpet sweepers, only totals 47.2 per cent, which checks with the total-carpet-sweeper figure shown.

— ★ —

EXAMINATION OF DATA FOR SIGNIFICANT RELATIONSHIPS

In the case of all data gathered by research which is presented in tabular form for the first time, the analyst's concern is with detecting and examining the significant relationships disclosed. Where a study is concerned with product use or product ownership, as the Bissell one is, it is normal to look first for variations and "pattern" in the economic-level or income breakdown.

It is normal to find either a negative or a positive correlation between product usage and income levels. Thus for automobiles, ownership would be expected to be relatively higher among high- than among low-income respondents. Some products exhibit the reverse pattern. Oleomargarine, for example, has sometimes been characterized by declining usage with each step up the income, or socioeconomic, ladder. In Table 17.2, the column headed "total vacuum cleaners" reveals a striking difference in product penetration by income levels. In the high-income sample, 93.0 per cent of respondents owned vacuum cleaners. In the upper-middle sample, 84.9 per cent owned vacuum cleaners. There was a drop-off in ownership to 60.9 per cent in lower-middle- and to 29.8 per cent in low-income respondents.

Note that the ownership of total carpet sweepers shows a generally similar pattern, but with sharply less marked differences. In the high-income group, the ownership level was at 47.2 per cent; it dropped off to 28.7 per cent in low-income families. The range between the lowest- and highest-income groups, however, was far less extreme than the span of more than 3 to 1 in vacuum-cleaner ownership from low to high income levels.

In the city-size breakdowns, a similar pattern of consistent variations is often disclosed. Some products—like cake mixes, for example—are more widely used in big cities than in small towns, while others (like corn syrup) have the reverse pattern. The carpet-sweeper ownership picture by city sizes shows only moderate variations, with no consistency to their direction. This would be described as a relatively flat city-size profile. Combined ownership of carpet sweepers and vacuum cleaners revealed an even flatter profile, with a slight dip in the "less than 10,000" group. (Remember that at the time of this survey electricity was less universally available than it is today, a factor which was probably related to the drop-off in the smallest city-size group.)

With the size of the major sample cells established, the results of the Bissell survey were analyzed further. Each question asked was tabulated for each major sample cell as well as in total. For example, the question was asked of carpet-sweeper owners (as reference to the questionnaire in Chapter 15 will remind you): "In general, what is your opinion of it?" That is a type of question which would today be handled by means of a rating scale or similar approach. In the case of the Bissell survey, it was necessary to establish various classifications of attitude, ranging from extremely favorable ones ("It's excellent," "It's very satisfactory," etc.) to extremely unfavorable ones ("It's terrible," "Cleans so poorly I almost never use it," etc.). This was an extremely time-consuming part of the tabulation process. Every response had to be read individually by an editor and translated into one of a number of numerical codes for machine tabulation.

Further, there was a constant problem of loss of accuracy in tabulation, since it was necessary for an editor to interpret the response of each carpet-sweeper owner into one of the established categories. The same type of classification could be established by handing respondents a card on which were listed a number of statements about attitude toward carpet sweepers and asking the respondent to select the one which most closely described how she felt. The questionnaire could then be *precoded* and the substantial editing and coding time eliminated with very slight loss in accuracy of attitude information.

(*Precoding* is the term used to describe one element in the physical design of a questionnaire intended for machine tabulation. The columns of the mechanical tabulating card which will be used for answers to specific questions are printed on the questionnaire, as are the numbers within that column which specific replies will be punched into. Thus if column 69 were to be used for a "Yes-No" type of question, the precoded number 69-1 might appear opposite the "Yes" blank or box, and 69-2 opposite the "No" blank or box. The interviewer simply checks the blank or box provided, to indicate the reply. The reply can then be readily punched into the planned-for space on the tabulating card, without the necessity of an intervening coding step.)

GUIDES TO THE ANALYSIS OF DATA

There is no cut-and-dried formula which can be supplied as a guide to the vital step of analyzing data. The analysis of data, whether gathered in the course of marketing research or otherwise developed, can and should be an essentially creative process. It is an art, a skill acquired through diligent practice and exercise. All that can be communicated in an introductory book like this are some of the general guides which have proved helpful to others.

The first step in the analysis of data is usually to pick that data to pieces. Make a lot of little problems out of the big problem. In the process of doing so, you as a research man are naturally concerned, first, with distinguishing between the known and unknown elements; and second, with distinguishing between what is and what is not relevant to the problem at hand. The practical value of separating known from unknown elements has been summarized by Charles F. Kettering: "The process of research is to pull the problem apart into its different elements, a great many of which you already know about. When you get it pulled apart, you can work on the things you don't know about."

The parallel between that approach and the one in which the objective is to identify and isolate the problem elements, described earlier in this book, is a close one.

One of the most important prerequisites for success as a marketing research man is an open mind. That is especially necessary in the analytical process. Those who are close to a problem are constantly prevented from seeing approaches to the solution of that problem because they "know too many things that aren't so." It is in precisely this area that a research man can often make his greatest contribution. He approaches a problem with a jaundiced eye. He has been trained to accept the firmly held beliefs of others as helpful guides, but only as guides. *Every opinion is a hypothesis* until it has been carefully evaluated in the light of the evidence and accepted, tentatively accepted, or rejected.

Another important characteristic of a marketing research man who is a competent analyst is a dual preoccupation both with the forest and with the trees. He begins by working down from the top of the problem —getting the big picture firmly in mind, as a background against which to examine the parts in accurate perspective. But he also builds up from the parts to the whole. He is constantly alert to the possibility that some new combination of elements, some ingenious reassembly of known facts, may add up to a promising new approach to an important old problem. It is partly because the Bissell case illustrates this point so aptly that it has been included and treated at such length here. Let's return to a re-examination of that problem.

RECAP OF KEY ELEMENTS OF THE BISSELL PROBLEM

The starting point in the research on the Bissell problem, you will recall, was an evaluation of the vacuum cleaner as a competitive threat to the carpet sweeper. Now put yourself in the role of the marketing research man who planned and analyzed the Bissell survey. Your job is to "put the pieces together" so that they make a coherent picture of the Bissell problem as it appears on the basis of the research in hand.

The first point which emerged clearly from the Bissell survey is that concern about the vaccuum cleaner as a competitor to the carpet sweeper was expressed a little late. Vacuum cleaners had successfully invaded the market for floor- and rug-cleaning devices and pretty much taken over that market, despite a substantially higher unit price and the depression-year timing of the problem situation. Total penetration of vacuum cleaners was near the 60 per cent level, far above the 37 per cent penetration of cheaper carpet sweepers. That penetration was especially high in the upper income levels—93 per cent of high- and almost 85 per cent of upper-middle-income families owned vacuum cleaners. The margin of superiority in penetration of vacuum cleaners over carpet sweepers extended to all city-size groups and to all sections of the country. Obviously vacuum cleaners represented a past and present, rather than a future, threat to the carpet sweeper.

This added up to a very dismal and discouraging picture, from the viewpoint of the Bissell management. They had long regarded "vacuum cleaners" as a "dirty word." Their advertising policy included a prohibition against any reference to the competitive product. It was apparent, however, that an invasion had been successfully accomplished. Considering the sales barriers which low depression-year incomes represented for higher-priced vacuum cleaners, the future—anticipating national recovery—seemed more likely to accelerate the adverse trend (viewed from the carpet-sweeper manufacturer's viewpoint) than to slow it down.

But the research analysis did not end with the mere reporting of the statistical findings. One aspect of the data examined with care was the age of appliances. This proved to be a further negative, from the viewpoint of the Bissell people. Carpet sweepers tended to be rather old—with an average age around 15 years—while vacuums were much newer. In other words, the rate of current sales of the two devices represented a far wider margin of superiority for vacuum cleaners than did the total-ownership figures, because of the backlog of long-owned carpet sweepers found in the sample.

Attitudes toward the two devices were examined. Attitudes toward carpet sweepers generally were lukewarm to mildly negative; those toward vacuum cleaners, lukewarm to mildly positive. Obviously no solution to the Bissell problem was going to be generated by the passage of time. Dissatisfaction was working against rather than for the carpet-sweeper manufacturer.

The digging process continued. Each key breakdown of data was examined for each of the major cells in the sample. The search for *actionable indications* was a ceaseless one.

Then a small ray of light broke through the clouds. Those families who owned *both* carpet sweepers and vacuum cleaners proved to be markedly more favorable in their attitudes toward both appliances than did owners of either device alone. What did this mean? The reasons for their attitudes were examined. The cleaning patterns of families in each type were broken out. The attitudes were re-examined, against the background of the cleaning patterns.

The final report on the Bissell study reported that:

1. Families owning both carpet sweepers and vacuum cleaners were much more favorably disposed toward both devices than were families owning either one alone.

2. Surprisingly, the carpet sweepers owned by families owning both devices tended to be substantially and significantly newer than were those in the remaining sample cells. This was an indication that those families owned both types *because they liked and used both types,* rather than because a vacuum cleaner had been sold into a home already owning a carpet sweeper.

3. When the reasons for the favorable attitudes were examined, it was disclosed that the families owning both types of devices had a basically different viewpoint from that of other families in the sample. *They regarded the two products as supplementary.* The woman who owned both a carpet sweeper and a vacuum cleaner said, "I use my vacuum cleaner for once-a-week heavy cleaning, and my carpet sweeper for quick daily touch-ups."

4. There thus emerged a pattern which could be interpreted as a sales opportunity for Bissell and other carpet-sweeper manufacturers. They couldn't "lick" the vacuum cleaner; the sales record showed that. But they *could join* the vacuum-cleaner manufacturer! They could merchandise their product—not as an obsolescent, old-fashioned way of cleaning rugs and carpets, but as a new and different device—as a supplement to the vacuum cleaner!

The Bissell management authorized the agency to proceed with advertising on that new approach: "A Bissell for quick, daily clean-ups, saving the heavy vacuum for once-a-week cleaning." The sales response was almost instantaneous. Bissell's sales volume rose to establish new peak levels, year after year. Successive surveys, with intervals of several years between them, confirmed the success of this advertising and marketing strategy. The greatest gains, year after year, were among the families who owned both—who bought a carpet sweeper as a supplementary cleaning device, in addition to their vacuum cleaner.

ALTERNATIVE MANAGEMENT COURSES OF ACTION ENTER INTO THE INTERPRETATION OF DATA

Throughout the analysis and interpretation of marketing research data, the marketing research man is continually and constantly asking himself: "What does this mean in terms of what the company should do about it?" At the outset of a major research project, two or more alternative courses of corporate action can usually be distinguished. Those courses of action are identified in the planning stage of the research. Each becomes, in effect, a hypothesis subject to evaluation and verification. Thus in the Bissell case, these two hypotheses were certainly present:

Hypothesis: *The most profitable course for the company to take is to get out of the carpet-sweeper business, because carpet sweepers are products which have been rendered obsolete by new-product developments.*

Hypothesis: *The most profitable course for the company to take is to move into the maufacture of vacuum cleaners, because the vacuum cleaner is going to (or already has) displaced the carpet sweeper.*

There are, of course, many other hypotheses which could be identified in the Bissell situation, including the one which emerged as the major recommendation following the interpretation of the research. The decision-making process would obviously be facilitated if the research interpretation led to the elimination of all hypotheses except one. It is usually not possible to prune the possibilities down to a single "winner." Factors other than research often enter into the selection of the final corporate course of action. Research ordinarily provides management with the alternatives and with the evidence supporting or limiting each. Management proceeds, in some cases, to add other alternatives and to arrive at a decision as to the most desirable course of action for the company to take.

In many cases, the selection of a single hypothesis by management represents merely the first step in a long program of marketing planning. This is illustrated by the second of the two hypotheses listed above. Suppose that the company accepted the second and decided to go into the vacuum-cleaner business. Should they make that move by developing their own vacuum cleaner or by buying a company already in that business? Evaluation of those two (and perhaps of other) courses of action would be a long and complex process, in all probability.

It should be emphasized that all the alternative courses of action which are apparent after the research is completed are not visible when the research is started. Consider the decision in the Bissell case to promote the carpet sweeper as a supplement to the vacuum cleaner. Such a course of action was not even considered before the research was completed. Additional hypotheses become apparent as the research progresses. The research man should have his mental radar tuned to identify any such alternative courses of action as soon as they are revealed. In most cases, such possible alternatives should be "flashed" to all interested executives without waiting for the completion of the research and delivery of the report. Such an approach ensures that each can be considered over as long a time as possible so that its full implications can be studied.

EVALUATING ALTERNATIVE COURSES OF ACTION IN THE CASE OF COMPLEX MARKETING PROBLEMS

The marketing problem which stimulated the Bissell research was a serious one, from the point of view of the Bissell management. From the marketing research standpoint, however, the Bissell case represents a relatively simple marketing research problem. A single marketing research study—using, in this case, the survey technique—was conducted to secure information helpful to the Bissell management in determining its future course of action. The research could and did proceed through all steps to the final interpretation. Where the marketing research conducted in the case of a single marketing problem is more complex—involving a number of different approaches, often utilizing different research techniques, requiring widely variable amounts of time for completion, and involving greater or smaller financial costs—the evaluation of alternative courses of action becomes, if possible, even more important.

We are here considering the problems which exist when a series of related marketing research projects have grown out of a single marketing problem. The importance of careful attention to the timing factor in the planning and scheduling of such research has already been pointed out. There is a further element of complexity which exists where the evaluation of alternative courses of action is concerned. The completion of any one project within the framework of a multiple-project research job may point clearly and unmistakably in a direction which makes some or all of the other elements in the research unnecessary. Major economies can sometimes be achieved by halting work on research which is no longer likely to be helpful.

Again we see the need for flexibility on the part of the research man emerging. In work on a complex marketing problem involving multiple research approaches, the research man must be continuously alert. A quick grab for the emergency brake, or a twist of the steering wheel, when indicated by the findings at any point in the research, can often produce marked economies and/or substantial increases in the value of the research program. To illustrate, let's now consider a case in which there were a number of marketing research approaches coordinated in an attempt to answer the single question of whether Standard Foods, Inc., should or should not continue to market packaged dry soup.

27. STANDARD FOODS, INC. (B)

The consulting organization working on the dry packaged-soup marketing problem for Standard Foods, Inc., began by reviewing the information which was available inside the company. That information proved to be largely fragmentary. Much of it was not completely current. It was considered generally inadequate as a guide to further research.

A search for relevant and useful data from external sources was next conducted. Some estimates of the size of the total market for soup were published by *Food Topics* magazine. In the case of many product categories, *Food Topics* estimates were widely accepted as accurate. In the case of soup, however, a grave question existed as to the accuracy of the figures. The soup industry was dominated by the Campbell Soup Company. That company had an extremely strict policy against the disclosure of any data, and estimates of the soup market which did not take into consideration the unknown Campbell volume were likely to be more "guesstimates" than estimates. Even if the figures were accepted as accurate in total, they left many aspects of the informational picture cloudy. They would not, for example, provide an indication of the sectional, city-size, or other variations in soup consumption.

Sources for additional data were explored. It was learned that the Market Research Corporation of America, through its National Consumer Panel, had been developing data on the size and composition of the soup market. Ordinarily contracts with MRCA or with the A. C. Nielsen Co. are made to cover an extended period of time. With the company's future in the soup business in question, such a long-term commitment would be inappropriate. The consulting organization therefore negotiated with MRCA for a special type of data purchase. The transaction involved what is identified as "back data"; that is, it covered time periods already completed. (Such data were already available in the files and records of the panel organization. It could therefore be secured without loss of time other than that required to prepare reports from the existing data.)

It was considered that substantially less information would be required to guide the basic decision of whether or not the company should stay in the dry packaged-soup business than would have been required if the service were purchased for the current and continuing guidance of operating management. Standard Foods, Inc., approved the data purchase which the consulting organization had negotiated with MRCA. The data from consumer-panel sources were ordered.

For additional guidance in determining whether the company's true product-type framework was *all* soup (i.e., canned soup plus packaged dry soup) or just the packaged dry soup, the consulting organization had the *Chicago Tribune* prepare a special analysis of its consumer-panel data covering the Chicago metropolitan area. This analysis was on a family-history basis, recording each individual soup purchase of each family in the *Chicago Tribune* panel for a full year. This made it possible to determine whether the same families used both canned and dry soup, the frequency of purchase of each type, brands and flavor used, etc. (The same kind of information could have been secured from MRCA. On a national basis, however, the cost would have been much higher. The time required to develop the data would have been substantially greater.)

The purchase of a special analysis of data of this type from a small one-market consumer panel is essentially similar to a pilot study in advance of a possible national study. If the single-market data prove useful and if a national extension of the same analytical approach seems likely to be worth more than its cost, you can proceed; if not, the value of the approach has been determined for a relatively moderate investment.

Attention was next turned to the question of product quality and consumer acceptance. Product research within the company purchased by Standard Foods, Inc., had been skimpy. A panel of six executives of the company were considered to be "soup experts." Their preferences determined product formulations offered to the public.

The consultant felt that a comparative product test among actual consumers was necessary to determine the consumer acceptance of the company's products. It was proposed to make that test against the leading competitive dry-soup brand.

An important supplementary value was sought as a by-product of the product test. It was planned to use a parallel or double sample of consumers. One sample would consist of current users of packaged dry soup. The other would include families who were former users and families who had never used the product. It was planned to use extensive additional interviewing subsequent to the product test on the latter group, in an attempt to determine what obstacles, if any, had to be removed to bring them into (or return them to) the dry-soup market.

Management of Standard Foods, Inc., had assigned primary responsibility for the evaluation and appraisal of the dry-soup marketing problem to the consulting firm. The partner in that organization who was in charge of the work had extensive marketing experience in closely related fields, substantial marketing research background, and a staff of marketing research specialists to aid and guide him. He developed an estimate of the total cost of the planned projects, secured approval on it, and proceeded to work on the primary task of answering the question as to whether the company should or should not stay in the dry-soup business.

— ★ —

ORGANIZATION PLAN ESSENTIAL ON A COMPLEX ASSIGNMENT

Now put yourself in the place of the consultant who has primary responsibility for the whole Standard Foods, Inc., assignment. One of the first things you must do is plan ahead. You must develop a specific and detailed organization plan for the whole complex assignment. That single assignment of yours already involves three major subassignments, and there are likely to be more before the job is finished. Note that all three of the subassignments involve different data sources. The data on market size and characteristics are being supplied by MRCA. The Chicago market consumer-panel data will come from the *Chicago Tribune*. The comparative product test will be executed by another source.

The problem you face, in a situation like this, is not unlike that of the individual responsible for scheduling production in an automobile manufacturing plant. There are certain major subassemblies which must be completed and fed into the production line at the right time and place, if the end result is to be a complete, finished, and functioning car. The major subdivisions of a complex marketing research assignment are like those subassemblies.

The timing aspect of this research problem has already been pointed out in general terms. Now it must be considered more specifically. There is a due date for the total assignment and for each of the major subassignments. Within the scheduling of each of those subassignments, there may be a number of individual due dates. Thus in the case of the comparative product test, preliminary estimates of the due date of each of these portions of the assignment would have to be established:

1. Date when merchandise to be used in the test should be received
2. Date by which that merchandise, suitably identified by code number or letters, should be available
3. Date by which forms, instructions to interviewers, etc., should be completed
4. Date by which field work on initial product placement should begin
5. Date by which field work on initial product placement should be completed
6. Date by which coding and editing of questionnaires, diaries, forms, etc., should be completed
7. Date by which field work on follow-up interview should begin
8. Date by which field work on follow-up interview should be completed
9. Date by which tabulation of questionnaires, diaries, forms, etc., from initial product placement should be completed
10. Date by which coding and editing of questionnaires from follow-up interview should be completed
11. Date by which tabulation of questionnaire data from follow-up interview, combined with preliminary data from initial placement, should begin
12. Date by which that tabulation should be completed
13. Date when preliminary report of the results of the placement should be ready for distribution
14. Date when charts for final report (if any) should be released to chart maker
15. Date when final report should go into typing or other publication process
16. Date when final report should be completed and available for review
17. Date when final report should be delivered to client

Maintenance of a detailed follow-up (or "traffic") system is an integral part of marketing research work. In most cases the individual responsible for work on a particular subassignment, or his secretary, would do the requisite follow-up or control work that is required. But the individual with responsibility for the entire assignment must also keep in close touch with progress against the approved timetable. Suppose, for example, that there was a delay in receipt of merchandise for the product-test placements. That delay might push delivery of the final report back, if no attempt to overcome the delay were made. Where an effective timetable is maintained, the delay would be detected early and subsequent steps taken to overcome it (perhaps through added personnel, overtime work, etc.) if it were serious enough.

The differences between the requirements of personal work organization in marketing research and in other areas of business administration are largely those of degree. Organization is stressed here because it is so important in marketing research, where a single detail overlooked may have an extraordinary influence on the quality of the total job.

You may choose the particular method of organizing material which suits you and which is the best "fit" to your own preference, aptitude, and temperament. *It is essential, however, that some definite organization plan be adopted.* Without such a plan, the danger of "dropping the ball" is great. Taking unnecessary risks is highly undesirable and not particularly typical of successful marketing research practitioners.

Some executives have found it helpful to adopt a dual-organizational approach in working on a complex assignment like the one described above. At the outset, while they are concerned primarily with breaking the big problem into its major subassignments, they separate material by subassignments. They collect cost estimates, due-date and progress-report information, preliminary findings, etc., under each major project category. Then as the various pieces flow toward completion and it becomes time to put the "subassemblies" together, a transition is made to an organizational framework which parallels the final report. That framework may be modified from time to time, as the final report crystallizes. One important advantage of this approach is that it requires the research man to devote a considerable amount of detailed, advance thought to the most effective method of organizing a complex mass of material into an integrated final report.

MAJOR ELEMENTS OF THE DRY-SOUP PROBLEM

As the data began to flow in from the various forces, the following information began to shape up on the dry-soup assignment.

1. *Size and Trend of Total Market*

MRCA reported that total consumer purchases of soup climbed from a little more than 27 million cases (with 36 units to the case) in 1943 to a peak of more than 46 million cases in 1948. There was then a moderate decline in consumption, followed by a leveling off at a level about 60 per cent higher than in 1943. Remember that these figures do not include nonfamily purchases, such as those of restaurants, boarding houses, etc.

2. *Canned-Dry Division and Trend*

Most of the increased consumption was on canned rather than dry soup. In 1943, canned volume was at a level which was 3.9 times dry volume on a unit basis. That figure climbed to a canned-dry division in which canned soup represented more than twelve times the volume of dry packaged soup.

3. *Are Canned and Dry Soup Different Products?*

In order to clarify the extent of overlap of use between dry and canned soup, the division of total families and of total soup volume was examined by types of soup purchased. Here is the result:

Type(s) of soup purchased	Per cent of families	Per cent of soup volume
Canned soup only.....................	44.0	32.5
Both canned and dry soup............	51.7	67.1
Dry soup only.......................	.8	.4
No soup purchased in 12 months........	3.5	
Total............................	100.0	100.0

It was found that 95 per cent of all dry soup was purchased by families that also purchased canned soup. In the aggregate, those were high-volume soup-consuming families. The conclusion on this point included these comments:

> The market-target of this business is the total soup market, and not just the existing market for packaged soup. Both dry soup and canned soup are in competition with each other for the "quick and easy" soup business (in contrast to the large volume of home-made soup, which is neither quick nor easy to make). Analysis of consumer purchasing habits and of a consumer attitude study suggests strongly that canned and dry soups are used *by the same families, for the same purposes.*

4. *What is the Market-share Picture in the Dry-soup Field?*

Examination of individual brands' shares of the dry soup market revealed the dominance of a leading brand, which had 69.3 per cent of total unit volume. The No. 2 brand had 18.8 per cent of the market. The brand made by the company which Standard Foods, Inc., had purchased was third in volume nationally, with 5.9 per cent of the total market. The figures are for the latest quarter covered by the MRCA data. It was evident from these figures that the company's starting point in the dry-soup picture was a very thin toehold in a market dominated by a single brand.

5. Purchase-frequency Picture on Dry Soup

When families buying dry soup at any time during a twelve-month period were analyzed, this picture of the division of families and division of dry-soup volume by number of purchases made was developed:

Number of units purchased	Per cent of families	Per cent of dry-soup volume
1	32.0	5.5
2–5	39.1	22.0
6–11	16.9	24.1
12–23	9.0	26.6
24 or more	3.0	21.8
Total	100.0	100.0

This adds up to a picture of a product class in which about one family in three buying during a twelve-month period makes only a single purchase. More than seven out of ten buying families (71.1 per cent) bought fewer than six packages in a year, or at an average rate of less than one package every two months.

6. Characteristics of the Market for Soup

Such characteristics of soup consumption as the influence of family size on purchase volume and variations by city sizes and geographic sections were explored. That facet of the research is detailed in Chapter 20, which deals with the problem of determining market size and characteristics.

7. Trend in Advertising Expenditures

The available sources of data on advertising expenditures for individual advertisers have some important limitations. They list radio and television expenditures for time, for example, but do not show the expenditure for talent which may represent a very high proportion of the total. They cover the space expenditures in newspapers in cities of certain sizes, but not in all cities. Figures on other media—outdoor advertising, for example—vary widely in availability and dependability. There is a strong tendency for the "traceable" advertising expenditures to represent a substantial understatement of the actual total expenditures. Recognizing these limitations, the consultant in charge of research on this assignment felt that a review of advertising-expenditure levels and trends was necessary and desirable.

Interest in advertising-expenditure figures was particularly stimulated by the desire to pinpoint the potential profitability of the packaged dry-soup product. Questions existed as to the variation, if any, in expenditure rates on canned and dry soup and in the expenditure rate of the two leading competitive firms in the dry-soup field.

This review disclosed a sharp rise in total soup-advertising expenditures in the years following World War II. From a 1939–1940 level of about 3 million dollars annually, soup advertising (for all companies combined) rose to a level well in excess of 8 million dollars. Because there was a substantial increase in the number of families in the United States over this period of time, those figures were reduced to a per-family basis. When so related, they showed that from a per-family expenditure of less than 9 cents in 1939 and 1940, soup advertising had risen to an average in excess of 20 cents.

The increase in advertising expenditures was recorded both by canned and by dry-soup producers. A disproportionate contribution to that increase was made by dry-soup manufacturers. Advertising of dry soup represented only 3.4 per cent of total soup advertising volume in 1941; shortly after World War II, that percentage exceeded 25 per cent. There had been over this period of time, as noted above, volume increases on canned soup far in excess of any dry-soup volume expansion.

The relationship between advertising costs for the two types of soup is illuminated by comparing the advertising costs per case over a period of years. In 1943, the average dry-soup advertising expenditures (all brands combined) were 18.1 cents per case versus a 15.2 cents per case figure for all brands of canned soup. By 1949, the per-case figure for dry soup was 57.6 cents, while the canned-soup expenditure rate per case was essentially unchanged.

8. *Results of Product Test Generally Favorable*

The blind product test against the leading brand revealed that consumer acceptance of the company's product was about on a par with that of the leading competitor. However, that product test was confined to those flavors of soup which both companies manufactured. The leading manufacturer of dry packaged soup had more flavors in the line than did the firm purchased by Standard Foods, Inc.

RESEARCH REVEALS AN OPPORTUNITY . . . IF

A preliminary report to the top-management team of Standard Foods, Inc., was prepared by the consulting organization, summarizing the indications from the research as those indications developed. This particular report was considered by the consultant to warrant top-management consideration. A meeting was arranged at which the consultant reported as follows:

1. The soup business is a big-volume business, in which there is at least in theory a substantial volume opportunity for Standard Foods, Inc.

2. But the shape of the competitive pattern in the market dictates the only scale upon which an attempt to exploit that opportunity can be successful. The canned-soup volume is dominated by the Campbell Soup Company. The packaged-soup volume is dominated by a leading competitive firm. *No small-scale attack on the soup market is likely to succeed* against such well-entrenched competitors.

3. The scale of advertising expenditures which would be required to mount an all-out attack on the soup market would be extremely high. Beyond question investment spending (i.e., spending of advertising money in advance of sales return, in the expectation that subsequent sales-volume growth will make the investment a paying one) would be required.

4. The flavor division of soup volume was such that several additional flavors would have to be developed and added to the line before reasonably complete coverage of consumer purchasing could be achieved. That would entail further expenditures, also on an investment basis.

5. In summary, then, the management of Standard Foods, Inc., faced a choice of alternatives. It could decide to launch an all-out attack on the soup market. This decision would commit the company to substantial and continuing expenditures in excess of income, over a period of years. It required, of course, an evaluation of the potential return from that course of action weighed against other uses of the same funds and management effort. Or it could decide to withdraw from the dry-soup market. In the latter case, there was a possibility that the company might be able to sell processing equipment, formulas, and trademarks to some other organization.

Further research was deferred until the basic decision as to the company's direction and intentions in the soup field had been made.

RESEARCH PROVIDES ONLY PART OF THE ANSWER

The above case illustrates the point which has been made several times in this book: Marketing research ordinarily provides only part of the answer or solution to a marketing problem. Research helps to narrow the area within which executive judgment must rely on intuition alone, by providing a foundation of facts for a major decision. The decision in the above case depended on many factors completely outside the scope of the research, such as the client company's financial situation, the existence of alternative ways of using the money the investment in soup would require (for example, to purchase some other small company in a field less competitive than soup), and many other considerations.

It is not unusual for a major marketing research project of a complex nature to end up much as this one did: with the development of two or more alternatives, each with its advantages and disadvantages detailed, from which management can make an informed and considered choice of direction. Thus the parallel between the case which follows and the preceding one is clear-cut.

28. FOREMOST PACKING COMPANY, INC. ★

This fictitious name identifies one of the largest meat-packing organizations in America. In the early years of World War II, the organization conducted an exhaustive re-examination of the volume and profit potential which margarine (then usually called oleomargarine and sold in uncolored form) represented.

The results of that re-examination were prefaced by a review of a series of facts supporting the viewpoint that there was then an important opportunity for Foremost margarine to build toward sharply increased volume and profit levels.

Fact 1 was that meat packers generally had been declining in importance in the margarine picture over a period of years. This decline was illustrated by the fact that in 1932, meat packers manufactured almost 41 per cent of all margarine. By 1939, that percentage had declined to less than 25 per cent. *Fact 2* was that Foremost margarine sales had followed the same trend. The company had 15 per cent of industry volume ten years before the analysis was initiated but dropped to less than 7 per cent at the time of the study.

Fact 3 was concerned with the margarine brand picture. It was pointed out that at that time there were literally hundreds of different brands of margarine available. Most were sold primarily on a low-price appeal. The brand name was much less important, for most of those brands—to the dealer or to the consumer—than the price. These are the so-called "cheap margarines."

Fact 4 noted that the cheap margarines, although numerous and collectively important, were far from the whole story. There were also a few "quality" brands of margarine (including Dell-O) which commanded a substantial price premium. Those brands were few in number. In total there were only five or six such brands at that time. But those brands together represented something like 25 to 30 per cent of the total amount of margarine sold.

Fact 5 was concerned with questions of product quality. It noted that in terms of the quality of the product, the differences between the "cheap" brands of margarine and the higher-priced "quality" brands were negligible, *except in the minds of consumers.* The corollary was that the manufacturing costs of a quality margarine were only slightly higher than manufacturing costs of a cheap margarine. Despite greater promotional and sales expense, quality margarines were *substantially more profitable to the manufacturer* than cheap margarines.

Fact 6 moved on to consider some of the causes of the meat packers' decline in competitive position in the margarine field. To a typical meat packer, margarine was then regarded as primarily an outlet for by-products. Most of the packer volume had been in the "cheap margarine" category, heavily in the private label or retailer-controlled-brand area. No packer up to that time had given the necessary "push" to a brand to lift it from the cheap to the highly profitable quality bracket which commanded a premium price. Another closely related point concerned the packers' approach to selling margarine. They added it as just another item to their full-line-salesmen's responsibility. The successful promoters of premium-priced margarine used specialty salesmen selling no other product or only one or two other closely related products, such as salad dressings.

Fact 7 considered the company's wartime situation in the margarine field. It could sell all the margarine it could make, without difficulty, by "doing what it had been doing." At the end of the war, it would emerge in much the same position as it had been in at the beginning. During the war years, the company could make a manufacturer's profit on margarine. The company's branches could make a wholesaling profit on margarine. But this was a temporary condition, resulting from wartime circumstances. As the analysis pointed out: "This profitable picture today is the result of war conditions. It isn't something we did—it's something that happened to us."

Fact 8 was concerned with a forward look at the company's prospects. It recognized that the company was still selling margarine much as it always had and concluded: "It seems extremely likely that unless we do something about it, our volume and profit will drop back to their former levels when the extraordinary war conditions are removed."

These and additional facts were "added up," and two different answers, each emphasizing a different combination of factors, were developed. Here are the two answers, with the underlying objectives of each, which were presented for management consideration:

Answer No. 1

Foremost should take advantage of the present situation to make as much immediate profit as possible from the manufacture and sale of margarine.

The objective of this policy would be to make as much money as possible from Foremost margarine right now. This could be described as the "let's make hay while the sun shines" answer.

Answer No. 2

Foremost should take advantage of the present situation to establish a strong foothold in the profitable "quality" section of the margarine field.

The objective of this policy is to use today's opportunities and part of today's profits to get Foremost's margarine operation on a higher plane of permanent profits so that when the war ends and the situation returns to approximately normal, we will be in a much stronger competitive and profit position than we were two years ago. This policy is one of building for *long-term* profits—building a roof over our margarine business in preparation for a rainy day.

It was pointed out that the selection of the second alternative would require a great deal of work on the part of the company and its marketing executives. A high-quality brand of margarine would have to be developed, and its acceptability to consumers established through blind-product tests. Quality-control standards would have to be introduced to be sure that product's quality was consistently uniform. Package redesign would be necessary. The beginning of a new specialty sales organization would have to be created, despite wartime manpower shortages.

Note this essential similarity in both the above two cases. A major policy decision, involving a selection of alternative courses of action, is required. If the company chose one course, no further research would be necessary. If it chose the other, a great deal of research would be likely to be required to implement that decision. In cases of this type, which are not unusual, the marketing research man must be diligent in scheduling and planning research. He must be careful to see that no avoidable major commitments for research expense are created until the key policy decision has been made.

WHERE DOES MARKETING RESEARCH STOP AND MARKETING BEGIN?

In examples like those in this chapter, the marketing research man's area of activities is relatively broad. He is fully informed by management as to its desires and interests. He has the confidence of management. He proceeds to plan and execute the research with a minimum amount of supervision and exercises a maximum amount of initiative. This picture of a skilled and experienced marketing research man in action is likely to raise some questions in your mind. Just where does marketing research stop and marketing begin? Isn't the marketing research man in these cases ranging rather far afield? Isn't he moving into the areas of responsibility of operating marketing executives?

To answer those questions, we must summarize the basic objective of this chapter. That objective was to underline the fact that marketing research today has moved far beyond the point at which it represented the narrow province of highly specialized technicians. It is today as broad as marketing itself.

The marketing research executive is one who knows the technique tools which can be used to gather facts and information helpful to operating executives at all levels in arriving at vital marketing decisions. But he must know more than those tools. He must know also the area within which they are applied. A seasoned and experienced marketing research man is in fact a marketing executive as well as a marketing research executive.

Marketing is his primary area of operations, and he must know the field thoroughly. In marketing, he is a specialist—a specialist, primarily, at problem solving. He almost always functions in a staff capacity. His findings are advisory. He does not trespass on the prerogatives of the operating executives with whom (and for whom) he works. They are free to accept or reject his findings or recommendations. When those findings and recommendations represent, as they often do and always should, the seasoned evaluation of a competent and objective marketing executive, arrived at after gathering and analyzing relevant facts, they become a vital contribution to marketing management effectiveness.

SUMMARY

1. This chapter extends the discussion of the analysis and interpretation of research findings into more advanced areas. The extent to which a marketing research man in a specific situation has an opportunity to extend the interpretive step as illustrated in this chapter varies with the state of development and acceptance of marketing research within an organization.

2. Often the smaller organization, which has had a shorter period of experience with marketing research, uses the techniques of research on a more limited basis and with less effectiveness than is characteristic of larger organizations.

3. There is a basic educational job which must be carried out in an organization in which marketing research is relatively new. Until that educational job is completed, the road of the marketing research man is likely to be a rocky one.

4. Responsibility for seeing that that educational job is accomplished successfully rests squarely on the shoulders of the individual in charge of market-

ing research. It is helpful to recognize that educating himself as to the needs and desires of those he works with is an important part of the educational process.

5. The outstanding characteristic of marketing research practice, in its early, nonproductive phase of development, is its fragmentary nature. The marketing research man typically works on specific marketing research assignments. He usually lacks an opportunity to review or to become fully acquainted with the marketing problem out of which the research assignments grew. He is often only partially informed as to his management's area of interest.

6. When marketing research is fully effective, it is marked by free access to top-management personnel and viewpoints; by widespread acceptance of research and recognition of its value by marketing personnel and other operating executives; and by a full-time marketing research man who is personally accepted and respected by his associates.

7. In the case of complex multiproject marketing research assignments, the marketing research man often emerges with two or more alternative courses of action. Selection of one of those alternatives is a policy decision, a management prerogative, with research contributing information but usually illuminating only part of the decision area.

8. A seasoned and experienced marketing research man must know the marketing field thoroughly. When he does, and operates in a corporate climate in which he has a maximum opportunity to use his technique tools to contribute to marketing management policy, he functions as a valuable and valued member of a marketing team.

QUESTIONS

1. What might be the difference in the way that the techniques of marketing research are used by small organizations versus the usage of these techniques by large organizations?

2. It is said that "Marketing research can grow and flourish and make a maximum contribution only in a certain climate." What is meant by this statement? What are the characteristics of that "climate"?

3. Why is it said that the educational process is a "two-way street"?

4. What is one of the biggest reasons why companies fail to get all they can out of marketing research?

5. What are the characteristics which are usually found in those situations in which marketing research is used productively, with something approaching maximum effectiveness?

6. What is meant by the term *precoding?*

7. In the vital step of the analysis of data, what are some general guides which have proved helpful?

8. How would you answer the question: Where does marketing research stop and marketing begin?

CHAPTER 18

Preparation of Research Reports

An experienced research man once reduced the subject of research reporting to a very few words. "Writing a research report is easy," he said. "I just tell 'em what the problem was, I tell 'em what I did about it, I tell 'em what happened or what I found out, I tell 'em what that means, and tell 'em what I think they ought to do about it." Those who lack his extensive experience are likely to feel that his comments somewhat oversimplify the subject of research reporting. The length of the present chapter will lend support to that viewpoint. His comments are included above because they provide a very brief description of what a complete research report ought to include.

We might note parenthetically that some research men would disagree that "what they ought to do about it" properly belongs within a research report. The pros and cons of conflicting opinions on this point are detailed later in this chapter.

THE FOUNDATION OF A RESEARCH REPORT

A research report requires, as a starting point, a firm foundation. That foundation should be a capable and complete analysis and interpretation of the results of the research. Unless the foundation is laid with care, erection of a durable report on it is likely to be far more difficult than it need be. When the job of analysis and interpretation is completed, the marketing research man moves into the preparation of his report. When he does so, he enters one of the most challenging and critical areas of all marketing research practice.

It is difficult to exaggerate the importance of the reporting step. You achieve some perspective on the importance of the research report when you note that all preceding steps in the research can be completely canceled out by a poor job of reporting.

Consider the situation when the analysis and interpretation step is completed. The *marketing research man* then knows what the research disclosed. But that information is still in his own head. Until it is translated into a form which other (usually non-research-trained) people can study and understand, it is unlikely to lead to the profit contribution which was considered to be implicit in the research at the time the cost was authorized.

Until a report of the results of the research has been prepared and presented to those who authorized it, the research is incomplete. The research was initiated in the expectation that it would make a contribution to profit. It cannot make that contribution until it is completed. Quite literally, then, the research report is the keystone of the entire research process.

REPORTING OFTEN A WEAK LINK IN THE RESEARCH PROCESS

In the opinion of many thoughtful students of the field, reporting represents the weakest link in the chain of steps which combine to represent the total marketing research process. Improvement in reporting is essential. A recognition of the inescapable importance of the reporting step is likely to stimulate that improvement. It therefore seems desirable to stress the fundamental importance of reporting and to note that the above viewpoint on the role of the report is shared by many authorities.

Thus the following quotation reflects the viewpoint on the importance of reports as a part of research as registered by a committee of the American Marketing Association:[1]

> The findings in marketing research remain valueless until they are communicated accurately and effectively to the persons who are responsible for policy decisions.

The same point was stressed in the excellent study of *Marketing, Business and Commercial Research* prepared by the National Industrial Conference Board[2] in these words:

> *Reports of Findings.* Unless a marketing, commercial, or business research department can analyze and synthesize the results of its research and present its findings to management in such a manner as to induce adoption and use, the work of the department is valueless. Management's

[1] *Preparation and Presentation of the Research Report,* a committee report of the American Marketing Association published in *The Journal of Marketing,* July, 1948, p. 62. Committee members were George W. Robbins, Roy S. Frothingham, Edward G. Reeves, Frederic A. Chase, Wallace H. Wulfeck, and Ray Jonason.

[2] Studies in Business Policy, no. 72, 1955, p. 21.

interest in the work and the support that findings and recommendations receive depend largely upon the effectiveness with which the department presents its reports. It is not surprising, therefore, to find most directors of research devoting considerable time and effort to report preparation and presentation.

Research directors seem to agree that regardless of the caliber of the research staff and the soundness of its reasoning, its work is of little value unless findings are presented clearly, simply, and in terms that can be understood and acted upon by management. Crispness, forcefulness, and writing from "mangement's slant" are essential to real success.

THE COMMUNICATION PROBLEM IN REPORTING

While the importance of the reporting step is widely recognized, some of the difficulties inherent in it are sometimes overlooked or underestimated. There is a very real problem in communication which must be solved by a research man before he can achieve the maximum clarity in reporting on and securing an understanding of the research findings.

Candor compels us to recognize that the communication problem mentioned is unsolved or only partially solved by many practicing marketing research men. This is not surprising. It occurs because the reporting step draws on a different set of talents from the remaining steps in the research process. The basic skills required for an exceptionally capable job of planning, executing, and analyzing research are not the same skills needed to prepare an interpretive report which presents the findings cogently, clearly, and understandably. The reporting problem remains an important one for many marketing research people. A lack of ability or limitations in their ability in the reporting of research results often retard their individual progress.

The American Marketing Association committee already mentioned recognized this problem. The following quotation[3] is a continuation of the comment quoted above:

> The preparation and presentation of the report deal with the arts of communication. If there is a weakness in this phase of marketing research, it may be accounted for by the divergence of talents essential to the art and science of communications and of research itself.
>
> In fairness to all concerned, the report of a research study should be prepared and presented in a manner that obtains proper understanding and recognition of the amount and quality of research work done.
>
> The process of research is largely one of the impact of facts and ideas on one mind (the researcher's), and is one of penetration. The process of communication, on the other hand, is one of presenting these facts and ideas to other minds; it is a process of interpretation by the written and

[3] *Preparation and Presentation of the Research Report*, pp. 62–63.

spoken word aided by the graphic arts. One may not always expect to find equal facility in both processes in every mind. It is therefore of great importance to the marketing researcher to study the needs of reporting as well as of fact-finding itself, and to devise means of achieving good reports, perhaps in spite of his own personal limitations. A persuasive attitude of mind is very helpful to research reporting, and while it may be true that people engaged in selling and promotion as a career should not engage in research, it does not follow that researchers should not use honest salesmanship based on tenable research methods. The fact is that this is just what they should do.

LEVEL OF WRITING SKILL REQUIRED FOR EFFECTIVE RESEARCH REPORTING

Research reports are usually prepared in writtten form, even in cases where the findings are presented orally. The basic medium of research writing is written English. The individual who would achieve competence in research reporting requires as a first and inescapable foundation of that competence an adequate command of English, coupled with minimum skill in self-expression.

That requirement is so obvious that it perhaps should not even be stated. Yet it is so important—and unfortunately, so relatively rare even among those with apparently adequate educational background—that it *must* be stated *and emphasized.*

Many people say, "I can't write." Because they never or rarely try, they prove themselves correct in that claim. The fact that an individual classifies himself as one of those who "can't write" does not mean that success as a research man and as a writer of research reports is barred. The level of writing skill essential for clear reporting of marketing research results should not tax the abilities of anyone with a college education or its equivalent in experience. It is essential to understand the *kind* of writing required. That kind of writing, fortunately, is within the grasp of almost everyone who can read this book.

Writing a research report does not require one to have a flowery vocabulary or a command of high-flown, polysyllabic words. Neither is the unusually developed imagination of the writer of creative fiction a prerequisite of success. What is required is an ability, first, to express ideas and thoughts directly and simply, in words and phrases that will be completely clear to all who read the report; and second, to so organize those thoughts that the reader can follow without difficulty the steps in an argument or summary of evidence.

The difficulties in reporting for many research men are increased by the tendency of technicians in any field to develop their own specialized terms and concepts. They build up a superstructure of jargon on those

terms and concepts. Their writing and conversation tend to become un-
intelligible except to others with similar technical interests and training. They read technical and professional journals, written in the same
often ponderous gobbledygook. Then when they are face to face with
the task of writing a report clearly and simply, so that it can be understood without difficulty by those who are not technicians, they face a
formidable hurdle before they can achieve communication.

Robert F. Elder, who was quoted in the preceding chapter, is one of
the pioneers in marketing research practice. He made the following
penetrating comments on this communication problem in the same
talk already quoted:[4]

> Perhaps it's a sort of unconscious defense reaction against this sort of
> interference that causes so many market research people to surround their
> work with a lot of statistical mumbo-jumbo, and to make some of their
> reports so awe-inspiringly bulky and complicated. Or perhaps it's just a
> carry-over from the school-day superstition that professors grade reports
> on a quantitative, rather than a qualitative basis. Whatever the cause, it
> does as much to retard the proper scope of management's use of market
> research as any other factor.
>
> I recall a case some ten or twelve years ago where the directors of a
> large corporation had employed a well-known market research consultant
> to study a rather vital problem. He did a good honest job. But he rendered
> a fifteen-pound report bound in leather covers, with gold lettering, replete
> with beautiful charts and tables. Each of the directors in turn took it
> home and pored over it for two or three evenings. Finally they held a
> meeting. They were all proud of the beautiful and impressive report, but
> when they got down to brass tacks it came out that nobody had been able
> to figure out from it what to do about their problems. They had pretty
> much decided that market research was a pretty but useless toy.
>
> I was called in and asked whether there was not some way to find the
> answers they needed. Buried in that voluminous report were all the
> necessary answers. It was not too much of a job to dig them out, relate
> the various pertinent figures to each other, and turn out a two-page
> summary showing the relation of the data to the problem. The directors
> were then able to act, and a report that was worth over half a million
> dollars in annual profits to the company was saved from smothering in its
> own complexity.

Mr. Elder's comment underlines the importance of tailoring a research
report to its audience. The report intended for a research man and the
report intended for executives who are not trained in research are
likely to be quite different in approach, length, detail, and in other ways.
This subject is discussed more fully later in this chapter.

---

[4] "Management Attitudes toward Market Research and Market Research Findings,"
a talk delivered to the American Marketing Association, May 16, 1948.

IMPORTANCE OF REPORTING ABILITY TO AN INDIVIDUAL'S PROGRESS IN MARKETING RESEARCH

Outstanding skill in communication, which is reflected in the effectiveness of their reporting, is characteristic of most successful marketing research men. Increased effectiveness in reporting is a constant goal of many practicing marketing research men who are ambitious and seek to progress in their field. His ability to prepare a clear and simple report of the findings of research exerts a vital influence on an individual's progress in marketing research practice.

In the closing paragraphs of the preceding chapter, it was pointed out that many marketing research men succeed in becoming *marketing executives who know and use research.* The area of their interest and activities extends far beyond marketing research per se, embracing instead the entire field of marketing. The broad-gauge capacities of such individuals and their ability to see that marketing research is planned and above all *applied* so that its profit contribution is maximized make them valuable members of the marketing team.

In their daily work such individuals tend to conform to a rather clear-cut pattern. They tend to work largely on a team basis. They *speak the same language* as the other members of the marketing team. While they have a vocabulary of terms comparable to that of a more specialized marketing research man, and a full understanding of the meaning of those terms, they do not use them extensively or unnecessarily in dealing with nontechnically trained coworkers. They are constantly aware of the importance of skill in communication and are alert to new developments in the field of communication which might be helpful to them in doing a better job in that vital area. They tend to express themselves well in speech or in writing. They are often more "outgoing" than average.

In contrast to such an individual, many in the field of marketing research are preoccupied with detailed matters of far narrower scope. Such an individual has a far more limited future in the field. The low ceiling which such an individual faces is often revealed by his reports. Those reports tend to be heavily loaded with highly technical terms. They are often poorly organized, parading a mass of unrelated details before the reader without a discernible organization plan. There is little awareness of the problems or interests of the reader revealed by their reports. Unfortunately for such individuals, it is not unusual to find that some executives "type" a man by the reports he writes. You write reports which are dull, poorly organized, academic in vocabulary or tone, or theoretical in approach? Then you are, to such executives, what your reports indicate you are.

Enough for the importance of ability in reporting. Now to brass tacks: What are the elements in that ability? What do you have to know how to do, or how not to do, in order to prepare an effective marketing research report?

STARTING POINT: ABILITY TO WRITE SIMPLY AND CLEARLY

The first requisite for effective reporting is far simpler to identify than to describe. It consists of the ability to write simply and clearly. Fortunately there are many excellent books which are helpful to the student in developing and/or improving skill in this area. One which is immensely important as an introduction to the process of writing research reports that can be easily understood is *The Art of Plain Talk*[5] by Rudolf Flesch. *The Art of Readable Writing*[6] by the same author may also be highly recommended. Additional readings in this area are listed in the bibliography contained in the Appendix. Here are some suggestions which may help you evaluate your writing. They can thus help you decide whether you need to do supplementary reading on this subject.

1. *Are Your Sentences Short and Simple?*

Vocabulary is often blamed when writing is dull and hard to understand. Research has revealed that sentences do more to interfere with communication than do single words. It is the ponderous sentence structure which should be avoided. Excessive sentence length is another symptom of hard-to-read writing. Flesch feels that an average sentence length much in excess of seventeen words is hard to read and understand. Long sentences are often complex sentences. Thus the length and complexity of sentences are often two sides of the same coin. Either problem reduces readability and imposes communication problems.

2. *Are the Words You Use Simple, Clear, and Concrete?*

There is a common tendency to use a fancy word where a plain one would do nicely. That tendency should be resisted in writing research reports. Every effort should be made to use words that are simple and clear. You want the reader of your report to understand exactly and precisely what you are trying to say. The best insurance against misunderstanding is to use words which are clear and unambiguous. Often this particular writing problem is one that is invisible to the writer. Take a sample of your writing to someone whose writing and judgment you admire. Ask him to edit it for you. Study the changes with care.

[5] Harper, New York, 1946.
[6] Harper, New York, 1949.

3. *Is Your Writing Grammatically Sound?*

It would be easy to overemphasize the importance of schoolbook maxims in grammar and to be pedantic on this subject. Grammatical writing is highly desirable in research reporting. Many of the principles of grammatical writing stressed in grammar and high school are actually aids in the communication process. When you write, such principles make your writing easier to understand. They also have an additional value. They make it less likely that some reader of your report will be so distracted by your grammatical errors that he overlooks or imperfectly understands some major finding of your research!

IMPORTANCE OF ORGANIZATION IN A RESEARCH REPORT

Your ability to write clearly and simply is assumed. We now move on to consider an extremely important element in the reporting process— the ability to organize material. This discussion is concerned with one of the most difficult aspects of research reporting to teach. It is also one of the most vital skills required in the preparation of effective research reports. A good research report presents the findings of the research in accordance with a carefully formulated and logical plan of development.

The test of the organization of a research report is relatively simple. If two questions can be answered affirmatively, the organization is likely to be acceptable. The first question concerns the relevance of the organization plan to the objectives of the research. Does that organization plan focus primary attention on the most important objective or objectives of the research and subordinate minor or fringe considerations? If it does, it has passed the first hurdle. The second question is concerned with the difficulties which the organization plan poses for the reader. Can an interested executive proceed directly through the report and emerge with a complete and clear mental picture of the research findings? If he can, the organization structure passes its second test. The contrast between a well-organized and a poorly organized research report is a striking one. A poorly organized report requires constant backtracking, detailed comparison of one section with another, and other energy drains *on the part of the reader.*

When you release a poorly organized report, you "pass the buck" on organization to the reader. You make it necessary for each individual reader to make up for deficiencies in the organization of the report by *organizing* the research findings mentally into a unified and coherent whole.

It is the responsibility of the *writer* of a research report to do the organization job *for* the reader. There are two reasons why that responsibility should be shouldered. The first is a matter of simple efficiency. It is far more efficient for one writer to organize the material once for all readers than to have each individual reader organize the material mentally, duplicating the effort output of all other readers. The second is concerned with aptitude. The individual with responsibility for translating the analysis and interpretation of the research into report form is, presumably, a skilled analyst who is also a capable communicator of the findings of research. In theory at least, such an individual can do a better job of identifying the major findings of the research and of organizing them into a coherent whole in the report than can a number of other individuals less well qualified.

One of the prices paid for failure to organize material effectively in a research report should be recognized. That is the tendency of each reader of the report to arrive at an individual judgment as to what the research disclosed and what those findings mean. The blind men and the elephant provide a parallel.

A FRAMEWORK IS REQUIRED

It is extremely difficult to describe the process of organizing material into an effective research report in general terms. As the preceding chapter indicated, the organization of material usually begins in the analytical and interpretive step. It may begin even earlier—in the planning phase of the research itself!

Skill and speed in organizing research material into a cohesive whole require considerable experience. Here are some suggestions which may prove helpful to readers who are in the process of acquiring that experience. The first point to remember is that *organization of material into a research report calls for and requires a definite organization plan.* The focus of that plan, to repeat a phrase from the preceding comment of Elder, should be an attempt to show "the relation of the data to the problem." It is worth recalling the point made in Chapter 1—marketing research is *problem-oriented.* More poor research reports result from failure to keep attention focused on the objective of the research than from almost any other single cause.

A well-organized research report is easy to read and easy to understand. It has a definite organization plan and uses it. The nature of that organization plan is usually communicated to the reader at the outset so that the relationship between the parts of the whole, or between different aspects of the research, is clearly defined. A well-organized research report *starts somewhere* and *goes somewhere* and usually takes the most direct route! The selection of the starting point depends on the particular situation. It may be a brief statement of the problem. It may be a brief review of previous research, which emphasizes the unanswered questions which led to the present research. It may be an outline of a favored management hypothesis, which the research was conducted to explore.

Whatever the starting point is, it typically establishes both the framework of the report and background for the material which follows.

"Where the research goes" is usually in the direction of a distilled and boiled-down essence of the research findings. Thus in the case of a product test, that might be a brief and simple statement that such-and-such a product was preferred by a given margin, among a sample of specified size, for these reasons. If there were important variations in preference among the participants, those might be identified.

REPORTS SHOULD BE TAILORED TO FIT THEIR AUDIENCE

The preparation of a research report does not take place in a vacuum. It is a step in the communication process. The participants in that process include the research man and the individual or individuals to whom the report is to be delivered. *The nature of the report should be determined primarily by the desires and characteristics of the individuals for whom it is prepared.* From the very beginning of his work in planning research reports, the research man should include careful attention to the requirements and characteristics of the audience for which a report is prepared as a major element in determining the nature of the report required.

An advertising agency research director had to deliver two reports, covering essentially similar research, to the presidents of two client organizations. In one case, the chief executive to whom the report was delivered had broad experience with research. He preferred and received a brief, visualized summary of the research findings. He asked some questions about the findings, reviewed them with his associates, and was then prepared to take the indicated action. The other president was an essentially insecure individual. He required a report presenting research findings in great and explicit detail. He refused to have the findings presented personally, for fear that he might be influenced by the persuasive powers of the presenter rather than by the research findings alone. He required a written report which he could study by himself, supplemented by subsequent discussion.

The nature of the relationship between the individual responsible for research and the individual for whom the research is conducted is often a major influence. An executive who required his advertising agency to present research findings in great detail might find a brief memo from his own research director a sufficient report. Cost considerations also enter into this question. A charted presentation of a research study might involve hundreds of dollars of additional expense for charts, art work, etc. Whether or not expenditure of the required time and money for a visualized presentation of a research report is desirable is a question which must be weighed on the same cost-versus-contribution scale as all other research-expenditure decisions. There is, however, one point of difference: The cost of *failing* to develop an effective report and of presenting that report must also be considered.

Thus the research has been completed. The major costs have been incurred. The data have been tabulated and analyzed. It is now ready to be translated into finished-report form. There is a danger that all the research costs up to and including the cost of reporting may be completely wasted if the research report is not effectively prepared and presented. Good research on which no action is taken because the research was poorly reported (as in the case described by Elder above) is bad research because it does not make a profit contribution equivalent to its cost. A little additional expense, as in the Elder summary of the above-described research, may be the difference between a total loss of research expenditures and a potent profit contribution. The cost of the research presentation in such a case is something like the cost of the horse-shoe nail, for want of which the shoe was lost.

CHANGING NATURE OF THE REPORTING PROBLEM

As marketing research has progressed from a "sometime thing" to a management tool in daily use, there have been major changes in many aspects of research practice. Few changes have been as great as those involved in the reporting of research results. A report of a major marketing research study, a score of years ago, was often in the form of a "production number." A large part of that report had to be devoted to the process of explaining what marketing research is before the findings of a particular study could be meaningfully presented.

It was not unusual to have two different research reports covering the same study. One was a long and detailed report, describing in great detail the methodology followed, often with a validation of that approach, incorporating a mass of fully detailed tables. Whether the tables were relevant to the objectives of the research was immaterial. Such a report was sometimes described as a technical report. It was intended for the perusal of technicians, who were expected to evaluate the methodological soundness of the research, the significance of statistical findings, and so on. The other report, sometimes described as a "popular" report, was often in the form of a visual summary of the results of the research. It was intended for an audience of executives who were *not* technicians.

That dual method of reporting was sometimes necessary, when each report had to be "sold." Techniques were not standardized, and considerable explanation of the techniques used was necessary. Changes in reporting practice have developed as a result of increasing familiarity with research on the part of those to whom research reports are directed. It is no longer necessary, in most cases, to spell out in great detail the minor decisions entering into the design of the research. Most research today, while possessing elements of uniqueness, tends to follow well-charted technique roads. Where two reports of a single major research project were once necessary, a single report usually suffices today.

Technical details, including methodological innovations, details of the sampling plan, questionnaires or other forms used, instructions, etc., are commonly included in the appendix to a research report. Subordination of such material does not represent an attempt at concealment or failure to disclose significant data. It represents instead a major shift in emphasis. What is important today is less often in the area of research methodology, more often in the findings of the research and the significance of those findings.

This change in reporting practice is another evidence of the increasing maturity of the research field. Most marketing research planned and executed by experienced people today is competently done. Qualifications of the organization or people responsible for the research were examined before the commitment was made. Attention in the report is focused on the pay-off area: *What did the research disclose, and what does that mean to us?*

TODAY'S EXECUTIVES READ AND RUN

Another important factor contributing to the change in research reporting is the increasing paper work and reading-matter load on today's executive. Despite attention to increases in reading speed, the typical executive today has to spend a great deal of time reading written material which is (or could be) important to his job. That reading burden has made it necessary for all who prepare reports—in marketing research or outside of it—to deliver the meat of the findings quickly and easily.

Today it is standard practice in marketing research reporting to prepare a written summary of the research findings. That summary is included as a major element in the report itself. It may be included either at the beginning or end of the report. In either position, it is usually flagged so that it can be located easily. (This may be done by using a different color of paper for the summary, for example.) Full details backing up and spelling out the summarized data are presented in the report, for those who have need (and time!) for those details. The summary of the research is all that most operating executives may realistically be expected to read.

This imposes on the marketing research man an added burden in the reporting process. He must be sure that the summary presents a balanced and complete picture of the research findings, supported in appropriate cases by conclusions from those findings and recommendations based on them.

To facilitate the rapid reading of a research report, and to aid the reader in locating particular portions of the report, it is desirable to use whatever typographical or other devices one can to provide necessary organization and emphasis. Thus even in a summary, a brief, telegraphic summary of each major point is sometimes used as a heading. Then a skimming of the summary provides a fast but relatively complete picture of the results of the research. Further details are at hand, often with their specific location flagged, so that any particular point can be explored further.

ILLUSTRATION OF A REPORT SUMMARY

For a specific illustration of the brevity and telegraphic style which are often favored in the summary of a research report, here is the full and complete summary of a product-test report on two formulations of Dell-O margarine—regular Dell-O and a proposed new formulation to which $\frac{1}{10}$ of 1 per cent of monosodium glutenate (MSG, a flavor-heightening agent) had been added:

1. *Margarine M—Regular Dell-O—was preferred*

Housewives preferred Margarine M—regular Dell-O—over Dell-O to which .1% MSG had been added. The ratio was 68 votes for M, 38 for O, and 31 with equal preference. *Details on page 6.*

2. *Preference of all family members was consistent with the preference pattern among housewives*

When the individual preferences of each family member were reported, the pattern was essentially the same as that of housewives alone. Here is the division of preferences among 536 individual family members:

	No.	Per cent
Prefer M—regular Dell-O............	252	47.0
Prefer O—with .1% MSG............	125	23.3
Like equally—no preference..........	129	24.1
No response on preference...........	30	5.6
Total............................	536	100.0

Details on page 7.

3. *Taste and flavor reasons for preference predominate*

Reasons for preference were largely in the taste and flavor category, with the consistency of the product ranking second. *Details on page 8 and facing table.*

4. *Housewives objected to the saltiness of Dell-O with MSG added*

Housewives indicated that the margarine to which MSG was added was "too salty." The number of comments of this type was not large, but consistency in this opinion is apparent. *Details on page 9.*

5. *Spread uses accounted for nearly half of all reported*

Almost half of all uses recorded for both margarines were as a spread on bread, toast, or rolls. An additional one quarter were as seasoning on hot vegetables. *Details on page 12 and facing table.*

6. *Test margarines well liked for all uses*

For all types of uses, the test margarines were liked much more often than they were disliked. Regular Dell-O was liked in 88 per cent of all servings, while Margarine O was liked in 79 per cent of all servings.

7. *Both margarines ranked lowest in spread-use likings*

For both margarines, the uses which were not liked clustered in the high-volume spread-use category. *Details on page 12 and facing table.*

8. *Allsweet Margarine was the leading brand in test homes*

Allsweet brand margarine was the top brand in regular use in test homes, with more than three times as many user families as the No. 2 brand. (This is consistent with the brand-share position in the test area, as reported by Nielsen.) *Details on page 17.*

9. *"More like butter" major reason for brand preference*

In giving their reason for using the brand of margarine they use regularly, housewives say "it is more like butter" in the majority of cases. This point should be noted in conjunction with the brand detail in the preceding paragraph. *Details on page 18.*

10. *Dell-O most frequently mentioned unsatisfactory brand*

Ten women named Dell-O as the brand of margarine they had tried recently and not liked. That was a larger number than mentioned any other brand. *Details on page 21.*

Note that the results of the research are presented briefly and succinctly in the above summary. Note further that the headings of the summary paragraphs are designed to deliver the highlights of the research even to those who read only the headlines in the summary. In each case, the location of additional detail on a finding is indicated, to facilitate cross reference between the summary and the more detailed body of the report.

WHAT SHOULD A RESEARCH REPORT INCLUDE?

What elements should a research report include? How should those elements be organized into a unified, coherent whole which communicates the research findings clearly and completely? These are questions which the marketing research man must answer anew on every major assignment. They are important questions. That is apparent from the fact that the profit contribution which a particular piece of research makes depends, to a considerable extent, on how well the questions are answered and the findings reported.

It would be desirable to provide the beginner with an outline which could be followed in reporting research findings. Unfortunately, it is not possible to provide a "stock model" blueprint of a research report which could realistically be expected to be widely useful. The variations present in marketing research practice are far too wide for that approach to be a helpful one. Those variations are influenced by many factors. The basic marketing research techniques involved are one major source of variation. The report of research conducted by one technique is likely to be very different in content and organization from the report of research utilizing a different technique.

Thus consider five research reports. One deals with quantitative research—a national consumer survey on usage of shampoos and home permanents. One reports on the results of a product test in which two shampoos were pitted against each other. One reports on a motivational type of study on attitudes toward shampoos. One is the report, based on panel research, of brand-share trends in the shampoo field as developed by the MRCA National Consumer Panel. The fifth is a report of sectional and city-size variations in territorial sales performance of a company manufacturing shampoo. These five reports have two things in common—all are concerned, in whole or in part, with the single product class of shampoo, and all represent research in the field of marketing. Yet the content and organization of the five reports vary so widely that almost no generalizations can be formulated which apply to all five. How, then, can a suggested organization plan be offered which will cover these five, plus other even more widely varying research-reporting situations?

It is possible, however, to outline the elements which are usually present in a complex research report. It is possible to point out the importance of some of those elements, in different reporting situations. By reviewing the following list of elements and selecting as many or as few as are relevant to a particular situation, a flexible approach to research reporting is possible. The organization of the chosen elements into the most effective over-all framework depends on the nature of the research and on the skill of the research man.

Title Page

Most research reports begin with a title page. That page usually presents the title of the report, supplemented by some additional material noted below. There are a number of different ways of handling the title-selection problem. It may represent simply a description of the research. Examples: *A national consumer investigation of the carpet-sweeper market; A survey of consumer attitudes and practices in feeding dogs.* Sometimes the title of the research is selected to reflect the objectives of the research and/or to identify the questions the research was expected to answer. An example would be: *How women feel today about premiums, promotions, coupons, and contests.* Sometimes a title is chosen which is intended to be provocative, or to serve as the "keynote" of a report which goes beyond the research heavily into recommended action. Examples: *What should Pabst do in New York in 1942? A five-year plan for doubling the Armour canned-meat business.* A title of the latter type is more likely to be used when the research report is supplemented by extensive additional material in the form of recommendations, etc., which is not typically within the marketing research man's primary area of responsibility.

In addition to the title itself, the title page often contains such information as the name of the organization or client for whom the research was conducted; the name of the organization or department by whom the research was conducted; the date the research report was prepared; and various identification material such as job number, purchase-order number, and so on.

Introductory Material: Purpose, Method, and Scope of the Research

There is usually a small amount of introductory material included at the beginning of the research report. A statement of the objectives or purposes of the research is almost always included and represents an extremely important element in the report. A brief description of the methodology of the research, if required, is often included. The scope of the research, in terms of such specifics as sample size, composition and characteristics of sample, time period covered, etc., is helpful.

The statement of the objective of the research is so important an element of the introductory material because it describes the problem the research was executed to help solve. It thus provides focus for the remainder of the report.

Statement of the Organization of the Report

In the course of developing the most effective organization plan for the research report, the research man typically considers and rejects many alternative approaches. He settles on one which seems to him to be best for the material he has to present. He should communicate briefly to the reader his over-all organization plan. An understanding of the organization plan is helpful to the reader in relating parts of the report to each other and to the objectives of the research as stated in the introductory material.

A Table of Contents

To supplement the general organization-plan description, a detailed table of contents is often provided. The research man wants the research report to be *used*. It is more likely to be used effectively if readers can find, quickly and easily, any specific finding or point in which they are interested. To aid that location, the table of contents should be relatively detailed and should be presented with the interests and viewpoints of the readers of the report as a guide.

A Summary of the Research Findings

Sometimes the summary of a research report is presented at the end of the report and sometimes at the beginning. The placement of a summary at the beginning is an aid to the reader, and is often preferable. Sometimes the summary is set apart from the body of the report by the use of a different color of paper or by some other device. The summary should be as brief and succinct as possible and should be keyed or cross-indexed in such a way to facilitate reference to more detailed evidence or discussion of any particular point in the body of the research itself. The example in this chapter will illustrate.

Whether the summary should or should not present *conclusions* and *recommendations* based on the research findings depends on the particular conditions present in each case. It is highly desirable to key the summary closely to the objectives of the research. When that is done, the finding or findings of the research relevant to each aspect of the objective(s) are set forth clearly. It is generally undesirable for a research report to include recommendations which go beyond the findings of the research itself, except where such recommendations have been specifically requested and/or authorized. Where included, such recommendations should be plainly labeled as opinion or as an extension of the research. A reader should be able to draw a sharp line between the research *findings*, which are presumably and usually *factual*, and *recommendations* based on those findings, which represent essentially an *opinion*.

Whether the research report itself includes recommendations or not, it should always include a clear and complete summarization of the research findings which are relevant to decisions on future action. The research man does not formulate recommendations, in some cases, because it is not his job to do so and because some of the considerations entering into decisions on action to be taken are not known to him. That does not mean that he should not complete his primary assignment, which is to distill from the research as much specific aid for those who must formulate recommendations as possible. Analysis and interpretation should be concluded *by* the research man *for* those to whom he reports. It should not be necessary for them to supplement his efforts by additional analyses or summarization, except in rare instances.

The Body of the Research Report

This section presents in considerable detail the findings of the research. The findings are so organized as to represent a unified whole, with the relationships of various parts to each other clearly and unmistakably designated. The body of the report of course varies with the technique used. If the research is quantitative, text and tables are likely to be combined; if the research is motivational or qualitative, the material will be almost all in text form.

One note of warning to the beginner in research reporting applies to this section, and to the summary as well. The typical executive who reads a research report is likely to have somewhat limited skill and facility at drawing out of a complex, multifaceted table the significant figures and the relationships between them. It is therefore desirable, in research reporting of quantitative data, to utilize relatively simple summary tables on which the key points are unmistakably revealed as well as more detailed tables providing additional detail for those who prefer it. This is sometimes accomplished by using a detailed table on a page facing the text description of it or discussion of its highlights. Then, within the text, the key figures can be shown and their relationships discussed.

Sectional Summaries

In the reporting of a large-scale or complex research study, it is sometimes helpful to include individual summaries at the end of each major section of the research report. Again the use of different-colored paper to make the location of the summaries easy is worth considering.

Appendices and Supplementary Material

It is usually desirable to include, entirely apart from the body of the research report itself, various types of supplementary material. These may be included in a single appendix or may be presented as a series of appendices. The forms, questionnaires, etc., used in the research will often be included here. More lengthy or technical discussions of methodology, sample design, etc., are often included. Illustrative material of various types is appropriate. Thus in a report of a motivational type of study, it is not unusual to include one or two typical interviews in full, along with the analyst's comments on the significance of material revealed in the course of those interviews.

The content of the research report is very strongly influenced by the specific characteristics and requirements of the audience for whom it is intended. The time dimension of the research also exerts a significant influence on the report size and nature. Other influences on the form and nature of the report are described in the following section.

FACTORS INFLUENCING FORM AND NATURE OF REPORT

The American Marketing Association committee pointed out[7] these influences which affect the form of a research report:

1. The instructions from the authority or client may indicate purely a statistical report on the one extreme or a fully elaborated recommendation on the other.
2. The nature and complexity of the problem will certainly dictate the manner in which the report must be presented.
3. The nature and variety of readers for whom the report is intended will vitally affect its form and content. If a report on the habits of buyers and users of a product is intended for the company's salesmen, it must certainly be less formal and technical, and perhaps briefer and more fully pictorialized than if it is solely for use of the sales manager.
4. The size of the report will influence its format, binding, and even the nature of the exposition of the findings.

[7] *Preparation and Presentation of Research Report*, p. 68.

5. The number of copies to be made will determine the types of reproduction and therefore the nature of the illustrative material. Where a small number of copies is made, the use of graphics and pictorial material may be restricted because of prohibitive costs.

6. The length of the useful life of the report may influence the expenditure of money and effort that is to be invested in presentation.

The above list provides a helpful illustration of some of the types of factors which enter into and influence the research man's decision on the nature and form of the report he prepares. That list should not, however, be considered to be either complete or exhaustive. There are many other influences on the reporting decision which are constantly present. Some of those influences should be recognized in addition to those listed above.

Since this book is concerned with the practical viewpoint toward marketing research, the first such factor is the ever-present problem of the time dimension of the research. It may be repetitive to say so at this point, but in a discouragingly large proportion of cases marketing research activities are initiated with an extremely "tight" time schedule and an optimistically early completion date. There are many contingent delays which require consideration in developing a research plan and which influence the time requirement for a particular research assignment. Where a number of those contingencies materialize in the course of a single major research project—and contingencies do seem to the harried research man to exhibit an unreasonable amount of gregariousness!—the timetable which was "extremely difficult" may become "almost impossible."

The reporting step is the last in the research process. When each earlier step is accelerated to its maximum and time is still inadequate, "something's got to give," and that something is often the research report. No competent research man willingly settles for less than the best report he can prepare, yet frequently he must choose the alternative of preparing the best report he can *in the time available* or miss a vital decision deadline.

This is a serious problem, which experienced marketing research men sometimes solve in a very practical way. They concentrate their attention less on the *form* than on the *substance* of the report. That concentration is sound because it is dictated, as so many aspects of research practice are, by the relationship between the cost of the research and the profit contribution which the research is expected to make. The research is expected to develop information and/or findings which, it is confidently expected, will make profit contributions to the organization sponsoring the research. The man with responsibility for the research has as his first task the *identification* of those actionable, profit-promising contributions. His next task is to *communicate* the nature of those research findings to the individual who has responsibility for translating the research into action.

The form of his report—which may be in a memo, a single paragraph, a single page, or even a telephone conversation—is far less important than its substance. A brief, distilled summary of the research findings received by management *in time* to make a key decision may be much more valuable than the most beautifully bound and artistically illustrated report in the world, received by management too late to take effective action on the problem!

TO ILLUSTRATE OR NOT TO ILLUSTRATE . . .

The last consideration listed in the quotation from the committee report above warrants further comment. Should a report be presented in which major findings are illustrated by visual material, charts, graphs, etc.? Or should the report be primarily a detailed, written one, without benefit of graphic devices? This question depends primarily on several influences: The first is the audience to whom the report is to be delivered. The preferences of that audience (which, remember, may be a single individual!) exert a major influence on the decision. The second is the budgetary factor. Preparation of a visual presentation of research results is a relatively expensive process, especially when finished charts prepared by professional artists and show-card people are used. It is not unusual to have a single chart of moderate complexity cost $50 or more. Whether the presentation is to be illustrated by charts or other graphic devices depends to some extent on whether the situation makes it economically desirable to make the required expenditure.

The importance of the decision to which the research is expected to contribute is more likely than the useful life of the research to determine the "expenditure of money and effort that is to be invested in presentation." Who is spending the money is another influence. A speculative presentation of research findings included in the solicitation of an account of a million dollars or more by an advertising agency is likely to be developed into an attractive and well-visualized form, the high cost of such a presentation notwithstanding.

Illustrating research reports is relatively expensive. This is true whether we are referring to the translation of the entire report into charts for visual presentation or to the development of illustrative charts or illustrations to be used within the body of a report not presented orally. The offsetting fact is that graphic devices contribute tremendously to the achievement of the communication of research findings, in many cases and with many people. Well-planned charts make it possible

PROFILE OF THE MARKET FOR FROZEN FOODS

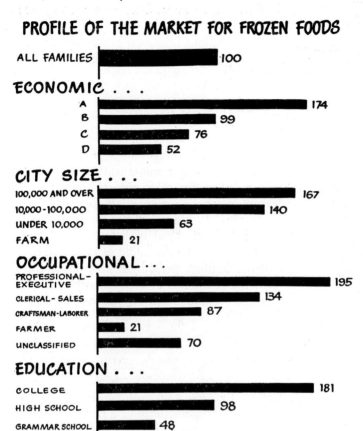

ALL FAMILIES — 100

ECONOMIC . . .
- A — 174
- B — 99
- C — 76
- D — 52

CITY SIZE . . .
- 100,000 AND OVER — 167
- 10,000 - 100,000 — 140
- UNDER 10,000 — 63
- FARM — 21

OCCUPATIONAL . . .
- PROFESSIONAL-EXECUTIVE — 195
- CLERICAL - SALES — 134
- CRAFTSMAN-LABORER — 87
- FARMER — 21
- UNCLASSIFIED — 70

EDUCATION . . .
- COLLEGE — 181
- HIGH SCHOOL — 98
- GRAMMAR SCHOOL — 48

Figure 18.1

to show relationships quickly and clearly, with a minimum amount of mental effort on the part of those to whom the report is delivered.

Consider, for example, Figure 18.1, which is from a report of a research study of frozen-food-consumption patterns. No extensive research background is required to get from that chart a clear picture of the frozen-food market (as of the time of that study) as being relatively well developed in higher-income homes, in larger cities, among professional-executive and clerical-sales occupational groups, and among those with high educational achievement.

Whether or not a marketing research man is at any particular time in a position to use visual devices extensively in developing his research reports, he should be alert to opportunities to learn as much as possible about the fundamentals of visual presentation and about sound charting procedures. Competence in translating research findings into visual form is a highly desirable skill, which an ambitious marketing research student should not overlook.

There are a number of excellent books on graphic presentation available. The listing in the appendix will guide further reading on this subject.

DANGER OF OVEREMPHASIS ON PRESENTATION

There is a danger present in the visualized research presentation which requires comment. The advantages of a graphic presentation of research findings, as an aid in the communication process, have been noted. There are some risks on the other side of that coin. Some individuals tend to interpret marketing research superficially. A polished presentation is taken as an indication that the research has been competently executed and is sound beyond question. In point of fact, the soundness of the research is quite independent of how well or poorly the report is prepared and the findings presented. To confuse the form of a fancy presentation with the substance of competently executed research is an ever-present danger. Some research, although presented in a beautifully illustrated visual form, is as phony as a Hollywood "set" of a Western town—front without substance.

A marketing research man has the specialized training required to cut through the window dressing of a "dog-and-pony-show" presentation and to examine the underlying research with a critical eye. His colleagues may be "taken in" by such a presentation of unsound, biased, or inadequate research. It is the responsibility of a marketing research man to see that no unsound conclusions based on inadequate research are made by his associates. Discharging that responsibility is sometimes difficult, sometimes embarrassing. It is not pleasant to be in a position in which one appears to be "sniping at" someone who is, at least ostensibly, a colleague in the marketing research field.

There is a tendency on the part of enlightened management to eliminate the danger of being misled by research, by adopting a very sound policy. All research to be presented to the management group must first be presented to and validated by the company marketing research staff. Only that research which is certified as sound and competent, without regard to how expensively it is "packaged," goes to the decision-making group.

SHOULD A RESEARCH REPORT INCLUDE RECOMMENDATIONS?

As earlier comments in this chapter have suggested, the question of whether or not recommendations should be included as part of a research report is a somewhat moot one. There are factors for and against the inclusion of recommendations, which we shall now examine. Further, variations in the specific type of research relationship involved influence the decision. There is a difference between the situation in which the marketing research director of a manufacturing organization is reporting on research to his superior, the marketing vice-president, and one in which an outside research organization or an advertising agency had primary responsibility for the research.

Let's first review the most important reason why the inclusion of recommendations is often considered undesirable. That reason has two facets. The first reflects the basic nature of the marketing research function, as described in Chapter 1. Marketing research is ordinarily a *staff, advisory* function. It exists to secure and supply information helpful to operating (line) executives in arriving at sound decisions. The second facet is the point made in the preceding chapter. Marketing research typically provides only part of the answer to a major marketing problem or decision. Other influences of which the research man has no knowledge often are key elements in the final management decision. Since the primary function of marketing research is to advise, and since that advice typically applies to only part of the problem area involved in a major decision, the conclusion is obvious. A marketing research man is not likely to be in a position to prepare sound recommendations as to the action to be taken, and should not do so.

Readers familiar with organization problems will recognize that the basic problem sometimes present here is common to many other line-staff relationships. The decision-making responsibility carries high status, because of its obvious importance. It is natural for some of those in a staff capacity to yearn for the right to make decisions and to trespass occasionally whether intentionally or unintentionally on the prerogatives of line executives. The danger of such a trespass occurring is present whenever recommendations formulated by a staff man are so definite and specific that, if accepted, they reduce the decision maker to the relatively routine task of executing the recommendations.

There is another side of the case. There is something to be said for including recommendations in a research report. A marketing research man has, in the course of extensive work on a complex problem, arrived at an intimate understanding of that problem. He is in a far better position to determine what should be done, in the problem area, than are most individuals who lack his intimate knowledge of the problem situation. If he fails to include in the report his considered judgments as to the desirability of alternative future courses of action, he may thereby reduce substantially the value of the research to management. As in so many controversial areas in the marketing research picture, this question of whether or not recommendations should be included must be answered: "It all depends . . ."

SUMMARY

1. This chapter deals with the preparation of research reports, one of the most important and one of the most difficult aspects of the research process.

2. As a result of the analysis and interpretation which were carried on in the preceding step, the marketing research man knows what the research revealed. The function of the reporting step is to communicate that information to others—clearly, completely, and objectively.

3. Reporting is often a weak link in the research process. This is in part a reflection of the fact that the communicating skills required for competent reporting are different skills from those which are required in the planning and execution of the research, in the opinion of some students of this problem.

4. The level of writing skill required for effective reporting of research results is easily attainable for one with a college degree or equivalent experience. What is required above all is the ability to organize thoughts and to communicate them in clear, simple language.

5. There are two major differences between a high and low degree of competence in research reporting. The highly competent research man will, first, develop a sound and carefully formulated organization framework for his report, and second, he will be sure that that framework is closely linked to the basic objectives of the research. The research man with less competence in reporting will neglect to develop a framework for a well-organized report in advance and/or will prepare a report not closely integrated with the primary objective(s) of the research.

6. The audience for whom a research report is intended is one of the most important determinants of the form and nature of the report itself.

7. Time pressure on executives today makes the summary a more important element in the total research report than it used to be.

8. Whether or not the research report should present recommendations which go beyond the findings of the research and enter into a selection of alternative courses of action depends on many factors. The responsibility of a research man to develop his report so that findings relevant to possible action are clearly presented, however, is always present.

QUESTIONS

1. What is meant by the statement: "A research report requires, as a starting point, a firm foundation"?

2. Many practicing marketing research men have not solved, or have only partially solved, the communication problem. Do you agree or disagree? Why?

3. What is the first requisite for effective report writing?

4. Some suggestions were included in this chapter to help you evaluate your own writing. What were these suggested check points?

5. What two questions should you be able to answer affirmatively if the organization of a research report is carefully planned?

6. It is said that research reports should be tailored to fit their audience. What is meant by this? How important do you feel it is?

7. Why was it not unusual in the past to have two different research reports covering the same study? What is more common today, and why?

8. What is the importance in reporting of the written summary of the research findings? What added burden does this place on the marketing research man?

9. What factors, pointed out by the American Marketing Association committee, influence the form and nature of a research report?

10. How do you feel about the question of whether or not recommendations should be included in a research report?

Major Areas of Research Application in Marketing

CHAPTER 19

Sales Forecasting

Sound management requires knowledge both of the present situation of a business enterprise and of the direction in which it is moving. As a guide to future planning, it is customary to prepare an estimate of anticipated sales volume extending into the future for six months, a year, or even a longer period. To evaluate actual sales achieved in any current time period, management then compares actual volume with the estimated or anticipated volume used in planning production schedules, cost budgets, and other commitments. An estimate of sales volume for a specific future time period is called a *sales forecast*.

Complete responsibility for or active participation in the preparation of sales forcasts represents a vital area of marketing research practice. This does not imply that all sales forecasts involve marketing research. Assume an executive "pulls out of the air" an arbitrary percentage figure by which he expects (or hopes!) next year's sales volume will increase. He uses that as the basis of his planning. His "guesstimate" is technically a sales forecast. Since it lacks the systematic, objective, and exhaustive search for the study of the relevant facts, such a forecast does not constitute marketing research as here defined.

This chapter deals with the problems involved in preparing a sales forecast and with the ways in which marketing research can help increase the accuracy of such forecasts. Sales forecasting warrants a separate chapter because it is one of the most widely performed of all marketing research activities.

GENERAL BUSINESS FORECASTS VERSUS SALES FORECASTS

It is desirable to distinguish between a *general business forecast* and a *sales forecast*. A general business forecast is usually an attempt to estimate trends in general business activity on a broad scale, as for the nation as a whole, or for a major segment, such as for all durable goods. Such forecasts are often made by economists. A sales forecast is narrower in scope, being confined to the sales expectations of an individual company or organization. It is usually developed primarily to guide management in planning future activities and in evaluating actual sales when they are achieved. General business forecasts are often one important element entering into a sales forecast.

This distinction is stressed because it is far more difficult to make a general business forecast than a sales forecast. The general business forecast is also less likely to be accurate within any given margin of error than is a sales forecast. As Arthur F. Burns commented while economic adviser to President Eisenhower, "Economists have not yet evolved, if they ever will, a technique for making dependable forecasts."[1] There are many dramatic cases of gross errors in general business forecasts prepared by economists, such as the prediction that there would be eight million unemployed in the United States shortly after V-J Day.[2] Between mid-1946 and 1953, J. A. Livingston[3] recorded forecasts by about fifty economists by means of semiannual questionnaires. He found that "Out of twelve forecasts, the economists' consensus could be graded 'right' only four times."

Past errors in forecasting general business activity have led some economists to question the soundness of economic forecasts which seek to pierce the curtain of the future. As the English economist John Jewkes commented:[4]

> A major error of economists is the belief that they can predict the future. It cannot be too strongly emphasized that there is nothing in economic science which enables us to foretell events. Those who claim otherwise are dragging their subject down to the level of astrology or some other of the many forms of divination that have, at various times, exerted their meretricious seductions. There is nothing in history to suggest that the expected will normally happen. . . .
>
> It would be unnecessary to repeat that truism were it not for the fact that economists have, in recent years, been disposed to overstep the limits of their discipline and to talk and act as if they knew enough about the future to advocate policy with confidence. The results have been unfortunate and are likely to bring the science into disrepute.

There is a natural tendency for the noneconomist to accept the forecast of an economist without sufficient recognition of the limitations and qualifications which are implicit in all such forecasts. Every general business forecast represents a "net-net" of many factors, some of which are active in one direction and some in the opposite direction. As the

[1] See "How Wrong Can Economists Be?" by J. A. Livingston, *The Management Review,* June, 1953, p. 344, (American Management Association, New York).

[2] That prediction was made by the Office of War Mobilization and Reconversion, of which Robert R. Nathan was deputy director and economist.

[3] *Op. cit.*

[4] Quoted by the late Robert P. Vanderpool, while financial editor of the *Chicago Sun-Times,* July 14, 1953.

Wall Street Journal commented, "Even the most learned of economists, trying to take every probability into account, often find that there is one they've forgotten and that it alone is sufficient to throw their calculations off badly."[5] The same article also pointed out that "there is a tendency for such often partially wishful projections to be taken by an equally wishful public as having at least some reasonable accuracy. And there is also a tendency for the majority of the soothsayers themselves to bolster each other up into a belief that, since they agree so closely, there must be a good deal of truth in what they are telling each other."

WHY FORECAST SALES?

The above comments which are intended to emphasize the inescapable hazards and risk of error present in all forecasting raise this question: If trained economists cannot accurately and consistently predict the trend of future business activity, how can anyone with less professional training hope to develop an acceptably accurate sales forecast? The answer to this question is largely one of scale. The sales forecaster operates within a far narrower field than the economist. In making a sales forecast, one is typically concerned first with the outlook for a single, individual industry, and second, with the expectations of a single, individual company within that industry. This is obviously a far simpler and less difficult problem than that faced by an economist whose concern embraces the entire national economy. Because a sales forecast ordinarily considers and is influenced by a far smaller number of forces or influences than the economist must weigh, the sales forecaster has an opportunity to make forecasts which are often relatively accurate.

This does not mean that in all company situations you can expect to prepare an accurate sales forecast, especially in the early stages of a sales-forecasting program. The point to remember is that some kind of sales forecast *must be made* to provide management with guides for future planning. Forecasts developed after a search for and study of relevant facts have proved in practice to be far more accurate than those lacking such a factual base.

INDUSTRY FORECASTS VERSUS COMPANY FORECASTS

The specific task of sales forecasting typically involves several stages. One stage involves a forecast or estimate of the trend of industry volume. Thus a manufacturer of soap or detergent products forecasting volume for the year ahead might begin by estimating total industry sales of all detergent and all soap products. A second stage is the delimitation of industry volume. This eliminates those segments of the industry

[5] "The Outlook," *Wall Street Journal,* Oct. 26, 1953.

which are irrelevant from the point of view of an individual company. Thus to a manufacturer of soap, but not of detergents, detergent volume trends would be less relevant than soap volume trends. Or if the manufacturer were interested only in industrial soap sales, rather than in the consumer market, that would influence the second stage. A manufacturer who made only conventional wringer-type washing machines and not automatic washers would be likely to estimate volume for just that portion of the industry within which he was competing. Sometimes this stage involves a restriction on a geographic basis. Such is the case with an organization operating regionally rather than nationally or with a retail organization serving a restricted geographic area.

A third stage in the forecasting process involves an estimate of company sales. This is made within the industry or subindustry trends determined in the preceding two stages. The fourth stage may involve further subdivision, as when forecasts are made for individual products or product lines. Further subdivision is also possible, as when sales to individual types of manufacturing customers are estimated in sales forecasting on industrial products or when sales within individual sales-territorial units are estimated. As subsequent discussion in this chapter will indicate, forecasting sometimes proceeds in two directions at once— down from the industry estimates and up from individual territorial or product estimates.

There are important differences in the accuracy with which forecasts can be made at the different stages mentioned. There is in particular a major difference in accuracy between industry-volume forecasts and company-volume forecasts. *It is almost always possible to make a more accurate forecast of industry volume than of company volume.* A little reflection will indicate why this is so. Within the industry's total volume, shifts are constantly occurring in individual competitive shares. An aggressive volume-expansion drive by a major competitor in an industry may depress the volume and competitive shares of all other firms in that industry. Obviously one cannot determine in advance how aggressive one or more individual competitors will be during a special future time period. The sales forecaster must work always with one large and influential variable classified as "unknown" and uncontrollable. That variable is *competition*. A significant new-product development by a competitor, or a sharply lower price by a competitor, can lead to a tremendous "error" in any sales forecast.

RESPONSIBILITY FOR SALES FORECASTING

The primary responsibility for developing a sales forecast is usually assigned to the chief marketing or sales executive. Since the marketing research man typically works for the chief marketing executive in a staff capacity, his role in sales forecasting is usually that of a specialist aiding his superior. A marketing research man is responsible to his superior for a sales forecast assigned to him. The chief marketing executive in turn typically must secure, from his superior or from an executive committee, approval of the sales forecast. It may be approved with or without modifications. Such modifications might reflect the views of the chief marketing executive himself or of any other member of the top-management group.

A sales forecast, when accepted and approved by top management and adopted for a given time period, is a vital operating tool for production and financial management, as well as for marketing management. Therefore it is not unusual for one or more representatives of those divisions of a company to participate in the sales-forecasting process. That participation may be informal. It may be confined to conversation and consultation with the marketing research man while he is working on the forecasting assignment. Or it may be formalized, as it is where a sales-forecasting committee has been set up.

The make-up of a sales-forecasting committee is likely to vary from company to company. It depends in part on the relative importance in any specific company situation of the various applications of the resulting sales forecast. In the financial division, a sales forecast is the basis of budgeting and is used for the planning of inventory levels, cash requirements, and estimates of income and disbursements. In the production division, the sales forecast is the foundation on which production schedules are built up. The production executives are likely to have an extremely keen interest in the accuracy of the forecast, since they often use it as the basis of planning production and employment on a uniform year-around basis, to iron out seasonal variations in work force, over-time requirements, etc. As the case study which follows illustrates, it is not unusual to have representatives of the production and financial divisions on a sales-forecasting committee, which is thus able to coordinate the varying views of the different divisions.

29. DODGE MANUFACTURING CORPORATION[6]

The Dodge Manufacturing Corporation, Mishawaka, Ind., makes and sells machinery and equipment to industry. Its products include equipment for the mechanical transmission of power, such as V-belt drives,

[6] This case has been adapted by permission of the author from a talk entitled "Forecasting Sales of Industrial Products" by Donald E. Gates, delivered at the National Conference of the American Marketing Association in Cincinnati, June 17, 1952.

mounted bearing applications, speed reducers, pulleys, take-ups, flexible couplings, and friction couplings. About 2 per cent of their products end up as consumer products, the other 98 per cent being bought and used as producers' durable equipment. Note that this company has no connection with any automobile firm. The Dodge Manufacturing Corporation was established in 1878 and in 1952 employed about 1,000 people.

Sales forecasting in the Dodge organization is largely the responsibility of the marketing research director, who is a member of and works closely with the company's Forecasting Committee. The committee consists of the Production Manager, the General Shop Superintendent, the Assistant Sales Manager, the Assistant Secretary and Treasurer, and the Marketing Research Director. The committee meets monthly to review a proposed monthly forecast, described below, and in special meetings as called.

One of the major functions of the Forecasting Committee is to reconcile the divergent viewpoints of the sales, manufacturing, and accounting departments and to reduce some of the conflicts of interest which naturally exist between those departments as a result of their divergent objectives. The problem at Dodge has been described as follows:

> The sales department wants immediate delivery of anything it may happen to sell. To insure this, it wants an inventory of finished goods big enough to cover any unusual order and a flexible shop which will work like mad to get out a rush job and then perhaps not have much to do. The manufacturing department wants a steady level of operation just comfortably below full capacity, without constantly having to hire and fire and scramble to meet emergencies. It agrees with the sales department that we should have a big inventory in the warehouse, but thinks that the sales department should do a better job of selling to ward off the demands for unusually quick delivery.
>
> The treasurer wants a reserve of cash in the bank to meet any and all contingencies, and hence wants a low inventory. He agrees with the sales department that the shop should be more alert and resourceful in meeting emergency delivery problems, and he agrees with the shop that a lot of these emergencies could be eliminated if the sales department would really get out and sell. Thus we have a situation where the interests of each department are opposed to those of the other two. When any two departments get together, they tend to gang up on the third one. And when all three get together, they jump on the forecasting committee.

That is right and proper, for with perfect forecasting these interdepartmental tensions could be greatly reduced.

It might be noted parenthetically that the functional viewpoints described above are found in most organizations. Those natural conflicts in objectives contribute to the ever-present need for coordination which enters into most sales-forecasting problems.

Sales forecasting at Dodge Manufacturing Corporation is difficult, because of the type of products involved. Volume of producers goods fluctuates more than production of consumers goods, and production of durable goods fluctuates more than production of nondurable goods. This point may be verified by reference to publications on business cycles by the National Bureau of Economic Research. The degree of accuracy attainable in sales forecasting in an organization in the producer's durable goods field is correspondingly less than is possible in consumer-goods forecasting. The scale of the fluctuations involved may be illustrated by considering the history of the producers durable equipment component of gross national product. That component fell from 6.4 billion dollars in 1929 to 1.8 billion dollars in 1932 and then rose to 24.9 billion dollars in 1951.

Sales of Dodge Manufacturing Corporation exhibit a similar pattern, with swings from 4 million dollars in 1929 down to less than $800,000 in 1932 and back up to 15 million dollars in 1951. Considering year-to-year fluctuation, this firm found that the average variation in billings from one year to the next over a twenty-two-year period was 28 per cent. In only three years was the variation less than 19 per cent, and those were the war years of 1942, 1943, and 1944. There were only three years when the year-to-year variation exceeded 38 per cent. Those were 1941 and 1951, when there was a transition to a defense economy, and 1932 when banks were failing. With those six abnormal years excluded, the fluctuations in the remaining 16 years were from 19 to 38 per cent, and usually were between 25 and 30 per cent. Against the background of this history, it is pointed out that a simple assumption that next year's sales will be the same as this year's sales may well be wrong by 25 to 30 per cent. In other words, cyclical trends must be considered very carefully when forecasting for a business that is subject to wide cyclical swings.

The forecasting problem is further complicated for firms like Dodge, which manufacture most of their products for stock and sell through dealers. There are fluctuations in the level of dealer inventories which influence sales volume. Those fluctuations are influenced by business outlook and by the anticipations of dealers with regard to price trends. Production must be scheduled in anticipation of sales, frequently anticipating sales by many months.

The marketing research and forecasting responsibility at Dodge is in the sales department. All the customary types of research for sales purposes are included, such as determination of territorial potentials, revision of sales-district boundaries, setting new sales quotas, and work on new-product development. In this organization, however, it is pointed out, "Our number one job is to maintain a very close and intimate relationship with the shop in scheduling production runs and controlling the overall levels of manufacturing activity."

The fact that most companies making equipment for the industrial market are relatively small in size has a strong influence on their approach to sales forecasting. They rarely have skilled economists in their employ. As Mr. Gates comments: "In the very nature of things they are forced to forecast, but whoever does it for them must probably do it on a part-time basis. He is likely to be a sort of jack-of-all-trades who knows a little about a lot of things, rather than a highly trained specialist who knows a great deal about a relatively narrow field." They do have access to consulting economists and other consulting services and can and should use these freely.

The approach to sales forecasting developed over a period of eight or nine years at Dodge involves these five steps:

> The first step is to determine what specific business functions require forecasting, and to organize our work to satisfy those needs. Secondly, we gather historical data on whatever it is we are forecasting. Practically everybody does this, whether they take any of the other steps or not. The third step is to refine the historical data statistically, correcting for seasonal variations and smoothing out random variations as much as possible. The fourth step is to apply principles of market research, to relate trends and outlooks in our own particular business and industry. The fifth step is to apply principles of economics and business cycle theory to our forecasts.

Sales forecasting at Dodge is keyed closely to the characteristics of the particular company situation. About 85 per cent of sales are of stock merchandise. More than 3,500 items are stocked. Lead times required to manufacture products vary from three to ten months, and that lead time itself varies with business conditions. The marketing research department at Dodge forecasts future sales of each of the 3,500 stock items, plus parts contained in them, considering lead time and cushions involved, and determines order points at which additional manufacturing orders should be placed. The detailed order to the production-control department come from marketing research.

The 3,500 stock items are grouped into about ninety commodity lines. Many of those commodity lines are relatively unimportant. The bulk of company sales are concentrated in about a dozen of them. In each of those lines a "sales pattern" is set up, which gives the distribution of sales, size by size, within that commodity line. The total for each sales pattern is set at some convenient figure, like 5,000 or 100,000. The sales pattern is revised once a year and is based mainly on average sales for the past three years, modified by judgment. Through the use of the commodity sales patterns, the problem is reduced to more manageable proportions. In addition, this tends to reduce the effect of random variations, a part of step 3 mentioned above.

Total unit sales are checked in each commodity line, month by month, and expressed as percentages of the base sales patterns. Based on this record of experience plus judgment as to market conditions and the economic outlook, a forecast is then set up for the product line. For example, the forecast of sales of Dual Duty Sheaves may be set at 130 per cent of the basic sales pattern. It is much more practical to expect a forecasting committee to agree on such broad goals than to ask them to review each one of the 150 sizes involved.

On a clerical basis it is then easy to translate the 130 per cent of the basic sales figure for each size into a specific forecast for that size. Also the forecasting committee may decide that the order point for that commodity line should be 35 per cent of the forecast annual volume, and again clerical extension of that decision into action is easy.

Each month the production department is notified what the desired rate of production for each of the ninety commodity lines should be for the next four months. This is determined by modifying forecasted sales by considering the company's actual warehouse-stock position on each commodity. If the warehouse stocks are considered too high on a product, the production rate set for that product would be below anticipated sales or bookings of orders, and vice versa. Thus forecasts are tied very tightly and specifically to operating procedures. When the company is "caught" with too much or too little inventory, responsibility can be pinned down. Either production failed to follow the production rate set, or the forecasting was faulty.

A number of different types of forecasts are included in the company's forecasting program. Each month a forecast is prepared and reviewed by the committee, covering changes in the commodity-line percentages, on which stock ordering is based. That forecast also includes for the next four months a forecast of dollars of gross bookings, cancellations, gross billings, and unfilled orders. It provides a comparison of actual and forecast figures for past months. Comments on general economic conditions and trends and special company and competitive conditions are included. In addition to annual forecasts, special forecasts are prepared on specific management request.

A forecast of bookings in dollars is calculated from a basic figure per working day, modified by seasonal correction factors and multiplied by the number of working days in the month. The forecast of order cancellations is based on the size of the order backlog and the phase of the business cycle. The forecast of billings depends on forecast bookings, cancellations, unfilled orders, shop capacity, and the phase of the business cycle. In boom periods when the order backlog is high and rising, billings depend largely on estimates of shop capacity. In depressed periods when the warehouse stocks are high, the billings forecast is based almost entirely on forecast gross bookings less cancellations. At other times, a combination of these considerations is used. Over a period of months when the order backlog is declining, it has been found that billings can be forecast rather accurately by taking forecast bookings less cancellations plus a fixed percentage of the backlog, but no one method has been found that will work at all times.

The forecast of billings is used by the Treasurer's Office in setting up budgets for the various shop and office departments and for projecting inventory-level changes and cash requirements. Daily average figures forecast for bookings, cancellations, and billings are incorporated into a daily progress report which permits major department heads to keep abreast of the relationship between actual performance and the forecast.

Each December the committee makes a forecast for the ensuing year used to set sales quotas. As part of the process of developing that forecast, each district manager estimates his district's volume for the coming year, both for the district as a whole and for individual major accounts. To guide him in those estimates, comparative information for past years is provided. As a general rule, district managers seem to assume that next year will be about the same as last year, except for a few particular accounts where he knows about some type of special situation. Because of the year-to-year fluctuations experienced in the past, forecasts indicating that next year will be like this year need to be modified for cyclical trends. The committee usually finds it necessary to adjust the forecasts sent in by the district manager to add up to the committee's considered opinion of what the national total should be. In setting 1951 quotas, the estimates of district managers were raised an average of 40 per cent. At the annual meeting at which quotas were distributed and discussed, some district managers complained and then went on to exceed the higher quotas by substantial margins. In setting quotas for 1952, in a period when order backlogs were declining and incoming business was at a lower rate, some of the district managers' estimates were revised downward.

Changes in dealer-inventory levels and policies are substantial influences in determining the scale of the year-to-year swings in sales. A group of thirty of the larger dealers provide a physical inventory of all Dodge items every three months. Forms for use in taking this inventory are sent out from the Dodge factory, and all calculations in summarizing the findings are done at the factory. Trends in dealer inventories are apparent from this dealer panel's reports.

EFFECTS OF BROAD PARTICIPATION IN FORECASTING

The foregoing comments about the departmental viewpoints in the Dodge case serve to underline one important advantage of the committee approach to sales forecasting. Such an approach has the effect of balancing individual departmental viewpoints and thus tends to achieve integration of the conflicting objectives of various functional executives. That result is desirable, even in situations where the forecasting process is not formalized into a committee setup. Experience has proved that it is highly desirable to achieve as broad participation as possible in the preparation of a forecast. Participation should especially include those executives who must work with the forecast after it is adopted.

One reason why that broad participation is beneficial arises as a result of functional temperament patterns. Sales executives often tend to be optimistic, while financial executives tend to be more conservative. By harnessing both tendencies to the forecasting task, the danger of excesses in either direction is reduced. There are also human-relations advantages. The fact that an executive actually participated, or was at least consulted, in the development of a forecast is likely to be helpful in getting him to accept that forecast. Much of the mental friction sometimes generated by a forecast may be avoided through even nominal participation. A knowledge of the considerations which influenced a given forecast is helpful, as is the effect of the responsibility which all who participate in the forecasting process inevitably share.

As an at least partial offset against the advantages achieved by broad participation in the forecasting process, some negative effects must also be recognized. From a review of a single company's forecasting practices, Irving Wallace noted some tendencies which are relatively widespread. He commented:[7]

> The industry divisions of the sales department of company "X" were given the responsibility of initiating the forecasts. The reason was the "common-sense" idea that the best authorities on sales should be the ones in charge of sales. The intangible nature of sales forecasting was recognized, and the job given to those who were supposedly in the best position to make informed judgments.

[7] Irving Wallace, "Individual Firm Sales Forecasting," *The Journal of Marketing*, October, 1948, p. 184.

Observation clearly showed that the resulting forecasts depended on (1) how the background of the "authority" enabled him to understand the economics of the product and industry. (2) The particular current information he happened to have digested. (3) The way his temperament and prejudices affected his evaluation. (4) The probable political effects within the company of various alternative forecast possibilities on the personal position of the forecaster and on the position of one agency vs. another.

The political effects were sometimes in one direction and sometimes in another. If an industry manager wanted more productive capacity, he sometimes purposely forecasted very high. If a checkback on performance vs. forecast was expected, he tended to forecast low to make a good showing. Or, if no checkback was expected, he tended to forecast high to make a good impression at the time of the forecast. Finally, if the general management were in a bullish or bearish mood, the division managers' forecasts usually followed suit.

In addition, sales department functionaries were obviously better suited to selling than to economic analysis. First, they simply did not know how to go about it. And second, the enthusiasm necessary for successful selling carried over into their forecasting and yielded a constant optimistic bias.

TWO TYPES OF SALES-FORECASTING SITUATIONS

Marketing research men participate in two different types of sales-forecasting situations. This classification base is very similar to the division of all marketing problems into those of a current operating type and those of a nonrecurring type, described in Chapter 3. One sales-forecasting situation is relatively routine. It occurs when a marketing research man who is working in a company finds that sales forecasting represents just one of the current operating problems which his boss faces and finds himself working on a sales-forecasting assignment as a relatively routine part of his job. The other situation is one in which it appears that there may be a sales forecasting *element* in a nonrecurring problem.

The Dodge Manufacturing Company case described above illustrates a routine sales-forecasting situation in which the preparation of a sales forecast represents part of the normal job content of a marketing research man. The Kessler Syrup Company case which follows provides an example of a marketing problem in which sales forecasting is a key element.

30. KESSLER SYRUP COMPANY ★ (A)

The Kessler Syrup Company was a small, family-owned concern located in a medium-sized city in a Middle Western state. The company bottled and marketed under its own Arco label a line of corn syrups generally similar to and competitive to those sold nationally under the Karo label. The company's operations were regional, confined to a group of Middle Western states roughly circular in shape with the company's headquarters town as the hub of the circular area.

In the six years prior to the entry of the United States into World War II, national consumption of "mixed syrup"—the basic commodity designation—was estimated to be at a level of about 250 million pounds annually. In the wartime years from 1942 onward, sugar was rationed and syrup consumption increased sharply as a result. While the expansion in syrup volume was strongly stimulated by the shortage of sugar, there were other factors in the wartime picture which also pushed consumption higher. There were, for example, wartime increases in home canning, in much of which syrup was used. There were also increases in the scale of home freezing, especially by farmers, which were also contributing factors. In the years from 1942 through 1947, syrup consumption was at an annual rate of about 467 million pounds.

Sugar rationing ended in the summer of 1947. Syrup volume which represented demand diverted from sugar vanished almost immediately. Consumers had at that time rather large stocks of hoarded sugar and other sweetenings. The decline in factory shipments of syrup precipitated by the end of sugar rationing was sharp and immediate. Kessler Company's sales of syrup dropped almost to the vanishing point.

As company executives reviewed the very low level of syrup sales which the company had achieved during the first six months of 1948, they recognized that they faced a most serious marketing problem. The very survival of the company was at stake. The company executives strongly suspected that their own sales volume was reduced more than that of their industry. If that suspicion was correct, it meant that the Arco brand had lost competitive position rapidly during the first half of 1948.

As with many relatively small companies, Kessler had a rather lean executive group. They were notably lacking in marketing experience. The president of the company had been trained primarily in financial management rather than in marketing. He decided to call on a consulting organization to aid in dealing with the marketing problem the company faced. A firm specializing in marketing activities was called in and asked to appraise the company's situation. The consulting firm was asked to recommend a course of action which might be expected to reverse the company's declining sales curve and expand its market share.

As a starting point in the analysis of the Kessler problem, the principal of the consulting firm who was primarily responsible for work on the assignment sought facts about the size of the total market. One of the questions he wanted answered concerned the size of the total consumer market and the trend in total consumption. It was known that volume had increased sharply while sugar was rationed. But what had the *trend* of consumption been in prewar years *before* rationing? Was this a growing, declining or static industry?

Thinking of the decline in manufacturers' sales which had occurred when rationing ended, there was a question as to whether that drop reflected shrinkage in consumer purchases and to what extent. It seemed

Table 19.1. Syrup-consumption Trend 1927–1947

(Industry Volume of Factory Shipments)

Year	Industry sales, lb. (000 omitted)	No. of families in the U.S. (000 omitted)
1927	244,313	29,270
1928	265,021	29,390
1929	241,119	29,456
1930	250,783	29,905
1931	201,062	30,427
1932	175,347	30,949
1933	231,638	31,471
1934	228,685	31,993
1935	218,712	32,515
1936	294,589	33,037
1937	212,228	33,559
1938	230,372	34,081
1939	268,034	34,603
1940	240,869	35,125
1941	248,283	35,850
1942	468,088	36,450
1943	458,587	36,875
1944	453,290	37,100
1945	469,475	37,500
1946	435,955	38,175
1947	519,695	39,100

likely that some inventory reduction by wholesalers and retailers might have contributed to a more drastic decline in factory than in consumer purchases. How long was it likely to take for the adjustment to "work off"? What consumption trend could be expected thereafter?

The problem of estimating the future volume of syrup consumption was of course a sales-forecasting problem, although at the industry rather than the company level. There was this further overlap between the

Kessler problem and ordinary sales-forecasting procedures: The basic data required to help diagnose the Kessler problem were essentially the same information which any marketing research man would have to gather in the early stages of work on any new sales-forecasting program in the consumer-goods field.

Table 19.1 shows basic data which permitted examination of the trend of syrup consumption both prewar and during World War II. Because the increase in the number of families in the country is likely to be an element in that consumption trend, the number of families in each year is also shown on that table. The figures shown reflect consumption of *corn syrup* only.

To determine what was happening to *consumer purchases* of syrup, especially in the period after sugar rationing had ended, the consultant

Table 19.2. Consumer Purchases of All Syrups, Lbs.

(000 Omitted)

Months covered	1946–1947	1947–1948
April–May	97,058	112,244
June–July	84,016	73,672
August–September	94,691	61,562
October–November	114,611	73,253
December–January	114,049	79,089
February–March	121,794	75,388

SOURCE: Nielsen Food Index of the A. C. Nielsen Company.

went to the A. C. Nielsen Company for information developed from the Nielsen Food Index, through the store-audit technique described in Chapter 9. Because the Kessler organization was a small-volume regional manufacturer, purchase of the full Nielsen Food Index service was not economically feasible. After some negotiation, arrangements were worked out which made available to the consulting organization on Kessler's behalf a limited amount of basic data about the size of the market for syrup as developed by Nielson. Table 19.2 shows the figures on consumer purchases of all syrups, as shown in the Nielsen data for twelve bimonthly periods. Note that "all syrups"—the Nielsen classification—includes other types in addition to corn syrups, such as maple syrups and blended syrups made from maple and cane sugars. The figures in Table 19.2 are therefore not directly comparable to those shown in Table 19.1.

In addition to the annual totals of factory shipments of corn syrup as shown in Table 19.1, figures for four individual months of 1948 were available from association sources. Those figures are shown in Table 19.3.

Table 19.3. Factory Shipments of Corn Syrup, Lb.

January, 1948............ 22,498,000
February, 1948.......... 20,647,000
March, 1948............. 22,713,000
April, 1948.............. 19,561,000

From figures provided by the three tables shown, it was possible to develop estimates of industry volume on corn syrup using three different and independent approaches:

1. From the data on prewar and wartime consumption levels, any trend in consumption could be determined. By making certain assumptions about the postwar consumption pattern and the relationship between prewar and postwar consumption, the volume level at which that consumption was likely to level off could be estimated.

2. The Nielsen data provided an indication of consumer-purchase trends. There was a sharp seasonal pattern present. The significant comparisons were those comparing the same bimonthly period in the two twelve-month periods, to establish the scale and direction of changes in volume.

3. From the data for the first four months of 1948, the approximate level of total 1948 volume could be projected. There was an absence of comparable past data on the seasonal pattern of factory shipments in a "normal" year. That would necessarily introduce some error into that approach. It was still possible to develop an approximate volume estimate from the data given.

Comment: When the available data make it possible to prepare two or more forecasts independent of each other, as in this case, the practical approach is to develop those forecasts and then to compare the indicated volume levels. As a general rule, a high degree of consistency between answers developed in quite different ways may be interpreted as a basis for increased confidence in the figures which are closely clustered. It is extremely important, however, to be sure that the data are in fact unrelated and the estimates actually independent. The existence of a single factor, causally common to all approaches, may lead to spurious correlation and a meaningless but misleading consistency. The earlier *Wall Street Journal* quotation points out the danger that consistency may be mistakenly interpreted as accuracy.

Now moving from the industry to the company level, historical factory-shipment figures for the years from 1927 through 1947 are shown in Table 19.4. Those figures are comparable to and are included within the industry figures presented in Table 19.1. For the first four months of 1948, Kessler sales were 1,712,720 pounds.

Table 19.4. Kessler Syrup Sales Trend, 1927–1947

(Factory Shipments)

Year	Sales, lb. (000 omitted)	Year	Sales, lb. (000 omitted)
1927	20,178	1939	11,253
1928	21,315	1940	10,537
1929	18,395	1941	11,053
1930	19,368	1942	18,680
1931	11,705	1943	18,069
1932	8,966	1944	18,642
1933	12,821	1945	21,951
1934	10,435	1946	24,182
1935	10,823	1947	28,540
1936	14,465		
1937	8,817		
1938	7,957		

The figures given made it possible to develop a forecast of 1948 volume both for the industry and for the company which could then be used as a workable base for developing future marketing plans.

— ★ —

STEPS IN SALES FORECASTING

The sales-forecasting problems to which a marketing research man is exposed are likely to have two characteristics: Each situation has some elements of uniqueness. But every sales-forecasting problem is likely also to include a number of elements common to most other sales-forecasting situations. The following comments have been prepared in the form of a step-by-step approach to sales forecasting, distilled from experience in a wide variety of different sales-forecasting situations. This step-by-step approach may seem to some readers like oversimplification. To others it is more likely to represent a helpful guide through the common elements of the sales-forecasting problems. It will thus enable them to conserve time and effort for the study and analysis of the vitally important elements unique to each specific sales-forecasting assignment.

Step 1. *Determine the Purposes for Which the Forecast Is Intended*

The purposes for which a forecast will be used influence the nature of that forecast. In many cases, they help to determine how detailed that forecast must be. The first way in which the objectives of the forecast influence the forecast itself is in the profit dimension of the problem it represents. That profit dimension of course largely determines the amount of time and expense the research man can afford to devote to the preparation of the forecast. The purpose for which the forecast is intended influences the amount of detail required in many instances, and the amount of detail in turn has a bearing on the time required to prepare a forecast.

A forecast which is intended to serve as a basic guide to management in estimating anticipated income and expenses in the year ahead for a company making cake mixes might well be confined to an estimate of total unit or case volume. However, if the forecast were to be used to guide the allocation of advertising emphasis between flavors, more detailed attention to trends in the relative importance of different individual flavors might be necessary. The objectives of a forecast also influence its form. Thus one for the guidance of the production division might be concerned primarily with physical volume, while one used by the financial division would almost certainly be on a dollar basis.

Sometimes the purpose for which a forecast is prepared will influence its magnitude. It is not unusual to find a company using one sales forecast as the basis of its sales quotas, and another—usually lower and hence more conservative—as the basis of its expense budgets, even within the sales division.

Again the purposes of a forecast influence emphasis devoted to different aspects of the forecast. If the forecast were to be used primarily as the basis for equalizing production the year around, while minimizing inventory accumulation prior to seasonal peaks in factory shipments, detailed attention to seasonal accuracy might be extremely important and worth the time it required. Or if the forecast involved trends in the importance of different areas of the country, because it was intended to guide construction of one or more individual warehouses, the forecaster might have to devote far more time to analysis of data on sectional trends than would be otherwise necessary.

In essence, the above comments underline this important fact: The preparation of a sales forecast by a marketing research man involves marketing research . . . with a definition of the problem as the first step, as in most marketing research. Where sales forecasting is concerned, it is especially important that the definition of a sales-forecasting problem should reveal the purposes for which a forecast is intended.

Step 2. *Subdivide the Forecasting Task*

A sales forecast, like any other type of sales statistic, represents a net-net figure in which the effect of various offsetting smaller figures is intermixed. Consider the case of a company making only two products, which

were equal in volume. A sales forecast for such a company might anticipate a 10 per cent sales-volume increase. Such a sales forecast could
prove precisely accurate if both products increased by 10 per cent, or if
one increased by 20 per cent while the other showed no change in volume, or if any of many other possible combinations of individual-product
trends occurred.

The sales forecaster in such a situation must ordinarily develop his
forecast in detail. He must estimate the rate of anticipated increase in
each product individually. The total estimated rate of increase is arrived
at by combining the individual-product forecasts. Even further detail is
often required, as in the common consumer-product case where a product is sold in two or more package sizes. It is not enough to estimate total
volume. Individual estimates for each package size must be made available or the purchasing department cannot determine how many containers or shipping cartons of each size to buy, nor can production prepare
its detailed schedules.

Most companies manufacture more than one product. The Dodge situation described above in which 3,000 products are stocked is unusual
but by no means unique, especially in industrial marketing. In subdividing the forecasting task where the number of products in question is
large, it is common practice to work toward a manageable number of
relatively homogenous groups of products. Again the Dodge case above
is illustrative, with products grouped into ninety commodity lines. The
process of grouping products for sales-forecasting purposes is sometimes
very similar to the grouping which precedes sales analysis of other types.
The discussion of grouping in Chapter 6 is relevant to the forecasting
grouping problem in many instances.

In successful sales forecasting, great flexibility in thought and approach
is required. For example, the research man should avoid the temptation
to make a single forecast for a group of products simply because that
group is used as an entity in analyzing territorial sales performance. A
building-product manufacturer divided products into groups on the
basis of the general ingredient type—all gypsum products together, etc.
Where some of those products within a group are sold through different
types of distribution channels than others, or are destined for distinctly
different end-use markets, the forecaster may well choose to subdivide
the group for forecasting purposes. That would make it possible to consider the anticipated trend in each end-use group. There may be situations in which the sales outlook for the group as a whole is not favorable
but that for one or more components of the group is extremely bright.

The latter situation was illustrated in the period following the post-
Korean War inventory build-up on television sets. Trade inventories at
wholesale and retail levels on combination sets (which combined tele-

vision with a radio and record player in a large cabinet at a high price) were extremely high. Inventories of lower-priced table-model TV receivers were substantially lower. That particular trade-inventory situation developed at a time when there was a sharp consumer trend away from combinations toward table models. That trend made the trade-inventory situation even more unbalanced, when it was translated into "months' supply" terms. In many cases a trend of the type described is related to a shift in price or price-line importance within the industry.

Step 3. *Prepare a Preliminary Sales Forecast*

A sales-forecasting program is often a progressively developing element in marketing management. The first efforts to formalize the forecasting process are typically relatively crude and slipshod, especially when viewed through the hindsight which a continually refined program makes possible. The first attempt to introduce a substantial reliance on facts into a forecasting program is often extremely time-consuming and difficult. This is true in part because of the time required to delve into historical data in great detail. That delving typically develops basic facts about industry trends which continue to be useful in future forecasts long after the pain costs of gathering them have been forgotten.

In the preparation of an initial sales forecast, one is concerned with company and industry sales volume and past trends. But the process of gathering the fundamental facts relevant to a sales-forecasting *program* (as distinguished from a single nonrecurring problem of the forecasting type) does not stop there. An attempt is often made to determine the factors which have influenced past sales and to establish the relationship between such factors and actual sales.

This type of analysis often involves correlation and other statistical techniques, often of an advanced type which requires that the non-specialist research man call on specialized assistance. The use of statistical techniques as forecasting tools is touched on briefly below. The time dimension within which the research man is working will often be the key determinant of the amount of analysis which will precede the initial forecast.

What is especially important in the preparation of an initial sales forecast is the detailed and careful scrutiny of all underlying assumptions. Such assumptions are often so widely held within a company or an industry that they represent corporate prejudices or industry blind spots.

One of the values of securing an outside point of view in the forecasting process is the reduced risk of being misled by such questionable verities. Two cases presented in this book illustrate that point. In the Dell-O case, the decline in butter prices was one "explanation" of the decline in the company's margarine sales. In the Shower-of-Stars case, the viewpoint that industry volume was declining was widely held in the company. Both hypotheses were proved false by objective research. Both cases illustrate the need for facts about the trend of industry volume, to which subject we shall return in the next chapter.

Step 4. *Relate the Forecast to Advertising, Selling, and Promotional Plans*

After a preliminary sales forecast has been developed, it should be carefully reviewed in the light of the company's advertising, selling, and other promotional plans. Those who work with sales statistics and particularly with trend data sometimes tend to overlook the influence on such trends of positive past actions. There is a need to integrate a forecast of future sales volume with the specific plans which have been developed to achieve that volume.

A planned promotional drive on a particular product will of course influence the sales level achieved on that product. A specific example is illustrative. The makers of Johnson's wax had purchased 5 million appliers and intended to offer those appliers as an in-store premium, free with each quart of Glo-Coat. The sales campaign of the six-month period was built heavily around that promotion. Note that both quart-volume and pint-volume forecasts would be likely to be influenced by the promotion. Quart volume would be increased, as the premium stimulated demand; and pint volume would be depressed as some pint purchasers were stepped up to the larger package size.

Changes in promotional pressure resulting from planned changes in the size of the sales force, or in major modifications in sales-coverage policies to permit the same number of salesmen to cover a larger number of customers and potential customers, are other examples of types of promotional influences on a forecast which must be considered. Not all such promotional-plan modifications are in a positive direction. A company with a single established television program had to modify its sales expectations downward to give effect to the television competition which the conversion of many single-station markets to multiple-station coverage created. Reductions in the advertising appropriation, in the planned advertising weight per unit of volume, or in a company's share of the total industry's advertising expenditures might similarly exert a downward pressure on a sales forecast.

In addition to the effect of planned promotion, the level of sales volume attainable may be influenced by other factors. There might be a production problem, reflecting an existing or anticipated shortage of some ingredient (such as of cans during a strike) or reflecting the limiting influence of machinery or manpower on production goals. Or there may be a financial problem involved, which would require the integration of divisional viewpoints.

Step 5. *Review Competitive Activities and Trends*

In addition to the effect upon sales volume of a company's own promotional plans, the actual or possible actions of major competitors must be taken into consideration. Trends in competitive share of market as reported by the Nielsen or MRCA services provide one clue for the companies using the services of those organizations. Various publicity releases in business publications often provide valuable indications of competitive plans. Such releases may involve test-market activities, which often precede expanded competitive promotion. For example, the news that a company whose previous advertising expenditures had been at a $750,000 annual rate had contracted to purchase a television program involving an annual commitment of $1,500,000 alerted competitors to the imminence of an intensified drive for expanded competitive position by that company.

Step 6. *Review and Revise in the Light of Experience*

A periodic and planned review of the sales forecast, both in retrospect for the full period covered and progressively during the period itself, is a key element in most sales-forecasting programs. The detailed and analytical review of the scale and nature of variations between estimated and actual volume, for each time period covered by the forecast, is standard operating procedure. Such a review provides clues to past errors in forecasting and thus helps increase the accuracy of future forecasts. Once standards have been set, the continuing comparison of actual volume with planned-for volume, territory by territory and product by product, can be handled on a routine clerical basis with a minimum amount of executive time.

STATISTICAL TECHNIQUES AS FORECASTING TOOLS

In their preparation of estimates of the future course of business activity in general, or of a major segment of that activity, economists often use relatively advanced mathematical and statistical techniques. Development of digital computers has stimulated the use of such techniques. The use of such techniques and the interpretation of the results often require mathematical and statistical training far beyond that of a typical marketing research man. As a consequence, the role of statistics in practical sales forecasting has tended to be a relatively minor one. Often that role has been confined to the use of rather elementary statistical approaches.

Mr. Gates's comment above provides perspective on this point. The Dodge Manufacturing Corporation, with its 1,000 employees, is a relatively large business enterprise. The fact that such an organization, in Mr. Gates's words, "relies on a jack-of-all-trades who knows a little about a lot of things, rather than a highly trained specialist who knows a great deal about a relatively narrow field" is helpful in understanding the practices of a vast number of smaller organizations.

A number of books about forecasting as a business management tool are available. Such books often try to make more widely available the techniques and approaches, often heavily statistical, which the authors have found useful in forcasting. Those books are typically not confined to *sales* forecasting. Some of them pay very slight attention to the subject of sales forecasting. The statistical techniques involved are sometimes useful in sales forecasting, however. The reader interested in more statistical approaches to forecasting may find the references in the Appendix helpful.

More extensive reliance on statistical approaches to forecasting is sometimes found in larger organizations. There it is one symptom of the advanced functional specialization characteristic of large-scale operations. In such situations a skilled economist is often available, either as a full-time member of the staff or on a consulting basis. Smaller organizations sometimes achieve much the same result by utilizing the skills and facilities of consulting services. Some consultants specialize in the analysis of relationships between economic forces and trends and the consumption of products of a specific industry or group of industries. For a moderate fee, such specialized organizations provide a generalized economic-analysis service to many companies that could not individually afford the full cost of such a service. Clients of such specialized organizations can often secure analyses focused more directly on their own specific problems, as an extension of the basic service. There is a trend toward the development of more and more skillful agencies specializing in economic aspects of forecasting. With the services thus made more available for moderate fees, an increase in the extent to which future sales forecasts are based on and use advanced statistical techniques is likely.

INTEGRATING DIFFERENT APPROACHES

The following description of a sales-forecasting program that has been developed over a period of years illustrates how one organization combines different sales forecasting approaches.

31. S. K. F. INDUSTRIES, INC.[8]

District sales managers, the "home office" and a commercial research staff mesh gears about the end of October to turn out an efficient and reasonably accurate sales forecast for SKF management. By January 1, the forecast is ready for executive action.

SKF must plan ahead from four to nine months. Unless the planning is fairly accurate, it runs into inventory or production problems.

Without a sound, dependable forecast the company would have to be unhumanly fast on its feet, ready at a moment's notice to speed up production cycles, or else be prepared to carry an expensive inventory. The system has evolved into an organization which in effect tests three types of forecasts against each other before coming up with a final, composite estimate. During the process of justifying, reconciling and defending, most of the kinks are ironed out.

An important figure in the SKF landscape is their sales manager. . . . The three streams of material initially flow to him and through him to the vice-president in charge of sales. In the forecasting area, however, the sales manager is more than an animated traffic light. His function is one of preliminary analysis. Each of the three forecasts must be checked for internal logic. In other words, he tries to ascertain whether or not the basic assumptions are probable—in forecasting, few experts ask more than this.

After analyzing the individual estimates, the sales manager usually proposes a single sales figure. This, as well as the original three, goes to the sales vice-president who makes an equally extensive check and re-vises before the forecast becomes official.

Behind the final estimate lies a chain of conferences with the sources of the original forecasts—Home Office Sales, District Sales Managers and Commercial Research. Because each department has a different point of view, reconciling the three is a vital and sometimes delicate step. For example, the Commercial Research staff prepares its forecasts on the basis of general and often aggregative material such as projections of the FRB production index of durable goods. On the other hand, the district managers receive and combine estimates from the sales force which are based on actual contacts with salesmen's clients. Because the approaches are so different, the final estimates are bound to differ.

SKF's management puts it this way: One forecast may assume that a customer industry is about to liquidate inventory and another fore-cast may assume steady purchases. Or the Sales Department may assume that the company will gain a larger percentage share of the market than

[8] Reproduced by permission from *Dun's Review and Modern Industry*, August, 1953, p. 44.

the analysts in Commercial Research think probable. Or the sales specialists may know that sales of a particular product will boom because a number of major potential customers are about to become actual buyers. But back in Home Office Sales, people preparing their forecast may be unaware of that new bloc of customers.

All of these differences in approach and background knowledge are taken into account and smoothed out in conference among the sales vice-president and the department managers responsible for the individual forecasts before the final estimate is formed.

Here's how the individual forecasts shape up:

Sales forecasts by District Managers: From their salesmen, the managers receive an estimate in terms of major accounts and sometimes by major product lines as well. The salesmen pick up this material quite informally from contacts with their customers.

The final district figures are an amalgam of what the clients say they expect and what the district manager, on the basis of past experience, thinks will happen. Managers ask for considerable detail from the salesmen, but what actually comes into the office depends, naturally enough, both on the salesman and his client.

Forecast by Home Office Sales: This area includes the six departments on the diagram, each of which forecasts total SKF sales by industry.

Industry specialists in Home Office Sales are pretty much in the middle between the statistical analysts in Commercial Research and the ear-to-the-ground techniques used in the district estimates. They are in close contact with district managers. They use many of the services of Commercial Research. And they have at their fingertips industry production, inventory and backlog data. In addition, they pay close attention to industrial information in the trade press.

Commercial Research forecasts: Two preliminary forecasts furnish the grist for the final estimates. One is a projection of general business conditions and the translation of this into an estimate of total antifriction bearing industry sales, together with an estimate of total SKF sales; and the other, a projection of conditions in major industries to whom the company sells and a summation of the resultant sales by industry.

These two groups are compared and reconciled within the department. Then they are converted into estimates by territory.

Every available source is combed to make the sales picture as complete as possible. Government is a major supplier of data. Trade associations furnish valuable new order and backlog material. Industry contacts fill in many gaps when material is not available in published form.

The company's economist belongs to most of the national professional groups, attends the sessions and does a lot of talking and "data trading" with his counterparts in other companies. Out of these meetings comes a residual "feel" which is invaluable as a balance for the statistical projections.

— ★ —

TIME PERIOD COVERED BY A FORECAST

What time period should a sales forecast cover? The optimum time period will vary from company to company. It depends in part on the length of the manufacturing cycle. The forecasts with which marketing research men are concerned are usually short-term rather than long-term in nature. That is, they typically cover time periods ranging from six months to a year. Occasionally they range upward to cover a two-year or three-year period. The time period most frequently covered by a sales forecast is a single year.

It should be noted that the time period covered by a forecast is often on a rolling basis, periodically revised and extended. Thus a one-year forecast for a given calendar year might be reviewed at the end of the first quarter of that year. As a result of the review, the forecast for the remaining three quarters of the original year might be revised in the light of experience and existing conditions. That forecast might be increased to a twelve-month one by adding a forecast for the first quarter of the following year. A company operating on such a basis has available an estimate of the volume in each calendar year which usually becomes progressively more accurate as it moves from a complete estimate to a combination of one quarters' actual experience, plus three quarters' forecast experience, and so on. In addition, there is available a forecast for at least three future quarters at any given time, providing management with an indication of expectations for a year ahead including the current quarter, at any time.

In any case, the review and revision of forecasts in the light of experience as the company progresses through the period covered provide insurance against too wide a gap between the forecast and actual volume.

HOW ACCURATE SHOULD A SALES FORECAST BE?

The answer will also vary from industry to industry and from firm to firm within an industry. Accurate forecasting is relatively easy for companies that are in stable industries. Utilities and many types of consumer products are examples. It is much more difficult where year-to-year swings like those described in the Dodge case are common. The accuracy which can be achieved depends in part on the extent to which company volume or industry volume is independent of or closely linked to changes in the level of general business activity. As a rough rule of thumb, it is of interest to note that participants in an American Management Association seminar on sales forecasting, representing eighteen different companies in as many industries, agreed that a sales forecast which was within 10 per cent above or below actual volume generally represented a successful and acceptably accurate forecast.

The accuracy of a company's forecast is likely to increase with that company's experience in forecasting sales. A continuing program under constant guidance can almost always achieve increasingly accurate forecasts, as sources of error in earlier forecasts are located and precautions taken to guard against repetition of past oversights.

WHY DO FORECASTS GO WRONG?

This brief discussion of sales forecasting should not be taken to mean that accurate forecasting is easy. Some sales forecasts, carefully prepared by competent and experienced people, are far wide of the mark. A case in point was a forecast by the marketing research director of an appliance firm. It was within five percentage points of predicting *industry* volume, but overestimated *company* sales volume by more than 45 per cent! That failure occurred because the forecaster failed to take into consideration announced and known plans of some competitors to increase production and promotion of the products made by the company. *Underrating competition* is a relatively common business error and is an important contributing cause in many poor forecasts. This sometimes involves failure to take into consideration the status of the industry and of the company's products in the industry and to give sufficient weight to the potential impact of competitive new-product innovations or promotional activities.

Changes in pricing, especially by competitors, frequently distort a company's sales-volume expectations to an extent that makes a forecast grossly inaccurate. In the pricing area, the depressing effect of an increase on volume expectations, or the volume stimulation produced by a price reduction, should be mentioned. *Shifts in consumer preferences* sometimes leave forecasters' estimates of volume high and dry. The shift in consumer preference to automobiles of the hard-top variety in the higher-priced models within the so-called low-priced segment of the automobile market is an illustration.

Intra-industry competition is another influence which should be considered when an attempt is made to reduce the error in forecasting. When automobile manufacturers in 1955 moved into an all-out battle for volume, their promotional efforts diverted consumer purchasing power to automobiles and away from other products such as color-television sets. A forecast of TV-set sales expectations which failed to consider such factors would be likely to err on the high side. *Nonrecurring demand and its saturation* may expand the errors present in forecasts where it is a factor. In the years after World War II, for example, the demand for durable goods such as appliances was made up of two components—normal demand, plus backlog of deferred (and nonrecurring) demand created by wartime shortages. In making sales forecasts, an estimate of the size of each of those components and of progress in liquidating the nonrecurring part of total demand kept forecasts of many firms relatively close to actual volume. Other organizations which failed to take that factor into consideration had to make radical revisions in forecasts.

Perhaps the single most important source of error in sales forecasting is failure to integrate the sales forecast with plans for achieving it. Until it is implemented by specific and detailed marketing plans, a sales forecast remains primarily someone's hope. Only when it is backed up by specific and detailed plans for achieving the volume estimate, coupled with a timetable for executing those plans, does a sales forecast become an attainable goal and a useful tool of marketing management.

SUMMARY

1. Sales forecasting represents an extremely important area of marketing research practice. To perhaps a greater extent than almost any other area, the sales-forecasting approach of an individual company is likely to reflect the individual characteristics of a company's business and to have elements of uniqueness represent a large proportion of the total activity.

2. It is important to distinguish between a forecast of general business activity, which might be prepared by an economist concerned with the entire economy, and a sales forecast prepared (usually) in whole or in part by a marketing research man. The sales forecast is usually restricted to a consideration of sales prospects for a single industry, or a major part of that industry, and for a single company within that industry. It is the relatively narrower scope of the sales-forecaster's concern which permits him to achieve, in many cases, greater accuracy than is possible in general business forecasts.

3. A multistage approach in sales forecasting is usual. The first stage involves an estimate of the outlook for the industry as a whole; the second for those segments of the industry within which the company is active; and the third for the company's own sales volume.

4. It is almost always possible to prepare a more accurate forecast of industry volume than of company volume. The explanation of this fact lies in the important influence of competitive activities, which may distort individual

competitive shares within an industry but which rarely influence materially the volume of the industry as a whole except in unusual cases.

5. Broad participation in the sales-forecasting process is highly desirable and has much to recommend it. A trend toward greater participation in forecasting is apparent.

6. A series of steps which can be followed in the preparation of sales forecasts are presented in this chapter. Those steps present a useful guide in initial sales-forecasting efforts.

7. It is extremely important for a marketing research man to view a sales forecast in realistic terms. So long as the forecast represents simply a series of numbers recorded on paper, it is accurately described primarily as someone's *hope* for future sales volume. *It is only when the forecast is carefully integrated with plans made to achieve the forecast volume that it becomes a management tool of practical and useful value.*

8. Increasing use of statistical techniques in sales forecasting, made possible by such data-processing developments as the electronic computers, is indicated for the near-term future.

9. The accuracy of a sales forecast varies widely with the stability or volatility of industry volume. Increased accuracy as a sales-forecasting program continues in effect over a period of years is a typical pattern.

10. A number of sources of error in sales forecasts, listed here, may be helpful as a precautionary check against the possibility that a major factor has been overlooked or underestimated.

QUESTIONS

1. How would you define a *sales forecast?* Why does sound management require sales forecasting?

2. What is the difference between a general business forecast and a sales forecast?

3. What is the multistage approach to sales forecasting described in this chapter?

4. It is almost always possible to make a more accurate forecast of industry volume than of company volume. Why?

5. Why is broad participation in the sales-forecasting process highly desirable and recommended? What are the advantages of broad participation in forecasting? Can you think of any limitations?

6. A series of steps was included in this chapter as a useful guide in initial sales-forecasting efforts. What were these steps? Discuss each briefly.

7. When does a sales forecast truly become a management tool of practical and useful value?

8. What time period should a sales forecast cover? What is meant when the time period covered by the sales forecast is on a "rolling basis"?

9. How accurate do you feel a sales forecast should be? What pitfalls or sources of error are there that could cause a sales forecast to go wide of its mark?

CHAPTER 20

Determining the Size and Characteristics of the Market for a Product

Of the thirty-seven marketing-research activities included in the questionnaire used in the American Management Association's survey of *Company Practices in Marketing Research,* there was one which was more widely performed than any other. The survey disclosed that that activity was performed by almost all—93.5 per cent—of the companies that do marketing research. That widely performed activity was listed in the AMA questionnaire as *studies of the competitive position of company's products (market share analyses, etc.).* In addition to the fact that it is widely performed, this activity merits attention because it is considered to be one of the most important of all marketing research activities. Only one of the thirty-seven activities in the AMA study was rated as *most important* by a larger number of participating companies.

It is with that extremely important area of marketing research practice that this chapter deals.

Another closely related activity included in the AMA questionnaire also proved to be widely performed: *analysis of the characteristics of the market for specific product.* A somewhat smaller proportion of companies in the AMA survey (75.6 per cent, versus the 93.5 per cent studying competitive position) reported performing that activity. That activity is also discussed in this chapter.

The two activities are combined into a single chapter because they are so closely related in marketing research practice. You want to know how big the market is, so that you can determine what your company's share is. But you want to know that share in specific rather than general terms. Your national market share is 20 per cent? Fine—but what is your share in the East, South, Middle West, and Pacific regions? What is your share in big cities, medium-sized cities, small towns, and on farms? What is your share among families with children as against families without children? How does that share vary with the age of children? In order to answer questions like these, you need to do two things: first, determine the characteristics of the market for your product, and second, determine your market share within market segments.

It should be stressed that the need for detailed information about market characteristics is not confined to consumer-product marketing. In industrial marketing, too, this knowledge is important. If you have 15 per cent of the fractional horsepower motor market, for example, you want to know whether your share is as high among half-horsepower as among three-quarter-horsepower motors. Or if you are selling industrial lubricants, you are interested in knowing your market share on each major type of lubricant you sell. You are also interested in knowing how that market share varies by industries. Do you do as well in metalworking establishments as among rubber-goods manufacturers? Is your market share higher among large than among small manufacturers? Questions like these, and some approaches to their answers, are the subject of this chapter.

IMPORTANCE OF A MARKET-SIZE ESTIMATE

In a wide variety of different marketing problem situations, an accurate estimate of the size of the market for a specific product is needed. Such an estimate is needed for sales forecasting, as we noted in the preceding chapter. It is needed also for many other aspects of sales planning. The question must be answered in the case of most new products, often rather early in the new-product-development program. It must also be answered on existing products.

Within a relatively static economy, or for a static industry in a dynamic economy, a question about the size of the market would have to be answered only infrequently. In American marketing since World War II, change of major scale has been the rule rather than the exception. New products have been developed which have reduced long-established industries to the status of buggy-whip manufacturers in trend and outlook. New developments within established industries, acting as the automatic washer acted on the washing-machine industry, have radically changed the size and composition of industry volume. In such a marketing climate, it is a continuing, or at least frequently reviewed, appraisal of the size and trend of industry volume that is necessary.

Assume a situation in which the entire economy is moving steadily upward. Different industries are participating in that growth to varying extents. The products that offer significant innovations are typically scoring spectacular gains. Other industries without major product improvements are showing moderate growth. Some industries, selling the same old tired products they have always sold, are just about holding their own. Within each industry, there are differences in trend for major subtypes. Within each subtype total, some individual brands are showing gains while others are showing losses.

This vital point must be recognized: When the economy as a whole or a single industry in that economy is showing growth, *an individual company may be losing competitive position even though it is showing sales gains in its absolute sales volume.* In such a dynamic situation, it is the relationship between the gains a company *is* making in its sales volume and those it *should be making* with industry growth considered that determines how a company is doing. Is it going ahead, holding its own, or falling behind the competitive parade? Thus a 1 or 2 per cent gain in total volume for the candy industry, while much larger gains were being scored by the food industry generally and by total consumer incomes, represents a loss in competitive position.

SOURCES OF DATA ON MARKET SIZE

Some consumer-product manufacturers have no problem in determining the size of the market for their products. Those are manufacturers which subscribe to one of the two major panel services—the Nielsen Food or Drug Index of the A. C. Nielsen Company or the National Consumer Panel of MRCA. For manufacturers of industrial products, or for manufacturers of consumer products not covered by those services, some one or combination of the following widely used sources may help provide similar information.

1. *Governmental Data*

Data available from governmental sources, particularly the Federal government, is one vital source for information on the size of the market for a specific product. All manufacturers are required by law to supply factual information to the Census of Manufactures. Comparison of the published (industry total) figures with those of the company is one elementary and basic step in keeping a "fix" on industry trends and on company position in the industry.

There are limitations of data from the census. One is the relative infrequency with which manufacturing censuses are conducted. Another is the fact that census data sometimes report only on broad aggregates of industry sales, rather than on the major divisions of those sales in which individual manufacturers would have greater interest.

For many industries, governmental sources supply much more detailed and frequent information than is provided by the periodic censuses. The following case is illustrative.

32. CONFECTIONERY SALES AND DISTRIBUTION

Since 1927, the U.S. Department of Commerce in cooperation with the confectionery industry has published an annual report of detailed trends in the sale and distribution of volume of various types of confectionery products. The scope of this annual report is indicated below. It is described here in detail because it represents a specific illustration of the type of data useful in marketing research which can be developed through industry-governmental cooperation.

The annual report begins with an estimate of total national confectionery volume, in dollars and pounds. A table going back to 1927 lists for each year the industry's production, in millions of pounds; per capita consumption; manufacturers' sales value in millions of dollars; and average value of that volume, in cents per pound.

The various kinds of candy which represent major subtypes within the industry are shown separately. Five major subtypes are distinguished: bars; package goods; bulk goods; 5 and 10 cent specialties; and "penny goods." Within the package-goods total, which is second to bars in total importance, the production is divided into four different price groups, with average retail price per pound less than 50 cents, from 50 to 99 cents, from $1 to $1.49, and $1.50 or more.

The manufacturers of confectionery products are divided, for the purpose of reporting sales of homogeneous groups, into two major types: manufacturer-wholesalers, who are the mass producers of the candy industry marketing their products through sale to jobbers, chain stores, or independent retailers; and manufacturer-retailers, a smaller segment selling boxed chocolates direct to the consumer through manufacturer-operated store. Manufacturer-wholesalers are further divided into six subgroups:

1. *General-line houses:* producers making a variety of goods with no one type of candy predominating

2. *Bar-goods houses:* producers whose output is chiefly candy bars, frequently chocolate-covered or solid chocolate bars

3. *Five-and-ten-cent-specialty houses:* producers whose output is principally items (exclusive of bar goods) such as rolls, bags or packets of mints, fruit drops, caramels, etc., intended to retail at the prices indicated

4. *Package-goods houses:* producers whose output is predominantly candy (frequently chocolates) marketed in boxes, cans, bags or other containers

5. *Bulk-goods houses:* producers whose output is largely candy marketed in bulk, frequently hard candies, panned items, or unpackaged chocolates weighed out at retail for sale by the pound or fraction

6. *Penny-goods houses:* producers whose output is mostly candy intended to retail at 1 cent or 2 cents per unit, or possibly several items for 1 cent

A table is presented to show the proportion of total sales of the manufacturers in each group which the group designation represents. Thus of the bar-goods houses, 82.5 per cent of tonnage represents bar goods in the case of the 1954 survey.

Comparative sales by type of producer are presented. The number of firms in each group, tonnage of such firms, and dollar value of their products are reported. This breakdown is based on a sample of 386 firms, whose volume represents (1954 survey) about 76 per cent of industry volume. Within each group of firm types, a further separation is made to show those which showed gains and those which showed declines over the preceding year. Volume of the gainers and losers is shown separately.

A breakdown by sales-volume group is also included. This divides manufacturers into five different sales-volume groups. Within each volume group, the manufacturers with sales gains and losses versus year-ago sales are again broken out.

Monthly and annual sales are charted for three major types of manufacturers. The chart shows volume both with and without seasonal correction, so that trend may be examined with seasonal influence eliminated.

Distribution of sales by customer type is also reported. Significant trends in that distribution are noted. Thus in a year of relatively level to moderately declining total sales, the report commented: "Sales of manufacturer-retailers to department stores increased 18 per cent, more than offsetting the decline in sales to these outlets by manufacturer-wholesalers. The net increase was over five per cent."

Distribution of the sales of confectionery manufacturers by states are reported, along with the consumption of selected ingredients such as sugar, cornstarch, etc. Export volume is also reported.

— ★ —

COOPERATIVE APPROACH HAS MAJOR VALUES

The above example of industry-governmental cooperation has some important marketing research implications. The industry involved is one which is made up for the most part of extremely small manufacturers in terms of total volume. If the use of marketing research by individual confectionery manufacturers were determined on the normal expenditure–sales volume ratio, no more than a dozen firms in the confectionery field, in all probability, would be large enough to do much marketing research. What those firms did do, within relatively limited budgets, would be likely to involve a considerable degree of duplication, as individual marketing research directors in individual confectionery-manufacturing organizations worked individually on the problem of determining market size. The cooperative effort of the industry, through the U.S. Department of Commerce participation, provides accurate and detailed estimates. Thus even extremely small confectionery manufacturers can guide their marketing plans on a factual base of knowledge of industry trends.

The larger organizations in the industry also benefit. They secure basic and fundamental information, which they would otherwise have to develop as well as they could. They can develop marketing research activities beyond that point, to the practical limit of their respective budgets, without duplication of effort. This approach is open to other industries, including many which now have essentially no bench-mark data on industry trends. The governmental participation is not a requisite of a successful cooperative research program. As Chapter 28 and comments later in this chapter will indicate, trade associations also perform much the same service for their members that the U.S. Department of Commerce performed for confectionery manufacturers in this example.

2. Association Data

Many industries have trade associations which gather individual-member production and/or sales data and combine them to develop a figure for the entire industry. Typical of such industries are those in the appliance field, the carpet industry, the wax-paper industry, and many others. An individual manufacturer in such an industry reports his own sales figures. He receives back from the association a figure on total industry volume. The relationship between the two tells him his share of market. Comparison of the same data for the preceding year indicates the trend in that market share.

This helpful source of vital marketing research data is available to many more industries than use it. It represents a natural and valuable extension of trade-association activities of service to association members.

One of the barriers to a wider use of this type of marketing research approach is in the viewpoint of the members of any particular industry group. In some industries, the individual companies are preoccupied with each other. Each is afraid that information reported to a trade association will somehow "leak" to a competitor. The potential damage from such a leak offsets the potential value of the figures. This viewpoint is a narrow one, characteristic of industries in which competitive pressure from *outside* of the industry is reducing the actual and potential volume of *all* industry members.

As the experience of countless industries has repeatedly demonstrated, the danger of disclosure of confidential data need not impede this type of cooperative industry-volume reporting. Reports are ordinarily sent by individual companies to some independent outside organization, often in the public accounting field. The accounting organization protects individual reports from disclosure, as an extension of its normal professional practice of holding financial data of its clients confidential.

A key element in determining the desirability as well as the usefulness of this type of cooperative approach is the competitive division of volume within the industry. It is least likely to work where the industry is dominated by a single brand with a very large market share—say 40 per cent or more. Such a firm typically is large enough to do its own marketing research, and may often prefer to do so rather than disclose data more valuable to other industry members in some cases than the data it secures in return. Where the industry volume is divided among a large number of brands, with the industry's largest competitive share at a 35 per cent level or below, this approach is likely to find acceptance because it is of value to all.

Note the importance, in the case of trade-association data, of distinguishing between the size of the *total market* on one hand and the total sales of *association members* on the other. There are often one or more large organizations which shun association activity in an industry. In such a situation, the need to expand volume reported by association members to allow for that represented by nonmembers is always present. In practice, this is not particularly difficult, especially over a period of time. Periodic census data provide an indication of the extent of coverage in census years. Comparison of the pattern for two or more census years indicates the trend. Large individual organizations within the association which have their own marketing research facilities can often provide an accurate estimate of the relative volume of specific nonmember companies.

The idea that an individual manufacturer is concealing his volume from competitors by failing to join an association is often a delusion. In the case of a washing-machine manufacturer, this approach was taken. The total volume of the nonreporting member was known to the association, because reports were filed by the company selling electrical motors to the washer manufacturer!

In the case of data from trade associations and similar sources, there is always a need for evaluation of the accuracy and completeness of the data reported. Caution should be exercised in using data from such sources until the data have been validated by experienced marketing research men. One source of inaccuracy is an attempt by an association to secure data in more detail than the bulk of the member companies ordinarily maintain them. This has a tendency to result in "by guess or by gosh" estimates and may carry over to influence accuracy with which other data—which *could* be reported accurately—are compiled.

3. Published Data

Many published estimates of the volume of specific industries are helpful to those who can find them and validate or adjust them. One of the prominent sources of such data is the group of business or trade publications serving the industry in question. For example, *Electrical Merchandising* magazine publishes each January a statistical issue that serves during the ensuing twelve months as the statistical bible of the appliance industry. Similarly, *Food Topics* magazine publishes in great detail annual estimates of the volume of specific types of products sold through food outlets. *Drug Topics* provides similar estimates on products moving through drug and related channels.

The research departments of publishers of industrial publication groups can often provide specific data of this type. For example, the research department of McGraw-Hill has an extensive library of fundamental data on the industries served by its publications.

A little detective work can often uncover a dependable source of data that might otherwise be overlooked. For example, doctoral dissertations (usually available only through university libraries) are often helpful. So are university research bureau publications in some instances. Careful reading of such business publications as *Business Week* magazine, the *Wall Street Journal,* and *Fortune* often discloses the existence of basic data or completed research studies which might otherwise be overlooked.

Particularly in the area of published data, a distinction should be noted. Some of the data referred to in this section—such as the estimates of confectionery volume developed by the U.S. Department of Commerce—represent estimates of industry volume in what might be roughly described as finished form. The only research involved in the use of such data is the task of locating them. Other published sources can be used to develop estimates of the size of industry volume, although that application is far from obvious. For example, a government study showed the distribution of consumer expenditures within a sample of families. Working from the published figures on a specific type of product, a research man was able to develop estimates of total consumption on those products. The resulting figures led a company's management to reappraise the opportunity represented by a market it had previously considered too small to warrant cultivation. Subsequent studies confirmed the accuracy of the estimates thus ingeniously developed.

In the case of all published data, the underlying research techniques should be carefully appraised before figures are accepted as warranting management's confidence. Consider as a case in point the estimates of industry volume published by *Food Topics.* Those estimates are based on a study of returns to questionnaires sent to manufacturers, advertising agencies, and retail organizations. The dependability of the estimates varies from product to product, with the particular competitive pattern in the industry in question as one determinant. This point was made earlier in a discussion of the Standard Foods, Inc., dry-soup case. A single dominant company in the soup field controlled most of the volume of that industry. That company had policies which made their participation in the *Food Topics* survey, or their disclosure of such confidential data, very unlikely. Therefore, the estimates of soup volume were almost certainly less dependable than estimates of a product class like soap or detergents. A strong association which publishes figures cn total soap and detergent volume provides a bench mark increasing the accuracy of *Food Topics* estimate.

4. Sampling Data

Data developed through the application of sampling methods, using either the survey or the panel approach, are often used in estimating the size of the market for a particular product. Thus Pillsbury Mills, Inc., conducts continuing audits of movement of a number of different product types through grocery outlets in all parts of the country. By auditing the movement of a product class in which it was interested—like frosting mixes or frozen waffles—and relating the volume on that product to the volume on other products whose national volume they knew, the marketing research department at Pillsbury can make a rough estimate of volume on any grocery product rather quickly and inexpensively.

Sometimes a survey by a manufacturer provides information on market size. This is typically a rather expensive approach. Sometimes the survey is made by an outside source, such as a publisher of an individual magazine or a group of magazines, consumer or industrial. Or it may be conducted by a research organization, with various companies each contributing part of the cost. A jointly sponsored study of television-set movement and retail-level inventory trends, paid for by a group of competitive television-set manufacturers, is typical of this type of approach.

In industrial marketing, a sample of large-volume customers is sometimes used to determine the size of the market for a particular type of product, such as an abrasive. The results of the sample study are then projected to industry volume. In any of these sampling approaches, a capable marketing research man belongs in the picture. He can identify pitfalls in the statistical morass which would be invisible to a less trained eye. In appraising research techniques and the findings of research, a superficial knowledge (which is typically all the nonresearch man has at his command) can be a very dangerous thing.

WHAT IS THE COMPANY'S POSITION IN ITS INDUSTRY?

As soon as the size of the market for a specified product, or total industry volume, is determined, it becomes possible to establish the company's position within that industry. What is the company's share of industry volume, or *market share* as it is often described? A picture in at least approximate terms of the relative market share of major competitors is desirable also.

Facts about a company's position in its industry are a vital element in marketing-management planning. They often influence decisions on basic marketing strategy. For example, some marketing programs have as their specific objective an expansion in the size of the total market for a product. The goal, in short, is to expand *industry volume*. Such a program is likely to be executed by a firm with a dominant share of existing industry volume. The decision to move in that direction is based on the judgment that it is likely to be easier to increase a company's sales by boosting industry volume and selling an expanding share of that additional volume than by competitive gains. In contrast, other marketing programs are completely competitive in their emphasis. Their goal is to take business away from one or more competitors. Such a strategic approach is often taken by a company with a relatively small share of existing volume. A company in that position is far below the ceiling of industry volume.

DATA ON COMPETITIVE MARKET SHARES ARE ALSO NEEDED

Facts about competitive market shares and trends in the competitive picture can be developed from many sources. Often such facts are *not* secured. One reason for what might appear to be an oversight is the confidence of management executives that they "know" the situation, hence need spend neither time nor effort confirming what is already known. This is an area of great potential contribution by marketing research. Some of marketing research's most spectacular contributions to company profit and progress have been achieved when facts have been developed and substituted for erroneous executive opinions.

Two examples are illustrative. One is from Johnson's wax experience. The company had long had in its line a product known as Cream Wax, on which annual volume was about $300,000. The National Consumer Panel of MRCA indicated that the market on that type of cream polish was much larger than the company suspected. The corollary was that the company's market share was relatively low. The finding was challenged. One sales executive commented: "The panel can't be right. Our salesmen are in stores all over America every day. If that much cream polish were being sold, they'd report it to us." The research finding had to be re-examined.

At that time, Johnson's Cream Wax was sold primarily in small bottles, retailing at around 25 cents, and primarily through variety outlets. The panel recheck revealed that the competitive volume was in pint and quart bottles, selling for about $1 and $2, respectively. The reason why the Johnson's salesmen had not reported the volume was also revealed. It was moving largely through house-to-house marketing channels, like Jewel Tea trucks, Stanley parties, etc. As far as the Johnson's sales organization was concerned, that was *invisible* volume! The company packed larger package sizes without delay. It put together a merchandising program with a very substantial increase in advertising. It also used its research findings as the basis of a sales portfolio. The portfolio pointed out to retailers that a substantial volume was going to their customers, but not through their cash registers. It suggested a partnership between the retailer and the Johnson's wax organization to get that volume back into normal retail channels. In less than eighteen months, volume on that product had been *multiplied by ten!*

A second example was in the cosmetic field. A cosmetic manufacturer was completely positive that his product controlled a dominant share of market in a particular portion of the industry. Research revealed that it was the sixth-ranking brand! The key element here was the manufacturer's emphasis on different types of retail outlets. Heavy sales emphasis on a type of retail outlet that actually controlled a very small share of industry volume gave the manufacturer a completely distorted view of his standing in the market.

IMPORTANCE OF DATA ON MARKET SUBDIVISIONS

Moving into the area of determining the *characteristics* of the market for a product, the first characteristic which is of unquestioned marketing significance is the division of the total market into major market subtypes. The total market for dentifrices, for example, consists of two major subdivisions—the market for dentifrices in powder form and the market for dentifrices in cream form. Similarly in the case of shampoos, there are relatively solid cream shampoos, liquid shampoos, and an in-between classification known as liquid-cream shampoos. A manufacturer must know how the total industry volume is divided into major subtypes or he can hardly be considered to know the size of his total market.

Suppose that in the shampoo market, for example, you were the Toni Company back in 1948 or 1949. You had only one product in the shampoo field—Toni Creme Shampoo. Volume on that market was so low that it was disappointing. Industry data indicated steady growth in the total shampoo market. Why, then, was the sales trend on Toni Creme Shampoo downward? Was that entirely a competitive problem? Not in the usual sense of the word, for there was a decline in the relative importance of cream-type shampoos, caused by growth among liquid shampoos. Toni Creme Shampoo was expanding its share of total cream-shampoo volume, but was being squeezed by the contraction of that *part* of the market. In this case, clearly, the *size of the total market* which was of primary interest to the folks at Toni was the size of the market for *cream-type* shampoos.

In cases like those cited, movement back and forth between different market segments is sometimes extensive. Therefore a manufacturer who makes products going into an industry marked by one or more major subdivisions should watch total market volume, trend in product-type division of that market, and company share both of type total and of total market. The significance of watching the type-total trend is pointed up by the Shower-of-Stars experience. When a company's only product in an industry is in a part of that industry, and when there is a trend away from that part, it is common to aim new-product development at the expanding market-segment. That way, the company is in a position to profit on one product from the trend that is adverse to its volume on another closely related product.

Another illustration of the subdivision of a market by subtypes was provided by the case on confectionery sales and distribution earlier in this chapter. A manufacturer of candy bars would require a knowledge of the trend in consumption of such bars, rather than of consumption of all types of candy, to guide marketing planning. Entering a new product in a major subtype of the same industry, we might note, is often much less difficult and hazardous a decision than entering an entirely new product category. In one case the new product begins with a heavy backlog of factors in its favor. Thus the characteristics of the industry being entered are known. Often the company has an established reputation within that industry and ready and easy access to the normal channels of distribution serving it. For example, suppose that a major manufacturer of candy bars like Mars, Incorporated, should decide to supplement its line—which already includes a number of established brands like Milky Way, Snickers, etc.—with an additional bar. That type of volume and line expansion is relatively easy. It is a very different and far more difficult marketing problem for a company like the Parker Pen Company to decide to launch what is for the company a completely different type of product, such as a camera.

THE VOLUME-CONSUMPTION PATTERN

In elementary statistics, the normal curve and a "normal" distribution are introduced. That type of a distribution represents the basis of a considerable part of statistical theory. It is important to note that marketing has its own "normal" distribution, which is very different from the statistical concept. In statistical terms, marketing populations tend to be heavily skewed. Thus a small proportion of all the markets and/or counties in the United States represent a very large proportion of the national total population, retail sales, buying power, etc. The comment is often made about an individual company that a small proportion of the total customers represents a very high proportion of total business. Marketing literature is full of references to situations in which 10 per cent of the customers contribute 80 per cent of the business, or 20 per cent represent 90 per cent, and so on.

Since that type of a concentration of volume among a small proportion of a population is common in marketing, that represents a marketing characteristic which it is often important to establish in quantitative terms. Figure 20.1 illustrates this type of concentration pattern in specific terms. It is based on the soup analysis described in Chapter 17, on a consumer-panel approach. The base of the two bars shown is total soup-buying families (which comes very close to being total families, since those families which do not buy soup are a very small share of the total). The right-hand bar shows how the physical volume of the consumption groups was divided. The heavy-volume soup consumers represented a group only slightly smaller than the light-volume consumers, yet contributed volume which was more than ten times that of the light-soup consumers.

A similar type of analysis, in which a total population of customers is divided on the basis of volume purchased or volume consumed, is often a rewarding approach. Once a concentration pattern like the one illustrated is disclosed, the next step is usually an attempt to identify the characteristics of high-volume consumers. In the soup example, an

CONCENTRATION OF SOUP CONSUMPTION

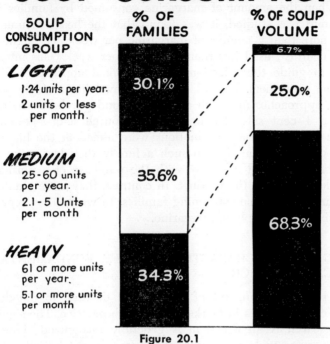

SOUP CONSUMPTION GROUP	% OF FAMILIES	% OF SOUP VOLUME
LIGHT 1-24 units per year. 2 units or less per month.	30.1%	6.7% 25.0%
MEDIUM 25-60 units per year. 2.1-5 Units per month	35.6%	68.3%
HEAVY 61 or more units per year. 5.1 or more units per month	34.3%	

Figure 20.1

examination of consumption variations by income levels was made. Was the high-volume soup-consumption family a high or low family on the income scale? This analysis disclosed that the highest income group purchased only 13 per cent cent more soup per family than the average family. Obviously the soup volume-consumption division of families was on some basis other than an income or socioeconomic grouping.

Every effort is made to isolate and identify the characteristics of high-volume consumers or users of a product. Once identified, such characteristics are useful in many aspects of marketing planning. A local brand of beer was established through research as having a relative weakness among high-volume beer drinkers. The same research disclosed that the high-volume drinker was a user of bottled beer, while the light-volume drinker was the primary consumer of beer in cans. A shift in advertising emphasis from canned to bottled beer was one step in the direction of overcoming the weakness mentioned. Changes in media and in other aspects of the advertising program were also made.

Even though it is not always possible to pinpoint the high-volume consumer, this type of analysis is often helpful in strengthening marketing aimed at him. In the case of margarine research, for example, it was disclosed that a sharp concentration pattern such as the one charted existed. When the amount of margarine consumed by families in each volume group was studied, it was found that the heavy-volume family averaged more than 2 pounds of margarine per week. The light-volume family, in contrast, used less than ½ pound per week. This information was used to guide the selection of promotional approaches aimed at high-volume consumers. Instead of "deals" involving a single pound of margarine, approaches in which a 2- or 3-pound purchase was required (such as a 1 cent sale, 1-pound-free-with-purchase-of-2-pounds deal, etc.) were adopted. Those promotions were aimed at the high-volume margarine-consuming family. To such a family they had great appeal, because they combined economy with the purchase of a normal week or week-plus supply of the product. In contrast, they were uninteresting to low-volume margarine-consuming families, to whom they represented a four to six week's supply of margarine.

DEFINING MARKET CHARACTERISTICS IS A FUNDAMENTAL ANALYTICAL APPROACH

A very substantial amount of attention is devoted to the definition of market characteristics in marketing research practice. The significance of such research is greater than is generally recognized. Those characteristics vary so widely in nature that you may not initially recognize the essential similarity of research concerned with different types of product characteristics. This research area is so broad and important in part because it represents a fundamental analytical approach. When you seek to determine the characteristics of the market for a product you are simply applying the approach recommended earlier: Subdivide the problem to help isolate the problem elements. Some examples of the types of characteristics subjected to research may be helpful in suggesting the range of research carried on in this area.

Extent of Overlapping Usage of Product Types and Subtypes

An illustration of this type of research on product characteristics was provided by the Standards Foods, Inc., case in Chapter 17. The question there was whether the same families used dry and canned soup. That question had to be answered in order to define the market target in that case. The same question is constantly arising. It has great marketing significance.

Thus if two types of products (like canned and dry dog food, for example) are used by different customers, then they are in competition with each other. The advertising and promotion should be and can be heavily competitive, in the direction of the other type. On the other hand, if a high proportion of consumers use both types (as they do, in the example cited), then different advertising approaches would be desirable. Similarly, if the overlap in usage between two products is great, the use of one as a carrier for coupons promoting the use of the other would be relatively expensive if the goal were to persuade new nonusing customers to sample it.

At a time when the major categories of frozen foods were three—frozen vegetables, frozen fruits, and frozen juices—research was used for one large packer of frozen foods to pinpoint the overlap between the three types of products in consumer usage. That research disclosed that less than one-third of the families using any frozen foods used all three types. It also disclosed, incidentally, that the users of three types represented about 60 per cent of total tonnage (all brands) of frozen vegetables, more than two-thirds of tonnage of frozen fruits, and 70 per cent of the tonnage of frozen juices. The opportunity to expand volume by persuading the one-type users (who used vegetables alone, for the most part) to try the other two types was an inviting one.

The same frozen-food research was also concerned with identifying the promising growth items in a relatively complex product line. In the frozen-vegetable field, this research disclosed that four varieties out of a far larger number were growing at a tremendously accelerated rate. These four were spinach, Brussels sprouts, broccoli, and cauliflower. Over a two-year period, those four items increased in tonnage by 280 per cent, while all other items showed only 38 per cent growth. Consumer research revealed that those items—which were collectively identified as "the stinkers"—had advantages over their fresh counterparts which were not shared by other vegetables. Used fresh, all involved cleaning, relatively long cooking time, and a tendency for cooking to develop odors to which many people objected. The advertising appeals on these varieties were sharpened, with competitive growth as a result.

Scale of Sectional and City-size Variations in Consumption

General background on the characteristics of the American market for all products provides only the starting point in developing marketing and advertising plans for a specific product. It is necessary to determine the variations which set that product apart from other products, in terms of marketing significance. Sectional variations in consumption of different products vary widely. City-size variations also exhibit a marked pattern on some products.

Thus the chart in Chapter 18 showed that the average family in a city of 100,000 or greater population had frozen-food consumption about eight times as great as that of the average farm family. Three families out of four in the Southeastern states baked biscuits once a week or oftener, compared to a figure less than half that high for the remainder of the United States. Consumption of fish and sea-food products is higher in the New England states than elsewhere. Research to pinpoint such significant variations is often required as the basis of a marketing plan tailored to fit an individual product's market efficiently.

"Thin" versus "Thick" Market Patterns

There is a basic difference between two quite distinct market patterns which enters into many marketing decisions. Some products have a "thick" market, consisting of a high proportion of total usage. Canned soup is one example. Other products have a "thin" market, with a very low proportion of all people or families as prospects. A powder to hold false teeth in place, or an ointment to relieve hemorrhoids, are examples. Some products with less obvious reasons develop a thin market. Their consumption is contributed by a small, thin slice of high-volume users.

Establishing the market pattern is necessary in determining the value of a customer to a product or brand. That value in turn influences how much a company may profitably spend to secure such a customer. There are obvious advertising applications also. Thus if most families already use a product, but with very low frequency, advertising with a "news" approach on the advantages of the product aimed at persuading people to try it is not likely to be effective. They have tried it, and consider themselves users. Shifting the focus of the advertising to increase frequency of usage is likely to be a more productive approach. An illustration was the development of a new area of application—use in a frosting recipe—for Philadelphia brand cream cheese by the Kraft organization.

Penetration within Market Segments

Particularly in the case of a relatively new product, or one showing striking growth, research is often harnessed to the task of locating the most promising target areas. Is the product progressing uniformly through all market segments, or are sharp variations revealed? What are those variations? Which of them can be effectively exploited?

An illustration is provided by an extensive analysis of the characteristics of purchasers of frozen pies and precooked meals which was conducted by MRCA, based on their national consumer-panel data. The individual product-usage variations and the consumer characteristics listed below will suggest the scope and direction of research of this type. Here are the market segments examined, with the range in variation from low to high in each:

Geographic regions. The highest region in consumption had a purchase rate 2.2 times that of the lowest.

City sizes. Consumption in largest cities was more than ten times as high, per family, as consumption on farms.

Television ownership. These products, which had been advertised extensively on television, were consumed at a rate more than three times as high among TV owners as among families living in areas not reached by television at the time of the analysis.

Employment of housewife. The variations, if any, existing between families in which the housewife is employed outside the home and those in which she is a full-time housewife are often relevant. If there is a sharp peak in consumption among working-housewife families, different advertising-media patterns are desirable. Variations in the case of this analysis were very slight.

Occupational groups. Variations in consumption between families in which the head of the household is in a professional-executive job, versus clerical-sales families, skilled laborers, unskilled laborers, etc., are often explored. Excluding the farm category, the range in consumption in different occupational groups on frozen products was about 3 to 1.

Family income. These products tend to be in a luxury category, with the result that the purchase rate in high-income families was more than five times as high as among the lowest income group.

Educational levels. When the consumption of these products was examined for families with varying educational achievement by the head of the household, there was a range of more than 3 to 1 from the lowest to the highest consumption rate.

Family size. In general, per-family consumption of food products tends to increase with the size of the family, simply because there are more mouths to feed. In the case of these products, however, large families had a per-family consumption rate far lower than that of smaller families.

Age of housewife. This is a vital marketing characteristic, particularly for products in transition—new products entering broad usage or traditional products declining in use. Older housewives tend to be the last to accept innovations and the last to give up traditional practices. The frozen-food analysis showed that older housewives were lagging in their use of these products.

Presence of children, by ages. The influence of children on consumption varies by products. A marked pattern of influence in the case of this product class was disclosed, with wide variations in consumption level revealed.

Importance of Different Uses, Etc.

It is often important to establish the relative importance of different usage classifications on a product, to guide advertising or marketing emphasis. Thus the extent to which margarine is used as a spread for bread, versus its usage as a seasoning for vegetables, for ingredient usage, etc., would influence advertising appeals and emphasis. The extent to which a food drink like Ovaltine was consumed hot or cold, as a drink with meals or at bedtime, by adults versus children, would be vital in marketing and advertising planning.

CHARACTERISTIC ANALYSIS AS A DIAGNOSTIC TOOL

Sometimes the analysis of market characteristics is made in the course of an attempt to diagnose a problem situation. An illustration may be drawn from a Johnson's wax experience. Sales analysis disclosed that there were major differences in sales performance in different districts. To provide clues to characteristics which might help explain those performance differences, a considerable amount of additional analysis was executed. In that analysis, emphasis was placed on a comparison of the patterns existing in strong districts versus those in weak districts.

When the division of volume by customer types in strong and weak districts was examined, wide variations were found. One characteristic pattern was common to all the strong districts. Another quite different pattern was found in the case of weak districts. The explanation in this case was that a major change had occurred in customer preference for different types of retail outlets as a source of their wax-polish purchases. The strong Johnson districts were "on top of" this trend and were putting heavy sales emphasis on the growing customer types in their day-to-day selling. The weak districts, by contrast, were still selling in the traditional way. A revision of sales emphasis resulted in an almost immediate improvement in the level of sales performance in weak districts.

MARKET-CHARACTERISTIC ANALYSIS AS THE FOUNDATION OF A MARKETING PLAN

While the definition of market characteristics sometimes exerts only a minor influence on a company's marketing and advertising planning, there are other cases in which that type of analysis becomes the very keystone of planning. The following case is illustrative.

33. PURITY FLOUR AND FEED COMPANY ★

This organization, with headquarters in Omaha, Nebr., had a large national volume on bulk flour products and on feeds of various types for livestock, etc. Seeking diversification by entering additional markets for which its manufacturing facilities and experience would be useful, the management examined the growing market for ready-to-eat (RTE, in trade parlance) cereals. The company was considering adding to its line one or two cereal products, which had already been developed in its laboratories. The decision to move into the highly competitive cereal market was recognized as an extremely important one, and extensive marketing research was used to appraise the problems and opportunities which such a decision would involve.

Three large and successful companies dominated the RTE cereal field —Kellogg's, General Mills, Inc., and the Post cereals manufactured by General Foods Corporation. While Purity Mills had been successful in achieving substantial sales volume, it was nowhere near as large as those three firms, and there was understandable concern as to whether or not Purity could compete successfully for a share of the cereal market against such experienced and able competitors.

The marketing research exploration of the cereal market revealed that all three of those organizations were concentrating heavily on the "kid market." Through television programs aimed primarily at children, through the extensive use of such promotional devices as premiums, etc., all three firms were aiming major efforts at juvenile consumers. Their preoccupation with the younger consumer suggested the possibility that there might exist a market opportunity for Purity. Could the concentration of promotion on adult consumers provide an avenue for Purity to build a profitable cereal brand at lower cost than by adding its own promotion to that already aimed at children?

There was a fundamental need to determine the relative importance, within the total cereal-consumption field, of the various age segments of the market. How much of the total cereal market did adults represent? How much cereal was consumed by families with children of different age groups, and how much by families without children?

A question was raised as to whether data from the national consumer panel of MRCA could supply a dependable answer to that question. Prices for a "package" of back data on cereal consumption were quoted by MRCA. That organization felt that the key question above could not be answered by the use of their data. They pointed out that their data reflected only the total consumption of families and that individual consumption figures were not available.

The marketing research man with responsibility for answering this question had had considerable experience in the analysis of consumer-panel data. After considerable study, he concluded that the question about *individual* consumption *could* be answered by analysis of *family* data. He planned an analysis, which MRCA made possible by a special tabulation of data.

In analyses of data by age of children from the consumer panel, breakdowns were usually made with all families of specific age composition combined. Thus all families in which there was a child in the five-or-under age bracket were combined and compared with those in which there was a child in the six-to-twelve age group. This type of analysis was often somewhat fuzzy, because many families had children in *both* age groups, hence were in both group totals.

To answer the question about individual cereal consumption, a special tabulation of consumer-panel family data into eight *mutually exclusive* age-of-children groupings was ordered. Here are the categories:

Families in which there were no children 20 or under
Families in which all children were in the 5-or-under age group
Families in which all children were in the 6-to-12 age group
Families in which all children were in the 13-to-20 age group
Families in which there were children in both the 5-or-under and the 6-to-12 age group
Families in which there were children in both the 5-or-under and the 13-to-20 age group
Families in which there were children in both the 6-to-12 and the 13-to-20 age group
Families in which there were children in all three age groups

Before ordering this tabulation, the composition of the panel by age groups was determined. The question here concerned the size of the sample in each of the above family-composition "cells." It was found that for two of the age groups listed, the sample size would be relatively small—those in which there were children both in the 5-or-under and 13-to-20 groups and those with children in all three groups. With the sample-size limitation recognized, the tabulation was made.

The total cereal consumption for each of the groups was needed. So were data on the average number of family members in each grouping.

The analysis began with an examination of the data for family groups in which the children were all in one age bracket or in which there were no children. Here is one of the basic working tables:

Table 20.1. Variations in Per Capita and Per Family Consumption of Cereals in Families without Children, or with Children in Only One of the Three Age Groups

Ages of children in family	Per cent of panel families in group	Group total RTE consumption, lb. per M capita	Average family size	Average RTE poundage per M families
None....................	42.8	5,824	2.4	13,978
5 or under only........	11.0	4,260	3.8	16,189
6–12 only.............	9.0	5,719	4.0	22,876
13–20 only............	14.4	5,474	4.1	22,443

In the above table, the proportion of families in the group is shown as an indication of relative sample size. The group total per-thousand-capita consumption of RTE cereals was arrived at by dividing the total tonnage of the group over a full year by the number of family members in the group and multiplying by 1,000. Thus the individual family-member consumption averaged a little more than 5 pounds. The average number of family members in the group is the factor used to convert the per-thousand-capita figures to a per-thousand-family basis.

With the above table as a starting point, an attempt was made to estimate the consumption rate of individuals of different ages. That estimate was developed by a combination of inference and assumption. The table shows that the individual consumption per 1,000 adults (in adult-only families) was 5,824 pounds. That was a consumption rate which represented 107.6 per cent of the all-age average of 5,415 pounds.

Now the assumption was made that in families in which there were children in the 5-or-under age group there were two adults. At least biologically that assumption seemed reasonable. The further assumption was made that adults in such families consumed RTE cereals at the same rate as did adults in adult-only families. That assumption was perhaps more tenuous. Note, however, that prior to the advent of the child in such families they were members of the adult-only group.

On the basis of the assumptions indicated, consider now the 16,189 pounds of cereal consumed in the 5-or-under-only families. That consumption includes the contribution of two adults, each at the adult-average rate of 5,824 pounds per thousand for an adult total of 11,648. There remained for (presumably) child consumption, 4,549 pounds; and there remained unaccounted for on the average 1.8 family members. If the 1.8 family members are assumed both to be in the 5-or-under category, then the consumption rate for that age group can be determined at least approximately by dividing the remaining consumption by the number of family members. The resulting figure was 2,522 pounds, indicating consumption for that age group which was at a rate representing 46.6 per cent of the all-age average. That average figure may seem low, especially to the parent of a youngster of four or five years. It should be remembered that for the first year or two of that age group, infants consume primarily baby foods and cereals rather than adult foods like RTE cereals.

By a similar reasoning process, the consumption of the individuals in the other two age groups was estimated. Here were the figures which resulted:

Age group	Average per M capita consumption	Consumption index
Children 5 or under	2,522	46.6
Children 6–12	5,614	103.3
Children 13–20	5,140	94.9
Adults 21 and over	5,824	107.6
All-age-group average	5,415	100.0

It was felt that if these figures were approximately accurate, they should check out with approximate accuracy in the family groups made up of multiple-age-group members. There was a further problem in those cases, since the age of the "fractional members" was not known. By averaging the consumption rate of those age groups from whom the fractional representation had to be drawn (by the definition of the groups), that problem was bypassed.

In this "checking" process, the estimated consumption per 1,000 families in the group including those 5-or-under plus those 6-to-12 was within 3 per cent of actual consumption. In the 5-or-under plus 13-to-20 age group, the estimates were within 3.6 per cent of total actual consumption. In those in the 6-to-12 plus 13-to-20 group, the estimated consumption was within 1.7 per cent of actual consumption. For the relatively small sample of families with children in all three age brackets, the estimate was 10 per cent below actual consumption.

With these individual age-group consumption figures developed, it was a relatively simple matter to weight the consumption rates by the number of individuals in each age group and thus to estimate the contribution which each age group made to total RTE cereal consumption. The company's decision on whether or not to launch cereals as new products was strongly influenced by the results of this analysis.

— ★ —

SUMMARY

1. An estimate of the size of the total market (i.e., of industry volume) for a product type is often required for marketing management decisions. Prepar-

ing such estimates is part of marketing research practice. A number of different sources are commonly used. Where a dependable indication of the market size can be drawn from existing data, no problem exists beyond locating the data. Where the information is unavailable, it can sometimes be developed through the use of any of a number of marketing research technique tools.

2. All companies require such an estimate. Cooperative effort, through the medium of a trade-association or other mutual-interest group, is one approach to developing an estimate of market size. That approach is being used more widely as its value and relative ease are more widely recognized.

3. Of particular interest in the case of industries whose volume is divided by major subtypes is an indication of the size and trend of the product-type division of the total market. For a manufacturer making only one or two of the product types in a complex industry total, it is the size of his *part* of the market that is important.

4. The use of marketing research to establish the relative importance and pattern of various market characteristics is relatively common. This represents an application of the problem-solving approach of subdivision, mentioned earlier. Examples in this chapter illustrate some of the types of characteristics to which research is often devoted.

QUESTIONS

1. It is true you want to know how big the market is so that you can determine what your company's share is. But you want to know that share in specific rather than general terms. What is meant by the latter statement?

2. Why is it so important to have an accurate estimate of the size of the market for a specific product?

3. Your company has been striding along, showing sales gains in its absolute sales volume in the past few years. What danger is there, if any, in knowing this but having no further knowledge of the market?

4. What sources are available that may help you determine the size of the market for your product?

5. What is meant by the statement: "Moving into the area of determining the *characteristics* of the market for a product, the first characteristic which is of unquestioned marketing significance is the division of the total market into major subtypes"?

6. What is the practical importance of knowing the volume-consumption pattern of consumers of your product type?

7. What types of market characteristics is marketing research often called on to define?

CHAPTER 21

Estimating Territorial
Sales Potentials and Measuring
Territorial Variations
in Sales Effectiveness

The one activity designated *most important* by a larger number of companies than any other, in the American Management Association study of *Company Practices in Marketing Research,* was *analysis of territorial sales opportunities or potentials.* Ranking fifth in its frequency of selection as most important in the same study was this closely related activity: *measuring territorial variations in sales yield, market share, sales effectiveness.* This chapter is concerned with both of those important and widely performed marketing research activities. It represents an extension of the discussion in Chapter 6, on the analysis of internal data. A review of that chapter is highly recommended as preparation for this one.

PRELIMINARY CONSIDERATIONS

The two areas of marketing research activity under discussion here are of fundamental daily importance to effective marketing management today. The areas are closely related, in that the first—analysis of territorial opportunities or potentials—is necessary before the second is possible. Thus the analysis of territorial potentials may be considered as a means to the desired end result of measuring existing variations in the company's own marketing effectiveness in different areas or territories. Action to correct the weaknesses disclosed by such measurement follows. Such remedial action is assumed here. Before that action can be taken intelligently, facts about the existing situation must be devel-

534

oped and analyzed. It is with the development and analysis of those facts that this chapter is concerned.

The fundamental importance of this area of marketing research activity stems from the fact that all sales and marketing management constantly faces two vital needs. The first is for dependably accurate information about the size of the sales potential or volume opportunity in different territories and geographic units. The second is for a basis of evaluating the company's *actual* level of sales performance in each territorial unit against the *potential* that territory represents. As later discussion in this chapter will show, the opportunity to add profitable volume by finding and correcting existing territorial weaknesses is an ever-present one. Marketing research can and does make an important contribution to increased marketing management effectiveness by increasing the precision of territorial potential estimates and of sales-performance measurement.

A MARKET INDEX IS THE BASIC YARDSTICK

How do you measure the potential which different sales territories represent? Usually that potential is measured by the use of a yardstick which is called a *market index*. A market index may be defined as a yardstick which can be used to measure the *relative* sales opportunities in different geographic or territorial units.

The use of a market index is far from new in sales management practice, although the term itself is relatively new. Consider the problem of a sales executive a decade or two ago. He had two salesmen in different sales territories. Each sales territory produced, say, $100,000 in annual sales volume. His problem, like that of today's marketing manager, was to determine which of the salesmen was doing a better job and which territory represented the greater opportunity for further volume expansion. In those days he probably tackled this problem by having his secretary get out census reports on population and add up the population in the two territories.

Suppose that the totals she developed indicated that there were 1 million people in one territory and 2 million in the other. From those figures alone, and the actual sales volume in the two territories, that long-ago sales executive concluded that the salesman in the territory with 1 million people who sold $100,000 in merchandise for the company was doing about twice as good a job as the one who got the same sales volume from a territory with twice as many people. This is a crude illustration of the use of a market index. The market index here was *population.*

POPULATION AS A MARKET INDEX

On purely logical grounds, population had (and has) considerable appeal as a market index. That appeal is based on the observation that *people are markets.* Population is not widely used as a market index today. The reason why it has been discarded is not hard to find. Buried within the observation that *people are markets* and that population therefore represents a good market index is an assumption that was not always recognized. The assumption implicit in the use of population as a market index is that *all people are equal* as markets for a product. That assumption is incorrect. There have always been and there are today major variations in buying power in different sections of the country, different city-size groups, and so on. Because of those variations, different segments of the total population represent widely varying sales potentials.

Drop back to 1929. The income per person in that year in the southeastern United States was at a level just a little above half as high as the national average. At the other extreme, income per person (or per capita, as it is usually expressed) in the Middle Atlantic states of New York, New Jersey, and Pennsylvania was more than 40 per cent higher than the national average. That meant, in broad terms, that any given number of people in the Southeast represented only a little more than one-third as good a "market" for most consumer products as the same number of "average" people in the Middle Atlantic states.

Moving forward to 1953–1955, there was sharp improvement in the relative income level in the Southeast. However, it remained low man on the national totem pole in per capita income. The Middle Atlantic states moved down toward the national average figure while the Southeast moved up. The spread in per capita income between the highest and lowest region had narrowed, and it has since continued to narrow and even today there remains a significant variation in income levels from region to region. And within a single region, there are sometimes greater variations from state to state than there are between the region and the national level.

Now return to the old-time sales manager in the illustration above. It is possible that his judgment about the relative performance of the two salesmen could have been completely in error. Suppose the salesman with 2 million people to sell to was covering the southeastern United States, while the salesman with 1 million people had a Middle Atlantic territory. In that situation, the salesman with per capita sales only half as high as the other could have been doing a better job against the actual potential in his territory than the other salesman!

Thus when population is used as a market index, there are elements of possible distortion present. *Low* per capita sales may represent a *good* sales job in territories like the Southeast where the opportunity to make sales is lower than population alone would indicate. And *high* per capita sales may represent a *poor* sales job in territories like the Middle Atlantic states or the state of California, where there is a higher level of buying power and hence of sales opportunity than population figures alone would suggest. Let's use a brief case example to illustrate this in more specific terms.

34. SHEAHAN MANUFACTURING CO. ★

This organization had total sales volume just below 9 million dollars. Their products were household products of a rather wide variety of types. The company's area of operation was national, with a relatively large sales organization covering the full United States. The only measure of territorial variations in sales performance that had been made was with population as a market index, on a per capita basis. Marketing research was set up as a separate function, and a man with four or five years' experience was hired to fill the newly created job. He began by examining the existing levels of sales performance in the company as the previous per capita analyses had disclosed them.

Here is how a group of specific sales districts compared with the national average in per capita sales:

District	Per capita sales, cents
Seattle	10.81
San Francisco	8.55
Chicago	6.66
National average	6.48
Los Angeles	6.47
Boston	5.45
Atlanta	4.51

The analyst decided to establish the relative levels of buying power in the different districts, as indicated by existing levels of retail sales in them. Then he used those buying-power differences to weight the population factor and reanalyzed sales performance. Here is what he found in the case of the six districts listed:

Seattle per capita sales of 10.81 cents was 67 per cent above the national average. When the higher buying power in that portion of the Pacific Coast was taken into consideration, the margin of Seattle's performance over the national average proved to be only 17 per cent instead of 67 per cent. *San Francisco* per capita sales were 32 per cent above average. With buying power introduced as a factor, San Francisco's volume proved to be 4 per cent *below* average. *Los Angeles* had sales which were almost exactly at the national-average level on a per capita basis. With the buying power of that area taken into consideration, Los Angeles sales proved to be 22 per cent *below* the company's national average.

Chicago sales appeared to be about 3 per cent above the national average. After adjustment, they were about 4 per cent below average. The change in this case was slight because people in the Chicago district had purchasing power which was very close to that of the national average. *Boston* sales appeared to be about 16 per cent below the national average on a per capita basis. When the above-average buying power in that district was considered as a factor, Boston sales proved to be 30 per cent below the national average. *Atlanta* appeared on a per capita basis to have the lowest level of sales performance. A full 30 per cent gap separated the per capita sales in Atlanta from the national average of the company. After adjusting for buying-power differences in the Atlanta district, the picture was quite different. Atlanta sales were found to be 5 per cent above average instead of 30 per cent below.

The analyst recommended a change in the traditional per capita basis of measuring territorial sales performance. He pointed out the existence of major variations between sections of the country in per capita buying power. Those variations exist between broad geographic sections like the North, South, and West. Even greater variations exist between subdivisions of those broad areas into census regions, between individual states in one region or in different regions, and between market areas in the same state. The use of population as a market index failed to take those variations into consideration. As a result, judgments about the level of sales effectiveness in different parts of the country could be grossly in error. Comparisons of the apparent and actual level of sales performance in the six districts mentioned above illustrated this point. His recommendations were approved.

— ★ —

"PEOPLE WITH MONEY TO SPEND ARE MARKETS"

Instead of the old-time concept that "people are markets," marketing executives today whose products are sold to consumers have substituted this one: "People *with money to spend* are markets." But when you define a market as "people with money to spend," you face a problem. How are you going to measure how much money people have to spend?

An empirical approach is to recognize that one indication that people have money to spend is the fact that they *do* spend it. The end result of their expenditures shows up as a volume of *retail sales*, that is, sales made at retail through all types of retail outlets. Total retail sales, or retail sales of specified types (such as drug sales, food sales, etc.), either in adjusted or unadjusted form, are widely used as a market index today. They tend to overcome the major drawback of population and to give effect to variations in buying power.

As a source for detailed data about retail sales which can be used in determining the total for any given sales territory, region, or district, most marketing men today rely on a publication which has been described as the statistical bible of the marketing executive. That source is the annual *Survey of Buying Power* issue published by *Sales Management* magazine. Published annually during early May, the Survey summarizes in great detail estimates of retail sales for the preceding year. Thus the May, 1957, issue covers 1956 retail sales, and so on. Beginning with July, 1957, *Sales Management* added an additional publication which represents a survey of *industrial* buying power. That publication offers industrial marketers many of the advantages of the consumer-market publication.

Developing the estimates published in each annual issue of the Survey is an immensely complicated and time-consuming task. Each time official figures from a retail-trade census are released by the government, the *Sales Management* figures are adjusted to match the official data for the base-line year. In bringing figures up to date each year between the sometimes irregular governmental censuses, carefully developed projections are made which take into consideration population migration, sales-tax receipts, bank debits, figures developed from cooperating retailers in many states by the U.S. Department of Commerce, Federal Reserve Board data on department-store sales, and many other sources.

The estimates developed by *Sales Management* are not perfect; few estimates are. They have been repeatedly demonstrated over the years to be sufficiently accurate for all practical purposes to serve as a market index for sales- and advertising-control purposes. The estimates are current. They are readily available, on a dependable publication schedule. They are sufficiently detailed for almost any marketing management need.

GENERAL AND SPECIFIC MARKET INDEXES

There are two major types of market indexes: *general* market indexes and *specific* market indexes.

A general market index reflects the presence or absence of market factors like population, buying power, etc. Such factors influence the market opportunity for all consumer products combined. Any quantitative information which makes it possible to estimate the relative sales opportunities in different territorial units might be used as a market index. The 1956 issue of the *Survey of Buying Power* included detailed figures on all the following factors, which might be used, individually or in combination, as a general market index:

Number of families
Total population
Retail sales: in total and for nine different types of stores
Effective-buying-income estimates
Number of spending units in each of five different income groups (i.e., under $2,500, $2,500 to $4,000, etc.)
Various industrial-potential indices, such as number of employees, value of products shipped, etc.

A specific market index is one which has been developed or constructed to reflect the market opportunities for a specific product or for a group of related products. A specific market index is sometimes based on a single source of data. Thus you might decide to use automobile-registration figures as a market index, if you were selling car polish. Or a specific market index may be developed by modifying a single index, or by combining two or more indexes. Suppose the product you were marketing was antifreeze for automobiles. You might start with automobile-registration figures as a base. Judgment would warn you that such an index could be misleading because of the strong influence on antifreeze sales potentials of the weather factor. Obviously a thousand cars in Minnesota represent more potential antifreeze volume than do the same number of cars in Florida, Mississippi, or Texas.

Many specific market index figures are developed by the cooperative efforts of the manufacturers within an industry. A trade association is most frequently the medium through which such figures are gathered, or influential in initiating the cooperative effort even when it operates through some other type of organization. Many industries have a setup in which each individual company reports its own figures confidentially to an impartial organization, such as a firm of certified public accountants. The figures of all reporting firms are totaled, and the total reported back to all participating organizations. No individual-firm detail is disclosed.

Companies using the panel services of the Nielsen Food Index or of the MRCA National Consumer Panel have an excellent source for a specific market index in the detailed data on sectional and city-size consumption variations reported by such services.

Other specific market indexes have been developed by involved and advanced statistical techniques. Sometimes a number of factors are correlated in developing a specific index. Most of the companies using specific market indexes have developed them by modifying, adjusting, and combining general market indexes. Before discussing the question of when a specific market index is necessary and when a general market index will suffice, let's examine the most common use of a market index —the measurement of territorial variations in sales performance.

MARKET INDEX VERSUS MARKET-INDEX BASE

A distinction should be drawn between a market index (whether general or specific) and the base of that market index. Suppose that the market index which is going to be used in a particular situation is based on the distribution of total retail sales. From *Sales Management's Survey of Buying Power,* the base figures are built up by combining the total retail sales in each county, building toward market area and/or territorial totals. Then those totals are similarly combined. If the company in question is operating on a national basis, the total of the total retail sales figures will be the same as the total shown in *Sales Management.* If the company's operations are regional or of any other type involving less than national coverage, it will develop a total for its operating area—in effect for its own "United States."

With that total figure as 100 per cent, detailed percentage figures are then calculated. Those figures show the proportion or percentage of the market-index base (i.e., total retail sales) which each of the company's geographic or territorial units represents. It is those percentage figures— adding up in each case to 100 per cent for the company's operating area —which represent the *market index.*

Step. 1. *Determine Territorial Division of Potential*

The first step in determining territorial potentials and then evaluating sales performance is to use the market index chosen to see how total potential is divided among major territorial units. As a generalization, it is desirable for a company's major territorial units (these may be sales territories, districts, etc.) to be *as nearly equal in potential as possible.* Inequality in potential division among territories poses a wide variety of problems for marketing management. The territory where potential is unusually large, in comparison to the average territory, is likely to be one in which high-spotting is necessary. There is too much potential for a salesman to cover as intensively as is possible in other territories with lower potential. As a result, the salesman is likely to take the path of least resistance and do a superficial job of coverage. The territory at the other extreme, with potential substantially smaller than average, has a different sort of problem. There, there is not enough potential to keep a salesman fully and productively occupied, on the same sales-coverage pattern established for an average (larger-potential) territory. If compensation is keyed to volume, as it often is, the salesman in the latter territory is likely to be dissatisfied with his earnings. High sales turnover is the result.

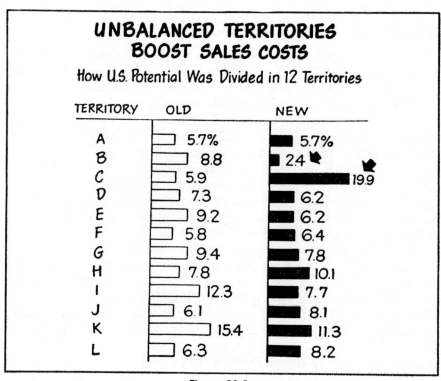

Figure 21.1

Figure 21.1 illustrates how the potential of a company covering the nation with twelve salesmen was divided. The "old" territory designation was one in effect at the time a sales executive took over. He revised the territories to "equalize" potential. The "new" potential division in the twelve territories is illustrated also. This company had at that time no marketing research man. The figures shown were developed subsequent to the territorial revision.

At the time of the territorial revision, it was considered that the territory with the largest potential (K) was about three times as large a territory in potential volume as the smallest, territory A. These figures were for the revised distribution of potential. Actually as the chart shows, the range between the largest and smallest territories in potential was more than 8 to 1, and neither A nor K were at the extremes. Note the very low potential in territory B. That was the territory in which turnover of salesmen (compensated on a straight-commission basis) was highest. The right-hand profile makes the explanation obvious. Territory C was consistently a "quota buster." No matter how high the volume sights were set in that territory, the salesmen seemed to be able to make it. Again the chart provides part of the explanation.

Step 2. *Determine Division of Actual Volume*

The second step is a determination of the division of the company's actual volume, territory by territory, and a reduction of that division to the same kind of a percentage figure used for the market index.

It is assumed in the discussion which follows that the comments made in Chapter 6 about preparation of a company's sales records for analysis have been observed. That means, for example, that all volume is credited to the point as close to its final point of use as possible and that the territorial units to which volume is credited do not divide logical marketing units. Violation of either principle introduces distortion and reduces the value of the data and the subsequent analysis.

Step 3. *Calculate Sales Par*

Evaluation of the existing sales volume in any territory requires two figures. The first is the actual sales-volume figure itself. The second is some kind of *standard* against which that figure can be compared. The figure which has been widely and effectively used for this purpose is known as *sales par.* That figure can be defined as follows: *The sales par of a territory or other geographic unit is the volume figure which that unit would contribute to the company's total sales if it were doing a just-average selling job against the potential of that territory— no better and no worse than the average of the company itself.*

The sales par is calculated by multiplying the percentage of potential in a territory (as indicated by the market index) by the company's total sales volume. To illustrate, assume you are analyzing territorial sales performance for a company whose annual volume in the year just ended was 10 million dollars. The market index tells you that the company's New York district represents 10.0 per cent and the Chicago district 6.0 per cent of national potential. What are the sales pars of the two districts? Multiplying, we get 10 per cent of 10 million dollars for a New

York district sales par of 1 million dollars; and 6.0 per cent gives a Chicago district sales par of $600,000. It's as simple as that.

Step 4. *Measure Territorial Variations in Sales Performance*

The next step is to measure territorial variations in sales performance. What is needed here is a method of relating actual sales—what you *did* sell—to the sales par—what you *should have* sold. The figure which expresses that relationship in the most practical and useful way is an *index of sales performance*. This is often referred to as a PI (for performance index).

The PI relates actual sales to par on an index basis. It is calculated by dividing actual sales by par. If actual sales and par are exactly equal, then the PI is 100. If the par figure is higher, then sales are below par and the PI figure is something less than 100. If actual sales are higher than par, the PI is something less than 100. Let's illustrate with the following tabular example.

MEASURING TERRITORIAL VARIATIONS IN SALES PERFORMANCE

(Assumed Company Volume in Year Analyzed: $10,000,000)

Sales district	Cleveland	Cincinnati	Chicago
Per cent of U.S. potential in district (from market index)	5.324	4.333	8.791
Sales par (market index times sales)	$532,400	$433,300	$879,100
Actual sales (from company records)	$330,620	$446,304	$721,741
Index of sales performance (PI)	62	103	82

This table tells you that of the three sales districts illustrated, only one—Cincinnati—had sales volume which was above par. The PI of 103 for Cincinnati indicates that sales there were 3 per cent above par. Chicago had a volume of sales which was 18 per cent (100 minus the Chicago PI of 82) below par. Cleveland had a PI of 62, indicating that sales there were 38 per cent below a level which would indicate a just-average job of sales performance.

Step 5. *Calculate the Sales Deficit*

In a practical program of sales control, it's a good rule to keep attention focused on the dark side of the picture. Accentuate the negative. Keep attention directed to the problem districts, the problem situations. The objective in a program of that sort is to keep your above-par territories and districts strong, while you build up strength by overcoming existing weaknesses in subpar districts. It is apparent that as a program of this type moves forward through time, each step forward in problem districts boosts the company's average performance level—which is the base line for measuring individual territorial performance. Thus the goal is constantly moving forward, and individual territories have to keep pace to maintain their individual PI levels.

It has been demonstrated that progress in overcoming territorial weak spots can be achieved more rapidly by concentrating on a small number of selected problem situations than by any general approach. Those carefully chosen problems become high-priority objectives. It is necessary to select a limited number of problem situations and to assign priorities to them, for a very practical reason. Diagnosing and correcting a territorial problem requires in most cases a variable but usually substantial amount of sales-supervisory attention. Every organization has as one inescapably scarce commodity the amount of sales-supervisory manpower available. Since that amount is limited, it must be concentrated where it will do the most good. That is the reason why the assignment of priorities to problems of a sales-territorial-weakness nature is essential.

What is the basis for assigning priorities to some selected problem situations out of the large number of candidates? That assignment should be made, in most instances, on a basis which is both objective and sensible. The marketing executive appraises the various sales-territorial weaknesses. About each weakness, he asks himself this question: How many dollars of lost sales volume does this problem territory represent? He then assigns the highest priority to the territory which represents the greatest number of lost sales dollars, the No. 2 priority to the second largest, and so on.

That question can be answered very simply *by subtracting the actual sales volume in each subpar territory from that territory's sales par.* The resulting figure—which we identify as the *sales deficit*—shows how many dollars of lost sales the problem represents. In the example above, the Chicago deficit is $157,359 and the Cleveland deficit is $201,780.

SIGNIFICANCE OF USE OF COMPANY PERFORMANCE AS BASE

In the above approach to measurement of territorial variations in sales performance, the yardstick used is a sales-par figure. That figure was arrived at by multiplying the market index figure for a territory by the company's own actual national total volume for the period being analyzed. That actual sales figure is reduced to a percentage figure also. The total of the market-index percentage figures for all territories is, of course, 100 per cent. The total of actual sales percentage figures for all territories is also 100 per cent. The company's own level of sales performance, therefore, is always at 100.

The significance of this use of the company's performance as the base line against which individual territorial performance figures are measured should be underlined.

Consider first the year-to-year variations which may occur in the company's sales volume. In one year the volume was at, say, $10,000,000. The following year there was a 10 per cent volume increase, and total sales rose to $11,000,000. Then another gain of 10 per cent to make the total sales $12,100,000. Then a decline to, say, $9,600,000. No matter what the level of the company's volume is on a dollar basis, the company's PI remains at 100. For an individual territorial PI to remain constant from year to year, it must change exactly as much (on a percentage basis) as the company's total sales, and in the same direction. If company volume dropped 10 per cent, an individual territory with a PI of 100 could have a 10 per cent decline in its territorial volume and yet retain its 100 PI. If the territory held its volume constant, or had a decline of less than 10 per cent, while the company volume dropped 10 per cent, the territorial PI would increase.

When a company adopts this approach to sales-performance measurement, it says this to its sales organization: "Our company volume will rise or fall, in total, as the result of the influence of many factors. Some of those factors are under your control, and some are not. We expect you to contribute to the company's volume a share of our total which is as large as the share of our national potential which has been assigned to you." This is a fair and equitable viewpoint, which salesmen can and do accept and appreciate.

There are other values in this approach, as compared to the use of per capita figures, for example. The base line against which territorial performance is measured is always 100. That PI figure takes into consideration differences in potential in different territories. The problem of a salesman transferred from a high per capita income territory to a low one is eliminated. His concern is on a constant 100 goal, rather than the 10.8 cents in Seattle or 4.5 cents in Atlanta. Further, with the use of per capita figures, there is a constant need for upward revision of the goal. The index approach eliminates that problem of a changing base.

NORMAL PATTERN OF SALES-PERFORMANCE VARIATION

This analytical approach uses as its base line for evaluating territorial performance the company's over-all performance. That company performance is, of course, simply a form of average of the individual territorial performance figures. As with all averages, some of the components are normally higher and some lower than the central value. But what is the normal pattern? When a company conducts analysis of this type for the first time, what may it expect in terms of a range of performance levels? The following observations, intended to provide some base line for evaluating individual-company patterns, are distilled from the results of introducing this approach into scores of different organizations. Those organizations varied widely in size, as reflected by sales-volume level. They varied also in the nature and complexity of the company's product line.

An initial analysis may be expected to disclose a range of at least 3 to 1 between the performance level of the weakest and strongest sales territory. This is the *closest* range revealed in analyses conducted in organizations which had not previously had a planned and detailed program of sales control utilizing marketing research approaches. Ranges of 6 to 1, 10 to 1, and 20 to 1 are not uncommon. A range as high as 800 to 1 has been uncovered!

Referring to the 3 to 1 range mentioned, the pattern is likely to have these characteristics. With the company's over-all average performance level (i.e., PI) as 100, the *strongest* territory is likely to have a PI of 150 or higher. The *weakest* territory is likely to have a PI of 50 or lower. Thus there is a range, from weakest to strongest, of *at least* 3 to 1.

The significance of that range in sales-performance levels should be appreciated. It means that for every $1 which the company is ringing up in sales in one territory, *per unit of potential,* the company is scoring $3 or more in another territory!

PAST WEAKNESSES REPRESENT PRESENT AND FUTURE OPPORTUNITY

The importance of concentrating sales-supervisory attention on the weaknesses disclosed by territorial analysis was indicated above. The above comment indicates why that is a sound approach. An analysis of this type can only be made in the past tense, covering a time period which is completed. Such an analysis discloses existing patterns of territorial sales strength and sales weakness. But a past weakness represents, in the present and future tense, an opportunity. It is because of that opportunity, inescapably inherent in existing weaknesses on a territorial basis, that the approach which accentuates the negative makes such sound sense.

The experience of countless companies has demonstrated that there is no way to throw a transfusion of highly profitable sales volume into the veins of a company faster than by identifying existing sales weaknesses and taking action to correct them. The profitability of the volume developed by this approach should be stressed. The company is already paying many of the costs of doing business in the areas in question: It has a salesman there, for example; its advertising is probably covering the territories. But the company is *not* securing from those territories the volume the potential of the territories would lead the company to expect. When plus volume is secured from them, it is high-profit volume because the incremental costs of achieving the volume are relatively low. Most of those costs have already been paid.

RELATIONSHIP BETWEEN PI AND MARKET SHARE

There is another reason why the approach of concentrating remedial attention on subpar territories is a sound one in the marketing sense. That reason has its roots in the relationship between a company's PI in a territory and the company's *market share* in that territory. That relationship is a close and direct one, which can easily be overlooked.

Assume a company has a market share nationally of 10 per cent. The company's own PI nationally is (as always) 100. The PI of 100 equals a 10 per cent market share. Now consider three territories in which the PI figures are, respectively, 50, 100, and 150. What is the company's market share in those three territories? The answer is that the *territorial* market share bears the same relationship to the company's *national* market share as the territorial PI bears to the national PI which is a constant of 100. Look at it in terms of these proportions.

Territorial market share : national market share : :
territorial PI : national PI (100)

Thus if the company's market share nationally is 10 per cent, as in the above example, the three territorial market-share figures will be 5 per cent, 10 per cent, and 15 per cent, respectively. This relationship exists because the *market index* which is one factor in determining the PI allocates to the individual territory a proportion of the national industry volume which is as accurate as possible. The company's territorial volume, related to the territorial industry volume, determines the market share. This relationship between territorial market share and territorial PI is an important one which should be remembered.

That relationship is, of course, of only academic interest to a company that does not know even approximately what its national market share is. Even in the case of such an organization, however, there is a significance in this relationship which should be recognized and which represents another reason why the approach of concentrating remedial attention on low-performance territories makes good marketing sense.

LIKELIHOOD OF COMPETITIVE COUNTERACTION REDUCED

There is in every industry a competitive *status quo*. Some brands are industry leaders, with large market shares; other brands are important in the industry, but have far smaller slices of the industry total than do the leaders; and still other brands are unquestionably marginal, with very slim slices of the total market. The latter group are unimportant minnows in a big pool. There are marked differences from industry to industry in competitive pressure and in the speed of competitive footwork. Some industries are characterized by very fast counterattacks whenever any one company moves to disturb the competitive *status quo*. Others appear sleepily unaware of what's going on.

The relationship between PI and market share makes the concentration on improvement of market share in below-par territories a sound approach. In those below-par territories, the company's market share is substantially lower than its national market share. An effort by the company to build its market share in problem territories up to the national level is not so much a threat to the *status quo* as an attempt to restore and preserve it! Such an action is therefore far less likely to provoke competitive counteraction or counterattack than would be a more overt attempt to expand market share and increase the company's market share. From the viewpoint of the management of the company, of course, there is no difference.

Either approach represents an attempt to increase the company's sales volume and market share. If successful, either approach will achieve both objectives. But the approach suggested here is a less conspicuous one. It might be likened to infiltration, rather than frontal attack. It is therefore less likely to stimulate competitive retaliatory action than is a more overt approach. As a result, the desired objectives can more easily be achieved. The cost of achieving them is less than would be necessary if one or more competitors were "slugging it out" to keep the company from expanding its volume and market share.

The dynamics of this approach are too obvious to require much comment. As the volume in the weakest territories moves up faster than that of the company as a whole, the PI in those territories increases. The company's PI remains at 100, but it represents an ever-higher volume level. Other territories, which were not initially in the problem category, find they have to run fast to stand in the same place in PI terms. The range between the strongest and the weakest territory narrows. Solution of the problem in some of the territories created openings for the reassignment of priorities to other areas which have not been keeping up with the company's accelerating pace. The company's volume and market share expand. A substantial toning up of the company's marketing muscle is a usual result.

TENDENCY FOR WEAK TERRITORIES TO GET WEAKER

There is a very strong force in the sales-performance area which is so pervasive that it warrants recognition and classification as a fact of marketing life. It may be briefly boiled down to this: If no positive action is taken to diagnose and correct the situation, there is a tendency for strong territories to get stronger while weak territories get weaker. Strong and weak are used here as synonymous with high and low in PI.

It is not too difficult to see why that tendency should be so marked. The strength of a strong territory did not "just happen." It represents the net-net of the influence of many factors. Those factors were heavily inclined in a positive direction. To be specific, such elements as these may be present in a strong territory: a strong salesman; unusually effective distributors or retail and wholesale support; an unusually good "fit" between the company's products and the needs of customers there; unusually heavy and/or effective advertising; and so on.

Unless specific action is taken, those elements of strength remain present and operative. A weak territory, in contrast, is usually characterized either by the presence of elements conducive to weakness or by the absence of elements of strength. In either case, if no action is taken to diagnose and correct the situation, the deterioration in the company's sales performance already evidenced by the low PI is likely to continue.

The company which has an extremely wide range in its level of sales strength in weak and strong territories faces a grave danger which is far from obvious. The danger is that such a company may be forced, in effect, into two distinct marketing situations. It may be forced to market its product in effect as though it were two different companies. Or it may be forced to develop marketing plans which are a compromise between the requirements of strong and weak territories, and therefore less effective than they could be in either type.

Consider a specific company, in the margarine business. In its factory market, that company had a market share in the 15 to 20 per cent range. Such a market share put it at or near the position of the best-selling brand in the market. It had high distribution there, a large number of user families, and substantial advertising weight. Now consider the contrast in fringe markets many miles from the factory—markets in which the brand's market share is on the order of 1 or 2 per cent of industry volume. In such markets, it is definitely an "also-ran" brand. Its distribution is likely to be spotty. It has insufficient volume to warrant much advertising. It is vulnerable to any tendency on the part of retailers to reduce the number of brands stocked. A company in that position is, in effect, in two different businesses. Its marketing effectiveness is reduced by the need to straddle dissimilar marketing situations in its planning.

The tendency of weak territories to grow weaker where no concentrated attention has been paid to them warrants comment for two additional reasons. That tendency, it should be noted, is one additional reason why the approach of concentrating on the more serious problem situations pays rich dividends. It thus serves as an insurance policy against further widening of the range between strongest and weakest territory. It guards against the risk that a company, through inactivity, might be drawn into the position of the company described in the above paragraph.

The other reason why that tendency is important lies in its influence, under some circumstances, on the assignment of priorities to problem territories. Assume a situation in which there are three or more territories with sales deficits of about equal size. Which should receive attention first? A consideration of the level of sales performance and of the trend in that sales performance would be relevant to that decision. The territory whose PI was showing the strongest adverse trend would be likely to warrant more immediate attention than another territory with an equally large sales deficit in which no sharp deterioration of the company's position was evidenced by the trend in PI.

PRACTICAL APPROACH TO INDEX-SELECTION DECISION

In the measurement of territorial sales performance, and particularly in the initial phases of a program of performance measurement, two quite dissimilar approaches deserve comment. An individual embarked on the first approach recognizes the desirability of measuring sales performance by territories. When faced with the decision on market-index selection, however, he hesitates. Maybe the market index under consideration is something less than perfect. Maybe he should spend a number of months refining and re-evaluating the market-index alternatives, before putting the program into action.

The second approach is a more direct one. The individual taking that approach chooses (with what the first individual might perhaps consider intemperate haste!) the best available market index and proceeds to go to work on the program. Performance variations are measured. Priorities are assigned. Spot research is conducted to aid in the diagnosis of the weaknesses uncovered. Then, while those activities are in progress, further work on the refinement of the market index is undertaken.

What is the difference between these two approaches? Two differences can be distinguished. One is in the speed with which the two approaches may be expected to contribute a profit payoff to the company. The second approach is far more likely to achieve such a profit contribution at an early date than the first. It is "on the road" while the other is still getting ready.

The practical desirability of proceeding with sales analysis using the best available market index, rather than of delaying analysis until the "perfect" index is developed, can hardly be overstated. The soundness of that approach can be illustrated by referring back to the preceding section on the normal pattern of sales-performance variations. It was there pointed out that it is extremely rare to find, in an initial analysis, that the weakest territory is at a performance level as high as one-third of that of the strongest territory. To illustrate, assume that an analysis of sales performance was conducted. The weakest territory had a PI of 50, the strongest of 150.

Now assume further that there was some question about the "fit" of the market index used. The weakest territory had, say, 5 per cent of the company's sales versus 10 per cent of potential according to the market index. The PI of 50 represents the result of dividing 5 (per cent of actual sales) by 10 (per cent of potential, according to the market index). Now suppose the market index were felt to be in error by as much as 10 per cent. That would put the "true" potential figure some-where between 9 and 11 per cent. When the 5 per cent is divided by 9, by 11, or by any figure in between, the result is a PI in the range between 45 and 56. The market index is thought to be in error by 20 per cent? Fine—now the PI range is somewhere between 42 and 62. By 30 per cent? That puts the PI range from 38 to 71. But even if the market index were in error by as much as 30 per cent, that territory would still be subpar in PI and would still represent a problem territory!

Most market-index possibilities that might be adopted, even as the basis for preliminary analysis, can be expected to be accurate within much closer limits than the examples given. This being the case, *they are entirely adequate tools for identifying the major problem territories,* even though the exact level of performance deficiency may be indicated with only approximate accuracy. The most practical approach is to *use* the best available index and identify the problem territories. Then *while* analysis and research are being used to determine the problem elements in each such territory (as it was in the Boston district problem in the

Allied Products, Inc., case in Chapter 13); additional work can be done on refining the index.

RELATIONSHIP BETWEEN SIZE OF TERRITORIAL UNIT AND RANGE OF PERFORMANCE VARIATION

There is a natural tendency in sales-performance measurement which should be pointed out. As a general rule, the variations which exist in sales-performance levels increase as the size of the territorial units decreases. Thus in a comparison of sales-performance levels for the four regions of the country, the variation between the highest and lowest region would be substantially less in most cases than in a comparison of the performance of the twenty or thirty districts in those regions. There are two reasons for this tendency. The first is that a regional performance figure is a net figure, combining some strong and some weak districts. It is, in effect, a regional *average* performance. As with all averages, some of the components are above and some are below the average value. Thus in the low region in performance there are districts with lower performance levels than that regional average. Similarly, in the high region in performance, there are districts with performance higher than the regional average.

The same tendency is present when the subdistrict units such as sales territories, marketing areas, etc., are considered. *The smaller the territorial unit for which performance is examined, the greater the range in variation in performance.*

The second reason for that tendency is mathematical. As the territorial units get smaller, so do the percentage figures for each unit's proportion of potential. At the same time, the range above which variation in performance is possible increases almost astronomically. Suppose there were two regions in a company's operation, each with 50 per cent of potential. The highest possible regional performance figure would be 200, and that could be achieved only if one region had all and the other none of the company's volume. Suppose that each region consisted of ten districts, each with 5 per cent of the national potential. The possible range in district performance would then be 2,000 as a PI, which of course would mean that that district contributed all of the company's volume and the remaining nineteen none. These examples will illustrate this point.

NET VERSUS GROSS DEFICITS

In analyzing sales-deficit figures, there is a problem which arises because there are deficits only in the subpar territorial units, and those deficits are offset by above-par volume in other units. It is essential to maintain *gross* deficit figures, so that the full opportunity present in sub-par territorial units can be examined. Extending the above comments, you often find a sales region in which the regional PI (which, remember, is an average for the region) is above par, but in which there are one or more sales districts with substantially weak sales performance and resulting deficits. For the region as a whole, there is no net deficit (because above-par sales in other districts offset and hide the weak-district performance). For the problem districts within the region, however, there are sales deficits, which should be carried through analysis in gross form without reducing them by offsetting them with strength from other districts.

WHY TERRITORIAL-POTENTIAL FIGURES ARE THE STARTING POINT IN MUCH PROBLEM DIAGNOSIS

There are a wide variety of different problems in the area of sales management which stem in whole or in part from faulty design of sales territories and from failure to develop accurate estimates of territorial potential. The following case will illustrate some of the ways in which territorial-potential figures enter into sales-management thinking and planning and will suggest why an examination of those potential figures is often a sound starting point in the diagnosis of a complex sales-management problem.

35. ASSOCIATED DRUG SPECIALTIES, INC. ★

Associated Drug Specialties, Inc., is an organization marketing a number of varied drug products including cold remedies, headache remedies, and similar products. The company's annual sales volume at the time of this case was $14,123,000. The company had sixty-three sales territories, divided into four regions. Three regional managers had fifteen sales territories (each manned by a single salesman) as their responsibility, while the fourth had eighteen sales territories under his supervision.

The company had continuing difficulty with some aspects of its sales-coverage problem and called in a consultant to examine its approach and to suggest ways in which some of the problems could be eased or solved. The consultant began work on this assignment by developing territorial-potential figures. As an index for this preliminary work, drug sales as estimated by *Sales Management's* annual *Survey of Buying Power* were used.

In discussing the results of this analysis of variations in territorial potentials, the consultant pointed out that the company's average territorial-potential figure was simply a function of the number of territories, representing the result of dividing 100, or the national total potential, by 63—the number of sales territories. Thus that meant that the average potential per territory for the country as a whole was 1.587 per cent of the national potential.

Next the division of national potential into the four sales regions was examined, and the average per region calculated. Here are those figures:

Sales region	Total regional potential, %	No. of territories in region	Regional average: potential per territory, %
A	24.08	15	1.605
B	24.58	15	1.639
C	25.88	18	0.943
D	25.46	15	1.697
U.S. total.........	100.00	63	1.587

The fact that the potential of sales region *C* was about the same as that of the other three regions, while that region included three more territories, had an obvious effect on the regional average. The average was extremely important, in the case of this company situation, because the company paid its salesmen on a straight-commission basis. The amount of potential in a territory therefore represented in effect a ceiling on the earning power of the individual salesman in the territory. Wide variations in territorial potential were undesirable, because they provided individual salesmen with widely varying earning potential.

The division of the United States into four or five regions is relatively common in sales-management practice. Drawing on his experience with other companies using a four-regional framework, the consultant pointed out one unusual feature of the division of potential shown on the above table. It is relatively unusual for a company to have four divisions as equal in potential as those shown. The reason for a less equal division of potential by regions is geographic. The Pacific Coast and Mountain states together represent, for most product types, about 15 per cent or a little more of the national potential. For the regional manager with Pacific Coast responsibility to have 25 per cent of the national potential therefore implies that his territorial responsibility includes some states east of the Rockies. Distances are so great that such a regional assignment is rarely a practical one.

Subdividing the regional potentials shown in the above table, this range of territorial potentials within the regions was revealed:

Sales region	Regional average: potential per territory, %	Largest territorial potential in the region, %	Smallest territorial potential in the region, %
A	1.605	2.071	0.952
B	1.639	2.382	0.960
C	0.943	1.916	0.783
D	1.697	3.554	0.894
U.S. average............	1.587		
U.S. range...............		3.554	0.783

One of the problems which had prompted the management of Associated Drug Specialties, Inc., to seek outside assistance was the difficulty they were having in keeping some of their territories staffed with salesmen. At the time of this study, eight of the sixty-three territories were without salesmen. Salesman turnover was relatively high. An examination of the eleven territories which individually represented less than 1.25 per cent of the national potential (versus the company average of 1.587 per cent) disclosed that all eight of the unfilled territories were included.

The likelihood that it was the low potential in those territories that was responsible in a large measure for the company's inability to keep them staffed with salesmen was inescapable. Since the company's sales compensation was based on a straight percentage of sales volume achieved, with the salesmen paying their own expenses out of their commissions, the situation added up like this:

1. Some territories had very low potential volume. This made it far more difficult for a salesman to achieve high volume (and high personal income) than in a territory with larger potential.

2. Because those territories had been rather consistently unmanned over a period of years, sales performance there was generally low.

3. On a straight-commission compensation plan, this meant that a salesman in one of those territories would have to work far harder for much less money than would a salesman in an adjoining territory with larger potential which had been continuously staffed. Salesmen were hired, stayed just long enough to find out "what the score was," then left.

In order to solve the company's problem, it was necessary, first, to revise territorial boundaries to equalize potentials, and second, to set up an equitable basis for compensation of salesmen who assumed the difficult assignment of representing the company in a run-down territory and rebuilding the company's volume there.

SUMMARY

1. The analysis of territorial sales opportunities, or potentials, which is the subject of this chapter, is an extremely important area of marketing research practice. Closely related to that activity is the measurement of the company's territorial sales performance, against the potentials established.

2. The basic yardstick used in measuring potentials is a market index. There are two major types: general and specific. A general market index applies to a wide variety of products. A specific market index applies to only one product or one group of similar products.

3. Once a market index has been chosen, it is possible to measure territorial variations in sales performance with the approach outlined in this chapter.

4. In that approach, the level of sales performance is translated into an index figure, known as a PI, for performance index. A sales deficit is developed for each subpar territory. That deficit figure shows the relative importance of the problems uncovered.

5. The extent of sales-performance variations has this normal pattern: The first analysis in any company situation usually discloses that the strongest territory has *at least* three times the sales volume per unit of potential of the weakest territory.

6. Concentration of diagnostic and remedial attention on the territorial weak spots is recommended, for reasons set forth in this chapter. That approach provides an avenue for adding profitable volume to the company's sales total.

7. Early use of any market index passing the evaluation of reasonableness is recommended. Refinement of the market index is possible in many cases, but sales analysis and attempts to convert sales deficits into sales gains should not be deferred until the perfect index has been developed.

QUESTIONS

1. How would you define a *market index?* Why isn't population widely used as a market index today?

2. There are two major types of market indexes. In your own words, describe each.

3. What is the first step taken to determine territorial potentials and then to evaluate sales performance?

4. What is meant by the term *sales par? PI?*

5. How would you go about the task of assigning priorities to some sales-territorial weaknesses out of a large number of candidates?

6. What is the significance of using the company's performance as the base line against which individual territorial-performance figures are measured?

7. What is the relationship, if any, between a company's PI in a territory and the company's market share in that territory?

8. Would you agree or disagree with the statement: "There is a tendency for strong territories to get stronger and weak territories to get weaker." Why or why not?

9. In the selection of a market index to be used in the measurement of territorial sales performance, two approaches are open to choice. What are these two approaches? What is the difference between them?

10. As a general rule, the variations which exist in sales-performance levels increase as the size of the territorial units decreases. Why is this tendency present?

11. Why is it important to differentiate between net- and gross-sales deficit figures?

CHAPTER 22

Product Research

One of the most important and most widely performed of marketing research activities, according to the American Management Association survey of company practices, involves *comparisons of the consumer or customer acceptance of existing products or services with that of similar competitive products or services.* This field of marketing research activity, usually described as *product research,* is the subject of this chapter.

Some minor matters of terminology, which might be confusing, should be clarified before we move into the subject of product research. First, the question of *products versus services* should be clarified. From the marketing research viewpoint, there is essentially no difference between a product or service which constitutes the major item "for sale" by an organization. When a manufacturer finishes his production process he ends up with a tangible product for sale. That is his product, the subject of any product research he does. When a service organization such as a bank or an insurance company finishes its particular "productive process," the end result is a *service* which that organization has to sell. The service of the service organization is a product, which requires research just as more tangible "products" do.

The distinction between *consumer* and *customer* also deserves a brief comment. In consumer-product marketing, it is the consumers—who are the customers—whose preferences are studied. In industrial-product marketing, however, it is customers rather than consumers who are important. Those customers may be manufacturers, processors, etc. Whatever their classification, they provide the population, or universe, among which the product research is conducted.

CUSTOMER'S VIEWPOINT NOW RECOGNIZED AS MOST IMPORTANT

The day is not too long past when production management and marketing or sales management were coordinated much less closely than they typically are today. In those days, the factory made products it thought consumers or customers ought to want to buy, and then it was up to the marketing or sales team to sell them. Sometimes the selling job was especially tough because customers didn't want the products the factory wanted them to buy. Relatively high sales costs and expensive price concessions were often incurred in moving the products of that production-oriented approach.

Today the picture has changed. It is widely recognized in management circles that it is easier and cheaper to sell what people want to buy than to persuade them to buy a product just because you want to sell it. There are constant changes in competitive products and constant changes in the tastes and/or needs and requirements of customers. Marketing research, which determines those needs or requirements and reports them to management as a guide to the product-development or product-improvement program, is a vital force in keeping a company's product line up to date.

It is only realistic to emphasize that the basic viewpoint here—that it is the customer's viewpoint rather than the factory's viewpoint that is important—has not been universally accepted. Smugness on product quality and unwarranted confidence in the company's "knowledge" of what customers want (or would want if they weren't so blankety-blank ornery!) is a deeply ingrained characteristic of many companies. Marketing research can often make major contributions to a company's sales and product growth in this area, provided it can overcome the obstacle posed by that smugness and gain a hearing.

DANGERS IN A TECHNICAL VIEWPOINT

Two distinct types of product research should be recognized. One often has nothing to do with marketing research. It involves *technical research* or *research and development* activities. The other is in the field of marketing research. It involves research among consumers or customers. The difference between those two areas is in their approach. Technical research is typically concerned with physical characteristics of the product, like wearing or abrasion resistance, length of life and stability, etc. The customer research is concerned with the attitude of consumers or customers toward a product. The dangers in a too-expert viewpoint were pointed out in the earlier discussion of the informal investigation. The same dangers are present in this research area, as the following illustration will show.

The makers of Johnson's wax products were moving out of a period when raw-material shortages (during World War II) had forced formula changes, into one of relatively unrestricted raw-material supplies. As a result, those products which had been modified because of raw-material shortages during the war period were being reformulated. One of the most important products in the company's line was a self-polishing liquid floor wax trade-marked Glo-Coat. Technically, that was a water-emulsion wax polish. Glo-Coat was the leading brand of its type, with a market share more than 50 per cent larger than the second-ranking brand. But Glo-Coat's leadership was under attack. Serious questions were being asked, especially by executives in the company's marketing division, as to the level of product quality.

Consumer research among housewives who had switched from Glo-Coat to competitive products revealed that there was substantial dissatisfaction with the water-spotting resistance of Glo-Coat. Women reported that they waxed their floor with Glo-Coat, splashed clean water on the floor in the course of doing the dishes, and ended up with a spotty-looking floor. To investigate this problem, a two-man team was appointed. One member was the representative of the technical research division of the company. The other was the marketing research director, representing the marketing division.

The two men reviewed evidence on the point under discussion. Consumer research evidence indicated that Glo-Coat had water resistance inferior to at least two major competitive products. Technical research confirmed the judgment of consumers. Glo-Coat did have less water resistance than the two products in question. Why not simply increase Glo-Coat's water resistance? Could that be done? The technical research man assured the marketing research man that it *could* be done. He also pointed out that in the combined judgment of the technical research staff, it *should not* be done!

An increase in water resistance, which would reduce the water-spot problem, would also make it more difficult for the housewife to remove Glo-Coat from the floors by scrubbing. As a result, the wax would tend to "pile up," especially in nontraffic areas, leaving an unsightly brownish stain. The technical research people were opposed to a formula modification because they were afraid of the pile-up problem. To illustrate this problem, the technical research man took the marketing research man to his own home. Sure enough, Glo-Coat had piled up in nontraffic areas in an unsightly and undesirable way.

After further consideration of this problem, the marketing research man decided to purchase a special tabulation of data from the MRCA National Consumer Panel, to which service the company subscribed. The objective of the tabulation was to secure a quantitative indication of the average quantity of self-polishing waxes like Glo-Coat which the typical buying family used in a year.

The tabulation showed that the average family buying any self-polishing wax averaged about a quart every six months. This meant perhaps two waxings of a kitchen floor in a six-month period with, presumably, a much larger number of scrubbings between waxings. The technical research man was consulted—how much Glo-Coat did he use? His consumption was about a half gallon every five to six weeks—many times the average consumption level of the typical family. Therefore the premises on which the technical-research judgment rested were unsound. The product was modified to give it additional resistance to water spotting. The company's market share expanded as soon as the new formulation had been worked into retail inventories and could be supported by advertising which stressed its new water resistance.

PRODUCT RESEARCH IS A FORM OF INSURANCE

Product research is carried on extensively today in part as a form of sales-volume insurance. Recall the Crisco-Spry competitive struggle described in Chapter 12. That struggle illustrates a principle of wide applicability which is nearly timeless. What was Crisco's position when Spry appeared on the scene? The Proctor & Gamble Company is one of the nation's leading manufacturers, guided by a management team of outstanding ability. P&G's marketing research department was and is one of the nation's largest. That department and its staff of competent and experienced personnel is constantly active in many fields including product research.

Crisco as a product was well liked by consumers generally. It had many users, and continuing promotion kept winning new users. Against the background of those elements of strength, Crisco had one important weakness. The product had some limitations and shortcomings of which consumers were aware. Lever Brothers' marketing research identified those shortcomings. The findings of that research were confirmed by the spectacular success of Spry.

The marketing principle involved is apparent. Despite many elements of strength, the existence of product weaknesses was alone enough to create a vulnerability in Crisco's position. An alert competitor could (and did!) recognize that vulnerability and effectively exploit it. What was true of Crisco was and is true of *every* product, consumer or industrial, provided there is no patent or other artificial barrier to bar a competitor from developing and introducing a superior product. *A product which has shortcomings of which its users are aware is inherently and inescapably vulnerable to a competitive challenge.* The way to remove that vulnerability is to use research to find the weaknesses in your own products and to correct those weaknesses without delay.

That vulnerability is far more widely recognized today than it was in 1936. Today most well-managed manufacturing organizations use product research continually. They research their own products to find limitations which can be overcome and to guide improvements. When used in this way, product research is sales-volume insurance. It is relatively inexpensive insurance, but so important that product research in which products are compared objectively with leading competitive products is one of the most widespread and productive areas of marketing research today.

GUIDING PRINCIPLES IN CONSUMER-PRODUCT RESEARCH

In research on consumer products, techniques have been relatively standardized. The following list of guiding principles for consumer-product research represents a distillation of the experience of many research practitioners, working on a wide variety of consumer products.

1. *Test Products Only Among Qualified Users*

The fact that a woman with naturally curly hair who would never ordinarily use a home permanent does not like the name or perfume of a new home permanent is of little interest or marketing significance to a manufacturer of home permanents. What the manufacturer wants to know is how the women who *do* use home permanents feel about his products. If you are a manufacturer of a given type of consumer product, it is the opinion of consumers who are users of the kind of product you make (and the kind of product you want to test) who are important to you. This does not mean that the average manufacturer has completely mature market penetration and that he is therefore uninterested in the opportunities to expand volume which can be developed by bringing nonusers into the market. It does underline the importance of testing *first* among users of the type of product under study. If present users of your kind of product prefer your product over a leading competitor, you have some basis for confidence that the new users you sell will also prefer it.

For another example, consider the product-testing problem of the marketing-research director of an organization which manufactures and sells a low-sudsing detergent designed primarily for use in automatic washing machines of the tumble-action type. You are that research man. You are about to conduct a product test. You would be concerned almost entirely with the reactions of women who own and use such machines. It is their reaction that is important to you, because it is their reaction which will determine the marketing success or failure of your product.

2. *Test No More Than Two Products at a Time*

When a single test product is placed with a consumer or a family, it is obvious that the test sponsor is interested in reaction to that product.

There is a very strong tendency for the tester to give the answer he or she knows is desired—what the research man calls an "accommodating answer"—the "opinion" that the test product is wonderful . . . or something more than wonderful. The validity of such a reaction is, at best, questionable. A single-product test is never made where a practical alternative is available. It is far sounder research procedure to present the tester with two products and to determine *which* of the two is preferred and the reasons for that preference. If the differences between the products are slight, as they often are, some guesswork enters in; but there are statistical techniques which a competent research man can use to measure whether a reported margin of preference is or is not significant.

The use of three or more products in a single test has rarely proved to be feasible in practice. Confusion between the products often develops, with a resulting drop in research validity. Further, there is a tendency for combinations of characteristics within products to make it difficult for a consumer to arrive at a single choice in the case of three products. In a food study, one product might be preferred for ease of preparation, and another for the end result. A choice equating such "mixed preferences" in which the number of products being compared exceeds two has a tendency to develop a large "no preference" or "like equally" response.

3. *Remove All Identification from the Products, Except for Identifying Code Letters or Numbers*

You are concerned with determining whether or not there is a difference between two *products*. Since that is the only variable you are interested in studying, you try to hold all other variables constant. Some people feel strongly favorable or unfavorable toward different *companies*. If the name of the company producing either or both of the products under test were shown on the package or product, or were otherwise made known to the test participants, the result would be only confusion. Suppose in that case a significant product preference emerged. As the research man interpreting that "preference," you would have no way of telling whether it was in fact a *product* preference, or a preference between *companies*, or some combination.

Especially where the differences between products are relatively slight, care must be taken to be sure that no biasing variable in the identification area is present.

4. *Eliminate All Variables in the Packaging, Color, Etc., of the Products Being Tested, Unless Those Variables Represent Intrinsic Features of the Products Being Tested*

This is really an extension of the point made above. It involves a separation of product features, to focus on those which are unchangeable and intrinsically part of the product under test. Suppose, for example, that a taste test were being made on orange juice. The objective of the test is to determine preference in flavor and texture between two products. There happens also to be a difference in *color*. Such a taste test would ordinarily be conducted with colored lights on the products in an enclosure so that the difference in depth of color of one juice could not influence reaction to flavor and texture.

Your objective is to be sure that no *unimportant* external characteristic influences reaction to the product itself. Thus in the case of a leading manufacturer of make-up products developing a new product, a comparative product test was planned against the leading brand of that type of product. The company's own formulation was first developed for test purposes in exactly the same skin tones as the competitive product. This was intended to eliminate preferences for different colors from a test primarily concerned with satisfaction with the wearing qualities of the product. This was done although consumer research had revealed some limitations of the colors of competitive products and although it was the company's intent to introduce its product in colors somewhat different from those used in the test.

After the test in question had been completed with color eliminated as a variable, improved colors were developed and retested before the product moved into test marketing.

5. *Have the Product Tested under Normal Usage Conditions*

The objective of product research is to see which of two products consumers like better. The opinions and preferences which are important are those which are developed under actual usage conditions. It is not the performance of the product in a laboratory that determines its sales success or failure; rather it is its performance when it is used *as consumers use it*. Because of inadequate consumer education, sheer laziness on the part of consumers, or for any of a dozen other reasons, the way consumers *do* use products often varies widely from the way they *should* or the way *manufacturers think they do*.

This points up the fact that there are important corollary values to product testing which go considerably beyond the simple determination of preference. One of those values is an indication, for example, of whether directions are adequate. Another is evidence as to whether the product's characteristics provide a wide enough "margin of consumer error" range. For example, a pie-crust-mix product test revealed extensive failures when women made pies in their own way in their own homes. When the product had been tested in the manufacturer's own test kitchens, there had been no failures. In this case it was demonstrated that failure of the women to follow directions exactly as to amount of liquid added, length of time worked, etc., had led to the failures. The product was modified to permit of wider variations in those directions.

6. Remind Test Participants That a Test Is in Progress

A product test is important to a manufacturer, to whom a successful new-product introduction may represent hundreds of thousands of dollars in volume. It is far less important to the test participant. Usually test participants are not compensated for testing, except that they receive quantities of the products tested without charge. Where a test is made in the consumer's home and is therefore removed from the direct supervision of the research personnel responsible, it is desirable to use reminders to keep the test participants' attention focused on the test.

This reminder is sometimes in the form of a phone call to the test participants, or it may be accomplished through a postcard or a letter. It is especially important where the test is supposed to start on a definite day, which day is some time in the future at the time the placement of the product is made.

7. Get Reactions Immediately after Use

In making a product test, it is desirable to provide some basis for recording reactions immediately after use of the test merchandise. This is accomplished by providing a questionnaire or similar form to be filled out immediately after use. The information developed on that questionnaire is typically supplemented by additional information gathered in a personal interview at the end of the test period.

There are two reasons why this is an essential element in sound product research. The first is because it guards against the substantial memory loss which inevitably is a factor in so much research. Suppose in a test of a food product, there was a very mild but unpleasant aftertaste from one of the products. That taste would last only as long as would be required to replace it with some other taste, perhaps from cigarette, cup of coffee, etc. Recollection of such a minor element might be fleeting, yet it could be an important element in preference. The second reason for immediate recording of reactions is to guard against the confusion as to which of the two products was or was not preferred. Since as part of the test design all identifying characteristics except the code letter or number are removed, the possibility of confusion is always high.

8. Check Early in the Test for "Bugs" in Instructions or Procedure

The problem of communication is especially important in product tests, because there is no opportunity to correct misunderstandings until it is too late. The test participant must understand exactly what and how he or she is to proceed; what reactions to record; when to make the test, etc. It is highly desirable to check to be sure that there is complete understanding of test procedures by participants. Sometimes that can be done as part of the reminder step, mentioned above. Another approach is to pretest the forms and procedures on a small scale before going into the test itself.

Product research is one area of marketing research practice in which the build-up of experience is vital. Each product test made within a particular product class becomes part of the foundation of experience for subsequent tests. Limitations of forms or procedure which are revealed by the analysis and reporting of one product test should be carefully noted and preserved, in anticipation of subsequent tests.

In terms of the cost-result equation, product research is usually a sound value. It represents an inexpensive form of insurance. That does not mean, however, that product testing is cheap. On the contrary, some product tests are relatively expensive. Even more important than the monetary costs—especially in new-product development—are the time costs involved. Time is often a scarce commodity in research. If a product being tested "flunks" its test, it must usually be returned to the lab for further development. That is unavoidable, one of the hazards of the trade. It is a very different thing to have the time consumed by a product test wasted through some oversight or error on the part of the marketing research man in planning or executing the research! No research man wants to be in the undesirable position of having responsibility for a "foul up" in his lap. As a precaution against such an eventuality, careful attention to detail in the preparation and testing of forms used, and checking the communication achieved by directions, is desirable.

9. *Let the Test Continue for a Substantial Period of Time on Continuing-use Products*

Some products, like some people, make a favorable first impression but don't wear well. It is highly desirable in the case of products which are in continuous use to get reactions over a long enough period of time to be sure the preference reported is a lasting one. In the case of research on ready-to-eat cereals, for example, General Mills, Inc., customarily uses a procedure called a "taste-tiring test." This test involves an extended period of time—from twelve to sixteen weeks. The proportion of all cereal servings which a cereal represents is measured, week after week. The company has found that some products, especially those with a novelty element, develop high initial liking but decline sharply in acceptance after a few experiences with them. Similarly in the case of product research on beer, the results of a single taste often differ markedly from preference developed over a period of time.

10. *Test Your Product against the Market Leader*

As a control product in comparative testing, it is desirable to use the best competitive product you can find. The selection process is easy, in the case of new-product development. You identify the leading brand in the field you plan to enter, as Lever Brothers identified Crisco, and then you use that product as your control. In the case of existing products the purpose of the research often determines the product to be used. Thus a comparative test conducted to evaluate the threat to your established business by a new or improved product in the field would be made against that product.

There is a very practical reason why the test should be made against the best competitive product you can find. If your product can equal or exceed in consumer acceptance that of the leading brand in a field, you can develop aggressive plans to promote that product with confidence. It is a marketing axiom that no promotion can sell a bad product more than once!

If there is no product on the market like the one which you want to test, you can use duplicate products—actually identical—so that consumer attention is focused on the products. That way, the danger that you will get an "accommodating answer" is avoided. In this (relatively rare) situation, there is an opportunity which should not be overlooked. Instead of making the product test with two actually identical products, introduce a moderate variation into one of them. This permits you to explore the value of some slight product variation within a product test as a sort of "free goods."

11. *Eliminate All Irrelevant Variables—Be Fair!*

Finally, at the risk of being repetitious, it is necessary to emphasize again the importance of being on guard against "invisible biases." For example, in a test of canned boned chicken, one of the brands used in the test came in an enameled can of distinctive color. In order to eliminate what could otherwise have been a clue to identification (and hence a violation of points 3 and 4 above), it was necessary to spray all the cans with enamel so that the distinctive color was concealed. Similarly, in a product test on beer, it was necessary to use a special type of liner for the cap to match that of the competitive product against which the test was made.

As a particularly important variable in many types of products, especially food products, the age—the interval between packing and testing —must be carefully watched. If you were making a cereal product test, for example, and used product fresh from your production line against competitive product purchased in the market, you would be introducing a substantial bias in your favor. Your product would be fresher, since it would be tested prior to the inevitable flavor loss which occurs over the period of weeks (or perhaps months!) it takes to move through trade channels, from wholesaler to retailer to pantry shelf and finally into bowls!

WHEN SHOULD PRODUCTS BE TESTED?

In general, product research is typically carried out on a continuing basis. Periodic and regularly scheduled checks of the consumer acceptance of a major product are standard practice in many companies. In addition to such regularly recurring tests, there are certain specific occasions when product research is usually desirable. Among the most important of these is the occasion when a competitor introduces a new (and theoretically, at least, improved) product. The problem here is that it is typically difficult to tell when such a change has been made, in many instances. This is one vital reason why tests are made regularly. It takes time for a product improvement to work its way through to the end of the pipeline. Only then can it safely be advertised, as in the Glo-Coat example above.

The strategic aspects of this problem are apparent. Consider two alert competitors with essentially similar products. For example, Procter & Gamble with Drene shampoo and Colgate with Halo. Assume that P&G develops an improvement giving it a performance advantage over the Halo product. By the time that improved formulation has worked its way down to retail and can be supported by advertising, Drene is in a position to achieve major competitive gains. For it will take time for Colgate to develop a similar improvement, and then more time for *that* improved product to work *its* way down to retail! Actually this rarely happens, because *continuing* product tests reveal the improvement in a competitive product before that improvement can be translated into a sales gain in most instances.

A second occasion when product research is especially desirable is when a company has developed an improved product or product modification that it wishes to introduce. Product research confirms that the improvement is really an improvement, in the eyes of customers.

A third influence which leads to accelerated product research is any basic change in the nature of the market. For example, a strong growth in the do-it-yourself trend made it necessary for manufacturers of power tools to reconsider the design features of those tools against the requirements of users who were not skilled craftsmen. Added safety features and some simplifications of design were the result. Another example of the same type would be any significant change in the economic climate. With a general increase in income levels, there was a considerable amount of upgrading in consumer purchases. A product which had been satisfactory might not fit the new trend toward better products and might lose market position to one previously in the luxury bracket.

SAMPLE SIZE REQUIRED FOR A PRODUCT TEST

There are wide variations in the sample size used for product tests. Some companies stress the quantitative aspects of product testing. They use a relatively large sample size—sometimes in the area of 1,000 to 1,200 participating individuals or families. Others use a smaller sample, often in the area ranging from 150 to 250 maximum, and rely on more intensive questioning to develop significant results. The larger sample size is sometimes used with a mail-panel approach. The smaller sample is usually used in personal interviewing. The superiority of personal interviews over mail as a basis for the kind of information which can be developed by the probing of a skilled interviewer tends to cancel out the apparent advantages of the larger sample size.

Cost considerations and availability of product often enter into the decision on sample size for a product test. Thus it is not unusual to find one of the test products a pilot-plant run available only in limited quantities. That is obviously a major influence on the sample-size decision. Or if the value of the product being tested is high, the added value of expanding the sample and increasing costs must be weighed carefully.

In product research it is usual to find that the total sample size at the end of the study is smaller than the total number of placements made. A family has illness or death, which interferes with their plan to test a product. A vacation takes them out of town at the time of the callback, hence they don't get into the final sample. A playful toddler loses or breaks the test merchandise—scratch one sampling unit! Provision for some excess in the initial sample is therefore necessary to deliver a planned-for sample size of a specified number of completed tests.

DETAILED REACTIONS OFFSET HALO TENDENCY

In product research, attention must be devoted to the problem of a *halo* reaction. That is, test participants who like a product claim to like everything about it; test participants who dislike a product claim to dislike everything about it. One way to dig through that reaction is to get a general reaction and also to get preference on specific features of each test product. This enables the respondent to register the initial over-all preference, without having that preference obscure specific reactions for or against different product characteristics in either product.

Here is an example of the halo tendency completely invalidating a product-test result. Two hair rinses were tested against each other. The perfume of one of the two was strongly disliked. As a result, all other features of that product were also rated negatively. When the perfume disadvantage was overcome, the same product (but with a different perfume!) acquired tremendously improved performance in areas which apparently had nothing to do with the scent.

ILLUSTRATION OF A NORMAL PRODUCT-TEST PATTERN

Table 22.1 illustrates the normal pattern of a product test on a consumer product. In this case a whipped salad dressing (G) was tested

Table 22.1. A Typical Product-test Pattern on a Consumer Product

	General preference	
	Prefer product G	Prefer Miracle-Whip
Total................................	67	76
Reactions to product G		
Taste reactions:		
Too bland.....................	1	30
Too sharp.....................	...	29
Too sweet.....................	...	7
Too oily......................	2	28
Too salty.....................	...	3
Consistency reactions:		
Too thick.....................	3	34
Too thin......................	2	6
Reactions to product H (Miracle-Whip)		
Taste reactions:		
Too bland.....................	20	1
Too sharp.....................	37	1
Too sweet.....................	5	1
Too oily......................	14	...
Too salty.....................	3	...
Consistency reactions:		
Too thick.....................	18	12*
Too thin......................	10	...

against Kraft's Miracle-Whip, the leading whipped dressing. The table illustrates the halo tendency which pervades much product research. Those who like a product tend to like everything about it. This tendency is so strong that the deviation marked with an asterisk (12 "too thick" ratings of Miracle-Whip among those who preferred it) signals the opportunity for a product improvement. The sample size in this case was 150, with 7 preferring the two products equally.

In consumer-product research, it is usually necessary to consider the conditioning effect of established habits. In a food-product test, for example, you would ordinarily determine the brand regularly used as part of the qualifying (placement) interview. In tabulating and analyzing results, a breakdown of preference to split preference by those who do and do not regularly use the brands tested is helpful.

ILLUSTRATION OF A PRODUCT-RESEARCH CONTRIBUTION

Sometimes product tests reveal that both the products tested are in need of improvement in some particular. Table 22.2 illustrates this point

Table 22.2. Product Research Identifies a Competitive Weakness

	General preference	
	Prefer product K	Prefer product R
Total......................	64	54
Reactions to product K		
Too thick............	11	33
Too thin.............	1	2
Reactions to product R		
Too thick............	54	14
Too thin.............	...	...

as it was revealed in a test of two mayonnaise products. Both the products tested were too thick, in the opinion of consumers. The value of this finding becomes more apparent when you know that product R in the test was the leading mayonnaise brand on the market. The manufacturer who was developing product K as a new product was trying to make that product as thick as the established brand. The test revealed that product development was working in the wrong direction. It incidentally revealed a weakness in the best-selling brand which the new brand could overcome and exploit successfully in sales promotion and advertising.

Incidentally, the process of making the product thicker had a substantial inflating effect on raw-material costs. A lower-cost product with higher consumer acceptance was thus developed as a result of this particular product test.

SAMPLING ASPECTS OF PRODUCT RESEARCH

Decisions as to sample are extremely important in product research. Those decisions include, of course, the ever-present one of determining the size of the sample to be used. Even more important are related decisions as to the characteristics of the sample to be used. Probability sampling is not possible in product research, because the cooperation of respondents is essential. The refusal rate in attempts to do product research on a sample selected by probability methods is so high that the test sample cannot be accurately described as a probability sample. The costs involved are also relatively high. Most product tests are made with judgment samples.

The point made above regarding the identification of users of the product influences the sample design. Where extensive information on the characteristics of users versus nonusers is available, that information is often helpful. It is applied to select sampling areas in which the incidence of users to the total population is relatively high, so that the total research cost is reduced by minimizing the proportion of nonqualified respondents contacted.

It is often desirable in product research to have a sample made up of light-, medium-, and heavy-volume consumers of the product under test. The reactions of those consumption groups often vary widely. Another approach to this same aspect of the product-research problem is to secure data on consumption at the time of qualification, classify respondents into volume groups, and examine the reactions of the groups individually without making an attempt to secure any known proportion of respondents in each group. Where this is done, the size of subsamples must be considered. It may be necessary to supplement the test sample to compensate for underrepresentation or too small a sample of heavy-volume consumers.

In general, the sample among whom a product is tested should be representative of the total population of users of the product. Controls are often established to be sure that those sample characteristics relevant to the product test are represented in approximate proportion and in adequate number. Thus when a product test was made for a cake-mix product aimed at the small-family market, careful control of the test sample by family size was required. Because small families often include two adult working members, they are difficult to find "at home" during the working day. Week-end and evening interviewing was required to secure an adequate sample of small families in that cake-mix test.

GEOGRAPHICAL DISPERSION OF SAMPLE

Is it necessary, in making a product test of a product to be sold in all parts of the country, to use a sample of test participants which is similarly geographically dispersed? In theory at least, the answer to that question is an affirmative one. That is the answer which leads to the use of relatively large samples of families, in testing consumer products, usually through the facilities of a mail-panel firm. In practice, many consumer-product tests are made in a single market, or in two to four markets. The result of the research in those limited areas is expected to indicate acceptance of the product on a national scale.

Whether those expectations are warranted depends to a considerable extent on the product involved and on what is known about the existing consumption pattern on that product. Begin with some extreme samples: If you were researching an improved product with an essentially regional consumption pattern—like hominy, for example—you would obviously have to test it where it was known and consumed. Or if you were testing an improved baking powder, you would require a sample drawn from small-town and farm homes where usage of that product is high. Moving on to less obvious illustrations, a biscuit mix would almost certainly require both a Southern and a non-Southern subsample. Products with a racial or religious background require special consideration. Thus a spaghetti sauce intended for volume usage would have to be tested, in all probability, among families that were and were not of Italian racial stock, with the preferences of each group considered separately.

Consumption of fish is high among families in New England and along both coasts and lower inland. Fish consumption is higher among Roman Catholic families. A test of an improved fish-stick product therefore required a four-cell sample. Both high- and low-consumption areas had to be represented, with subsamples of adequate size. Catholic and non-Catholic families also had to be represented to provide a dependable sample base.

Apart from those products on which there is known to be a sharp and distinctive consumption pattern, is geographical dispersion necessary in product research? A substantial body of evidence indicates that such dispersion is not required in the case of many consumer products. This is in part a relatively recent development, reflecting the "homogenization" of the national market for consumer products. Wartime migration and the advent of television have both contributed to the erosion of regional and city-size variations in taste, attitudes, etc., which once required representation of many geographic areas in a product test.

RESEARCH ON INDIVIDUAL PRODUCT CHARACTERISTICS

Most of the comments up to this point have been concerned with the total test of a completed product. The relatively long time required for such tests and the not-inconsiderable expense involved disqualify that approach in many situations. That is particularly true where the number of product alternatives is large. An illustration is provided by a new cereal developed by General Mills, Inc. The product—subsequently named Trix—was a corn cereal in puff form. The puffs were in different colors, were sugar-coated, and had a fruit flavoring. The concentration of fruit flavoring used could vary anywhere within a range of from 1 to 10, different amounts of sweetening could be used in the coating, different colors used, and so on. The permutations and combinations of product characteristics in that case were almost endless.

When a single product characteristic—such as the strength of the fruit flavoring in Trix—is being researched, other product characteristics are held constant. A somewhat different research approach is often used in such a case. The following case is illustrative.

36. JIFFY MIX AND FLAVORING CO. ★

The Jiffy Mix and Flavoring Co., located in Chicago, had developed a line of frosting mixes. Consumer research on those products in which they were compared with leading competitive products, along the lines described earlier in this chapter, had indicated that the proposed line of frosting mixes had high consumer acceptance. Many decisions remained before the product line was ready for launching. One vital decision was in the packaging area.

Two methods of packaging the new frosting mixes were under consideration. One involved the use of a metal-foil envelope, within a cardboard package. The other used a waxed-paper wrapper for the inner portion of the package. The metal-foil package was substantially more expensive. The executives of the company were concerned about whether that cost was justified. The product, if packed in metal foil, would retain its flavor better over the period of time required to move through trade channels. The time required for that movement, including allowance for time on the pantry shelf after purchase, was estimated. The question was whether or not the loss in flavor over that period of time was great enough to be noticeable to the consumer. If it were, the more expensive package might be desirable.

In this case, the chocolate-frosting mix was considered to be the most important flavor. Two formulations of frosting mix were used in the test. The only difference between those two "different products" was in age. One had characteristics of freshness such as the foil envelope could provide. The other had undergone the flavor loss which would result from the shelf-life time factor in the less expensive package.

In developing the research plan for this problem, it was considered desirable to have the company's home economist supervise the mixing and frosting of cakes with the products in a commercial kitchen. This made available frosted cakes which could be used in the research. A sample including 400 respondents was considered necessary, with each respondent tasting both formulations. All variables were carefully controlled. Half the respondents tasted one formulation first, and the other half tasted the other. Respondents were asked to rate each product. Water was provided to permit rinsing of the mouth between tastes. The two cakes were identified with code numbers 375 and 573 to eliminate designation bias between letters and of odd over even numbers. Adults were interviewed in their homes. Children were interviewed one at a time, with a tasting setup made near a school or playground. Table 22.3

Table 22.3. Frosting Rating Scale

NOTE: IT IS IMPORTANT THAT THE TASTER CONCENTRATE
ONLY ON THE FROSTING

You will be given two pieces of frosted cake. We want to know about each how much you *like it* or *dislike it*. Eat as much of each piece as you need to before making up your mind. Drink some water after you have finished with the first sample and then wait for the next. There will be approximately two minutes between samples.

When you have decided how you feel about the frosting, use the scales below to indicate your attitude. Check at the point on the scale which best describes your feeling about the frosting. Also your comments are invited as they are generally meaningful.

Keep in mind you are the judge. You are the only one who can tell what you like. Nobody knows whether this frosting is good, bad, or indifferent. An honest expression of your personal feeling will help us to decide.

SHOW YOUR REACTION BY CHECKING THE SCALE

Code: 375	Code: 573
_____ Like extremely	_____ Like extremely
_____ Like very much	_____ Like very much
_____ Like moderately	_____ Like moderately
_____ Like slightly	_____ Like slightly
_____ Neither like nor dislike	_____ Neither like nor dislike
_____ Dislike slightly	_____ Dislike slightly
_____ Dislike moderately	_____ Dislike moderately
_____ Dislike very much	_____ Dislike very much
_____ Dislike extremely	_____ Dislike extremely
Comments:_____	Comments:_____

illustrates the rating scale and instructions used. In the case of children, the instructions were read by the interviewer.

Table 22.4 illustrates the results of this research. The loss in flavor occurring through time was reflected in a significantly lower level of liking, and the decision was made to pack the product in the foil container.

The relatively high costs involved in this research led the company into a considerable amount of research-technique experimentation. One approach used was the development of a panel of "tasters" recruited from the factory of the firm. Continuing experiments were conducted to determine the minimum difference in taste which could be detected by a trained panel. The company's panel developed an ability to repeat

Table 22.4. Scale Responses

Assigned value	Scale-point description	Foil-packaged	Paper-packaged
9	Like extremely	88	38
8	Like very much	154	118
7	Like moderately	96	104
6	Like slightly	36	80
5	Neither like nor dislike	4	16
4	Dislike slightly	10	16
3	Dislike moderately	4	14
2	Dislike very much	6	12
1	Dislike extremely	2	2
Total responses.............		400	400
Mean rating.............		7.50	6.80
Dislike responses, %........		5.5	11.0

tests on identical formulations at different times and to develop identical ratings for them. A total of 25 different "difference" tests were used in establishing the discriminatory powers of panel members. A total of thirty employees were finally chosen for a continuing taste panel.

In the experimental work, sometimes one product was tested and rated and sometimes two were used. Satisfactory ratings were secured on a single product, but testing two products was considered to represent a more efficient use of research time. Where the number of products was three or more, considerable taste fatigue became evident. The possibility that the test panel might become conditioned through time was considered, and repeated checks on control products to be sure their rating level on those (constant) products were unchanged were used.

This employee panel provided guidance in subsequent consumer research. Where two or more formulations of a product were under consideration, the test panel first established that there was in fact a difference which could be detected by trained tasters. Only when the existence of such a difference had been established was a large-scale consumer study, such as the one described above, conducted. Note that the company in this case applied these two product-testing approaches in the reverse of a logical order. In the study described, it was quite possible that no difference which trained testers could distinguish existed. The employee panel, in such a case, would have been able to reach that finding in a minimum amount of time and at low cost. If that had been the case, the research described would have ended in a tie. That finding might have led to the opposite packaging decision, since the higher price of foil was not equated with consumer-acceptance advantages.

— ★ —

PRODUCT RESEARCH IN INDUSTRIAL MARKETING

The comments above apply primarily to research on consumer products. A great deal of product research in industrial marketing is required, but that research is often far more difficult than is consumer-product research. One source of difficulty lies in the multiplicity of influences which enter into industrial marketing. In the consumer-product field, it is necessary to secure acceptance of a product by consumers. In industrial marketing, the product must meet various sets of specifications as to initial cost, maintenance cost, and performance standards. Often those specifications are developed by different individuals, or individuals in different functional positions. What the operator of a machine wants, for example, may be in conflict with what the maintenance engineer demands, and there may be other desires or needs in conflict with both of those sets.

An additional complexity is posed by the relatively high cost of developing a physical product for test purposes in many industrial-marketing situations. The bulk of the product makes it impossible to take a physical product to the individual whose reactions are sought in many instances. Often blueprints or sketches of proposed products or of product modifications are developed for product research in industrial marketing.

In industrial marketing as in consumer marketing, however, it is what the customer wants that is important, rather than what someone in the factory thinks the customer *ought* to want. Jerome Fitzsimmons has described some work on a filling pump for bulk service stations which is illustrative. The assignment began with a request to evaluate an advertising appeal to be used. The pump in question was much quieter in operation than competitive pumps. An advertisement presenting the "quiet" appeal was used in interviewing in bulk service stations. The research disclosed that such stations are inescapably noisy. Whether a pump did or did not make a small contribution to the total din was relatively unimportant to the operator. However, the filling load was great at some times in the day. The result was that considerable lost time resulted, as trucks awaited their turns. What the operator needed was not a quieter pump, but one which would fill trucks faster! It developed that the new pump had superior speed. Research among customers, to guide product development, would have been helpful in focusing product-development time on capacity, where it was vital, rather than on quietness of operation.

Much industrial-product product research requires an extremely intimate knowledge of the product characteristics or processes involved. As a result, much of that research is conducted by research and development people rather than by marketing research personnel. As a generalization, it would often take less time to indoctrinate an engineer or design executive with principles of marketing research applicable to product testing than it would to indoctrinate a research man with the background he would require for a particular product study. The approach indicated therefore has efficiency to recommend it.

SUMMARY

1. The current great importance of product research reflects a growing recognition of the fact that it is the viewpoint of the customer that is important in designing and developing products today. It is easier and less expensive to make the kind of product people want to buy, and then to sell it, than to make a product without specific reference to consumer desires, and then perhaps incur very great marketing costs trying to move it.

2. Experience in product research has revealed that there is an ever-present danger in accepting without question the viewpoint of technically trained people. They are sometimes too close to the product and have an *expert* viewpoint which is quite different from that of typical customers or consumers.

3. A series of guides to consumer-product product research are presented in this chapter. Those guides have this as a common aim: to eliminate biases arising from factors irrelevant to the single variable under consideration, and to secure information as accurately as possible.

4. A *continuing* program of product research is found in most well-managed organizations. Sporadic product testing is likely to end up as "too little, too late."

5. In product research, attention should be directed to the problem posed by the halo tendency. As a result of that tendency, people tend to like everything about a product which is generally liked and to dislike everything about a product that is generally disliked. By careful exploration of reactions to specific product characteristics, as well as to the products as a whole, valuable information can be secured despite a general preference which is relatively strong.

QUESTIONS

1. In your own words, how would you describe product research? From a marketing research viewpoint, is there any difference in the terms *products versus services* and *consumers versus customers?*

2. How would you account for the current great importance of product research?

3. What is the danger, if any, in accepting without question the viewpoint of people trained and skilled in technical research?

4. What were the guides to consumer-product product research presented in this chapter? What is the common aim of these guides?

5. When should product research be conducted? What is the reason for your answer?

6. What are your attitudes toward the sample size used for product tests? What influences these attitudes?

7. Of what importance are the decisions as to the characteristics of the sample to be used in product research?

8. What is meant by the term *halo tendency?* What problems does this pose to the researcher?

CHAPTER 23

New-product Development

In the development of new businesses and new industries, and in the growth and diversification of old ones, innovation has been a major competitive weapon. One aspect of that innovation has been the *new-product-development* activities which have been playing an increasingly important role in American marketing. New-product development in the broad sense is an extremely large and complicated field, which could easily serve as the subject of a larger book than this one.

In the area of new-product development, marketing research participates in many ways and many forms. The objective of marketing research in this field as in others is essentially to provide guidance to executive judgment. There are many vital decisions in the course of developing and launching a new product. The importance of marketing research contributions to those decisions is indicated by the fact that two distinct marketing research activities in this area were included among the group of *most important* and *most widely performed* marketing research activities in the American Management Association study of company practices. One of those activities involved *estimates of the demand for new products.* The other was concerned with *the measurement of consumer or customer acceptance of new products.*

This chapter provides a broad overview of the new-product-development area, with emphasis on marketing research participation in that area. In the interests of perspective, note that other chapters in this section also deal with aspects of new-product development. Thus the process of estimating demand for a proposed new product and of estimating the size of the market for an existing product are closely related. Chapter 20 applies to both areas. Also the process of determining the consumer or customer acceptance of a proposed new product overlaps substantially with comparative studies of customer acceptance of existing products versus competitive products. Chapter 22 on product research thus has many contributions to make to your knowledge of the role of marketing research in new-product development.

STEPS IN THE PROCESS OF NEW-PRODUCT DEVELOPMENT

There are tremendous differences from company to company and from industry to industry in the relative emphasis placed on the development of new products. In some organizations, new-product development is the primary responsibility of technical-research people outside the company's marketing department or division. In others, it is a primary area of marketing management responsibility. The trend appears to be toward increasing participation by marketing management executives in the new-product program.

Regardless of where within the organization chart new-product development is assigned, the following ten steps are likely to serve as the basic framework of new-product activities:

Step 1. *Decision on New-product Idea*

What kind of new product are we considering, or should we be considering?

Step 2. *Preliminary Evaluation of the Opportunities That New Product Represents*

What are the positive and negative elements which the production and sale of such a product would involve, for this company?

Step 3. *Detailed Study of the Size and Characteristics of the Market for the Proposed New Product*

Step 4. *Decision to Launch the Proposed New Product*

Step 5. *Actual Physical Development of the Proposed New Product, Usually to Match Specifications Developed in Part through Marketing Research among Customers or Potential Customers for the Product*

Step 6. *Customer or Consumer Acceptance Checks of the Developed Product*

These may be against a leading competitive product, if there is such a product on the market. Or they may be between two or more possible variants or variations of the proposed new product itself. The latter approach is sometimes part 1 and a competitive check part 2 within this particular area of the new-product–development activities.

Step 7. *Development of Detailed Marketing Plans for the New Product*

These would normally include crystallization of decisions on sizes, varieties, prices, area of introduction, sales methods and policies, and all other decisions required before a new product can be placed on the market with a reasonable expectation of success.

Step 8. *Actual Market Testing, Including Perhaps a Regional or Small-scale Introduction of the Proposed Item*

Chapter 25 on Test Marketing applies here and will contribute to understanding of this step.

Step 9. *Full-scale Launching of the New Product*

Step 10. *Follow-through and Reappraisal of the Progress of the New Product*

Primary emphasis in this step is on a comparison of the anticipated and actual volume and profit achievements of the new product. A revision of plans to take into consideration any major changes in competitive activities or in the competitive climate within which the product is marketed is sometimes required.

While these steps are listed numerically, the listing is primarily as a matter of convenience. In any particular new-product-development program, the sequence of these steps may vary. Also, any two or more of the steps might be carried on at the same time. Occasionally one of the steps listed is omitted from the development process on a specific new product. The omission may be planned or unplanned. Where it is a planned omission, it implies either that the step is considered unnecessary in the case of that particular product or that it is omitted as a calculated risk. Since all new-product development is inherently and inescapably risky—it has been estimated that four out of five new consumer products which are launched prove failures in the market place—omission of a step which increases the risks is hazardous indeed. Where the omission is unintentional, it is likely to represent, at least potentially, a point of vulnerability, perhaps of far-reaching consequences.

SEARCH FOR AND DECISION ON NEW-PRODUCT IDEA

What is involved in this first step is a preliminary determination of the type of new product to be launched. A decision here has the effect of narrowing and delimiting the area within which the subsequent steps in new-product development take place. Sometimes there is a tendency to keep the area of exploration relatively broad. This in turn often multiplies many times over the amount of work which must be done in each subsequent step. The objective in this step should be primarily one of narrowing the field of search. It may involve the selection of the industry or general-product field into which the new product will be entered. It need not, and in fact should not, at this point, go so far as to define the product's specific characteristics.

Sometimes this step is of minor importance or is unnecessary. This occurs, for example, where the new item involved is simply a modification of an existing one or is merely an extension of the existing line of products. When Jell-O adds a new flavor to its line, for example, there is no need for this step. The same thing applies when the Johnson's wax organization develops a new formula or type of self-polishing floor wax, or decides to develop its cream wax into a product called Jubilee and sell it for a more specialized range of wax and polish applications.

Ideas for new products flow in from many sources. Suggestions from company personnel are one source. Particularly valuable are the suggestions from the sales force or from sales executives. Salesmen who are in daily contact with customers and prospects can often determine what customer needs are not being satisfactorily supplied. They are also keenly interested in competitive activity and in competitive new-product development. Lost orders often alert them to the threat posed by a new competitive product more quickly than a desk-bound executive could perceive that threat. Customer complaints about existing products sometimes stimulate new-product thinking. Business and trade publications stimulate much new-product activity, as they report facts about the volume in expanding fields and the promotional plans of industry leaders.

OBJECTIVE OF NEW-PRODUCT ACTIVITY GUIDES SEARCH

Often it is the objective of a new-product-development program which serves as a guide in this step. Why is management so vitally interested in new-product development? There are many reasons, which vary in importance from firm to firm. Some companies seek new products because they want added volume to spread fixed costs, often including the cost of maintaining a sales organization. Others are interested in replacing the volume lost when other, older products declined in relative popularity. The Shower-of-Stars Cosmetics case provides an illustration. Others are seeking to push production closer to capacity by utilizing idle plant facilities.

Others are seeking diversification for any of a number of reasons. They may be trying to reduce the likelihood that a decline in activity in a particular industry may find the company's volume and profit vulnerable. Companies which were initially primarily in a dependent position with regard to another industry—such as those supplying some part of the needs of the automotive industry, for example—have been especially active in new-product development. They may be seeking to offset a painfully seasonal business. An illustration is the manufacturer of Christmas-tree lighting sets who moved into the manufacture of lawn-sprinkling equipment.

Often it is the marketing need for a "full line" which stimulates new-product development. When there are strong competitive disadvantages for a part-line manufacturer in competition with full-line firms, new-product development is stimulated. Often an apparently great or expanding potential in an industry motivates firms outside of it to move in and "cut themselves a slice."

OBJECTIVES LIMIT AREA EXPLORED

The specific objectives of a company's new-product development narrow the area within which product possibilities would be explored. If the objective is to fill up unused plant capacity, the company would be likely to use the characteristics of the unused facilities as a starting point. If the objective is to spread sales costs more efficiently, the new-product search would be likely to be confined to products which in general are sold to and through the same types of customers or through the same distribution channels. If the objective is to move from a part-line to full-line position, the relative volume of the products not included in the line would have an influence on priorities in the new-product program. Diversification to introduce a stabilizing effect on volume would be likely to confine a company's interests to products of the same general type as those manufactured. Or it might stimulate interest in crossing the barrier separating consumer products from industrial products.

Some specific illustrations: Bendix Home Appliances, Inc., which pioneered the automatic washing machine was vulnerable when full-line appliance manufacturers like Frigidaire, General Electric, and Westinghouse moved forcefully into the automatic washing machine field. Bendix added refrigerators and ranges to its line, without marked sales success. The makers of Maytag conventional washers similarly moved in a full-line direction by adding freezers and other products. Procter & Gamble, entrenched in the soap and shortening field, moved into drug marketing with shampoos, home permanents, and dentifrices, attracted in part by the substantial volume and relatively wide profit margins in those product lines. Sylvania moved into the manufacture of fluorescent lighting fixtures, as one way of increasing its sales of fluorescent lights. Most of the large milling firms moved aggressively into the cake-mix field, in part to replace volume lost through the long-continuing decline in flour consumption.

This step in the process of developing and launching a new product must often be highly selective. The number of new-product avenues open for exploration is limitless. The amount of time required to develop and launch a single new product may be as long as five or ten years. Obviously there is a need for some basis for screening ideas and assigning priorities to the surviving product projects. Marketing research is helpful in that screening process. Remember that often what is a new product for one firm is an old established product for another. Thus when P&G introduced Gleem tooth paste, it was a new P&G product in what was for other firms such as Lever Brothers Co. and Colgate an established and important industry. Analysis of the size, trend, and characteristics of the dentifrice industry would represent new-product exploration for P&G's marketing research department. The same type of work would be part of the continuing, operating assignment of the Lever Brothers and Colgate marketing research staffs.

PRELIMINARY EVALUATION OF OPPORTUNITIES

Once one or more new-product possibilities have been selected, marketing research is used to appraise each opportunity in more specific terms. Is the volume of the industry which the new product would enter increasing or decreasing? This is a key point because in a declining industry excess capacity often exists or develops. That leads in some instances to extremely difficult price competition and reduces the profit attraction of a particular field. A close look at the composition of the industry, through an informal investigation, is often indicated. How many manufacturers represent the "competitive population" of the new industry under consideration? Is the number increasing or decreasing? Why? Often special tabulations of data from the Census of Manufactures are helpful in pinpointing the volume composition of the industry where the number of manufacturers is large.

This step flows naturally into the next one and serves primarily as a form of insurance policy. If it discloses some major reason why the new product is extremely unlikely to achieve its objective, this step may serve to terminate activity while the company's investment of time and effort is still moderate. An example will show how the objectives of the activity serve as a continuing check point. The Toni Company was seeking one or more new products with a strong winter seasonal peak in sales to share its television programs with products peaking sales in summer months. One product considered was a hand lotion. Toni's interest in the hand-lotion field was diminished, at least temporarily, when marketing research disclosed some peculiar sectional and city-size characteristics of consumption which made hand lotions a poor "fit" with the television medium.

If the preliminary evaluation discloses no strong negative factor, the development program is likely to move on into a more detailed study of the market and its opportunities.

DETAILED MARKET STUDY FOLLOWS

The relationship between this step and the one which preceded it is something like that between a distance shot and a close-up in photography. A company first makes a preliminary examination of the market for a new product it is considering. In that examination it generally uses information that is already available from published or other sources or information that can be secured inexpensively. The expense factor is important because a company may be exploring many different industries or product types, seeking the ones which seem most attractive and most suited to the company's objectives.

In the detailed market study, a company moves in for a closer look. Now it fills in details where it was previously concerned largely with broad outlines. In the preceding step, for example, a company considering a new product in the hand lotion or fractional-horsepower motor field might check the trend of industry volume for the entire product class. In the detailed market study, however, it would begin to consider such specifics as the division of hand-lotion volume between creams and liquids and trends in that division. In the motor field, it would examine the division of total market by motors of different capacity or by purchasing industries.

The detailed market study often includes an appraisal of the strengths and weaknesses of competitors. It examines the relative importance of different channels of distribution or customer types. It studies existing price levels and discount structure and the characteristics of the customers or users of the product. There are many specific questions which management must have answered in order to be able to plan an intelligent marketing program for a new product. It is the function of this step to answer such questions.

PROFIT IS A KEY FACTOR

A key factor in the detailed market study often is an attempt to determine the *profit* as well as the *volume* opportunity a new product represents. Estimates of the production costs of leading competitive products often play a part in that determination. In industrial marketing, in particular, where the length of production runs may be relatively short, this cost-of-manufacture study may carry costs to several decimal places. Studies of sales costs and of advertising expenditures are also typically included. Two important applications of data on advertising expenditures are worth noting. First, the expenditure for advertising on a particular product or brand, when compared with that of other brands, often provides a useful "fix" on sales volume by items. Second, the level of advertising expenditures is a key element in determining profitability.

It is not unusual to find that a product under consideration may appear to represent an inviting profit potential, because the production cost is far below the manufacturer's sales price. If most of the difference is soaked up by the advertising and sales costs required to move the product, the net profit opportunity is likely to be far lower than it might at first appear.

Sometimes this step discloses that the opportunity for a new product is unattractive because of existing price policies. A consumer-product manufacturer was considering entering a market dominated by a single brand. When detailed cost estimates were developed, it was found that the price policy of the dominant brand was one in which an extremely narrow unit margin was maintained. Profits were substantial, because of total volume. Such a price policy makes it almost impossible for a newcomer to enter the market without heavy spending. That is, of course, one reason for such a policy. In this instance, the company's new-product interests were transferred to other products.

Note again that a company's new-product objectives again are a factor in this step. They provide a yardstick useful in measuring the various characteristics of the market about to be entered. The Johnson's wax organization was considering the addition of shoe polish to its line. The objective of the addition was to spread sales and advertising costs over a longer line of products and over additional volume. The detailed market study revealed that an extremely large part of the volume of shoe polish moved through entirely different distribution channels than the company's main line of products. While there was a volume opportunity, there was a questionable profit opportunity because of the added costs of covering additional outlet types. There was no fit between the product and the company's objectives, so it was decided not to enter the field.

EXAMPLE OF DATA IN A DETAILED MARKET STUDY

The scope of a detailed market study for a consumer product may be illustrated by this subject outline of the market study which preceded the development and introduction of an extremely successful consumer product in the food field:

1. Size of the market for this kind of product nationally.
2. Recent trends in market size.
3. Division of the market by major product subtypes and trends in that division.
4. Data on how the industry volume is divided by the types of outlets through which it is purchased.

5. Detailed characteristics of the market for this product on a geographic section basis.

6. Seasonal variations in consumption of this type of product.

7. Special market characteristics affecting sales. (In this case, the primary emphasis was on family size and family composition. Other examples would be climatic factors, water-hardness variations, electric-gas rates, etc.)

8. Characteristics of purchasers by sex, age, socioeconomic status, etc.

9. Estimated competitive division of market by companies and by brands, with detail for each major product subtype.

10. Size and price composition of industry, with trade-discount practices, promotional allowances, etc.

11. Advertising expenditures by brands, with details as to advertising media used, etc.

It is not suggested that all companies dig into the marketing facts of life to this extent before deciding to go ahead with a new product. If they did, the success batting average would certainly be higher than one out of four! This type of detailed, planned digging, however, is standard operating procedure in many well-managed companies. The interesting corollary to the fact that not all new-product launchings are preceded by detailed market study is the undeniable fact that many new products never seem to "get off the ground." The cost to a company of a new-product failure, both in dollars and in prestige, can be tremendous. The observation has been made that under today's tax laws, only a big, well-financed company can afford to have a marketing failure in the new-product field. This approach can be used by any organization large enough to have its own full-time marketing research department.

DECISION TO LAUNCH THE NEW PRODUCT

Once the decision has been made to go ahead with a new product, emphasis shifts from *if* to *when*. This is not a decision to be entered into lightly. The findings of the detailed marketing study are reviewed, often by various divisions of the company such as production, sales, finance. Estimates of the cost of producing and marketing the new product are similarly reviewed and re-examined. This step often overlaps and is closely related to the one which follows, which is concerned with the physical development of the new product. The relationship is a natural one. If a company has developed a product with an outstanding advantage or point of superiority over competitive products, its chances of success are far greater than if it is a "me, too" product in the field.

Careful consideration of the financial aspects of the proposed new-product launching is necessary. What production facilities, if any, will have to be acquired? How much will they cost? What advertising, sales-promotion, or other marketing costs will be involved? Can the product be launched on a "pay as you go" basis, or will investment spending be necessary? If investment spending will be required, how much, and how soon will the product be on a profitable basis?

Consideration of timing also enters at this point. What, if any, are the seasonal characteristics of the sales or consumption of the new product? How much time will it take the company to build stocks adequate to make launching possible? Can that be accomplished in time to take advantage of the seasonal peak that may accelerate the introduction? If not, is it preferable to defer the introduction or to risk a contraseasonal introduction?

DEVELOPMENT OF THE NEW PRODUCT

Where this step falls in the sequence of new-product development steps varies widely. It is influenced in part by the length of time it is estimated will be required to develop a new product ready for marketing. Certain practical considerations are worth underlining. Sometimes new-product development really begins when the product has already been created. This is the case occasionally in the chemical industry. Another example is provided by the new-product acquired by purchase of a company or by acquisition of a patent or process. In such cases, there is an ever-present danger that the product in being is not the one the company *should* introduce. If the decision to launch a product is made before the development period begins, the risk of wasted development time is reduced. By contrast, however, if it takes so long to develop the product that the facts upon which the decision to go ahead was made are obsolete, it may be necessary to review the decision when the product is ready.

Research and development of a product can consume a fabulous amount of time. That time span can often be shortened by marketing research, which can provide specific guidance *from the viewpoint of the consumer or customer* as to desired product characteristics. This is sometimes accomplished by moving into the following step—consumer or customer acceptance checks—while the product is not yet in its final form.

CUSTOMER OR CONSUMER ACCEPTANCE CHECKS

Once a new product has been developed, it is typically subjected to product research. As already noted, this does not differ significantly in most instances from product research on existing products. All of Chapter 22 on product research can therefore be considered to be a guide to this step in the new-product developmental process. The comments made in that chapter need not be repeated here. The guiding principle of product research, whether on new or existing products, is this: The preferences and acceptance of typical customers or consumers of this type of product are much more important than the viewpoint of technical or factory people. What is important are the features and performance characteristics which the customer likes and looks for, not the ones you think he *ought* to look for.

Minimum standards in product testing for a new product vary widely. In general a useful guide is to note that any product which has a demonstrable measure of superiority over the leading competitive product, in the eyes of the customer, has the odds in its favor. One which is at least as good as the leading competitive product has a fair chance of success, provided pluses in the form of marketing muscle, promotional ingenuity, etc., can be provided. A product which consumers consider to be inferior to competitive products is almost certainly doomed and should not be introduced.

DEVELOPMENT OF DETAILED MARKETING PLANS

Once the decision to proceed with a new product has been made, and the product itself is "in sight," a timetable is needed for the remaining steps in the new-product program. That timetable typically starts with the date of the proposed introduction and works backward. Each of the scores of subordinate decisions which must be made is included. Key dates on each are indicated. When must the product name be decided? When must the package design be approved? When must packaging machinery be ordered or adapted? When must the pricing decision be made?

With a timetable set, detailed marketing plans must be developed. Marketing research provides factual guidance at many points in the development of marketing plans. The scope of such a marketing plan is suggested by the following outline of a new-product marketing plan for the Proctor & Gamble Company:

1. Estimate of industry volume for Year I (for Introduction).
2. Estimates of industry volume for years I $+1$ and I $+$ 2, etc.
3. Estimates of the company's target market share of industry volume which represents the sales objective for Year I. (If there is provision for "pipeline" stocks for wholesale and retail inventory purposes, representing non-recurring volume, that detail is provided here.)
4. Estimates of market share of industry volume that is the sales objective in subsequent years.
5. Reduction of the above estimates, which are on a dollar basis, to physical quantity in units, dozens, cases, etc.

6. Reduction of those specific quantities to further specifics in terms of counts of sizes, varieties, etc.

7. Outline of long-range marketing strategy.

8. Outline of short-range strategy in specific detail, closely integrated with a timetable.

9. Detailed plans for achieving the volume objectives noted above.

10. Detailed estimates of all costs—production, selling, advertising, and promotion—applied to the estimated volume over the several years covered by the plan.

11. Profit-and-loss estimates, showing investment required if any, length of "payout period" required to reach a cumulative net profit on the product, amount of that profit, subsequent profit expectations, etc.

SMALL-SCALE EXPERIMENTAL MARKET TESTING

To minimize risks and to "get the bugs out" of a marketing plan, it is often desirable to introduce a completely new product within a limited area. Its sales achievement under actual marketing conditions can there be observed and analyzed. Sometimes several individual market or sales territories are chosen for test purposes. This phase of new-product development coincides exactly with the *test marketing* which is the subject of Chapter 25. That chapter, therefore, should be considered as a part of the description of this step in the new-product program.

As Chapter 25 points out, the role of marketing research in such market tests is relatively complex. Normally it is used to set up tools to measure the success of the new product in achieving its planned-for market share. It may also be used, in consumer or customer studies, to determine acceptance of the new product under actual marketing conditions. It may also be used to evaluate the differences in sales return which result from different advertising approaches, advertising or sales-cost expenditure levels, and so on.

The market test is to marketing what the pilot plant is to production. Its major contribution often is in the improvements it suggests in the original plan or in details of the execution of that plan. There are often differences between test marketing and broader-scale marketing, just as there are often differences between pilot-plant and full-scale production runs. Marketing research is helpful in appraising such differences. As Chapter 25 points out, market tests are relatively complex. Despite those complexities, their contribution to the reduction of the risks in a new-product introduction is often far in excess of their costs.

FULL-SCALE LAUNCHING OF THE NEW PRODUCT

With the marketing plan modified to apply the experiences added in test marketing, the new-product launching on a broader scale follows.

This step involves the application of the revised marketing plan on a broader scale. It involves careful attention to any differences in effectiveness or productivity which appear when the scale of the introduction is expanded. Of particular significance, always, is the influence of changes in competitive climate which may reduce the validity of experience gained in the small-scale test.

FOLLOW-THROUGH VITALLY IMPORTANT

Under today's dynamic competitive pressures, no marketing plans long remain up to date. A continuing process of study, evaluation, and re-evaluation is typically required, in the years after a new product is introduced, to be sure that changing competitive or market conditions do not invalidate, or require modifications in, the new-product program. It is almost impossible to overestimate the importance of this follow-through step.

A new competitive product, a major improvement in an existing product, a change in price levels by a major competitor, a spectacular development in the interindustry competitive picture—any of these might signal the need for a significant change in the promotional weight or policy in new-product introduction. The effectiveness of the introductory program itself may dictate changes in strategy. For example, one new consumer product was launched on a basis which called for the expenditure for promotion and advertising of the company's full gross-margin return from the product. Sales volume reached higher levels in the national introduction of this product than had been anticipated on the basis of test results. This in turn led to constant upward revisions both of sales forecasts and of promotional budgets. If the expenditure rate had not been revised upward, the profit in the initial period would have been higher. On the other hand, the sales-volume levels attained would almost certainly have been far lower than were actually achieved under this dynamic approach.

It is sometimes helpful, in planning a new-product introduction which involves a short-term profit return at less than normal levels, to remember that not all profits are alike. An operating profit is sacrificed; but an *asset profit* is created in the process of building the big new business which a successful new-product introduction sometimes develops.

TERMINATION OF RESEARCH NOT UNCOMMON

In considering the series of steps through which a new-product development often moves, it should be noted that *all* these steps are taken only in the case of the product which actually gets on the market and achieves at least a modicum of success. The new-product-development field is fraught with difficulties. Some estimates indicate that the proportion of failures among new products is as high as four out of five products introduced. We may safely postulate that in the case of many of those failures in the market place, marketing research precedent to the introduction could have predicted the failure and reduced the loss. Where a new-product development program utilizes marketing research effectively, it is normal to find that the results of any step in the process may indicate the desirability of "killing" the proposed product.

As the results of each step in the new-development process are reviewed, those who have responsibility for evaluating the research face this question: Does this evidence make additional steps in the development of this product desirable? There is always a possibility that a negative answer may lead to substantial savings in the case of products foredoomed to failure. Major limitations in the product itself sometimes are disclosed. Or the opportunity may be pre-empted by the introduction of a competitive product in the same field, leading to the same "stop-work" decision. Additional evidence on market size and characteristics may lead to the same decision.

Unfortunately most published data on new-product activities are concerned with successes in the field. There is more to be learned from failures, which are typically interred quietly in the graveyard of company mistakes. Here is an example.

37. PARKER PEN COMPANY (B)

The Parker Pen Company is one in which considerable emphasis is placed on product research and product development. The company's organization chart reveals that emphasis. A product-research and product-development division in the company has an equal voice with sales, production, and financial divisions in determining future merchandising activities. The company's interest in expanded volume is pursued in two ways: in depth, by attempting to capture as much of the market as possible for existing products; and in breadth, by adding new products either under the company's own name or by the acquisition of new companies.

In the company's research and development activities, considerable freedom is exercised by the firm's research people, within the following general framework of interests. Not all the research activities involving Parker's several dozen technicians in the physics, chemistry, metallurgical, and electronics laboratory were concerned entirely with pens and inks. The specialists roam also into other fields. This element of variety in their explorations stems from a scientific kinship and a merchandising kinship between the many hand-operated or mechanical items of personal utility. That includes cameras, cigarette lighters, compacts, and many other possibilities.

New-product candidates were carefully screened by the company, against the following brief check list of characteristics essential to a new Parker product, as summarized by Daniel S. Parker:

1. We have wanted products which required precision manufacture, so that our manufacturing and production skills could be applied to their development and assembly.

2. We have wanted products that were sold—or *could* be sold—through essentially the same types of retail outlets that sell Parker pens. That means not only products that can be sold through stores such as jewelry and department stores; it also means products that can compete successfully in a world-wide market rather than in just one or two countries.

3. We have wanted products with prices strong enough to pay for the rather high costs of excellent quality in manufacturing and, at the same time, to support vigorous promotion.

4. We have wanted products which offered elements of uniqueness, so that they might be suitable companions to the distinctive products in our line.

One of the products which gave promise of fulfilling these requirements was a small camera, referred to subsequently in this case as the Parker camera. The starting point in the consideration of this product was a recognition of an unsatisfied need. The function of a camera is to record memorable incidents, places, and occasions.

A camera can best serve that purpose if it is always available, because the subjectively selected occasions for picture taking do not always occur according to plan. The size of most cameras militates against that constant availability. The Parker people reasoned that if a camera with satisfactory performance features could be developed within size limitations which would make it small enough to fit, say, into a man's shirt pocket, the desired element of uniqueness might be achieved.

This involved the development of what was known technically as a subminiature camera. "Miniature" in the camera and photographic field identifies cameras using 35-mm. film. A camera using smaller film would be required to achieve the Parker size objectives. In the memo which initiated the company's activities in the camera area, Daniel Parker wrote:

Although it is true that other cameras of sub-miniature size have been developed and marketed, each has had certain deficiencies in either technical development or merchandising that were serious enough to impede their progress. The two most important deficiencies have been (1) unsatisfactory performance, and (2) lack of reputation of manufacturer which causes doubts in the minds of consumers and distributors as to quality and warranty.

The company by policy would not launch a new product until satisfactory objective evidence had been developed that the product exceeded by a comfortable margin the maximum requisites of satisfactory performance. There was reason for confidence that a product bearing the name and warranty of the Parker Pen Company would overcome the second limitation mentioned above.

The product was developed fully, where technical product research was concerned, and was ready for evaluation in the market place by marketing research techniques. Plans to research the new product went forward in two phases. The first phase was a small-scale study among fifty consumers, using all available pilot models of the camera. Assuming that this test would prove the camera satisfactory, plans were also going forward for a one-market test of the camera under actual sales and promotional conditions.

In selecting the sample of people to use for the initial product test, it was reasoned that the best indication of interest in a subminiature camera was provided by the actual purchase of such a camera. There ensued a needle-in-a-haystack search for fifty owners of subminiature cameras, who were recruited for the test. Because the camera used a special size and type of film, facilities for processing that film had to be provided. The cameras and an initial supply of film were placed with the product-testing panel. Cloth sacks in which the exposed film were to be mailed special-delivery to the processor were provided. Finished pictures were delivered to the picture taker by the interviewer, who interviewed each respondent on each batch of pictures.

With the permission of the individuals participating in this product test, the Parker Pen Company had a duplicate print made of each picture taken with the Parker camera. Both black-and-white and color film were supplied, and duplicates of both types of pictures were secured for analysis.

The primary objective of this research was to determine whether there were any product limitations so great that they would make the relatively high cost of the market test an unsound business risk. The cameras used in the test were pilot models. Product improvements were therefore possible if the research indicated they were desirable, prior to the production-line manufacture of cameras for the market test.

Every attempt was made, in developing the Parker camera, to incorporate features which contributed to simplicity of operation. One such feature was in the nature of a fixed-focus setting. The camera was "in focus" over a wide range of distances, without the need for individual focusing by the camera operator. The short focal length of the camera made that a possibility. There was, however, a point at which the focus was sharpest. That point was set at a distance of about 15 feet from the camera.

Analysis of the first group of pictures revealed that the camera was used mostly for photos of people—typically from a distance of just a few feet. Many of those photos were fuzzy in focus. This led the company to modify the fixed-focus feature. Two positions were established, one for close-up photos and one for distance shots as of mountains, etc. Marked improvement in the photographic "batting average" of the test participants was evident as soon as the cameras they received initially were replaced by modified two-focus models.

One feature of the camera was a daylight-loading magazine. The operator could switch from color to black-and-white film at any point during the exposure of a roll, without difficulty. A substantial amount of difficulty with this magazine developed. Despite careful instruction, a substantial number of users depressed a center plate in the magazine, exposing and ruining the film.

During the course of the research a question developed about the sample. Was a group of consumers all of whom had had experience with subminiature cameras a representative group to evaluate the camera? It was eventually decided that the sample should be modified. Half of the original group were dropped and replaced by others who were "shutter clickers" and therefore representative of the numerical mass of camera users. This change in sample proved to have been a sound one. The original group were aware of the limitations of subminiature cameras and as a result were more tolerant of the limitations of the Parker camera than were the less experienced group.

At the end of a period of five months, the test was terminated. The attitudes of users toward the product were determined, in a terminal interview. The problem was of course complicated by the favorable bias inescapably present. The consumers had been using a novel camera for months, with all film supplied free. They were naturally inclined to be generous in their appraisal of the product's performance. One approach to the evaluation of their attitudes was an attempt to sell the camera in each case to the test participant, with the participant setting the price either for the camera used in the test or a brand-new model.

Over the period of the test, a rash of miniature and subminiature cameras of poor quality and low price had developed, mostly on an import basis. The prices of those products were apparently used as a basis of evaluating the value of the Parker camera. The resulting price estimate was substantially lower than the minimum price for which the product could be profitably produced, promoted, and sold. Difficulties with the handling and processing of the odd-sized film also proved substantially greater than had been anticipated.

Another organization, like Parker an outsider in the camera field interested in diversification, introduced a somewhat similar camera in a test market. Consumer interviews in that market were conducted as part of the research on the Parker camera. They were an important part of the appraisal of the market opportunity on the new product.

After careful review of the research evidence, The Parker Pen Company management decided not to market the Parker camera. That decision, it should be emphasized, did not preclude entry by the company into the manufacture and sale of a photographic product at some later date. The decision was not to introduce that specific product at that time.

— ★ —

NEW-PRODUCT RESEARCH FOCUSES PRIMARY ATTENTION ON PRODUCT WEAKNESSES

The camera which the Parker Pen Company considered as a possible addition to its line was a generally satisfactory and attractive product. That fact is implicit in the careful consideration which the proposed new product received and in the thoroughness with which its marketability was explored. Many companies, less aware than the Parker Pen Company of the importance of sound marketing research, would actually have introduced the product. Many new-product failures could be predicted with near certainty if adequate research were used before the product was launched. Increasing recognition of the value of adequate marketing research on proposed new products seems likely to contribute to a higher success batting average in the future.

In new-product research, primary emphasis by experienced research men is often placed on the identification of major product limitations or weaknesses, if any. There is a very good reason for that emphasis. A new product which is close to "being born" is the idea of some individual or group of individuals. Objectivity about one's own brain children is almost as rare as objectivity about one's natural children. Each child is a beauty to its parents, and each proposed new product is a sure-fire success to the man who thought it up or who approved the idea. Because a strong natural bias in the direction of optimism is present in many appraisals of a new-product's promise, the marketing research man must lean in the opposite direction. He must be on guard against the common tendency to minimize the importance of faults or limitations in the product. He must be very sure that his research presents those faults or limitations objectively and in accurate perspective.

Once a product enters the market place, its success or failure is largely dependent on the degree to which it satisfies existing wants. It is going to be appraised by customers or consumers in terms of their own judgment of their needs. Marketing research which precedes new-product introduction should be aimed at determining with all possible objectivity whether the proposed product is or is not satisfactory. The following case describes another new-product situation in which research led to a decision not to launch a product.

38. PARAMOUNT PAPER CO. ★

The Paramount Paper Company, with mill and offices in a medium-sized city in Wisconsin, was an important producer of paper products. Most of its products were aimed at the industrial market. Many of them were products which had grown out of developments in the company's own extensive technical-research laboratories.

One development of the company's research was being considered as a possible new product. The company had developed a cohesive sealing coating for wax paper. With a sheet of wax paper so coated, a perfect seal could be achieved simply by pressing the surfaces of the paper together. It was felt that this would be a great convenience to house-wives, for such applications as wrapping sandwiches, etc.

The company explored the marketing potentials of the new product. Several marketing courses were open. One was to market the product as a consumer product, under the company's own name. That course would require that the company set up a marketing organization for consumer-product selling. Another was the production of the product for some other organization, which would market it through some existing facility. For example, such a product might have been sold to the Johnson's wax organization and marketed as a Johnson's wax product through that company's existing sales organization.

Before going very far in the exploration of marketing alternatives, the company felt that an objective test of the product by consumers was necessary. The objective of the test was to determine how well consumers liked the product. Particular attention was focused, in the research, on the question of price. Did consumers like the product well enough to pay a substantial premium for it? The coating and processing were relatively expensive. If the product could not command a premium over ordinary wax paper, the outlook for it was dim.

In the research, a panel of 200 housewives who had purchased wax paper within the two weeks prior to the qualifying interview was recruited. Identical cartons of the leading wax paper and of the proposed new product—tentatively known as Seeltite—were placed with the panel. The feature of Seeltite was explained and demonstrated. The women were asked to use the two products as they normally used wax paper. Two callbacks were made to determine reactions. One was made a few days after the original placement; the other was made two weeks after the first. Additional supplies of both papers, if needed, were delivered at the time of the first callback. A total of 193 of the 200 women carried through the three interviews. The following highlights of the research report are based on those 193 women.

1. *Seeltite Generally Preferred by Narrow Margin*

Housewives were asked at the conclusion of the test: "All things considered, which of the two products do you like better?" Here is how they replied:

Response	Number	Per cent
Prefer Seeltite	101	53
Prefer regular wax paper	80	41
Like equally, no preference	12	6
Total	193	100

2. *Six Out of Ten Women Disliked One or More Characteristics of Seeltite*

Housewives were asked to identify any characteristics of either product which they had disliked. In answer to questioning on the regular wax paper, 172 of the 193 women said there was nothing about that product they disliked. By contrast, only 76 of the 193 said there was nothing they disliked about Seeltite. That means that about six out of ten women disliked one or more feature of Seeltite.

3. *Primary Dislikes: Sticks to Itself, Tears Too Easily*

The 117 women who disliked something about Seeltite named a total of 178 "pet peeves." Here is how their objections to the product were divided:

Feature disliked	Number	Per cent
Sticks in rolling or to itself	70	40
Tears too easily	54	30
Trouble opening, starting roll	15	8
Container objections	10	6
Baking or heat difficulties	6	3
Unfamiliarity	4	2
Sticks to other things	2	1
Miscellaneous	17	10
Total	178	100

An attempt was made in the research to explore the extent to which women who had used Seeltite felt they would repurchase it if it were on sale in a store. That is an extremely difficult subject to research, because the respondent knows the interviewer is interested in the product and is likely to give an accommodating answer which is unrealistically favorable. In the Seeltite research, about seven women out of ten said they thought they would buy the product if it were on sale in the store where they usually shopped. However, most of those women indicated they would also continue to use regular wax paper. That indicated that they were considering the use of Seeltite only for specialized uses, representing therefore something less than the total wax-paper consumption of buying families.

Asked to state the price they would expect to pay for the product, the overwhelming majority indicated they would expect it to cost the same as ordinary wax paper or to carry a very slight price premium. Since the costs of the process precluded marketing the product except on a basis in which the pricing was substantially higher than regular wax paper, the consideration of Seeltite as a new consumer product was terminated.

— ★ —

THE PROBLEM OF PRIORITIES

In organizations which are active in new-product development, there are usually far more new-product ideas clamoring for attention than the company has time, money, or manpower to explore. In such a situation, some basis for determining priorities is required. Ideally that basis should be objective. The best yardstick would be the comparative profit contribution which the new products might make. That kind of a comparison is of course impossible, far in advance of the development of the products.

An interesting approach to this question in the industrial marketing field was developed by executives of American Alcolac Corp., described in *Business Week*, Mar. 31, 1956. That firm has a formula for calculating the relative attractiveness to the company of different possible new-product projects. The factors in the formula were the estimated chances of technical success in developing the product, estimated chances of commercial success, estimated annual volume, price-cost relationship, estimated life of the product, and total costs. All those factors except total costs were in the numerator of a fraction; total costs were the denominator; and the total led to an assignment of priorities. The following quotation from the *Business Week* article is illustrative:

One of the first things Blinoff found was that some of his management's pet new product ideas registered so low in the project number scale that they should never be considered.

That's the case of a commercial laundry detergent that, at first glance, looked like a potential goldmine. It seemed to have a good market— 3 million lb. a year, and a fine profit—5¢ a lb.

Here's how Blinoff put it through the paces:

The research director estimated that his department's chance of producing the detergent in a form suitable for commercial laundries was between 100% and 80%.

Translated into mathematical terms, this meant that the chances of technical success were 1 to .8—an average of .9.

The sales manager estimated that Alcolac's chances of getting the detergent into production—figuring on the basis of potential customers, and market conditions—were about 60%. Thus the chances of commercial success were rated at .6.

Next, the sales manager predicted he could sell an average of 3-million lb. of the product a year; that he could sell it at an average of 18¢ a lb.; that it could be made at an average of 13¢ a lb.; and that the life of the product—the number of years it could be sold at the 3-million-lb. a year volume—averaged out at 3 years.

Those estimates filled in the top line of the equation. And to fill in the bottom line—the total cost of making and selling the detergent—Alcolac's management made these estimates: research, a median of $20,000; market development, $40,000; engineering and pilot plant work, $40,000. So the total costs were $100,000.

All this time, Blinoff and his management kept regarding the detergent as a good new line—after all, there seemed to be a profit of $150,000 a year in it if they could sell 3-million lb. and make 5¢ on every lb.

But they set up the left-hand-side of the formula:

$$\frac{.8 \times .6 \times 3.0 \times 10^6 \times (18¢ - 13¢) \times \sqrt{3}}{\$100,000}$$

And the answer they got as the project number—the gauge of the detergent's profit potential—was 1.2.

This was so low that Blinoff saw it as a warning signal that it would be extremely hazardous for his company to press its development any further.

This rather novel approach to the assignment of priorities in new-product development is presented here because it illustrates the direction in which much marketing research in the new-product field is moving. There is a continuing attempt to calculate ever more precisely what the profit contribution of a proposed new product will be or could be. That profit contribution then determines to a considerable extent how much marketing and other research can be devoted to the product on a profitable basis. In the case of many products, the intangible cost of failure of a product—in terms, for example, of loss of prestige and perhaps volume of other products in the line—belongs in the calculations.

SUMMARY

1. In the dynamic and competitive American marketing scene, new-product development plays an increasingly significant role. Many promising new products prove to be failures. Marketing research participation in the development of new products is increasing, as management seeks to screen out the products which are unlikely to succeed.

2. Many different types of marketing research activity are included in new-product research. Two particularly important types are estimates of the size of the market for a proposed new product and measurements of relative consumer or customer acceptance of the product under consideration.

3. The overlap between new-product research and other marketing research areas, in today's integrated practice, is extensive. Thus a marketing research man working on a new-product assignment would be likely to participate in most of the activities described in this section. He would estimate the size and characteristics of the market, the subject of Chapter 20. He would use product research, described in Chapter 22. He might engage in test marketing, as discussed in Chapter 25, and in advertising research, which is covered in Chapter 24.

4. There is a widespread tendency, in considering a new product, to overestimate the advantages and underestimate the difficulties and/or limitations involved. Marketing research contributes to the sound consideration of new-product possibilities by reducing the difficulties to specific form and presenting them objectively.

5. An estimate of the profit contribution of a potential new product is usually required before the decision to launch it is made. Marketing research can and does contribute to making that estimate more accurate.

QUESTIONS

1. What is the primary objective of marketing research participation in the field of new-product development?

2. Where within a company's organization chart does the assignment for new-product development typically fall?

3. What were the steps presented in this chapter to serve as the basic framework of new-product activities? Discuss each step briefly.

4. Why is it important to know the trend of the volume of the industry which the new product would enter?

5. As part of the detailed market study for a new product, what key factor was discussed that has a most important bearing on the new product's opportunity? What areas would this phase of the investigation cover?

6. Once a new product has been carefully developed, why is it typically subjected to product research?

7. What part does small-scale experimental market testing play in new-product development?

8. It is said that under today's dynamic competitive pressure no marketing plans long remain up to date. What innovations or changes might take place that would signal the need for a significant alteration in the promotional weight or policy in new-product introduction?

9. In new-product research, where is the primary emphasis often placed by experienced marketing research men? What is the reason for this emphasis?

CHAPTER 24

Advertising Research

In this chapter we examine a major subdivision of the field of marketing research which is concerned with *advertising research*. Advertising plays an important role within the broad picture of American marketing. Advertising costs represent a substantial part of all marketing costs. Those costs are increasing at a spectacular rate. *Printers' Ink* magazine has long prepared carefully compiled estimates of the level of total advertising volume. In 1945, advertising volume was at a 2.8-billion-dollar level. Ten years later, 1955 volume topped 9 billion dollars, more than treble the 1945 total. The trend upward is continuing.

The estimate of advertising volume incidentally illustrates a marketing research problem in evaluating available data. The *Printers' Ink* estimate of advertising volume includes most but not all advertising cost elements. For example, the art and mechanical costs of preparing advertisements are excluded. So are the substantial costs of talent for radio and television programs. The level of total advertising volume, therefore, is even higher than the figures cited.

Marketing management executives are responsible for the effective expenditure of those billions of advertising dollars. Many questions must be asked and answered before an executive can approve a proposed advertising program or appropriation with confidence that it will achieve maximum effectiveness. Marketing research has long been used to contribute all or part of the answer to many key questions concerning advertising. The importance of advertising research is likely to increase, as larger expenditures increase the cost of a mistake in judgment.

FACTORS IN ADVERTISING RESEARCH

In order to understand fully the discussion of advertising research presented in this chapter, you should be familiar with the principal types of organizations which are factors in advertising and in advertising research. The most important and primary factor is the *advertiser*. The advertiser supplies the money spent for advertising. The billions of dollars of advertising volume within the *Printers' Ink* total represent the aggregate expenditures of a very large number of advertisers.

In most cases, an advertiser is a manufacturer. There are, however, some important exceptions. Some advertisers are sales organizations, often wholly owned subsidiaries of manufacturers, who purchase the products of manufacturers and resell them. Some advertisers are trade associations, like the American Dairy Association. The trade association permits an industry or group made up of a large number of individually small units (dairy farmers, for example) to pool their facilities and accomplish an advertising objective. They are discussed at greater length in Chapter 28. In the above comments and in this chapter generally, we are concerned principally with what is called *national* advertising. National advertising is distinguished from *local,* or *retail,* advertising. Retail advertising includes the advertising of food chains, department stores, and other merchandising organizations. The terms include some elements of confusion. Thus a large regional brewery, using newspaper, radio, and television advertising in four markets around the brewery, is included in national advertising figures, although the advertising in question is so limited in geographic scope that it might more accurately be described as local. While the discussion in this chapter is principally concerned with national advertising, much of it applies also to local advertising. It thus supplements Chapter 27, in which the marketing research activities of retailers and wholesalers are discussed.

The second important factor present in the national advertising picture is the *advertising agency.* An advertising agency is a specialized service organization, appointed by an advertiser, to prepare or help prepare the advertiser's advertising. Some advertising agencies have additional functions making them almost marketing agencies. Those functions are examined in Chapter 29 and need not concern us further at this point.

The compensation basis traditional in advertising agency–advertiser relationships requires brief comment here. The comment should be prefaced by the observation that although the compensation of agencies has historically and traditionally been on the basis described below, that basis is being searchingly re-examined by advertisers and agencies alike as this book goes into production. Agencies have traditionally received as payment for their services a sum roughly equivalent to 15 per cent of the advertising appropriation they spend for their advertiser clients. That compensation is known as *agency commission.* It has often been supplemented by fees and other special charges, including in some cases charges for research conducted for clients. The compensation of agencies is relevant here because the agency's commissions represent (usually) the agency's gross income. It is out of that gross income that the agency's expenditures, including those for research, must come. The nature of the limiting factor here is obvious.

The advertising which is prepared *for* advertisers *by* advertising agencies is released, when approved by the client, to *advertising media*. The major advertising media include individual newspapers and magazines (both consumer and trade or industrial), groups or chains of newspapers or magazines, radio and television stations and networks, outdoor advertising posting services, and so on. Advertising media do a substantial amount of marketing research, as we noted in Chapter 2 on the organization of marketing research activities. The research activities of advertising media are considered in detail in Chapter 29.

There are within the advertising research portion of the marketing research field a considerable number of specialized service organizations. One is the Advertising Checking Bureau, which provides data and tear sheets on advertising of various types, measures lineage, and so on. There are a number of different services offered in checking various types of advertising, in measuring advertising audiences, and in other areas of advertising research. Some of the more important services of those types will be described in greater detail later in this chapter.

The Advertising Research Foundation, a nonprofit organization supported jointly by advertisers, advertising agencies, and advertising media, deserves special mention. The activities of the ARF are detailed in Chapter 28.

ADVERTISER AND AGENCY VIEWPOINT IDENTICAL

In this chapter we are concerned primarily with research used to develop or to evaluate advertising. Our viewpoint is that of the advertiser—typically the manufacturer who makes a product and who appoints an advertising agency to prepare effective advertising which will sell the product at a profit. In the following discussion, we are also looking at the problem from the viewpoint of the advertising agency, because in theory at least the agency and the advertiser face an identical problem and have a mutual viewpoint. The advertising agency is the agency of the client or advertiser and is therefore essentially an extension of the advertiser's own organization. In a sound advertiser-agency relationship, both organizations share a common interest in developing the most effective possible advertising. Their viewpoints as to objective are therefore identical.

There is one aspect of the agency-client relationship which has an important bearing on advertising research. That aspect is implicit within the designation *agency*. The agency-client relationship is sometimes described as a partnership. If it is a partnership, it is one within which there is one junior and one senior partner. There is never a question as to which organization is "the boss." The client organization is the dominant partner and sets the tone of the relationship. If there is a basic disagreement between agency and client, there is never any question as to whose views will prevail. It's the client's money, and the client is entitled to see it spent as he wants it spent. The agency has the alternative, in the case of such a disagreement, of resigning from work on the account. Such resignations growing out of a policy disagreement are not uncommon. In most situations the agency develops its recommendations and presents them, along with the reasoning (and perhaps the research evidence) on which they are based. The client accepts the recommendations in whole, accepts them as modified, or rejects them. Many agency-client relationships span a score or more years, although there are many advertisers who have had anywhere from two to a dozen agencies over the same length of time.

The particular relevance of the above comment to this chapter lies in this fact: It is the manufacturer or client organization that usually establishes the extent to which research does or does not enter into the development of advertising. An advertiser's advertising appropriation establishes a commission total which represents the gross income to the agency from the account. The agency is entitled to retain part of that gross income as profit. The remaining portion represents in effect a "service bank account." The client or advertiser can and does determine to a considerable extent whether any of that service shall be of a research nature or not. There are some agencies recognized as strong research agencies, with excellently staffed research departments, who do little or no research on *some* of their accounts. The client does not want research and therefore doesn't get it.

There is one area within which the viewpoint of the agency and that of the advertiser are not identical. The two organizations are (usually) completely separate entities, with no overlap in ownership. Each is in business to make a profit. The agency can maximize its profit by giving the client as little service as the client will accept. The client can maximize the value it receives from its advertising appropriation by securing as much service as possible from the agency. The conflict in viewpoint is inescapable. Each agency has the problem of holding the service demanded of it at a level which permits it to make a profit on each account. Where the required service is in excess of income, the alternative of resignation is always open to the agency. If the amount of service delivered by the agency is considered inadequate by the client, termination of the agency's appointment is always possible.

VARIATIONS IN AD PERFORMANCE STIMULATE RESEARCH

There are two major reasons why advertising research is today an increasingly important part of marketing research practice. The first has already been identified. It is the great magnitude and uptrend in scale of advertising expenditures. The second reason for increasing attention to advertising research lies in the now widely recognized fact that there are big differences in the effectiveness of different advertisements.

A unit of white space in a large-circulation magazine costs a lot of money. By making an expenditure for a unit of white space in a magazine like LIFE, an advertiser can buy the privilege of addressing his sales message to the readers of that publication. The price of that privilege is equal to all. But some advertisers *deliver* their sales ideas at a very small fraction of the *cost per thousand prospects reached* that other advertisers pay. This represents, in effect, an advertising fact of life. In any issue of any consumer magazine, you will find both good ads and bad ads. Some ads do many times as good a job of *delivering sales ideas* as do other ads.

This question of advertisement performance boils down in essence to the buying power of advertising dollars. Let's illustrate it in more specific terms, by drawing from two studies of two issues of a Sunday "supplement" (a magazine section distributed with a week-end paper). This particular study was based on *Parade*. Other publications in the same media category are *This Week* and the *American Weekly*. Here are the variations in the recall levels of different advertisements among a sample of women interviewed:

	Study no. 1	Study no. 2
Number of advertisements (one-half page and larger) studied	11	14
Total recall, highest ad, %	59	59
Total recall, lowest ad, %	7	2
Total recall, median ad, %	29	16.5*

* The central values were 21 and 12 per cent.

If the median value in terms of recall as shown is taken as representing delivery of a dollar's worth of recall for each space dollar invested, then this pattern is revealed: Some advertisers got as much as $2.03 and as little as 24 cents for each dollar they spent in one issue, as much as $3.58 and as little as 12 cents in the other. Actually the range from top to bottom in buying power of a space dollar is substantially greater than even those figures indicate. In one instance a half-page black-and-white ad achieved the highest recall level, while a four-color full-page ad with a much higher space cost was at the bottom of the range. The above comments are not intended to suggest that the proportion of respondents recalling an ad represents an adequate measure of advertising effectiveness. The figures are illustrative. The existence of such wide variations in advertising performance has been repeatedly confirmed by many different research approaches. Some of those approaches are discussed in detail later in this chapter.

THE PROBLEM OF THE INDIVIDUAL ADVERTISER

The existence of such wide variations in advertising performance is a matter of keen concern to an individual advertiser. Suppose that you were the advertising manager of a company making a consumer product. Your advertising budget is x dollars. If your ads are among the top-performing ads, you may buy $2x$, $3x$, or more advertising for your expenditure. But if your ads are near the bottom of the performance range, you will be buying perhaps $\frac{1}{3}x$ dollars or $\frac{1}{6}x$ dollars worth of advertising for your expenditure. The range from top to bottom represents an expansion in advertising power of anywhere from 6 to 1 on up to perhaps 18 to 1!

You as the advertising manager are going to be mighty sure—if you can!—that your ads are top-performance rather than low-performance ads. You cannot long afford to let a competitive firm buy many times as much advertising per dollar as your firm buys! No firm can! Any advertising research which promises to provide an individual firm with an insurance policy against subpar performance is going to appear to be highly desirable and economically sound research when it is evaluated on the cost–versus–profit contribution scale.

It is further apparent that effective advertising research is likely to have to be *comparative* research, and comparative in more than one direction. Return to your position as advertising manager of the company mentioned above. Your advertising agency has presented for your consideration two proposed advertising campaigns. (In practice they are much more likely to submit only a single compaign, but that's irrelevant at this point.) As you examine the two recommended campaigns, you have two questions in your mind. Both involve comparatives. Here they are:

—Which of the alternate advertising campaigns under consideration will do the most effective job of delivering the message we want our advertising to deliver?

—How does that superior advertising campaign, out of the two under consideration on our product, compare with campaigns of our principal competitors?

Thus you have the problem, in other words, first of deciding which of the two campaigns is better, and second of determining whether the better campaign is good, fair, or poor in comparison with the campaigns of your competitors.

The remainder of this chapter is concerned with some of the ways in which marketing research—or advertising research, which is a subdivision of marketing research—can and does contribute facts helpful to executives in arriving at sound judgments regarding such questions as those stated above.

CAN ADVERTISING EFFECTIVENESS BE MEASURED?

Those questions are involved explicitly or implicitly with the effectiveness of the advertising under consideration. It might be well to preface a more specific discussion of advertising research with a brief statement on the subject of advertising effectiveness and the ability or inability of existing marketing research techniques to measure it.

The ultimate goal of advertisers is a yardstick to measure advertising effectiveness. Such a yardstick represents the Holy Grail which much advertising research has long pursued. The desirability of such a yardstick is obvious. If you had one, you could determine on a factual and objective basis whether a given advertising appropriation would produce more sales volume per advertising dollar spent on magazines, newspapers, radio, television, or some combination of those media. Or you could use it to answer such subordinate but important questions as whether a magazine advertising campaign using four-color pages would produce more or less sales volume per advertising dollar than one using black-and-white pages or some other space unit.

What progress is advertising research making toward that goal? The answer is at least initially disappointing. Unfortunately there is not even a promising approach to an *approximate* measurement of advertising effectiveness visible on the farthest horizon. This may largely be attributed to the inherent and inescapable complexities of the American marketing process. Research workers in the physical sciences carefully control all important variables in their experiments. Theoretical development in social sciences such as economics often proceeds from the assumption that "all other things are equal." In advertising today, however, the variables are so numerous and their combined influence on any experiment so pervasive that progress toward acceptable tools for measuring advertising effectiveness has been almost nonexistent.

Consider one of the very important variables in any marketing situation: *competition*. In order to test a number of approaches to your advertising problem, you would have to conduct a series of experiments in which competitive effort was held at least relatively constant. But alert and aggressive competitors are singularly noncooperative. They simply will not "hold still" and allow you to make such tests. The results might be a powerful competitive weapon in your hands, and they're not going to let you get that weapon if they can help it. They usually can help it! This point is documented in specific detail in the following chapter on test marketing.

But while no promising approach to the measurement of *total* advertising effectiveness is visible, promising progress has been and is being made in the field of advertising research. That progress has been achieved by using an approach which you will now recognize as basic in marketing research. It began by subdividing the problem. Then it proceeded to work on what seemed to be the most important subdivisions. This is the isolation of problem elements which has been discussed in earlier chapters in this book. The progress has been greatest, within the advertising research area, in developing ways of evaluating and pretesting and post-testing advertising copy.

SOUND ADVERTISING BUILDS UPWARD
FROM A FOUNDATION OF FACTS

We are here concerned primarily with advertising research. It should be emphasized, however, that effective advertising research in most cases presupposes that there has been a considerable amount of detailed and competent marketing research in areas other than advertising research.

Preparing effective advertising and advertising and marketing plans is the end result of a long process of fact gathering and fact digesting. An advertising agency tackling a new and difficult problem product today ordinarily begins with a substantial amount of factual material, which must be digested *before* advertising research itself can begin. What kind of factual information should be included? That question can be pretty well answered by reviewing the chapter headings in this section of this book. It is almost certain to include detailed data on the size of the total market for the product; on the characteristics of that market; on the division of that market by major subtypes if there are such divisions; on the trend in that subtype division; on territorial variations in sales potentials and, for the company itself, on territorial variations in sales effectiveness and market share.

Chapter 29 on the research activities of advertising agencies will provide you with additional insight into the division of responsibility between the advertiser, or client, and the advertising agency, in gathering such information of the preadvertising-research type. In the following discussion of advertising research procedures, it is assumed that that prior research has been executed and that the requisite information is available. If it has not been executed adequately, the agency may have to supply part of it before it can proceed with its advertising research. That would be likely to involve considerable library research, exploration of existing data, and so on.

THREE MAJOR PHASES OF ADVERTISING RESEARCH

Advertising research which has as its objective the fact finding required in the development of an effective advertising campaign can be subdivided into three major phases. The first involves, in most cases, qualitative or motivational research, often supplemented by quantitative research. The quantitative research may be confined to one or more major or key points disclosed in the qualitative research. The objective of this first phase of the advertising research is to help those responsible for the advertising—and particularly members of the creative departments in the advertising agency—arrive at a sound decision on *what story the advertising should tell.*

For the benefit of readers unacquainted with advertising-agency nomenclature, it should be pointed out that the *creative* departments in an advertising agency are those primarily concerned with the creation of advertising. The copy, art, and radio and television commercial writing departments make up the creative departments in an advertising agency. By elimination, all other functional groups in the agency become "noncreative." Included are such service functions as production (of engravings, type, etc.), traffic (the scheduling function), and the mail and mimeograph rooms. Also included in that "noncreative" group are members of departments who do a considerable amount of creative advertising work—the account supervisors and managers, merchandising executives, and research executives. This pre-emption of the "good" word creative might be described as a victory in semantic "gamesmanship"!

When the research in the first phase of the advertising research program has been completed, creative personnel proceed to study and digest the research findings. They are looking for guidance in the vital decision on: *What story should the advertising tell?* In practice a review of the phase 1 research is likely to result in the development of a considerable list of alternative creative avenues which the advertising might take.

After the phase 1 research has been reviewed, a detailed discussion usually takes place between the research and creative departments in the agency. That discussion is focused around the alternatives which the research seems to open up. It almost always includes a discussion of a number of questions which the phase 1 research stimulated or raised but did not answer. Is additional research needed to answer those questions, or can they be "dug out of" the already completed research by reanalysis? At the end of this discussion, the research proceeds into the second phase.

The objective of the second phase of the research is to explore the avenues mentioned and to provide some guidance on the relative importance, in terms of consumer interest, of various possible advertising approaches. Sometimes this phase of the research is described as *selling point* or *sales idea* research. When it is completed, the creative personnel of the agency have the information they need to develop their *copy platform*. They know what story the advertising should tell. They know, in addition, the relative importance of various sales ideas or subpoints in that story. That latter knowledge is necessary in order to guide emphasis in the finished advertisements.

With the copy platform developed, and the specific objectives of the advertising campaign reduced to writing, the translation of that copy platform into actual advertisements or radio or television commercials follows. The third phase of advertising research is concerned with the evaluation of those advertisements or commercials. The key criterion is: How well does this advertisement deliver the sales ideas which it was created to deliver? As indicated earlier, this is likely to be comparative research of a two-directional nature. One involves the comparison of various ads for the product the company or agency is advertising. The other involves the comparison of the better or best ad developed with competitive ads. Thus an attempt is made to answer the two questions raised earlier.

The discussion up to this point has been concerned primarily with the advertising itself. There is an important additional area for research, certainly significant in determining the net effectiveness of the advertising. That area involves *media*—determination of the types of media which should be used in the advertising, and selection from within those types of specific magazines, radio or television networks or programs or time periods, and so on. In the following section, we examine the three major phases of the advertising-research job in more detail. Media research activities are discussed in Chapter 29.

THE HIGH COST OF KNOWING THINGS THAT AREN'T SO

There is a major pitfall in advertising research which every research man encounters sooner or later. That pitfall is the danger of accepting without objective support various opinions about a company's customers, products, and the uses of those products.

Fundamental to all advertising research is this basic premise: *It is the viewpoint of the customers or consumers that is important, rather than the viewpoint of the manufacturer of the product.* In this area of research above all others there is a grave danger in accepting an incorrect assumption.

You are working on the early phases of an advertising research program on a product to which you are a stranger. Your basic task is to plan research for the first phase of an advertising research program. You are planning how to gather information and what types to gather, to guide the decision on *the story to tell* in the advertising. You are informally interviewing an executive in the manufacturing organization that makes the product. Ask him why or how people buy or use his kind of product. He is likely to respond with a speech of considerable length. That speech will be enlightening to you, but *you should learn to accept no such statements without substantiation.*

Probe a bit. *How does he know* that the things he tells you are true? What are the sources of his information? Can you examine the individual data, to arrive at a judgment as to their validity? Is he giving you facts or are the statements merely opinions? If they are opinions, are they your respondent's own opinions arrived at independently, or are they part of the "gospel" he learned when he was indoctrinated into the organization's policies and beliefs?

You should be warned that probing of that type is likely to prove a bit irritating to some of your executive respondents. Presence of irritation may be a vital clue to you. There are some things, you see, that he *knows* so well that research on them would be an unnecessary waste of time and effort. Why, he may say, "everyone knows" that such-and-such is the case! What he really means is perhaps that he is stating a corporate or industry prejudice so widespread that it is never questioned. That viewpoint, experienced marketing research men have learned, is more likely to be wrong than right!

TWO EXAMPLES OF UNQUESTIONED FACTS

Two examples may be illustrative. One is from the heating field. Back twenty years or so, the early residential warm-air heating was of the gravity type. It was basically not very satisfactory. It was displaced to a considerable extent by "wet heat"—steam or hot water, with radiators or convectors as the heat-distributing unit in individual rooms.

A company in the plumbing and heating equipment manufacturing industry in 1940 was instructing its new advertising agency in background about that industry. The discussion was confined to "wet heat" —steam and hot-water heat. What about warm-air heating? The company was not in that field. It had no interest in making equipment which was essentially unsatisfactory and with which consumers were dissatisfied. How did the company know that warm-air equipment was not satisfactory? "Everyone knows that," the executives in the firm responded. Informal consumer interviews revealed that the development of *forced* warm-air heating had reversed the trend mentioned earlier. Consumers who lived in homes heated by forced warm air were typically quite pleased with it.

The disadvantages of warm-air heating listed by executives in the plumbing and heating firm were found to exist, but at the consumer level they were relatively unimportant. The consumer considered the wet-heat radiator—an unsightly, dust-catching pain in the housewife's neck!—to be so great a disadvantage of wet heat that the technical limitations of forced warm-air heating faded to insignificance beside it!

This research, expanded to provide a dependable quantitative base, led to two actions by the company. The first was the development of some equipment designed for warm-air heating, which had previously been shunned completely. The second was a "crash" program to develop satisfactory substitutes for radiators. The latter took the direction of convectors, which could be set inside the wall and yet perform satisfactorily, "baseboard heating" which had previously been considered an undesirable substitute for the (to the engineer) efficient radiator, and "radiant heat" in which hot water was piped through tubes set in the floor or ceiling.

The second example was in the wax field. A number of different wax products were on sale, all aimed primarily at the maintenance of floors and furniture. These products were technically differentiated, each being aimed at a particular type of maintenance situation. Through careful sales training, the Johnson's wax organization had succeeded in indoctrinating its sales organization with an understanding of the differences between products. The company's corporate viewpoint was that the dealer and consumer, too, understood the differences between the products. No problem was felt to exist in this area. Dealer research indicated a complete lack of awareness of the product distinctions. Since the dealer did not know what the difference was between Johnson's liquid wax and Johnson's Glo-Coat, which was also a liquid product, the consumer who turned to the dealer for advice got no satisfactory information. Product complaints were received from time to time, which were traced to the use of one product for a condition requiring the other.

When the research clearly demonstrated the high level of confusion existing at dealer and consumer levels, the problem received attention. The products were differentiated in many ways. Distinctive product names were used, packages were markedly different although retaining a family resemblance, and advertising was separated so that individual products were individually advertised. In distinguishing between Johnson's Glo-Coat and Johnson's liquid wax, the first step was to add identifying phrases to the can. Glo-Coat was identified as a self-polishing wax for floors. Liquid wax was described as a cleaning and polishing wax for floors and furniture. Additional steps were also taken, with research continuously used to check progress. The wax which had to be polished was eventually renamed Johnson's Beautiflor, with a descriptive designation also included on the can.

Many assumptions are explicitly or implicitly included in advertising planning. The research contribution which results from an objective re-examination of the evidence on which each assumption rests is often an extremely significant one.

APPROACH IN DETERMINING STORY TO TELL

Now let's consider in more detail the first phase of the three-phase advertising research program presented above. The primary objective of that phase of the research is to secure information to guide the decision on what advertising message or story should be used in the case of a specific company or product. The assumption that there is a substantial amount of marketing research prior to this advertising research activity has already been stated and is implicit in the comments which follow.

In most advertising research programs, this first phase of the research represents a separate, distinct, and important marketing research problem. In working on such a problem, in advertising research as in other specialized areas of marketing research, the steps outlined in Section Three of this book serve as a guide. It is necessary, first, to define and refine the problem. Then it is necessary to develop a research plan. The execution of that plan and the analysis and interpretation of the research follow. A report must be prepared. It would be unnecessarily repetitive to review all those steps at this point. Our emphasis here is on those special aspects of a typical advertising research problem which should be considered as you proceed through that basic framework of steps.

It might be well to emphasize that in most advertising research it is desirable to work from the general toward the specific. Before effective advertising can be prepared on a particular branded product, it is necessary to know something about the *industry* in which that product is sold. Then moving in the direction of the more specific, knowledge about *the particular product type or subtype* is necessary. Finally, the individual *company* or *brand* may enter into the research as a major influence on the story-to-tell decision.

Two illustrations of the latter point may be of interest. One demonstrates the company variable in action. Consumer research on the subject of tampons, a product designed to provide internal sanitary protection for women, developed a strong competitive story. Most of the sales advantages of tampons are related to product advantages in comparison with the product disadvantages of sanitary napkins, the major competitive product. At the time of this research, the total sanitary-protection field was divided on a 90-10 basis, with napkins representing 90 per cent of dollar volume. A strong anti–sanitary-napkin campaign might represent a sound advertising approach for a firm making only tampons. It was unlikely to be approved by the management of a company which already controlled a dominant share of the sanitary-napkin business.

STORY-TO-TELL RESEARCH ON A FOOD PRODUCT

To bring the discussion of advertising research into focus on a specific product area, consider the problem of a ready-to-eat cereal like Kellogg's Corn Flakes, Wheaties, or Post's Sugar Crisp. The product category is made up of foods which are quickly and easily served at a busy time of the day. They are therefore a time-saving convenience for the housewife. They are available in a wide variety of different forms, flavors, and grain bases. They therefore have a variety story, to which there were two facets. One is that there is a cereal available to suit any taste. That could be translated in advertising into an important appeal to the mother of a number of children with dissimilar tastes. The other is that variety permits serving different brands of cereal, retaining the quick-and-easy advantages without the risk of family fatigue with any one. That could be translated into a variety appeal, especially for a new or relatively unknown brand.

The base of cereals is grain, which is highly nutritious food. Therefore, nutrition represents one possible advertising appeal. Or, from the general concept of nutrition, advertising might single out the specific consumer benefit of *energy*, provided by the cereal. In comparison with other foods commonly served for breakfast, ready-to-eat cereals represent a relatively inexpensive food. Should the economy of serving cereals be stressed? When served either by themselves with cream and sugar or with fresh fruit, ready-to-eat cereals are a pleasant, appetizing food. Should they be advertised with the appetite-appeal approach, with major emphasis on illustrating and describing how good they taste when eaten? Or should some two or more of these alternatives be combined? If so, which, and with how much emphasis on each? Answering questions like these represents one of the first phases in advertising preparation. Marketing research can contribute guidance and is frequently called upon to do so.

There is in advertising always the need to discriminate between advertising which sells a *type* of product (like a ready-to-eat cereal) and advertising which sells a *brand* of that type (like Corn Kix, Cheerios, or Sugar Jets). Advertising for an industry may be effective if it sells use of the product type; advertising for a company is unlikely to achieve acceptable levels of effectiveness unless it is sharply focused on the advantages of the specific brand in question. In this phase of advertising research, that means that the most effective advertising story for a type of product (for example, for a ready-to-eat cereal or a shampoo) is not likely to be the most effective story for a single brand within those types.

In research which is designed to guide the advertising decision on what story to tell, the state of development of the product is an important variable. Another brand entered into a known product-class field—another soap or detergent, for example—has one problem. A new, improved form of a product which has once enjoyed substantial sales success but has since declined from that level has a very different problem. Then reasons for discontinuing use loom large in the researcher's mind, in planning, executing, and interpreting the research.

One of the most difficult types of problems in the advertising research area is the one which exists where a product is essentially unique. There the problem of creating experience with the product often exists, as in the following case.

39. GENERAL MILLS, INC.

General Mills, Inc., Minneapolis, Minn., a leading manufacturer of a wide variety of food products including cake mixes, cereals, etc., in 1953 developed and perfected a new product in the cake-mix field. This new product—called product *B* to preserve "security" on it until it could be put into production and on the market—combined three major ingredients. The first ingredient was a cake mix. There was no question as to the consumer acceptance of the cake mix in question, since it was identical with the Betty Crocker cake mixes which had been marketed nationally in great volume for many years. The second ingredient was a frosting mix. To this frosting mix it was only necessary to add a tablespoonful of boiling water and mix briefly. The result was a frosting which research had demonstrated had consumer acceptance equal or superior to homemade "cooked" frostings made with far greater expenditures of time, effort, and ingredients (some of which were expensive). The third element in this proposed new product was an aluminum-foil baking pan in which the cake could be baked and frosted. The pan could be thrown away after use.

All three of the ingredients were packaged in a cardboard container the same size as a standard cake-mix package. The two mixes were in sealed envelopes within the pan, which was within the carton. The disposable pan filled the carton. Thus the size of the cake which the new product was intended to bake was relatively small. The maximum size of the cake was determined by the size of the cake-mix carton, within which the baking pan had to fit.

This new product conformed to the established policy of General Mills, Inc., in new-product development, in that it was designed to create new business rather than simply to divert to a General Mills brand business previously enjoyed by a competitive firm. Standard cake mixes, which were selling in substantial volume, made a two-layer cake. While a cake of that size was perfect for medium-sized and larger families, it was a rare two- or three-member family that could consume one before it had grown stale. The new smaller cake which product *B* made was aimed specifically at the small-family market. Thus the new product combined both a different market target in terms of family size and a multiple-feature product of extremely great promise.

The task of advertising the new product posed a number of problems, some usual and some unusual. On the essential elements of determining product name, designing package, etc., there initially appeared to be no unusual elements. But the advertising of the new product posed major problems for which there was no precedent. Obviously this new product should be advertised with a "news" approach. But from the consumer's point of view, what was *the* news in the product? Was it the fact that this new product would make it possible to make a completely frosted cake of very high quality quickly and easily? Or was it the new size—the fact that this product made the convenience of cake mixes available to the small family? Of the features of the product, which should be stressed?

In the case of a new product entering an established industry, consumer research on the importance of specific features and characteristics of existing products is possible. That research can guide the "story-to-tell" decision. In this case, however, there was no comparable product available. This General Mills creation had characteristics of many products, but no other product combined all its characteristics. Under ordinary circumstances with a new-product idea, the advertising-research approach would involve two steps: Place the product with consumers, and let them use it. Then go back and determine from detailed interviews with them which features are most important and least important.

In the case of product *B* there were real problems, in part because of the security aspect. There was nothing patentable about the General Mills idea. Any cake-mix manufacturer could combine the same ingredients (and after General Mills had demonstrated the market opportunity awaiting such a product, some of them did!). It was decided that the only realistic basis for deciding which feature or combination of features the advertising should emphasize was a look at the product through the eyes of women who had used it. A limited quantity of product was developed, placed in plain white cartons, and made available for research.

In the research, the first step with each respondent was an interview about her cake-baking and cake-mix-using practices. Next, because of the security aspect of the problem, the occupation of the head of the household was determined. Then the potential product tester was asked whether she or her husband had any relatives in the grocery business or in the food-processing field. (An affirmative answer terminated the interview.) Respondents who seemed to be "safe" from security angles were then told about the product and invited to participate in testing it.

Placements of three different packages were made with each qualified respondent. (The variety was required to guard against the possibility that some families might not like some flavors of cake, frosting, or both.) Directions were reviewed. Each test participant was asked to save all packages, mix foil envelopes, and a piece of the cake for a callback. (This was partly as a guard against the possibility that one of the boxes placed might "leak" to a General Mills competitor.)

The panel of families used in the product test was deliberately restricted to an absolute minimum in size, because of the security problem. However, the family-size question was considered so important as a determinant of reaction to the cake that it was necessary to have an adequate sample of respondents among two-, three-, four-, and five-or-more-member families.

After the test panel had baked the cakes with product B, detailed re-interviewing took place. The reactions to various characteristics of the product were determined, both in general and in detail. Diaries for recording individual family-members' reactions were used to supplement the results of the interviewing. The end result of this research was a report, "How Families Who Tried It Feel about Product B," which became the guide in the development of advertising copy on the product.

This product was introduced as Betty Crocker's Answer Cake. The Answer Cake designation developed out of research. Prior to the introduction of General Mills' product, and its subsequent imitators, all cake mixes had shown a frosted cake on the package. Women were conditioned to the idea that although frosting was illustrated, it was not in the package. Shown a package variously identified as a Cake Kit,

3-in-1 Mix, etc., they uniformly identified it as "a cake mix." The name Answer Cake was disclosed by research to have interrupting qualities. Women did a "double-take" when they saw it, asked themselves "Answer to what?" and looked at the package long enough to register its truly new-product nature. When the product was introduced in test markets, its sales volume was sensationally high.

THE ROLE OF QUALITATIVE RESEARCH

In research to determine what advertising story to tell, qualitative, or motivational, research usually plays a major role. This is true on industrial as well as consumer products. In many cases that research is supplemented by quantitative research. Thus in the example above, quantitative research determined the number of families in the United States in various family-size groups, and thus contributed to accurate interpretation of the results of the research described.

Chapter 26 is devoted to qualitative and motivational research. Because so much research of the qualitative and/or motivational type is planned to guide advertising policy and direction, that chapter might well be considered as part of and an extension of this discussion of advertising research. The extent to which qualitative research is necessary as part of the determination of what story the advertising should tell varies rather widely. One influence is the amount of previous basic research available. A second is the extent to which the product has elements of uniqueness which would make general findings inapplicable to its advertising problem.

SUMMARY COMMENTS ON FIRST PHASE
OF ADVERTISING RESEARCH

The first phase of an advertising research program is of fundamental importance. That phase of advertising research is also widely misunderstood. Despite those two facts, extensive additional discussion of that phase of advertising research does not seem necessary here. Why not? Because all the other chapters in this book contribute to your knowledge of that subject.

When you approach the first phase of an advertising research program, you face a marketing research problem. Your approach to that problem is essentially the same as your approach to any other marketing research problem of similar magnitude. First you define the problem. Defined, the problem is: What should our advertising say about this product? Before you can determine what additional research is required, you must summarize what is already known on the basis of past research. You then proceed to extend the research to fill in the missing links, if any, in your knowledge of the advertising problem at hand.

Experience has demonstrated that the most efficient approach to the advertising research problem of a specific product is to move from the general toward the specific. You begin with the general area of industry usage, attitudes, etc. You move on to consider the product subtypes involved—for example, automatic washers versus wringer washers. Finally you focus on the specific product and brand characteristics which distinguish the brand you are advertising from competitive products. Which of those differences are most important? What consumer advantages or consumer benefits do they make possible?

A specific illustration may be helpful. Betty Crocker cake mixes, made by General Mills, Inc., require the addition of a fresh egg by the housewife at the time the cake is baked. In contrast, Pillsbury offers a line of *complete* mixes to which no egg need be added. At a time in the early 1950s when Pillsbury enjoyed a substantial market-share lead over Betty Crocker, the pros and cons of the complete mix versus one to which eggs had to be added were thoroughly researched. Much of that research was planned to guide advertising. The research involved lengthy interviews with women who used both types of mixes. What advantages did the housewife feel the added egg provided? How important were the limitations, in terms of reduced economy as against a mix which was complete without the added cost of an egg?

This research disclosed that women felt the egg added moistness to the cake and made it stay fresh longer. The economy point was especially interesting. Economy-minded cake bakers were not essentially mix users. Instead, they made their cakes "from scratch," using a recipe, flour, and other ingredients. Thus the product advantages in terms of moister cakes which stayed fresh more than offset the loss of economy. The eggs were also felt to add to the certainty that the cake would be a perfect cake. Cake failures from recipes were a major element in the growth of the cake-mix industry. Aggressive promotion of the advantages of a cake containing the moistness only a fresh egg could impart and of the dependable results Betty Crocker cake mixes provided soon pushed Betty Crocker cake mixes into leadership in the cake-mix industry by a substantial margin.

In this phase of advertising research, the research man has a slightly different orientation from that which exists in most research. In general, as the chapter on reporting emphasized, the objective is to boil down the findings so that busy executives can get them quickly. The objective of this phase of advertising research is to provide the creative personnel in the agency or the company's advertising department with a broad and detailed look at their products through the eyes of consumers. A single phrase in a consumer interview may "spark" a great creative concept. Therefore it is desirable to keep the research report more complete and detailed in this type of research than in many other types. The objective of this research is to provide "thought starters" for the creative process. Because it is so difficult to determine what elements in the research might "start" a "thought," care not to eliminate promising clues must constantly be exercised.

SECOND PHASE: SALES-IDEA RESEARCH

After the creative group of an agency have reviewed the research executed in the first phase of an advertising research program, they are likely to have far more ideas than they can use. A vast panorama of possible advertising directions is open. Which path should we take? It is at this point that the second phase of an advertising research program begins. We might note parenthetically that that stage is often subdivided into a number of subphases. Essentially the problem in this phase of the research is to secure a quantitative indication of the relative importance of an often substantial number of sales ideas about the product.

Sometimes this phase of the research follows the preceding phase. That is the rule with a new product, or with a product which represents a new assignment to an advertising agency team. At other times, however, this phase begins when there are indications that the advertising which has been used is becoming "tired," losing effectiveness, or has been eclipsed by some new competitive development either in the product or advertising area.

There are many different techniques which can be used in this phase of an advertising research program. One simple and direct approach is simply to place the individual selling ideas on cards and to use those cards as the focus of the interview.

DISADVANTAGES OF THE CONSUMER-JURY APPROACH

Sometimes the various ideas are developed into advertising form (often with identical layouts and illustrations and only the headline or copy appeal as a variable). Such layouts or "almost ads" are then used in the research. Typically a consumer is given two or more ads and asked some such question as "Which one of these two (three, etc.) advertisements do you think would be most likely to make you buy this product?" Occasionally a straight *liking* reaction is sought, with such a question as: "Which one of these two advertisements do you like better?" A variation is to ask which of the advertisements the respondent thinks "most people" would like better.

The observation is a somewhat controversial one, but relatively few experienced practitioners in the field of advertising and marketing research attach significance to the consumer-jury approach. The disadvantages more than offset the advantages. The primary disadvantage is that the consumer, who is not an expert on advertising, is asked to become one for the purposes of the research. The validity of such "quasi-expert" judgments is open to considerable question. In an attempt to "expert" the selection, respondents often choose advertisements which they themselves do not like or do not react favorably to, as subsequent questioning has revealed. A second disadvantage, particularly of the liking approach, is this: There is no evidence that liking for an advertisement is essential to its effective performance. An irritating, disliked advertisement may be more effective than a bland, well-liked one which says relatively little about the advantages of the product. In this case, it is the lack of validity of the criteria (liking) that makes the research approach questionable.

Despite those disadvantages, an approach which bears a resemblance to a consumer-jury test is often used in sales-idea research. Individual selling points for the product are typed on small cards. Those cards are then presented to consumers, ideally qualified prospects for the product in question, and their judgments about them are solicited.

In order to attempt to defeat the "advertising-expert" aspect, the points are often presented as though they were describing different products. The consumer is told that a manufacturer is considering making a product in such-and-such a category and has a number of product possibilities in mind. The respondent is then given (usually) a pair of cards and asked, "Which one of these *products* do you think you would be more likely to buy?" Whether this does in fact flow around the "expert" problem is perhaps somewhat moot. It is an approach, however, which has been widely used, often with excellent results. It is customary to probe on the reasons for the preference, after each choice. That probing has important values.

Thus suppose that of a pair of proposed products *J* and *K*, consumers widely choose *J*. It is important to know whether it is the positive values of *J* that produce the preference or whether *J* is chosen as the lesser of two evils because some aspect of *K* is strongly disliked! Where a larger number of possibilities than two are exposed in a single interview, the usual approach is to ask for a "liked most" or "most likely to make me buy" choice, perhaps a second choice in that area, and also for negative reactions. The latter are determined by the frequency with which various "products" (sales ideas, really) are chosen as "liked least" or "least likely to make me buy." In reporting the results of research of this type, it is occasionally desirable to use net scores as the basis of rating. Those choosing a particular sales idea as desirable are reduced by the number who chose it as undesirable.

ILLUSTRATION OF SALES IDEAS EXPLORED

Here is a listing of the selling points under consideration for a campaign advertising a shampoo:

This shampoo makes hair look younger.
This shampoo eliminates static so hair stays manageable.
This shampoo keeps hair fresh-smelling and sweet.
This is a one-rinse shampoo that's faster, more convenient.
This is a hormone shampoo that helps keep hair vigorous.
This is a shampoo like softest rain water that leaves hair sunshine-bright.

In the research, these sales points were converted into uniform form. Each of the above statements was followed by "Buy Shampoo K today," or the same statement with a different code letter.

In this area of advertising research, the research man is often at the mercy of the copy writer. As a competent research man, you want to eliminate all variables. You want the research to be scrupulously fair. You would probably fight against the inclusion of a "romance phrase" like "sunshine-bright" in one of the shampoo descriptions, when there was no such "plus" present for the other "nominees." And you would probably lose! As a trial run on this series of six statements, fifty interviews were conducted. Here is how the results shaped up on a liked-most–liked-least basis:

Shampoo theme	Number liking most	Number liking least	Net score
Soft as rain water............	21	1	+20
Fresh-smelling..............	15	...	+15
Eliminates static............	3	5	− 2
One-rinse shampoo..........	4	8	− 4
Hormone shampoo..........	6	17	−11
Younger hair...............	1	18	−17
No choice..................	..	1	
Total interviews..........	50	50	

In addition to selecting a first and last choice, respondents were asked to indicate whether their attitude toward each of these shampoos was favorable, neutral, or unfavorable. Here is how their replies were divided:

Shampoo theme	Number of respondents who were:			Don't	Total
	Favorable	Neutral	Unfavorable	know	
Soft as rain water...........	46	3	1	...	50
Fresh-smelling..............	39	9	2	...	50
Eliminates static............	23	14	12	1	50
One-rinse shampoo..........	22	9	18	1	50
Hormone shampoo..........	12	12	24	2	50
Younger hair...............	13	10	24	3	50

VALUES IN REASON TABULATIONS

The reasons for preference or for disliking specific product characteristics, as disclosed by the various *why* probes in this type of research, are extremely valuable. Sometimes those reasons disclose an immovable obstacle in the path of the effective use of a sales appeal. In other cases, a clue to a different and far-stronger approach may be provided. The reason comments are especially valuable as a guard against discarding an appeal when it was not the appeal but the way it was stated that was rejected.

Thus in research on dog-food sales ideas, the economy appeal as presented was uniformly rejected. The initial interpretation was that consumers were reluctant to admit to a socially unacceptable motivation in the selection of the food for their dog. Examination of the reasons for rejection made it clear that it was not economy which was being rejected, but the method of stating it. The claimed saving over another form of dog food was so great that it was rejected as unbelievable. Economy was an important element in the dog-food advertising-claim picture.

The above interpretation of the pattern revealed on reaction to economy suggests another limitation of this approach which should be remembered. Some appeals with heavy emotional charges may be rejected, even though they would be very effective in practice. Thus consider "Even your best friend won't tell you" or "Often a bridesmaid, never a bride" as headlines of famous ads for products designed to overcome bad breath. It may safely be predicted that this particular technique approach would have failed to identify those potent appeals. Consumer reaction to them on cards, as in ads, would have been likely to be strong; but the likelihood of consumers admitting an interest in such a subject to a stranger in an interviewing situation would be relatively slight.

We may thus conclude that in this, as in some other advertising research areas, there are blind spots where this relatively simple and inexpensive technique cannot be used effectively.

Major value of this type of research is as a guide to emphasis. Many of the points indicated can and would be combined in a single ad. It is important in this type of research to see that each sales point is isolated and presented separately. If a single statement combined two sales points, the interpretation of the research results would thereby be complicated to a considerable extent. Thus in the shampoo illustration above, it would have been better to have separated "soft as rain water" and "sunshine-bright" for a fix on the contribution to total appeal made by each component.

APPLICABILITY OF RESEARCH FINDINGS

The advertising research of phase 1 and phase 2 as described above is widely applicable. It is research which is focused around advertising ideas growing out of the product itself and the way potential users feel about that product. It can and does contribute to the creation of advertising for all forms and media. Thus the findings of the research might contribute to the development of an outdoor billboard design; to a radio or television commercial; or to a print advertisement, whether intended for magazine, newspaper, or other form of reproduction.

In the third phase of the research, the focus and the area of application are narrower. The objective of that phase of the research is to determine how well a specific advertisement—whether print, radio, TV, or whatever—does in fact communicate the ideas which it has been decided, on the basis of earlier research, to communicate. Because it combines relative simplicity, in the technique sense, with wide applicability in its usefulness both for consumer and industrial advertising, let's begin by considering the research approaches useful in studying print advertising.

RECOGNITION METHOD OF ADVERTISING RESEARCH

Since it was developed by George Gallup in the early 1930s the recognition method of research on advertisements has been one of the most important areas of advertising research, if the total amount of money invested in it and the number of organizations using it may be accepted as criteria of importance. That method is now most commonly associated with a continuing service which has been offered since 1931 by Daniel Starch & Staff. A "Starch check" or "Starch rating" of a printed advertisement, to use two familiar terms in advertising research, is the numerical score developed through an application of the recognition method of advertisement research as applied by the Starch organization.

The recognition method is used primarily to measure variations in attention and interest of various advertisements which have appeared in actual publications. The interviewers for the Starch organization, for example, locate readers of the particular issue of a magazine in question. They then go through the publication, page by page, with the respondent indicating those advertising (and sometimes editorial) elements which he or she *recognizes* as having read.

Various questions are asked to determine the extent of readership. The Starch reports show "noting," "seen associated" and "read most" figures. The same technique, used by the Advertising Research Foundation in a *Continuing Study of Newspaper Reading*, develops simply a "read" score for each item and each page in newspapers checked in the course of a study which began in 1939.

The scores developed by the recognition method indicate the proportion of qualified readers of a publication who claim to have seen (noted) and read individual advertisements and other elements. The normal sample size for Starch and many similar checks is 200 respondents (i.e., qualified readers) of each sex.

GALLUP AND ROBINSON'S ORIGINAL "IMPACT"

After he developed the recognition technique, George Gallup joined Young & Rubicam, Inc., a large advertising agency, as research director. While with Y&R he operated a continuing service using the technique he developed, with some improvements and modifications. Unfortunately the results of that research were confined to Young & Rubicam's own organization and client list, so they are not generally available. Subsequently he left Y&R and went to Princeton, N.J., which became the headquarters of his famous Gallup poll.

As an outgrowth of his continuous experience with the recognition method, George Gallup became aware of some major limitations of that method. Chief of those limitations was the fact that it measured only quantitative data. It did not provide an indication of what consumers got out of ads they recalled seeing. Nor did it separate readership of relevant from irrelevant material, from the advertiser's standpoint. Thus an ad for spark plugs might, through featuring a scantily clad model, develop a high "noting" score without registering anything about the product which the advertisement was created to sell.

In partnership with Claude Robinson, who had been doing some parallel research in advertising penetration, Gallup formed Gallup and Robinson, Inc., and announced an "impact" service for measuring advertisement penetration. In the original concept of impact, a special "magazine" called *Impact* was used. That magazine combined editorial material gleaned from Canadian publications with actual advertisements, some of which were being studied. The initial approach was to place the publication with a family, and then call back a week later, to pick up the magazine and interview family members on their recall of advertisements in the magazine.

In their initial approach, three levels of recall of advertisements were used. The first was *unaided recall*. Respondents were simply asked: "What advertisements do you remember seeing in the magazine?" The recalled advertisements were then described, product advertised indicated, and so on. The second level of recall was *commodity-aided* recall. If the issue being studied had included a Goodyear tire advertisement, which the respondent did not recall unaided, the interviewer asked: "Do you remember an advertisement for automobile tires?" If that aid did not develop recall, the third level was used. A direct question was asked: "Do you remember a Goodyear tire advertisement?"

In an experimental duplication of the original Gallup and Robinson technique, conducted to provide a basis for a client recommendation as to the purchase of the service (which would have cost more than $100,-000), the average recall levels were 1 per cent unaided, 7 per cent commodity-aided, and 7 per cent brand-aided. That means that out of 100 interviews, an average of 15 respondents would recall an ad of half-page or larger size. Detailed examination of the recall at the three levels disclosed that the brand-aided recall was almost meaningless. Thus the practical average recall figure was about 8 per cent, indicating that 100 interviews would have to be made to find 8 people who recalled an average ad.

PLAYBACKS AS AN ADVERTISING RESEARCH TOOL

The most significant contribution to advertising research growing out of the initial Gallup and Robinson, Inc., impact service (which has long since been discontinued) was a device called the *playback*. A playback is simply a verbatim report, in the respondent's own words, of everything he or she can recall about an advertisement. To illustrate what a playback looks like, let's use some specific examples. The advertisement in question was for Kix cereal. The ad showed two pictures of stenographers at their desks. One was bright-eyed and chipper, obviously alert and happy; the other had her head on her hands and looked dopey and groggy. Readers were invited to guess which girl had the breakfast including Kix. The girls were named "Lupe" and

"Droopy." Here are four actual playbacks illustrating the range of content from the same ad:

1. It was a Kix ad. I just looked at it to see if I was interested or not.
2. Kim or Kix cereal. There were two pictures of the same lady, but I don't remember what she was doing or what the ad said.
3. Kix cereal. Difference in woman who had it, the pep and energy it gave her, and how sluggish the other one was that didn't have it. Package of Kix with a dish on it showing what it looked like.
4. There was an ad with two girls on it. It said which one is Loop and which one is Droop. It was for a breakfast food, but I don't remember what brand. I just skimmed the ad. I noticed one girl was alert, and one was looking the other way.

This range of playbacks illustrates the analytical problem. If all respondents reacted like the one in playback No. 1, you'd junk the ad. If they were all like No. 3, you'd be delighted. This illustrates the quantitative and qualitative problem involved in analyzing playbacks. It is necessary in evaluating an advertisement first to set up meaningful frameworks for groups of playbacks; and then to determine quantitatively how many playbacks fall into each group. In comparisons of ads, both the quantitative and qualitative aspects of the playbacks would guide your appraisal.

SIGNIFICANCE OF THE PLAYBACK

The introduction of the playback as an advertising research tool was a major step forward. In the traditional consumer-jury approach, people were asked to determine *subjectively* which ad they liked better or considered most effective. With the switch to playbacks as an analytical tool, people are exposed to an ad. They report what they can recall about the ad. Then on the basis of differences both quantitative and qualitative in the extent to which two ads delivered the ideas they were created to deliver, an *objective* judgment about the comparative effectiveness of the ads could be made.

Playbacks revealed that in many cases the ideas consumers were getting out of ads were not the ideas the ads were created to deliver. Thus they provided a basis for looking at ads through the eyes of consumers they were intended to reach. That was an important milestone in advertising research.

DEVELOPMENTS STIMULATED BY IMPACT

With the widespread recognition of the potential value of the play-back as an advertising research tool, technique experimentation took off in all directions. Gallup and Robinson shifted to a different service in which they check a number of different magazines regularly. They use a card listing the advertisements in the issue as a basis of stimulating recall. That approach is now known as the *aided-recall* technique, as distinguished from the recognition technique, and it is available as a syndicated type of service.

The Advertising Research Foundation conducted an experimental duplication of the techniques used by the leading firms in the recognition field (Starch) and aided recall (Gallup and Robinson). Alfred Politz Research, Inc., did the field work on that research. The total cost was in excess of $200,000. Among the findings of the ARF study of Printed Advertising Rating Methods (PARM) was the level of recall of individual ads. That is important because it indicates the approximate sample size available on an average ad. For a four-color page in LIFE magazine, the PARM study showed the median level of recall using aided-recall techniques was only 1 per cent of qualified readers. That means that the average number of playbacks developed by the service using aided recall would be about 2 since the sample size was 200 interviews. (Since both sexes are interviewed, the total would be 4, 2 men and 2 women.) That finding raised some serious doubts as to the practical value of the aided-recall technique as a method of studying ads comparatively.

The low level of ad recall, and therefore the small sample size on number of playbacks, which the usual aided-recall approach develops can be traced primarily to two factors. The first is that the interview concerns a full publication, within which the volume of ads is sometimes substantial. That diffuses recall of any one ad or other element. The second is the memory loss between the time of exposure to the ad and the interview. There have been many attempts to retain the objectivity which the playback provided and to overcome those influences depressing the total sample size per interview.

One approach of this type is of interest because it reflects a continuing advertising research program spanning nearly ten years and because it is now in relatively widespread use. This approach utilizes a folder of ads rather than a complete magazine. It thus reduces the competition for attention and raises the total level of ad recall. It involves an interview immediately after ad exposure. If thus secures information before the memory-loss factor has a chance to become operative. This particular approach to advertising research has been widely publicized, as reference to the Appendix will confirm. It was honored by the American Marketing Association in a national award as a contribution to research-technique knowledge.

The primary disadvantage of this approach is its artificiality. The respondent looks through a folder of ads, rather than a complete magazine. There is an offsetting advantage in that many of the variables present in research in an actual magazine are eliminated. Each ad in this technique is on a right-hand page, facing a blank page. In the case of two-page spreads, there is of course no blank page. The influence on "ad performance" of the accidental positioning of an ad opposite high-interest editorial material is thus eliminated.

In its experimental development, this technique involved a series of ten ads. Nine were control ads, and one was the ad being studied. The procedure was to make a series of interviews; substitute one test ad for another and make another series; and so on. The test ads were compared both with each other and with the control ads in the flight. When so operated, the technique revealed two major limitations. First, nine-tenths of the work dealt with (and nine-tenths of the costs involved) the control ads that were of very little interest. Second, the variable of *product interest* proved decisively influential. This meant that for ads in an average product-interest level, two alternatives were possible: If they were tested against high product-interest "control" ads, they looked very bad; if the control ads were low in product interest, the test ads looked good by comparison.

Over a number of years of technique experiment, this approach to advertising research was developed into a form which is widely useful and relatively economical. Five ads are included in a folder. The position of the ads is rotated to eliminate position bias. One ad is kept constant from flight to flight, to check against major variations in ad interest from sample to sample. An indication of how this technique works is provided by the following case.

40. THE TONI CO. (C)

Earlier cases have introduced the problem of research on Bobbi home permanent, manufactured by the Toni Co. (A review of that introductory material—Case 10 in Chapter 12 and Case 21 in Chapter 15—might be helpful at this point.) The earlier discussion didn't emphasize that the Bobbi problem was in the area of advertising research. With the discussion up to this point in this chapter as a guide, you will now have no difficulty in recognizing the problem type. This is an advertising research problem in which initial attention must be devoted to determining what advertising story Bobbi advertising should tell.

Reviewing briefly, the product appeared to be a "natural" for a "quick and easy" approach. That advertising approach had been tried, without noticeable success. Product disadvantages were inescapable in a bobby-pin type of home permanent. The wave was not so tight as with a conventional home permanent and did not last so long. As a reflection of those product disadvantages, consumer satisfaction with the product was revealed by research to be relatively low and repeat-purchase intentions were far lower than for other brands.

In executing the phase 1 advertising research, the agency's research department moved from the general toward the specific, as suggested earlier. General attitudes toward home permanents were explored. Differences by type of home permanents were reviewed. In this phase of the research, some exploratory interviews were conducted. Past research by the Toni Co.'s research department was summarized, with emphasis on those points relevant to the Bobbi problem. Detailed interviews with former and present users of Bobbi were executed. The results of this research were made available to the agency's creative personnel, who had the responsibility of deciding what story Bobbi advertising should tell.

After exhaustive study and consideration of the available research evidence and of the advertising problem in this case, the agency's creative team developed this analysis and conclusion:

1. Although it is the obvious approach, we believe that advertising Bobbi as a quick and easy home-permanent would be dangerous and undesirable. When so advertised, Bobbi competes with all home permanents. Most purchasers are former users of curler-type home-permanents. They will use their own most recent experience as a standard for evaluating Bobbi performance. By that standard, Bobbi will be found unsatisfactory because it does not give such a tight wave, and the wave does not last so long. We think some other approach must be found to advertise Bobbi, or the brand is destined for failure.

2. Studies of the Toni Co.'s research indicate that a considerable number of women give themselves a conventional type of home-permanent and then follow—apparently by habit—this pattern: The woman dislikes her "new" permanent—it's too tight, and her hair is too frizzy. She proceeds to shampoo it frequently and "beat it up" until it gives her a softer wave. If Bobbi could be creatively interpreted to such women as a home-permanent that gave them the kind of wave they wanted without the necessity for that "self punishment," that approach might be desirable.

3. Style experts indicate that there is a trend at this time toward shorter hair, and toward less formalized and fussy hairdos.

4. Our conviction is that if Bobbi is advertised specifically at a segment of the market rather than at the whole market, its opportunity is expanded. We propose to advertise Bobbi to those women who want the kind of a softer wave Bobbi gives. We believe that in that way the expectations of the consumer and the performance delivery of the product can be brought together. Satisfaction and repeat-purchase intentions should rise.

5. We therefore recommend creative exploration of the possibility of advertising Bobbi with an appeal intended to pinpoint out of all home-

permanent users those who want the kind of a wave Bobbi will give. We believe the style trend mentioned will provide a "news hook" for that approach. We believe that such advertising can sell Bobbi in increased volume, and that Bobbi's market share can be expanded by increasing the repeat-purchase intention.

The agency's creative department developed a print ad for Bobbi which was intended as the "pattern" of the proposed new campaign. The ad featured one large photo and five smaller photos of hair styles, with a picture of the package in a sixth small photo. The format of the ad was like that of a black-and-white editorial page in LIFE magazine. Here is the headline and subhead in the ad:

Swing to Casual Hair Styles Demands New Kind of Home Permanent

Tight, Bunchy Curls from Ordinary Home Permanents Won't Do!
But Now There's a Happy Answer . . . Bobbi Pin-Curl Permanent!
The Only Permanent That Waves So Softly . . . So Permanently . . . So Easily

The ad was studied, using the single-ad technique with forced reading. Primary emphasis in that research was on *comprehension*. Did the women who read the ad understand the copy message? Did this ad deliver the desired sales ideas about Bobbi? Because there was some disagreement about what the word "casual" meant, within the agency group, a specific question about that word was included in the research. There were also questions as to whether the major points in the story—a style trend to casual hair styles and a softer wave with Bobbi—were believable. Belief of those two points was also explored.

The results of that research were considered encouraging. The ad was therefore researched in competition with four other ads in a folder, using the technique outlined above. The results of the study of the ad in this way were rather disappointing. A lack of comprehension of the complete story was revealed. Analysis suggested that part of the answer might lie in the relatively large number of elements in the basic advertising story. Recapping, these ideas in this sequence constituted the story as illustrated by the copy above:

1. There is a trend toward a less formal type of hair style.
2. Tight, bunchy curls are inappropriate to that kind of hairdo.
3. Ordinary home permanents deliver tight, bunchy curls.
4. But the happy answer to this problem is Bobbi home permanent.
5. Bobbi is the only home permanent that waves so softly, permanently, easily.

A reworking of the copy with the research as a guide developed a much more streamlined story. One characteristic of that story was that it registered the brand name Bobbi far earlier than as the fourth in a sequence of ideas, as in the above example.

In format, the new approach involved a small "preheadline" and a single three-line headline as follows:

NO TIGHT, FUSSY CURLS ON THIS PAGE!
These Hairdos Were Made with Bobbi
. . . The Special Home Permanent
For Casual Hair Styles

The following table summarizes the performance of the original and revised Bobbi advertising approaches. In the table, the term *pictorial recall* identifies recall of a picture or other pictorial element such as a package, which did not require reading of the ad. *Meaningful copy recall* is the classification used for playbacks which reflect unmistakable reading of some part of the copy.

(In Per Cent)

	First ad: "Swing to . . . "	Second ad: "These hairdos"
Base: total interviews	100	100
No recall of ad	6	4
Total recalling of ad	94	96
Meaningful copy recall	35	79
Pictorial recall	94	96
Pictorial recall *only*	53	15

The revised approach more than doubled the proportion of women exposed to the ad who registered one or more sales ideas. Further, there was an increase in the believability of the ad. In the case of the first ad, 42 per cent of those interviewed felt the ad was "probably true"; the figure for the revised ad was 66 per cent.

— ★ —

In any discussion of advertising research, the question of whether the ad which researched well "sold any merchandise" is likely to arise. A note on that point may be of interest. The Bobbi sales curve shot upward when this approach was adopted, with no change in product or other significant variable. The brand's market share climbed from around 3 per cent of all home permanents to a figure in excess of 15 per cent. Procter & Gamble brought out Pin-It home permanent to try to cut a slice of the pin-curl volume Bobbi had developed, and Richard Hudnut launched Pin-Quick, another competitive product. The rate of repeat-purchase intention among Bobbi users rose spectacularly, because Bobbi users had been sold on the basis of a product performance the product could deliver. The lack of a long-lasting wave became a somewhat mixed blessing. Research indicated that Bobbi users bought more home permanents per year than did users of longer-lasting home permanents. From the viewpoint of the Toni Co., that was certainly a desirable trend!

COMPREHENSION CHECKS

Reference in the Bobbi case above was made to a single-ad check. This type of research is sometimes described as a comprehension check. A consumer is handed an ad and *asked* to read it. This differs from testing in a folder of ads, in which the respondent is free to read as much or as little of any ad as he or she likes. Then the ad is taken away, and the respondent tells the interviewer everything that can be remembered about the ad: what the ad said, the product advertised, what was pictured, and so on. This approach is useful as a way of being sure that the message of the ad is being delivered clearly. It is also helpful as a check against the possibility that there may be a strong negative factor present, which could be eliminated before subjecting the ad to research in a folder of ads, which is often more expensive.

The same approach—exposure of an advertisement to a consumer and recording the recall, recollection, or impression which resulted—is possible with radio commercials, television commercials, and outdoor billboard designs. Some services specialize in research on television commercials. Others offer a service in the outdoor or magazine-advertising field.

OTHER ADVERTISING RESEARCH APPROACHES

There are many other specialized research techniques and approaches which are currently being used in advertising research. Space does not permit a description of those techniques here. Readers especially interested in advertising research should familarize themselves with *Advertising Psychology and Research* by Darrell Blaine Lucas and Steuart Henderson Britt.[1] That definitive book was honored by the American Marketing Association with a national award. The fact that it devotes more than 750 pages to the subject illustrates why advertising research cannot be completely covered within the limits of a single chapter of this book.

[1] McGraw-Hill, New York, 1950.

MEDIA RESEARCH

A major area of advertising research not touched on in this chapter is concerned with advertising media. What is the size of the audience reached by a particular publication? What are the characteristics of that audience? To what extent do the audiences of two or more media overlap? Questions like these form the subject matter of media research.

A considerable amount of media research is conducted for and/or by the advertising media themselves. For that reason, a discussion of media research has been deferred to Chapter 29, where it is discussed as part of the research activities of advertising agencies and advertising media.

SUMMARY

1. This chapter deals with advertising research, which is a major subdivision of marketing research.

2. A considerable amount of marketing research of other types usually precedes and forms the foundation for advertising research. The foundation of facts developed through marketing research becomes the platform on which advertising research builds.

3. There are three major phases to a complete advertising research program for any product or brand. First there is research to determine the story the advertising should tell. This is usually research which stresses qualitative approaches described in Chapter 26. It is often supplemented by quantitative research as well. Second, there is research to determine the relative importance of various appeals, approaches, sales points, or sales ideas. That is usually quantitative research, although there are qualitative overtones, especially to the analysis of reasons for preference. Third, there is research to determine how well the planned advertising succeeded in delivering the basic message.

4. There is a limited amount of specific "how-to" information on advertising research in this chapter, for two reasons. The first is the great complexity of the subject. The second is that advertising research is primarily an area of application of marketing research. The approach to marketing research problems, including those in the advertising research field, is the subject matter of this entire book. A more specific "how-to" discussion would therefore tend to be unnecessarily repetitive.

QUESTIONS

1. What is the area within which the viewpoints of the agency and of the advertiser are not identical in advertising research? What is the reason for this difference?

2. What two major reasons are there for advertising research's increasingly important role in marketing research practice?

3. What is meant when it is said that effective advertising research is likely to have to be comparative, and comparative in more than one direction?

4. How would you comment on the progress advertising research is making in developing a yardstick to measure advertising effectiveness? In what area has progress been greatest?

5. It is said that advertising research has as its objective the fact finding required in the development of an effective advertising campaign. What three major phases can advertising research be divided into as it strives to reach its objective? Discuss the part each phase plays in this research.

6. What disadvantages should you be aware of in the "consumer-jury" approach? In sales-idea research, how has the consumer-jury approach been modified in an attempt to defeat some of its disadvantages?

7. How would you describe the "recognition method" of research on advertisements? Also, describe Gallup and Robinson's "impact" method. What was the most significant contribution to advertising research growing out of the initial Gallup and Robinson service?

8. What is a comprehension check?

CHAPTER 25

Test Marketing

When a new product developed in the laboratory is thought to be ready for the market, the first step toward full-scale production is usually manufacture of a limited quantity of the proposed product. The manufacturing facility which is used for such small-scale experimental or test runs is known as a *pilot plant*. A pilot plant is set up to facilitate the small-scale experimental production of proposed and/or modified products. The pilot plant makes a major contribution to increased manufacturing efficiency. It enables a company to "get the bugs out" of a proposed new product or contemplated product improvement. With a minimum investment of time and effort, the pilot plant makes it possible to reproduce most of the conditions likely to be found in full-scale production. This approach thus serves as an insurance policy against large-scale mistakes or errors in manufacturing.

What the pilot plant is to production, test markets are to marketing. Test marketing identifies a rather wide range of marketing activities which have a common objective: They all seek to determine, through the medium of a small-scale experimental reproduction of a large-scale marketing step, what the effect of that large step would be *if* the company chose to take it. Thus in test marketing, a proposed marketing step or action is reproduced experimentally on a small scale. Test marketing makes it possible to determine on a relatively small investment of time, money, and effort and at minimum risk what the effects would be of carrying out essentially the same action on a broader scale.

The technique of test marketing has been developed to a far more advanced degree in consumer-product marketing than in the marketing of industrial products. Most of the material in this chapter is therefore drawn from the consumer-product field.

EXAMPLES OF TEST-MARKETING PROBLEMS

The Toni Co. was considering the addition of a new shampoo to its line. (This case occurred before the company was purchased by Gillette.) Toni already marketed Toni Creme Shampoo, a thick cream product packaged in jars. The portion of the shampoo market under study was the liquid-cream product-type subdivision. Products in that category were thicker and heavier than the liquid-clear shampoos like Halo and Drene, but lighter than cream shampoos like Toni Creme Shampoo.

Toni's research and development efforts had produced two possible shampoos that might have been marketed as liquid-cream shampoos. One was a white, creamy product. The second was identical in formulation, except that it included an additional ingredient. The extra ingredient was a deodorant. The product containing the deodorant was slightly brownish in color, with a pearly appearance when in a transparent bottle.

The Toni management faced the problem of deciding on its marketing course with the two products. *Which one* of the two should be marketed—or should *both* be launched as new products?

Many experienced marketing research men would consider this to be the type of problem which calls for test marketing. That was the course Toni chose to follow. One product was introduced into a group of test markets; the other was introduced into a different group of markets, carefully chosen to "match" the first group in major marketing characteristics. Each shampoo was advertised in its group of test markets as it would have been if it were being launched in a normal (rather than an experimental and limited) way. One shampoo was advertised with claims for the product which its performance would support. The other placed major stress on the deodorant feature, which was at that time a product exclusive.

The research department of the Toni Co. set up a panel of stores in each market. The store-audit approach (described in Chapter 9) was used to determine the relative rate of movement and the share of the total shampoo market achieved in each group of test markets. On the basis of this test-market approach, it was decided to drop the deodorant shampoo and launch the other product. The brand name chosen was White Rain Shampoo.

Another situation in which the test-market approach was indicated revolved around the selection of an advertising approach. A consumer-product advertising problem could be solved in a number of different ways. One was by the use of black-and-white newspaper advertising. A second was through the use of color comic advertising, in week-end newspaper comic sections. A third way was by the use of rotogravure advertising, in the picture sections of week-end newspapers. Which of those three approaches would produce the greatest total sales of the product? Which would achieve the highest sales volume per advertising dollar?

To answer these questions, test markets were used. One group of markets was set up in which black-and-white newspaper advertising was scheduled. Another group of matched markets was chosen for color-comics advertising. A third group was selected for rotogravure advertising. *In addition, a fourth group of matched markets was required.* Those were *control markets.* A panel of stores was set up in each of the four groups of markets. Sales of the product were determined by auditing movement through the panel of stores.

THE FUNCTION OF CONTROL MARKETS

In test marketing, the objective is usually to measure experimentally the effect of a single variable. In order to do so, it is necessary to have two basic types of data. One type reflects results in a situation in which the variable under study was present. The other reflects the "normal" results, in which—in theory, at least—"all other things are equal" *except* that the variable being studied is absent. The "normal" or base-line data required for the evaluation of test-marketing approaches are secured through study of a group of *control markets* or *control stores.*

Returning to the advertising-approach selection problem above, the product in question was already on the market. The problem of the company was one of evaluating the relative effectiveness of the three different advertising approaches. Each approach would involve advertising costs. In each case it is the relationship between the *extra* sales volume produced by the advertising versus the cost of the advertising that is important. In order to determine what incremental volume the advertising contributed, it is necessary to have a base line. What would the level of sales have been if the advertising in question had not been introduced? The control markets perfom the function of answering that question.

Marketing is a field in which it is always extremely difficult to assign a causal relationship to any single factor. In test marketing, an attempt is made to establish a causal relationship. The research man tries to establish that the addition of variable A was the *cause* of a greater increase in sales volume, or a more profitable sales-volume expansion, than the addition of variable B. In order to do so, he needs to be sure that the increases in question would not have occurred *without* the addition of either variable. Almost always this type of research takes place through time. With time, dynamic influences other than the one(s) under study might affect the "normal" trend. It is therefore essential to have a base line *covering the identical time period* in which the pattern without the addition of the variable in question is revealed.

A CLASSIC ILLUSTRATION OF TEST MARKETING

The notion that test marketing is a relatively recent development in the marketing field is rather widely held. It may be new in so far as general use is concerned, but it was used in essentially its present form as a marketing management tool many years ago. The September, 1956, issue of *Fortune* contained this description by Gerard B. Lambert of the way in which Listerine was built, through tested advertising, to its present status as a household word.

41. THE LAMBERT PHARMACAL CO.

As early as 1922, I instructed our sales manager to set up a system in drugstores that would permit us to count the sales response to the (advertising) appeals I wanted to test. . . . In general, this is how our testing worked. We picked two groups of small towns with a population of about 10,000. One group was to be left alone as a control to show the results without advertising. In the other we could test the relative effectiveness of different appeals.

Before starting the test our men went into a town and saw every, and I mean *every*, retail outlet. They arranged to have an excessive shipment of the product [Listerine] sent to these retailers. In this way the retailer could not reorder from a wholesaler and so confuse the figures. The retailers accepted our big shipment because we guaranteed the sale of it.

Once a week our men would personally count the stock at that time in each store. The difference between the amount in stock on the previous week and the next count would show *the sales over the counter*. This is quite different from psychological guessing. In those towns the sales manager was absolutely forbidden to install any window displays, counter displays, or to give any special discount. No good chemist would add several ingredients while carrying on a single experiment.

With this setup we first let all towns run along as usual for several weeks. In this way we got a norm or base from which to start. When we had the norm established we broke with advertising in all towns except the control towns. This advertising was confined to local newspapers. In all cases the amount of advertising in dollars was made four times higher per capita than the amount that could be risked in a national campaign. This exaggeration was to make it easier to read results, and to save time.

Results show up very quickly in weekly checks. When these early findings come in, it is wise to cross-check by setting up a different set of towns in a different part of the country. If this is done thoroughly, you will eliminate any chance for accidental error. In my own case, at least, I have never known the final national campaign to run counter to the results of the tests.

— ★ —

ELEMENTS IN TEST MARKETING

The above description of a test-marketing approach circa 1922 represents a surprisingly up-to-date picture of sound test-marketing practices today. A review of the elements in an effective test-market program will confirm that observation.

The starting point in test marketing is a number of groups of markets. One group represents the control markets. As many additional groups are needed as there are variables to be tested. In the above example, a small town with a population of about 10,000 was used as a "market." There have been some changes in market-size thinking which have grown out of test-market experience which are noted below. Whatever size of market is chosen today, however, it is likely to consist of a complete marketing area. That might be a standard metropolitan area or a wholesale trading area of some type.

Since the control markets and the test markets are going to be compared with each other, every effort should be made to secure sets of markets which are truly comparable. Comparability depends in part on the product for which the test is being conducted. The test and control markets should be the same size. They should also be alike, or as alike as is practicably possible, in such relevant marketing characteristics as per capita buying power, per cent of urbanization, and so on.

The second element in market testing is to divide the test into time periods. If an advertising approach or a promotion (such as a 1 cent sale, etc.) is being tested, it is customary to divide the duration of the test into three different time periods. The first might be identified as the *prepromotion* time period. This is the time which is allowed to establish a norm, or base line, as in the Listerine illustration. The second is the *promotion* time period, in which the variable factor under study is added to the marketing "mix" in the test markets. No promotion is added in the control markets, of course. The third time period is the *postpromotion* time period. This is the time after the effects of the advertising, promotion, etc., under test have had a chance to wear down. As the comments on test-market interpretation later in this chapter will indicate, the appraisal of the effectiveness of the variable is often influenced by the relationship of volume or market share in the prepromotion and postpromotion periods.

The third element in test marketing today is some basis for measuring the movement of merchandise both in the test and in the control markets. That may take the form of a store-audit approach, and often does. The Listerine example illustrated an almost identical approach. One difference between common practice today and the example described is that no attempt is usually made to "load" the dealer in order to simplify the research. Instead, a record of additions to available stock from wholesale and other sources is maintained. This introduces one further step into the calculation of sales. Opening inventory plus additions to stock equals amount available for sale. That figure, minus closing inventory, provides an indication of physical movement of merchandise. Today, as in 1922, it is "sales over the counter" that are the ultimate determinant of the results of the test.

One important distinction between the example above and present practice can be drawn. Today the selection of stores in which a count of movement is made is almost always on a *sampling* basis. Instead of auditing the movement of merchandise in every outlet, as Mr. Lambert did, today's marketing research man would audit movement only through a carefully selected *sample* of the outlets in a test market. There is a great deal more information about the distribution of retail population today than there was in 1922. That distribution is heavily skewed; that is, a relatively small proportion of total outlets represent a relatively high proportion of total dollar or unit volume in most product categories. That type of population lends itself to sampling very well and makes it possible to get almost as much information from a sample as from a full census, at a small fraction of the cost.

The fourth element in a test-marketing operation is the controlled application of the variable under study. In the Listerine illustration, that variable was advertising. The application of advertising funds at a rate four times that anticipated nationally, on a per capita basis, was decided on in the test-planning stage for Listerine. Some comments on current thinking in that area will be presented in the course of this chapter.

WHAT CAN BE TESTED?

What constitutes sound test-market procedure depends to a considerable extent on the objective of the test. What are you trying to test? In the Listerine illustration, as additional comments not reproduced above indicate, the primary distinction was between the relative sales effectiveness of different advertising appeals. Some experimental exploration of the effectiveness of different types of timing advertising was also included.

The answer to the question: "What can be tested?" today is "Almost anything." Test marketing activities today are widely used for purposes like the following:

Determining the potential of a new product. Test marketing is standard practice among organizations that are active in new-product development. In the case of a proposed new product, the test-market experience makes two significant contributions. First, it provides an indication of the sales potential or volume expectation on a new product. Second, it provides a small-scale opportunity to review under something approximating dress-rehearsal conditions the proposed introductory marketing plan. That review typically leads to refinements which strengthen the introductory approach.

Selecting a new product from a number of possibilities. Where a company has two or more alternative forms of a new product under consideration, test marketing can pick the one with the greatest potential. This was illustrated in the Toni example of a shampoo with and without a deodorant ingredient.

Determining the optimum price of a product. There are often a number of different pricing alternatives open. A higher price may involve reduced volume but increased profit. Similarly, a price reduction is likely to increase volume, but the question of its effect on profit is unanswered. Test marketing can provide specific guidance in the selection of the price-volume relationship which fits the company's objectives.

Determining the most effective advertising appeal. The Listerine case illustrated the use of test marketing to determine which of a number of different advertising appeals would move the product in greatest volume.

Determining the most effective advertising media. As in the case of the black-and-white newspaper versus color comic versus rotogravure advertising problem described above, the test-marketing approach can often help with key decisions in the area of advertising-media selection.

Determining the most effective promotion or premium. Where a number of different promotional approaches—a 1 cent sale versus a two-for-one sale, versus a 5 cent off sale—are being considered, a small-scale test can usually determine which will do the best job of achieving the objective of the promotion. Where several different premiums are under consideration, tests can usually identify the one with superior appeal.

Predetermining promotional costs. Many times an advertising or promotional approach—such as couponing, for example—seems to be desirable, but there exists a question as to how much it will cost. That cost depends on the rate of redemption of the coupons. A small-scale test can answer the question.

Evaluating alternatives in the area of sales methods and policies. General Foods Corporation after World War II was selling an expanding line of food products through a single sales organization. Controlled market tests demonstrated that separate sales forces—one for coffee products, for example, and one for the company's Birdseye line of frozen foods—would more than pay for themselves. Questions involving policy (such as guaranteeing prices on floor stocks in the event of a price change) can also be resolved more safely with testing than by the usual approach which borders on guesswork.

This list could be expanded almost indefinitely. The test-market approach, in which a small-scale reproduction of a proposed change of any kind is first tried out, lends itself to a wide range of marketing applications. The cost of a market-test program is sometimes relatively substantial. That cost must be weighed on the same cost–versus–profit-contribution scale as any other decision involving marketing research expenditures. In the case of test marketing, however, there is a negative aspect of the cost relationship which should be noted. The decision *not* to launch a new product after a market test demonstrated that the product's future was not bright does not make a direct contribution to profit. It does make an indirect contribution, however, by saving the company the loss (both of time, money, and sometimes prestige) which *would have* resulted *if* the decision had been to go ahead without a test and the product had proved unsuccessful, as the test predicted.

WHAT TYPES OF TESTS ARE MADE MOST FREQUENTLY?

Sales Management magazine in the course of one of its studies of test-marketing practices asked 134 executives in advertising agencies about the purposes of test marketing they had done in the preceding six months. Here is how the replies were divided:

Purpose of test	Number of mentions
Base: number of respondents	134
Introducing a new product	106
One copy theme versus another	69
One medium versus another	63
Use of new medium (especially TV)	58
Securing new dealers	36
One premium versus another	31
Testing a new package	30
Tests by market size	27
One layout idea versus another	27
Tests by income groups	17
Proposed price change	13
Tests by age groups	13
Tests by racial or religious groups	13
Large product size versus small	10

Other purposes mentioned by fewer than ten respondents were: product evaluation (taste, new uses, etc.), merchandising offers (combination deals), saturation tests, name tests.[1]

Since the results in the table above were developed by a survey covering advertising agency executives, the replies are biased in the direction of tests in which advertising was an element. They are, however, illustrative of the relative frequency with which test marketing is applied to different types of problems.

HOW ARE RESULTS DETERMINED?

The same study asked how the results of the tests were evaluated. The replies showed that in 82 cases out of 134, retailer sales or inventory records were the basis for evaluating test results. That would involve in most cases a sample of outlets and the store-audit approach to the measurement of movement. Often that is not the only way in which an appraisal of results is developed. Slightly more than half the executives conducted opinion surveys among retailers to help appraise the test results, and almost the same proportion also used opinion surveys among consumers as a source of information.

In some instances the surveys in question were made by advertising media. Almost one-fifth of the respondents mentioned such surveys as part of their test-market-evaluation experience. Sometimes, when coupons are a part of the test, coupon redemption is one criteria used. About one-third of the respondents in the *Sales Management* study mentioned coupons as an aid in evolution of a test.

CONTRASTING POLICIES TOWARD COMPETITIVE TEST MARKETING

One of the most significant indications of the potential power of test marketing as a competitive weapon is provided by the reaction of competitive firms to a market test. When General Mills, Inc., launched a test-market exploration of the relative value of two promotional approaches, four major competitors countered with intensified activity of their own in the test markets within a three-week period. What should you do if a competitive firm launches a test-market campaign? The answer of course depends on the circumstances. Two quite opposite viewpoints are worth noting. Those viewpoints can perhaps best be illustrated by example.

---

[1] "Experts Pick Best Test Markets by Regions and 5 Population Groups," *Sales Management*, Nov. 10, 1950, p. 99.

The first approach is to take immediate and strong competitive counteraction to each test. That approach might be illustrated by what happened in 1953 when the Colgate Palmolive Company launched a test-market campaign for a proposed new product—Lustre Creme home permanent. The test markets used were Atlanta, Ga., Grand Rapids, Mich., and Beaumont, Tex. The Toni Co., with a dominant share of the home-permanent market, was anxious to discourage the potential entry of another strong competitive firm. They took immediate and strong counteraction to "foul up" the Colgate market test. The activity was identified in company memos as "Operation Snafu."

One part of the foul-up effort was a very substantial increase in advertising expenditures for all existing Toni Co. brands of home permanents—Toni, Prom, and Bobbi. The second part was the introduction into those three markets with heavy advertising and promotion of an entirely new Toni home permanent called Epic. The characteristic of Epic was that it included a plastic rod to be used in rolling curls. The rod was identified in Epic advertising as a *magic wand*. Several months after the test had been completed, research by the Toni Co. indicated that Epic had outsold Colgate's Lustre Creme home permanent in two of the three markets and had equaled its volume in the third.

Note the strategic aspect of this activity. Suppose the market test had proved that Lustre Creme could be successfully marketed. Toni would then have had an important new competitor. By taking action to muddy up the test, Toni moved in the direction of two objectives. First, there was the chance that the Toni foul-up might lead the Colgate management to decide not to go ahead with Lustre Creme home permanent. (That decision was made, although the extent to which factors other than the test results contributed to it is difficult to assess.) Second, even if the decision to proceed to market Lustre Creme home permanent nationally had been made, the Toni activities would almost certainly depress the volume levels achieved in the test towns. Those volume levels would be the basis of sales forecasts for national expansion. The advertising-expenditure rate was linked to the volume forecast. By depressing test-market volume levels, Toni had a chance to influence the advertising expenditures of Colgate downward, in the event of a national introduction of Lustre Creme home permanent.

In contrast to the above militant counteraction approach is another which merits consideration. That approach is one of noninterference, usually supplemented by research. A test-market activity is planned to provide information for the company sponsoring the test. Marketing research, adroitly planned, can often provide the same information *for competitors*. Thus a company is enabled to learn directly from the experience of its competitors, at a minimum cost to itself.

When General Mills, Inc., introduced Answer Cake into test markets, Pillsbury Mills, following this approach, immediately set up a panel of stores in the test markets. By auditing movement of merchandise in that panel of stores, Pillsbury was able to determine that there was in fact a tremendous opportunity for a product with the characteristics of Answer Cake. Those characteristics, to save reference to the earlier discussion of this product, were a small cake, aimed at the small-family market, and a product which combined cake mix, frosting mix, and throw-away foil pan all in a single package. The result of Pillsbury's research in the Answer Cake test markets led to a speedy duplication of the product by Pillsbury. When Answer Cake was introduced on a broader scale, Pillsbury's Kit Cake was not far behind.

FLEXIBILITY OF SCALE POSSIBLE

In many instances, test marketing involves the use of whole markets as the testing ground. That is particularly true where advertising is concerned. Since the advertising usually covers the entire market area, the product or variable under test is usually similarly distributed. It should be emphasized, however, that a controlled experiment—which is what test marketing represents—is possible on almost any scale. Thus in the case of a market test of a premium, a sample of stores in a market was chosen and subdivided. Premium A was put into one part of the sample, premium B into another part, and no premium was used in the control portion. In a case of that type, it is usual to rotate the premiums or other variables being tested. It is also desirable to use such devices as a traffic count to be sure that both were exposed to equal opportunity.

Some retail food chains customarily test proposed new products for volume in a panel of stores before adding them to their full store population. The Jewel Tea Company in the Chicago area, for example, has long used that method of evaluating the market size of a proposed new product.

Moving in the other direction, it is not unusual to find whole sales districts used as "test markets." General Mills, Inc., for example, customarily conducts a test on a district-wide basis. The advantage of this approach is that it eliminates problems of having part of the salesmen in a given district active on a test about which the remaining salesmen know nothing. That eases the problem of district-manager supervision of a test activity.

HOW BIG SHOULD A TEST MARKET BE?

Later in this chapter the characteristics considered in selecting test markets are reviewed. Size is one of those characteristics. It warrants individual attention because it is a subject on which there is a great deal of disagreement among men with test-marketing experience. Two approaches are illustrated by cases in this chapter. In the Listerine example above, markets of about 10,000 population were used for test purposes. While that test took place a long time ago, some current tests use markets of that size. In the more recent Swift & Company case presented later in this chapter, markets with a population of about 100,-000 were chosen. That approach, too, has many adherents.

The important influence of the A. C. Nielsen Company on test-market thinking should perhaps be noted here. Companies that were advanced in their use of marketing research were likely to be among early A. C. Nielsen clients. Nielsen set up expanded samples of outlets, as a supplement to their regular national sample, in a group of carefully selected test markets. All Nielsen test markets initially were in a population range between 75,000 and 115,000 population, with the 1930 census as the base. Among the cities chosen were Erie and Harrisburg, Pa., Utica, N.Y., Manchester, N.H., Peoria, Ill., South Bend, Ind., Charlotte, N.C., Shreveport, La., Sacramento, Calif., and Spokane, Wash. Those markets usually turn up with high frequency on any list of "best test markets."

Nielsen's preference for cities in the size range indicated is primarily a reflection of the sample size required for coverage using Nielsen's store-audit technique. To quote an intraoffice memo of the Nielsen organization on that subject: "We prefer test cities of about 50–100 thousand population. This makes it possible for us to maintain a high coverage with a sample of approximately fifty food stores and 15–20 drug stores. In addition to population, other characteristics of size such as the number and sales volume of retail stores, food stores and drug stores must be considered."

Another influence on the selection of markets near the 100,000 population level lies in the fact that most Nielsen clients are relatively heavy advertisers. The advertising costs are lower, in terms of total dollar expenditures, in small than in large cities. Thus the economy of selecting relatively small cities is a factor favoring the selection of markets near the lower limits of metropolitan centers in size.

There is an opposed viewpoint on the size of test markets which should be stated. That viewpoint is that test markets should be representative of the national market and should be, generally, substantially larger than those mentioned above.

That viewpoint is based in part on the fundamental characteristic of the American market which is one of *concentration*. A small number of markets represent a disproportionate share of the national potential on most products. A breakdown by the J. Walter Thompson Company is illustrative. Using their classification, eight *A* markets represent 24.3 per

per cent of the national total population and a higher percentage of retail sales in most categories. The next thirty-five markets, classified as B markets, aggregate 16.9 per cent of population. The next seventy-two markets, in their C category, add 12.0 per cent of the population. Finally their D^1 markets, forty-seven in number, add only 3.5 per cent of population. The latter group is in the population range from 50,000 to 150,000 and thus embraces most of the Nielsen test cities.

Competition is sharply intensified as you move up the city-size scale. If the objective of the test is to provide an indication of what will happen nationally, then this school of thought holds that your test markets should include some large enough to provide a true indication of the reaction of a large metropolitan center. There is much to be said for that point of view. The primary argument against it is in the costs involved. When major metropolitan centers are used as test markets, the costs are relatively high and some of the theoretical advantages of market testing—reduced costs, in particular—are washed out.

The decision on the size of city to use is often strongly influenced by the objective of the test. If the purpose is to determine which of two advertising appeals is stronger, there is presumably no reason why markets in the 100,000-population area cannot answer the question as well as larger markets could. If the purpose is to determine what market share a new product can achieve, then generalizations from experience in smaller markets where the competition is less intense may provide a pretty shaky guide to future action.

The same cost–versus–profit-contribution equation which extends through all marketing research decisions is prominently present here. To a considerable extent the judgment of those responsible for a test as to its likelihood of "success" is a factor also. A small-scale test, duplicated elsewhere as in the Listerine example, may be fully as effective (and far less expensive) as a large-scale effort.

The following case illustrates how the objectives of a research project influenced the nature of the test-market activity which was a major part of that research.

42. SWIFT & COMPANY

Swift & Company packs a diversified line of food and other types of products, extending far beyond the traditional concept of the activities of a "meat packer." A substantial part of the growth of the firm's volume may be attributed to their development of new products. One such new-product idea, in which test marketing played a major part, was the development of meat for babies.

Preliminary consideration of the possibility involved a review of infant-feeding practices and requirements. Specialists in nutrition in the Swift research laboratories checked the possibility. It was decided that it would be nutritionally sound, provided the meats were prepared with a minimum fat content and with very little salt. One nutritional value in meats for infant feeding was the fact that they provided certain essential minerals lacking in milk and had high vitamin content. Many babies allergic to milk were able to tolerate meat-based preparations. Leading nutritionists were checked for guidance on permissible fat levels and salt content.

Characteristics of the market were examined, including various estimates of market size. One relatively unique feature of the market for baby food was the continuous turnover of consumers as they outgrew the need for infant foods. Thus it was not possible to count on the momentum contributed by a growing backlog of users, characteristic of other types of food products.

For test purposes, it was decided to produce seven varieties—beef, lamb, veal, pork, liver, heart, and chicken. These were all made to fit rigid nutritional specifications, from specially selected and trimmed meats. Following the pattern of established baby-food packers, they were developed in two consistencies—strained and chopped. Daily intake for minimal and optimum feeding requirements was considered in determining package size. There were, at this stage, many unknowns in the picture, such as the relative acceptance of the different varieties, attitudes of mothers toward meat for babies, and so on.

A home-feeding test was conducted among a sample of Swift employees who had babies in the proper age range. Different items were fed on a rotating basis. Mothers noted down observations as to reaction and amount consumed on a record card. A home economist working on this project called each week to pick up the record card and supplement it with an interview. Actual feedings were observed in many instances. A new supply of product was left weekly.

At the end of the home-feeding test, the acceptance of the product by both mothers and babies was assured. Minor modifications in the product were recommended. Decision as to package size was made possible. The product or product line was ready for test marketing.

The objective of the test marketing was to answer certain questions about commercial aspects of the new product's future. The product was priced substantially higher than fruit and vegetable baby foods. How many mothers would spend the higher price for an initial purchase? How many would repeat-purchase? There were problems of distribution and of servicing stock which were not present in other Swift products which had to be explored. In addition, the important question of the doctor's influence on feeding practices entered the picture. It was necessary to detail doctors. The men who serviced stocks in stores maintained records of the movement of the product, in total and by item (flavor).

Three markets with population near the 100,000 mark were selected. In those markets, an organization specializing in consumer diary work set up panels of families in which there were infants in the required age group. The panel members were asked to record their purchases of a number of different packaged food items, so that they were unaware that the research was focused on the baby-food portion of their reporting.

At the end of a six-month test period, accumulated data permitted Swift & Company to identify the types of families buying (as to economic status, occupational and educational level, etc.). The quantities purchased per buying family were known. The frequency of purchase and the repeat-purchase ratio were established. The relative popularity of different items in the line was determined.

After the consumer panels had served their purpose, the families who had purchased the product were identified and were extensively interviewed. In this interview, emphasis was on how they had happened to start using the product (was the doctor a primary influence?), attitudes toward the product, whether it was fed alone or in combination with other foods, and other information. Panel families which had not bought the product were also interviewed. What had they heard or read about it? Was there any particular reason why they hadn't bought it?

On the basis of this test-market experience, the company was able to launch the product on a national scale. The approximate volume expectations were known, and marketing plans could therefore be tailored to realistic volume goals.

— ★ —

FACTORS CONSIDERED IN SELECTING TEST MARKETS

Sales Management magazine publishes an annual *Survey of Buying Power* issue giving current estimates on many types of vital statistics entering into test-market selection. The publication also devotes considerable editorial attention to test marketing. It publishes frequent articles about market tests and occasionally conducts a mail survey of advertising and marketing executives in which "the best test markets" are chosen. In conjunction with their studies on that subject, they developed the following list of the "ten most important factors influencing the choice of test market."[2] The major list of factors influencing the ex-

---

[2] "Sales and Advertising Experts Pick the Best Test Markets of the Country in 3 Population Groups," *Sales Management*, Sept. 1, 1947.

perts' choice of test markets is shown, in which the factors are listed in order of frequency with which they were given.

The test city should:

1. Be a cross-section of population, contain typical population, have a diversified population.
2. Be a relatively isolated community, independent of other large cities.
3. Have good advertising media available and willing to cooperate.
4. Have diversified industry and business.
5. Be of average income per capita.
6. Have good or typical distribution facilities, outlets, channels.
7. Be a stable market.
8. Have a good record as a test city.
9. Be an area where, if successful, the advertiser knows his product will sell anywhere.
10. Have good transportation facilities.

The emphasis on advertising media (radio stations, newspapers, television stations, etc.) in the above list and the use of the word "advertiser" in point 9 underlines the frequency with which test-marketing activities involve advertising or are related to advertising questions.

It is necessary for a test market to be physically separated from other markets and relatively independent, in order to be able to react to the variable under test without the likelihood of external influences upsetting the test. Where a single market is part of a "twin" situation (as in the case of Duluth, Minn., and Superior, Wis.), the entire market should be used or an alternative chosen. Diversification of industry and of employment is an important factor. Without such diversification, the market is unlikely to satisfy the requirement of representativeness. This rules out for most purposes markets which are atypical, like state capitals (where the proportion of governmental employees, and hence of clerical personnel is unusually high) and markets dominated by a college or university.

Some marketing research men have learned through sad experience the necessity of examining the extent to which a proposed test market is dependent on a single industry or factory. Surprisingly enough, some markets popularly accepted as "good test markets" are heavily so dependent. A market test running in Peoria over a long period of time was rendered almost completely useless by a prolonged strike at the Caterpillar plant in that market.

HOW MANY TEST MARKETS SHOULD BE USED?

The question of how many markets should be used for a test-market study is another on which there is considerable variation. A one-market test is occasionally used, but the decision to rely on a single market is always a hazardous one. Some factor like the strike mentioned in the case of Peoria may develop which will "foul up" the test and make interpretation difficult if not impossible. A practical minimum on number of cities per cluster is two. That is, in the case of a test of a single variable there would be four markets—two test markets and two control markets. The use of three or more markets per cluster is widely recommended by marketing research men, but cost considerations sometimes make that a difficult concept to "sell." With three markets in a cluster, one can be "washed out" by some unforeseen circumstance without leaving the interpretation of the test dependent on a single market.

As a general rule, the smaller the number of markets involved the greater need for careful study in their selection. That study should be sharply focused on the question of whether the markets are or are not representative *in the case of the product for which the test is being conducted.* The following comment by Peter Hilton[3] suggests some of the difficulties which may crop up:

> In one-market testing, you must be prepared for hazards, because of the amazing consumer variations posed by different geographical areas. A distiller, for example, should know that in Cuyahoga County, Ohio, more liquor is consumed than in any one of 25 states. A coffee manufacturer must take into account the fact that southern consumers drink 77 per cent of their tea during the five warmest months. In addition, the favorite size of package varies widely. For example, over the nation as a whole, 59 per cent of root-beer sales are in small bottles. But in the South Central area, 95 per cent of sales for this product are in small bottles.

THE DANGER OF OVERTESTED MARKETS

With the increasing use of test marketing as a management tool, there has developed an awareness of the danger of using the same markets for repeated tests. When markets are used repeatedly for tests, there is a tendency for them to become less and less typical. That developing atypicality involves the reactions both of consumers and of trade factors —wholesalers and retailers. Through repeated exposure to promotional activities on new products, consumers and retailers alike may develop indifference which makes their reactions far from typical.

Closely related to that factor is the danger of "wearing out" a company's own sales organization in a market or area by repeated tests and special assignments. The likelihood that the regular assignments may be neglected in favor of the novelty of a test activity is also present as a

---

[3] Peter Hilton, "How to Pick a Test Market," *The Management Review,* April, 1954, p. 255.

factor which should be considered in evaluating sales-force test-market participation.

COMMONLY ENCOUNTERED PROBLEMS IN TEST MARKETING

The process of planning and executing an effective test-marketing operation calls for an extremely high level of marketing research skill and competence. It is by no means as easy as it sounds when it is described briefly. A test-marketing operation to have real significance must usually extend over a substantial period of time—three months, six months, or a year or more. Marketing executives tend to be impatient, with the competitive pressures which are a part of their job as a contributing factor. There is often a problem in securing authorization for a test long enough to be dependable.

Often the key statistic in the case of a test-market operation lies in the relationship of prepromotion volume or market share and postpromotion volume or market share. The kinds of things that are often tested tend to be expensive. (It is that high cost, in many instances, which makes the research cost of the test-marketing operation a sound business risk.) The key marketing-management decision as to whether to extend the variable under test—to introduce the new product nationally, to extend the 1 cent sale to other areas, etc.—often rests on the relationship between the cost and the increased volume developed. It is a natural mistake to underestimate the length of time it takes to make a sale, allow time for the product to be used up, and allow time for a repeat purchase. Failure to continue the test over a long-enough time period is a common source of failures or disappointments in test-marketing activities.

Setting up a panel of stores for a market test takes a great deal of time, much of it high-priced executive time. The market must be studied. A sample of stores must be developed which is truly representative of the market. That is expensive. After the original setup, the cost involved is essentially a function of two factors—sample size and audit frequency. There is natural pressure, as a result, to reduce the number of stores in the panel and/or to audit movement less frequently. That tendency is in a direction opposed to sound research evaluation of the test results.

Sampling errors are present. There are chance variations which influence volume movement (weather, for one). The danger when a small sample of stores is used in a test market is that the inescapable chance errors involved may be greater than the difference in influence of the variable being measured. From this we may generalize that the smaller the difference (estimated in advance) between the two variables being measured, or the smaller the likely influence of something being tested on the sales rate, the larger the number of stores that must be included in the panel.

Careful attention to the test markets on a continuing basis is necessary throughout the test. Only in that way can the effect of unanticipated factors which might otherwise ruin the test be detected. Carl Henrikson of Crossley S-D Surveys, Inc., cites these examples:[4]

> Then there are the uncontrollable, unpredictable things that can knock the best planned sales test askew. Here are a few examples:
>
> 1. A competitor can mess up your test, unwittingly, by springing a big local promotion in one or more of your test areas.
>
> 2. Some of your sample stores may run out of stock or decide not to stock an important competitive brand during your testing period.
>
> 3. One or more of your sample stores may close or have a change in proprietors who won't cooperate.
>
> 4. A spell of bad weather may occur in some of your test areas.
>
> 5. Major strikes of several weeks duration in one of your test areas can cause abnormal consumer purchase patterns. Big war contracts, crop failures, floods, storms and fires can also throw your test out of a normal balance.

In the same talk, Mr. Henrikson made these comments about "things that gum up sales tests":

> When the director of research submits a proposal for a sales test project, the usual reaction of those with whom he must deal is that the plan is unnecessarily complex, too costly, and takes too much time. Account executives and clients quite often are ready with suggestions to simplify the plan and to cut down costs and time. If the suggestion is made to reduce the sample of areas and stores, the statistical sampling error is all too often larger than the differences achieved between the factors tested.
>
> Sometimes it is suggested that costs can be brought into line by using sales personnel instead of field research workers. Experience has shown that even the best salesmen do not have the training nor the attitudes that make for accuracy and objectivity in reporting. Using sales personnel for store-check reporting can, and usually does, snarl up an otherwise well planned sales test.

ADVERTISING-EXPENDITURE POLICY IN SALES TESTING

In the Listerine example earlier in this chapter, the comment was made that "the amount of advertising dollars was made four times higher per capita than the amount that could be risked in a national campaign." That approach—of using substantially increased advertising weight in

---

[4] In a talk to an American Association of Advertising Agencies regional convention, Oct. 31, 1951.

order to secure quick results from a market test—is still generally used. Sometimes the costs involved are substantial. A reluctance to risk so much in so limited an area is often noted in test-market discussions. In the case of some tests, the variable under study is the effect on volume of varying advertising-expenditure rates. The interpretation of such tests would be almost impossible if the "forced-draft" theory of expanded advertising volume were introduced.

We have already noted that economy often suggests the desirability of using small markets for test purposes. It is an established fact that advertising rates per unit of population are higher in smaller places than in the large metro markets. Today it is considered sounder to determine the *advertising weight* rather than the *advertising cost* of a proposed national effort, and then to duplicate the weight rather than the cost in the test market. Suppose, for example, a new product is to be introduced in a test market. The national campaign plan calls for, say, thirteen four-color pages in LIFE magazine. In the test markets, color pages in local newspaper magazine sections are to be used to simulate the LIFE impact. How many such pages should be used? One approach would be to determine the level of LIFE circulation in the market and run enough to duplicate that weight in the test. Thus if LIFE's circulation covered 30 per cent of the households in the test market and if the local medium used covered 60 per cent, roughly half as many pages would duplicate the proposed national weight.

It costs as much in terms of art work, mechanical reproduction of advertising, etc., to prepare an advertising campaign for national use as it does for use in a limited number of test markets. Most companies that do extensive testing remove the extraordinary and nonrecurring cost components from a test-market activity from the cost picture, before examining the cost-profit relationship of the test-market results. Thus the cost of conducting the research is usually excluded. Where local-media costs are excessive, they are often reduced to an equivalent of a national-campaign cost in evaluating test-market volume-and-profit arithmetic.

FREQUENCY OF AUDITING MOVEMENT

How often should audits be conducted, in the case of a test-market campaign? Again the Listerine example provides one extreme, with weekly auditing of sales. The A. C. Nielsen Company regularly audits movement once every two months. Test-marketing practice today falls somewhere between those two extremes. One influence on the audit frequency is the movement rate of the product. On a fast-moving item like a cake mix, audits weekly or every two weeks would be likely to be necessary. On a slower-moving item, an audit every four weeks might be considered to suffice. This is a key question, because of its direct bearing on cost. Weekly audits cost almost four times as much as every-four-week audits, because of the time involved.

There is a flexibility in a brief auditing period which deserves mention. Consider a test-market situation on a cake-mix product. Store-auditing on an every-four-week cycle was being used. In the middle of the month, a big promotion—a "Silver Dollar Deal"—was used. Was that promotion effective? If there had been weekly audits so that the movement in the two weeks prior to the deal were known, an approximate answer could be developed. When it was simply buried within the average movement rate for the full four weeks, no guidance was provided.

TEST MARKETING AND THE SALES DEPARTMENT

Experience suggests the desirability of keeping the local salesman or sales organization "in the dark" as to how many and what stores are being audited. The objective in most tests is to get an idea of how the entire market reacted, from a sample of audited stores. Where the names of the stores are known to the sales representative, he may concentrate attention on them, thus developing an entirely misleading picture of what is happening in the market. For example in one test on a floor-wax product, the list of stores was released to the sales department "by mistake." In audited stores, the new product had almost 100 per cent distribution. In a matched sample of nonaudit stores, distribution achieved was in the 10 to 20 per cent range!

SUMMARY COMMENT ON TEST MARKETING

Test marketing is a marketing research approach of established value. In test marketing, long experience suggests that the safest guide is: "If a thing's worth doing, it's worth doing well." A skimpy, inadequate job of test marketing has often proved to be grossly misleading. Hindsight indicates that in some such cases it would have been far sounder to proceed without the market test. This powerful competitive weapon, carefully used by experienced people, can do much to reduce the risk in major marketing decisions. It is not inexpensive, and it is not and cannot be accomplished under forced-draft timetables.

SUMMARY

1. This chapter described the test-marketing approach which is to marketing management what the pilot plant is to production management. It is a way of conducting a controlled marketing experiment on a small scale with reduced

cost and risk, as a way of determining the soundness of proposed action on a broader scale.

2. In new-product development, test marketing is widely used. It provides insurance against a failure through product rejection by consumers under normal conditions of use. It provides guidance to the strengthening of the marketing plans which would be used if the test proved successful and the test area was expanded to regional or national distribution.

3. Control markets provide the base line against which the results of the variable being tested can be evaluated. They are essential to test marketing, especially where the product involved is already in the market place.

4. A practical minimum number of markets for testing is two to each cluster, i.e., two control markets and two test markets if a single variable is being studied.

5. Time is required to establish a normal or base-period movement rate, before the variable under study is added. It is usually desirable to continue the test for a substantial period of time, to get the trend picture in sharp focus.

6. The versatility of test marketing is greater than is generally recognized. It can be used to test almost any major marketing variable—price, product, policy, etc. Its limitations are essentially two: It is neither quick nor easy; and it requires careful supervision by experienced personnel.

QUESTIONS

1. Although test marketing identifies a rather wide range of marketing activities, what common characteristic do these activities have?

2. What is a control market? What is the function of control markets in the test-market operation?

3. What were the elements in an effective test-marketing program as described in this chapter? Discuss each briefly.

4. It is said that test-marketing activities are used for a wide range of purposes today. What are some of these marketing applications?

5. How are the results of a test-market operation evaluated?

6. One of the most significant indications of the potential power of test marketing as a competitive weapon is provided by the reaction of competitive firms to a market test. What courses of action are open to you if a competitive firm launched a test-market campaign?

7. There is a great deal of disagreement among men with test-marketing experience when size of the test market is considered. What are these differing viewpoints?

8. *Sales Management* magazine developed a list of the "ten most important factors influencing the choice of test markets." What are these factors?

9. How would you answer the question: How many markets should be used for a test-market study?

10. What are some of the most commonly encountered problems in test marketing?

11. How would you decide how often audits should be conducted in a test-market campaign?

CHAPTER 26

Qualitative and "Motivational" Research

Marketing research men have long drawn a distinction between two fundamentally different approaches. One is essentially *quantitative* and is concerned primarily with developing information or data of a numerical type. The other is *qualitative* in nature and emphasis. It deals primarily with subjects like attitudes, characteristics, reasons, motives, and other related matters.

It should be emphasized that these two approaches to marketing research are not mutually exclusive. Most research combines both quantitative and qualitative approaches, often within a single study.

The direction emphasized depends in a large measure on the questions the marketing research seeks to answer. Thus quantitative approaches are indicated when one wants to know *"How many?"* or *"What proportion?"* When the key question is *"What kind?"*, *"How?"*, or *"Why?"* a more qualitative emphasis is indicated.

There are often differences between research using primarily quantitative or primarily qualitative approaches on an intensive-extensive basis. Quantitative research using the survey technique often involves questioning a relatively large number of people. Often a simple questionnaire is used, or a rather limited subject matter area is explored. Qualitative research, by contrast, often digs more deeply and intensively into the feelings, viewpoints, attitudes, or practices of a smaller number of people.

Qualitative and quantitative as terms applied to research often pose problems in communication. The tendency is for those lacking extensive research experience to think of them as describing mutually exclusive research areas. There are almost always qualitative aspects to essentially quantitative research, and vice versa. The terms as used in this chapter are intended to distinguish between research which is *primarily* focused on questions of the "How many?" or "How much?" type, as distinguished from research *primarily* on the "What kind?" and "Why?" questions typical of qualitative research.

662

Some experienced research men are gravely concerned about the semantic problems posed by the use of quantitative and qualitative as terms to describe types of research. Thus J. Stevens Stock wrote in a letter to the editors of the *Harvard Business Review:*[1]

> I think it is a dangerous kind of dichotomy to make in research. Any research, to be valid, has to be qualitative; any research, to be accurate, has to be quantitative. Therefore, all acceptable research should be both qualitative and quantitative. I can't see how marketing research can be meaningfully classified in this way. (I am not thinking here of "statistical reporting" like that of the A. C. Nielsen Company or such as is done in much audience research for magazines.)

IN INFORMAL INVESTIGATIONS, QUALITATIVE RESEARCH IS USED TO HELP DEFINE THE PROBLEM

Qualitative research is widely used in the problem-defining phase of the research process. It is a vital tool in conducting an informal investigation. Research men often utilize a small number of qualitative interviews in which different aspects of each respondent's attitude toward, knowledge of, and experiences with a particular type of product are explored, as part of the problem-defining phase of their research.

Let's illustrate this in specific terms. You are the research director of an advertising agency which has just been appointed by an organization that processes and packs poultry of many types. The firm produces frozen and canned chicken and turkey products. There are five or six different major types of canned-chicken products alone—canned boned chicken, canned chicken à la king, canned chicken fricassee, canned whole chicken, and so on. Before the advertising agency you work for can develop sound advertising and marketing recommendations for this new client, there are many basic questions which must be answered. It is up to the research department of the agency to supply those answers.

Where should research begin in a situation like this? First you consult the client's sales figures. Those figures show that the canned part of the business represents the bulk of the company's volume and the major source of the company's total profits.

You begin with almost complete ignorance of the canned-chicken market. The client's executives have certain opinions on the subject of who uses the products, for what, and so on. Because of experience with situations like that described in the Dell-O case, you accept such opinions with some reservation.

What do you want to know? Well, almost everything. What kinds of

[1] On page 147 of the May–June, 1956, issue of that publication.

families use canned-chicken products? Are all canned-chicken varieties used by the same types of families and for the same purposes, or is the canned-chicken business several businesses of essentially dissimilar nature all lumped together? Considering major products within the canned-chicken total individually, you have these questions about each: What kind of families use this product? Do a small proportion of families use the product with high per-family frequency, or do a large proportion of families use it rather infrequently?

Why are these products used? Is it primarily convenience which leads a housewife to buy and use them, or is it the economy the product represents, or the appetite appeal of the product, or what? (You are constantly on guard against the danger of overgeneralizing about these products. You recognize always the possibility that answers which apply to a 16-ounce jar of chicken with noodles selling for 23 cents might not apply to a 7-ounce package of canned boned chicken selling for 65 cents.

So you tackle the research problem by going out yourself and interviewing some housewives on their knowledge of, usage of, and attitudes toward canned-chicken products.

You move into a lower-middle-class neighborhood, where you interview Mrs. Henry P_____. Here are your notes on your interview with her:

Mrs. P_____ said her serving of chicken "would average out about one and a half times a week." The family had chicken on the day preceding your interview with her and had served it also a week earlier. "We often have chicken on Wednesday night," Mrs. P_____ commented.

She buys fresh chicken—"both fryers and stewers." The family likes chicken served both fried and stewed. Mrs. P_____ said she thought "stewing chickens go further. You're fuller. It's a more satisfying meal." When she prepares a stewing chicken, she first browns it, then makes gravy, adds onions, and serves over dumplings.

She has bought frozen chicken, but she has discontinued buying it because it's too expensive for her family. "I think it's more economical to buy the fresh and I think they are better tasting. With the number in my family, one package of the frozen chicken didn't do it. It would run too high-priced to have it often and we eat quite a bit of chicken."

Mrs. P_____ keeps a canned whole chicken on her pantry shelf at all times "just in case." At the time of the interview, she had a can of Corn Blossom on hand, but she said that was the first time she had purchased this brand. "I buy just whatever they happen to have at the store and usually look for a special-price sale. Once in a while I get Banquet or College Inn." She serves canned whole chicken as chicken à la king or as creamed chicken on toast. She also occasionally ("but not often") buys canned boned chicken which she uses in salads or sandwiches. She has never used canned whole chicken for a meal for her family—"I just get it for entertaining." She regards it primarily as an insurance policy in the case of unexpected company.

She has bought packaged chicken à la king, both in canned and frozen form. She did not remember the brand of frozen chicken à la king she tried, but she did know they didn't like it. "You don't seem to get much of it. You get more in the cans," she said. She always buys College Inn brand canned chicken à la king and has tried no other brands. She says she serves chicken à la king for lunches "probably once a week or so."

She has never bought or served canned chicken fricassee. "I just imagined it's all soft and gooey inside and I don't think we'd like it."

She estimates that she uses about one can of boned chicken ("or turkey if it's cheaper") each month. She uses it "just for salads now, with maybe once in a while a sandwich." At first she said she had no favorite brand of boned chicken and bought "whatever brand they happened to have on the shelf." Later she commented that "College Inn is probably the best brand of boned chicken." Of other brands tried (names not recalled) she complained: "There's too much gelatin and not enough chicken in some of it. Some of it doesn't seem to have much of a turkey or chicken flavor."

When asked specifically about X brand, she said she had used X-brand boned chicken at one time. "I didn't like it any better than those others. College Inn is more white meat than the X brand and it has more of a flavor."

Lower-middle-class family in deteriorating neighborhood. Husband is an hourly-paid factory worker who attended one year of college. Respondent's education terminated after three years of high school.

After you thank Mrs. P_____ for the thirty-five minutes she has given you out of her busy day, you move on down the street. You don't want to make interviews too close together, because of the danger of a loss of representativeness among respondents. You start ringing doorbells on the next corner. The neighborhood is one in which many of the housewives work during the day. It's a Thursday, and many of those who don't work are shopping. The lady is home in the fourth house from the corner, but she "can't be bothered." The fifth house has no one at home. In the sixth one—finally!—Mrs. Steven J_____ comes to the door and invites you in. Your notes on your interview with her were a bit thin. Here they are:

Mrs. J_____ could furnish very little information about chicken and chicken products because she and her husband do not especially care for chicken and she serves it very rarely. It was "over three months ago" that she last served chicken.

When she does serve chicken, she buys a fresh, whole chicken "at the feed store down on the corner." She always serves chicken fried.

She has never bought or tasted any canned-chicken product that she can recall. She has heard friends talk of serving and liking canned chicken, but she can't recall the kind or brand of chicken they were discussing.

She never buys any canned meat. She has never heard of *X* brand of canned-chicken products.

Her family consists of herself, her husband who is a cab driver, and one son, two years old. When she mentioned the age of her son, she commented: "We were married fifteen years before our son came. I wish he'd come when I was younger. He really keeps me hopping!" She lives in a modest frame house on a rather well maintained mid-block lot in a lower-middle-income neighborhood.

CHARACTERISTICS OF EXPLORATORY INTERVIEWS

Interviews like the two described above are illustrative of some qualitative research. Interviews of the type quoted, when conducted in the problem-defining phase of the research process, may most accurately be described as *exploratory interviews*. Certain common characteristics of research situations in which exploratory interviews are conducted can and should be recognized.

The first such characteristic is concerned with the part such interviews play in the over-all research process. Exploratory interviews typically have as one major objective the gathering of information *for the education and guidance of research people in planning subsequent research*. In other words, such exploratory interviews are usually conducted *as part of the process of developing a research plan,* rather than as part of the *execution* of planned research. (As a qualification to this generalization, you will recall that sometimes research begins and ends with an informal investigation. This was illustrated by the Pabst case in Chapter 13.)

It may be helpful to think of exploratory interviews as one of the raw materials of the research process. They are often consumed in the process of the research and rarely survive as one of the end results of the research.

A second characteristic of exploratory interviews is a corollary of the first. The exploratory interview is conducted because the research man wants and needs information. His objective is to secure that information. Mechanical details as to how the information is secured are relatively unimportant. Therefore he may begin by asking a question. That question draws only a blank look from the respondent. The question is rephrased and asked again. This time it elicits an answer, but one which is in the judgment of the research man a fragmentary one. He follows up that question with one or more probing questions, exploring each response in detail. He is watching the respondent's face, rather than observing the specific phrasing of each question asked.

Thus exploratory interviews have a relatively high degree of individuality to them. Such interviews are expected to provide the research man with a consumer's-eye view or a respondent's-eye view of the subject under discussion. That subject will be seen and interpreted differently, with varying perspective and emphasis, by each respondent. The researcher is preoccupied with the task of securing as much information as possible relevant to the subject of the research from each respondent. Because respondents are so highly individual, it is impossible to standardize the questions asked and the approach taken in exploratory interviews.

A third closely related characteristic of exploratory interviews is that the shape and content of each is strongly influenced by the individual respondent interviewed. The objective of the research man in all such interviews is to pump each respondent dry of information which will help him sharpen focus on the problem area. The breadth and depth of the picture each interview develops depend primarily on the respondent. As the two interviews above illustrate, some respondents have much more information and/or experience in the area of a particular subject or product than others. The research man cannot secure more information from a respondent than that respondent brings to the interview. A considerable variation in the length of individual interviews, and in the meatiness in terms of helpful information provided from interview to interview, should be expected.

DEPTH INTERVIEWING: TWO APPROACHES

One of the important research tools which is widely used in qualitative research is an interviewing approach which is known as a *depth interview*. The reader should be warned at the outset that this particular term is one which is widely used by different writers and organizations to describe a rather wide range of research approaches. Most of the variations in the meaning of the term represent refinements or subdivisions of two quite dissimilar approaches to depth interviewing. Those approaches involve concepts as to the purpose and nature of a depth interview which vary widely. The concepts involved warrant a brief examination here.

A committee of the AMA undertook the task of developing a manual of sound practice in the field of depth interviewing. The efforts of that committee were rather unproductive because they found it impossible to secure agreement as to what a depth interview is. As the committee reported:[2]

[2] "Depth Interviewing," an American Marketing Association committee report, *The Journal of Marketing*, April, 1950, p. 721. The committee was a subcommittee of the Marketing Research Techniques Committee. Julian L. Woodward was chairman; other members were David Hoffer, Fred Haviland, Herbert Hyman, Jack Peterman, and Harry Rosten.

Among the A.M.A. members interviewed, there appear to be two basically different ways of viewing depth interviewing, and consequently two recurring and fundamentally different emphases in the varying definitions of the term. There is, first, the group of people who stress the word "depth" rather than the word "interviewing." They emphasize the end or purpose or objective of depth interviewing, which they believe is somehow to get below the surface of the personality of the individual being interviewed, to get down to his "basic" underlying motivations, the reasons why he says what he says or does what he does.

For this first group, depth interviewing is simply any kind of research that goes deeper into the personality than conventional fixed-answer questionnaires succeed in doing, and it does not matter how this additional depth is obtained so long as some kind of "interviewing" is involved. Information about sub-surface factors may come from the type of interviewing whose prototype is the cathartic "seance" with the clinical psychologist, it may come from some laymen's modification of the psychiatric interview characterized by extensive and skilled probing by the expert interviewer and free response from the interviewee, it may come simply from a relatively informal, unstructured interview by a highly trained reporter. There is also no reason to exclude some other methods of getting "depth" that also use a kind of interview as a means of collecting data. One of those methods would be the use of projective techniques (like the Rorschach), another would be a carefully designed closed-answer questionnaire from which inferences or motivation or "reasons why" are drawn by cross-tabulation and analysis.

The second group's definition of depth interviewing stresses not the word "depth" but rather the word "interviewing." For this group of marketing researchers depth interviewing is not a particular end, but a technique that is employed to reach a variety of ends. It is a special type of interviewing in which there is less rigidity of structure than in ordinary interviewing, more probing of the respondent, and a more complete record of his responses obtained. This more informal type of interview may be used to get "depth," it may be used to get "frame of reference" (which is not the same thing as depth), or it may simply be employed to get better rapport where the interviewing is on a subject where good rapport is essential.

For the second group, depth interviewing connotes a tool that can be employed for a variety of purposes, some of which involve no more "depth" in the psychological sense than is yielded by the most conventional fixed-answer questionnaire.

The committee report continued with the following comments which suggest why the usefulness of *depth interview* as a meaningful term is somewhat limited:

Different market researchers combine the elements of these two viewpoints in different ways when formulating their own personal conceptions of what the term "depth interviewing" means to them. Some are consistent in holding a group one position, some equally consistent in group two emphasis, but many combine parts of both and end up with a hybrid that is either so inclusive as to make the term almost useless to describe any specific part of the researcher's armamentarium, or so personal as to have little current meaning for the profession as a whole. In general the core of unanimity is so small as to raise seriously the question whether the use of the term does not do more harm than good. The term has already acquired so many meanings as to be inaccurate for scientific description, and it appears that so many different research products are being sold as "depth interviews" that it is also a term of doubtful utility in explaining research to clients.

The Committee has therefore come to the conclusion that the term could well be abandoned by market researchers and replaced by new terms that do not have to carry the freight of confusion that it now carries. The term "depth interviewing" needs to be laid away on the shelf along with such other now largely discarded bits of terminology as "instinct," "social forces," and "free market" which over the years finally come to mean all things to all social scientists.

QUALITATIVE APPROACHES BYPASS OBSTACLES WHICH QUANTITATIVE RESEARCH ENCOUNTERS

The increasing importance of qualitative research in the over-all marketing research picture has been strongly stimulated by a recognition of certain limitations which are inescapably present in conventional quantitative research approaches in which a fixed questionnaire is used.

An interviewer is face to face with a respondent. The interviewer asks a question, exactly as phrased on a conventional questionnaire. The respondent replies, and the reply is recorded on the questionnaire. That respondent's reply is coded, edited, and tabulated, along with those of hundreds or thousands of other respondents interviewed in the course of that quantitative study. Is the tabulation of replies to that question an accurate and dependable reflection of "the fact," on which management may safely base major decisions? That is a question which cannot be answered categorically: It may be, or it may not be—it all depends!

Suppose the question concerned a factual matter like ownership of a gas versus an electric refrigerator. Answers secured would be likely to be reasonably accurate. Such a question explores an area in which two things are true. First, the respondent knew the answer to the question, hence was *able* to answer the question accurately. Second, the respondent was *willing* to answer the question accurately. Many research projects involve areas in which respondents are either unable or unwilling to supply accurate answers. It is in such areas that a qualitative approach is likely to be more effective. Marketing research men have learned to recognize situations in which personal bias on the part of respondents would lead to inaccurate and/or incomplete replies and to take appropriate steps in terms of qualitative techniques to secure dependable answers in such areas.

EXAMPLES OF PERSONAL BIAS

Lucas and Britt[3] point out that there may be both conscious and unconscious mental limitations, which they describe as examples of personal bias, present even in a fully cooperative respondent. They note that respondent bias exists where a respondent is motivated to provide replies to an interviewer which are either incomplete or distorted. An example is provided by surveys seeking to determine readership of different magazines. Respondents tend to exaggerate their readership of magazines which are relatively high in prestige and social acceptance (*National Geographic, Ladies Home Journal,* and *Good Housekeeping,* for example). Readership of publications at the other end of the social-acceptance scale (such as *True Story, True Confessions,* etc.) is consistently understated. Another example of this tendency was mentioned in Chapter 8 on the survey technique when the inflationary bias in a question about deodorant usage was mentioned.

The type of personal bias mentioned above is familiar to all experienced marketing research people. It requires consideration whenever there is a possibility that a particular question might present a respondent with the need to choose between the right answer, which would involve some loss of prestige or social acceptance in the eyes of the interviewer; and remaining silent or volunteering some inaccurate but more socially acceptable response which might enhance his ego.

Closely related is the problem which arises in the case of socially unacceptable motivations. If an accurate response to a question might require the respondent to admit that he acted because of some socially undesirable motivation, the accuracy of replies is questionable. People continually rationalize their own actions. They substitute socially acceptable "reasons" and "explanations" in the case of actions which were actually triggered by some other motive.

Often the actual motive operative in a particular situation has been concealed by respondents even from themselves. Thus the owner of a new car is likely to have a logical-sounding explanation of his decision to make a trade-in of his late-model car. He is unlikely to admit that his (or his wife's!) desire to keep up with a neighbor exerted a strong influence on his decision. In situations of this type, it is desirable to dis-

[3] Darrell Blaine Lucas and Steuart Henderson Britt, *Advertising Psychology and Research,* McGraw-Hill, New York, 1950, p. 121.

tinguish between two types of situations. One is the case in which the respondent knows the "true" reason or answer yet substitutes a rationalization. The other is one in which the respondent does not know the true reason, either because it has been repressed or because the actual motivating force was operative at a level of consciousness too low to permit articulation.

HOW EGO INVOLVEMENT DISTORTS REPLIES

Sometimes the questions asked about a product do not develop accurate answers because the questions are received and interpreted by respondents in ways other than those intended. The likelihood of distortion is particularly great if the respondent's extension of the question involves the ego or self-esteem of the respondent. Mason Haire illustrated this tendency when he wrote:[4]

> When we approach a consumer directly with questions about his reaction to a product we often get false and misleading answers to our questions. Very often this is because the question which we heard ourselves ask was not the one (or not the only one) that the respondent heard. For example: A brewery made two kinds of beer. To guide their merchandising techniques they wanted to know what kind of people drank each kind, and particularly, what differences there were between the two groups of consumers. A survey was conducted which led up to the questions: "Do you drink _____ beer?" (If *yes*) "Do you drink the *Light* or *Regular?*" (These were the two trade names under which the company marketed.) After identifying the consumers of each product it was possible to find out the characteristics of each group so that appropriate appeals could be used, media chosen, etc.
>
> An interesting anomaly appeared in the survey data, however. The interviewing showed (on a reliable sample) that consumers drank *Light* over *Regular* in the ratio of 3 to 1. The company had been producing and selling Regular over Light for some time in the ratio of 9 to 1. Clearly, the attempt to identify the characteristics of the two kinds was a failure. What made them miss so far?
>
> When we say "Do you drink *Light* or *Regular?*" we are at once asking which brand is used, but also, to some extent, saying "Do you drink the regular run-of-the-mill product or do you drink the one that is more refined and shows more discrimination and taste?" The preponderance of *"Light"* undoubtedly flows from this kind of distortion.
>
> When we ask questions of this sort about the product we are very often asking also about the respondent. Not only do we say "What is _____ product like?" but, indirectly, "What are *you* like?" Our responses are often made up of both elements inextricably interwoven. The answers

---

[4] Mason Haire, "Projective Techniques in Marketing Research," *The Journal of Marketing,* April, 1950, p. 649.

to the second question will carry cliches and stereotypes, blocks, inhibitions and distortions, whenever we approach an area that challenges the person's idea of himself.

LEVELS OF AVAILABILITY OF INFORMATION

A research man brings to work on a particular problem an often unconscious recognition of the fact that there is a wide range in what we might call the availability of different types of information required of individual respondents. The highest (and in research terms, the easiest) example is illustrated by the interviews on chicken usage presented earlier in this chapter. In those cases, we noted, the respondents were both *able* and *willing* to provide the information needed. Often research is not that easy. There are different degrees of inability and unwillingness to supply information required for research purposes. The marketing research man must appraise the difficulties which must be overcome to secure the desired information and select appropriate research approaches with the scale of those difficulties as a key influence.

George Horsley Smith has formulated[5] a useful three-level classification of the availability of information in terms of what he describes as "levels of awareness." The following comments draw on that classification framework.

1. *First Level: Material Can Be Discussed*

Examples of information falling within this level are numerous in this book. We might include the preference of women for one of two different margarines, a product research problem in the Dell-O case; and the varying carpet sweeper and vacuum cleaner cleaning rituals developed by women who do and do not own both types of cleaning devices. Smith notes that many feelings, beliefs, and attitudes can be verbalized fairly accurately. Even at this level, however, there are problems for the research man. Smith comments:[6]

> Even at this level, consumers' lack of training in introspecting may make it difficult for them to give complete information. They may fail to note and remember important things. They often lack the right words or the right concepts to express themselves, may confuse apparent with real determinants, may hold contradictory views which they do not disclose in full, may assume one frame of reference when talking to an interviewer and another when reading a magazine or making a purchase, and their answers may depend on how the question is phrased or who does the asking. They may talk in terms of platitudes, but behave by different

[5] *Motivation Research in Advertising and Marketing*, an Advertising Research Foundation publication, McGraw-Hill, New York, 1954, p. 18.
[6] Ibid, p. 19.

standards. There is also a reluctance to discuss views on religion, sex and politics with strangers.

It is widely recognized today that the total area represented by information which is completely accessible by direct approaches at this first level is far smaller than it was once thought to be. There have been many demonstrations of the fact that unsuspected influences are sometimes active in distorting or withholding information which one might expect to find respondents both able and willing to disclose. Mason Haire described such a situation in the following terms:[7]

For the purposes of experiment a conventional survey was made of attitudes toward Nescafé, an instant coffee. The questionnaire included the questions "Do you use instant coffee?" (If *No*) "What do you dislike about it?" The bulk of the unfavorable responses fell into the general area "I don't like the flavor." This is such an easy answer to a complex question that one may suspect it is a stereotype, which at once gives a sensible response to get rid of the interviewer and conceals other motives. How can we get behind this façade?

In this case an indirect approach was used. Two shopping lists were prepared. They were identical in all respects, except that one list specified Nescafé and one Maxwell House Coffee. They were administered to alternate subjects, with no subject knowing of the existence of the other list. The instructions were "Read the shopping list below. Try to project yourself into the situation as far as possible until you can more or less characterize the woman who bought the groceries. Then write a brief description of her personality and character. Wherever possible indicate what factors influenced your judgment."

Shopping list I	Shopping list II
Pound and a half of hamburger	Pound and a half of hamburger
2 loaves Wonder bread	2 loaves Wonder bread
bunch of carrots	bunch of carrots
1 can Rumford's Baking Powder	1 can Rumford's Baking Powder
Nescafé instant coffee	1 lb. Maxwell House Coffee (Drip Ground)
2 cans Del Monte peaches	2 cans Del Monte peaches
5 lbs. potatoes	5 lbs. potatoes

Fifty people responded to each of the two shopping lists given above. The responses to these shopping lists provided some very interesting material. The following main characteristics of their descriptions can be given:

1. 48 per cent of the people described the woman who bought Nescafé as lazy; 4 per cent described the woman who bought Maxwell House as lazy.

[7] *Op. cit.*, p. 651.

2. 48 per cent of the people described the woman who bought Nescafé as failing to plan household purchases and schedules well; 12 per cent described the woman who bought Maxwell House this way.

3. 4 per cent described the Nescafé woman as thrifty; 16 per cent described the Maxwell House woman as thrifty. 12 per cent described the Nescafé woman as spendthrift; 0 per cent described the Maxwell House woman this way.

4. 16 per cent described the Nescafé woman as not a good wife; 0 per cent described the Maxwell House woman this way. 4 per cent described the Nescafé woman as a good wife; 16 per cent described the Maxwell House woman as a good wife.

We shall return to this interesting experiment later in this chapter. Continuing with George Horsley Smith's classification of levels of awareness, here is the second level in his framework.

2. *Second Level: Material Rarely Discussed*

The types of information which fall in this zone are illustrated by Smith as:[8]

> Examples in this zone are the desire to impress one's neighbors with a bigger TV set, moving into a better neighborhood as a means of social climbing, reading a certain newspaper in order to feel like a big shot, driving a high-powered car rapidly in order to let off aggressive impulses, drinking a Coke as a reward after frustrating circumstances, smoking cigars in order to feel more masculine.

The motivating forces present in the actions described above are, Smith notes, "only slightly outside awareness, and psychologically sophisticated people can penetrate them easily enough." He points out, however, that for most respondents interviewed this is not the case. The result of questioning on reasons for actions like those indicated would be likely to develop rationalizations, intellectual discussions often quite irrelevant to the subject matter of the research, and a mass of half-truths.

They tend to provide what Smith describes as "partial or pseudo explanations" like these:[9]

> They insist that they buy the new TV because the old one had a flicker, move into the tony neighborhood because it represents a better real-estate investment, read the uppity newspaper because it contains more news, drive rapidly in order to save time, drink the Coke because it "tastes good," and smoke the cigar because it has a pleasant aroma.

[8] *Op. cit.,* p. 20.
[9] *Ibid.,* p. 20.

Smith comments on the profitable opportunities for research at this second, or "preconscious," level and notes some characteristics helpful in exploiting those opportunities:[10]

Good training in the social sciences, plus experience on the job, will often enable the investigator to spot rationalizations as they show up, formulate hypotheses that can be checked by varied probing, and infer general frames of reference and motives from cues that are turned up. A clinical skepticism of pat and obvious answers is an attitude which the researcher needs to cultivate in himself.

This brings us to Smith's third "level of awareness," and into an area of considerable unresolved controversy.

3. *Third Level: Material Unanalyzed, Not Discussed*

This level in Smith's classification includes material, particularly in the area of motivation, which is not consciously recognized and which would be likely to give rise to anxiety and other forms of disturbance if it were brought to conscious awareness. Among the examples Smith cites of material in this level are:[11]

. . . The origin of some "common colds" in the need for attention and the loss of security; the pathologic gambler's unconscious wish to lose as self-punishment for equally unconscious aggression; the favorable response to polite and flattering advertising because it "offers a substitute for the (childlike) desire of the customer merely to walk in and get what he wants without paying"; bargain hunting as the need to outsmart others and to express aggression toward a substitute of the bad, refusing mother; chronic psychogenic constipation as a symbol of withholding from the world ("not giving"); homosexual and Oedipus tendencies; repressed hostilities toward minority groups; numerous personal experiences, sexual and otherwise.

Smith comments in a footnote to this listing that "some of the preceding statements represent hypotheses based on clinical observations and should not be widely generalized without empirical verification."[12]

We shall return to a consideration of the research problems and opportunities encountered at these three levels and appropriate research approaches to them, later in this chapter. As a postscript to the above listing, this comment by Smith on the educational requirements of effective work with material at this third level is worth underlining:[13]

[10] *Ibid*, p. 21.
[11] *Ibid.*, p. 21.
[12] *Ibid.*, p. 21, footnote.
[13] *Ibid.*, p. 23.

In order to do profitable work at this level, the motivation researcher should be familiar with the major concepts of psychiatry and abnormal psychology. He should have experience in gathering and interpreting complex personality data. As consumer analyst, he will not ordinarily have the opportunity to get direct evidence of deeper motives; certainly he cannot carry on his probing of the same individuals for months or years as the psychoanalyst does. Hence, he must be alert to interpret such cues as do come to hand and to utilize techniques (e.g., word association) which may give indirect evidence of repressed material.

PROJECTION: THE BASIC CONCEPT

A relatively large proportion of the information which the marketing research man seeks lies at the second or third level in Smith's classification framework. Such information is approached by indirect rather than direct avenues. The approach in question utilizes the basic concept of *projection*, originated by Freud. In possibly oversimplified terms, Freud found that characteristics and attitudes which were denied or repressed, within one's self, were sometimes revealed when they were attributed to (or *projected upon*) others. This concept underlies a great deal of qualitative and motivational research today. When the information sought may have an emotional charge, particularly of a negative nature, an indirect approach is more likely to be productive than a direct one. Instead of asking a respondent how he or she feels, the analyst draws inferences about those feelings from the way in which the respondent describes or talks about *other* people, events, or situations.

This fundamental concept of projection can be and is applied today to a wide variety of different marketing research problems. An illustration of its application was provided in the instant-coffee research described by Mason Haire in a quotation earlier in this chapter. Women would not (or perhaps could not) tell an interviewer that the reason they did not use instant coffee was because they feared being considered a lazy housewife. The way respondents talked about "another" woman—identified only by her grocery selection—provided additional insight into the obstacles that had to be overcome before instant coffee could achieve the volume levels it has since attained.

ORIGIN OF PROJECTIVE TECHNIQUES

Today various avenues to information at Smith's second or third level are widely used by marketing research men. All those approaches utilize the basic concept of projection. Collectively those approaches are described as *projective techniques*. Projective techniques are more widely used, it seems, than understood. To provide an indication of the ad-

vantages as well as the limitations of those techniques, it seems desirable
to pause briefly for a backward look at the origin of those techniques.

Projective techniques were developed originally as clinical instruments.
They were designed to help identify abnormalities in thinking processes
and emotional reactions. Those abnormalities in turn provided clues
helpful in identifying the nature of the personality problem or disturbance of an individual patient. Before one can recognize the abnormal, however, one must first be able to decide what is "normal." That
is especially difficult in the case of mental abnormalities because often
the particular manifestations are a part of normal development. Thus
the interpretation of those manifestations as normal or abnormal depends
upon the stage of growth of the person revealing them. It is also worth
emphasizing that certain cultures emphasize characteristics which are
not accepted as "normal" in our culture. Thus the interpretation of what
is normal and what is abnormal must be made within the known context
of the individual's background.

This is an important point which is worth remembering: *Projective
techniques were developed for individual evaluation.*

INFLUENCE OF STRUCTURING

The rationale behind the projective techniques goes something like
this: When an individual is confronted with an unstructured stimulus,
structure will be imposed (or projected) on the basis of the individual's
own past experiences and present "set," or wants. The less structure the
stimulus provides, the more the person must turn within himself or herself to provide the missing structure.

This can be illustrated with an extreme example. Suppose an individual were handed a blank card and told to tell a story based on that
card. That story would have to come entirely from the individual's own
thoughts, feelings, memories, and experiences. The story would be
unique, quite different from the stories told by other individuals in response to the same unstructured stimulus. Now shift to another extreme:
Suppose an individual were shown a picture which was recognizably a
photograph of a Hollywood party in which there were three widely
known and easily recognized movie stars who had recently figured in a
headlined triangle-divorce situation. The story told in response to that
stimulus would be largely determined by the picture itself. The individual would have to supply very little structure. Stories told by
many persons in response to that stimulus would tend to be quite
similar.

The fact that the focus of a projective technique is on an individual
respondent is in a way somewhat of a limitation on that approach.

Whether the marketing research approach being used is quantitative or qualitative, we are seldom concerned with a single, individual respondent. However, we are often concerned with the significant differences in feelings and attitudes of different *groups* or *types* of respondents. From individual respondents chosen to represent a particular group, we can determine the responses, attitudes, feelings, etc., which are characteristic of members of that group. We can thus compare and contrast the views of different groups, building upward from the responses of individual representative samples of each group.

Projective techniques are rarely used alone. They are almost always used in conjunction with an interview, which may range from relatively structured to relatively unstructured. That interview almost always develops information about the respondent which enables the analyst to identify him or her as a member of one or a number of groups. The groups in question may be users, former users, or nonusers of a particular product; or they may involve the classification of the respondent into one or another socioeconomic group, or stage in the life cycle (i.e., bride-to-be, newlywed, "young married," mature housewife, or "deserted housewife," the latter designation being applied to women whose children have grown and left home).

MODERATE STRUCTURING TYPICAL IN MARKETING RESEARCH

In a typical marketing research situation, the research is not concerned with the attitudes, feelings, wishes, and motives of people *except as they relate to the specific product or company sponsoring the research.* Projective techniques can be readily adapted and modified to fit whatever product or subject area is being explored. This is done in most cases by introducing into the projective techniques a moderate amount of structure. This was illustrated by Haire's instant-coffee example.

The structuring introduced into projective techniques used in marketing research is usually as little as possible, provided that the general product or subject area is indicated or suggested. Sometimes the structuring is not in the projective itself but is provided by the accompanying interview. After a long discussion of how she feels about the general subject of soup, with particular reference to the nutritional qualities of that soup, a respondent may assume that soup is an element in a subsequent projective approach. The particular stimulus chosen and the degree of structure provided will tend to define the limits within which a respondent is likely to project.

IMPORTANCE AND INFLUENCE OF THE ANALYST

There is one major difference between qualitative research which combines detailed, probing interviews and projective techniques and the older and more conventional marketing research approaches which are the subject of all other chapters in this book. That difference is concerned with the relative importance of the analyst and the extent to which he or she influences the findings of the research.

This should be regarded as a note of caution. It is often cited as a major limitation of research which relies heavily on projective approaches.

No projective technique, and no research utilizing such a technique or combination of several such techniques, is any better than the individual who analyzes it.

To see this point in perspective, let's consider first the normal relationship between the research man and his research. In most marketing research, the research man gathers information, data, and evidence in the field. He then proceeds to summarize, tabulate, analyze, appraise, and interpret the information the research provided. *The findings of the research stem directly from what the research itself uncovered.* In theory at least, another research man of equal skill and experience could duplicate the research and develop essentially similar, consistent findings.

In the case of research using projective techniques, however, the analyst plays a far more dynamic and important role in determining what the "findings" of the research were. All projective techniques allow great freedom and latitude to the analyst in the interpretive process. The analyst's imagination has free reign. The analyst has an opportunity, quite literally, to project his own pet theories and/or complexes into the research and its interpretation!

To a considerable extent the results of research using projective approaches is influenced by the analyst's own background and training. It has been said, perhaps ungenerously, that submitting the same research assignment to two analysts with quite different educational backgrounds is something like submitting a column of figures for addition to an inexperienced clerical employee: "I added them up twice . . . and here are the two answers!"

The criticism is often made of qualitative and motivational research that the "findings" of the research come from within the analyst, rather than from the evidence gathered among those who were the nominal subjects of the research. That criticism applies with varying force to different approaches to the analysis of qualitative research data. One suggestion has been made that it could be overcome by this approach:[14]

> Have at least two research analysts interpret at least part of the interviews independently of each other and then compare results in the presence of a third analyst. The latter would be of general use as a buffer

[14] Robert Ferber, *Projective Techniques from an Analytical Point of View,* a paper presented at the 1955 Marketing Symposium, University of Illinois, Urbana, Ill., *University of Illinois Bulletin,* 1955, p. 112.

force in case of disagreements of opinion in addition to providing a broader perspective on the specific problem at hand.

EXAMPLES OF PROJECTIVE TECHNIQUES

1. *Sentence Completion*

A widely used projective technique of considerable value in the case of marketing problems is known as *sentence completion*. This technique in use involves the exposure of a respondent to an incomplete sentence (called a *stem*). The respondent is asked to complete the sentence with the first thought that comes to mind. There is usually moderate pressure for speed, accomplished by using a group of sentence stems which are read quickly, with a new stem following promptly on the respondent's completion of the preceding one.

The purpose of the time pressure is to secure the respondent's thought in the particular words or phrasing that come first to mind. It is meant to contribute to the spontaneity of the replies and to make the respondent less wary and "careful" of the replies given.

Here are some examples of sentence stems used in the sentence-completion portion of a study of attitudes toward synthetic sweeteners like saccharine, Sucaryl, etc.:

Exercising to lose weight . . .
Looking in the mirror . . .
Whenever the going gets rough . . .
Synthetic sweeteners . . .
Overweight people . . .

Note that the sentence stems quoted above represent just a few of those used in the sentence-completion portion of this study. Note further that they are not listed above in the sequence followed in the actual administration of the projective technique.

These sentence stems were especially designed to elicit attitude indicators toward the subject of overweight and dieting. Synthetic sweeteners are one aid in dieting. In this case as in many other situations where projective techniques are utilized, the researcher is interested not only in finding out about the product area under study but also about the personalities of the respondents. It was anticipated that there might be significant differences between users and nonusers of synthetic sweeteners, even though both groups had similar overweight problems. The research was used in part to explore that hypothesis.

Thus consider the sentence stem: "Whenever the going gets rough. . . ." That item was designed in an attempt to detect differences in the kinds of defenses used under such circumstances. As the following examples illustrate, there were marked differences in the completions supplied by users of synthetic sweeteners and by nonusers who were also in the overweight category:

Representative completions to the sentence stem:
"Whenever the going gets rough . . . "

By nonusers of synthetic sweeteners	*By synthetic-sweetener users*
" . . . smile."	" . . . I go to sleep."
" . . . grin and bear it."	" . . . I start to pray."
" . . . you just make up your mind to keep going."	" . . . I splurged."
" . . . I thought of the outcome and was encouraged."	" . . . I eat from nervousness."
" . . . that's the time to sit down and relax and think a bit."	" . . . I just give up."

As the above completions indicate, the users of synthetic sweeteners are characterized by their absence of a realistic means of attacking the problem. They rely on the defenses of withdrawal, self-indulgence, and helplessness (with appeal to the superior power of others, e.g., God). This presents a sharp contrast with the more realistic and goal-oriented reactions to stress evidenced by those who do not use synthetic sweeteners. The latter group does not seem to give in so readily to pressure from outside. They expect to show greater fortitude. From this the inference may be made that those who use synthetic sweeteners are those with relatively less faith in their own ability to overcome difficulties (including the problem of overweight). They tend instead to rely on others to help them. The synthetic sweetener, sanctioned by the authority of a pharmaceutical manufacturer, promises to do for them what they cannot do for themselves.

Considering now the level of information which is most likely to be tapped by the sentence-completion approach, note that the completions quoted above are representative of information from Smith's second level of awareness. They identify tendencies which appear in thought in typically undisguised form. They are thoughts of a type which an individual respondent might prefer to conceal from others, because they tend to reflect adversely on the respondent. Sentence completions are often helpful in eliciting information of that type.

The sentence-completion approach is also used frequently to provide a more spontaneous and less inhibited access to material from the first level of awareness. Many questions which could be asked directly of respondents are asked instead (or in addition) through the sentence-completion approach. Here are some examples, chosen from sentence stems used in a variety of studies:

Husbands who get corned-beef hash for dinner . . .

People who drive Cadillacs . . .

The woman who saves trading stamps . . .

Children who won't eat ready-to-eat cereals . . .

Sentence completions like those quoted are useful for ascertaining quickly the cultural stereotypes which exist in certain product and product-use areas. One limitation of the sentence-completion approach lies in the fact that that approach is useful primarily in dealing with information at the first and second levels of awareness in Smith's classification. They are of little value in trying to tap feelings or attitudes toward information of the type which is strongly repressed. Sentence completions can only develop information which the respondent is *able* and *willing* to give. They represent a somewhat indirect approach, which is useful because it expands the area which might be explored by direct questioning.

2. *Thematic Apperception Test* (*TAT*)

The thematic apperception test, more familiarly identified as the TAT approach, consists of the use of a picture about which respondents are asked to "tell a story." Directions to the respondent used in the administration of this technique, repeated for each picture in a series, take essentially this approach:

> I want you to look at this picture and tell me a story. I want you to tell me what is happening now, what led up to it, and how it will end. I want you to tell me what the people in this picture are thinking, feeling and doing. You can make up any kind of a story you please.

This technique was originally devised for clinical use by Henry A. Murray. It consists of 30 cards illustrating scenes with varying degrees of structure or ambiguity. The pictures represent interpersonal situations. Some are situations with a single picture, and some do not include any people. One is a blank card. The power of this approach to disclose data which would evade a more direct approach is suggested by the following comment from the test manual prepared by Murray:[15]

> The fact that stories collected in this way often reveal significant components of personality is dependent on the prevalence of two psychological tendencies: the tendency of people to interpret an ambiguous human situation in conformity with their past experiences and present wants, and the tendency of those who write stories to do likewise: draw on the fund of their experiences and express their sentiments and needs, whether conscious or unconscious.

[15] Henry A. Murray, *Thematic Apperception Test Manual*, copyright 1943 by the President and Fellows of Harvard College, Cambridge, Mass.

If the pictures are presented as a test of imagination, the subject's interest, together with his need for approval, can be so involved in the task that he forgets his sensitive self and the necessity of defending it against the probings of the examiner, and, before he knows it, he has said things about an invented character that apply to himself, things which he would have been reluctant to confess in response to a direct question. As a rule, the subject leaves the test happily unaware that he has presented the psychologist with what amounts to an X-Ray picture of his inner self.

As its name suggests, the TAT approach was developed as a test of apperception rather than perception. It was intended for use in uncovering covert (second-level) information. When interpreted by analysts

Figure 26.1

trained in psychoanalytical theory, it can sometimes provide clues to the nature of repressed information at the third level of awareness.

An illustration of a TAT picture used in marketing research is reproduced as Figure 26.1. A woman is shown in a supermarket, in front of a section which consists of family flour on one side and cake mixes on the other. When cake mixes were less widely accepted, this picture elicited responses which tended to cluster around areas of conflict. The women's desire was to bake a cake which her family would rave about and praise her for as a good cook and homemaker. She was tempted to use a cake mix which would be faster and easier. She was inhibited in her tendency to use a mix because she feared the same type of "lazy housewife" interpretation mentioned earlier in the case of instant coffee. With the exception of extremely experienced housewives, the likelihood of "success" in cake baking represented a major "plus" for the mix.

Parallel research at a time several years later when cake mixes had become a more accepted element in the normal homemaking pattern disclosed an almost complete shift of focus. The only conflict remaining in the situation, the more recent research disclosed, was centered around the selection of one brand and/or flavor of cake mix from the wide variety available!

Here are some of the stories told in response to the TAT picture shown as Figure 26.1:

> This woman is shopping in the Food Fair, and she's probably said to herself "What will I do? Shall I make a cake or get a cake mix?" So she thinks about it for a while and thinks she doesn't have much time because she has to go into town one day this week, and she feels her family doesn't know the difference anyway, and even though the mix is more expensive, she buys it.

> She's a young woman looking at cake mixes instead of the flour to bake her own cake. She's going to pay more for the cake mix, but she might be having company and is rushed for time, or she might have a lot of tasks to do. She's about 35 and has about three children. (The respondent is also 35 and has three children.)

> She's gonna make a cake if she is looking at cake mixes and flour. If she makes it with a mix it will be delicious. I never make any from scratch. (Why delicious?) I don't see how anyone can go wrong with a mix, it's all done for you. She's a regular type housewife and maybe with all the kids around and under foot all the time she can't make one from scratch. With all the disturbances they cause, she forgets to put something in or forgets she did and puts it in twice and then it's a flop or maybe she doesn't always have all the stuff on the shelf to make a cake from scratch and then she has to run out to the store to buy it, so she thinks if she has a cake mix in the house on hand, she won't run into all of those troubles.

These stories are typical of the positive identification respondents reveal with the woman who buys a cake mix. There is general awareness that a cake mix represents a more expensive way of baking a cake than use of individual ingredients. Yet they are quick to suggest justifications for the purchase of a mix, and to deny that there is any reason to feel guilty about using a mix. They feel that they can rely on a cake mix more than on a recipe-baked cake and that they deserve the convenience and expedience which cake mixes represent.

A TAT approach in marketing research opens up a considerable range for decision, in terms of the amount of structuring to be included in the stimulus picture. Experience has indicated that pictures which are too highly structured (i.e., well defined and unambiguous) tend to elicit only stereotyped responses. This point may be illustrated by a beer study. A picture was used in which beer was shown being served to an informal group of smiling, casually dressed adults. It brought forth little beyond the expected stereotyped responses referring to beer as a sociable beverage, suitable for informal entertaining. Similar information could be developed more easily and less expensively by direct questioning.

There are potential values in the TAT approach which are entirely apart from the projective effects. Although those values are widely useful in marketing research, they are sometimes overlooked. Thus a TAT picture may be used to increase rapport between an interviewer and a respondent and/or as a take-off point for more detailed questioning. Thus in the beer example cited above, an interviewer might go on to ask such questions as: "Under what other circumstances do you think beer should be served?" "Under what circumstances do you feel beer should *not* be served?" "Is there any special kind or brand of beer you think the people in this picture would be likely to be drinking?" "Why do you say that?"

One additional example of the usefulness of the TAT approach in eliciting second-level information helpful in marketing research may be helpful. The problem was one involving the appeals to use in an advertising campaign for home permanents aimed at diverting volume from beauty-shop permanent waves. In research on this problem, an attempt was made to contrast attitudes toward permanents given in beauty parlors and at home. Two TAT pictures were developed. One showed a scene in a beauty shop, with a woman sitting under a dryer reading a magazine. The other showed a home-permanent situation, in which one woman was giving another a permanent at home. In the stories describing the beauty-shop scene, there were frequent references to concern and anxiety about the carelessness of beauty operators. Women were afraid their hair might be damaged or left unsightly and kinky as a result of operator carelessness. In the home scene, the operator was expected to be friendly, careful, and sincere. Some minor questions as to the competence of the woman giving the home permanent were expressed.

3. *Cartoon Technique*

The cartoon technique is a widely used projective approach. It is an adaptation of the Rosenzweig picture-frustration test. That test was developed as a limited projective device, designed to elicit responses to stress situations. The test consists of a series of pictures in which a person is shown in a frustrating social situation. Often another individual is pictured. A cartoon "balloon" above the head of one of the individuals pictured sets up a stress situation by a remark. The balloon above the head of the other person is blank. The interviewer asks the respondent to "fill in" the balloon by supplying the response or answer the pictured individual would make. Then questions about the kind of person involved, etc., are asked. Usually the questioning terminates by asking the individual respondent how he or she feels about that situation, thus permitting a disassociation of the respondent from the previous discussion.

As used in marketing research practice, the cartoon approach represents a combination of a focused TAT and an elaborated sentence completion. A rather well structured, provocative situation is often represented. There is a suggested interaction between two or more persons pictured in the cartoon, involving an issue verbalized by one of them. In supplying material to fill in the empty balloon, respondents engage in a form of sentence completion. By describing the kind of people concerned, the respondent indicates with which (if any) concept he or she identifies personally. The cartoon technique is a hybrid approach best suited to develop material somewhere between the first and second levels of awareness. It is widely used in part because it is relatively easy both to administer and to interpret.

4. *Word Association*

Word association, or free word association as it is sometimes called, is one of the oldest techniques for bypassing the defenses of respondents. It is administered by reading a list of words to a respondent. The respondent is asked to tell the interviewer the first word thought of after hearing the stimulus word. Generally a reply requires three seconds or less. A respondent who hesitates for more than three seconds is assumed to have encountered some kind of emotional "blockage" in responding to the stimulus word.

In a typical list of words used with the word-association approach, there are some neutral words and some considered to be crucial or particularly relevant in terms of the research subject area. In this use of this technique in guilt detection, for example, words associated with the crime under investigation would be the crucial words. A guilty respondent could betray his guilt by "blocking," or delaying a response to some of those words.

In marketing research, word association applies to a relatively limited area. It is a useful tool in the selection of brand names, names for such developments as new synthetic fibers, etc. It provides clues to the value of some advertising claims or slogans by disclosing the associations with those claims. It is more often used as a technique within a larger framework of interviewing than by itself.

A closely related technique approach is *controlled association*. This has been used over the years in a variety of ways. It involves the use as a stimulus for association of a structured element like a slogan or the request for associations in a limited area. An example would be: "I am going to read you the brand names of a number of soaps. As soon as you hear the name, please tell me the *perfume* or *odor* that soap brings to mind." Lucas and Britt describe applications of this technique at some length.

ATTITUDES VARY WITH USAGE

Motivational research often succeeds in revealing the fundamental differences in attitudes toward a product which exist between light and heavy users of it. Often that information can be used to pinpoint advertising or promotion aimed at removing the obstacles which keep consumption low. To illustrate how the attitudes toward a product often vary with the usage level, and also to provide a sample of part of a depth interview for illustrative purposes, two quotations from a motivational study follow. This study was made for the Campbell Soup Company. Its primary objective was to determine how important nutrition is as an advertising appeal for soup. The material in bold type represents the question or probe used. Note that only a portion of the interview is used here.

An interview with a light-volume soup consumer

How does soup do at your house?

Oh, we don't have it very often. Maybe on a Saturday afternoon for lunch is about all.

How come?

Oh, I don't know. I usually don't bother.

Why then?

Oh, because it's about the only thing to serve my husband when he comes home. It's quick and easy and you get it over with, get him out of the way on Saturday. [Laughs]

Serve with it?

A sandwich. On Saturday that's enough for him.

Kind of soup?

I usually buy the cans.

Ever make your own soup?

Yeah, in winter; and I serve it before dinner, that's about all. My husband likes homemade soup, I guess that's why I make it.

Ever use soup as a meal?

No, it's not very much for a full meal.

Ever serve packaged, dry soup?

I've never used it. I don't know what they're like, so I never bought 'em.

Frozen soup?

Never tried 'em either. I don't know why, either. I've heard a lot of people say they're good and a lot say they aren't, so I don't buy 'em.

How do you feel about ease of preparing different kinds of soup?

I never tried the other two, but the canned is nice and easy.

Which kind offers more nutrition?

Oh, I suppose the homemade is about the best because you know how you make it and you don't know what's going into the other ones.

Think about nutrition in canned soup?

Oh, I suppose the canned—I don't know. I suppose they all got everything in they're supposed to have, but I don't know anything about 'em.

Who likes soup best at your house?

My husband. I don't know why, he just likes soup.

What other kinds of people do you think like soup?

Oh, I don't know. Lots of people like soup on a cold day and it fills you for the time being.

What do you mean by that?

It doesn't stay with you very long before you are hungry again—at least that's the way I've found it.

How do you feel about soup?

It's all right. I can do without it.

How come?

Well, I don't eat lunch and that's about the only time I'd bother with it. I just don't like to sit down and eat it with a meal, either. I'm just not too crazy about it. I'd rather have meat and potatoes instead of fooling around with soup. Eat and get it over with and get the dishes done—that's me!

Now contrast the attitudes and practices expressed by that light-volume consumer with the following interview with a woman in whose home soup is served with far greater frequency.

An interview with a heavy-volume soup consumer

How does soup do at your house?

Good—we eat quite a bit of it.

How often have it?

I guess I serve it at least twice a week. Of course the baby (age three) has it more often, especially for lunch. Soup is really the only thing she eats as well as she should. She isn't a good eater otherwise.

Why do you suppose that is?

Well, soup is a lot easier to manage. Just spoon it right up and it doesn't take any chewing. She is just a lazy eater, I guess.

How often would she have it?

About four or five times a week.

Do you have soup with her?

No, I'm not a soup eater. The only kind I like is homemade, but my whole family is great for canned soup.

Why don't you like canned soup?

I don't like the taste of it. I would rather have homemade, especially vegetable soup. I don't like the taste of the vegetable soup canned. I don't like the tomato they stick in there, it isn't a pleasant taste. I don't enjoy it. What I don't like I don't eat.

Why do you think the kids like canned soup best?

That's always been a problem to me. I can make a delicious chicken or vegetable soup, and spend a lot of time and put some really fine ingredients in it, and then the kids say to me "I'd rather have canned soup."

THE MR PROMOTIONAL TEMPEST

Motivation or motivational research, MR for short, was the subject of extensive promotion and considerable heated controversy in the period from 1950 to 1956. Early attempts to sell the approach, when it was known as *psychological research,* met with only moderate success. When it was renamed and interpreted as the key which could unlock the secrets of consumer motivation, MR became a subject of great interest to management. The publicity achieved for it, even in generalized publications, was tremendous. *Business Week* devoted a two-part report to the subject. *Fortune* covered it extensively. Interest in the promise of this "new" approach with its promise of panaceas reached great heights.

A sharp counterattack on the exaggerated claims of MR adherents was launched in 1955 by Alfred Politz, whose professional reputation in the marketing research field is outstanding. Politz charged that claims for MR were being grossly exaggerated; that its primary value was in developing hypotheses which then had to be quantified with conventional research techniques; and that much so-called motivation research had nothing to do with motivation. His attack had the effect of letting a considerable amount of hot air out of the MR balloon. Today perspective has been restored, and motivational research is widely regarded as one useful part—but only a part—of the marketing research technique area.

RELIABILITY OF MOTIVATIONAL RESEARCH

One of the major limitations of MR has already been touched on when the importance of the analyst was emphasized. That limitation is concerned with questions as to the reliability of some MR techniques. Steuart Henderson Britt commented[16] on this point in these words:

Not all techniques are reliable. In explaining why this is so, we shall have to refer to the statistical concept of *reliability.* In elementary

[16] "Four Hazards of Motivation Research: How to Avoid Them," *Printers' Ink,* June 17, 1955.

statistics, you learn that the word *reliability* refers to the precision with which a given test or technique measures a function.

For example, if you take your temperature each day, you want a thermometer that is reliable: one that will consistently give you the same measurement for the same set of conditions.

The problems we face in the use of projective techniques in marketing are also ones of *reliability*. What information do we have that projective techniques used by some organizations are as *reliable* as they should be?

Another way to put this is—how do we know if the same research techniques were used on the same people or a comparable sample, we would get essentially the same results? This kind of reliability has been demonstrated for a good deal of quantitative consumer research. It needs to be demonstrated by certain organizations with their projective techniques.

Related to this is the question: What about the reliability of the judgments of those who *interpret* the materials?

It should be emphasized that this is quite a different thing from the honesty of the judgments. This is not a question of sincerity of purpose, or honesty of intent. It is a question of consistency of interpretation from one person to another.

Would the same interpreter of the materials make the same interpretation if given the same set of data two weeks later? Or would a second interpreter of the materials give the same interpretation as the first one?

In a continuation of his remarks, Britt underlines the danger of bias on the part of the analyst interpreting the data:

Many years ago a well-known social scientist, Stuart Rice, reported information concerning interview records of social workers who had been engaged in interviewing 2,000 homeless men who were applying for free lodging. Since the average interviewing form used by social workers is well standardized, you might assume that the answers filled out would be completely objective. Yet Rice showed how the already formed attitudes of the social workers might affect their behavior in filling out these forms.

One of the interviewers was a strong prohibitionist, another was an ardent socialist. In analyzing the interview blanks turned in by the prohibitionist and socialist respectively, Rice found that the prohibitionist attributed 62 per cent of the cases to liquor and only 7 per cent to industrial conditions. On the other hand, the socialist attributed 39 per cent to industrial conditions and only 22 per cent to liquor. According to the information turned in by the prohibitionist, 34 per cent of the applicants themselves had mentioned liquor as a reason for their downfall, whereas the socialist reported that 60 per cent mentioned industrial conditions as the principal reason!

This study is an excellent illustration of the way that already acquired attitudes may affect what is done in a supposedly objective manner. Applying this analogy to the area of projective techniques, the question is: To what extent will two different interpreters of projective materials give the same interpretation of the same materials? Or, better still, to what extent are two different practitioners of motivation research likely to give the same interpretation to projective data?

There are a few instances in which an identical assignment was given to two different organizations active in the MR field. The results reflect to a considerable extent the orientation and training of the heads of the organization in question, rather than of the respondents' comments. Thus in the case of an appraisal of Betty Crocker, General Mills' corporate personality, one firm with a basically Freudian orientation developed a report full of "mother images" and other Freudian concepts. Another firm, with a background stemming from social anthropology, reported primarily in terms of the viewpoint of "middle majority housewives." Reconciliation of the two reports was a difficult and perplexing task.

This, incidentally, is one of the major criticisms heard about some work in the MR field: the charge that the report and findings come to a greater extent from the analyst's own past training and inclination than from the evidence gathered in the course of the research.

SAMPLING DEFICIENCIES

The charge is also made that the sampling base in the case of some MR is extremely slipshod. Evidence to support that viewpoint is available. Here for example is how the sample of respondents was distributed in the case of one of the two studies of the Betty Crocker problem:

State	Number of interviews
California	64
New York State	26
Kansas City area	36
Michigan	30
Pennsylvania	20
Maryland	8
Ohio	8
Indiana	8
Total interviews	200

It is likely that the availability of interviewers rather than any objective sampling design influenced the distribution of the sample in this case. Since the sample size in MR studies is often relatively small—ranging from 100 to 250 interviews in many cases—the distribution of the sample is an extremely crucial area. Probability sampling is not possible because respondent cooperation in a relatively long interview is essential. Even on a quota-sampling basis, however, the representativeness of a "national" sample on which one-third of the interviews were made in the state of California warrants consideration. The atypicality of Californians in many areas of attitude and behavior is well known. A sample design of the type indicated suggests that some aspects of marketing research knowledge—notably sampling—could profitably be injected into the planning of some MR work.

A BALANCED VIEW: LET THE PROBLEM DETERMINE THE APPROACH SELECTED

A balanced viewpoint toward motivational research and its role in the total marketing research picture has emerged after the sound and fury of the promotional tempest died down. That viewpoint, like the viewpoint toward other marketing research areas, is essentially problem-oriented. It recognizes that motivational research and the psychological techniques associated with it can make important contributions to the solution of many problems. It also recognizes that MR is no panacea. In the case of most major marketing problems, a combined approach is necessary. Both quantitative and qualitative research are called on. The sequence in which the two approaches are used, if they are used individually, varies with the problem as the major influence.

Sometimes a motivational approach is used, as in the soup example quoted above, to determine something about the kinds of people who fall into various usage categories. Subsequent research to assess the quantification of the groups so identified is usually necessary. Britt's comments on the relationship between the two approaches summarize the view held today by a great many seasoned and experienced marketing research men:

> The point is that there is room for both kinds of research. Both are needed to get as complete answers as possible to the *why?* of consumer behavior. The kind of problem determines the extent to which each is used.
> Recently when a client was bringing out a new food product, we recommended the double-barreled research method. One approach alone was not enough. This meant that we could give the client considerably more information about *why?* as well as *how many?* We found out not only how many people liked the new product, but what they liked about it . . . how various members of the family reacted to it . . . its role in family meals, etc.
> We left samples of the new product in homes in selected test markets and then called back a few weeks later to learn about consumer usage

and attitudes. Most of the interviews were strongly quantitative, with a standardized questionnaire involving several hundred people in each market. However, for a smaller sample (50 people) we used several qualitative methods: sentence completion tests, balloon tests, depth interviewing, hidden intelligence tests, etc.

A different man was in charge of each kind of research. And the qualitative man and the quantitative man wrote their reports *independently of each other.*

Information from the same kind of people—using these two different techniques—and with the reports written absolutely independently—produced many similar results. But there were differences: as to the kind of consumers who liked the product; their basic attitudes toward it; detailed information about various members of the family. So many clues were uncovered about the *why's* of consumer behavior that fundamental changes were made in the manufacture of the product, and, in turn, in the advertising and merchandising program.

The point is that each research technique provided a lot of information that the other did not. And each served as a cross-check on the other.

Also, we did something else different from run-of-mine research. *We carried out qualitative research that could be quantified* or added up. *And we carried out quantitative research that did not have to be qualified.*

This summary comment by Britt boils down the relationship of quantitative and qualitative research into relatively few words:[17]

The difficulty with a great deal of qualitative research is that it is rarely quantified or expressed in measurable terms. Too often the man who talks out the language of *psychologese* fails to make sufficient use of statistics so that one can have faith in his conclusions.

And the trouble with a great deal of quantitative research is that it has to be qualified. Too often, the man with the fancy charts fails to hedge or qualify his conclusions as he should.

But—with proper safeguards—the *combination* of qualitative and quantitative approaches is unbeatable for more complete and more valid information about consumer attitudes.

"INTERESTING INFORMATION" ISN'T ENOUGH

The observation is made about many reports on motivational research that they represented interesting reading but that no action was indicated or could be taken on the basis of them. This is a reminder that motivational research must also take its chances on the cost–versus–profit-contribution scale. Emphasis on the *actionable aspects* of the research findings is highly desirable. That usually requires that the final

[17] Steuart Henderson Britt, "Combination Research," *Printers' Ink*, Oct. 22, 1954.

motivational research report be developed jointly by a team of at least two people. The trained psychologist or social scientist is necessary as one member of the team to provide the specialized knowledge necessary to extract the buried meaning from the research. But the seasoned marketing research man must also be in the picture, to be sure that the findings of the research are translated from psychological jargon to everyday English and to be sure also that no important marketing implications are overlooked.

When motivational research is handled on that type of a team basis, it gives promise of becoming a tool almost as significant as the exaggerated claims of a few years ago suggested it might be.

SUMMARY

1. This chapter points out the differences between research which is primarily quantitative in its emphasis and objective and research which is primarily qualitative. In considering this division of research activites it is essential to remember that most quantitative research has qualitative aspects, and vice versa.

2. Exploratory interviews, which are commonly used in the problem-defining step in research, illustrate the qualitative type of research. Subsequent research establishes the quantitative importance of various divisions or groupings established through qualitative study. Thus the two approaches fit together to make a unified whole.

3. The term *depth interviewing* is one which means different things to different people. Some of the dissimilarities in viewpoint on this subject were presented in this chapter.

4. One way to distinguish between some qualitative research and much quantitative research is to consider how directly the desired information is sought. In qualitative research, indirect approaches are more common. The indirect approach is indicated whenever it seems likely that a direct approach may be blocked by emotional or other forces from securing dependable and accurate information.

5. The fact that some of the information which marketing research requires is located at different levels of awareness and/or availability in the respondent's mind leads to the use of qualitative approaches which can dig below the surface, or obvious (and perhaps inaccurate), answer.

6. Qualitative research is often more subjective than research taking quantitative approaches. The importance of the analyst is greater, and the analyst's influence on interpretations is great. That suggests the need for caution in accepting an interpretation of qualitative research as *the* interpretation, in the absence of the considered judgment of more than one analyst.

7. Projective techniques are useful aids in qualitatively oriented marketing research. They are rarely used alone. When used in conjunction with depth interviews (however that term is defined), they often add penetrating power to the research.

8. A problem-oriented approach in which quantitative and/or qualitative techniques are used, individually and/or in combination, is the balanced viewpoint toward motivational research which is recommended here.

QUESTIONS

1. What are the kinds of questions which qualitative, as opposed to quantitative, research seeks to answer? Give examples.

2. What are the two basic interpretations of depth interviewing?

3. What are the three "levels of awareness" used by George Horsley Smith to classify availability of information?

a. Give examples of the kinds of information available at each level.

b. For each level, what advantages might be provided by using projective questions or techniques?

c. What common projective techniques are best suited to obtaining information at each level? What makes them particularly suitable?

4. A manufacturer presents you with this problem: His laboratory has developed a new dentifrice with the following properties:

When used once a day, this dentifrice provides maximum tooth protection (against caries, etc.). It is superior to any other dentifrice on the market now. However, if it is used more often, the dentifrice may be irritating to gums.

The manufacturer wants to find out about potential consumer acceptance of his product before putting it on the market. As a research consultant, what do you recommend? Outline a research plan giving reasons supporting your choice of methods.

5. Suppose your recommendation included an exploratory study of the kind sometimes referred to as motivational research. You planned to interview 100 persons on the area of dental hygiene, using depth interviews and some projective techniques. The manufacturer is suspicious of motivational research, and he raises the following objections to this proposal:

How can I have confidence in any results based on a sample of only 100 respondents?

How can I be assured that your interpretation of the findings is reliable?

Projective techniques were developed to diagnose individual personality.

How can you justify their use in the research you recommend?

If you feel that the research recommended above can be defended against each objection, explain how. If you feel it cannot be defended, explain why not.

Research in Nonmanufacturing Organizations

CHAPTER 27

Marketing Research by Retailers, Wholesalers, and Other Service Organizations

Retailers and wholesalers who purchase the products of manufacturers and then resell those products to consumers or to industrial customers can use marketing research techniques in many of the same ways manufacturers can. For example, one of the most important areas of research by retailers and wholesalers corresponds closely to the *product research* of manufacturers.

There is this key difference: The products of a manufacturer are usually tangible. Those of retailers and wholesalers are typically intangible. They consist primarily of the service or services offered. Retailers and wholesalers represent, in effect, a special subdivision within the general area of service organizations. It is for that reason that their marketing research activities are grouped with those of such service organizations as banks, insurance companies, etc., in this chapter.

Most retailers and wholesalers are in competition with other firms of the same type. Comparative research on the consumer acceptance of the service offered therefore represents a logical starting point in the marketing research program of a retailer or a wholesaler. As in the case of manufacturers, that research should be primarily comparative. It should provide an indication of the relative consumer or customer acceptance of the service offered, as compared to that of one or more specific competitors. But that research should not be entirely comparative. Drawing on the experiences of manufacturers in product research, as described in Chapter 22, the research should go beyond mere comparisons. It should be planned with an awareness of the possibility that the services offered by *all* retailers or wholesalers may be markedly deficient in one or more ways, in the opinion of customers. The research should therefore explore the *general* attitudes toward the services offered, and then move into the *specific* strong and weak points of individual establishments.

ILLUSTRATION OF RESEARCH BY A RETAILER

The following description of a consumer-research project conducted by a large retail establishment illustrates some of the potential profit contributions which research of that type may be expected to make.

43. BERGDORF GOODMAN[1]

What do American women want for the $4 billion a year they spend on clothes? To find out, Manhattan's elegant Bergdorf Goodman sent detailed questionnaires to 7,000 New York housewives, career women, debutantes and students picked from the roster of a mailing-list firm. The 1,542 replies sent a storm of controversy whistling through the salons and cutting rooms of the sensitive women's-wear industry.

Chief objection of the women customers is the industry's topsy-turvy custom of offering June's clothes in January, January's in June. Cried one anguished woman: "Never in season can one find the clothes one needs. Bathing suits in July—never! Winter cocktail clothes after Christmas—never! You lose valuable trade because you do not cater to people when they need things." For this, manufacturers last week blamed the department stores: "The store buyer doesn't think ahead. If it's a cold spring, she gets panicky, concentrates on getting rid of what she had, and won't reorder fresh stock early." The stores blamed manufacturers: "Try to reorder anything in May. The manufacturers don't think ahead. They order only enough fabric to cover our first orders."

Here and there, however, signs cropped up last week that the customer criticisms were having some effect. Three top bathing-suit makers —Cole of California, Jantzen, Rose Marie Reid—reported that some New York stores had agreed to carry a complete line of swim suits to Aug. 1 instead of closing out after July 4. On the Fourth, Bergdorf defied usual custom, boldly featured several window displays of bathing suits.

Hats that stay. The questionnaire turned up other criticisms. Overwhelmingly, the women reported that it was impossible to find the basic, simple black dress that "isn't too hot in New York and can be worn morning through evening." They wanted blouses "with plenty of tail" that won't pull out of skirts, cottons that need no ironing, "hats that stay put." They disdained frills and gewgaws in favor of "simple, good classic lines," "feminine but not frilly romantic clothes."

One businesswoman who rides subways five days a week said: "We'd love dark cottons for summer—no white trim to get dirty long before the dress." Another pleaded for a "good girdle to work in, not requiring

[1] *Time* magazine, July 16, 1956, p. 86.

stockings." They suggested "stores arranged so that all coats are on one floor, same for dresses and suits. It's a nuisance running from one price-range department to another—always have a feeling that you haven't seen everything."

Slacks that slack. There was a long list of pet peeves: the big "buckety-baskety hats," "slacks that are too slack in the rear," sheath skirts "that make it so awkward to get in or out of taxis," dresses with petticoats that wilt after the first washing, the "no-ironing" synthetic fabrics that do need ironing, white collars and cuffs that are not detachable, the store that advertises a dress on Sunday and is "out of it" on Monday.

Most heartfelt gripe: store help that doesn't. The customers described sales clerks as "high-pressure, pseudo-snobs, impolite, disinterested," complained that they either "act like leeches or ignore you." Singled out for special mention were saleswomen who "call you 'dearie,'" have a superior attitude when you ask for something a little cheaper, or say: "But madam, it's the fashion; everyone is wearing it."

— ★ —

RANGE OF GUIDANCE PROVIDED BY A SINGLE STUDY

Note the very wide range of retailer operations which were touched on in the course of that relatively simple and inexpensive mail survey. First, the basic merchandising policy involving timing of emphasis on different types of clothing as related to the seasonality of those types was revealed to be essentially unsound in terms of consumer satisfaction. Unmistakable evidence that established trade practices were leading to lost sales through unavailability of merchandise at the right time was provided by the survey. Second, some specific deficiencies in the "product line" of the retailers were pinpointed—note the "basic black dress" comment.

Third, some improvements in products carried were advanced: Blouses with more "tail," dark cottons without white trim for summer, and detachable white collars and cuffs. Fourth, suggestions on the rearrangement of departments in the store to maximize consumer opportunity to shop thoroughly for a specific item like a coat or suit were advanced by the customers. Finally, some specific comments helpful in the training (or retraining!) of retail sales personnel were provided by the survey.

Another point of interest in the above quotation is the evidence that *something is being done about* the survey's findings. The "storm of controversy" mentioned is an indication that considerable study of the validity of the criticism was under way. The bathing-suit manufacturers mentioned had applied part of the research findings to lengthen their selling season. The Bergdorf Goodman bathing-suit windows on the Fourth of July were another evidence of the application of the research findings.

RETAILER RESEARCH HAS BEEN RETARDED

A very significant point which the above quotation reveals about research by retail establishments should be emphasized. What was described was a single, relatively small-scale mail survey by one retailer in one major market. The results of that survey in terms of impact on industry practices which had been largely unchanged for decades were apparently great. That fact clearly telegraphs this point: The findings of that survey came as news to the industry, which suggests that up until 1956 there was very little research of a very fundamental type conducted in the field of women's-wear retailing.

It was pointed out above that retailers *can* use marketing research, just as manufacturers can. That does not mean that retailers *do* use marketing research on a very large scale. Marketing research by retailers has been quite retarded, especially when compared with the progress which has been made among manufacturing organizations. While marketing research could make many contributions to increased management effectiveness in the retail field, it has so far had relatively little opportunity to demonstrate that fact. Marketing research among retailers is a promising field for future expansion.

One reason why the use of marketing research by retailers has been relatively minor in the past is provided by the distribution of retail establishments on a size basis. The average retail organization is a very small one. The relationship between the cost of research and the profit contribution of that research which has been repeatedly mentioned is just as important for the retailer as for the manufacturer. The typical individual retailer is too small to be able to afford much of a research expenditure and is too busy running his establishment to have time to find out much about what research could do for him. It is to the large multiple-unit and high-volume establishments in the retail field that we must look for an expanded application of marketing research techniques to the problems of the retailer.

PARALLEL BETWEEN RESEARCH REQUIREMENTS
OF RETAILERS AND OF MANUFACTURERS

Retailers represent one large and important segment of the national marketing structure. All the business of retailers is marketing. It follows that virtually all research carried on to guide the management of a retailing organization is almost by definition marketing research. What major differences exist between the ways in which research can contribute to the increasingly effective marketing management of retailers and the ways manufacturers use research for the same purpose? The answer is that differences are very slight. It is necessary to recast a specific activity in a somewhat different light, or to describe it in somewhat different terms, to make the retailer understand it as applying to his business. Once that slight translation has been accomplished, the ways in which research can be used effectively by retailers parallel closely the ways in which research can be and is used by manufacturers.

To illustrate this point and to suggest the direction of the translation required, let's re-examine the activities which were revealed to be most important in the American Management Association survey. The sample of respondent companies in that study was primarily a sample of manufacturing organizations. Do their observations apply to retailers? How much modification is necessary to achieve a "fit" for the retailer?

1. *Analysis of Territorial Sales Opportunities or Potentials*

This was the activity which ranked highest in importance in the AMA survey. It clearly applies almost without modifications to retailers as well. Before a retailer opens a new store, closes an old one, decides to invest in remodeling or renovation of an existing outlet, or decides to enter or not to enter into some proposed new shopping center, a detailed analysis of the sales opportunities or potentials of the area served is important.

In its usual sense, territorial applies to a description of the geographic unit covered by a single salesman or a team of salesmen. Translating into retailers' language, territorial potentials represent the potential of a territory served by a single store or a group of stores in the same market. This is an important area of research application for retailers. It is sometimes described by them as *store-location research*. It may involve both a study of available detailed data on population, buying power, trends, etc., and a traffic count of the particular locations under consideration.

2. *Studies of the Competitive Position of Company Products (Market-share Analyses, etc.)*

This ranked second in the frequency with which it was considered to be important by manufacturers. As noted earlier, the "products" of the retailer are usually the services offered. With this distinction in mind, research to determine what share of the total volume a given retailer or multiple-unit retail operator is securing is a valuable guide to management appraisal of performance. Often this is a relatively detailed study, distinguishing between the relative popularity of different outlets for different types of products, product lines, price groups of merchandise, etc.

Research among food retailers has disclosed major differences between key chains in the share they secure of different types of food business. Here, for example, are figures from a *Cleveland Press* study showing the proportion of total volume on a number of different product classes done by three leading food chains in that market:

(Per Cent)

Product type or class	Food chain's proportion of volume on:		
	Fisher	A&P	Kroger
White bread	8.5	11.6	2.3
Frozen vegetables	24.6	18.8	7.8
Soaps	33.5	30.1	2.8
Canned milk	26.6	27.6	5.4

The type of information shown can serve as an invaluable guide to individual chain managements in reappraising their opportunities and in determining the strength and weakness of their operations in various major departments. *Trend data* which reveal shifts in the division of volume between different retailers in a market, in as much detail as is relevant, are especially valuable in a volatile marketing field.

3. *Analysis of the Size of the Market for Specific Products*

Among manufacturers, this activity ranked third in the frequency with which it was designated as most important. In the case of retailers, it has a dual importance. First, remembering the previous comments on the need to recognize that the product of a retailer is a service, it applies in terms of measuring the total market size or potential open to a retailer. Second, if the retailer's line includes different types of products, then it applies to the determination of the size of the market for specific products and product types. It is particularly important in the case of multiple-unit retailers, where the size of the market for specific products (or the product mix in an individual retail outlet) must be studied individually. It is closely interrelated with the preceding point and is helpful in identifying the causes of a major weakness in market share.

Some examples will be illustrative. Should a candy-retailing chain open stores in all suburban towns surrounding the major metro center which is the heart of the chain's business? Or should stores be opened only in towns above a given potential, expressed either in population, number of families, buying power, or families with income above a certain figure? Or consider a large chain of food stores operating in a major market. For purposes of our illustration it does not matter whether that is a national chain, of which we are considering only the single market branch, or a chain operating only in that market. How should the individual store's lines be varied? Should stores serving a neighborhood made up primarily of rooming houses, tiny apartments, and apartment hotels devote major display space to baby foods or settle for a skeleton department as compared to a suburban store? In major metropolitan markets like Chicago, New York, and Philadelphia, there are neighborhoods made up primarily of families with a similar ethnic background. How much display space on spaghetti and related products should be set up in a supermarket serving a neighborhood of Italian-American residents? Should the price-line emphasis of department stores be varied to fit the level of income of major customers, branch by branch?

4. Determining Consumer or Customer Acceptance of Proposed New Products or Services

This is a vital activity for retailers, which lends itself easily to small-scale experimental test-market-type approaches. Before the A&P food chain launched candy departments in its stores nationally, the sales contribution and consumer acceptance of such departments were carefully pretested in a number of major markets, including Baltimore. The expansion of the A&P's private brand of bakery products—the Jane Parker line—was similarly pretested before it was expanded on a large scale.

In the case of department stores and department-store chains, various services such as special types of charge accounts, etc., can be and are subjected to preliminary pretesting on a small scale before they are introduced or offered on a broader scale. As Chapter 25 on Test Marketing pointed out, the contribution of such a test often goes far beyond guidance on the simple "should we or shouldn't we?" decision. Test experience provides a basis for identifying the elements of strength and/or weakness in a proposed addition or modification being tested. It thus contributes to the likelihood of success or to the scale of success in cases where the answer is affirmative.

5. Measuring Territorial Variations in Sales Yield, Market Share, Sales Effectiveness

This is a marketing research activity which is important in the case of all multiple-unit retailers. It can also be important for large department stores, which have an opportunity to analyze their volume (using addresses on sales slips) by portions of the area they serve. For a multiple-unit retailer as for a manufacturer, some units are likely to be strong and some weak. Pinpointing the weak units by objective measurement of their performance is one step in the direction of strengthening them.

6. *Advertising Research*

The general subject of advertising research is likely to be more important as a portion of total marketing research activity for a retailer than for a wholesaler. The retailer, as subsequent comments in this chapter will note, is in a much better position to engage in the objective measurement of the sales resulting from a particular advertisement than is the manufacturer. Continuing analyses of sales per advertising dollar, with such factors as weather considered, are standard operating procedure among many advertising retailers.

THE COST-RESULTS RELATIONSHIP LIMITS RETAILER RESEARCH

The research expenditures of retailers must be weighed as carefully as those of manufacturers on the scale of cost of research versus profit contributions of the findings. Because so many retailers are medium-sized to small, this evaluation has a critical urgency absent in the case of some manufacturers. In the case of relatively small units in the retail field—small local chains, department stores in medium-sized cities, etc.—marketing research recognized as such may be confined to the research which is conducted to evaluate a major problem of the nonrecurring (as distinguished from the current operating) problem type.

The following case illustrates a problem at the retail level. It involves a relatively small retail organization and a moderate expenditure for marketing research. This was a study made on what appeared to the management of the chain to be a major problem of the nonrecurring type. It will be recognized by readers as a current-operating type of problem if the classification base of a larger organization was used.

44. COZY COTTAGE CANDY COMPANY ★

The Cozy Cottage Candy Co. is a retail-chain organization which operates more than thirty candy stores in a large Eastern city. This organization is of a type known in the candy industry as a "candy-manufacturing retailer." It manufactures all its own candy, delivering it fresh daily to its chain of stores. The candy is sold to consumers mostly in 1-pound, 2-pound, and 5-pound boxes.

Most of the company's candy was chocolate-coated, a fact which contributed to a very sharply defined seasonal pattern of sales variation. Summer's high temperatures made for poor candy-eating weather. When temperatures soared during the summer, Cozy Cottage candy sales sagged. Apart from the summer months, sales were relatively even except that there were a number of very extreme seasonal peaks in sales at Thanksgiving, Christmas, Easter, Valentine's Day, and Mother's Day. The company's candy was relatively high in price, and a large proportion of its sales were for gift purposes.

Beginning in the summer of 1955, average daily and weekly volume per store in the Cozy Cottage chain began to run behind year-ago levels. The management could not immediately identify that as an adverse sales trend. Summer volume was subject to considerable variation, with temperature as a major influence. The summer of 1955 was unusually warm in the city where the company's stores were located. On through fall and through the Christmas season, however, sales continued to fall behind year-ago levels. A marketing research organization was called in to suggest ways in which research might contribute to a diagnosis of the company's sales problem.

In the initial meeting between the head of the research organization and the president of the candy firm, the president defined the research assignment in these terms: "We used to be the No. 1 candy chain in this market," he said. "We know that from a survey we had made five years ago. Now our sales per store are declining. We want to know three things. First, are we still No. 1 in this market, or has one of the competitive candy chains taken over or decreased our market leadership? Second, is it the increased dietary consciousness and the trend toward reducing diets that is cutting into our sales? Third, is the increasing sale of other types of candy through super-markets the explanation of our sales decline?"

The research man expressed the opinion that those questions could be answered without too much difficulty. He expressed the view that so specifically defined a research assignment might be undesirable. "We could answer all three of those questions," he pointed out, "and still leave the fundamental cause of your sales decline unidentified." The research assignment was redefined. The objective of the proposed research was to ascertain the causes of the sales decline in Cozy Cottage candy sales.

A two-phase research study was recommended. Phase 1 was concerned with a re-examination of the standing of the Cozy Cottage Candy Company as against its major competitors. That involved a qualitative exploration in depth of the type sometimes described as motivational. The approach taken was to begin with candy generally, move on to explore boxed candy and its role in conjunction with social conventions, and then to examine the individual company status and associations for major competitive organizations and for Cozy Cottage candy. In the course of this phase of the research, the effect of weight consciousness and dietary factors on the amount of candy consumed was studied. The supermarket as a source of candy and as an influence on candy purchasing was also included in that phase of the research.

The second phase of the research was an examination of marketing factors outside of the realm of consumer attitudes. It explored national trends in candy consumption, in total and by types. It examined the shifts occurring in the major metropolitan market where Cozy Cottage candy was sold. It examined locations of Cozy Cottage stores, as compared to competitive outlets.

The findings of the first phase of the research were, from the viewpoint of the management of Cozy Cottage Candy Company, extremely favorable. The company had not suffered a decline in prestige. On the contrary, the indications were that its margin of leadership over competitive firms had widened. No explanation of the loss in Cozy Cottage candy volume was disclosed by that phase of the research. Weight consciousness was disclosed to have exerted only a very slight downward influence on candy consumption. That influence should have been more than offset by increased population. The influence of supermarket candy was disclosed as almost nonexistent, because of differences in consumption patterns on the two types as disclosed by the research.

In the second phase of the research, however, the nature of the problem was revealed. There had been a strong movement out of the city itself to outlying suburbs. Considerable economic deterioration of many neighborhoods in the city followed. The neighborhoods affected were those including many Cozy Cottage candy stores. The company was in the position of trying to sell its fine, high-quality, and high-priced candy in neighborhoods where the majority of the residents were having difficulty in maintaining themselves much above a subsistence level.

The research findings pointed to the desirability of a more aggressive relocation policy on the part of Cozy Cottage Candy Company. By moving into a large number of newly developed shopping centers, the company was able to regain lost volume and to cash in on its existing leadership in the minds of consumers in its home market.

— ★ —

The above case illustrates the use on a nonrecurring basis of research approaches which are widely used on a continuing basis in larger organizations. In this case as in the Dell-O illustration, the organization with the problem had no marketing research department. It is instructive to note again, as we did in the Dell-O case, that the application of marketing research on a day-to-day basis, even if confined to the relatively few but important activities which stood out in the AMA study, would have been likely to have detected this problem long before it reached major proportions.

It was not the absolute decline in average sales per store which signaled the existence of a problem. The failure of the chain to keep pace with expanding volume in its market in total and of its type of products (using type here generally as to include all food sales) provided a much earlier indication that a problem situation was building up. Thus we have another illustration of the fact that it's the things you don't know that can hurt you and the research you don't do that can prove extremely costly.

Another important value of this case is as an illustration of the fact that many marketing problems, while quite different in appearance, often shake down to a relatively common type. It is skill in diagnosing the type present, in marketing research as in medicine, which makes it possible to get quickly to the cause of a major symptom.

THE RETAILER'S ADVANTAGEOUS LOCATION
FOR CUSTOMER RESEARCH

Because of his position in the marketing chain, the retailer is in a far more advantageous position than most manufacturers to conduct marketing research among his consumers or customers. Manufacturers typically sell their products to marketing middlemen of one type or another and are thus separated from their final customer by one or more levels of intermediaries. In contrast, the retailer sells directly to and is in continuing and close contact with the final consumer.

It is worth noting that the existence of that gap between manufacturer and consumer led directly to the creation of two of the most important of the syndicated services in the marketing research field. Both the consumer panel of MRCA and the store-audit technique which is the basis of the Nielsen Food and Drug Index were developed to permit manufacturers to secure information which bridged that gap. Note further that the Nielsen type of operation could not exist without the cooperation of a panel of retailers. Nielsen secures information, using the stores as the source of that information. What is done through the stores by Nielsen and others can be just as well accomplished by the retailer himself for his own information and guidance.

Recognizing that last opportunity, there has been an increasing tendency on the part of retailers to utilize their own facilities for various types of marketing research. Controlled experiment by individual chains of retail outlets is relatively easy. As the size of chains has increased, more and more of them have developed their own marketing research departments. Naturally those departments have conducted controlled experiments within the chain's own units, primarily for the benefit and guidance of the management of the chain itself.

45. STOP & SHOP, INC.

Stop & Shop, Inc., is a major regional chain of food supermarkets. William Applebaum and Richard F. Spears, while employed by Stop & Shop, Inc., published in *The Journal of Marketing*, January, 1950, under the title "Controlled Experimentation in Marketing Research" a discussion of the subject drawing on Stop & Shop, Inc., experience, from which the following material has been abstracted.

Reported experimental research at the point of purchase, Applebaum and Spears commented, "has in too many cases been conducted either in outstanding but definitely atypical stores, in settings which were abnormal or entirely artificial, or *without* control stores when such were requisite. In other instances no attempt was made to determine the *before* and *after test* conditions, without which the results were of little value. Or, no attempt was made to study the effect on competing products and the resultant *total effect* on the sales of the entire line. Similarly, no adjustments were made for seasonal trends, nor was there any effort to isolate and ascertain the effect of special promotion—advertising, price reduction, coupons, etc."

There is a mutuality of interest between manufactures and retailers which can stimulate progress in this area of retail research, as Applebaum and Spears point out:

> Over a period of years the authors have developed and used a methodology for controlled experimentation in marketing research. In part the progress of this work, especially since 1940, was stimulated and aided by the direct and practical interest of a number of leading national manufacturers of food and grocery products. Problems of mutual interest to these manufacturers and to Stop & Shop have been investigated on a cooperative basis under the direction of the authors. Various refinements in methodology were contributed by representatives of the cooperating companies.
>
> In all these studies the aim has been to ascertain at the point of purchase (1) the behavior and response of people to products, methods and devices, or (2) the performance of devices and materials. Results have been measured in terms of sales produced or work performed.

The following comment by Applebaum and Spears on the importance of controls has applications and implications which extend far beyond research by retailers:

Control in experimentation requires constancy or uniformity in all elements affecting the results, except the *one* variable which is being tested. Therefore, the reliability or accuracy of the results of such experimentation is largely dependent on the controls exercised. Since in marketing we are dealing with many elements (consumers, competition, weather, etc.) over which we can exercise no direct control, it becomes necessary to set up experimental conditions in such a manner that these "uncontrollable" elements will exist and will exert their effect simultaneously and to the same degree in two or several places. If this is achieved, then we actually obtain controlled conditions even though we do not control these elements. So long as the research environments remain continuously comparable, except for the one variable being tested, controlled experimentation is possible.

The various controls required can be grouped into ten categories, but not all of these are needed for every experiment.

1. *Experimental stores.* The stores in which a variable is to be tested may be designated as *test stores*. The stores in which the variable is not introduced, but which are used for comparison with the test stores, are designated as *control stores*.

Great care is required in choosing experimental stores. Not only should the test stores as a group be matched by a comparable group of control stores, but each test store individually should be matched by a comparable control store. This is essential not only for maximum comparability but also in interpreting results in case an unexpected event, such as a fire, should knock out one store from the test.

In the selection and matching of experimental stores, Applebaum and Spears recommended these criteria:

a. Type of store. Super markets vs. conventional grocery stores. Service versus self-service. (Certain tests can not be carried out in service operations because of the salesmen's influence.) Number and types of departments. Check-out systems.

b. Size of store. Total and departmental weekly sales. Number of weekly customer transactions. Store area and parking lot.

c. Trading area. Size of city. Type of location—business center. Origin of customers. Type of population (economic levels and ethnic background). Competition. Area coverage by major newspapers.

d. Shopping habits. Mode of travel. Frequency of store visits. Length of patronage. Average purchase per transaction.

This comment on the time factor in tests and its influence on the experimental design is of interest:

The number of experimental stores which will be required for a specific study will vary with the nature of the problem. Where two or more variables are to be tested simultaneously, a different group of test stores will be required to investigate each variable. In addition, a group of control stores will be necessary. For example, if the regular price of an item is 10¢ and the problem is to determine what sales results will be achieved at 9¢ and at 2/19¢, then three groups of experimental stores are required to carry out the test simultaneously—a group for each price, 10¢, 9¢, 2/19¢. The element of time cannot be controlled in any other way.

Of course in some experiments the element of time may be a very minor factor in the results, and each variable can be tested by successive steps. Also, in some experiments it is possible to test different variables by criss-crossing the tests between different groups of stores. A word of caution is in order here. The authors' experience indicates that to safeguard the validity of the results it may be worth spending the extra money required to set up an additional group of test stores.

This sample-size comment is especially interesting:

> In choosing experimental store groups, there also arises the question of how many stores to include in each test and control group. This is a type of sampling problem that is not easy to solve. The authors have used as many as 10 stores in each group. For most studies we have been using only 5 stores for each test and control group, and could probably get along with 3 or 4 per group for the vast majority of the tests; the larger number is an added precaution in sampling.

Applebaum and Spears make this helpful comment on the problem of measuring results:

> The results of controlled experimentation in marketing research are measured in terms of sales produced or work performed, or both, depending on the nature of the problem.
>
> Sales produced are measurable in monetary units or in physical units. But prices change, and hence equal monetary units do not necessarily denote equal physical units, and comparability is lost. On the other hand, physical units of one kind are different from physical units of another kind (apples vs. pears). The difficulty can be resolved by measuring sales in both monetary and physical units.

Table 27.1 reproduce examples of results of two controlled experiments. Here are the comments on those experiments made by Applebaum and Spears:

> Let us assume that an experiment has been conducted to determine what additional sales are produced by pre-packaging a certain staple vegetable sold by weight. For simplicity's sake, let us ignore here the cost of the packaging material and of the labor involved in packaging; let us also keep the retail price of the vegetable constant and let us ignore spoilage and markup profit.
>
> Assume the experiment shows that the vegetable tested produced greater sales when pre-packaged, as illustrated in Table [27.1].

Table 27.1. Results of Two Controlled Experiments Conducted in Stop & Shop, Inc., Stores

I. EXAMPLE OF RESULTS OF PRE-PACKAGING EXPERIMENT

	5 test stores			5 control stores		
	Pre-test 4 weeks	Test* 4 weeks	Per cent change	Pre-test 4 weeks	Test 4 weeks	Per cent change
Store sales	$300,000	$306,000	+2.0	$298,000	$304,000	+2.0
Fruit and vegetable sales	44,000	45,100	+2.5	44,400	45,300	+2.0
Sales of tested vegetable	2,000	2,600	+30.0	2,040	2,200	+7.8
Sales of tested vegetable, lb.	25,000	32,500	+30.0	26,500	22,500	+7.8

II. EXAMPLE OF RESULTS OF DISPLAY EXPERIMENT

	Pre-test 4 weeks	Test† 4 weeks	Per cent change	Post-test 4 weeks	Per cent change
4 test stores:					
Grocery sales	$144,100	$146,000	+1.3	$143,600	−0.4
Transactions	88,500	88,900	+0.5	86,500	−2.3
Total coffee sales, lb.	10,200	10,390	+1.9	10,100	−1.0
Test-brand sales, lb.	2,400	3,010	+25.4	2,250	−6.3
Share of market, %	23.5	29.0	+23.4	22.3	−5.1
4 control stores:					
Grocery sales	$144,700	$147,700	+2.0	$146,500	+1.2
Transactions	87,400	89,190	+2.0	87,800	+0.5
Total coffee sales, lb.	10,510	10,550	+0.4	10,300	−2.0
Test-brand sales, lb.	2,350	2,370	+0.9	2,320	−1.3
Share of market, %	22.3	22.4	+0.4	22.6	+1.3

* During these four weeks, the vegetable tested was sold pre-packaged in the five test stores only.
† During these four weeks the special display was up in the four test stores only.
SOURCE: William Applebaum and Richard F. Spears, Controlled Experimentation in Marketing Research, *The Journal of Marketing*, January, 1950, p. 511.

It will be noted that the sales of the tested vegetables increased during the test period (second 4 weeks) in both test and control stores, 30.0 per cent and 7.8 per cent respectively. Hence it follows that a *net* increase of 22.2 per cent is attributable to the pre-packaging.

In the above example the retail price of the item tested was assumed to be constant; therefore the results, whether measured in dollars or in pounds, are identical. But if an additional test were made, in which the cost of the pre-packaging were added to the retail price, then comparisons of dollar sales would be required.

Let us take another example, a test of a special display of one brand of a product line.

Here it will be noted that total coffee sales in pounds in relation to grocery sales and transactions remained virtually the same during the test and post-test periods, compared with the pre-test period, in both test and control stores. Sales of the tested brand likewise remained about the same in the control stores during all three stages, but increased greatly in the test stores during the test period, and the brand obtained a larger share of the market.

From this we can conclude that the *net* increase produced by the display was at the expense of the other brands of coffee, and that part of the gain was offset by a *net* decline during the post-test period because customers had "loaded up" on the displayed brand.

— ★ —

MAJOR AREAS OF RETAIL RESEARCH

Applebaum and Spears identify a number of areas within which research using the controlled-experiment approach can be profitably used by retailers. They include studies of packaging, displays, pricing, promotional plans, sales potential of new products, store equipment, store layout and design, and work simplification. In addition, many of the types of research discussed elsewhere in this book can be used effectively by retailers. Attitude studies in particular warrant attention as a possible research approach.

The Jewel Tea Company, a Chicago food chain, conducted extensive consumer studies which were then used both in developing increasingly effective store designs and in building a "store personality" in advertising. The Great Atlantic & Pacific Tea Company has used attitude studies and other surveys made among customers within the store to guide their key marketing decisions. One such study, focused on the problem of increasing sales of the chain's own brand of shortening, disclosed that a majority of shoppers did not know that the brand was an A&P brand bearing the chain's warranty and endorsement.

MARKETING RESEARCH BY WHOLESALERS

The marketing research activities of wholesalers follow those of manufacturers even more closely, if possible, than do the marketing research activities of retailers. Wholesalers tend to be somewhat larger in volume than the average retail unit, hence more able to afford both the cost and the specialized skills required for effective marketing research. It is often possible for a wholesale organization to lean on the marketing research facilities and findings of the manufacturing organizations for which it distributes. This is an entirely legitimate type of "borrowing" since increased sales by the wholesaler are likely to reflect increased volume for the manufacturer as well.

In some instances, manufacturers depend entirely on a relatively limited number of wholesalers for their volume. In such a situation, the sales organization of the wholesaler is, in fact, the manufacturer's "sales force." The fact that individual manufacturers must often compete with other manufacturers for "their" salesmen's times does not invalidate the description. In that type of situation, it is not uncommon for the manufacturer's marketing research activities—particularly in the area of sales analysis and territorial-effectiveness measurement—to be planned and executed primarily to fit the needs *of the wholesaler and his salesmen.*

One may wonder how it is possible for a manufacturer distributing through wholesalers to have basic data available for sales analysis and other purposes. This is achieved in a number of ingenious ways. One approach is to have the wholesaler send the manufacturer a copy of each invoice on merchandise shipped to a retailer. Then the manufacturer, building up from those invoices, can maintain detailed sales records and conduct sales analysis even though his own salesmen never see or visit the outlets in question. An effective framework of sales control, by a manufacturer operating through nonexclusive distributors, has two important values which should be noted. The first is that it tends to secure for the manufacturer a larger share of the time and attention of the management and sales organization of the wholesaler, for which he is in competition. The second is that it provides a vital service *to the wholesaler.* A manufacturer selling through nonexclusive wholesalers finds through his own analysis that there is a given area of geographic weakness—and opportunity!—and duly reports that finding to the wholesaler's management team. If the manufacturer in question represents one-fifth of the wholesaler's volume, the opportunity in question is likely to be on the order of five times as large as the manufacturer thinks it is! The explanation lies in the fact that a weakness of a wholesaler in territorial coverage on one line has been disclosed more often than not to represent a pervasive weakness in the wholesaler's entire operation.

MARKETING RESEARCH BY OTHER TYPES OF SERVICE ORGANIZATIONS

Figuring prominently in marketing research practice are a number of other types of service organizations, in addition to retailers and wholesalers. Among those types are banks, insurance companies, public utilities, and some trade associations. Research activities of trade associations are covered at some length in Chapter 28, which follows this one. In general, however, organizations of that type follow in their marketing research much the same pattern as do manufacturers.

The primary distinction between the manufacturer and the service organization has been pointed out earlier in this chapter: The manufacturer produces a tangible product, while the service organization's "product" is a service, hence usually intangible. Selling an intangible product or service is often just as difficult or more difficult than selling a tangible product. It involves just as many and just as serious marketing problems. There are just as many opportunities for the company in a service business to use marketing research effectively as there are for manufacturers. And the great importance of evaluating every proposed marketing research expenditure against an estimate of the contribution its results are likely to make to profit is just as vital for the service organization as for the manufacturer.

Services often do research on what aspects of their service (versus those of competitive organizations) are liked or disliked. This is product research, pure and simple. The size of the market for the service is estimated. Advertising research is often required to determine which aspects of the service to stress in advertising. The following case, reporting on a study by a service type of organization, reveals the similarities between service and manufacturer research in specific detail.

46. PHILADELPHIA SAVING FUND SOCIETY[2]

It's not so much what a bank is as where it is that attracts savings accounts. That's the conclusion culled from 1,001 savers in a survey conducted for the Philadelphia Saving Fund Society, third largest mutual savings bank in the nation.

The survey took in users of savings banks, savings and loan associations, and commercial banks. Every time, convenience turned up as the No. 1 reason for selecting a particular institution. At one bank, 72 per cent of depositors were moved by the where-is-it factor; the lowest percentage recorded was 30 per cent, still well ahead of any other motive.

Specialized accounts. Since it's hardly feasible to locate a branch on every corner, Philadelphia Saving Fund sought other means to increase its deposits. Noting that 38.8 per cent of all savers interviewed said they were doing the saving for specific purposes, PSFS this month started offering bait to attract the specialized squirrel. The campaign

[2] *Business Week*, Sept. 22, 1956, p. 64.

took the form of ten new types of "convenience" accounts, each named for its objective: automobile, hobby, home improvement, new home, education, bride's, stork, $500, $1,000 and catch-all rainy day account.

All these accounts operate in the same way as regular savings accounts, pay the same interest—2¾ per cent—and have the same withdrawal privileges. They do not have the set amount of Christmas and vacation clubs.

As a byproduct of its survey PSFS discovered that the customers were heartily indifferent to some of the lures heavily stressed in bank advertising. The depositor cared but little how old a bank was, how big it was, what it looked like, how many branches it had. More startlingly, there was evidence that the customer wasn't very avid for higher interest. Most of those interviewed knew what the rate their own banks paid, but few knew the other—and potentially higher—rates of competing banks.

Happy customers. The survey cast new light on what customers think of banks: Mostly, they think they are fine. Few found them stuffy or cold, fewer still had improvements to suggest and PSFS also discovered that a majority of the depositors are women—60 per cent on the average, 80 per cent in some branches. The big bank's reaction to this will soon be available. It's a bankbook covered in plaid.

— ★ —

SUMMARY

1. This chapter considers the differences between the marketing research practices and opportunities of retailers, wholesalers, and other service organizations, on one hand, and manufacturers on the other. It is necessary because of the primary emphasis on manufacturers throughout this book and because of the importance within the total marketing picture of retailers, wholesalers, and other service organizations.

2. The basic distinction which should be remembered is that the manufacturer typically produces a tangible product, while the service organization —including retailers and wholesalers—offers a service to the public. The service is less tangible, but it can be researched.

3. Research by retailers has been relatively retarded. This is true despite their advantageous position. The small size of the average retailer, with its cost-results implications, is one explanation.

4. Retailers are in a particularly advantageous position to conduct marketing research using controlled experimental approaches. Such research receives considerable emphasis in this chapter, as well as elsewhere in this book, because of its great future promise.

5. Differences between the marketing research opportunities open to retailers and those open to manufacturers are relatively minor. A moderate amount of "translation" is needed. With that translation accomplished, the practices of manufacturers become a useful pattern for retailers as well.

6. Wholesalers and other service organizations resemble manufacturers in their research approaches and requirements even more than do retailers.

QUESTIONS

1. Why has the use of marketing research by retailers been quite retarded?

2. Is there any parallel between research requirements of retailers and of manufacturers? What "translation," if any, is needed?

3. Why is the retailer said to be in a far more advantageous position than most manufacturers to conduct marketing research among his consumers or customers?

4. It is said that wholesalers and other service organizations resemble manufacturers in their research approaches and requirements even more than do retailers. Why is this so?

CHAPTER 28

Marketing Research by Trade Associations and Other Mutual-interest Groups

To provide background for this chapter and an indication of its significance, it is necessary to review and reconcile some comments and observations made in earlier chapters of this book.

The bulk of this book has been devoted to the marketing research activities of manufacturing organizations. The reasons for that emphasis on the role of the manufacturer in marketing research were detailed in Chapter 2.

The point has been made repeatedly that an expenditure for marketing research must give promise of making a contribution to profit far in excess of its cost, or that expenditure is of questionable soundness. The practical ceiling for a marketing research expenditure, the American Management Association disclosed, was at a level of 1 per cent of sales. That figure was reported by a company with relatively low sales volume.

When the distribution of manufacturing establishments in the United States by size is examined, it is apparent that a sharp concentration pattern exists. There are relatively few very large industrial giants. There are a multitude of middle-sized to small manufacturing establishments.

When the above factors are combined, a number of questions are raised. An individual small manufacturing organization which allocated 1 per cent or even 2 per cent of its sales volume to marketing research would have a total research appropriation too small for any major research activities. That appropriation, in many cases, would not even support a single full-time employee working on marketing research. Does this mean that marketing research is a management tool open only to the very large manufacturing organization? If not, how can a smaller organization secure the benefits of sound marketing research without spending a quite unreasonable sum for them, in relation to total volume?

It is to the answers to such questions as these that this chapter is devoted.

It has been established that a number of small organizations—typically manufacturers, but in some cases nonmanufacturers—can combine their individually small research expenditures into a respectable total. By the careful investment of that total in effective marketing research, they can secure all the advantage of large-scale research on a very small fraction of the cost. This is an opportunity to make a very productive investment of a relatively small research appropriation. It is an opportunity, as we shall see in this chapter, which is ever more widely recognized and acted upon.

TRADE ASSOCIATIONS PLAY A PROMINENT ROLE

Many industries and major subdivisions of industries are today served by trade associations. Typically a trade association is staffed at its headquarters by at least one full-time executive, plus clerical and other assistance. The primary objective of most trade associations is to represent the combined interests of their members and thus to further those interests. Trade associations are especially likely to be found in industries in which the membership is numerically large and average size of member companies correspondingly small.

Where an industry is served by a trade association, the use of that association as the focal point for industry-wide marketing research activities is a logical move. From the viewpoint of the association, marketing research represents a typical service function which the association can perform for its members. It is not surprising, therefore, to find that marketing research activities represent an important and expanding proportion of the service performed by member companies by trade associations.

When a trade association becomes active in the field of marketing research, it faces the same task as a manufacturer in determining which areas are most important and most in need of research. There is a surprising parallel between the decisions which are typically made by manufacturers, as to the relative importance of specific marketing research functions, and those of trade associations active in the field.

USUAL STARTING POINT: DETERMINATION OF MARKET SIZE

When a trade association moves into marketing research activities, its first step is likely to be an attempt to develop—usually on a continuing basis—data on the size of the total market for which its members are competing. This information is usually developed by a two-step process.

Step 1 is to have each association member report on a confidential basis its own individual sales for each month or other time period. The reports of individual companies are combined to develop a total which represents the total sales of all association members. Step 2 is to adjust that total upward to allow for the proportion of industry volume which non-members of the association represent.

Often some impartial outside organization, such as a firm of certified public accountants like Ernst & Ernst or Arthur Anderson & Co., receives the individual company reports and combines them. This step is sometimes necessary where concern that the confidential reports might "leak" is a factor which keeps association-member participation in this research activity below the 100 per cent mark.

Among manufacturers covered by the AMA survey on research practices, the most widely performed activity was determining the competitive position of the company's products. That would ordinarily be difficult and perhaps expensive for a small company. If that small company were a member of a trade association active in marketing research, however, the picture would be quite different. The association would secure figures from member companies and total them. It would adjust those figures to allow for production by nonmember companies. It would issue an estimate of industry volume periodically. Each company could then quickly and easily determine its competitive position and market share by calculating it from the industry estimate and the company sales which were part of that industry estimate.

There is a tendency, where a trade association takes this first (and obvious) step in the direction of providing marketing research service, for members to request and sometimes demand additional service of the same type. Thus if the figures in question were for refrigerator manufacturers, the need for individual figures on various sizes of refrigerators would be apparent. Or if the industry had any major variations in price lining (distinguishing between low-priced and high-priced merchandise), the need for a breakdown in the total figures by price brackets would be felt.

In extending its marketing research service in the indicated direction, trade associations occasionally "come a cropper." Where all or almost all association members make the same kinds of products and are interested in the same types of breakdowns on product detail, no problem exists. Where a single company wants a breakdown not useful to others, or where a breakdown would pinpoint the trend of a single company, resistance is almost certain to develop. Thus for a time the Easy was the only spinner type of washing machine made by a member company in the washing-machine manufacturers' association. In a type breakdown between conventional or wringer-type washers and other types, spinners had to be combined with automatic washers to avoid disclosure of the Easy production figures.

Where association membership is not complete or where the reporting organizations are not the full membership of the association, the need for careful adjustment of figures arises. Over a period of time, the periodic Census of Manufactures releases provide a check point on the accuracy of the association's estimate of coverage. There are problems present where the nonmembers have a radically different sales trend and/or pattern from members. This was illustrated in an earlier chapter when the vertical-horizontal freezer division of nonmembers differed from that of members. The association must be especially careful to spell out in detail its basis for this estimate.

TERRITORIAL POTENTIALS DEVELOPED COOPERATIVELY

Often in a trade association consisting of relatively small individual firms, some geographical differences in operating area exist. Thus total sales may be up for a product, but the manufacturer operating only in the New England area may have the feeling that in New England sales are not keeping pace. Can the association help him with figures covering just New England? That need is simply a reflection of the common problem discussed in Chapter 21—the problem of estimating territorial potentials, with its corollary of providing data useful in analyzing territorial sales performance. Trade association marketing research often covers this vital area as well.

In this connection, the pioneering work of Luke J. McCarthy, of the Hearst Magazines of the Hearst Corporation should be recognized. In the early 1930s, Mr. McCarthy developed a basic approach to territorial sales control which was published as *The Basis of Sales Quota Making Combined with the Trading Area System of Sales Control.* In its original publication (now long out of print) this was a mammoth atlas breaking down the markets of the United States into 626 consumer trading areas. A total of thirty-three factors were considered in determining the boundaries of the trading area of each market center. Maps were prepared and made available by the Hearst organization delineating each area. A "buying power index" for each area was also developed.

That development was a major contribution to marketing management practice.

One characteristic of the original Hearst areas was the fact that county lines were ignored in developing them. This meant that no data on specific characteristics of individual areas were available except from Hearst or from a detailed and painstaking analysis of data. That represented a major limitation of the Hearst breakdown, especially as the amount of governmental data on a county basis became greater. That limitation was overcome by a revision and a slight reduction in the number of Hearst areas. Those areas were redesignated as *durable-goods trading areas*. In the mid-1940s, trade associations—especially in the durable-goods field—began to use the Hearst breakdown of trading areas as the basis for developing detailed metropolitan-area and trading-area figures on sales potentials.

The National Electrical Manufacturers Association (NEMA) and a number of other associations began to have their member companies report sales for each of the 600-odd trading areas. Those sales were combined for all reporting companies. The combined total provided a very specifically pinpointed measurement of market potential, which was especially useful because it was in an industry subject to quite extreme variations. With NEMA data and that of such other associations as the Gas Appliance Manufacturers Association, the Institute of Cooking and Heating Appliance Manufacturers, and the American Home Laundry Manufacturers' Association, detailed market data are available through cooperative effort that it would be almost exorbitantly expensive for any single manufacturer to have gathered individually.

ASSOCIATION ACTIVITIES LIMITED BY DATA AVAILABLE FROM MEMBER COMPANIES

It should be pointed out that the advantages of a cooperative approach through the medium of a trade association as the fact-assembling, summarizing, and dispensing unit vary widely. One key influence on the value of this approach is the composition of the association itself and the relative development of their own record-keeping facilities. A trade association can easily secure from member companies data which the member companies already develop for their own use. In such a situation all that is required is a copying job. On the other hand, the trade association which tries to lead its association into marketing research so refined that a considerable amount of fact gathering *for the association alone* is involved is on questionable ground.

There is a key distinction here which should be noted. The kind of information which a trade association is in the best position to gather— data on distribution of sales by types, sizes, etc., by states, markets, or trading areas, etc.—is the kind of information which the well-managed manufacturing company needs for its own information. It is essential for trade-association executives who are contemplating initiating or extending marketing research activities in the directions indicated to work in two directions. They should begin with a clear picture of the kinds of contributions marketing research can and should make to a well-managed manufacturing organization. They should then develop a clear picture of the kinds of information essential to such contributions which are currently available or which can be rather easily made available within their member companies' operations. They then proceed to try to bring those two pictures into a common focus.

The danger is always present that a trade-association executive may "lead" his member companies too much and as a result get a fact-finding program of solid merit thrown out. The offsetting advantage is that by leading the companies' present practices, he can contribute to the improvement of their management practices and thereby increase the value of the association and the strength of its membership. It is apparent that where the initiative is taken by officials of the trade association, there is a two-edged sword present which might swing in any direction!

RECAP OF IDEAL TRADE-ASSOCIATION DATA

It may be helpful to consider briefly the components of a marketing research program operated by and through a trade association. We are leaning, in this discussion, in the direction of leanness of data. We are assuming a "normal" trade-association membership (with the recognition of the fact that there is no such animal) in terms of state of development of record keeping and internal-control information for medium- to small-sized companies. The items listed below are not beyond the reach of a trade association including firms which have an interest in extending their management knowledge into areas which have been demonstrated, in the case of larger organizations, to be extremely important to marketing success.

1. *A Monthly Report of Total Industry Volume, Often in Both Dollars and Units*

A monthly report is useful because it enables manufacturers to develop a sharp picture of the seasonal trend, if any, in their industry. It facilitates a comparison of the individual manufacturer's seasonal trend and emphasis with that of his industry as a whole. Almost all companies have monthly sales records, at least in total, so this kind of information is not difficult to secure.

The maintenance of detail both in dollars and in physical volume is highly desirable, because it enables manufacturers to separate the "growth" attributable to price increases, or the losses due to price declines, from shifts in the physical volume level. To cite just one application of this information: A carpet manufacturer does not have to re-examine his mill capacity when the industry growth reflects the higher prices caused by a tight wool market, but if expanded physical volume is moving up, the re-examination may be highly desirable.

Monthly data also make it possible to detect a shift in trend or direction in the industry with a minimum time lag. One problem sometimes arises: Some companies are operating on a calendar-month basis, and others are on a thirteen-"month" basis, with periods of a uniform four weeks' duration. The reconciliation problem involved is usually relatively minor.

2. A Subdivision of Industry Volume, Also Monthly, by Major Types

To prevent the growth in one segment of the industry's volume from being offset and hidden by the decline in another and to provide continuing guidance to management as to the major subtrends, industry volume should be reported for its major subtypes. What those subtypes are varies from industry to industry. In the carpet industry, for example, there were at one time four major subtypes which deserved attention: Axminster, Velvet, Wilton, and Tufted carpeting. A further subdivision of auto carpeting was also recognized, but because it was of interest to relatively few industry firms it was treated primarily by excluding it from the industry totals. In the refrigerator industry, breakdowns by capacity were once important. Price-class groupings of sales are significant in many industries. The detail shown in the report of confectionary sales in Case 32 in Chapter 20 is illustrative of another industry's classification base.

3. A Breakdown of Sales Volume by Geographic Units

In this area in particular, the amount of detail and the frequency of reporting are strongly influenced by the existing record-keeping practices of the firms that constitute the association's membership. One extreme in amount of detail is provided by practices in some appliance industry associations, already mentioned. They report unit sales for each of more than six hundred different geographical subdivisions of the national market. At the other extreme are the industries in which breakdowns are available only for states or groups of states.

The amount of useful detail provided by an approach like that of the appliance manufacturers is great. To illustrate, a manufacturer of electric ranges guided by data from his industry's association can appraise the potential of the Hempstead, Long Island portion of his New York branch territory as against the Westchester County portion.

State breakdowns may be indicated as the other extreme because they are almost always available. Tax laws require that division of volume by states be maintained in many instances. Because a state is usually not a meaningful *marketing* unit data by states pose some analytical problems not present with metropolitan-area or trading-area break-downs.

How frequently should trade associations report on breakdowns of sales by geographic areas? The answer "as often as necessary" sounds like an evasive response, yet it is very near the truth. The particular characteristics of the industry enter into this consideration strongly. If total sales data are reported monthly, the geographic breakdowns are typically required with less frequency, say, quarterly or twice a year. There is a clerical burden in some cases in developing such information, and there is a practical ceiling on how much and how frequently analyses of this type of data can be executed and the findings applied.

One important influence on whether frequent breakdowns of industry volume by areas are required is the extent to which the distribution of volume is changing. In a particularly dynamic industry, quarterly reports may be necessary and desirable. For most industries, a breakdown of volume by geographic areas for each six-month period is quite sufficient. In some cases, an annual breakdown is all that the association members are in a position to use. It is therefore all that warrants compilation.

The decision on frequency of reporting is one for which hindsight is almost a prerequisite. Until several such breakdowns have been developed and the change from period to period determined, the basis of a sound decision on required frequency is lacking. From the viewpoint of ideal marketing research practice, it would be sound to begin with breakdowns which are made more frequently than the marketing research man in charge thinks are necessary. When the scale of change from period to period has been determined, a cutback can be effected. On the other hand, that approach may result in a lack of cooperation from those association members who regard all record keeping as an unnecessary nuisance and too frequent reports as utter nonsense!

One value of frequent breakdowns should be underlined. It may be of aid in "selling" the need for such frequent reporting. The monthly data provide a guide to the seasonal pattern in the industry's business. But often the seasonal pattern in different sections of the country is widely variable. Reports by quarters make it possible to pinpoint the major variations in seasonal pattern. That information is highly valuable in many cases for effective planning of sales and promotional effort.

There are other types of helpful marketing research data which some trade associations develop and which have proved, in the case of those particular industries, to be almost as essential as those described above. Major variations in the characteristics of different industries make it difficult to describe those types of data meaningfully. We may note, however, that they often include cost data—data on various aspects of selling costs, for example, and other related information. When a trade association becomes active in gathering cost data from and for its members, it must generally tread lightly. The possibility that it may cross the line from legal to illegal trade association activities and become suspect as a partner to some kind of illegal price-fixing or price-setting activity is present and requires consideration.

ASSOCIATION ADVERTISING ACTIVITIES

Often an association or other organization representing the interests of a group of members may conclude that advertising is necessary to advance the common interests. Advertising by the association, on behalf of its members, often follows, with the cost of the advertising assessed to the membership on some equitable basis. Among the associations which are major advertisers are the American Meat Institute, the American Dairy Association, the United States Brewers Foundation, and many others. When an association embarks on a program of advertising, it faces the same problems as any other advertiser. What story should our advertising tell? What are the important sales points or ideas which we should register? How well does this proposed advertising campaign deliver the ideas we want delivered? How well does the group of media we have chosen to carry our advertising messages "fit" the audience we want to reach?

It is not unusual, therefore, to find that advertising research, in any or all of its phases, may sometimes fall within the area of the marketing research activities of trade associations or other mutual-interest groups.

MAJOR RESEARCH BY ASSOCIATIONS

On behalf of its membership, usually as a step following by a considerable time interval the basic data gathering indicated above, a trade association may embark on a major survey, study, or other type of marketing research project. In such research, the association is in much the same position as any manufacturer or other research sponsor. Most of the comments made in this book are relevant to the problem. It is especially important to keep such a cooperatively sponsored research project sharply focused on the problem at hand and to weigh it on the cost-versus-results scale we have mentioned so often.

The particular difficulty in many association-sponsored research projects is that there are a great many participating companies, each contributing to the cost of the research and each desiring a voice in the direction and emphasis of the project. "Too many cooks" is a very minor problem in contrast to one involving "too many researchers"! Another frequent characteristic of such research is that there may be a dearth of seasoned marketing research men among the association-member companies.

One pattern often seen in a proposed study of this type is that only the largest companies in the industry have marketing research men on their staffs. The smaller companies either distrust the larger organizations or have different problems or research objectives than those larger organizations. A committee approach is sometimes taken, but the difficulties of securing unified action through the medium of a committee of representatives of different companies with different objectives are too well known to require comment here. The effectiveness of association-sponsored research is often lower than it could and should be. On the other hand, some association-sponsored marketing research measures up to the highest levels of professional practice. The case which follows is illustrative.

47. UNITED STATES BREWERS FOUNDATION

The United States Brewers Foundation is a trade association representing the companies that brew beer, ale, and other malt beverages. Among the activities of the foundation is a continuing advertising campaign selling beer as "the beverage of moderation" and seeking to mold consumer attitudes in ways which would make a return of the prohibition experience following World War I unlikely. The foundation periodically has conducted nationwide consumer surveys to measure the level of sentiment for and against beer, individual variations in consumption, reasons for liking and disliking beer, and so on. Parallel studies were conducted in 1944, 1949, and 1954. The field work for those surveys was conducted by Crossley Incorporated (successor organization Crossley-S. D. Surveys, Inc.). The J. Walter Thompson Company conducted the analysis of the survey findings and prepared a visual report for and to the United States Brewers Foundation from which the following highlights have been abstracted. The total number of interviews in the three studies were: 1944, 8,882; 1949, 9,553; 1954, 10,097.

The three studies reflected a continuing growth in opposition to prohibition. In the 1944 study, 63.4 per cent of those interviewed were classified as "definitely opposed to prohibition." In the 1949 study the same figure was 70.4 per cent, and in the 1954 study it rose to 74.8 per cent. The remaining respondents were classified into two groups. One group was classified as "definitely in favor of prohibition." The third group refused to answer the question on this point. As a matter of interpretation, the latter group was assumed to be primarily opposed to drinking, hence was added to those definitely favoring prohibition to arrive at an "indicated maximum of prohibition sentiment." That maximum figure declined from 36.6 per cent of those interviewed in 1944 to 25.2 per cent in 1954.

While this survey covered various attitude questions, it was most emphatically a marketing research study designed to guide association members in planning more effective marketing approaches. It developed a volume consumption pattern, for example. Of all those interviewed, 14.3 per cent were classified as "regular" drinkers, averaging over fourteen glasses of beer weekly. Those 14.3 per cent of respondents represented more than two-thirds—68.7 per cent—of all beer consumed in the seven-day period prior to the interview. Variations in the consumption of male and female respondents were developed to guide advertising and promotional planning in terms of the different sexes as targets. Thus in the case of the 1954 study, women who represented 51.5 per cent of the total population made up only 40.0 per cent of total beer drinkers. Because of lower average consumption per drinker, women represented only 21.8 per cent of total gallonage consumed.

— ★ —

PIPELINE-TREND RESEARCH

Where the product sold by a manufacturer moves through one or more additional levels before reaching the ultimate consumer, trend data based on actual movement to consumers are essential for sound marketing planning. It was primarily to satisfy that vital need that such important continuing services as the Food and Drug Index of the A. C. Nielsen Company and the National Consumer Panel of the MRCA were created. The outstanding success of both services is an indication that the type of information they supply is an essential part of the informational requirements of marketing management under today's increasingly competitive market conditions.

To a considerable extent, those two services and other services of a syndicated type represent special cases of cooperative marketing research by mutual-interest groups. In the case of the clients served by such organizations, the mutuality of interest is, perhaps, somewhat moot. The organizations served have as their common goal a maximum market share. Thus their interests are mutually opposed. It would not be possible, within existing antitrust regulations, for competitive firms of major size to cooperate in securing information of the type supplied by syndicated services. The fact that the services are operated independently and offer the data to all make it possible for effective cooperation to take place without the violation of legal limitations. Where data on a single product class like cake mixes are sold to competitors like General Mills, Inc., Pillsbury Mills, General Foods Corporation, and others, the price each pays for the research is lower than it would be if the data gathering were for a single firm's exclusive benefit. Thus the competitive yet co-operative subscribers to such a service illustrate the value of cooperation without any intent to do so.

The services mentioned serve primarily a limited type of manu-facturer-client: Manufacturers in the food and drug field, especially those making low unit price products purchased with high frequency for family consumption. The same kind of information is needed—sometimes desperately needed—by other types of manufacturers. An example is provided by the manufacturers of radio and television sets. Periodically radio and TV manufacturers appear to work themselves into problem situations involving a peaking of inventories at wholesale and/or retail levels. Cooperative effort to avoid the recurrence of such problems is one obvious answer.

The Business Information Department of Dun & Bradstreet, Inc., pro-posed to the manufacturers of radio and television sets a marketing re-search approach of considerable promise. This would involve establish-ment of a panel of more than 450 representative radio and television retailers. From that panel, inventory and consumer-purchase data would be developed which could be purchased by individual manufacturers. The proposal envisioned data breakdowns to cover five ranges of man-ufacturers' list prices; four ranges of dealers' experience in the going market prices at which sets are actually being sold; five ranges of screen sizes; seven general types of sets; three style types and three finishes.

The following case illustrates the extension of research on one facet of the pipeline problem into a basic industry.

48. AMERICAN STEEL WAREHOUSE ASSOCIATION[1]

Steel mills keep close track of where their various products go. With each mill keeping tabs on how much steel goes to auto manufacturers or into construction, it's comparatively simple to get an over-all picture of such steel uses. And for many years, American Iron & Steel Institute has issued industry statistics of steel shipped directly from mills, broken down by end-use markets. This accounts for the great bulk of steel ton-nage.

But up to now there has always been one big blank spot in the picture. About 20% of the steel produced moves to steel warehouses, where it is resold. And warehouses don't maintain records showing where the steel goes.

Stainless steel. For stainless steel producers, this gap in the market statistics has been of special concern. Stainless, a high-value product, finds a multitude of uses in a wide variety of end products, not all as easy

[1] "New Light on Stainless Sales," *Business Week*, Sept. 1, 1956, p. 64.

to keep track of as autos. The tonnage of stainless passing through warehouses has been increasing—from 23.4% of the stainless tonnage shipped from mills in 1951 it rose to 29.4% of this tonnage in the first quarter of this year.

To gauge future expansion and plan promotional activities and market development (and stainless is promoted to a greater extent than any other type of steel), producers needed to know what happens to this tonnage shipped through warehouses.

As Richard E. Paret, stainless steel specialist for AISI put it, "Steel company people and others outside the industry were constantly coming to me for information about the market for stainless steel. I could give them figures relating to mill shipments. But there was always the quarter or so of total tonnage going to warehouses that I couldn't account for."

Filling the gap. Now, thanks to a market survey made as a joint effort of mills and warehouse people, data on warehouse sales of stainless are available for the first time. The result not only fills in the blank spot in the market picture for stainless, but shows that some of its uses have a much bigger place in the whole picture than steelmen had thought.

The survey got started when AISI's Committee of Stainless Steel Producers formed a special subcommittee, headed by Ralph L. Harding of Allegheny Ludlum Steel Corp. The subcommittee went to the American Steel Warehouse Assn. at Cleveland, and the two groups worked up a survey that would classify warehouse orders by type of product, number of tons shipped, and 31 end-use markets. Warehouse members of the ASWA were asked to participate.

During the first quarter of this year, more than 64,000 reports came in, providing this specific information for over 52,000 net tons of stainless steel. The subcommittee tabulated the results.

Differences. Many of the differences that emerged between warehouse and mill distribution had been suspected, but the survey substituted figures for guesswork. Steel people knew that, over-all, the automotive industry was the largest single consumer of stainless steel. The survey showed that little of this business goes through warehouses. Instead, the aircraft industry takes the largest slice of the warehouse stainless steel business.

When you add warehouse figures to mill shipments, a number of end-use markets take on a new importance in the total stainless market:

Mills shipped 6,339 net tons of stainless for construction and building maintenance purposes in the first quarter. Warehouse shipments boosted this total to 13,338 net tons—or twice as big a market as steelmen had thought. On this basis, it's an annual 53,000-ton market.

The chemical market, which uses largely plate and tubing, jumped from 908 net tons shipped from mills to a total of 3,357 net tons.

Stainless for restaurant and equipment use is largely sheet, a big warehouse item. With warehouse shipments added, this market took 6,500 net tons—three times what mills alone shipped.

Useful. Such data, exposing partially hidden markets for stainless, provide guides for redirecting promotional activities of the stainless steel industry and individual companies.

Warehouses, too, are finding it useful. Robert G. Welch, ASWA executive secretary, notes that the survey is the first instance of market analysis applied to the warehouse industry nationally. Participating warehouses get tabulations showing market classifications broken down by type of product and geographical location—and from these can see how they are doing in comparison with the national average.

ASSOCIATIONS PROVIDE KNOWLEDGE OF CURRENT PRACTICES

One important area of activity for association research is on the management practices and techniques of leading firms (or of all firms) in an industry or in a given technique area. Research of both types has been illustrated in the course of this book. Thus the American Management Association study of *Company Practices in Marketing Research* was conducted in part to provide smaller companies with an indication of what larger companies had learned about research from their own first-hand experience with it. Other areas have similarly been covered in American Marketing Association studies. This represents cooperative research in all cases, but cooperative marketing research in only some instances. Similarly, the American Marketing Association through committee activities and reports has helped to crystallize knowledge of advanced practices in marketing research.

GOVERNMENTAL PARTICIPATION IN COOPERATIVE MARKETING RESEARCH

Where an association or other mutual-interest group can interest a unit of the Federal, state, or local government, governmental participation in cooperative research can sometimes be achieved. There are many illustrations of such participation, especially by the Federal government. Many of them represent outstandingly competent marketing research. Here are some illustrative examples.

Confectionery Sales and Distribution Studies

Chapter 20 presented a detailed description of the type of annual studies of trends in confectionery sales and distribution which have been prepared over a time span of more than a quarter of a century by the confectionery industry in cooperation with the U.S. Department of Commerce.

Reports on the Distribution and Consumption of Fruits and Juices

The U.S. Department of Agriculture, in cooperation with participating fruit-industry groups, has conducted studies of the retail distribution of certain fresh citrus fruits and canned single-strength and frozen concentrated juices. In addition, continuing data on the trend of consumption of some products of the same type, including city-size, sectional, and other variations in consumption, have been purchased and distributed by the U.S. Department of Agriculture. In some research of this type, the USDA has purchased data made available by commercial marketing research organizations, notably including the MRCA.

Consumer and Trade Attitude and Opinion Studies

The U.S. Department of Agriculture has also conducted many opinion and attitude studies intended to aid the marketing of agricultural products. The type of study included in this category is suggested by the following random selection of titles from the files of a commercial research firm:

Rice Preferences among Household Consumers. This was a 2,450-interview survey with a special sampling to permit projection of Chicago-area results separately.

Citrus Preferences among Household Consumers in Louisville and in Nelson County, Kentucky. This study included 497 interviews in Louisville and 538 in Nelson County.

Opinions of Homemakers Regarding Fibers in Selected Items of Household Furnishings. This was a survey utilizing a probability sample of 2,223 women, distributed nationally.

Men's Preferences among Selected Clothing Items. This was a personal-interview survey including 2,508 interviews.

Potato Preferences among Restaurant and Hotel Buyers. This was a two-market survey covering restaurant and hotel buyers in Cincinnati and New Orleans.

Other departments of the Federal government are also engaged in research in areas relevant to their responsibilities. Thus the U.S. Department of the Interior through its Fish and Wildlife Service authorized Alfred Politz Research, Inc., to conduct a national study of consumer attitudes toward and usage of fresh and frozen fish and shellfish. This was a probability survey of 2,473 households distributed nationally. The study was conducted in October, 1951.

THE ADVERTISING RESEARCH FOUNDATION
RESEARCHES RESEARCH

No discussion of cooperative research activities would be complete which failed to recognize the activities of the Advertising Research Foundation. The Advertising Research Foundation is a nonprofit organization which is supported by advertisers, advertising agencies, and advertising media. Its basic purpose is to further scientific practices and promote greater effectiveness in advertising and marketing through objective and impartial research. Specifically, the foundation assists advertising media in developing research data, supervises and validates media research surveys, and appraises media studies. Further, the Advertising Research Foundation seeks to develop new research methods and techniques; to analyze existing techniques and define their proper application and limits of usefulness; and to establish research standards and criteria. The Advertising Research Foundation collects and disseminates advertising and marketing data for the benefit of subscribers. It is interested in exploring any research plan which might increase the industry's knowledge of how to make advertising more effective.

49. ADVERTISING RESEARCH FOUNDATION, INC.

In February of 1952, the Project Development Committee of the Advertising Research Foundation, Inc. (referred to hereafter as the ARF) set out to discover just what research projects were of primary interest to the organizations subscribing to the foundation. A mail questionnaire was used to secure that information. Excerpts from that questionnaire which follow illustrate the approach taken.

PROJECTS QUESTIONNAIRE

This questionnaire lists projects proposed for ARF consideration. They are divided into four general categories. Please give us your opinion on each of the classifications. Also please place a check before any specific activities you think should be conducted under ARF auspices.

1. *Research Techniques*

Please indicate how you regard ARF participation in the field of research techniques. Check one only:

Very important   _____
Moderately important   _____
Not of great importance   _____
Not in favor of doing   _____

1*a*. Here is a list of possible research technique projects. Please check *any* that you consider worthwhile. If you have any added starters, please list under "other."

1. Study of radio and TV rating methods.
2. Studies of the effectiveness and significance of the recognition techniques.
3. A study to determine the minimum samples needed for measuring readership by the recognition method according to various media.
4. Effect of call backs on business paper ad ratings.

[There followed eight additional projects within the research techniques area, followed by a blank for respondent write-in of other suggestions in that area.]

2. *Studies to Improve Advertising Craftsmanship*

How do you regard ARF participation in this field? Check one only:

> Very important   _____
> Moderately important   _____
> Not of great importance _____
> Not in favor of doing   _____

2*a*. Please check *any* of the following projects that you consider worthwhile:

13. Study to determine the optimum length of display for car cards and outdoor posters.
14. Experimental testing of the influence of each of the basic elements in the advertising layout.
15. Experimental research to determine the prominence (or frequency) with which product or advertiser identification should be used in both printed and broadcast advertisements.
16. Study to determine how long people remember, or how quickly they forget, advertising.

[Two additional projects within the advertising craftsmanship area were listed, followed by a blank for respondent write-in of other suggestions in this area.]

3. *Competitive Media Evaluation Studies*

[The four-point "importance rating" scale included in the above two areas was repeated.]

3*a*. Please check *any* of the following projects that you consider worthwhile:

19. Studies of depth or extent of reading of magazine articles.
20. The effect of television on magazine and/or newspaper reading.

[Twelve additional projects within the media-evaluation area were listed. No blank space for a write-in of additional projects in this area was provided.]

4. Basic Economic and Market Data Studies

[The four-point "importance-rating" scale included in the first two areas was repeated to determine the attitude of foundation members toward ARF participation in this field.]

4a. Please check *any* of the following projects that you consider worthwhile:

33. ARF to supply on continuing basis county-by-county index of sales potential in dollars according to actual location of the consumers.
34. Development of study to show historically the relationship of advertising expenditures to sales (by commodity classification); to national income.
35. Interpretation of data gathered by Federal Government Bureaus. [Provision for other projects in this area was included. The following important "Note" was then included.]

NOTE: Please indicate the ONE project which you would like to have the Advertising Research Foundation tackle first: No. _____

The questionnaire included provision for identification of respondent. If respondent chose not to sign the questionnaire, provision for identification as a media, advertiser, or agency subscriber was included. That permitted a classification of responses based on the tripartite membership of the ARF.

In terms of the rating of *areas* as to importance, the rank order of the four major areas was identical for all three types of subscriber where rating as *very important* was concerned. This table summarizes the findings of the study:

Research area	Type of subscriber		
	Media	Agencies	Advertisers
Research techniques..............	1	1	1
Media evaluation..................	2	2	2
Advertising craftsmanship..........	3	3	3
Economic-market data.............	4	4	4

Here are the top ten projects on the basis of the frequency with which they were designated as *very important* by ARF subscribers, without reference to classification of subscribers by type:

1. A study to determine if an adequate and practical method of accurately measuring the readership of magazine advertisements can be developed.
2. Study of radio and TV rating methods.
3. A study of magazine audiences and characteristics including magazine duplication.

4. The effect of television on magazine and/or newspaper reading.

5. Study to determine how long people remember, or how quickly they forget, advertising.

6. Composition of a new, up-to-date manual on copy testing and research methods.

7. Studies of the effectiveness and significance of the recognition techniques.

8. Development of study to show historically the relationship of advertising expenditures to sales (by commodity classifications) to national income.

9. A compilation of all existing audience research results in an attempt to produce a handbook containing the latest and best potential audience figures for every medium.

10. A study of audience duplication and audience totals for combinations of media.

There were, not surprisingly, some differences in the way different types of ARF subscribers rated the relative importance of the top five projects. Those differences are indicated in the following table. A shorter description of the project is used, to conserve space; refer to the fuller description above for specific identification of the proposed projects in question:

	Type of subscriber and rank		
Proposed project	Media	Agencies	Advertisers
1. Accurate measurement of magazine ad readership	2nd*	2nd	1st
2. Study of radio-tv rating methods	4th*	1st	4th
3. Magazine audience characteristics and duplication study	1st	3rd	2nd*
4. Effect of TV on magazine and/or newspaper reading	2nd*	5th*	5th
5. Study to determine how long people remember advertising	4th*	5th*	6th

* Denotes tie in ranking among subscriber group.

The results of this study were used as one of the major guides in assigning priorities to projects which had been suggested for ARF consideration.

— ★ —

THE FUTURE OF COOPERATIVE RESEARCH

The illustrations presented in this chapter indicate some of the ways in which it is possible for a cooperative approach to be used effectively in marketing research. Cooperative research simply applies the concept that "in union there is strength" to the marketing research problems of organizations or individuals with a common problem.

Cooperative marketing research can be used in a wide range of different situations with considerable effectiveness. The potential uses of this approach far exceed present practice. Continued growth in such research may therefore be predicted with confidence.

Such marketing research utilizes the same approaches described as applying to the research of individual manufacturers. All the subject matter of this book, therefore, is applicable. The major difference is that the cost of the research is spread among a relatively large number of sponsors or organizations. As a result, the cost to each is relatively small. In cooperative or any other marketing research, the key factor is the competence of the individual marketing research man with primary responsibility for it. It is essential in cooperatively sponsored research for an experienced research man to head up and coordinate the project.

SUMMARY

1. This chapter described the prominent role which trade associations and other mutual-interest groups play in marketing research practice. Such associations represent a focal point for marketing research by an entire industry. They are particularly important in the case of industries made up of a large number of relatively small companies.

2. The kind of information developed by trade associations and other mutual-interest groups corresponds closely to that developed by individual manufacturers. Reports of the trend and level of industry volume, of major subdivisions within the industry total, and of territorial potentials are often provided.

3. The amount and type of information gathered in the course of trade-association-conducted marketing research are generally limited by the types and kinds of information normally available within the association's member companies.

4. Major research using any technique may be conducted by a trade association, in addition to the more usual types of information provided. Where the association advertises, advertising research is often involved.

5. Governmental participation in cooperative research is often one way of implementing the informational needs of an industry. A wide range of types of marketing research stem from various governmental units.

6. The cooperative research approach is open to far more organizations and industries than use it. Growth of such research may therefore be predicted with confidence.

QUESTIONS

1. What is a trade association? What kinds of marketing research information do trades associations develop for an industry?

2. What factors could limit trade-association research activities and the amount of information they can supply to member companies?

3. In your opinion, a marketing research program operated by and through a trade association would ideally offer what kind of data to its membership?

4. When might advertising research activities fall within the scope of the marketing research activities of trade associations or other mutual-interest groups? What might these activities include?

5. How have trade associations aided their members in the area of pipeline-trend research ?

6. How do you feel about the future of cooperative research conducted by trade associations and other mutual-interest groups?

CHAPTER 29

Marketing Research by Advertising Agencies and Advertising Media

Advertising agencies are continually active in marketing research practice. They conduct directly, and participate in both directly and indirectly, an extremely large proportion of all marketing research activities.

The obvious approach to a discussion of advertising agency marketing research activities has the advantage of being relatively specific. That approach begins with a sharply focused picture of the marketing research activities of one or more specific advertising agencies. It moves on to develop the role of the advertising agency in marketing research practice from that base.

That approach has a major limitation which is not immediately apparent. It rests on an erroneous premise. It assumes that there *is* a pattern of marketing research activities in advertising agencies which is, with a few minor exceptions, fairly typical. A business lifetime working in and closely with a large number of advertising agencies has made it quite clear to the author that there is no such thing as a *typical* advertising agency research operation. Further, the description of the research activities of a single agency would be likely to be obsolete or obsolescent before a book could be produced. The rate of change, even within a single agency, is that great.

The differences from agency to agency in the relative importance of marketing research are so great that it would be difficult to impossible to exaggerate them. Further, the differences *within a single advertising agency* as it moves through a growth cycle and as the nature of its client list changes are almost as extreme. The reader who seeks a description of a typical or average advertising agency research department or function would be well advised to seek instead the pot of gold at the end of the rainbow—it's likely to be easier to find!

740

PRIMARY FUNCTION: TO SERVE THE ADVERTISING
AGENCY'S MANAGEMENT

A considerable amount of misunderstanding about the research activities of advertising agencies can be avoided by recognizing at the outset the basic reason why advertising agencies *have* research departments. An advertising agency is a service business. The research department in an advertising agency is a service department. That department is typically created and operated *primarily to serve the advertising agency.*

The parallel, in this respect, between the research department in an advertising agency and one in a manufacturing organization is perfect and complete. A research department in a manufacturing business exists primarily to serve the management of that business. It is an advisory function, which works by helping the managers of the business arrive at key decisions. It does that by gathering, analyzing, and interpreting information relevant to those decisions. Similarly, the research department in an advertising agency has as its primary function the task of contributing informational guidance to the management of the agency itself.

In Chapter 27, the basic distinction between the product of a manufacturing business and that of a service business was drawn. The inescapable similarity between those two types of "products" was also underlined. The product of an advertising agency, which is a service business, is advertising. The research activities within an advertising agency are usually focused primarily on areas which are most likely to contribute to the soundness and effectiveness of the advertising prepared by the agency.

KEY INFLUENCE: ATTITUDE OF AGENCY PRINCIPALS
TOWARD THE IMPORTANCE OF RESEARCH

Tremendous differences exist in the relative importance of the research function, even within advertising agencies of the same size serving essentially similar lists of accounts. The source of those differences is not visible to an outsider. That source can be readily identified by anyone who has spent much time working either in advertising-agency management or in advertising-agency research. Variations in the importance of research from agency to agency are primarily a reflection of differences in the attitudes of the principals, that is, the major stockholders, officers, or owners, of the advertising agency toward research. Those attitudes in turn will be heavily conditioned by the background, training, and previous experience of those executives.

It is an oversimplification to try to classify advertising agencies into a small number of groups or types, yet that approach is helpful in understanding advertising-agency research. Consider first the type of advertising agency which is familiar to most students of advertising. That is the *creative* agency. The head or heads of the agency have risen to leadership on a background of creative success in the copy, art, or radio or television commercial departments. Often the president of such an agency is widely recognized as a top-flight creative man. The agency of which he is the head develops many outstanding advertising campaigns. In such an agency, research is likely to play an extremely subordinate role.

At the other extreme, with few examples to make identification easy, there is the advertising agency which is known as a research, or merchandising agency. Perhaps the president of that agency moved upward from the research department. Perhaps the agency is known for its fact-finding, or merchandising, successes. In any case, such an agency emphasizes research to a much greater extent than do other agencies of the same size.

Somewhere between those extremes, most advertising agencies fall. In a new-business presentation, when they are soliciting a new account, such agencies preach the gospel of research in strong and strident tones. In their day-to-day operations in developing and executing the advertising and merchandising plans for their clients' products, the picture is quite different. The role of research in the actual, day-to-day operations of such agencies can be most accurately described by selecting a few items from any handy cliché catalogue. "Prophet without honor in his own country" and "The face on the cutting-room floor" spring most quickly to mind as appropriate.

THE COST SQUEEZE ON RESEARCH EXPENDITURES

The above comments should not be interpreted as being critical of the management of advertising agencies. In advertising agencies as in other types of organizations, the cost of research must be carefully weighed against the profit contributions to be expected from that research. Good research costs money. Agencies are under constant pressure to supply an ever-expanding spectrum of services to their clients. All those services cost money, too. The proportion of the total gross income of the agency which is devoted to research, in the case of any particular account, is largely determined by the decisions of the client rather than of the agency.

When an advertiser (client) hires an agency and commits a sum of money to advertising, that client in effect creates a service bank account. The agency's *gross* income is about 15 per cent of the amount committed. The agency, like the advertiser, is in business to make money.

Therefore there is a slice "off the top" of the indicated gross income which represents provision for the agency's anticipated profit on the account. Since Federal income taxes will take a slice off the agency's profits, both before-tax and after-tax agency profit margins enter into this calculation.

With provision made for the agency's profit, how is the remaining balance in the service bank account to be spent? This is a question to which there is no quick or easy answer. One aspect of that question, however, is quite clear. When it comes to determining how the income is spent by the agency, and the services which are provided within it for the advertiser, it is the advertiser who is unquestionably the boss. If the advertiser doesn't like the way an agency he has appointed spends the income his appropriation provides on service for him, he has (and uses!) the classic remedy of firing the agency and hiring another to come closer to his concept of what an advertiser-agency relationship should be.

In decisions about expenditures within the control of the management of the agency, there is a constant cost pressure which should be recognized. Costs keep rising. The range of agency services offered keeps expanding, and the added services bring new and additional costs. As a result, the agency's profits are in a cost squeeze. Any cost which can be reduced is expendable. Those costs which are most likely to be pruned are those which the client is least likely to miss. It's almost as simple as that. In that type of a cost climate, the costs of marketing research—and many other costs, which need not concern us here—are under pressure. The generalization that few advertising agencies spend more for research than their clients require them to is essentially a sound one.

TREND IN AGENCY RESEARCH EXPENDITURES

In a story on "Advertising: The Battle of 15 Per Cent," *Fortune* magazine included some information on the level and trend of advertising agency research expenditures. That information is quoted below, with an introductory comment which may be helpful in establishing the tone of the *Fortune* article:[1]

If agencies have, indeed, been offering clients more and more in the way of extra services—e.g., public-relations counsel, research, and advice on marketing problems—how have they been able to maintain their profit margins so well? To begin with, while more agencies are undoubtedly offering a full line of collateral services than was the case in 1930, advertising men probably tend to exaggerate how much those services cost them to provide. In 1955, for instance, according to figures prepared by

[1] *Fortune*, October, 1956, p. 206.

the 4 A's [the American Association of Advertising Agencies], agencies of all sizes were on the average spending only 1.94 per cent of their gross income on their research departments, which is less than the 2.45 per cent they spent in 1945 or the 2.35 per cent they spent in 1949. Even the largest agencies, which boast of their elaborate research facilities, are not spending a very large percentage of their income on research. For agencies billing $40 million or over, total research costs—payroll plus "unbillable" outside research—amounted last year to only 3.64 per cent of gross income, less than the 4.25 per cent agencies of this size were devoting to research in 1949, the earliest year included in this particular comparison by the 4 A's.

The very sharp increase in total advertising expenditures pointed out in Chapter 24 on advertising research should be considered in interpreting figures like those cited by *Fortune*. A lower percentage of a sharply increased total volume may still represent a significant increase in advertising agency expenditures for research. Even though those expenditures in total are increasing, however, they represent a declining share of all advertising-agency costs. The introduction both of new services and of new media (notably television) with a corresponding increase in the number of high-priced specialists on the typical agency's payroll is a factor in that trend.

The danger of generalizing or overgeneralizing from average figures should require no comment this late in a book which devoted so much space to problems in the interpretation of data. The average figures cited conceal a tremendous range of variations. If this thought is kept in mind, interpretation of them will be less hazardous: There are wide variations in the extent to which a single agency spends research funds (or does no research) on two accounts of essentially the same size. The inclination of the agency toward or against research is one influence in those variations; the desires of the client organization are another and more important influence.

BREADTH OF ADVERTISING AGENCY RESEARCH

It would be misleading to consider advertising agency research as something different and apart from the types of marketing research described in other chapters of this book. There are important differences between the marketing research activities of advertising agencies and those of manufacturers. Those are primarily differences in emphasis. To illustrate, consider an advertising agency which may be actual or hypothetical. Assume that advertising agency has a relatively large research department. The department is under the guidance and supervision of a competent and experienced marketing research director. Look in the "completed jobs" file of that agency's research department. There you are likely to find examples of almost every type of marketing research discussed in this book.

The breadth of activities carried on as part of the marketing research activities of advertising agencies today is much greater than is generally recognized. There are almost no types of marketing research which a department of the type described above cannot do. In the course of some of that research, outside research facilities would be called upon as required for supplementary manpower and muscles. There are few types of marketing research which such a department is not called upon to undertake at one time or another.

Because of the profit arithmetic involved in advertising-agency operations, such a research department is likely to be found only in an advertising agency with billings above a certain minimum in size. Relatively few advertising agencies with total billings much below 15 million dollars can afford the type of research department described.

EXAMPLE OF JOBS PERFORMED BY ONE ADVERTISING AGENCY

For an illustration of the range in research projects carried on within a single advertising agency, consider the capsule histories illustrated in Figure 29.1. Those capsule histories were prepared by Steuart Henderson Britt to illustrate the range of activities in one agency's research. The reader will find among those capsule histories examples of many of the types of marketing research which have been discussed in this book.

The listing of projects obviously raises some important questions as to what constitutes a reasonable division of research responsibility between the client (manufacturer) and his advertising agency. By way of background we should note that the client list of an advertising agency with large enough billings to be able to afford its own capable marketing research department is likely to include manufacturers who also have large and capable marketing research departments of their own. Since both the advertiser and the agency, in such a relationship, have research departments capable of executing almost any type of marketing research assignment, a duplication of facilities exists.

Careful coordination of the research activities of both the agency and advertiser is clearly necessary to guard against the risk that the duplication of facilities may lead to overlapping and wasteful duplication in research assignments. Let's consider how that coordination is achieved.

Figure 29.1.

Some "Capsule" Case Histories of One Advertising Agency's Research Projects

Type of research project	Problem	Method	Results
1. Agricultural research	What is happening to farmers' purchasing power?	Analysis of farm-census, farm-income, and farm-expense statistics and projections; a long-range prediction by the agency's agricultural technician, based on the findings.	The farm market is far from drying up. There is an increasing demand for farm products from a growing population. But farm income is concentrating in fewer hands, mainly because of increased productivity, resulting from technological improvements.
2. Analysis of market trends	Why has a certain industry had declining sales, in spite of increased population?	Investigation included analysis of Nielsen data, home-canning surveys, restaurant sales surveys, and discussions with leading doctors.	The decline in home canning, plus an unusually high consumption during the war, accounted for much of the decline.
3. Basic research studies	What is the economic outlook for the coming year?	The Department made a comprehensive analysis and interpretation of all available economic data of the past 20 years, from both governmental and private sources, and projected forecasts for the coming year from these.	On the whole, the prospects for 1955 were considered good. Business conditions should be at a slightly higher level than in 1954. Barring war and major strikes, no "boom" or "bust" was foreseen.
4. Brand-position determination	What is the historical pattern of brand shares in local markets for a particular product field?	Consumer analysis reports covering the product field over a four-year period were summarized to show changes in preference among leading brands in each market.	Considerable changes in brand shares had taken place in most of the markets studied. The one brand which had been doing the most promoting in these areas made gains in most of them at the expense of the other brands.
5. Competitive advertising expense analyses	What were the traceable advertising expenditures for all the major brands in one product field?	All published sources of advertising-expenditure data by products, brands, and media were carefully checked.	The figures were used by the agency and client in planning and budgeting a campaign on this particular product.
6. Consumer-preference studies	What are consumers' buying habits of a particular fresh food commodity, and what are their specific attitudes toward the client's products as well as competitive brands?	Comprehensive, pretested interviews were conducted with a number of housewives in a market where the client had good distribution.	Much new information on buying habits was obtained, and it was discovered that there is little evidence of brand loyalty in this particular food field.
7. Copy research	Has a given copy theme, based on one advantage of a certain product, outlived its usefulness?	Personal interviews were conducted with consumers.	Consumers thought that the particular product feature was an important one and that few competitive products had it. Continuation of the basic advertising theme was recommended.

Type of research project	Problem	Method	Results
8. Economic studies	What is the distribution of income in the U.S., and what changes have taken place in recent years?	Department of Commerce estimates of income payments to individuals were summarized, analyzed, and interpreted.	Noteworthy changes had taken place and were very useful in locating the best markets for various consumer products.
9. Market potential studies	What is the sales potential of a client's product by districts, trading areas, and markets, for use mainly in media and merchandising operations?	Per cents of national potential for all areas itemized in the client's territorial sales outline were analyzed and arranged in descending order of potential.	Lists were prepared showing the per cents of national potential arrayed by district; trading areas; market; districts, trading areas within districts, and individual cities within trading areas.
10. Media surveys	What is the status and future of radio as a national advertising medium?	All available data on national network and national spot radio were analyzed, and the four networks were consulted. In addition, information from Standard Rate & Data Service was helpful.	Although radio has been replaced by television as a primary national advertising medium, radio has a very important secondary role in specific situations.
11. Package testing	Was a proposed new plastic package for a client's product better than the old cardboard one?	One of each kind of package was given to a panel of housewives, who were then interviewed in person a week later.	About 70% of the women preferred the plastic package for over-all qualities, ease of opening, and storing utility.
12. Premium tests	Would stainless-steel tableware make an effective premium?	A comparative study was made of the market for stainless steel, silver plate, and sterling.	Stainless steel was gaining wide popularity, according to buyers and trade journals; therefore its use as a premium was recommended.
13. Price analyses	Are price brands a serious threat to quality brands?	Available consumer panel reports were carefully analyzed.	In many—but not all—commodity fields, price brands (particularly chain-store house brands) are capturing more and more of the market.
14. Product tests	How would consumers react to the taste and other properties of a client's experimental product?	Housewives were given unidentified packages of the new product and a well-established competitive one. They were asked to serve both at the same meal in the same way.	The majority of women considered the new product easier to prepare and better-tasting. There was no difference in preference on the basis of texture.
15. Psychological (motivational) research	What are the psychological factors behind the public's buying of the type of service offered by a certain client?	Psychological interviews were conducted with men in a number of cities around the country.	Recommendations, based on findings of this research, led to important changes in the client's marketing and advertising strategy.

Type of research project	Problem	Method	Results
16. Public opinion and attitude surveys	What does the general public think of one of the agency's clients?	A public opinion survey was made, and the findings compared with similar studies made in earlier years.	Results helped the company understand its customers and prospects better; and the information was also helpful in setting advertising objectives.
17. Readership surveys	What general criteria might be used for gauging the value of each publication as an advertising medium for a specific product?	In cooperation with the Media Department, data from Starch Consumer Magazine Report were studied.	The resulting report was one of the factors in the determination of a magazine schedule on this product.
18. Sales analyses	What per cent of sales of a certain kind of product are in TV homes, and what per cent in non-TV homes?	Pertinent data were obtained from MRCA, and then summarized and interpreted.	Sales were split about equally between TV and non-TV homes, indicating that our client's extensive TV advertising of a product in this field should be backed up with advertising in other media reaching non-TV homes.
19. Sales tests	Would consumers purchase and repurchase a certain new product?	Store distribution, backed by heavy advertising, was set up in five markets, and careful watch kept on the movement of the product.	Initial purchases were relatively high, repurchases low, indicating either abandonment or changes in the new product.
20. Store audits	How would sales of a particular product in an advertised area compare with those in an unadvertised area?	A series of audits in representative stores in each of the two types of markets were conducted over a period of time.	Sales effectiveness of the advertising was dramatically demonstrated. Client also got much factual information about product movement, competitive prices, etc.

SOURCE: Reprinted from August, 1956, issues of Standard Rate and Data Service, Inc.

HOW RESEARCH RESPONSIBILITY IS OFTEN DIVIDED BETWEEN ADVERTISER AND ADVERTISING AGENCY

In the following comments we are concerned with the situation in which both the advertiser or manufacturer and the advertising agency have complete and competently staffed research departments. In such a situation, the coordination so obviously necessary is achieved in a number of ways, with certain common characteristics which may be identified. One of those characteristics is usually a very close working relationship, typically at the research-director level, between the research departments of the advertiser and of the agency. Frequent consultation between the research directors of the advertiser and of the agency serves to keep each informed of the nature and scope of activities in progress or under consideration in areas of mutual interest. That helps to reduce the risk of duplication. Regularly scheduled meetings of the full department of the agency and advertiser, sometimes as often as monthly, serve the same purpose. An advance agenda, widely distributed, is helpful in keeping all interested parties informed of work in progress and major findings.

A second precaution against waste through overlapping or duplication in research is the specific and definite delineation, usually in writing, of the areas of research responsibility of the agency and of the advertiser.

In such a division of research responsibilities, the advertiser often assumes responsibility for *market* research (not marketing research), while the agency assumes responsibility for *advertising research.* Information about the size and characteristics of the market for the advertised product, competitive division of the market, etc., is gathered and supplied to the agency by the manufacturer. Working from that information, the agency goes on to gather whatever additional information is needed to develop sound advertising and marketing plans. That research may take the form of attitude studies, qualitative or motivational research, etc. An illustration of this division of responsibility in a specific situation was provided by the Toni case involving Bobbi home permanent.

Research on specific advertisements or radio or TV commercials, commonly called *copy research,* is typically the responsibility of the advertising agency. Chapter 24 described some research of that type. There is sometimes a distinction drawn between pretesting and post-testing advertising. It is not unusual to find the advertising agency responsible for the execution (and the cost!) of pretesting, while the advertiser assumes the burden of post-testing advertising.

ONE MAJOR ADVERTISER'S POLICY ON ADVERTISER-AGENCY DIVISION OF RESPONSIBILITY

While he was director of marketing research for General Mills, Inc., Gordon A. Hughes prepared an interesting statement of that organization's policy on this advertiser-agency division of responsibility. His statement reflected company policy at the time this book went into production, according to A. W. Harding, who succeeded Mr. Hughes as the head of General Mills' marketing research activities.

50. GENERAL MILLS, INC.[2]

At General Mills, we believe that it is very important to have close coordination of all parties involved in marketing a product. To say

[2] Gordon A. Hughes, "The Relationship of Advertisers and Agency in Research," *The Journal of Marketing,* January, 1950, p. 579.

the opposite, in our opinion, would be almost parallel to ignoring the need for close coordination between advertising, merchandising, production, etc. The advertising agency in General Mills' plan of operation is a partner in the business. Its job is to know the operations of General Mills so well that its recommendations for advertising will fit perfectly into the over-all merchandising and promotion plans of the company.

This is not unique with General Mills. I am sure it is duplicated, with only individual variations, among most successful advertisers. The counsel and advice of your advertising agency is important not only in the fields of media and copy but also in research.

Research is a vital part of this program in General Mills. We have in the company a department of 24 people each of whom is qualified in some phase of marketing research, thus affording a marketing research service capable of meeting the varied needs of the company's operations. Advertising research is a major part of our regular activities, and our advertising agencies have an important place in much of that work.

We have not attempted to set up policies governing the flow of work and sharing of responsibility. My experience, first with an agency and later with the advertiser, would indicate the inadvisability of doing that. Rather, we have adopted two simple rules which help us in deciding each project as it is being planned. The first of these rules is to encourage or assign agency research only in the fields directly affecting the creation of advertising. The second is to discourage or refuse agency research which concerns the evaluation of their own efforts.

Generally we classify research projects in two categories insofar as their relation to our advertising agencies is concerned. The first type, such as copy testing, media and duplication studies, premium tests, radio commercials, package design studies, etc., are related to the basic function of the advertising agency and as such are agency responsibilities. In the delegation of research responsibility for these types of work we proceed about as follows. Regardless of where the problem originates, it comes first to the attention of our Market Analysis Department. The problem is studied here and our library files are searched to check any research findings previously done that may have a bearing on the subject. We then release the assignment to the agency, possibly with observations concerning the areas of information that should be covered, extent of sampling, etc. and a request that they submit a plan for research along with a schedule and estimate of costs. At the time the plan is received in our department we again study it to make sure that all of the interests of General Mills are covered insofar as that particular problem is concerned, and that it conforms with accepted research procedures and techniques. If approved the project is then assigned to the agency for completion.

Sometimes we continue with the agency in jointly completing the research. In any event, however, the final report must clear through the Market Analysis Department before reaching the operating department of the company for which the work was done. This practice assures each department in General Mills that the research findings submitted to them are accurate in all matters of procedure and interpretation and are complete insofar as the problem is concerned.

A second type of research project concerns the product itself, its market position, its sales volume, etc. These, in our opinion, are projects which should be done by the advertiser rather than its advertising agency. Research in these areas is the responsibility of the advertiser, usually does not relate to the job of creating advertising and would involve the agency in the evaluation of its own efforts.

While we do not encourage this type of research among our advertising agencies, we do solicit their advice and consider it carefully, and we distribute copies of the findings to the agencies.

The advertising agency is a service organization. Its plant facilities are people, and its output is "ideas that sell." The agency spends large amounts of money in acquiring people with experience and proven ability. They must also spend substantial amounts to maintain the production of "selling ideas" through research.

At General Mills, we are constantly urging more financial investment on the part of our agencies in pre-testing printed word copy, radio commercials, special merchandising promotions, premiums, etc., but we do not require that the agency assume the financial responsibility of post-checking these activities.

Except for this single rule, our procedure is to consider each project by itself to determine first the agency responsibility on the project and finally the extent to which the agency should share in or assume completely its costs.

— ★ —

"GRAY AREAS" IN RESEARCH RESPONSIBILITY

As might be expected, there are some gray areas in the division of responsibility between advertiser and agency. Each major project in such an area is likely to require individual examination and consideration. Such areas are too numerous to list, but two major ones merit identification. The first is in the area of research on a new product which is being considered for launching and on which the agency must prepare advertising. In many cases there is a lack of market information on such a product. The agency often is required to enter into areas of research on new products which extend beyond the normal limits which exist on established products.

The second major gray area concerns test-market activities. Agencies are active in test-market research. The selection of test markets is often dictated by advertising factors (such as the availability of color in the newspapers, number of television channels, etc.) to a considerable extent. The responsibility for the test-market research is sometimes assumed wholly by the agency, sometimes by the advertiser, and sometimes shared by both. Even in a single, specific agency-client relationship, different test-market programs are likely to be handled with different assignments of responsibility. Specific objectives and characteristics of the individual market tests are likely to determine the extent to which the agency participates in the research with major responsibility.

CLIENT POLICY DETERMINES EXTENT OF ADVERTISING AGENCY RESEARCH

It must be emphasized, however, that tremendous variations exist in the nature and scope of advertising agency research activities between agencies. Basic decisions on whether research is to play a major or a minor role arc likely to reflect the policies or wishes of the client or manufacturer-advertiser. The agency's position is a subordinate one. This is entirely sound and natural. It is implicit in the agency-client relationship.

The advertiser—usually a manufacturing organization—plans its own research activities. In doing so, the relationship between the cost of the research and the profit contribution of that research is considered. The advertising appropriation includes compensation to the agency for its services, including the research provided, if any. It is only natural, then, that the executives within the advertiser or client organization, who have primary responsibility for authorizing the advertising expenditure, should have the major voice in determining how that money is spent.

Variations in agency emphasis on research thus tend to reflect the preferences of the agency's client list. Some agencies have large research departments, with many experienced technicians on their full-time payroll. Other agencies, including some of equal size, may have no research departments or only a single research director without any full-time staff to assist him. Some accounts receive a great deal of research within the advertising agency; other accounts, including perhaps some of equal size in the same agency, may receive little or no research as part of their total package of advertising agency service.

RESEARCH IS IN A SUBORDINATE ROLE IN ADVERTISING AGENCY OPERATIONS

It should be emphasized that research plays a relatively subordinate role in almost all advertising agency operations. This is not a reflection on advertising agency research personnel. There are many skilled, competent, and experienced marketing research men today who are employed by or were formerly employed by one or more advertising agencies. All those research men have had firsthand experience with the inescapable limitation of advertising agency research. In the advertising hierarchy, it is the "creative" personnel and those in the "contact" or "account management" categories that have the greatest voice and weight. Marketing research, even when represented by an outstandingly competent man, is likely to be subordinated.

There is no reason why a competent research man or a research team, employed by an advertising agency, cannot do as competent and objective a job of research on a major marketing problem as any other equally competent man or group could do. Some of the cases in this book illustrate instances in which advertising agency research made outstanding contributions to the solution of marketing problems. Despite that fact, it would be foolish not to recognize that research conducted by advertising agencies is often viewed by the clients for whom it is done with suspicion or worse. This is especially likely if the findings of the research point toward action which coincides with the agency's own interests.

The agency-client relationship is a tenuous one. A client can fire an agency at any time, for cause or without cause. Research which results in a reflection on the client's products, or which shows that a decision made by a client executive was unsound, is likely to endanger the agency's status on the account. That being the case, it is well to recognize that the reporting of agency-conducted research—often as "guided" by nonresearch personnel within the agency—may be less forthright than would be the case if the research man were not subject to the instructions of his superiors in the agency. A research man can and often does prepare a straightforward report for the information of his associates within the agency. Whether that report is or is not forwarded to the client organization, and if forwarded whether in original or "modified" form, is often a question decided *for* rather than *by* the agency's research personnel.

The following quotation from the National Industrial Conference Board study of marketing research practices[3] summarizes the viewpoint

[3] *Organization for Market Research*, National Industrial Conference Board, Studies in Business Policy, no. 19, p. 28, 1946.

of a sample of manufacturers' marketing research directors on this point:

> The majority of directors do not regard advertising agencies as a good source of outside marketing research assistance and few seek help from that quarter. The general attitude is that the advertising agency research should be confined to matters relating to the effective prosecution of campaigns, and that the cost of this research should be borne by the agency.
>
> In the opinion of some directors, the advertising agency should also check the effectiveness of its own campaigns, although the majority reported that they preferred to make independent checks.
>
> Although some companies believe that their agencies' research departments are good instruments for general marketing research and that this service should be provided at the standard agency fee or at cost, the majority fear that interpretations of such research are inclined to be biased by an agency's natural desire to promote its services or prove the value of its campaigns. This situation is recognized by some leaders in advertising who advocate the removal of the sales influence from agency marketing research. As a result, those employing advertising agency research generally devote considerable time to cross checking. The fact remains evident, however, that some of the best research minds of the country are found in advertising agency marketing research departments.

SUMMARY COMMENTS ON ADVERTISING AGENCY RESEARCH

It is extremely difficult to summarize the advertising agency research picture because of the wide variations which exist, from agency to agency, and from time to time within a single agency. These summary comments, however, are possible: As the NICB quotation above noted, some of the outstanding marketing research men in the country are on advertising agency payrolls. For the agencies that employ them, and for the clients of those agencies in some instances, those research men engage in a wide variety of marketing research activities. There is almost no type of marketing research excluded from the advertising agency research area, as the list of capsule items supplied by Britt illustrated.

Advertising agency research can be very good research, or something less than excellent. The same quality range exists, we might note, for research by manufacturers. There are forces present in an agency-client relationship which tend to exert what might reasonably be described as "undue influence" on some marketing research in some advertising agencies. The existence of those forces makes the careful examination of agency-conducted research desirable. In this as in so many other areas of marketing research, the judgments made about research boil down to one's confidence in the marketing research man with primary responsibility for the assignment. Access to that individual, and an opportunity to discuss the findings with him personally in specific detail and in the greatest frankness, should make possible an objective evaluation of any specific advertising agency research project.

MARKETING RESEARCH BY ADVERTISING MEDIA

The rising flood of advertising volume noted in the introduction to Chapter 24 on advertising research reflects the increase in the amount of advertising. That advertising is first created and then distributed. It is created by advertising agencies or by the advertising departments or manufacturing organizations or of large retail stores. It is distributed by utilizing some one or combination of advertising media. The major advertising media are magazines, newspapers, radio stations and networks, television stations and networks, outdoor advertising, direct mail, and so on. Those media sponsor and/or conduct a substantial volume of marketing research. It is with that media research that the remainder of this chapter is concerned.

Let's begin a consideration of the characteristics of media research with a key question: Why should advertising media engage in marketing research?

Advertising media are service businesses. They are extremely competitive. That competition is both general, between different types of media (television versus newspapers, for example); and specific, between individual media of the same type, as between the *Chicago Tribune* and the *Chicago Daily News* for a share of newspaper-advertising volume in the Chicago market. The sale of advertising space or time represents the major source of revenue for advertising media.

Advertising media must evaluate their proposed research on the same cost–versus–profit-contribution scale that applies to manufacturers. In the case of an advertising media, an increase in profit can usually be achieved only by an increase in sales volume of advertising. Therefore most marketing research which is under consideration by advertising media is examined in the light of the answer to this question: Is the result of this research likely to increase our sales of advertising space substantially? If the answer is in the negative, the research is unlikely to be authorized.

To sum it up, then, the objective of most marketing research by advertising media is *promotional*. In point of fact it is not suprising to find that the marketing research function in the case of many media is a part of and reports to the promotional department or promotional director of the media.

This is an extremely important point to remember. In most cases, the marketing research sponsored by advertising media is conducted *with the expectation that it can be used as a sales tool* by the media sponsoring the research.

Much of the marketing research conducted by advertising media is published. With the above comment in mind, *it would be unrealistic to expect to find any media publishing research findings which do not show that media in a favorable light.* Obviously not all the research conducted by advertising media does present "evidence" which can be used as sales ammunition by the media. The research which is unfavorable toward the sponsoring media is quietly interred without publication. An alternative is to publish "selected facts" disclosed by the research, suppressing or deleting those findings which were unfavorable.

The greatest care is required in evaluating the soundness and validity of media-conducted research.

One of the important values contributed by the ARF has been its influence in the direction of soundly conceived and accurately and completely reported research by advertising media. The ARF reviews the proposed research while it is still in the planning stage and suggests modification of approach if those modifications are required to ensure dependable and accurate research findings. The ARF also reviews the report of some research to be sure that it conforms to the foundation's high standards. A full and complete report of ARF evaluation of specific studies is often published, to guide interpretation and analysis of media-sponsored research.

The fact that much research sponsored by advertising media is promotional should not blind one to the fact that a great deal of that research often supplies information helpful to marketing research practice. The Curtis Publishing Company is credited by many as the birthplace of marketing research on an organized basis. Charles Coolidge Parlin established a Division of Commercial Research as a part of the Advertising Department of the company in 1911. Curtis has continued to conduct a great deal of competently executed research. *Marketing Research Practice,* edited by Donald M. Hobart,[4] contains many examples of media-sponsored research of which any marketing research man might be proud. Some research services offered by advertising media are also outstanding. The consumer panel conducted by the *Chicago Tribune* is an example.

SUMMARY

1. If it is remembered that the primary function of advertising-agency research is to render a service to the management of the agency, it is much easier to see agency research in accurate perspective.

[4] Ronald, New York, 1950.

2. Many competent marketing research men work for advertising agencies. Within the agency framework, they perform a wide variety of types of marketing research.

3. There is a cost squeeze on advertising-agency research, which tends to restrict the amount and type of work that is done. In the relationship with any individual client, the amount of research work performed is determined largely by the wishes and inclination of the client.

4. There are in fact no limits on the kind and type of marketing research which advertising agency research departments *can* perform.

5. A common basis for dividing up marketing research responsibility and avoiding wasteful duplication of research efforts is to have the client assume responsibility for all research on the *market* for the product, and the agency responsibility for all *advertising* research. To the latter responsibility one exception is sometimes made. The client may choose to do the work concerned with evaluating the effectiveness of the advertising or other agency recommendations. This pattern is especially popular in cases where the manufacturer is a large one, with a sizable advertising appropriation.

6. The essentially subordinate nature of research in an advertising agency situation is a more important limiting factor on the application of agency research than is generally recognized.

7. Marketing research by the advertising media is primarily promotional research. It often contains by-product values for marketing research men, quite apart from the intended promotional applications. Some service research by advertising media is excellent.

QUESTIONS

1. What is the basic reason why advertising agencies have marketing research departments?

2. What is the key influence in the tremendous differences which exist in the relative importance of the research function among agencies?

3. How are the research responsibilities often divided between an advertiser and its advertising agency?

4. What are the "gray areas" in research responsibility discussed in this chapter?

5. What is the objective of most marketing research conducted by advertising media? Is there any value for marketing research men in this research by media?

CHAPTER 30

Consultants in Marketing Research Practice

A wide variety of different types of organizations exist to offer varied services to the manufacturer, retailer, wholesaler, or service organization that requires marketing research advice, counsel, aid, or assistance. Those organizations may be collectively identified as consulting firms or consultants. The objective of this chapter is to identify the major types of consultants active in the field of marketing research practice. Some background material helpful in understanding both the contributions that may be expected from consultants and the limitations which exist in dealing with them is included.

In the preceding chapter, the essentially promotional nature of marketing research sponsored by advertising media was underlined. The likelihood that research sponsored and published by any advertising media might reflect unfavorably on the sponsor, it was noted, was relatively slim. In the chapter on evaluating available data, the need for considering the possibility of bias on the part of the author or source of the data was underlined. The relevance of the above comments to the information which follows lies in this fact: While this chapter is intended to present an objective picture of the role of consultants in marketing research practice, the possibility of bias exists. The views which follow are those of one whose chosen occupation is consulting in the field of marketing and advertising management and research.

MANAGEMENT CONSULTANTS REPRESENT A GROWTH INDUSTRY

Consultants in marketing research represent a specialized subdivision of the management-consulting field. A review of the growth of general management consultants as a factor in today's management picture, written by Perrin Stryker, was published in the May, 1954, issue of *Fortune* under the title "The Ambitious Consultants." Some of the material which follows is drawn from that article, by special permission of the publishers of *Fortune*.

Fortune pointed out that in terms of total charges for their services management consultants by 1954 had achieved substantial volume. The continuing rate of growth in consultants' volume gave the field some of the characteristics of a growth industry. A survey was conducted by the Association of Consulting Management Engineers (ACME) in cities of 100,000 population and over. In such cities, 1,915 consultant firms were found (some of them, as *Fortune* noted, one-man operations), employing a total of 44,000 people.

Fortune reported:

Of the 1,915, 39 per cent were "specialists," i.e., offered only one kind of technique or service, and 61 per cent met ACME's own definition of a "management consultant," i.e., offered two or more services.

Fortune continued:

But the big statistic in ACME's census was this: for all their services this group of 1,915 firms last year collected some $426 million from management, and roughly three-fourths of this ($311 million) was collected by "management consultants." Compared to the long-established legal profession, whose 222,000 members annually gross about $1.4 billion, the consultant trade is surprisingly large.

Later in the same article, *Fortune* commented:

And the business of advising management is indeed a growth industry. Many consulting firms report their billings have doubled or tripled since 1950. So far as past history indicates, an occasional economic recession may only increase the demand from the U.S. business for consultants' help in cutting costs. It is still too soon to know what effect the elimination of E.P.T. [the federal excess-profits tax] may have on clients' purse strings, but the effect may be slight, for many managements have long since acquired the consultant habit.

COST BACKGROUND OF THE CONSULTING FIELD

Consultants are in a service business, with some rough parallels with other service businesses like advertising agencies and firms of certified public accountants. The primary costs of consultants, in the operation of their own businesses, are for payroll and such overhead items as rent, telephones, etc. Travel costs are often a major component as well, but since those costs are typically billed to the client for whom the traveling was done, those costs may be disregarded for the purposes of the present discussion. Detailed breakdowns of the financial operations of a consulting firm with gross income of $225,000, reported in *Fortune*, showed that 49.0 per cent of the income was distributed as consultants' salaries, an additional 9.1 per cent for office salaries, and 4.0 per cent for bonuses distributed quarterly. That represents an aggregate of 62.1 per cent for salaries and bonuses. Other expenses including rent and maintenance (2.5 per cent) and travel and entertainment (6.5 per cent) left an after-tax net profit of 11.7 per cent of sales.

The above figures are presented not as typical of consultants' level of retained income but rather to emphasize this point: The consultants' service consists primarily of the ideas and production of the people on the staff. Those people are typically relatively high in caliber and in price.

Since what consultants have to sell is essentially the time of their people, most charges for work done by consultants are on a time basis. Often the basis of charging a client for work done is on a straight cost per day per man, or a *per diem*, as it is sometimes called. As *Fortune* notes, this method of charging clients has some very important practical limitations:

A large part of their suspicion may be traced to the size of the consultants' fees. For one man's services these fees may run from $75 up to $500 a day, the most common figure being $150 a day for a junior staff consultant. To an executive earning $100 a day ($30,000 a year), the fees of a senior partner of a big consulting firm (usually $250 to $350 a day) naturally seem extraordinary. The client-executive, to be sure, will usually understand that these fees are the consultant firm's gross take. Yet he still may conclude either that his company is being robbed, or that the consultant doesn't know how to run his own business. Both conclusions are likely to be wrong. But it will be hard for the client to find out whether such fees are in line with the services performed. For practically all consultants have made trade secrets of their own management practices and policies.

One of the great advantages which consultants offer to their clients is the availability of able and experienced specialized help, when that help is needed. The client pays only for as much of the time of the consultants as his particular job requires. That represents a substantial saving, in most instances, over the costs of having similar talent on the payroll on a full-time basis. But the maintenance of the type of "stand-by manpower" which consultants make available involves costs which must be borne and which must be included in the fees charged to the client. This additional excerpt from the *Fortune* article provides helpful background on understanding the cost problems of consultants, which are reflected in their fees:

Many other firms, however, figure that to make money they must bill from two and a half to three times or more what they pay out in staff consultant salaries.

One important reason for this ratio of salaries to fees is that consultants can figure on billing only part of the potential working time of their staffs. A fairly common estimate is that a firm can count on billing only about 60 per cent of a man's time, or 150 days out of 260 working days a year. The rest will be idle time and travel to and from jobs (and, of course, vacations, sick leaves, and holidays).

Therefore, taking $150 a day as an average fee, and assuming 150 working days as the maximum billable time of each consultant, each man might be expected to produce a maximum of $22,500 in annual billings.

Remember that that billing figure represents *gross income*, out of which must come rent, heat, light, and other expenses in addition to the salary of the man involved.

One of the cost factors which is often overlooked by clients purchasing consulting service is the cost of selling time. In August, 1955, the maximum fees charged by the partners of one large consulting firm were $250 per day, while another large firm charged a top fee of $300. In the course of developing a proposal covering a project for which their services are considered, partners in the consulting firm might spend a substantial number of days for which there was no income. If the amount of selling time to actual working time were 50 per cent—perhaps a high ratio, but no higher than some jobs involve—then the actual realized per diem charge in terms of return to the consulting firm is only half of the quoted figure.

Ironically enough, it is often the small manufacturer whose lack of familiarity with consulting services runs up the selling costs, as repeated conferences, meetings, etc., are required before the job is finally approved.

There is an implication of the selling-time cost which should be underlined. In the consulting field, expenses are so daily—rent and payroll must be paid, etc.—and income is somewhat erratic. This puts a premium on dependable income and on income which does not involve any or involves only a minimum of selling time. A retainer type of arrangement with a consulting firm can, therefore, represent a sound value for the client. From the consultant's viewpoint, the income is regular and dependable, and does not involve selling time. Therefore a consulting firm can deliver a relatively high amount of service per dollar on a retainer arrangement which makes such an arrangement a real bargain for the client.

In the case of a retainer or any other expenditures for consultants' services, the now familiar yardstick of cost–versus–anticipated-profit contribution applies.

HISTORICAL BACKGROUND OF THE PRESENT IMPORTANCE OF CONSULTANTS IN MARKETING RESEARCH

The consultant plays an extremely important part in the total marketing research picture. The importance of the consultant's role is in part a historical accident. The background of that importance is worth brief attention by any student of marketing research.

One of the characteristics of marketing research as an area of specialization today is that there are many more good jobs seeking experienced men then there are men looking for jobs. This is entirely natural development, since marketing research is a relatively new area of specialized management skill. It has been expanding its base, in terms of the proportion of companies making use of it, rather rapidly. That expansion has had to be accomplished from a relatively narrow numerical base.

Think back to 1940 and 1941, as the United States moved into the transition to a wartime economy. In those days there were relatively few people active in marketing research above a clerical-statistical level. How many? In a talk to the Boston Conference on Distribution in 1944, T. G. MacGowan estimated the number at less than 1,000. That number included all those who were, in his words, "both available for and interested in marketing research work."

With the war, emphasis shifted heavily to production. Relatively few companies opened up marketing research as a new area of specialized activity during the war years. During those years, of the fewer than 1,000 individuals mentioned, some died, others retired, and many were promoted into other areas of management responsibility. The net result was that during the years of World War II, the pool of trained and experienced marketing research manpower contracted sharply.

In the transitional period following World War II and in the early postwar years, marketing began to resume a far more important role. New marketing research departments were created in countless companies. The manpower pool from which such new departments could draw an experienced director was a small and well-fished one. The higher the level of skill sought, the fewer candidates available for consideration. This relationship between number and size of fish has a parallel familiar to all bass fishermen!

Before World War II, marketing research was not a very well paid field. With the shortage of skilled personnel and the intensified competition for such personnel after the war, the price tags began to rise sharply and they are still rising.

After World War II, America's colleges and universities poured out a flood of graduates with bachelor's and master's degrees. Many of those men moved into marketing research. The very small number of men with experience going back fifteen or twenty years were supplemented, in the marketing research manpower pool, by a much larger number of men of increasing experience. The high compensation levels of the more experienced men in the field contributed to accelerated salary progress for less experienced men.

In comparing x years experience acquired subsequent to World War II with the same experience acquired before it, one significant difference should be noted. The old-timers in the field worked pretty much as general practitioners. They were active in all areas of marketing research practice. As the length of this book indicates, the areas are numerous. The younger men have sometimes had to settle for rather highly specialized experience. The result is that a comparison of "years of experience" is sometimes rather misleading.

The limited number of thoroughly seasoned and experienced veterans of marketing research have tended, at an accelerated rate in recent years, to move into consulting work. Their broad experience, used to supplement and guide the efforts of men with less experience within the companies served, has been far more productively applied when it has been spread over a relatively large number of companies, problems, and situations. Those veteran marketing research men who have remained active in what might be described as the "private-practice" portion of marketing research have tended to gravitate toward positions in one of a very few categories. They are marketing research directors of large manufacturing organizations. The diversified product line of such an organization provides a wide variety of challenging problems. Or they are at high levels of responsibility in the marketing research area within an advertising medium or media association. Or they are serving as marketing research director or equivalent in a large advertising agency. Attrition of that limited number of men through promotion continues unabated.

EFFECT OF THE SHORTAGE OF EXPERIENCED RESEARCH MANPOWER ON MARKETING RESEARCH PRACTICE TODAY

The peculiar distribution of marketing research manpower, classified on a years-of-experience basis, is what statisticians would describe as bimodal. There is a small peak, followed by the World War II–induced valley, followed in turn by a relatively large peak made up of post–World War II research men. That distribution has had a profound effect on the developing pattern of marketing research practice. It is important and relevant here both for its contribution to understanding the role of consultants in marketing research practice and as an indication of the opportunity the field still offers the individual who cares to take the not-inconsiderable pains required to achieve outstanding competence in it.

There has been a spectacular increase in compensation levels within the field. That increase was the natural result of supply and demand, as seasoned, experienced marketing research men recognized and took advantage of their scarcity value. As a result, there are some marked distortions between the compensation enjoyed by a marketing research man and that of, say, an accountant of equal skill and equivalent years of experience. There are more accountants; and the flow of men (and women) into the field was not interrupted by the war. It is not unusual, as a result, to find accountants and other staff specialists paid substantially less than their "opposite number" in marketing research.

The scarcity-inflated price tags of experienced marketing research men have had the effect of pricing such men out of the market for all but the largest companies, in terms of full-time employment. Even a large organization could in most instances afford to hire only one or two men of that caliber and cost. Most other organizations have had to choose from the larger number of less experienced men. Large organizations have had to staff their research departments, below the very top level, with men in the same category.

The result has been a situation which combines opportunity with problems. Marketing research men with relatively brief experience in terms of years find themselves as marketing research directors of small, medium-sized, and even some fairly large companies. That adds up to a very important opportunity. But it is often accompanied by a whole bevy of associated problems. Those problems arise almost inevitably from the specifics in the situation. A man young both in years and in his field finds himself working with executives of far greater experience. He faces a challenging necessity: to sell himself, and to sell also the specialized activity for which he is responsible, along with his competence in that area. The magnitude of the sales task involved, especially in some companies which have done fairly well without marketing research, is difficult to exaggerate. "We've always done it this way, Junior" old-timers are likely to say. The task of achieving acceptance as a *senior* and important member of the marketing team must be met and mastered.

The same problem existed a decade or two earlier, for men who currently have had much longer experience in the field. They learned, often the hard way, how to solve that problem. The difficulty is that most of their experience is not a matter of record. Must the younger man repeat their trials and errors? Or can he somehow borrow from and apply the lessons they learned and benefit from the mistakes they made? It is into this experience gap that the seasoned and experienced marketing research man can step. His years of experience are available in many cases as one by-product of the use of a consulting firm in the marketing research field. While employment of the consultants is likely to be on a specific assignment, the opportunity to secure guidance in other areas such as those mentioned exists.

WOMEN IN MARKETING RESEARCH TODAY

One further effect of the manpower shortage mentioned warrants attention. Throughout this book, "marketing research man" and "he" have been used repeatedly—largely to avoid the repetitiveness of "man or woman" and "he or she." The usage of those terms should not mislead the reader as to the importance, in marketing research practice today, of women who are *de facto* "marketing research men." Women hold many positions of importance in marketing research practice. There are probably few fields in the semiprofessional area within which the opportunities for women to achieve substantial "man-sized" income levels are greater.

A great deal of marketing research, especially on consumer products, involves interviewing women. The interviews are usually conducted by women. Interviewers of unusual intelligence and aptitude often progress onward to become supervisors of field work, tabulating supervisors, analysts, and eventually directors of marketing research. Women with college degrees involving a marketing major often move into marketing research work and achieve rapid advancement in the field. It would be unrealistic not to recognize that in some firms a prejudice against a woman in an executive position exists. The outstanding competence of so many women in marketing research, in positions of executive level, is doing much to eliminate some lingering pockets of prejudice against them. Specifically in consulting organizations, many of the most responsible positions are held by women.

MAJOR TYPES OF CONSULTING ORGANIZATIONS IN THE MARKETING RESEARCH FIELD

In the following section we are expanding on the comments about specialized marketing research organizations which were made in Chapter 2. Here are the major types of consulting organizations active in the marketing research field:

Complete Marketing Research Service Organizations

These are organizations headed by one or more individuals with broad experience in the marketing research field. Their activities, like the marketing research field itself, are problem-oriented. They are called in for aid with a marketing and/or marketing research problem. They recommend the approach which, in the light of their experience, seems to offer the client the greatest promise of making a profit contribution far in excess of its cost. They work in a world in which the three dimensions of the problem—the time dimension, the profit dimension, and the facilities dimension—are extremely important guides in their day-to-day activities.

Within this category there is a size distinction to be noted. A very few relatively large organizations belong in this grouping, along with a much larger number of middle-sized firms. In the case of the very large organizations—such as Alfred Politz Research, Inc. in New York or Alderson & Sessions in Philadelphia—a single assignment is likely to be handled on a team basis. The team will be under the guidance of one of the principals or partners in the firm but will represent the allocation to a single client or client's problem of only a moderate proportion of the organization's total personnel. In the case of middle-sized firms, a single major assignment would be likely to be handled by what might be described as a "team of the whole." In other words, most of the manpower resources of the organization would be thrown into work on the particular assignment. Organizations in this middle-sized group, representing anywhere from five to twenty-five full-time employees, exist today in most of the major markets of the country.

Limited-service Marketing Research Organizations

Consultants in this category are usually smaller than those in the full-service group, typically specializing, as we noted in Chapter 2, in a limited area of the marketing research service spectrum. Among the major types are organizations which specialize primarily in the execution of field work on surveys and other field studies. Another major type specializes in the application of a single technique or technique area. Thus some firms primarily active in the field of motivation research would fall into this category. (A case could also be made for calling such firms "specialized" and including them in the following grouping.)

Specialized Marketing Research Organizations

Organizations of this type run the gamut in size from the largest in America (the A. C. Nielsen Company, with its Nielsen Food Index and Nielsen Drug Index services) to the very smallest. A characteristic of the organizations of this type is that they typically offer a "research package" or research packages. The package, which may be subject on occasion to minor modifications, is one with which the consulting firm has extensive experience and in which they have confidence. In this group fall firms selling a major service (like Nielsen's Food or Drug Index, or MRCA's National Consumer Panel); firms selling work in a specialized area such as the operation of store-audits for test-market purposes; and firms specializing in a particular research area like the Horace Schwerin organization, which concentrates on radio and television program and commercial evaluation, and Daniel Starch & Staff, who supply a continuing evaluation service covering print ads.

Individual Consultants

A considerable amount of marketing research advice and counsel is provided by individuals who serve as consultants, either on a full-time or part-time basis. Some of those individuals are primarily college professors, who supplement their income and keep their class subject matter attuned to the dynamic realities of competitive marketing by doing a variable amount of consulting. Others are simply individuals with a broad background in the field who have chosen to consult, without the development of an organization or the acquisition of overhead to provide themselves with a challenging variety of problems in an occupation which leaves them with considerable freedom of action and control over their own schedules and activities. Many individual consultants are outstandingly competent; others have far less solid backgrounds. In this area, obviously, no generalizations are possible.

FACTORS INFLUENCING THE SELECTION OF A CONSULTING ORGANIZATION IN THE MARKETING RESEARCH FIELD

What factors enter into the selection of a consulting organization in the marketing research field? This is a two-stage decision. The first stage is a decision as to the *type* of consultant organization to be used. The second is the selection of the specific candidate from within that group. One of the most important factors influencing the selection either of a type of consulting organization or a specific firm is the size as measured in sales volume of the organization seeking consulting assistance.

Partly because of the cost factors mentioned earlier, there is a tendency on the part of consultants to attempt to build lasting relationships with the clients they serve. The fruit of that tendency, as well as a commentary on the general level of client satisfaction with consultants' services, is suggested by the *Fortune* comment: "Among the clients of well-established consultant firms, it would appear that about three out of four return for more advice."

The larger consulting jobs, in terms of total cost, are likely to be beyond the means of any but very large companies. There is a natural tendency, therefore, for the larger consulting firms to work closely with the larger manufacturers, and vice versa. The same relationship exists between marketing research consultants and their clients. Thus *Fortune* commented in an article on "Motivation Research" in the June, 1956, issue that "Last year Politz grossed $2,500,000 from his small group of eleven big customers."

Clients like those served by Politz typically have large and well-staffed marketing research departments of their own. The definition of the problem and guidance on research approach tend to be rather well crystallized before the consulting firm moves into the picture. The consultant's contribution is usually confined to a possible refinement of some aspect of the approach under consideration and to the execution of the research with competence and dependable quality achieved through careful supervision at all stages in the data-gathering and data-processing process.

Companies in what we might call the middle-sized-volume bracket (with sales ranging, perhaps, from 75 million dollars down to perhaps 10 million dollars) are unlikely to have the internal facilities required to do the problem-defining themselves. They require in most cases the services of a marketing research consulting organization which can do that task for them and guide them in the direction of a sound research approach to the problem. Because the nature of the problem is not known, a complete rather than a specialized organization is likely to be the soundest type of choice. (The danger in the case of a specialized organization is that the full dimensions of the problem will not be recognized and/or that it will be fitted into a too-rigid technique framework of the firm's specialty. *The problem* should dictate the research approach taken.) Because the potential in terms of total consulting-service requirements of such firms is likely to be relatively low, a better "fit" is likely to exist with a medium-sized consulting organization than with one of the larger firms.

For smaller companies, with sales volume below the 10-million-dollar level—and especially for firms far below that level with total annual volume ranging from 1 million to 3 million dollars—a smaller consulting organization or an individual consultant is likely to represent the sounder choice. The comment above about the selling-cost problem and the desirability, from the consultant's viewpoint, of a continuing relationship involving a retainer, however, tempers that choice. A modest retainer from a small company may be sufficient to provide all needed consultation on marketing research and marketing management problems and may be of interest to well-qualified individual consultants or consulting firms.

Moving beyond the influence of company size, the second consideration affecting the choice of a consultant is geographic. Travel takes time and costs money. Therefore a consultant who is closer to the head-quarters city or problem point may be a sounder value even though in terms of specific competence he or his firm is felt to rank somewhat below "the tops."

A third influence is the nature of the problem. Some consulting organizations do an outstanding job in one or more areas of marketing research practice, while they lack competence and/or experience in other areas. This may be the case even with firms that provide what is at least nominally a complete service. An important limitation on the exercise of this influence should be underlined. Often, as earlier chapters in this book have indicated repeatedly, the true nature of the problem was not what it at first appeared to be. Therefore, selection on this basis involves an assumption that the nature of the problem is known, hence "fit" between problem and experience established. That assumption, like many others in marketing management, is often open to serious question.

A fourth influence boils down to a matter of personalities. Not all types of people can work effectively together. The personal relations of the partner or principal in a consulting organization and client execu-tive(s) with whom the consultant must work most closely are an ex-tremely important influence on the caliber of the consultant's work and therefore on the profit contribution to be expected from the research. This can usually be established in initial discussions, prior to the devel-opment of a specific proposal. The organization seeking a consultant would be well advised, in such initial discussions, to probe as deeply as possible for objective indications of the basic operating philosophy of the consultant or consulting firm under consideration. Charm is no sub-stitute for competence!

PROBLEM AREAS IN DEALING WITH CONSULTANTS

The NICB study previously referred to cited some disadvantages of outside consulting organizations in the marketing research field, as seen through the eyes of the marketing research directors with whom they work closely:

> The principal disadvantage noted by those cooperating in this study was the lack of familiarity of the agencies with the peculiar problems of the client's business and industry. This problem was most serious in the industrial products field, where considerable technical knowledge and ex-perience is generally regarded as necessary to the conduct of sound re-search. An agency serving a variety of customers usually lacks the time to develop a broad knowledge of the problems of any one of them. The following statement from an industrial manufacturer is a typical descrip-tion of this experience: "Outside consulting organizations are used only in

rare cases because the technical nature of the company's products makes it necessary to spend too much time in educating the consulting firm personnel."

There is an interesting parallel to that viewpoint which might be drawn. Consider the situation of a department head in a business who is grossly overworked. He finally demands of his boss, in despair, that additional personnel be provided. The boss accedes, but specifies an unrealistically low salary ceiling. To get someone within the salary ceiling set, the department head has to hire a beginner. The effect of that action is not to relieve the overloaded situation, but instead to add a training problem to those problems already existing! It is in part because of the value of a knowledge of an industry, a company, and the company's policies, as background for effective marketing research, that there is a strong trend in the direction of a continuing association between a manufacturing organization and one or more marketing research consulting firms. The background is acquired either once or gradually and remains available for subsequent assignments. It is certainly not realistic to expect a marketing research organization given a relatively narrow assignment for (typically) a relatively tight cost figure to invest substantial overhead in acquiring a background on industry and company trends not necessary to the accomplishment of the assignment in hand.

This additional comment from the NICB study detailing a disadvantage of marketing research consultants is of interest:

> Some companies have noted a tendency for marketing research agencies to sell a "research package" which may not be the best possible solution to a company's problem and may be a more expensive answer than can be obtained by some other means. There has also been noted in some quarters an occasional tendency to do a more thorough and expensive job than situations actually require.

The latter criticism in particular would be avoided if the time, profit, and facilities dimensions of the problem were clearly established at the outset of work on an assignment.

SUGGESTIONS TO GUIDE THE SELECTION OF AND WORK WITH MARKETING RESEARCH CONSULTANTS

Now let's consider some specific suggestions which may be helpful in increasing the effectiveness of marketing research in which consultants participate. Let's begin with the situation in which a company which has not previously used consulting organizations faces a marketing and/ or marketing research problem on which there is a feeling that consultants might be able to make valuable contributions.

The first problem in that type of situation is the construction of a list of candidates from which the consultant might be chosen. As earlier comments have indicated, this is a two-stage decision. It involves, first, selection of the type of consultant to be used; and, second, selection from among the nominees of that type of the specific consultant or consulting organization with the best "fit" to the company's needs. As a starting point in building a list of candidates, executives with the responsibility indicated would be well advised to consult their "opposite numbers" in other companies. The companies consulted could be those in the same industry, in the same line of trade (e.g., wholesaling, etc.), or in the same sales-volume-size bracket. From the comments of such firms about their experiences with marketing research consultants, it should be possible to compile a list of candidates without much difficulty. Additional references on the subject in the Appendix of this book might also be helpful.

In discussing the possible assignment with consultants or consultant organizations, it is highly desirable to develop in writing as clear and complete a statement of the problem (or of the known symptoms of the problem) as possible. That statement should, to the extent that it is possible to do so, establish the limits within which it is felt likely that research might be helpful. It is important that such a statement be complete and specific. It is also important that it provide direction but not inhibition to the consulting firm. In other words, it should say something like this: "In our judgment, this problem can perhaps best be approached by taking thus-and-so a research approach. It is not our objective here, however, to 'fence in' the thinking about this assignment on the part of consulting firms which are being considered for it." The specifications which indicate in as much specific detail as possible what the objectives of the research are and what information is needed, *without* intruding to tell how the consultant should go about the actual assignment, are likely to be most effective.

The contribution of this step is essentially a laborsaving one. It avoids misunderstandings. It provides a common framework or starting point for consultants to use in developing a proposal. In some cases, it will have the immediate effect of screening some of the nominees from the list. Organizations which feel that the assignment in question is not one they feel qualified to tackle should have the privilege of withdrawing without prejudicing their consideration for some future assignment from the same firm. Sometimes the organizations which withdraw can suggest additional candidates for the list.

A *written proposal* covering the assignment in question should be requested. That proposal should have in it most of the elements described in the chapter on the preparation of the research plan. It should tell what will be done and what will not be done. The technique tools to be used should be described in specific detail. Limitations of the findings, particularly with reference to projectability, should be spelled out. A timetable should be included, and the assurance of the consultant or consulting organization that it is a realistic and dependable one should be insisted on. Costs should be specified. The variation, if any, between the final cost to be billed and the estimate should be specified in detail. If payment should be made during the course of the work (i.e., before the assignment is completed), that point should also be specified.

Each consultant or consulting organization under consideration should be asked to supply the names of other clients for whom essentially similar types of assignments have been carried out in the past. If the consultant or firm has not been experienced in the specific research area in question, the basis for the consultant's confidence as to qualifications, etc., in that area should be spelled out. It should be understood that the prospective client is free to contact former clients and discuss with them the qualifications of the consultant and the level of quality of past work done by the consultant.

Translating the above comments to fit the situation of a firm which has used consultants in the past, and/or which has one or more consulting firms with which it has done business on a more or less continuous basis, these modifications should be noted: The problem should still be specified in writing. Any boundaries or limits should also be specified. A written proposal in complete detail should be insisted on. Only with such a written statement of the problem and written proposal, experience has indicated, can misunderstandings be avoided, communication problems bypassed or at least minimized, and essentially satisfactory relations be maintained.

Sometimes familiarity breeds a type of problem which is painful for both sides. Oral instructions are relied on, and a gap develops between what the client wanted and the consultant understood he wanted. The results can best be summarized in one word: Ouch! This is a problem which develops so frequently, and sometimes with such painful symptoms, that it should be carefully avoided.

POLICY ON NONCOMPETITIVE CLIENTS SHOULD BE CLEARLY UNDERSTOOD

One question which often arises in dealing with any outside facility, especially including consultants and consulting firms, is this one: Will the information we have gathered, often at considerable expense, "leak" to one or more of our competitors? Will some of the highly confidential background information on our company's present or planned operations, products, profits, pricing, or plans get into competitors' hands by way of the consultant or consulting firm? Questions in this area are so important, in the viewpoint of many executives and many companies, that they deserve attention.

It might be well to begin a consideration of this problem at a little different level. One of the major shortages which American business faces today is a shortage of skilled and experienced manpower. That shortage extends through all areas but is particularly acute in some. The situation in marketing research, particularly where long experience is required in a position, has already been noted. A similar type of shortage exists to a somewhat lesser degree among other types of marketing management personnel. As a result, the turnover of personnel and the extent to which executives change jobs are very high in marketing and in advertising.

Each executive who moves into a new job brings to it all his previous experience. Included, inevitably, is some information which former employers would rightly consider to be highly confidential. Ethical practice in management protects a company against leakage of information which might be damaging. The integrity of the individual is sufficient protection in most cases against disclosure of information which might be adverse to the interest of a former employer.

Most companies have continuing or intermittent relationships with outside organizations which also involve disclosure of information of a confidential nature. Attorneys and certified public accounting firms are examples. Therefore, in addition to the risk of possible leakage of confidential information through loss of one of its own executives, each company continually and inevitably faces certain risks as a result of turnover of personnel within those organizations.

The risks of loss or disclosure of confidential information in dealing with marketing research consulting firms are very similar to those involved in working with a CPA organization. In either instance, there is a further possible hazard: that a consultant organization after serving one firm in an industry may have the relationship severed and subsequently serve a competitor in the same industry. It is that latter hazard which requires consideration here, since the problem of a single executive's defection is simply an inescapable "hazard of the trade."

Most consulting organizations will not accept simultaneous assignments from competitive firms. Most have as part of their standard policy a specified interval between the completion of an assignment with one firm and the date when they will accept an assignment from a competitive organization. In marketing research practice that interval might be three months or six months, rarely longer. Because of the repeat-business ratio mentioned earlier, it is common practice for a consultant or consulting organization considering an assignment for a competitor of a former client to clear that assignment with the former client.

The desirability of that practice may not at first be apparent. Let's illustrate it with a specific example. Suppose a consultant did a comprehensive study for a firm in an industry. A specified time period after completion of the study—say three months or six months—the same consultant is invited to submit a proposal covering an assignment for a competitor of the former client. If the consultant accepted the assignment from the competitor and the former client then came back for additional guidance growing out of the original study, the former client would be the one in conflict and would in effect be "bumped" from the consultant's client list. The possibility that additional work from a former client may be pending or imminent and consideration for the rights of that former client to priorities on the consultant's services make the practice indicated highly desirable.

The importance of this competitive-service angle increases directly with the intimacy of the relationship between consultant and client. Thus a marketing research organization specializing in conducting field work (interviewing, store-auditing, etc.) is often in the position of a public carrier—it serves all firms which seek its service. However, some firms in the interviewing field do so much work for a single important client that as a matter of policy they will not serve a competitor of that client. Work involving access to and analysis of a client's sales records typically involves a pledge as to the exclusivity of the consultant's services for a specific time period after completion of the job.

In some cases, exclusivity is confined to work of a certain type. For example, a consulting firm in the marketing research field proposed to conduct a continuing, experimental test-market activity for a large multiple-product firm. A condition of the proposal was that if it were accepted no competitor would be served. However, the same firm had a continuing advertisement-checking service, open to all on a so-much-per-check basis. The proposal specifically excepted from the exclusivity commitment the ad-checking service.

Because it represents a potential source of friction between the marketing research consultant and client, this matter of the exclusivity or nonexclusivity of a service arrangement warrants attention and specific agreement in the negotiation period of a relationship or assignment involving a marketing research consultant.

ECONOMIC FORCES STIMULATE THE GROWTH
OF CONSULTANTS IN MARKETING RESEARCH

As a factor in the total marketing research picture, consultants and consulting organizations have been growing. That growth has been stimulated primarily by the economic advantages they have to offer. It is likely to continue. Through the consultant's facilities, the small manufacturer who cannot afford (and in truth does not need) a full-time marketing research man can secure as much or as little service as required. The medium-sized or large manufacturer can tap the consultant's pool of skilled manpower when needed, to expand their own facilities. There are some marketing research skills which are not required often enough to warrant maintenance of a full-time specialist even by a large manufacturer's marketing research department. The consultant, spreading that skill over the needs of many different clients, can supply it.

Beyond the economic aspects, however, lies an additional factor which is stimulating the growth of consultant services in marketing research practice. The consultant with broad experience brings objectivity to each assignment which it would be difficult if not impossible to duplicate from within the company. Further, the lessons and mistakes of other companies become part of the client's own backlog of experience, as the consultant brings them to focus on each new assignment.

SUMMARY

1. There is a growing trend toward the use of management consultants. Consultants and consulting firms in the marketing research field represent one important part of the over-all consulting population and are sharing in the growth.

2. The cost arithmetic of consulting services, as outlined in this chapter, is not widely understood. It is helpful in appraising the value represented by a quotation from a consultant.

3. A relative scarcity of seasoned and experienced marketing research men has contributed to a situation in which the services of such men can most economically be utilized by spreading them over a relatively large number of different companies. Each company pays only for the proportion of time actually used. This reduces the competition for full-time service of such men which has contributed to a relative inflation in their salary levels.

4. The use of consultants in marketing research has economic advantages which make it likely that the expansion of marketing research consultants and consulting organizations will continue.

QUESTIONS

1. How do most consultants in marketing research charge their clients for services rendered? What practical limitations does *Fortune* cite concerning this method?

2. What is one of the great advantages which consultants offer to their clients? What bearing, if any, does this have on the manner in which a client compensates a consultant?

3. How did the historical background of the present importance of consultants in marketing research develop? Include in your discussion pre–World War II, World War II, and post–World War II periods.

4. What are the major types of consulting organizations active in the marketing research field? Include a brief description of each type.

5. What factors would influence your selection of a consulting organization in the marketing research field? What bearing would these factors have upon your choice?

6. The National Industrial Conference Board cited some disadvantages of outside consulting organizations in the marketing research field, as seen through the eyes of the marketing research directors with whom they worked. What were these disadvantages?

7. What specific suggestions were presented in this chapter to aid in increasing the effectiveness of marketing research in which consultants participate?

8. What do you feel the policy of a consulting firm should be with regard to the subject of serving competitive clients?

Suggestions for Supplementary Reading

The bibliographical task of the writer of a book about marketing research is relatively simple. A single source provides a comprehensive listing of most of the important biographical material in the field which would be of interest to a student. That source is a book entitled *A Basic Bibliography on Marketing Research* (American Marketing Association, Chicago, June, 1956, 164 pages) compiled by Hugh G. Wales and Robert Ferber. It is an extremely well organized compilation, in which each reference item is supplemented by brief comments of the compilers on that reference.

The following suggested readings are those relevant to each chapter which are likely to be of interest to the serious student of marketing research.

Chapter 1. Nature and Scope of Marketing Research

1.1. 1948 Report of the Definitions Committee, American Marketing Association, *The Journal of Marketing*, October, 1948, p. 211. (Also available in McNair and Hansen, *Readings in Marketing*, McGraw-Hill, New York, 1949, p. 1.)

> This listing and definition of marketing terms will be especially helpful to those who bring to the study of marketing research little familiarity with marketing practices.

1.2. Richard D. Crisp, *Company Practices in Marketing Research*, American Management Association Research Report 22, 1953.

> This 64-page paperbound booklet summarizes in detail the marketing research practices of a sample of 180 companies which were members of the AMA. The sample consists of firms which tend to be relatively advanced in their use of marketing research. The report is in two major parts: a 37-page summary of the findings of the survey, and a discussion of "Marketing Research in Action" which describes major areas of research activity.

1.3. Paul E. Holden, Lounsbury S. Fish, and Hubert L. Smith, *Top-management Organization and Control*, McGraw-Hill, New York, 1951.

This outstanding book provides a detailed discussion of the trend to the increasing use of staff specialists, and of the advantages and limitations of using such specialists, which is helpful in understanding some of the organizational problems of marketing research.

1.4. Harry H. Tosdal, *Introduction to Sales Management,* 2d ed., McGraw-Hill, New York, 1957.

"Sales management," as Tosdal uses the term, is an extremely broad concept, very nearly synonymous with marketing management as currently used. This case book is a helpful reference source and a splendid introduction to marketing problems.

Chapter 2. The Organization of Marketing Research Activities

2.1. *Marketing Research in American Industry,* National Association of Manufacturers, 1946 (mimeographed).

A report of the results of a survey of 4,786 companies which were members of the NAM, prepared by William W. Heusner, Charles M. Dooley, Gordon A. Hughes, and Percival White. It was reprinted in slightly condensed form in *The Journal of Marketing,* April, 1947, pp. 338–354, and July, 1947, pp. 25–37. It is perhaps more readily available in McNair and Hansen's *Readings in Marketing* (see Ref. 1.1). This study and the one in Ref. 1.2 are roughly parallel in objective, with a time-interval separation which suggests some trend relationships.

2.2. *Marketing, Business and Commercial Research in Industry,* National Industrial Conference Board, Inc., Studies in Business Policy, no. 72, 1955.

This 88-page booklet is a revision and combination of two earlier studies on the same subject. The earlier studies were identified as *Organization for Market Research.* Part I, published in 1945 as no. 12 in the Studies in Business Policy series, reported the results of a survey of 145 companies. It was essentially quantitative in approach, but with considerable amplification of the quantitative findings. Part II, no. 19 in the same series, was published in 1946. It presented a discussion of the operating methods of a substantial number of firms, many of which were identified by name. This is a helpful and detailed guide to a marketing research director in such areas as organization, procedures, etc.

Chapter 3. The Marketing-problem Base of Marketing Research

3.1. Richard D. Crisp, *Company Practices in Marketing Research* (see Ref. 1.2).

The list of specific activities, pp. 22–23, is relevant here.

3.2. *Marketing Research in American Industry* (see Ref. 2.1).

The report develops information on specific activities, but only in those companies with a full-time assignment of marketing research responsibility. When the base is the full sample of respondents, major shifts in emphasis become apparent.

3.3. W. W. Heusner, "How to Double Your Returns from Dollars Spent for Sales Research," *Sales Management,* May 1, 1946. (Reprinted in Hugh G.

Wales and Robert Ferber, *Marketing Research—Selected Literature,* Wm. C. Brown, Dubuque, Iowa, 1952.)

Of particular interest in this reference is a chart showing the relationships of marketing research functions to problems and decisions in various management areas.

Chapter 4. Introduction to the Problem-solving Process in Marketing

4.1. Marion Harper, Jr., "Making Business Decisions," *The Journal of Marketing,* July, 1950, pp. 57–60.

Mr. Harper moved from marketing research to the presidency of a large advertising agency. In this reference he presents the viewpoint of the decision maker toward information supplied by research. The reference is relevant here because an understanding of what the research is expected to contribute is helpful in planning the problem-solving approach with a minimum amount of waste motion.

4.2. Donald F. Mulvihill, "An Aid for Problem-solving in Business Situations," *The Journal of Marketing,* January, 1955, pp. 263–265.

This brief article presents an approach to the problem-solving process which the author has found helpful in securing an understanding of the process.

Chapter 5. Introduction to Sampling in Marketing Research

5.1. Robert Ferber, *Statistical Techniques in Market Research,* McGraw-Hill, New York, 1949.

This is the definitive book in the field. While it goes far beyond sampling alone, its discussion of sampling within a marketing research framework is excellent.

5.2. Morris H. Hansen, William N. Hurwitz, and William G. Madow, *Sample Survey Methods and Theory,* 2 vols., Wiley, New York, 1953.

These two volumes present a complete coverage of both the theory and practice of probability sampling. Volume II is likely to be difficult reading for those lacking a very substantial background in mathematical statistics.

5.3. William G. Cochran, *Sampling Techniques,* Wiley, New York, 1953.

Sampling principles and sample design are discussed lucidly by the author. Heavily mathematical and theoretical in orientation.

Chapter 6. Analysis of Internal Data

6.1. Donald R. G. Cowan, *Sales Analysis from the Management Standpoint,* University of Chicago Press, Chicago, 1938.

This little book remains one of the milestones in the field. It was far ahead of its time when published.

6.2. Richard D. Crisp, *How to Reduce Distribution Costs,* Funk and Wagnalls, New York, 1948.

Presents a detailed step-by-step approach to sales analysis, largely based on experience of S. C. Johnson & Son, Inc.

6.3. R. P. Eastwood, *Sales Control by Quantitative Methods,* Columbia University Press, New York, 1940.

Discusses the use of accounting and statistical approaches in dealing with sales and marketing problems.

Chapter 7. Locating and Evaluating Available Data from External Sources

7.1. *Current Sources of Information for Marketing Research*, American Marketing Association, Chicago, 1954.
A broad coverage of sources of statistical data useful in marketing research.

7.2. Philip M. Hauser and William R. Leonard, *Government Statistics for Business Use*, Wiley, New York, 1956.
An excellent survey of governmental data sources.

7.3. Marian C. Manley, *Business Information*, Harper, New York, 1955.
A guide to the location and use of business information. Part I explains the use of available information resources. Part II presents a bibliography of business periodicals and books, trade-association reports, governmental studies, business publications, and industrial directories. Part III is a cross-referenced index.

Chapter 8. The Survey Technique

8.1. Mildred Parten, *Surveys, Polls and Samples: Practical Procedures*, Harper, New York, 1950.
This 600-page book covers the entire field of social surveys, with primary emphasis on public-opinion studies. It includes a bibliography of 1,145 references. It is a well-organized and lucidly written description of the survey approach, in exhaustive detail.

8.2. Herbert H. Hyman et al., *Interviewing in Social Research*, University of Chicago Press, Chicago, 1954.
This book is described on the jacket as "a systematic analysis of sources of error in the personal interview." The description identifies its area of emphasis.

8.3. Stanley L. Payne, *The Art of Asking Questions*, Princeton University Press, Princeton, N.J., 1951.
A readable discussion of problems of communication arising in surveys through question wording, use of ambiguous words, etc., illustrating the complexity of the survey process today.

Chapter 9. The Use of Panels in Marketing Research

9.1. Richard D. Crisp, *How to Reduce Distribution Costs* (see Ref. 6.2).
Chapter 18 presents a detailed discussion, with a number of illustrations, of the Nielsen store panel and MRCA consumer panel. Applications of panel data are also discussed in detail in chap. 21.

Chapter 10. Observation and Experiment in Marketing Research

10.1. William Applebaum and Richard F. Spears, "Controlled Experimentation in Marketing Research," *The Journal of Marketing*, January, 1950, pp. 505–517.

This article describes controlled experimentation primarily within a grocery-store universe. It points out problem areas which in the authors' judgment are likely to arise in other types of experimental work in marketing as well.

Chapter 11. Practical Aspects of Sampling in Marketing Research

11.1. George H. Brown, "A Comparison of Sampling Methods," *The Journal of Marketing*, April, 1947, pp. 331–337.
An excellent, nontechnical discussion of alternative sample designs.

11.2. H. M. Hansen, W. N. Hurwitz, and M. Gurney, "Problems and Methods of the Sample Survey of Business," *Journal of the American Statistical Association*, June, 1946, pp. 173–189.

11.3. P. G. Peterson and W. F. O'Dell, "Selecting Sampling Methods in Commercial Research," *The Journal of Marketing*, October, 1950, pp. 182–189.
This discussion of sampling approaches emphasizes the viewpoint of the practitioner.

11.4. W. E. Deming, "Some Criteria for Judging the Quality of Surveys," *The Journal of Marketing*, October, 1947, pp. 145–157.
A critical review of the advantages and limitations of different sampling methods.

Chapters 12 and 13. Defining and Refining the Problem

As an examination of various bibliographies in the field will confirm, this vital area of research practice has been largely bypassed in the literature of the field. There are no references of outstanding interest. Note, however, that the subject is closely related to the design of research. References on the subject of research design will be found below under Chapter 14.

Chapter 14. Developing the Research Plan

14.1. William J. Goode and Paul K. Hatt, *Methods in Social Research*, McGraw-Hill, New York, 1952.
This is an excellent introductory treatment of many important aspects of research design.

14.2. Russell L. Ackoff, *The Design of Social Research*, University of Chicago Press, Chicago, 1953.
This book introduces some useful concepts in research design. It is rather heavily preoccupied with the statistical analysis of data developed through sampling.

Chapter 15. Executing the Research Plan

Parten (Ref. 8.1) and Hyman (Ref. 8.2) provide helpful information on interviewer bias and some other sources of bias.

Chapters 16 and 17. Analysis and Interpretation of Marketing Research Data

16.1. *The Technique of Marketing Research*, American Marketing Association, McGraw-Hill, New York, 1937.

This book—and particularly chaps. 3 and 4—provides some helpful guidance in this area. Chapters 11, 12, and 13 are also relevant.

16.2. Hans Zeisel, *Say It with Figures,* Harper, New York, 1950.
A small (250 pp.) but extremely meaty book on the interpretation of data and on some commonly encountered problems in data arrangement and analysis.

Ferber (Ref. 5.1) also has some significant contributions to the area of statistical-data analysis and interpretation.

Chapter 18. Preparation of Research Reports

18.1. "Preparation and Presentation of the Research Report," an American Marketing Association committee report, *The Journal of Marketing,* July, 1948, p. 62.
A discussion of what research reports should include, in the judgment of a group of practitioners. It illuminates a number of controversial points in the report-preparation area.

18.2. R. O. Hall, *Handbook of Tabular Presentation,* Ronald, New York, 1946.
Adequate coverage of this area of reporting.

The National Industrial Conference Board study (Ref. 2.2) also includes much helpful information about the preparation of research reports.

Chapter 19. Sales Forecasting

19.1. Adolph G. Abramson and Russell H. Mack, *Business Forecasting in Practice: Principles and Cases.* Wiley, New York, 1956.
Combines contributions by a number of well-qualified individuals. It is concerned more with general business forecasting than with sales forecasting for an individual firm.

19.2. *How to Make Sales Estimates More Accurate,* Research Institute of America, Research Institute Study 2, 1954.
This 78-page mimeographed report describes and illustrates a number of approaches to sales forecasting. Unlike most literature on forecasting, it is sharply focused on the problems of the individual firm.

19.3. "Business Forecasting," a special report in the Sept. 24, 1955, issue of *Business Week.*
A discussion of the major approaches to forecasting with emphasis on the advantages and limitations of each.

19.4. *Sales Forecasting: Uses, Techniques, and Trends,* Special Report No. 16, American Management Association, Inc., 1956.
This special report reproduces more than a dozen papers on sales forecasting presented at a two-day special conference. In addition, it includes the results of a survey of sales-forecasting practices among 297 companies. Because it deals with sales forecasting rather than with general business forecasting, this report is likely to be of considerable interest to those working in the forecasting field.

Chapter 20. Determining the Size and Characteristics of the Market for a Product

This subject is discussed at some length, primarily for consumer products, in Crisp (Ref. 6.2), chaps. 17, 19.

Chapter 21. Estimating Territorial Sales Potentials and Measuring Territorial Variations in Sales Effectiveness

21.1. *Measuring Sales Performance,* National Industrial Conference Board, Inc., Studies in Business Policy, no. 31, 1948.

An interesting study of current practices in measuring salesmen's performance. It is of interest primarily as an indication of how retarded progress in this important area has been.

Chapter 22. Product Research

22.1. D. M. Phelps, *Planning the Product,* Irwin, Homewood, Ill., 1947.

This book discusses product planning in a broad frame of reference and provides helpful background on product research. It is particularly helpful in underlining the importance of thinking of "product" as a broad rather than narrow concept.

Chapter 23. New-product Development

23.1. *Developing and Selling New Products, A Guidebook for Manufacturers,* 2d ed., U.S. Department of Commerce, Small Business Administration, 1955.

A 100-page booklet, packed with specific and detailed data including many specific case examples. It is an outstanding reference source on new-product development.

23.2. *New Product Development,* National Industrial Conference Board, Inc., Studies in Business Policy, nos. 40, 57, and 69, 1950, 1952, 1954.

Number 40 in this series presents part I dealing with Selection-Coordination-Financing; no. 57 presents part II covering Research and Engineering; no. 69 presents part III covering Marketing New Products. Together the three booklets offer a great deal of excellent information, including many specific case illustrations, on the planning of new-product-development activities. Included is considerable information on the research and development (as distinguished from marketing) aspects of the problem.

23.3. *New Product Introduction for Small Business Owners,* Small Business Management Series, no. 17, 1955.

This 69-page booklet is an excellent and comprehensive treatment of the subject.

Chapter 24. Advertising Research

24.1. *Copy Testing,* a study by the Advertising Research Foundation, Ronald, New York, 1939.

This is a review of the methods then in use and of the advantages and disadvantages of each.

24.2. Darrell B. Lucas and Steuart Henderson Britt, *Advertising Psychology and Research*, McGraw-Hill, New York, 1950.

The outstanding book in this area, presenting a comprehensive coverage of the field.

24.3. Richard D. Crisp, *A Case Study in Copy Research*, 2d. ed., Richard D. Crisp and Associates, Chicago, 1957.

This is a revision of a discussion of advertising research experimentation honored by the American Marketing Association with a National Award in 1954.

Chapter 25. Test Marketing

25.1. "How to Check Sales Results by the Paired-city Method," *Sales Management*, Jan. 15, 1952, p. 98.

A discussion of the "market-matching problem."

25.2. Lawrence M. Hughes, "Can Tests in Four Markets Tell How All Major Markets Will Buy?" *Sales Management*, Nov. 10, 1951, p. 37.

An unusually detailed case study of the use of test marketing by Lever Brothers Company in developing Chlorodent tooth paste.

Chapter 26. Qualitative and "Motivational" Research

26.1. George Horsley Smith, *Motivation Research in Advertising and Marketing*, an Advertising Research Foundation Publication, McGraw-Hill, New York, 1954.

This is the definitive work in the field. It includes an extensive bibliography. In addition, the ARF publishes from time to time expanding bibliographies of references on this topic.

Chapter 27. Research by Retailers, Wholesalers and Service Organizations

See Applebaum-Spears (Ref. 10.1) for study in this field.

Chapter 30. Consultants in Marketing Research Practice

30.1. *Directory of Consultant Members*, American Management Association, New York, 1956.

This is a listing of consulting organizations, with their fields of activity indicated. It is introduced by an excellent article on selecting and working with a consultant by Robert F. Dick.

Case Index

Page references in **boldface** type indicate main discussions. Multiple-unit cases are designated by the letters (A), (B), (C), and (D) as in the text.

Name Index

References are to names of individuals, firms, products, associations, and publications. Because of space limitations they are confined to major discussions.

ACME (Association of Consulting Management Engineers), 759
Admiral Corporation, 32
Advertising Checking Bureau, 607
Advertising Research Foundation, Inc., 173–177, 240, 633
Alderson & Sessions, Inc., 766
American Alcolac Corp., 601
American Dairy Association, 727
American Home Laundry Manufacturers Association, 723
American Iron & Steel Institute, 730
American Management Association, 23–27, 59–67, 733
(See also Company Practices in Marketing Research)
American Marketing Association, 21–23, 97, 130
(See also Subject Index)
American Meat Institute, 727
American Steel Warehouse Association, 731
Andersen, Arthur, & Co., 721
Applebaum, William, 242, 710–714
ARF (see Case Index, case 49)
Association of Consulting Management Engineers, 759
Avco Corporation, 57
Avon Products, Inc., 139

Battey, Edward, 173
Bendix (see Case Index, cases 20, 23)
"Betty Crocker," 32
Bishop, Hazel, 56
Bosch, Leon A., 10
Britt, Steuart Henderson, 187, 637, 670
Brown, Lyndon O., 14

Brown, Theodore H., 98, 118, 247
Burke Marketing Research, Inc., 32
Business Week, 601

Campbell Soup Company, 33, 438, 687–689
Carpet Institute, Inc., 33
Cascino, A. E., 347
Chicago Daily News, 755
Chicago Tribune, 439, 755, 756
Clements, Forrest E., 37
Cleveland Press, 705
Cochran, William G., 408
Company Guide to Marketing Research, A, 27
Company Practices in Marketing Research, 8n., 23–26, 29–30, 59–67, 510, 534, 559, 581, 719, 733
Conant, James B., 15–16
Congoleum-Nairn, Inc., 59
Crisco, 285
Crisp, Richard D., and Associates, Inc., 33
Crosby, John, 363
Crosley appliances, 57
Cross, John H. A., 271
Crossley S-D Surveys, Inc., 241, 658, 728
Curtis Publishing Co., 757

Deming, W. Edward, 120
Donham, Richard, 10
Drug Topics, 517
Dun & Bradstreet, Inc., 730
Dun's Review and Modern Industry, 504–506

787

Subject Index

Date Due